S0-ADO-263

Dictionary of Judaism in the Biblical Period

Editorial Board

Dictionary of Judaism in the Biblical Period

450 B.C.E. to 600 C.E.

VOLUME 1

Jacob Neusner, *Editor in Chief*
William Scott Green, *Editor*

MACMILLAN LIBRARY REFERENCE USA
Simon & Schuster Macmillan
NEW YORK

Simon & Schuster and Prentice Hall International
LONDON MEXICO CITY NEW DELHI SINGAPORE SYDNEY TORONTO

Simon & Schuster Macmillan
866 Third Avenue, New York, NY 10022

PRINTED IN THE UNITED STATES OF AMERICA

printing number
1 2 3 4 5 6 7 8 9 10

LIBRARY OF CONGRESS CATALOGING-IN-PUBLICATION DATA

Dictionary of Judaism in the biblical period : 450 B.C.E. to 600 C.E.
Jacob Neusner, editor in chief : William Scott Green, editor.
p. cm.
ISBN 0-02-897292-9
1. Judaism—History—Post-exilic period, 586 B.C.-210 A.D.—Dictionaries. 2. Judaism—History—Talmudic period, 10-425—Dictionaries. 3. Rabbinical literature—Dictionaries.
I. Neusner, Jacob, 1932- . II. Green, William Scott.
BM50.D525 1996 95-31543
296'.09'01—dc20 CIP

This paper meets the requirements of ANSI/NISO Z39.48-1992 (Permanence of Paper).

Contents

Preface

The "biblical period" of the title of this Dictionary refers not to the time of which the Bible speaks but to the era during which the sacred writings of both Judaism and Christianity were formulated and canonized, in other words, from about 450 B.C.E., when the Pentateuch as we know it was formulated, to the closure of the Babylonian Talmud around 600 C.E. The Dictionary therefore covers the age in which the Dead Sea Scrolls were composed, the Jewish philosopher Philo wrote his books, the Jewish historian Josephus composed his histories, the books comprising the New Testament were written and the Christian Bible, covering the Old and New Testaments, was canonized, and the time in which the classical writings of Judaism beyond the scriptures took shape: the Mishnah, Tosefta, the two Talmuds, and a score of Midrash collections.

Users will find here definitions of words likely to turn up in the Bible and related writings of the biblical period as just now defined, places that are commonly mentioned, and kings and emperors of this period. We cover writings on the Jews written in Hebrew, Aramaic, Greek, and Latin; translations of the Hebrew scriptures into Aramaic; the Dead Sea Scrolls; and the entire corpus of writings of "our sages of blessed memory," the authorities of Judaism in ancient times. Concepts, religious rites, and theological categories come to simple, lexical definition. Insofar as important Christian and pagan writers refer to the Jews and Judaism, we present lexical information to make sense of what they say. By defining words in their historical, literary, religious, and archaeological settings, the editors answer many questions that until now have found no ready and convenient explanation. We give only lexical definitions, for this is a dictionary, not an encyclopedia. We mean to provide a convenient, ready reference to guide reading in the Bible and related books. What one will not find is extensive articles, complete with bibliographies. That is a separate task.

Strictly speaking, the "biblical period" should close at about 400 C.E. The New Testament and, with it, the Bible as a whole, reached closure at that time, after a long process of writing and reflection. But since, in this Dictionary, we address both Christianity and Judaism in the formative age of the two great religions of the West, we extend our closing date beyond the closure of the Bible to encompass the final redaction of the Talmud of Babylonia, the complete, authoritative statement of Judaism at the end of its formative age.

The religion that the world calls "Judaism" is defined by its followers as the Torah, or Teaching, understood as the full and complete account of God's self-manifestation and the authoritative statement of what God wants from humanity and especially from Israel, the holy people that stands in a covenanted relationship with God. In antiquity a variety of Judaic religious systems came to expression, each framed by a community that called itself "Israel" and set forth its statement of "the Torah," which not only included the ancient Israelite scripture but also additional writings, whether they were the library found at the Dead Sea, the New

Testament, or the rabbinic writings, to name three bodies of writing that represented communities of Judaism.

All of the Judaisms of ancient times contributed words for definition in these pages. But the most important one requires special attention. Rabbinic Judaism, also known as Classical Judaism, Talmudic Judaism, or Normative Judaism, in ancient times competed with other Judaic systems but emerged as paramount from late antiquity to our own day. That Judaism represents the way of life and the worldview of Israel, the holy people, as set forth in the Torah, part oral and part written. By its own account, the Pentateuch was revealed by God to Moses at Mount Sinai. The Torah furthermore encompasses teachings by God to Moses that were not written down but orally formulated and orally transmitted in a chain of tradition. So, from the viewpoint of Judaism, when the Torah, oral and written, is properly explained, people who practice Judaism, called "Israel," therefore know what God has to say to them and wants them to do.

The written part of the Torah. The Torah means first of all the Pentateuch or the Five Books of Moses (Genesis, Exodus, Leviticus, Numbers, and Deuteronomy). Part of the Torah as well, and read in the synagogue along with the Pentateuch, are the Prophets—Joshua, Judges, Samuel, Kings, Isaiah, Jeremiah, Ezekiel, and the Twelve Minor Prophets. A third part of the Torah is the Writings: Psalms, Proverbs, Job, Song of Songs [Song of Solomon], Ruth, Lamentations, Ecclesiastes, Esther, Daniel, Ezra, Nehemiah, and Chronicles.

The oral part of the Torah. Along with the Torah in written form, corresponding to what Christianity knows as the Old Testament, Judaism affirms God's revelation to Moses at Sinai in oral form, meaning a form of the Torah formulated and transmitted not in writing but in memory, in oral form, from master to disciple, from Moses on down into the early centuries of the common era.

The written form of the oral Torah. These originally oral traditions reached written formulation in the Mishnah, around 200 C.E., a philosophical statement in the form of a law code; the Tosefta, a compilation of rules formulated in the period in which the Mishnah was taking shape as well as afterward, around 300 C.E.; two Talmuds, or systematic commentaries to tractates of the Mishnah: the Talmud of the Land of Israel (the Jerusalem Talmud or Yerushalmi), around 450 C.E., and the Talmud of Babylonia (the Ba<u>b</u>li), around 600 C.E.; as well as compilations of exegeses of various books of the Hebrew scriptures. These compilations of exegeses, or midrashim, occur, in particular, in Sifra to Leviticus, around 350 C.E.; Sifrei to Numbers and Sifrei to Deuteronomy, of the same period; Genesis Rabbah and Leviticus Rabbah, around 450 C.E.; Pesikta deRab Kahana, on passages of scripture read in the synagogue at high points of the liturgical year, about 500 C.E.; and the later readings of the scrolls of Esther, Lamentations, Ruth, and Song of Songs (Song of Solomon), Esther Rabbah, Lamentations Rabbah, Ruth Rabbah, and Song of Songs Rabbah, from about 500 to 600 C.E. In this same period, the prayerbooks of Judaism—Siddur for daily and festival occasions, and Maḥor for the Days of Awe—took shape.

Since we direct this work to an English-reading audience, we have tried to represent Hebrew words in the form in which they are likely to appear in English-language publications. The aim of transliteration is to provide access to reliable pronunciations of foreign words as well as the ability to cross reference additional materials as a point of departure for further study and research. To that end, prevailing English usages—Bethlehem and Melchizedek, for example—have been retained since they are ubiquitous and have become English words in their own right. Similarly, where virtually every citation of the Dead Sea material is labeled *Q*, the reader will find Qumran rather than Kumran throughout the text.

As in the word "Sheol," double vowels are pronounced separately rather than blended. "Baal," then, is Ba-al and not Bail. Other constructs of note include the following:

Weighted syllables. When *h* appears at the end of a word (as "aggadah"), it indicates stress on the ultimate syllable.

Y or I. In both "hoshayah" and "Akabiah," the transliterated value is that of *yod,* the distinction reflecting the presence or absence of an untransliterated value, such as a breath (*aleph*) or a glottal stop (*ayin*).

Double consonants indicate "dagesh," which doubles the consonantal value in Hebrew and shortens the preceding vowel. "Long" vowels as found in English do not exist, and their equivalents (e.g., Pirkei Abot) require a diphthong.

Diphthongs combine two vowel sounds to produce the characteristic English vowels ā (= ei) or ī (= ai).

Double Y. The Talmud contains several instances of doubling in proper nouns, which have thus been transliterated, although they are not phonologically significant.

Th does not exist in either Hebrew or Aramaic. Wherever this transliteration remains (e.g., Bethlehem, Asenath), it reflects anglicization and the prevalence of this attestation among the sources.

In speaking of "the Bible," meaning the Old and New Testaments, we use language familiar to everyone likely to use this Dictionary. Depending on the context we refer to the Holy Land as both "the Land of Israel," as it was known up to the second century C.E., and "Palestine," the name given to the country by the Romans later on. Where either phrase is used, we intend no political statement of any kind. "Palestine" is a necessary geographical term in some contexts, "Land of Israel" a required theological term in others.

The editors took responsibility for these areas, respectively: the history of the Jews and of Judaism before 70: George W. E. Nickelsburg; the history of Judaism after 70, in Hebrew and Aramaic sources: Jacob Neusner, William Scott Green, and Alan J. Avery-Peck; the Targumim (Aramaic translations of the Hebrew scriptures): Paul V. Flesher; the Jews and Judaism in Greek and Latin sources: Lester L. Grabbe; the history of the Jews after 70: Anthony J. Saldarini and Gary G. Porton; the archaeology of the Jews and Judaism in the Land of Israel in the biblical period: James F. Strange.

The area editors called upon numerous colleagues for the preparation of specific entries, and the names of our collaborators are listed on page *xv*. We take pride in the fact that in the United States, Canada, Britain, continental Europe, and Israel, scholarship on Judaism and Christianity is carried on by Jews and Christians in close harmony, and among the editors are Jews, Protestants, and Catholics.

In the formation of the entry lists, the editors consulted Professor Louis H. Feldman, Yeshiva University, and we express thanks for his help in compiling the lists of words and phrases treated here. He checked our original entry lists, made numerous suggestions of items we had not yet included, and offered valued advice.

The skilled and professional staff at Macmillan Reference made possible the production of this Dictionary. Special thanks go to Philip Friedman, Publisher, and Elly Dickason, Associate Publisher. During the six years in which this project took shape, we worked closely and in harmony, and as a result, the task was a happy one. We speak for all the editors in paying tribute to Macmillan's first-class staff.

John Kutsko and Patricia Biagi served as copy editors for the Dictionary and made matters as consistent and accurate as is humanly possible in a project of such formidable complexity and dimensions as this. We thank them as well.

Jacob Neusner
William Scott Green

Abbreviations Used in This Work

Abod. Zar.	Abodah Zarah
Abot deR. Nat.	Abot deRabbi Natan
abbr.	abbreviated; abbreviation
abr.	abridged; abridgment
Abr.	*De Abrahamo (On Abraham)*
Acts	Acts of the Apostles
Add. Esth.	Additions to Esther
Aet.	*De Aeternitate Mundi*
Ag. Apion	*Against Apion*
Agr.	*De Agricultura (On Agriculture)*
amend.	amended; amendment
annot.	annotated; annotation
Ant.	*Antiquities of the Jews*
Apoc. Abr.	Apocalypse of Abraham
Apoc. Bar.	Apocalypse of Baruch
Apoc. Moses	Apocalypse of Moses
Apoc. Zeph.	Apocalypse of Zephaniah
app.	appendix
Arab.	Arabic
Arak.	Arakin
Aram.	Aramaic
art. (pl., arts.)	article
Assyr.	Assyrian
ASV	American Standard Version
b.	born
B.	Babli (Babylonian Talmud)
B. Bat.	Baba Batra
B. Kam.	Baba Kamma
B. Metz.	Baba Metzia
B.C.E.	before the common era
Bar.	Baruch
Bekh.	Bekhorot
Ber.	Berakhot
Bik.	Bikkurim
bk. (pl., bks.)	book
c.	*circa,* about, approximately
C.E.	of the common era
CD	Damascus Document
cf.	*confer,* compare
chap. (pl., chaps.)	chapter
Chron.	Chronicles
Chron. Jer.	Chronicle of Jerahmeel
cm	centimeter(s)
col. (pl., cols.)	column
Col.	Colossians
comp. (pl., comps.)	compiler
Conf.	*De Confusione Linguarum (On the Confusion of Tongues)*
Congr.	*De Congressu quaerendae Eruditionis gratia (On the Preliminary Studies)*
cont.	continued
Copt.	Coptic
Cor.	Corinthians
d.	died
Dan.	Daniel
Decal.	*De Decalogo (On the Decalogue)*
Der. Er. Rab.	Derekh Eretz Rabbah
Der. Er. Zut.	Derekh Eretz Zuta
Deut.	Deuteronomy
DSS	Dead Sea Scrolls
e.g.	*exempli gratia,* for example
Ebr.	*De Ebrietate (On Drunkenness)*
Eccles.	Ecclesiastes
Ecclus.	Ecclesiasticus
ed. (pl., eds.)	editor; edition; edited by
Ed.	Eduyyot
Eng.	English
enl.	enlarged
Eph.	Ephesians
Erub.	Erubin
Esd.	Esdras
esp.	especially
Est.	Esther
et al.	*et alii,* and others
etc.	*et cetera,* and so forth
Eth.	Ethiopic
EV	English version
Exod.	Exodus
exp.	expanded
Ezek.	Ezekiel

f. (pl., ff.)	following	*Leg.*	*De Legatione ad Gaium (On the Embassy to Gaius)*
fl.	*floruit,* flourished	Let. Arist.	Letter of Aristeas
Flacc.	*In Flaccum (Against Flaccum)*	Let. Jer.	Letter of Jeremiah
frag.	fragment	Lev.	Leviticus
Frg. Tg.	Fragmentary Targum	lit.	literally
ft.	feet	LXX	Septuagint
Fuga	*De Fuga et Inventione (On Flight and Finding)*	m	meter(s)
		M.	Mishnah
Gal.	Galatians	Maas.	Maaserot
Gem.	Gemara	Maas. Sh.	Maaser Sheni
Gen.	Genesis	Macc.	Maccabees
Gen. Rab.	Genesis Rabbah	Mal.	Malachi
Ger.	German	Mart. Isa.	Martyrdom of Isaiah
Gig.	*De Gigantibus (On the Giants)*	Matt.	Matthew
Gitt.	Gittin	Meg.	Megillah
Gr.	Greek	Meil.	Meila
Hab.	Habakkuk	Mekh.	Mekhilta
Hag.	Haggai	Melch.	Melchizedek
Ḥag.	Ḥagigah	Menaḥ.	Menaḥot
Ḥal.	Ḥallah	mi.	miles
Heb.	Hebrew, Hebrews	Mic.	Micah
Hor.	Horayot	Mid.	Middot
Hos.	Hosea	*Migr.*	*De Migratione Abrahami (On the Migration of Abraham)*
Ḥul.	Ḥullin		
ibid.	*ibidem,* in the same place (as the one immediately preceding)	Mikv.	Mikvaot
		Moed Kat.	Moed Katan
		MS (pl., MSS)	*manuscriptum,* manuscript
i.e.	*id est,* that is		
intro.	introduction	MT	Masoretic text
Ios.	*De Iosepho (On Joseph)*	*Mut.*	*De Mutatione Nominum (On the Change of Names)*
Isa.	Isaiah		
Jdt.	Judith	n.	note
Jer.	Jeremiah	n.d.	no date
Jon.	Jonah	Nah.	Nahum
Jos. Asen.	Joseph and Asenath	NASB	New American Standard Bible
Josh.	Joshua	NEB	New English Bible
Jub.	Jubilees	Ned.	Nedarim
Judg.	Judges	Neg.	Negaim
Kall.	Kallah	Neh.	Nehemiah
Ker.	Keritot	Nez.	Nezikin
Ketu<u>b</u>.	Ketu<u>b</u>ot	Nid.	Niddah
Kidd.	Kiddushin	no. (pl., nos.)	number
KJV	King James Version		
km	kilometer(s)	Num.	Numbers
l. (pl., ll.)	line	Obad.	Obadiah
		Odes Sol.	Odes of Solomon
L.A.	*Legum Allegoriarum (Allegorical Interpretation)*	Ohal.	Ohalot
		On Abr.	*De Abrahamo (On Abraham)*
LAB	Book of Biblical Antiquities (Liber Antiquitatum Biblicarum)	*On Agr.*	*De Agricultura (On Agriculture)*
		On Migr. Agr.	*De Migratione Abrahami (On the Migration of Abraham)*
Lam.	Lamentations	*On Rew.*	*De Praemiis et Poenis (On Rewards and Punishments)*
Lat.	Latin		

Opf.	*De Opificio Mundi (On the Creation of the World)*
Or.	Orlah
p. (pl., pp.)	page
P. Oxy.	Papyri Oxyrhyncus
Pal.	Palestinian
Pal. Tgs.	Palestinian Targums
para. (pl., paras.)	paragraph
Pers.	Persian
Pesaḥ.	Pesaḥim
Pesik. deRab Kah.	Pesikta deRab Kahana
Pesik. R.	Pesikta Rabbati
Pet.	Peter
Phil.	Philippians
Philem.	Philemon
Phoen.	Phoenician
pl.	plural
Plant.	*De Plantatione (On Noah's Work as a Planter)*
Post.	*De Posteritate Caini (On the Posterity and Exile of Cain)*
Pr. of Man.	Prayer of Manasseh
Praem.	*De Praemiis et Poenis (On Rewards and Punishments)*
Prep. Gos.	*Preparation for the Gospel*
Prov.	Proverbs
Prov.	*De Providentia (On Providence)*
Ps. (pl., Pss.)	Psalms
pt. (pl., pts.)	part
Q	Qumran
1Q, 2Q, 3Q, etc.	Qumran caves: Cave 1, Cave 2, etc.
1QapGen	Genesis Apocryphon
1QH	Hodayot
1QM	War Scroll
1QpHab	Habakkuk, Pesher on
1QS	Community Rule
1QSa	Rule of the Congregation
1QSb	Benedictions
3Q15	Copper Scroll
4Q169	Commentary on Nahum
4Q504	Words of the Heavenly Lights
4QFlor	Florilegium
4QPhyl	Phylacteries
4QPrNab	Prayer of Nabonidus
4QShirShabb	Songs of the Sabbath Sacrifice
4QTestim	Testimonia
4QTLevi	Testament of Levi
11QMelch	Melchizedek, Pesher on
11QPs[a]	Psalm Scroll
11QtgJob	Targum to Job
r.	reigned; ruled
Rab.	Rabbah
rev.	revised
Rev.	Revelation
Rom.	Romans
Rosh. Hash.	Rosh Hashanah
RSV	Revised Standard Version
Sacr.	*De Sacrificiis Abelis et Caini (On the Sacrifices of Abel and Cain)*
Sam.	Samuel
Sam. Tg.	Samaritan Targum
Sanh.	Sanhedrin
sec. (pl., secs.)	section
Sem.	Semaḥot
ser.	series
sg.	singular
Shabb.	Shabbat
Sheb.	Shebiit
Shebu.	Shebuot
Shekal.	Shekalim
Sib. Or.	Sibylline Oracles
Sifrei Deut.	Sifrei Deuteronomy
Sobr.	*De Sobrietate (On Sobriety)*
Somn.	*De Somniis (On Dreams)*
Song of Sol.	Song of Solomon
Sotah	Sotah
Spec. Leg.	*De Specialibus Legibus (On the Special Laws)*
sq.	square
st. (pl., ss.)	stanza
supp.	supplement; supplementary
Sus.	Susanna
Syr.	Syriac
T.	Tosefta
T. Yom	Tebul Yom
Taan.	Taanit
Ter.	Terumot
Test. 12 Patr.	Testaments of the Twelve Patriarchs
Test. Abr.	Testament of Abraham
Test. Jacob	Testament of Jacob
Test. Jud.	Testament of Judah
Test. Moses	Testament of Moses
Tg.	Targum
Tg. Isa.	Targum to Isaiah
Tg. Ket.	Targum to the Writings
Tg. Neb.	Targum to the Prophets
Tg. Neof.	Targum Neofiti 1
Tg. Onk.	Targum Onkelos

Tg. Ps.-J.	Targum Pseudo-Jonathan
Tg. Yer.	Targum Yerushalmi
Thess.	Thessalonians
Tim.	Timothy
Tob.	Tobit
Tohar.	Toharot
trans.	translator, translators; translated by; translation
v. (pl., vv.)	verse
Vg.	Vulgate
Virt.	*De Virtutibus (On the Virtues)*
Vita Con.	*De Vita Contemplativa (On the Contemplative Life)*
Vita Mos.	*De Vita Mosis (Life of Moses)*
vol. (pl., vols.)	volume
War	*The Jewish War*
Wisd. of Sol.	Wisdom of Solomon
Y.	Yerushalmi (Jerusalem Talmud)
Yad.	Yadayim
Yebam.	Yeb̲amot
Zebaḥ.	Zebaḥim
Zech.	Zechariah
Zeph.	Zephaniah
Zer.	Zeraim
×	by; multiplied by
+	plus
–	minus
=	equals; is equivalent to
?	uncertain; possibly; perhaps

List of Contributors

Philip Alexander
Oxford Centre for Post-Graduate Hebrew Studies, England

Robert T. Anderson
Michigan State University

Harold W. Attridge
University of Notre Dame

David Aune
Saint Xavier College, Chicago

Alan J. Avery-Peck
College of the Holy Cross

Mordecai Aviam
University of Rochester

Jason BeDuhn
Indiana University

Itzhaq Beit-Arieh
Tel Aviv University

Theodore Bergren
University of Richmond

Moshe Bernstein
Yeshiva University

Joseph Blenkinsopp
University of Notre Dame

Oded Borowski
Emory University

J. Patout Burns
Washington University

Marilyn J. Chiat
Minneapolis, Minnesota

R. J. Coggins
King's College, London

John J. Collins
University of Chicago

Nina L. Collins
The University, Leeds, England

Jamess Crenshaw
Duke University

Mary Ann Donovan
Jesuit School of Theology at Berkeley

Robert Doran
Amherst College

Tamara C. Eskenazi
Hebrew Union College

Alysia Fischer
Tucson, Arizona

Paul V. Flesher
University of Wyoming

David Frankfurter
Institute for Advanced Studies, Princeton

Sean Freyne
Trinity College, Dublin

Lester L. Grabbe
The University of Hull, England

William S. Green
University of Rochester

Dennis E. Groh
Garrett-Evangelical Theological Seminary

Ithamar Gruenwald
Tel Aviv University

Daniel J. Harrington
Weston School of Theology

Judith Hauptman
Jewish Theological Seminary, New York

E. Glenn Hinson
Baptist Theological Seminary
at Richmond

Yizhar Hirschfeld
Israel Antiquities Authority, Jerusalem

Larry Hoffman
Rye, New York

Richard Horsley
University of Massachusetts, Boston

Charles Kannengiesser
Montreal, Quebec

Howard Clark Kee
Boston University

Joan Keller
Clearwater, Florida

Judith Kovacs
University of Virginia

Nancy Lapp
Pittsburgh Theological Seminary

Amy-Jill Levine
Swarthmore College

Thomas R. W. Longstaff
Colby College

C. Thomas McCollough
Centre College of Kentucky

Sara Mandell
University of South Florida

Richard Mitchell
University of Illinois,
Urbana-Champaign

Frederick Murphy
College of the Holy Cross

Jacob Neusner
University of South Florida
Bard College

George W. E. Nickelsburg
University of Iowa

J. L. North
The University of Hull, England

Naomi Pasachoff
Williamstown, Massachusetts

Birger Pearson
University of California, Santa Barbara

Gary G. Porton
University of Illinois,
Urbana-Champaign

Gary A. Rendsburg
Cornell University

Lucille Roussin
New York, New York

D. T. Runia
University of Utrecht, The Netherlands

Anthony J. Saldarini
Boston College

Alison Salvesen
Oxford Centre for Postgraduate
Hebrew Studies, England

Eileen Schuller
McMaster University, Canada

Ephraim Stern
The Hebrew University, Jerusalem

Elizabeth Strange
Sarasota, Florida

James F. Strange
University of South Florida

James R. Strange
Tampa, Florida

Thomas Tobin
Chicago, Illinois

Pieter W. van der Horst
University of Utrecht,
The Netherlands

James C. Vanderkam
University of Notre Dame

Andrew G. Vaughn
Princeton Theological Seminary

Shelley Wachsmann
Texas A & M University

Sidnie Ann White
Albright College

Donald F. Winslow
Episcopal Divinity School,
Cambridge, Massachusetts

Benjamin G. Wright III
Lehigh University

Tzvee Zahavy
University of Minnesota

Maps

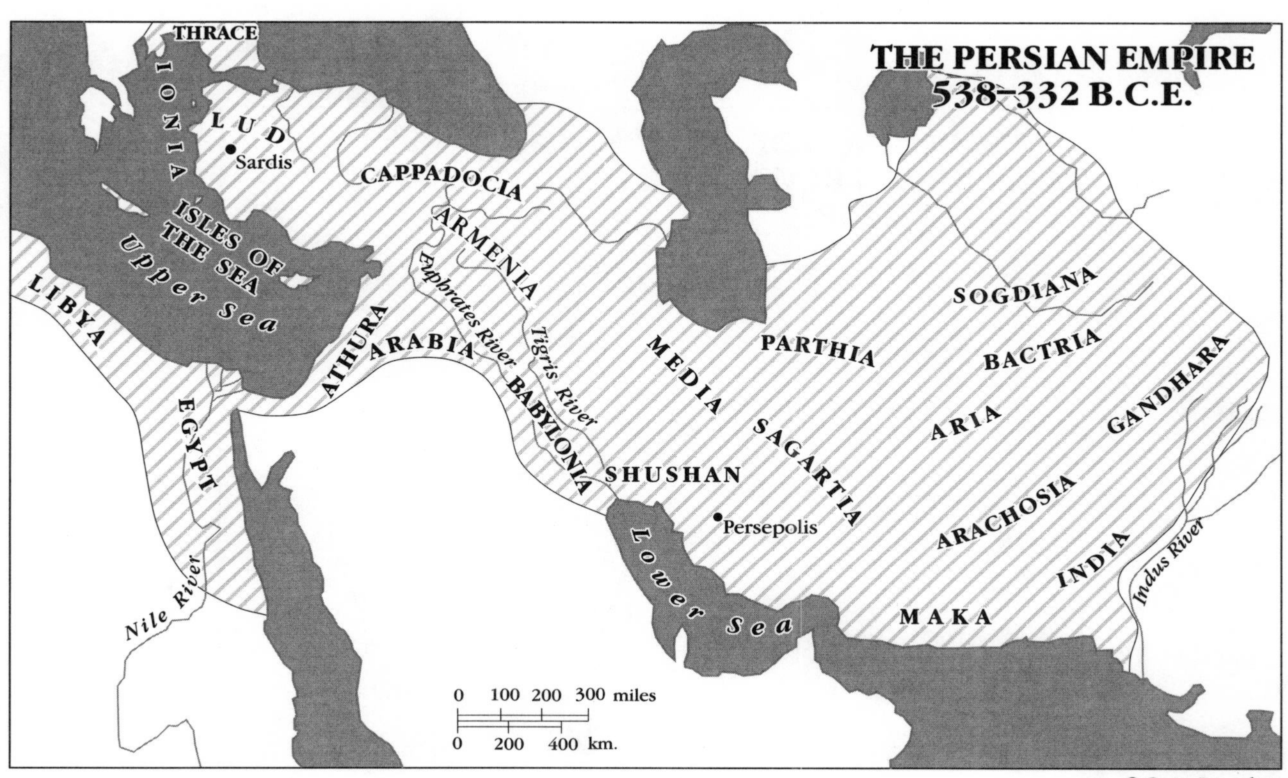
THE PERSIAN EMPIRE
538–332 B.C.E.
THRACE
IONIA
LUD
Sardis
CAPPADOCIA
ISLES OF THE SEA
Upper Sea
ARMENIA
LIBYA
Euphrates River
Tigris River
ATHURA
ARABIA
BABYLONIA
MEDIA
PARTHIA
SOGDIANA
BACTRIA
ARIA
GANDHARA
EGYPT
SAGARTIA
SHUSHAN
Persepolis
ARACHOSIA
INDIA
Indus River
Nile River
Lower Sea
MAKA
0 100 200 300 miles
0 200 400 km.

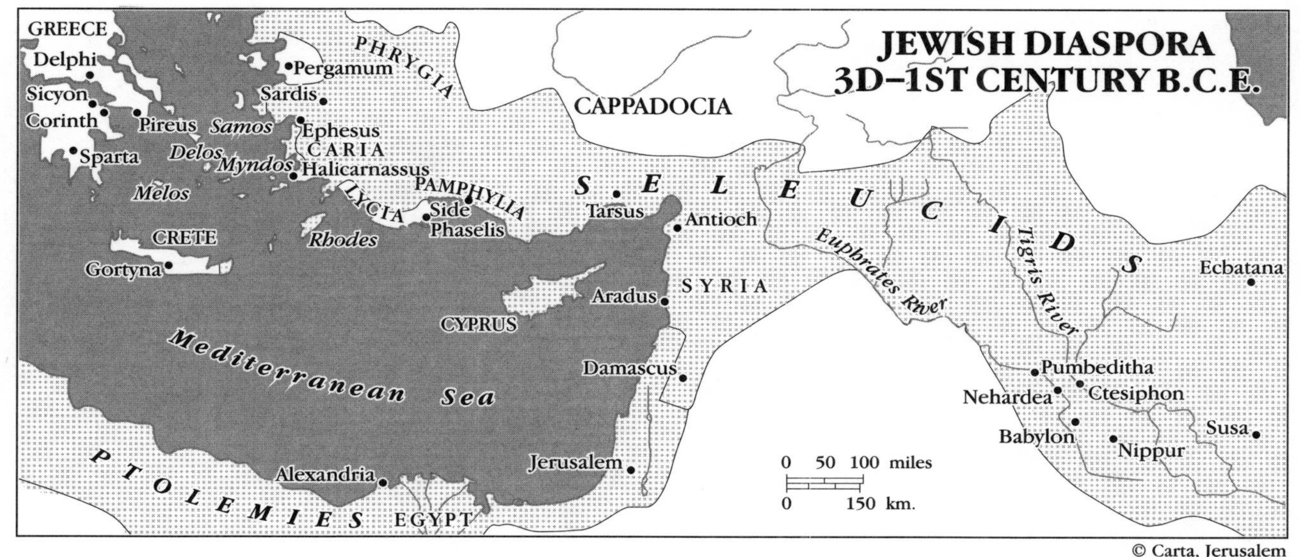
JEWISH DIASPORA
3D–1ST CENTURY B.C.E.
GREECE
Delphi
Sicyon
Corinth
Pireus
Sparta
Pergamum
PHRYGIA
Sardis
Samos
Ephesus
CARIA
Delos
Myndos
Halicarnassus
Melos
PAMPHYLIA
LYCIA
Side
Phaselis
CRETE
Rhodes
Gortyna
CAPPADOCIA
S E L E U C I D S
Tarsus
Antioch
Euphrates River
Tigris River
Ecbatana
SYRIA
Aradus
CYPRUS
Mediterranean Sea
Damascus
Pumbeditha
Nehardea
Ctesiphon
Babylon
Nippur
Susa
PTOLEMIES
Alexandria
Jerusalem
EGYPT
0 50 100 miles
0 150 km.

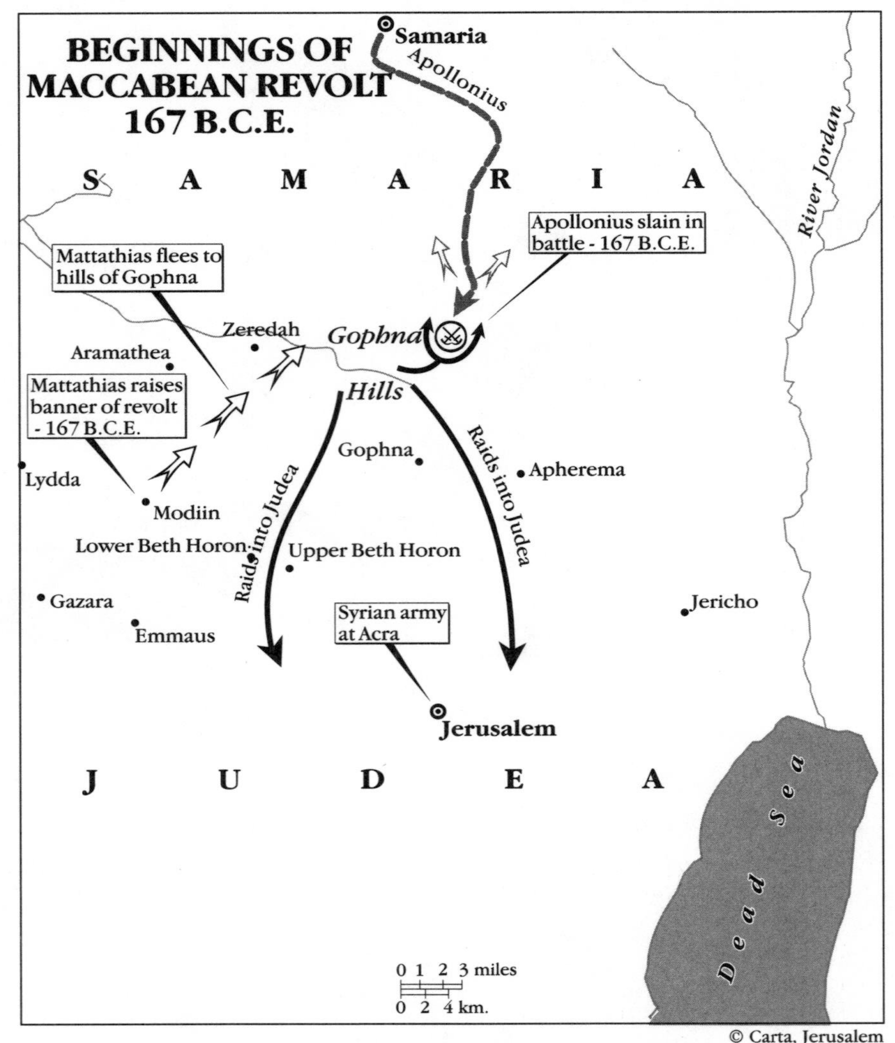
BEGINNINGS OF MACCABEAN REVOLT 167 B.C.E.
Samaria
Apollonius
S A M A R I A
River Jordan
Apollonius slain in battle - 167 B.C.E.
Mattathias flees to hills of Gophna
Zeredah
Gophna
Aramathea
Mattathias raises banner of revolt - 167 B.C.E.
Hills
Gophna
Apherema
Raids into Judea
Raids into Judea
Lydda
Modiin
Lower Beth Horon
Upper Beth Horon
Gazara
Emmaus
Syrian army at Acra
Jericho
Jerusalem
J U D E A
Dead Sea
0 1 2 3 miles
0 2 4 km.
© Carta, Jerusalem

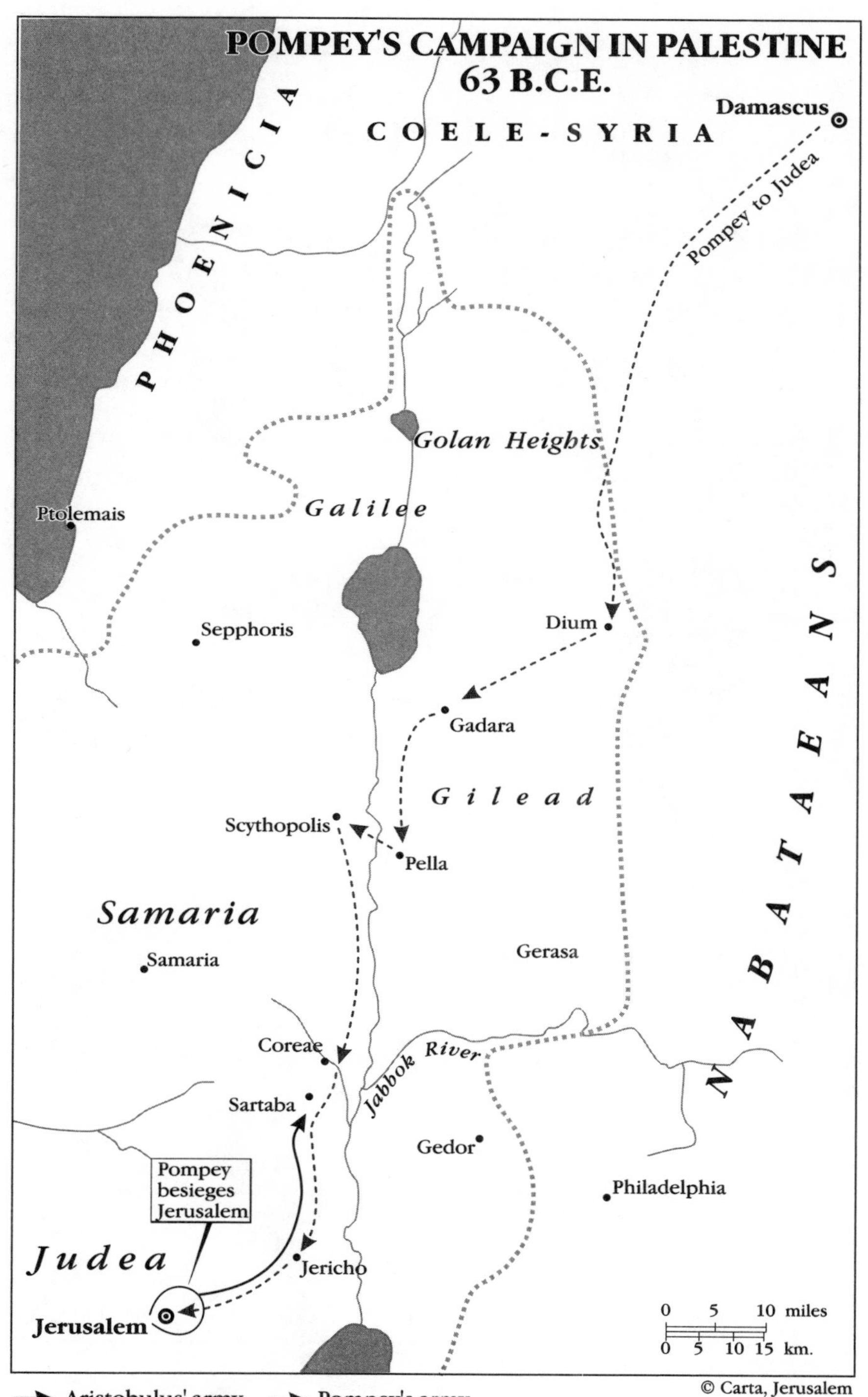
POMPEY'S CAMPAIGN IN PALESTINE
63 B.C.E.
Damascus
COELE-SYRIA
PHOENICIA
Pompey to Judea
Golan Heights
Galilee
Ptolemais
Sepphoris
Dium
Gadara
Gilead
Scythopolis
Pella
Samaria
Samaria
Gerasa
NABATAEANS
Coreae
Jabbok River
Sartaba
Gedor
Pompey besieges Jerusalem
Philadelphia
Judea
Jericho
Jerusalem
0 5 10 miles
0 5 10 15 km.
© Carta, Jerusalem
Aristobulus' army
Pompey's army

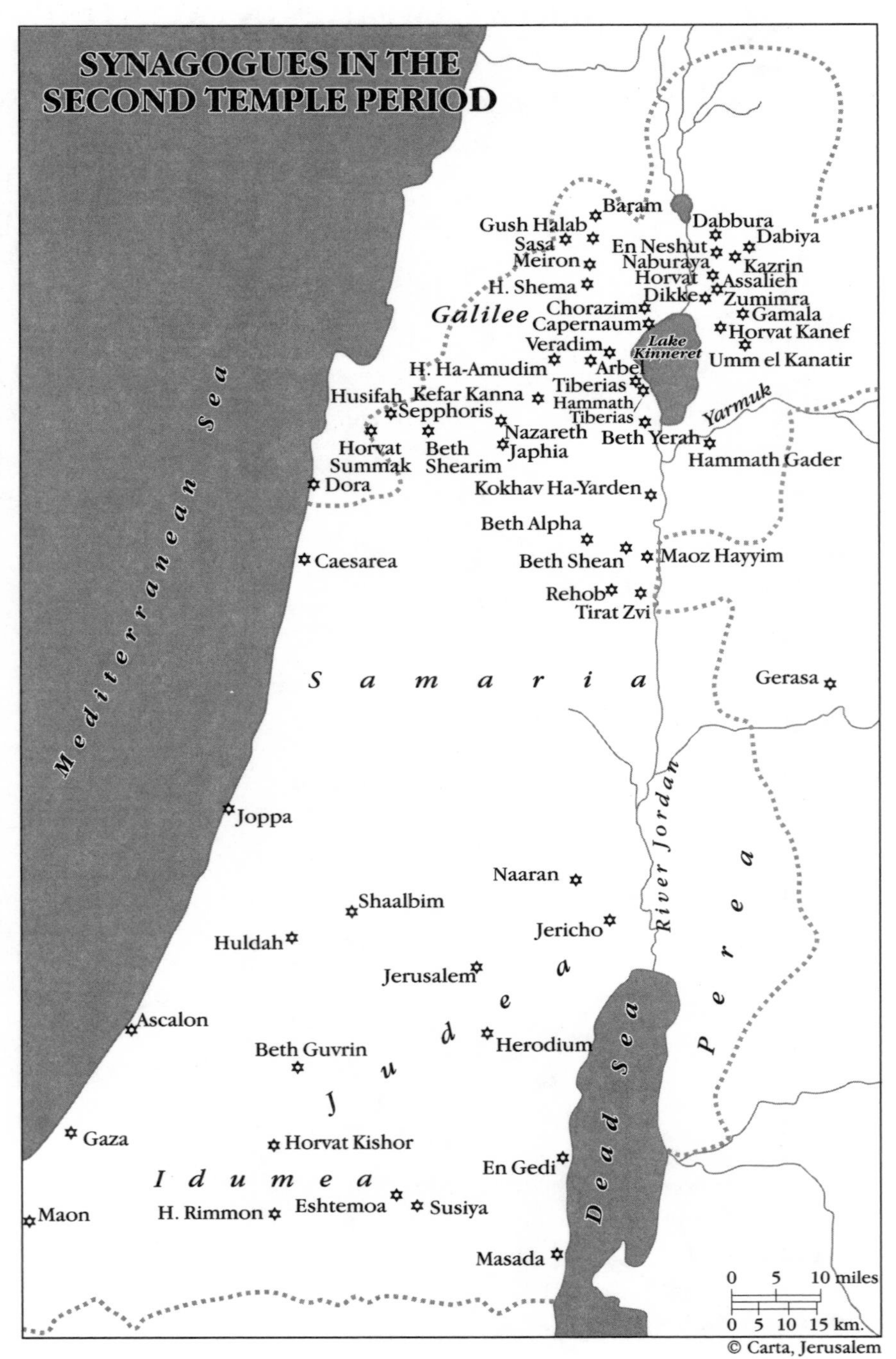

SYNAGOGUES IN THE SECOND TEMPLE PERIOD
Baram
Gush Halab
Sasa
Meiron
H. Shema
Dabbura
Dabiya
En Neshut
Naburaya
Kazrin
Horvat
Assalieh
Dikke
Zumimra
Gamala
Galilee
Chorazim
Capernaum
Horvat Kanef
Veradim
Lake Kinneret
Umm el Kanatir
H. Ha-Amudim
Arbel
Tiberias
Husifah
Kefar Kanna
Hammath Tiberias
Sepphoris
Yarmuk
Nazareth
Beth Yerah
Horvat Summak
Beth Shearim
Japhia
Hammath Gader
Dora
Kokhav Ha-Yarden
Mediterranean Sea
Beth Alpha
Caesarea
Beth Shean
Maoz Hayyim
Rehob
Tirat Zvi
Samaria
Gerasa
Joppa
River Jordan
Naaran
Shaalbim
Jericho
Huldah
Perea
Jerusalem
Judea
Ascalon
Herodium
Beth Guvrin
Dead Sea
Gaza
Horvat Kishor
En Gedi
Idumea
Maon
H. Rimmon
Eshtemoa
Susiya
Masada
0 5 10 miles
0 5 10 15 km.
© Carta, Jerusalem

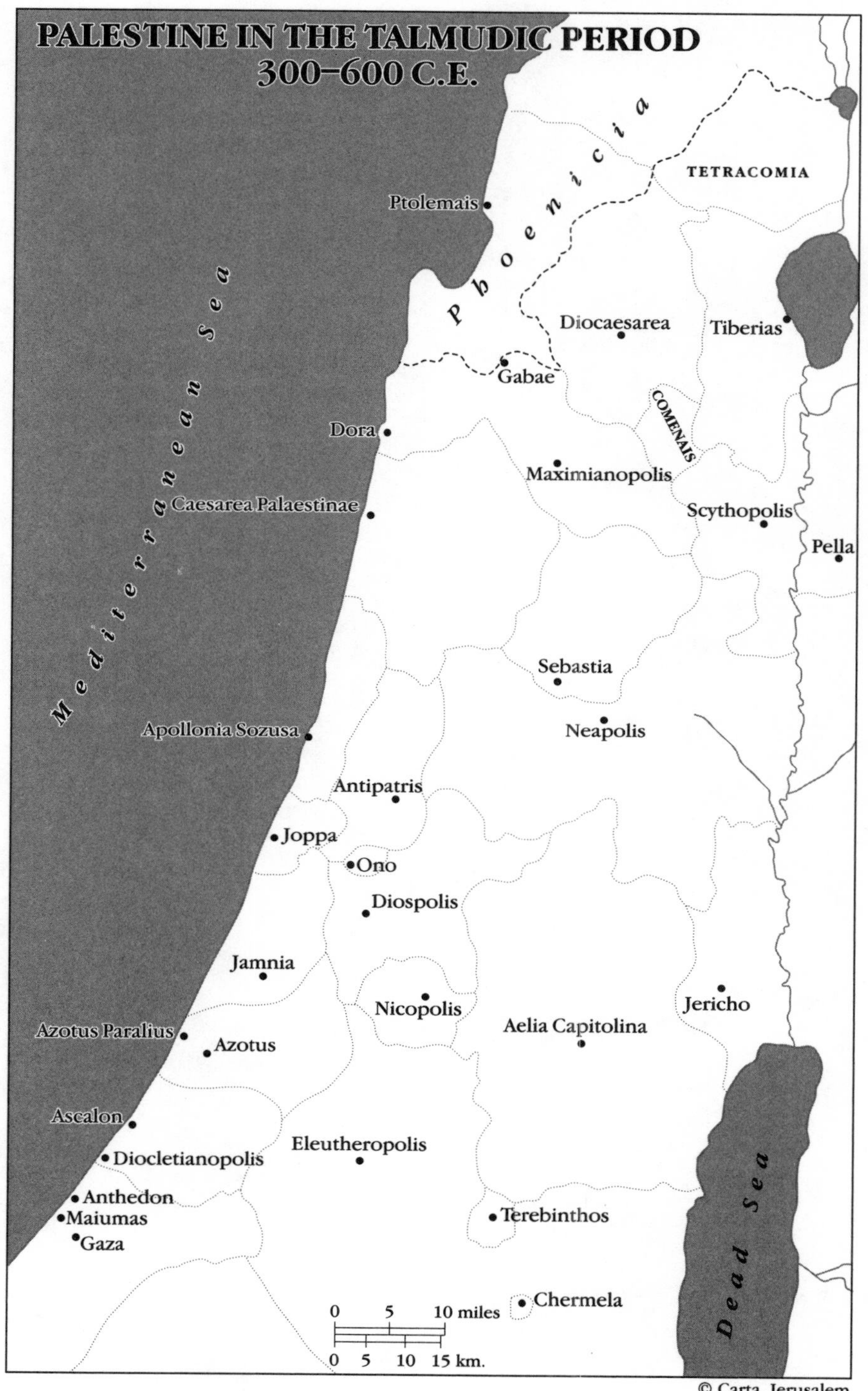
PALESTINE IN THE TALMUDIC PERIOD
300–600 C.E.
Phoenicia
TETRACOMIA
Ptolemais
Mediterranean Sea
Diocaesarea
Tiberias
Gabae
COMENAIS
Dora
Maximianopolis
Caesarea Palaestinae
Scythopolis
Pella
Sebastia
Neapolis
Apollonia Sozusa
Antipatris
Joppa
Ono
Diospolis
Jamnia
Jericho
Nicopolis
Aelia Capitolina
Azotus Paralius
Azotus
Ascalon
Eleutheropolis
Diocletianopolis
Dead Sea
Anthedon
Maiumas
Gaza
Terebinthos
Chermela
0 5 10 miles
0 5 10 15 km.

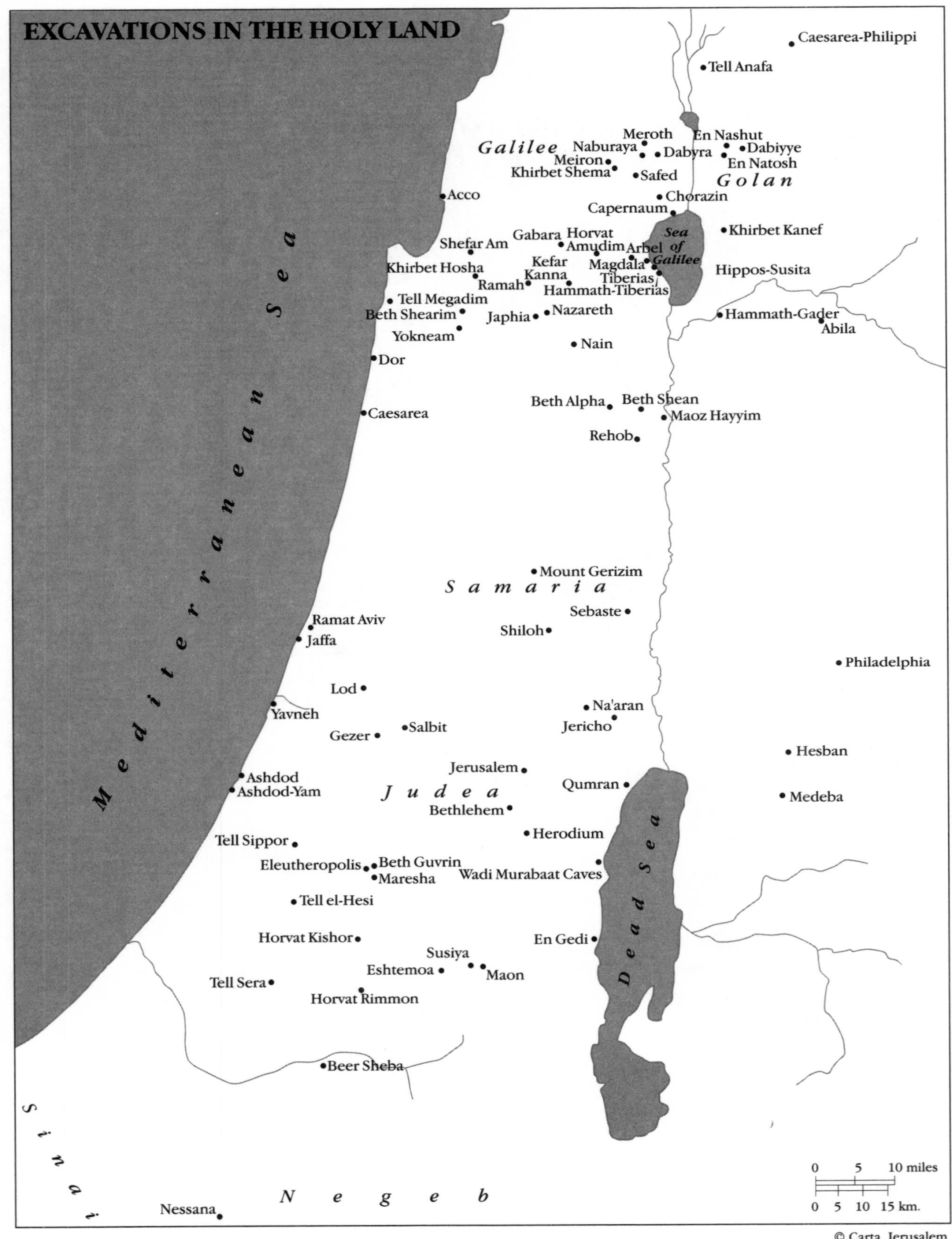

EXCAVATIONS IN THE HOLY LAND
Caesarea-Philippi
Tell Anafa
Meroth
En Nashut
Galilee
Naburaya
Dabyra
Dabiyye
Meiron
En Natosh
Khirbet Shema
Safed
Golan
Acco
Chorazin
Capernaum
Khirbet Kanef
Sea of Galilee
Shefar Am
Gabara
Horvat Amudim
Arbel
Khirbet Hosha
Kefar Kanna
Magdala
Tiberias
Hippos-Susita
Ramah
Hammath-Tiberias
Tell Megadim
Beth Shearim
Japhia
Nazareth
Hammath-Gader
Abila
Yokneam
Nain
Dor
Mediterranean Sea
Caesarea
Beth Alpha
Beth Shean
Maoz Hayyim
Rehob
Mount Gerizim
Samaria
Sebaste
Ramat Aviv
Shiloh
Jaffa
Philadelphia
Lod
Na'aran
Yavneh
Jericho
Gezer
Salbit
Hesban
Jerusalem
Ashdod
Qumran
Ashdod-Yam
Judea
Medeba
Bethlehem
Herodium
Tell Sippor
Dead Sea
Eleutheropolis
Beth Guvrin
Maresha
Wadi Murabaat Caves
Tell el-Hesi
Horvat Kishor
En Gedi
Susiya
Eshtemoa
Maon
Tell Sera
Horvat Rimmon
Beer Sheba
Sinai
Negeb
Nessana
0 5 10 miles
0 5 10 15 km.
© Carta. Jerusalem

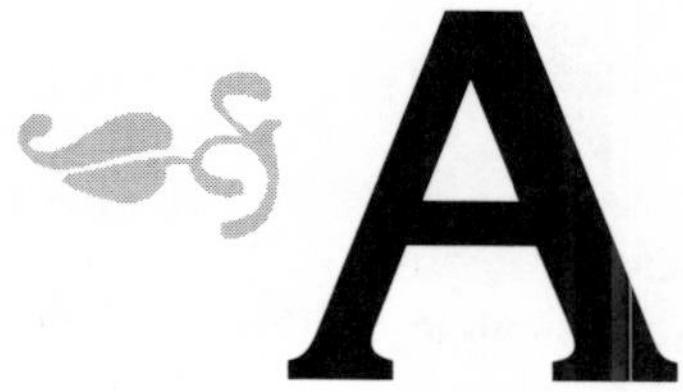

Aaron ancient Israel's first high priest and the patriarch of its priesthood. Where the pentateuchal accounts depict Aaron performing nonpriestly roles, he is Moses' subordinate. In other texts, the action turns on his priestly calling, status, and activities (Exod. 28–29; Lev. 8; Num. 16–17). As first high priest, he is the patriarch of the priesthood, and "the sons of Aaron" and "Aaron and his sons" are cliches that serve as metonyms for future Aaronic priests and high priests. Psalm 115:10, 12 mentions the priests as "the house of Aaron" alongside the laity, "the house of Israel."

Second Temple Jewish texts highlight the priestly status and functions of Aaron and his sons. Ecclesiasticus 45:6–22 emphasizes God's everlasting covenant with him and his descendants, and 50:1–21 glorifies Simon who presides over the cult and "the sons of Aaron." In 1 Maccabees 7:13–14, the Hasidim make peace with Alcimus because he is "a priest of the line of Aaron." The Qumranic combination of "Aaron" and "Israel" parallels the usage in Psalm 115 (1QS 8:5–6; CD 1:7), and several texts anticipate the coming of "the anointed one(s) of Aaron and Israel" (1QS 9:11; CD 12:23–13:1, 19:11, 20:1).

Several texts emphasize Levi rather than Aaron. Testament of Levi 2–6 describes Levi's call, and chapter 12 traces his genealogy back only to Amram. Although Jubilees 30:18–19 recounts Levi's call and 31:13–15 refers to his descendants, the book never mentions the brother of Moses, its alleged author. The omissions are odd in literature preserved at Qumran, where other texts feature Aaron and his descendants. Perhaps they are testimonies to the obscure history of the levitical priesthood.

The Epistle to the Hebrews portrays Jesus as a "priest after the order of Melchizedek," whose activity supersedes the Aaronic priesthood and its covenant (Heb. 7–9). Postbiblical Christian texts draw on this motif, and some interpret Jesus' anointing at his baptism with reference to his priesthood.

A<u>b</u> eleventh month of the Jewish calendar, corresponding to July/August

A<u>b</u>, Ninth of fast day commemorating five disasters that fell on that day: the divine decree that those in the Exodus from Egypt should not enter the promised land; the destruction of the First Temple in 586 B.C.E.; the destruction of the Second Temple in 70 C.E.; the taking of Betar, where the rebels against Rome in 135 C.E. had made their last stand; and the razing of Jerusalem in 13 C.E. after that same war. The day stands for Israel's national disasters and is observed through fasting, prayer, and reading of the Book of Lamentations.

Abaddon (Heb., destruction) the disintegration of the human being caused by death. In the Hebrew Bible it stands in parallel to Sheol or is a metonymy for it. In the Hodayot (1QH 3:19), one is rescued from Sheol Abaddon when one enters the Qumran Community. Revelation 9:11 identifies Abaddon as the angel of the abyss, translating it "Apollyon" (Gr., destroyer).

Abadim (Heb., slaves) title of one of the so-called minor tractates of the Talmud. It consists of a collection of tannaitic sources in three chapters, containing primarily rules about the purchase, manumission, and sale of slaves.

abandoned woman (Heb.: *agunah*) a woman not free to remarry, held in a marital relationship although separated from her husband because the husband cannot be proved to be dead, because his whereabouts are unknown, or because he is unwilling to give her a writ of divorce. She is abandoned in that she cannot enter into a legal marriage. Under Jewish law, only the husband can provide a writ of divorce to the wife; if he is unavailable or unwilling, the woman has no recourse. Absence of proof of the husband's death may impose the status of *agunah* on the putative widow.

Abayye (d. 339 C.E.) Babylonian amora; raised by his uncle, Rabbah bar Naḥmani; student of his uncle and of Joseph b. Ḥama, successive heads of the academy at Pumbedita. After Joseph's death in 333 C.E., Abayye took over that position, which he held until his own death. Abayye is known for his disputes with Ra<u>b</u>a, which were deemed so important that, anachronistically, even Yoḥanan b. Zakkai was reputed to have known of them (B. Sukkot 28a).

Abayye's father, Kaylil, died before he was born, and his mother died in his birth. He was raised by his uncle, who early on recognized his intellectual strengths (B. Berakhot 33b). In his youth, Abayye took care of his fields at night in order to be able to study by day (B. Gittin 60b). Later in life, he apparently had greater wealth, employing tenant farmers (B. Ketu<u>b</u>ot 60b) and trading in wine (B. Berakhot 56a).

Abayye's disputes with Ra<u>b</u>a comprise such an important element of the Babylonian Talmud that the phrase "debates of Abayye and Ra<u>b</u>a" is commonly used to refer to talmudic dialectics in general. Except for six specific cases, the law follows Ra<u>b</u>a's view. In contrast to Ra<u>b</u>a's independent reasoning, Abayye preferred to develop arguments based upon statements of earlier sages (B. Eru<u>b</u>in 3a), which he would reduce to general principles. Abayye also cited popular maxims and recognized the practice of the common people as an appropriate indicator of the correct law. He frequently mentioned his foster mother's folk remedies and dietary principles, arguing that whatever was done for the sake of health was exempt from the prohibition against pagan practices.

Abayye is recognized as the first authority to distinguish between the unembellished meaning of a verse of scripture and its interpretation (B. Ḥullin 133a). He learned Palestinian biblical interpretations from Dimi, whom he frequently asked to explain how a verse was interpreted in the "west," that is, the Land of Israel.

Abayye Kashisha Babylonian amora of the third century C.E.; designated Kashisha (the Elder) to distinguish him from the later, better-known amora Abayye. Abayye Kashisha is known for his statement comparing controversy to the planks on a bridge, which become fixed in place through constant treading (B. Sanhedrin 7a).

Abba **1.** (Aram., father) Some assert that "Abba" is unique to Jesus and displays a special intimacy (i.e., daddy), but neither claim is supported by textual and philological evidence. Of the three early occurrences of the Aramaic term in the Gospels and Epistles, one (Mark 14:36) is otherwise unattested and plausibly redactional rather than authentic to Jesus, and the others (Gal. 4:6; Rom. 8:15) are liturgical cries suggesting heirs of the Spirit, not little children in relation to their father. The "father" (Gr.: *ho patēr*) in Matthew 23:9 may indicate the Aramaic title as found in rabbinic sources (e.g., Abba Saul). *See also* FATHER, GOD AS.

2. amora of the late third and early fourth centuries C.E. A disciple of Ḥuna and Judah, he settled in Palestine, living first in Caesaria and then in Tiberias. He frequently revisited Babylonia, transmitting Babylonian teachings in the Land of Israel and vice versa. Abba is referred to in Babylonian academies as "our teacher in the land of Israel" (B. Sanhedrin 17b).

Abba Arikha (d. 247 C.E.) Babylonian amora; designated "the tall" on account of his height, but generally known simply as Ra<u>b</u>. Abba Arikha followed Ḥiyya, his uncle, to Palestine, where he studied with Judah the Patriarch; later, he founded the academy at Sura, in Babylonia. Several talmudic passages indicate that he is accounted as a Tannaitic authority, such that he can dispute opinions stated in the Mishnah (see B. Ketu<u>b</u>ot 8a). His name appears in the Tosefta (Besah 1:7), where he is referred to as Rabbi Abba.

Abba Arikha's importance is signified by his designation as Ra<u>b</u>, which reflects his status as "the teacher [*ra<u>b</u>*] of the entire diaspora" (B. Besah 9a). In addition to his distinguished family, which traced its origins to Shimei, brother of King David (B. Sanhedrin 5a), and alongside his position in his uncle Ḥiyya's household, Abba Arikha frequented the house of Judah the Patriarch (B. Berakhot 46b) and was a member of Judah's academy (see B.

Ḥullin 137b) and court (B. Gittin 59a). Judah himself granted Abba Arikha rabbinic ordination.

Rab̲ is generally credited with establishing the characteristic literary style and interests of the Babylonian Talmud, its focus upon the Mishnah as a foundational text, its use of supplemental Tannaitic teachings, and its concern for the theoretical explanations and practical applications of the law. Rab̲'s disputes with Samuel, who brought high repute to the academy at Nehardea, form the backbone of numerous talmudic passages. Additionally, Rab̲'s numerous disciples, many of them also students of Samuel, amplified his teachings and ensured that his thinking would be a central component of all talmudic law.

Alongside his legal statements, Abba Arikha is responsible for a vast array of exegetical and homiletical sayings, preserved in the Jerusalem Talmud and in the midrashic compilations of the Land of Israel. In his public discourses he spoke of the importance of study and of the value to humans of ritual observance, which he saw as improving people's morals. Through such exhortations and, in particular, through his legal study, Abba Arikha raised the status of the Babylonian community and its academies to a leading position within Jewry. He was mourned by the entire Babylonian community and, understanding him to have a special power, people took dirt from his grave for medicinal purposes (B. Sanhedrin 47b).

Abba b. Abba rabbinic authority of the early third century C.E., at the nexus of the Tannaitic and Amoraic periods; always referred to in the Babylonian Talmud after his famous son, as "Samuel's father." A native of Nehardea, he spent time in the Land of Israel, where he studied in the academy of Judah the Patriarch. Upon his return to Babylonia, he was a colleague of Levi b. Sisi, with whom he reportedly experienced a revelation in the synagogue at Nehardea (B. Megillah 29a).

Abba b. Ḥana *see* RABBAH B. ḤUNA

Abba b. Ḥiyya b. Abba Palestinian amora of the early fourth century C.E.; the son of Ḥiyya b. Abba. He transmitted sayings of Yoḥanan that he had learned from his father, who had been Yoḥanan's student (Y. Sotah 9:16, 24c; B. Ḥullin 86b).

Abba b. Ḥuna *see* RABBAH B. ḤUNA

Abba b. Kahana Palestinian amora of the late third century C.E. A student of Rab̲, best known for his interpretations of scripture, he indicates the relationships between biblical personalities (e.g., Dina as the wife of Job; Gen. Rabbah 19:12), identifies geographical sites (e.g., at B. Kiddushin 72a), and embellishes biblical narratives with stories and tales. His teachings often reflect contemporary hardships (e.g., Lev. Rabbah 15:9, referring to heavy taxation), and he speaks with expectation of the coming of the Messiah (Lam. Rabbah 1:41).

Abba b. Memel Palestinian amora of the late third century C.E., active in the circle of Ammi at Tiberias. Reputed as a legal authority, he argued for severe limitations on the use of verbal analogies in scripture as a foundation for deciding the law (Y. Pesaḥim 6:1, 33a).

Abba b. Ulla Babylonian amora active in the fourth century C.E.; often referred to as Rab̲a Ulla. He is cited in legal contexts in conjunction with Ulla (B. Yeb̲amot 77a), Rab̲a b. Joseph b. Ḥama (B. Erub̲in 21b), and Pappa (B. Ḥullin 91a).

Abba b. Zab̲dai Palestinian amora of the third century C.E. He studied in Babylonia under Rab̲ and Ḥuna, and then settled in Tiberias, where he was a colleague of Ammi and Assi. The Talmud reports that he prayed in a loud voice (Y. Berakhot 4:1, 7a).

Abba Eleazer b. Gamla Tannaitic authority; a contemporary of Judah the Patriarch in the late second and early third centuries C.E.

Abba Ḥalafta *see* ḤALAFTA

Abba Ḥanin Tannaitic authority active in the mid-second century C.E., sometimes cited as Abba Ḥanan. He was active in the circle of Eliezer b. Hyrcanus, whose teachings he transmits in all of his preserved statements. Abba Ḥanin's name appears exclusively in the legal midrashic compilations.

Abbahu Palestinian amora of the late third century C.E. He studied under Yoḥanan, Simeon b. Lakish, and Eleazar b. Pedat and ultimately became head of the academy at Caesaria. Abbahu knew Greek and was influential with the Roman government (see B. Ḥagigah 14a, which refers to the favor Abbahu brought his people in the court of Caesar). Among his prominent students were Jeremiah, Jonah, and Yose. He had two sons, Zeira and Ḥanina.

Abbahu is recalled as wise, handsome, and wealthy (B. Bab̲a Metzia 84a). In light of his knowledge of Greek and his secular learning, he was influential with the proconsular government (B. Ketub̲ot 17a). At the same time, he was known for his modesty, which, following his ordination, led him to decline appointment as head of the academy in favor of Abba of Akko, who was in debt and who Abbahu felt needed the position more (B. Sotah 40a). He lived by his understanding that it is better to be one of the persecuted than a persecutor (B. Bab̲a Kamma 93a) and that the world endures on account of those who abase themselves (Y. Berakhot 5:1, 8d).

Abbahu was a distinguished haggadist who engaged in disputes with both Christians and sectarians of his day. Regarding Christianity, he said, "If a man should tell you, 'I am God,' he is a liar; [if he says,] 'I am the son of man,' he will regret it; [if he says,] 'I shall go up to heaven,' he said it, but he cannot do it" (Y. Taanit 2:1, 65b). Similarly, Abbahu ostracized the Samaritan priests in his town, explaining that, unlike their ancestors, whom prior generations of Jews had treated as Jewish, this generation of priests followed corrupt practices (Y. A̱bodah Zarah 5:4, 44d).

Abba Issi *see* ABBA YOSE B. ḤANIN

Abba Joseph *see* ABBA YOSE B. ḤANIN

Abba of Akko Palestinian amora of the late third and early fourth centuries C.E., known for his modesty. At B. Sotah 40a, Abbahu reports that Abba of Akko was so humble that he did not even take exception when, after he said one thing, the amora who repeated his teaching for the students stated a different position. No legal statements are preserved in Abba of Akko's name.

Abba Saul Tannaitic authority of the mid-second century C.E., possibly a student of Akiḇa, whom he quotes several times. He appears in dispute with Judah b. Ilai and Meir. He reports that his occupation was as an undertaker (B. Niddah 24b; see also T. Niddah 8:7). By contrast, Abin b. Aḥa reports in Isaac's name that Abba Saul was a baker in the house of Judah the Patriarch (B. Pesaḥim 34a).

Abba Saul b. Batnit Tannaitic authority active in the late first and early second centuries C.E. A Jerusalem shopkeeper reputed for his honesty, he would fill measuring vessels with oil and wine, to be picked up on a festival (M. Besah 3:8). He once brought as a gift to the Temple 300 jars of oil, accumulated from drops left in measuring vessels, to which he believed he had no right (T. Besah 3:8). T. Menaḥot 13:21 reports a diatribe that he and Abba Yose b. Ḥanin recited against the conduct of the priesthood in the last years of the Second Temple.

Abba Yose b. Dostai Tannaitic authority active in the mid-second century C.E. He does not appear in the Mishnah, but is found in the Tosefta, as a tradent (transmitter of statements) for Eliezer and Yose the Galilean. In Sifre Numbers 42, Judah the Patriarch cites in his name homilies reconciling conflicting biblical passages.

Abba Yose b. Ḥanan *see* ABBA YOSE B. ḤANIN

Abba Yose b. Ḥanin Tannaitic authority active in the second half of the first century C.E. He describes the location and number of the gates of the Temple court (M. Middot 2:6) and details the order of the Temple service (T. Sukkot 4:15). In conjunction with Abba Saul b. Batnit, he also speaks against the high priests of the final years of the Second Temple (T. Menaḥot 13:21). His name alternatively occurs as Abba Joseph, Abba Issi, Abba Yose b. Ḥanan, and Abba Yose b. Yoḥanan.

Abba Yose b. Yoḥanan *see* ABBA YOSE B. ḤANIN

aḇ beit din (Heb., father of the court) in the Talmudic period, the vice president of the rabbinic court. The office is first referred to at M. Ḥagigah 2:2, where it is explained that, of the individuals listed as "pairs" (*zugot*) at M. A̱bot 1:1–15, the first person listed was the president of the court and the second listed was the "father." Talmudic tradition, followed by some contemporary scholars, asserts that the institution is ancient. The Talmud explains that while the biblical Saul was the president of the court, his son, Jonathan, served as the "father."

The rabbinic literature enumerates the duties of the *aḇ beit din,* specifies the method of appointment (this was to be done orally), and notes limitations on his authority (he could not render judgment in the presence of the president of the court). In the gaonic period, the title of *aḇ beit din* designated the deputy to the gaon of the academy.

Abdimi *see* DIMI

Abel second son of Adam and Eve who was murdered by his brother, Cain, because God had accepted Abel's sacrifice but not Cain's (Gen. 4:1–16). Tradition sees Abel as a prototype of the martyred righteous one. In his vision of the mountain of the dead, Enoch sees the spirit of Abel pleading for vengeance on the descendants of Cain (1 Enoch 22:5–7). The scene plays on Genesis 4:10, with the spirit corresponding to the *nefesh* (soul, or life) that resides in Abel's blood (cf. Gen. 9:4). According to the Testament of Abraham 12–13 (A), Abel is enthroned as the heavenly judge of all humanity. The role builds on the image of Abel as avenger, nuancing it with the notion that the persecuted and murdered righteous one will judge his enemies (cf. Wisd. of Sol. 5:1–2). Perhaps also related to Wisdom of Solomon 2 and 5 is the version of the Genesis 4 story in Targum Neofiti Genesis 4:7–8, where the quarrel between Cain and Abel involves a dispute about the reality of retribution after death. In the New Testament, typical of its contrast between the old and the new covenants, the Epistle to the Hebrews emphasizes that Jesus' efficacious blood speaks more graciously than the avenging cry of Abel's blood (Heb. 12:24).

Abel-Main site in Upper Galilee to be identified with biblical Abel-Beth-Maacah, present Tell Abil, 7 kilometers west-northwest of Tell Dan; also known as Abel-Maim. In 1 Enoch 13:9 the fallen watchers sit there mourning their fate. The 1 Enoch text plays on the double meaning of *abel* (Heb., meadow; Heb. and Aram., to mourn), identifying Abel-Maim (literally, "the meadow of waters") as the place whose waters are the watchers' tears. Abel-Main is mentioned in a Qumran Aramaic fragment of a related text, Testament of Levi 2:3, where the Greek translation has corrupted the name to Abel Maoul.

Abgar V (4 B.C.–50 C.E.) king of Edessa. Eusebius claims that Abgar exchanged letters with Jesus in which he requested that Jesus travel to Edessa in order to cure him of a disease. Jesus responded that his mission was limited to Palestine but that he would send an apostle to heal the king. Eusebius continues that after the Ascension, the apostle Thaddaeus traveled to Edessa, healed the king, and evangelized the kingdom. Some scholars claim that Abgar V allied with Gotarzes, a member of the Parthian nobility, against the Jews in Nisibis and that this led Eusebius to assume that he was Christian. Others claim that Eusebius has confused Abgar V with Abgar IX (179–216 C.E.), who did convert to Christianity.

Abidarna identified in the Babylonian Talmud, Ab̲odah Zarah 64b–65a, as Rab̲ Judah's gentile friend. Although Jews were forbidden from interacting with Gentiles on the latter's holy days, Judah sent Abidarna a gift on the day of a gentile festival, claiming that Abidarna did not worship idols. This indicates the flexibility of Jewish law.

Abimelech character in the Paraleipomena of Jeremiah who is identical with Ebed-Melech, the Ethiopian eunuch who befriended Jeremiah (Jer. 38:7–13, 39:15–18; cf. Par. Jer. 3:12–13). In the apocryphal story, Jeremiah gives him special consideration for his kindnesses, and he functions as a bridging character in the narrative, which spans sixty-six years.

Ab̲imi (contraction of Abba Immi) **1.** Babylonian scholar of the third century C.E., always referred to without his father's name

2. Babylonian amora of the fourth century C.E., a student of Rabbah b. Naḥmani. In the Jerusalem Talmud, he is called Ab̲imi, brother of Hefa; in the Babylonian Talmud, he is Ab̲imi b. Raḥba.

Ab̲in **1.** Palestinian amora of the third century C.E., a student of Rab̲, referred to in the Babylonian Talmud as Rab̲in Saba

2. younger contemporary of the above-mentioned authority, referred to in the Palestinian Talmud as a colleague of Measha, Jeremiah, Isaac Nappaḥa, and Ḥanina b. Pappa

3. frequently cited Palestinian authority of the late fourth century C.E., possibly the son of the first Ab̲in described above, who was a student of Jeremiah, traveled often to Babylonia, and is referred to in both Talmuds

Ab̲ina II b. Huna *see* RAB̲INA II B. ḤUNA

ab̲odah *see* SERVICE

Ab̲odah Zarah (Heb., alien form of divine worship) Mishnah tractate devoted to idolatry. The tractate supplies rules and regulations to carry out the fundamental scriptural commandments about the destruction of idols and all things having to do with idolatry, with special reference to commercial relationships, matters pertaining to idols, and the prohibition of wine of which part has served as a libation to an idol. Anything a Gentile is not likely to use for the worship of an idol is not prohibited. Anything that may serve not as part of idolatry but as an appurtenance thereto is prohibited for Israelite use but permitted for Israelite commerce. Anything that serves for idolatry is prohibited for use and for benefit. Certain further assumptions about Gentiles, not pertinent specifically to idolatry, are expressed. There are three parts to the tractate: (1) commercial relationships with Gentiles (1:1–2:7); (2) idols (3:1–4:7); and (3) libation wine (4:8–5:12). Gentiles are assumed routinely to practice bestiality, bloodshed, and fornication, without limit or restriction. Jews may not sell to Gentiles bears, lions, or anything else that is a public danger. Jews may not help Gentiles build a basilica, scaffold, stadium, or judges' tribunal. Jews may not make ornaments for an idol, sell produce that is not yet harvested to Gentiles, or sell land in the Holy Land to Gentiles. Jews may not leave cattle in Gentiles' inns, because Gentiles are suspect in regard to bestiality. The following items belonging to Gentiles are prohibited, and the prohibition extends to deriving any benefit from them at all: wine, vinegar, earthenware that absorbs wine, and hides pierced at the heart. Both Talmuds address this tractate.

abomination (Heb.: *sheketz, shikutz, shakatz*; Gr.: *bdelyssomai, bdelygma*) sacrilege, something abominable or detestable to YHWH, and hence to Israelites. The term has cultic connotations and applies to idols and unclean foods and to one's condition through association with these. A specific and notorious example was the Abomination of Desolation or Desolating Sacrilege that Antiochus IV installed in the Jerusalem Temple.

Abomination of Desolation objects that desecrated the Jerusalem Temple in 167 B.C.E. The Hebrew phrase *shikutz meshomem* (Dan. 11:31, 12:11) is also translated as "abomination which makes desolate" (NRSV) or "appalling abomination" (JPS); in Greek, it is *bdelygma eremoseos,* translated as "desolating sacrilege" (1 Macc. 1:54; cf. 2 Macc. 6:2). In Hebrew, "abomination" is often used in reference to an idol (1 Kings 11:5; Jer. 4:1); in this case, the Near Eastern chief sky-god, Baal, is probably meant. "Abomination" is a pun on Baal's most common epithet, *shamayim* (of the heavens). Abomination of Desolation refers to the cult objects placed in the Jerusalem Temple by order of Antiochus Epiphanes IV in 167 B.C.E., during the Maccabean persecution. The abomination was probably an altar to Baal or upright stones placed on the altar (*massebot*), symbolizing Baal, his consort, and their offspring. The removal of these cult objects and purification of the Temple in 164 B.C.E. is celebrated by the Feast of Hanukkah.

abortion *see* FETUS

A*b*ot (Heb., The Fathers) tractate of five chapters containing sayings attributed to sages, attached to the Mishnah; probably compiled around 250 C.E. The tractate begins: "Moses received Torah at Sinai and handed it on to Joshua, Joshua to elders, and elders to prophets. And prophets handed it on to the men of the great assembly" (1:1). Chapter 1 sets out the chain of tradition from Sinai to the major authorities who form the earliest layer of sages in the Mishnah, thus claiming that the Mishnah sets forth the oral tradition that began in God's revelation to Moses at Sinai. Five pairs of authorities, ending with Hillel and Shammai, link the Mishnah to Sinai. Chapter 2 carries the chain of tradition in two directions: first, to the house of the patriarch, via Judah the Patriarch (c. 200 C.E.) and his sons, Gamaliel and Hillel; second, to the sages, via Yoḥanan ben Zakkai and his five disciples. Chapters 3 and 4 present sayings attributed to second-century authorities. The most famous sayings are attributed to Hillel: "If I am not for myself, who is for me? And when I am for myself, what am I? And if not now, when?" (A*b*ot 1:14). Other important sayings appear in chapter 2, as follows:

> Rabbi says: What is the straight path which a person should choose for himself? Whatever is an ornament to the one who follows it, and an ornament in the view of others. Be meticulous in a small religious duty as in a large one, for you do not know what sort of reward is coming for any of the various religious duties. And reckon with the loss [required] in carrying out a religious duty against the reward for doing it; and the reward for committing a transgression against the loss for doing it. And keep your eye on three things, so you will not come into the clutches of transgression. Know what is above you. An eye which sees, and an ear which hears, and all your actions are written down in a book (2:1).
>
> Rabban Gamaliel, a son of Rabbi Judah the Patriarch, says: Fitting is learning in the Torah along with a craft, for the labor put into the two of them makes one forget sin. And all learning of the Torah which is not joined with labor is destined to be null and causes sin. And all who work with the community—let them work with them [the community] for the sake of Heaven. For the merit of the fathers strengthens them, and the righteousness which they do stands forever. And, as for you, I credit you with a great reward, as if you had done [all the work required by the community] (2:2).
>
> Be wary of the government, for they get friendly with a person only for their own convenience. They look like friends when it is to their benefit, but they do not stand by a person when he is in need (2:3).
>
> He would say: Make his wishes into your own wishes, so that He will make your wishes into his wishes. Put aside your wishes on account of his wishes, so that He will put aside the wishes of other people in favor of your wishes. Hillel says: Do not walk out on the community. And do not have confidence in yourself until the day you die. And do not judge your companion until you are in his place. And do not say anything which cannot be heard, for in the end it will be heard. And do not say: When I have time, I shall study, for you may never have time (2:4).
>
> He would say: A coarse person will never fear sin, nor will an am ha-Aretz ever be pious, nor will a shy person learn, nor will an ignorant person teach, nor will anyone too occupied in business get wise. In a place where there are no individuals, try to be an individual (2:5).
>
> Also, he saw a skull floating on the water and said to it [in Aramaic]: Because you drowned others, they drowned you, and in the end those who drowned you will be drowned (2:6).

A*b*ot deRabbi Natan *see* FATHERS ACCORDING TO RABBI NATHAN, THE

Abr. *see* DE ABRAHAMO

JEWISH DIASPORA IN THE FIRST CENTURY C.E.
ITALIA
Rome
Aricia
Puteoli
Neapolis
Pompeii
MACEDONIA
Thessalonica
Philippi
Beroea
GREECE
Delphi
Athens
Corinth
Sparta
Lesbos
Samos
Delos
Paros
Melos
Cos
Miletus
Halicarnassus
Rhodes
CRETE
Gortyna
ASIA
Adramyttium
Pergamum
Sardis
Philadelphia
Ephesus
Tralles
Laodicea
Antioch
Apamea
PHRYGIA
PAMPHYLIA
Perge
Side
Heraclea
PONTUS
Ancyra
GALATIA
CAPPADOCIA
Iconium
Derbe
Tarsus
COMMAGENE
Antioch
SYRIA
Seleucia
Apamea
CYPRUS
Salamis
Paphos
Aradus
Tripolis
Berytus
Sidon
Tyre
Ptolemais
Palmyra
Damascus
Jerusalem
JUDEA
ARABIA
MESOPOTAMIA
Tigris River
Euphrates River
ADIABENE
Ecbatana
Ctesiphon
Pumbeditha
Nehardea
Babylon
Nippur
Susa
Mediterranean Sea
CYRENAICA
Alexandria
EGYPT
Pelusium
Athribis
Bubastis
Leontopolis
Memphis
Theadelphia
Philadelphia
Arsinoe
Heracleopolis
Tebtynis
Oxyrrhynchus
Nile R.
0 50 100 miles
0 75 150 km.

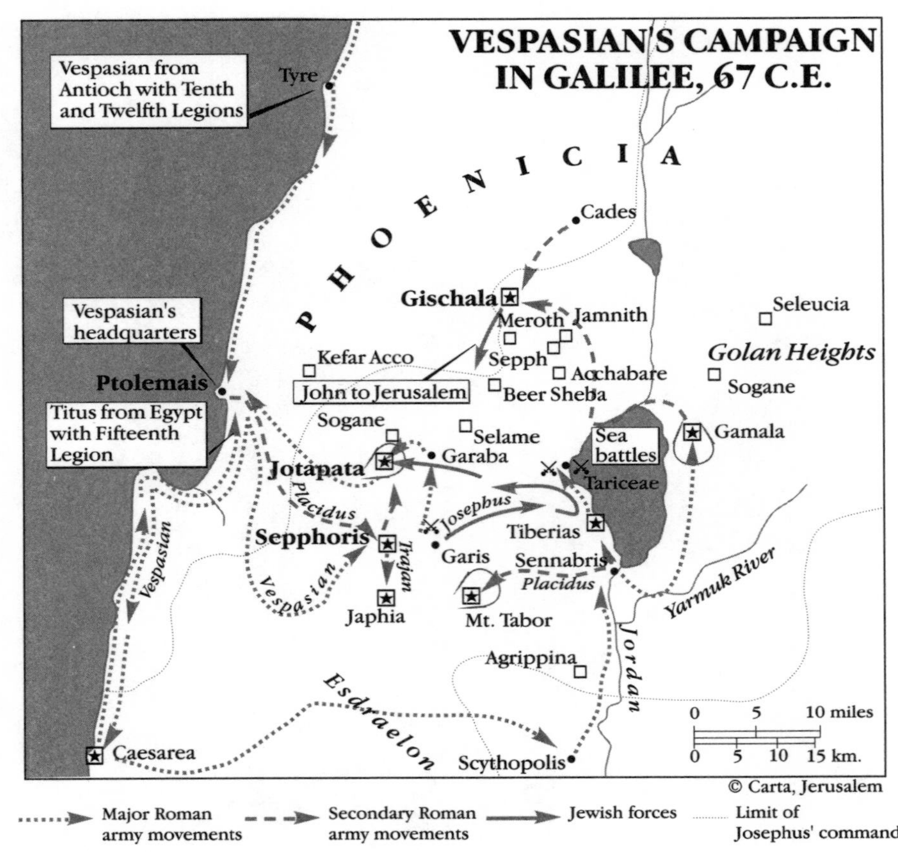
VESPASIAN'S CAMPAIGN IN GALILEE, 67 C.E.
Vespasian from Antioch with Tenth and Twelfth Legions
Tyre
PHOENICIA
Cades
Gischala
Meroth
Jamnith
Seleucia
Golan Heights
Vespasian's headquarters
Kefar Acco
Sepph
Acchabare
Ptolemais
John to Jerusalem
Beer Sheba
Sogane
Titus from Egypt with Fifteenth Legion
Sogane
Selame
Sea battles
Gamala
Jotapata
Garaba
Tariceae
Placidus
Josephus
Tiberias
Sepphoris
Trajan
Garis
Sennabris
Vespasian
Vespasian
Placidus
Yarmuk River
Japhia
Mt. Tabor
Jordan
Agrippina
Esdraelon
0 5 10 miles
0 5 10 15 km.
Caesarea
Scythopolis
© Carta, Jerusalem
Major Roman army movements
Secondary Roman army movements
Jewish forces
Limit of Josephus' command

Abraham Israel's patriarch, whose name was changed from Abram in Genesis 17:5. The events recounted in Genesis 11–25 provide the basis for a rich and innovative tradition in Judaism and Christianity. Although the Bible is silent about the circumstances of Abram's departure from Mesopotamia, a major stream of the tradition identifies his rejection of idolatry as the reason for his election. According to Jubilees 10–12, the young Abraham came to understand the folly of idolatry and the uselessness of astrological prognostication. The name Ur (Gen. 11:31), interpreted as "fire," plays an important role here and in related texts. Abram flees from Ur after burning an idolatrous temple in which his family served as priests (Jub. 12:12–14). The Apocalypse of Abraham elaborates: Abraham mocks the stupidity of his father Terah, an idol maker and priest, and searches for the true God, who sends him out of his father's house before it is struck by a lightning bolt (Apoc. Abr. 1–8). Abraham's search leads God to call him "beloved" (9:1–6; cf. Isa. 41:8) and provide the epiphany in Genesis 15 (Apoc. Abr. 10–32). In the Book of Biblical Antiquities 6, Abraham is thrown into a fiery furnace because he refuses to help build the Tower of Babel, and God rescues him from the fire (cf. Dan. 3). These stories interpret Abram's faith as knowledge of God that leads to trusting action, rather than as trust in God's promise of progeny (Gen. 15:1–6). The interpretation of Abram's conversion from idolatry is suggested already in Joshua 24:2, but his status as prototypical convert may have developed in gentile contexts among Jews seeking to make converts. The stories about Abram's rejection of idolatry and astrology also appear in Josephus (*Ant.* 1.7.1:154–156), Philo (*On Migr. Abr.* 176–186), and rabbinic tradition (Gen. Rabbah 38:13). A related countermotif makes Abraham the discoverer of astronomy (Pseudo-Eupolemos in Eusebius, *Prep. Gos.* 9.17, 6–8; cf. Gen. 15:5). In the Qumran Genesis Apocryphon 20:28–29, his skill extends to exorcistic healing.

Although the Bible ties Abraham's faith explicitly to the promise of progeny, Jubilees 17:15–19:9 finds it epitomized in the sacrifice of Isaac and generalizes it as faithful endurance through a series of ten trials. The tradition interpreting the *akedah* as an act of faithful obedience recurs in Ecclesiasticus 44:20 and 1 Maccabees 2:52. The Testament of Abraham, however, parodies the traditional Abraham; the patriarch refuses God's command to "Go forth" from this life (Test. Abr. 1 [A], cf. Gen. 12:1) and displays a self-righteousness that is the dark side of his celebrated righteousness (Test. Abr. 10 [A], cf. Gen. 15:6).

Abraham's status as Israel's patriarch of Israel is essential in the Apocalypse of Abraham 9–32, which explores the disparity between Israel's status as heir of the Abrahamic covenant and its situation after the destruction of Jerusalem (cf. also LAB 9:3, 18:5). Following late biblical and postbiblical notions that "the chosen" are the faithful of Israel, 4 Maccabees 15–18 emphasizes the martyrs' obedience as evidence of their status as Abraham's children.

Christian interpretations emphasize Abraham's faith and his role as patriarch, but often invert the notions and depict him as the forebear of believers in Christ, which means, in fact, primarily Gentiles. Paul's revolutionary exegesis is most prominent in this respect. Galatians 3 interprets the promise of offspring (Gen. 15:1–6) with reference to Christ rather than Isaac, and Abraham's blessing on the Gentiles (Gen. 12:3) occurs when they share Abraham's faith in that promise (Gen. 15:6). Romans 4 interprets Genesis 17:5 to refer to Abraham's status as patriarch of Jews and Gentiles. Genesis 15:6 is a key passage for Paul, who states that Abraham's faith in the promise of offspring was a faith in the resurrection, by definition, the resurrection of Christ (Rom. 4:16–25). Especially striking is Paul's use of Abraham's faith in an argument against the requirement for gentile circumcision (Gal. 3; Rom. 3–4). Justification by faith (Gen. 15:6) is opposed to justification by the deeds of the law (especially circumcision). Abraham believed and was justified before his circumcision; that is, Genesis 15 precedes Genesis 17. Paul's exegetical irony is particularly evident in Galatians 4:21–31; Christians are the children of Sarah the free woman, while unbelieving Jews are children of Hagar the slave. These innovations notwithstanding, Paul's matter-of-fact use of the Abraham tradition in an epistle to the gentile Galatians may indicate that his missionary preaching had employed other traditions about Abraham the convert (cf. Rom. 4:5; 1 Thess. 1:9).

Matthew 8:11–12 and Luke 13:28–29 attest an inversion of Jewish Abraham traditions similar to Paul's; the Gentiles rather than "the sons of the kingdom" will share the eschatological banquet with Abraham, Isaac, and Jacob. A saying attributed to John the Baptist strikes a similar motif (Matt. 3:8–9; Luke 3:8–9) but is also reminiscent of 4 Maccabees: Abraham's true children are those who repent in the face of the coming judgment.

Other New Testament texts indicate closer consonance with some Jewish traditions. In Hebrews 11, faith in general, and Abraham's faith in particular, involve obedient trust that is realized in daring actions, for example, the *akedah* (Heb. 11:17). For James faith that does not issue in deeds does not justify, and Abraham was justified because his faith was complemented by his action in sacrificing Isaac (James 2:23–24). *See also* ABRAM; AKEDAH.

Abraham, Apocalypse of extensive first person account of Abraham's break with idolatry in Chaldea, his ascent to God's throne, and his vision of Israel's future. Like the Book of Daniel, the Apocalypse divides into two major sections (chaps. 1–8, 9–32), the first in narrative form, and the second with features similar to the apocalyptic visions in 1 Enoch 12–16 and 17–33. References to the destruction of Jerusalem and similarities to 2 Baruch and 2 Esdras indicate a date of composition in the decades after 70 C.E. The Apocalypse is preserved in the fourteenth- to sixteenth-century manuscripts of a Slavonic version that stems from an original composed probably in Hebrew.

According to chapters 1–8, Abraham's father Terah is a maker of idols. Abraham recognizes that the idols cannot be gods, chides his father for his folly, and searches for the true God. God responds to Abraham's prayer by calling him out of his father's house (cf. Gen. 12:1) before destroying it and the idols with a thunderbolt, an interpretation of the Hebrew *ur* (fire; cf. Gen. 11:31). From start to finish, the story is a piece of biblical interpretation that takes elements in Genesis literally and puts them and other motifs from prophetic polemics against idolatry into narrative form, employing a mocking style that parallels the Letter of Jeremiah and Bel and the Dragon. Similarities in Jubilees 12 indicate that the story of Abraham the convert stems back at least to the end of the third century B.C.E.

Abraham's search for God is rewarded by a vision of the enthroned deity and by his being chosen as Israel's patriarch. The theophany in Genesis 15 provides the setting for his ascent to heaven (Apoc. Abr. 9–20). While many details in the throne vision are reminiscent of Ezekiel 1–2 and 1 Enoch 14, the hymn of the angel Yaoel (Apoc. Abr. 17) parallels similar features in accounts of mystical ascents in the later Merkabah and Hekalot literature. Abraham's vision of the future (chaps. 23–29) emphasizes the disparity between Israel's status as God's chosen people, the descendants promised to Abraham in Genesis 15, and its fate at the hands of the Gentiles in 70 C.E. Differing from contemporary explanations in 2 Baruch and 2 Esdras, the author employs the story of Manasseh to suggest that the first-century Temple cult had reverted to the idolatry that Abraham rejected. When this capitulation to the demon Azazel is renounced, their gentile conquerors will be punished and the nation will achieve the destiny promised to Abraham.

Abraham, Testament of fictitious account of the events leading up to Abraham's death. Its name notwithstanding, this text is not cast in the traditional genre of a testament, but is a narrative about Abraham's refusal to make a testament and, hence, to assent to God's decree that it is time for him to die. Although it is preserved only in manuscripts written by Christian scribes, it appears to be Jewish in origin, composed in Egypt in the first century C.E. The text is extant in two major forms with many parallels in content and wording, but significant differences in the order of events. The so-called Recension A seems to preserve the more original order, but Recension B contains some original wording and narrative elements. The language of composition was probably Greek, and a rich manuscript tradition attests both text-forms in Greek and includes Slavonic, Coptic, Arabic, and Romanian versions of one or the other text form.

Although written in a humorous style, the Testament treats serious topics. Central is Abraham's inability to accept the inevitability of his impending death. In the first half of the narrative (chaps. 1–15), the patriarch employs a series of delaying tactics that force Michael, the messenger of death, to shuttle back and forth to the heavenly throne room for new orders about how to deal with Abraham. In the second, parallel half of the story (chaps. 16–20), God sends personified Death, who tricks the patriarch into surrendering his soul. In the course of this action, Michael takes Abraham on a chariot ride across the inhabited world, during which Abraham repeatedly calls down death on a variety of sinners. As the epitome of a righteous person, he cannot understand the deeds of sinners. In order to deal with the self-righteous dark side of the patriarch's celebrated virtue, God orders the chariot up to heaven to view the judgment process. Abraham now finds himself interceding for a person who is in risk of damnation; inadvertently, he has learned about the mercy of the God who does not want sinners to perish.

The Testament of Abraham is a remarkable piece of didactic literature that makes its point through parody. The traditionally obedient Abraham refuses to "go forth" from this life (chap. 1; cf. Gen. 12:1), and his haggling with God is thoroughly self-centered (contrast Gen. 18). His intolerance of the sins of others, which serves as a warning against the excesses that the New Testament attributes to the Pharisees (Luke 18:9–14), is noteworthy in a document that is most likely Jewish in origin.

The judgment scene in chapters 11–13 employs features found in a number of apocalyptic texts (two angelic witnesses, books of deeds, and enthroned judge), but also contains unique features, notably Abel's role as judge and a graphic portrayal of the souls of the righteous and the wicked being taken along the two ways toward eternal life and eternal destruction. Remarkable is the author's use of motifs attested in the Egyptian Book of the Dead. The tradition of Abraham's refusal to accept death recurs with reference to Moses in the midrashim (Sifrei Deut. 305; Deut. Rabbah 11:5, 10; cf. Test. Abr. 7:12, 9:3–6).

Abraham's bosom place of repose and honor at the banquet table in heaven or paradise (Luke 16:22). In the view of some, Abraham, Isaac, and Jacob were already enjoying the heavenly banquet (4 Macc. 13:17; Matt. 8:11). Association with Abraham is granted Lazarus in compensation for his wretched life, and it designates him an Israelite in contrast to the rich man who suffers in Hades for not caring for the poor.

Abram (Heb., exalted father) name of Israel's patriarch according to Genesis 11:27–17:4. His name is changed to Abraham in Genesis 17:5 in connection with the promise that Abraham would be "father of a multitude" (Heb.: *ab-hamon*). The distinction is maintained in the Book of Jubilees and the Book of Biblical Antiquities.

A<u>b</u>talion prerabbinic sage of the first century B.C.E.; in the chain of tradition at M. A<u>b</u>ot 1:1–18, listed along with Shemayah as a pair, directly preceding Hillel and Shammai. He is quoted as saying: "Sages: watch what you say, lest you become liable to the punishment of exile, and go into exile to a place of bad water, and disciples who follow you drink [bad water] and die, and the name of heaven be thereby profaned" (M. A<u>b</u>ot 1:11). Within the later talmudic literature, the story of his life and teachings is considerably developed.

A<u>b</u>udimi *see* DIMI

Abul Fath fourteenth-century C.E. author of one of the Samaritan Chronicles, also known as Chronicle 6, which drew on a number of earlier works, such as the Samaritan Book of Joshua and lists of priests similar to those in the Tolidah and the Adler Chronicle. It is written in Arabic in narrative form.

A<u>b</u>un *see* A<u>B</u>IN

A<u>b</u>unah deShmuel *see* ABBA B. ABBA

Abydenus Greek author of *On Assyrian History,* a work quoted by Eusebius but otherwise unknown. He mentions a flood with some resemblances to the Babylonian version, though Eusebius connects it with the biblical Flood. Abydenus also mentions a story similar to that of the Tower of Babel of Genesis.

abyss (Gr.: *abyssos*; Heb.: *te<u>h</u>om*) originally, the bottomless watery deep on which the dry land is set. In this sense it carries with it the fearful and chaotic connotations of the related word "sea" (Gen. 1:2; Jon. 2:5). Later it also denotes the deep fiery chasm into which the rebel angels are cast (1 Enoch 10:13, 21:7). In the Book of Revelation the abyss is the pit of hell into which Satan is hurled (20:1), the lake of fire where all the wicked are punished (20:14); it is presided over by the angel of destruction, Abaddon (9:11).

academies in Palestine and Babylonia *see* SCHOOL

Academy on High rabbinic school in heaven where sages and other righteous persons attend after dying. It is a mirror image or projection of the rabbinic academy on earth. The sages who went there for their eternal reward continued to study and to debate the fine points of rabbinic law. God himself participated in the discussion, presented novel interpretations, made reference to rabbinic teachings, and taught the Torah to others. Rabbis took their positions according to rank and sat in an eternal semicircle. Exceptional Babylonian masters who merited it occasionally communicated with the members of the Academy on High. At the Kol Nidrei service on the Day of Atonement, worshipers in synagogues call on the authority of this Academy on High to sanction their prayers.

Acco, archaeological survey of an underwater archaeological survey of the ancient port city of Acco in the Bay of Acco and north of modern Haifa. It appears that the first construction of the southern breakwater of the ancient port is to be ascribed to the Persian period, more specifically to about 500 B.C.E. This breakwater was about 330 meters long and 12 meters wide and protected by 25 acres of water to its north. The breakwater served both as a pier and as a quay. The small island and structure that can still be seen in the harbor today, called the Tower of the Flies, probably dates to the Hellenistic period. It is about 60 meters long and about 18 meters wide. It appears to have served as a free port for foreign trading vessels similar to the island found in the port north of ancient Sidon. In the Roman period there is evidence that the breakwater was raised about 1.5 meters by the addition of huge stones laid across it.

Waves swept between the stones and flushed the bottom of the bay back to the sea. The large amounts of first-century C.E. pottery found during dredging of the port in 1983 suggests a first-century date for this renovation of the harbor. On coins of Acco from the second century C.E., a monumental, arched pier appears in the harbor scene, which implies that the Roman pier was already a monument. It may be that the emperor Claudius or Nero contributed to the harbor's repair. No further constructions or additions to the port were made until the ninth century C.E. *See also* ACRE.

accused wife (Heb.: *sotah*) wife accused of adultery, who is subjected to the ordeal described in Numbers 5. *See also* SOTAH (*Mishnah tractate*).

Achaemenids dynastic line of the kings of Persia from Cyrus (r. 559–530 B.C.E.) through Darius III (r. 336–330 B.C.E.). Also included in the line are Cambyses (r. 530–522 B.C.E.), Darius I (r. 522–486 B.C.E.), Xerxes I (r. 486–465 B.C.E.), Artaxerxes I (r. 465–424 B.C.E.), Xerxes II (r. 424–423 B.C.E.), Darius II (r. 423–404 B.C.E.), Artaxerxes II (r. 404–359 B.C.E.), Artaxerxes III (r. 359–338 B.C.E.), and Arses (r. 338–336 B.C.E.).

Achaeus Roman judge in Palestine under Gallienus in the mid-third century C.E. According to Eusebius (*Ecclesiastical History* 7.15.3), Achaeus ordered the execution of Marinus, a Roman soldier due military honors who refused to abandon his Christian beliefs and sacrifice to the emperors.

Achior Ammonite leader in the Book of Judith. His advice against attacking Bethulia and his accompanying summary of Jewish history from Abraham until the Babylonian exile (Jdt. 5) prompt Holofernes to exile him from the enemy camp. When Judith displays to him the head of Holofernes, Achior faints. Reviving, he praises Judith, expresses belief in Israel's God, is circumcised, and joins the covenant community (contrast Deut. 23:3, which forbids Ammonite conversions).

Acilius Glabrio *see* GLABRIO, MANIUS ACILIUS

acquisition of property (Heb.: *kinyan*) all acts through which a person voluntarily acquires proprietary or contractual rights. The term *kinyan* applies to acquisition of that which is ownerless or lost (when the owner has abandoned hope of recovery); acquisition through sale or gift; and acquisition of personal rights, such as debts or contracts, including hiring of workers. As in other types of acquisition, these latter, contractual rights entail one individual's conveying of a right to another, in order to be appropriately encompassed by the general rules for acquisition.

Acquisition of what is ownerless or lost requires proof that the individual acquiring the property possesses it and intends to use it. In the case of a sale, gift, or contract, by contrast, to be effective, the act of acquisition must additionally encompass proof that the seller intended to complete the transaction. In these cases, the individual acquiring title performs a symbolic act, known as *kinyan,* which represents the taking of possession, and the seller orally or otherwise expresses approval. The symbolic act representing transfer of ownership provides physical evidence of the transfer and demarcates the actual moment at which the transfer took place. This precludes later disputes regarding who owned the property at a particular moment.

Three methods of acquisition apply to movables: (1) the placement of the property to be acquired within the acquirer's courtyard (*kinyan ḥatzer*), where it is under his possession and control; (2) placement of the property within 4 cubits of the acquirer, again, so that he has control over it; and (3) lifting (*hagbahah*), pulling (*meshikhah*), or physical transfer (*mesirah*) of the property. As noted above, in the case of a purchase or gift, the transfer of property is effective only when accompanied by the expressed assent of the seller or donor. Immovable property is acquired by an act through which the acquirer indicates that he has possession, for example, through the construction of a fence or some other act of improvement, such as weeding, hoeing, or setting out a place to sleep (B. Kiddushin 26a, 53b, and 54a).

The seller's or donor's agreement to the transfer, and hence the completion of the transaction, frequently is represented by an exchange of an article of property between the two. Usually a kerchief owned by the buyer is pulled away from him by the seller, who may then return it (*kinyan sudar; kinyan ḥalifin*). This symbol of purchase is first explicitly mentioned in the Talmud (B. Ba<u>b</u>a Metzia 47a), in a dispute regarding whether the object to be pulled should be owned by the buyer or seller. In time, *kinyan sudar* became so commonplace as to represent the preeminent mode of acquisition. It often is denoted by the unqualified term *kinyan*.

By the end of the Tannaitic period, payment of the agreed-upon purchase price alone was not deemed in itself to effect purchase. While payment was understood to be a necessary condition of purchase, final acquisition needed to be indicated by one of the above-mentioned methods, which physically represented the transfer of the property and thus precluded disputes regarding the point at which ownership changed hands.

Acre (also known as Acco) coastal city in northern Israel, 14 miles north of Haifa, at the northern end of the Bay of Haifa. Acre is first mentioned in Egyptian texts dating to c. 1800 B.C.E. The Greeks related the name to *ake* (healing) and associated it with the legend of Heracles. Under Ptolemy II, the city's name was changed to Ptolemais, by which it was known until the Arab conquest.

The city's geographic location made its occupation vital to armies engaged in campaigns in Syria and Palestine. Under Persian rule, it served as a military and naval base in campaigns against Egypt. Under Seleucid control, the city was hostile to Galilean Jews. In 164 B.C.E., Simeon the Hasmonean had to repel attacks from there. Later, the city was held by Antiochus VII Sidetes, under whom it acknowledged only nominal suzerainty to Ptolemaic rulers. In 39 B.C.E. Herod the Great used the city as a base of operations, and, in 67 C.E., Vespasian made the city the center of his operations against the Galilee. Under Nero, Acre became a Roman colony. By this time, its port was overshadowed by Herod Agrippa's new port at Caesaria.

After 70 C.E., Jews reestablished their community there, and the city served as the port of embarkation for rabbis who were traveling to Rome. M. A̱bodah Zarah 4:3 reports that Gamaliel II visited a bath dedicated to Aphrodite there. Y. A̱bodah Zarah 1:4 (39d) comments on the volume of fish produced by the city's fisheries. *See also* ACCO, ARCHAEOLOGICAL SURVEY OF.

Acta Alexandrinorum work from the first or second century C.E., known as the Acts of the Alexandrian/Pagan Martyrs. The contents concern Greek citizens condemned and executed by Roman emperors because of their defense of the rights of Alexandria. Because the work is preserved only in fragments, its full character is still unclear; a wholesale attack on the Alexandrians by Roman emperors is not known. However, a few of the episodes relate to the incident of 38 C.E. in which riots broke out over conflicts between Jews and Greeks and each community sent a delegation to Rome.

acts of loving kindness *see* GEMILUT ḤASADIM

Actium, Battle of climactic battle for control of the Roman Empire, fought between Antony and Octavian (the future Caesar Augustus) on September 2, 31 B.C.E. In a land and sea engagement at Actium, on the western coast of Greece, Octavian defeated Antony, who fled to Egypt, where he committed suicide a year later.

A.D. the abbreviation for Anno Domini, "in the year of our Lord [Jesus Christ]." In the Christian calendar, years are counted from the nominal year of Jesus Christ's birth, as established by Dionysius Exiguus in the sixth century C.E. *See also* C.E.

Adam (in the tradition) Adam and Eve receive extensive treatment in extrabiblical Jewish and early Christian sources. Although all of these sources reflect to some degree material also found in Genesis, many of them also feature traditions not explicitly present there.

The earliest sustained treatment of Adam and Eve outside the Bible appears in the Book of Jubilees (2d c. B.C.E.), in a historical review. Jubilees 2–4 narrates a story similar to that of Genesis, but includes a few new details, focuses on the halakhic implications of the story, and sets the whole within a time frame of "jubilees" (periods of 49 years).

Another text that treats Adam and Eve in the context of a historical review is 2 Enoch (chaps. 30–32). Again, the basic story line is similar to Genesis, but much new material is present: Adam is created from seven components of the world, his name is an acronym of the four directions, and his glory at creation is extolled.

The most extensive extrabiblical treatment of the first couple appears in the Books of Adam and Eve, a series of interrelated literary works. These books describe Adam's and Eve's attempts to repent by standing neck-deep in water, Eve's second deception by Satan, Satan's story of his expulsion from heaven, and Adam's death and elevation to the third heaven.

Both 2 Enoch and the Books of Adam and Eve depict Adam's status before the "fall" in a highly glorified manner. Similar treatments appear in Sirach 49:16, Pseudo-Philo 26:6, Sibylline Oracles 11:154, rabbinic literature, and the Quran (2:35–36).

There are, on the other hand, many traditions that focus on the disastrous consequences for later humanity of Adam's and Eve's act of disobedience. Prime examples are the apocalypses 4 Ezra (3:21, 7:118) and 2 Baruch (23:4, 48:42–43). Other important references to Adam in early Jewish literature include Testament of Abraham (Recension A) 11; Apocalypse of Abraham 23–24; and 3 Baruch 4:8–13.

The most significant references to Adam in early Christian literature appear in the letters of Paul, who portrays Adam as an antitype of Christ (Rom. 5:12–21; 1 Cor. 15:20–22, 45–50). 1 Timothy 2:13–14 cites the Genesis Adam story to justify the submissiveness of women in the church; in Testament of Adam 3:2–4, Adam's final words to Seth include prophecies about Jesus. Other important notices in early Christian literature include Ascension of Isaiah 9:28; Testament of Simeon 6:5; and Greek Apocalypse of Ezra 7:2. The Apocalypse of Adam, an early Gnostic writing, depicts Adam/Eve as an androgynous being, which, when separated into two, loses its primeval glory and begins to serve the creator God.

Adam receives extensive treatment in rabbinic literature and throughout the medieval Jewish and Christian traditions.

Adam, Apocalypse of Gnostic text of the first centuries C.E. found at Nag Hammadi in Egypt. It claims to be a revelation by Adam to his son Seth to pass on to his descendants. Although the text was previously unknown, there are many parallels with Jewish literature. Many scholars argue that it is an example of Jewish Gnosticism.

Adam and Eve, Books of a broad term for a whole range of narrative traditions about the first parents after their expulsion from the Garden. The two major forms of these narratives are attested in the Apocalypse of Moses, extant in Greek manuscripts from the twelfth to the seventeenth centuries, and the Life of Adam and Eve, preserved in Latin manuscripts from the ninth to the fifteenth centuries. The two forms differ from one another in the events that they include or exclude and in the order of events. Versions in Armenian, Slavonic, and Georgian follow the Greek or the Latin with some variations. There is no scholarly consensus as to which text form is original, when they may have been written, and whether the books in roughly their present literary forms originated in Jewish or Christian circles. Clearly they preserve some pre-Christian Jewish traditions also attested in Christian, later Jewish, and Gnostic literature.

The Apocalypse of Moses is primarily an account of Adam's (especially) and Eve's deaths, their cause and their cure. The framework for the main part of the narrative is the traditional form of the testament (Apoc. Moses 5–42). Different from other exemplars of this genre, Adam and Eve's narrative does not deal with particular vices (or virtues) exemplified in the lives now coming to a conclusion, but with the fact that their deaths are the inevitable consequence of their initial sin and with details of the circumstances that led to that sin. Several episodes not found in Genesis 1–5 emphasize the author's message. Seeking to forestall his death, Adam sends Seth and Eve to the Garden to obtain the oil of mercy from the tree of life (Apoc. Moses 9:3–13:6). Michael prevents them, emphasizing that Adam must die, but also that Adam will obtain the oil at the time of the resurrection of all flesh. Although the testament is really Adam's, the heart of the retrospective narrative is spoken by Eve (Apoc. Moses 15–26), who describes the events recounted in Genesis 3. Satan coopted the serpent, and then in the form of an angel he deceived Eve into committing her sin (cf. 2 Cor. 11:14). As Adam and Eve are expelled from the Garden, God shows them mercy by providing them with the seeds necessary to grow food to sustain them and spices for the incense of sacrifice.

The testamentary form, with many of the same motifs, is also central to the Life of Adam and Eve, although Adam rather than Eve is the main narrator. The story begins after the expulsion from the Garden (chaps. 1–22). Adam and Eve are seeking food and decide to express their penitence by submerging themselves in the Tigris River. The detail may indicate an origin in a religious community that practiced ritual ablution. Satan deceives Eve a second time and then explains to Adam the reason for his first temptation (chaps. 12–16). He had been an angel, but when he and his followers refused Michael's command to worship God's image in Adam, they were expelled from heaven (cf. Isa. 14 and Rev. 12:7–9). The temptation was their revenge on Adam. A second major difference from the Apocalypse of Moses (and Genesis) is Adam's two revelations to Seth (Life of Adam and Eve 25–29). According to the first, Adam ascended to the heavenly paradise, where he received the sentence of death. The account parallels ascent narratives like 1 Enoch 14. In the second revelation, Adam transmits to Seth information about future events that he had learned after eating the fruit of the tree of knowledge. This section parallels historical summaries in Jewish apocalypses such as the Apocalypse of Weeks in 1 Enoch 93. The emphasis on revelation and Seth as its mediator recur in Gnostic Adam traditions.

Adar sixth month of the Jewish calendar, containing twenty-nine days in ordinary years and thirty days in leap years and corresponding to February 12–March 11 at the earliest and to March 2–30 at the latest. The festival of Purim and four special Sabbaths, Shekalim, Zakor, Parah, and haḤodesh, fall in this month.

Adar Sheni intercalary month, added in leap years to keep the lunar and solar calendars synchronized; *see also* CALENDAR

Adda b. Ahabah Babylonian amora of the late third and early fourth centuries C.E.; a student of Ra<u>b</u> and teacher to numerous students at Pumbedita. He is known for his piety, and numerous stories relate his ability to move God to action, for example, to avert a drought or to prevent weakened buildings from collapsing. This name also refers to a student of Raba and, later, Pappa, rebuked by the former as portraying "empty-headed stupidity" (B. Taanit 8a).

Addai Christian apostle to the kingdom of Edessa. He is also known as Addaeus, which may be a corruption of Thaddaeus, the person whom Eusebius says converted the king of Edessa to Christianity. Eusebius provides stories about the conversion of Edessa under Abgar V, and these seem to form the basis of the Doctrine of Addai, written about 400 C.E. In the Doctrine, Judas sent Addai, one of the seventy-two disciples, to Edessa to preach the Gospel after Jesus' ascension. Abgar was so amazed by his preaching that he converted. A detailed description of Addai's activities in Edessa appear in which we are told that Emperor Claudius's mother, Protonice, found the cross. We are also told that after his conversion Abgar asked Tiberius to punish the Jews for crucifying Jesus. We are also told that part of the Jewish merchant community in Edessa converted at the same public meeting at which Abgar became a Christian. Addai is followed by Aggai, who was martyred by Manu, Abgar's son. Paulit followed Aggai, but the Doctrine's chronology seems to be flawed at this point, for it claims that Paulit was ordained by Serapion, bishop of Antioch, 190–212 C.E.

Adiabene district in the upper Tigris region; during most of the Hellenistic period, a vassal kingdom within the Parthian Empire. From 36 to 60 C.E., Adiabene was ruled by Izates, the son of Queen Helena. Later it was ruled by King Monobaz, Izates' older brother. Under Izates, Adiabene achieved power and influence within the Parthian Empire. Izates restored a deposed Parthian king, Artabanus II, to his throne, in return for which he was given the territory of Nisbis and its surroundings, which contained substantial Jewish populations. Izates later played a central role in the dynastic struggles within the Parthian Empire that followed the death of Artabanus III. Adiabene is best known for the conversion to Judaism of its rulers, Izates, Queen Helena, and King Monobaz.

Adiabene, Jews of Early in the first century C.E., the Adiabene royal house converted to Judaism. Izates, heir to the throne, had been sent to Charaz-Spasinu, on the Persian Gulf, where he would be safe from the envy of his half-brothers. There he was converted to Judaism by a Jewish merchant, Ananias. In the same period, his mother was converted by another merchant, Ḥananiah. Josephus reports that, against the wishes of Helena and Ananias, Izates chose to be circumcised, having been convinced by a Galilean Jew named Eleazar that failure to do so would be a grave offense against the law (Josephus, *Ant.* 20:34; Gen. Rabbah 46:11).

The Adiabenians took great efforts to impress Palestinian Jews with their piety and generosity. King Monobaz II, Izates' brother, had gold handles made for the vessels used in the Temple on the Day of Atonement. His mother, Queen Helena, set a golden candlestick over the door of the sanctuary and made a golden tablet, on which was written the scriptural passage of the accused wife (M. Yoma 3:10). Josephus reports that when Helena visited Jerusalem in 46 C.E., during a famine, she had her attendants bring grain and dried figs from Alexandria and Cyprus to the needy. Izates is reported also to have sent a considerable sum to fight the famine. Talmudic sources state that during this famine, Monobaz used his entire fortune to purchase food for those in need. He responded to criticism by declaring, in part, "My fathers collected treasures below, but I have collected treasures above [that is, in heaven]" (B. Baba Batra 11a). The piety of the royal family also is indicated in reports of Monobaz's installation of a mezuzah even on temporary lodgings (T. Megillah 4:30), and the story that in Lydda, Queen Helena erected a large sukkah, frequented by rabbis (T. Sukkot 1:1).

The Adiabenians took an active part in the Jewish war against Rome in 66–70 C.E. Josephus (*War* 2:520) reports that, among the Jewish ranks, the most distinguished fighters were "Monobaz and Cenedaeus, kinsmen of Monobaz, king of Adiabene." While Parthia did not openly participate in the conflict, it made no effort to prevent the Adiabenian Jews from assisting in the revolt.

By the late second century, Abiadene had become Christian. Since Christianity frequently spread in existing Jewish communities, this may indicate that by this date, the kingdom was largely Jewish.

Adler Chronicle one of the Samaritan Chronicles, also known as Chronicle 7. It is mainly a list of the various Samaritan high priests, along with brief descriptions of events during their time of office, extending from Adam to 1899. Although late in its present form, it seems to have a more antique chronicle behind it. *See also* SAMARITAN CHRONICLES.

admission *see* HODAAH

Admon judge, named at M. Ketubot 13:1–9 as a judge of robbery cases in Jerusalem, alongside Ḥanan b. Abishalom. B. Ketubot 105a names a third judge, Ḥanan the Egyptian, and gives Admon's father's name as Gadai. The fact that at M. Ketubot 13:9, Yoḥanan b. Zakkai discusses these individuals' decisions suggests that they lived while the Temple stood. Little more is known about them.

Adonai *see* GOD, NAMES OF

adoption the assumption of responsibility for another. Adoption in Esther 2:7 and 2:15 is prompted by the death of the heroine's parents; in the Book of Aḥikar, the title character adopts his sister's son Nadan in order to provide himself an heir (cf. Gen. 15:2–3). One example of adoption appears in the Elephantine papyri. Paul employs adoption (*huiothesia*), sometimes translated as "sonship," to indicate the Christian's present as well as future relationship to God as mediated through Jesus or the Holy Spirit (Gal. 4:5; Rom. 8:15, 23; Eph. 1:5). This metaphorical usage may derive from language concerning the adoption of household slaves and/or from the covenantal adoption of Israel and its kings (cf. Exod. 4:22, 6:7; 2 Sam. 7). *See also* ORPHAN.

adultery in Hellenistic Judaism, intercourse between a married or betrothed woman and any man not her husband, a capital offense (Lev. 20:10; Deut. 22:22–24; Sus.; John 7:53–8:11; see also Prov. 6:26, 32; Ecclus. 23:22–27). In contrast to Exodus 20:13–14 and Deuteronomy 5:17–18 (MT), the Book of Biblical Antiquities (Liber Antiquitatum Biblicarum) 11:10 lists adultery before murder in its version of the Decalogue (also LXX; Luke 18:20; Rom. 13:9; James 2:11). The plot of Susanna pivots on the heroine's choice of actual adultery with the vile elders or death prompted by their false charge. Psalms of Solomon 8:10 presents widespread adultery among the reasons for Pompey's capture of Jerusalem, and the Vision of Ezra describes the horrendous final judgment of both male and female adulterers (12–18). Metaphorically, adultery indicates the covenant community's infidelity to God (Hos.; Matt. 12:39). Jubilees 39 and the Testament of Joseph comment on Potiphar's wife and her desired adultery with Joseph.

The Gospels extend the definition of adultery from action to intention and proclaim that intercourse with anyone not one's first spouse constitutes adultery (Matt. 5:27–28, 32; Mark 10:11–12; Luke 16:18). In John 7:53–8:11, Jesus forgives a woman caught in the act.

Rabbinic Judaism uses the same definition of adultery as does Hellenistic Judaism. Rabbinic application of the term "adultery" to a betrothed woman reflects the understanding that betrothal is tantamount to marriage and that a betrothed woman requires a writ of divorce if she is to marry a different man. While a man who has intercourse with another man's wife is subject to punishment, his infidelity to his own wife is not in the category of adultery. This is because, in the biblical and talmudic systems, there is no prohibition against polygamy. Only in medieval times was the wife's right to enforce her husband's sexual faithfulness recognized, a function of the formalization of the prohibition against polygamy. The child of an adulterous union is a *mamzer,* excluded from membership in the Israelite people (Deut. 23:2) or from marrying a Jew of untainted lineage (M. Kiddushin 3:12).

The rabbis listed adultery along with idol worship and murder as one of the three acts that a person may not commit even at the cost of his or her own life (B. Sanhedrin 74a). Scripture, for its part, designates adultery a capital crime, for the commission of which the adulterous woman as well as the man must die (Lev. 20:10; Deut. 22:22). Rabbinic law holds that execution for this offense is by strangulation (M. Sanhedrin 11:1, referring to the punishment of the man), which always applies when scripture does not explicitly indicate the means of execution. A priest's daughter who commits adultery is executed by being burned (B. Sanhedrin 66b).

Numbers 5:11–31 describes "the ordeal of the bitter waters," a procedure through which the guilt or innocence of a suspected adulteress was tested. Moved by jealousy, her husband brought her to the tabernacle, where, in an elaborate ritual, a priest administered a potion of water and dust. If she had acted unfaithfully, the water caused bitter pain, swelling, and ultimately death. If she was innocent, it had no impact whatsoever.

Even while detailing the procedure through which the bitter waters were administered, the rabbinic literature profoundly limits the application of this rite. Only if there were witnesses to the woman's actions, if she understood the laws relating to adultery, and if she had been warned regarding her contact with this specific man (M. Sotah 1:1–2) could the ordeal of the bitter waters be carried out. In most cases, in place of this rite, a suspected adulteress is simply to be divorced (M. Sotah 6:1). The rite in all events was nullified by Yoḥanan b. Zakkai, the result of the increase in the number of adulterers in his day (M. Sotah 9:9). In light of the destruction of the Temple, where the needed rite was performed, it could not in any event be carried out.

The rabbis held in the greatest contempt a man who had intercourse with another's wife. No matter what his other virtues, he could not escape Gehenna (B. Sotah 4b). The adulterer was subject to flagellation and was forbidden from marrying a woman with whom there was any suspicion that he had engaged in an adulterous relationship, even after her divorce.

Adversus Judaeos writers phrase adopted since at least the 1930s to describe a genre of early Christian apologetic and polemical literature written against Jewish history and Jewish and Jewish-Christian practice. The phrase "Adversus Judaeos" (Against the Jews, or In answer to the Jews) is first found in the last quarter of the second century C.E. as the title of monographs written by Pseudo-Cyprian (c. 175) and Tertullian (197). On the Latin side, other significant writers are Cyprian, Augustine, and, on the edge of our period, Isidore. Important Greek contributions are made by Justin, Hippolytus(?), Eusebius of Caesarea, and John Chrysostom, and by works wrongly attributed to Barnabas, Gregory of Nyssa, and Gregentius. A completely different but equally "anti-Semitic" line was taken by Marcion. Syriac authors include Ephraem, Aphrahat, Isaac of Antioch, and Jacob of Serug.

These Christian writers should be put into context. Before the rise of Christianity to literary prominence, Jews had been polemicizing against Gentiles (Old Testament prophets; Philo, *Hypothetica*; Josephus, *Against Apion*), and Gentiles had been polemicizing against Jews; after the rise of the Jesus movement, both Jews (Celsus's Jew) and Gentiles (Celsus; Porphyry; Julian) had directed their artillery onto the church. In turn, Christians (e.g., Tatian; Tertullian; Arnobius; Orosius) wrote against Gentiles and against Jews. Members of all three groups frequently engaged in serious debate and acrimonious vilification. This literary engagement was part of a wider confrontation, which might include physical violence. Josephus clearly shows the vigor of Gentile "anti-Semitic" feeling and writing, and Christian Adversus Judaeos writers must be seen, at least in part, as belonging to that tradition.

Whatever the contribution of the Old Testament to this disputation, few will deny that of the New Testament. Some writers are apparently very critical of the Jewish heritage (cf. Matthew; John; Stephen; and the author of Heb.), and some have been criticized for being "anti-Semitic." This is a crude and simplistic assessment, just as "anti-Semitic" is itself an imprecise word, but some statements cannot be ignored: for example, "His blood be on us and on our children"; "You are of your father the devil"; "You stiff-necked people, uncircumcised in heart and ears, you always resist the Holy Spirit"; "In speaking of a new covenant he treats the first as obsolete. And what is becoming obsolete and growing old is ready to vanish away." Such authoritative statements would very readily come to mind as the Church was removed from its Jewish roots, was increasingly "gentilized," and was perhaps heckled and hounded here and there by Jewish groups. The Jewishness of Jesus and Paul and their frequently positive appreciation of their heritage could be easily forgotten in an alien land. With such ammunition as that quoted above, the next fifteen centuries are not difficult to imagine.

But if the New Testament provided precedent, the main struggle concerned the Old Testament. To whom did it belong? To whom did it refer? Adversus Judaeos writers were in no doubt about the answer—to the Church. Speaking of the covenant, Pseudo-Barnabas says, "Ours it is, but they [the Jews] lost it in this way [through idolatry] forever." Allegory was the exegetical tool that made the most unpromising material eloquent of Christian faith and practice, so that the Old Testament prophesied every detail of the career of Jesus, who was Christ and God, even his rejection by the Jews and the displacement of the Synagogue by the Church as heir to the promises of God. The bulky Old Testament was made manageable for debate and dialogue by being ransacked for particular texts that "proved" particular Christian dogmas. These texts were classified and in that form became the handbook of every preacher and writer (cf. Cyprian's Testimonia). Their ultimate purpose was to mark out the Church's identity and prove its distinctiveness from and superiority over Judaism.

advocate (Gr.: *paraklētos,* one who is summoned to aid another) heavenly figure who serves as the helper and defender of the righteous, especially when they suffer injustice. In the construct of the two spirits, which pits two figures against one another in the heavenly court, the accuser (Satan) is opposed by a defending attorney who looks after the interest of the righteous by pleading their just cause before God and protecting them from evil in a variety of ways. In the Community Rule, 1QS 3:18–25, that figure is called the prince of light, the angel of God's truth, and the spirit of holiness and is probably identified with the angel Michael. This spirit leads the righteous on the path of right conduct, defending them from the onslaughts of the evil angel and thus ensuring them of the reward of eternal life. In the Testament of Judah 20, this figure is known as the spirit of truth and opposes the spirit of error.

The Greek term *paraklētos* appears nowhere in the Septuagint or Greek pseudepigrapha, but is employed four times in the Gospel of John (14:16, 26; 15:26; 16:7), where it refers to the spirit whom Jesus and his Father will send after Jesus' resurrection. (The KJV wrongly translates the word as "comforter," from Gr. *parakalein,* to comfort.) Identified as the "holy spirit" and the "spirit of truth," its function is to "be with" Jesus' followers, leading them in the right path by revealing to them the meaning of the words that Jesus spoke during his life. The spirit is also seen as Jesus' advocate, witnessing concerning him and convicting the world of unbelief (John 16:7–11). The expression "another advocate" (14:16) implies that John sees Jesus himself serving this function (cf. 1 John 2:1, where this is explicit). The close association between Jesus and the "advocate" is duplicated in Romans 8, which identifies the Spirit of God with the Spirit of the risen Christ and attributes to this figure the angelic role of interceding for the children of God (vv. 26–27). While Christian theologians cite these passages in John and Romans with reference to the Holy Spirit, the third person of the Trinity, the actions ascribed to this spirit derive from the Jewish notion of a high angel who carried out legal and ethical functions in behalf of God's people. The principal difference is the spirit's association with the risen Jesus. *See also* SPIRITS, TWO.

Aelia Capitolina name given to the city of Jerusalem in 135 C.E., in the aftermath of the failed Bar Kokhba revolt, after the emperor Hadrian (Aelius Hadrianus) and the god Jupiter Capitolinus. The change in the city's name represents the actualization of a plan, almost certainly conceived before the war, to turn Jerusalem into a Roman colony and to obliterate forever its Jewish character. In line with this plan, after the war, Jews still residing in the city were driven out, and no Jews were permitted to enter the city area, upon pain of death. Gentile colonists were settled in the Jews' place. The city's constitution was that of a Roman colony, and the image of a pig purportedly was carved on the southern gate of the city, facing Bethlehem. The main cult of the city was that of Jupiter Capitolinus, to whom a temple was erected on the site of the former Jewish Temple. Alongside Jupiter, Bacchus, Serapis, Astarte, and the Dioscuri appear on coins as deities of the city.

Aelius Restitutus *see* RESTITUTUS, TITUS AELIUS

Aelius Sempronius Lycinus *see* LYCINUS, PUBLIUS AELIUS SEMPRONIUS

Aelius Statutus *see* STATUTUS, PUBLIUS AELIUS

Aemilianus, Sextus Attius Suburanus procurator of Judea, early 90s C.E. In 84 he served with Julius when he was prefect of Egypt. He then was procurator of the Cottian Alps, Judea, and Belgica. At the beginning of Trajan's reign, he became the prefect of the Praetorian Guards. Nothing is known of his time in Judea.

Aemilius Bassus *see* BASSUS, MARCUS AEMILIUS

Aet. *see* DE AETERNITATE MUNDI

Afastia an undisclosed location referred to at B. Erubin 100b ("But did Rab not come to Afastia and forbid use of a stripped tree?")

afikoman the larger half of the middle piece of three pieces of *matzah* (unleavened bread) placed on the seder plate at the Passover table. The middle piece of *matzah* is divided into two pieces, the larger of which is called the *afikoman,* meaning either "postprandial entertainment" or "dessert." Its eating marks the end of the meal.

Afrahat (270?–345? C.E.) dignitary of the Syrian Church. One of the earliest leaders of the Syrian Church, he was part of the ascetic movement known as the "sons of the covenant." These were not monks but ascetics who stayed in the world, yet chose to remain celibate. He was also a high-ranking dignitary of the Syrian Church, perhaps a bishop, at Mar Mattai, north of Nineveh, near the present-day Iraqi town of Mosul. Apparently all of his writings have survived. Among them are twenty-three treatises, letters, or homilies, entitled *Demonstrations,* in a fifth/sixth-century manuscript. Originally there must have been twenty-two, corresponding to the number of letters of the Syriac alphabet. He wrote number twenty-three at the time that Shapur II began his bloody persecution of the Christians in 345. Numbers 1–10 were written in 337 and deal with Christian asceticism. Numbers 11–23 were written between 343 and 345 and, with the exception of number 14, are a polemic against the Jews. The Jewish-Christian argument was important to Afrahat because the Iranian church included a significant number of converted Jews. Furthermore, the Jews enjoyed a good deal of prosperity during Afrahat's life. Afrahat's work is scripturally based, and the debate is carried along exegetical-historical lines. His writings evidence little if any hatred for the Jews. While he analyzes and rejects Jewish beliefs and practices and criticizes the Jews' past and present actions, he does not vilify them as did many of the other church fathers. Afrahat's arguments rely on historical facts accepted by both Jews and Christians; he does not employ biblical interpretations accepted by Christianity but rejected by Judaism. His exegeses of the Bible are presented in a rational and reasonable manner; he avoided traditional Christian interpretations of scripture that were generally repudiated by Judaism. Afrahat often cites scripture to support his historical claims, but he seems to be most interested in establishing historical facts. Unlike many of his Christian contemporaries who wrote on Judaism, Afrahat does not attempt to allegorize the Bible. Like the Jews, Afrahat believed that the Bible's commandments spoke of concrete things, and not in allegory. Afrahat dealt with circumcision, the Passover sacrifice, the Sabbath, the dietary laws, the Jews as the chosen people, and the messiah. He also identifies specific Jewish criticisms of Christianity, such as the fact that adherents worshiped Christ, that they were persecuted, and that many were celebate monks and nuns. The underlying theme of Afrahat's writings about Judaism is that God has rejected the Jews and called the Christian church in their place because the Jews rejected Jesus. He also claims that Jewish religious practices do not lead to salvation, nor had they in the past. They had been imposed upon the Jews because of their sins. It is of interest that Afrahat focused his attention on Judaism and virtually ignored Mazdaism, the religion of the majority of the Iranian population. Afrahat's audience consisted of recently converted Christians who interacted daily with a vital Jewish community. Afrahat saw his task as strengthening the faith of his community in their belief that they—not the Jews—were God's chosen people and that the Christians, not the Jews, had the proper understanding of the Bible and of what God expected of them. There is little evidence that Afrahat was familiar with rabbinic exegeses of the Bible or that the rabbis were aware of Afrahat's critique of Judaism. When the rabbis and Afrahat share a religious view or ethic, there is no common exegetical tradition upon which they draw. The few parallels that occur between Afrahat and the rabbinic texts point to a common environment and not to actual borrowing from each other.

Africanus, Sextus Julius (d. c. 240 C.E.) Christian chronographer. He was born in Jerusalem and lived most of his life in Palestine. His *Chronicle* (only partially preserved) was the first Christian synchronic world history; it attempted to coordinate dates from the Hebrew Bible and Christianity with those of Graeco-Roman historians. He made use of a 7,000-year plan of history, with the birth of Jesus in the year 5500. The work includes a good deal of information on Jewish history, possibly from Justus of Tiberias.

afterlife existence after physical death. With few exceptions, biblical authors believed that "life" was lived now, in this world, and that death was followed by one's descent to a gloomy semi-existence in Sheol (Isa. 38:9–20). The Book of Ecclesiastes may suggest something effectively closer to annihilation, perhaps following strains of Greek skepticism. Two exceptions to the rule are Isaiah 26:19 and Daniel 12:2, which posit a resurrection of the dead. It is sometimes argued that Psalm 16:11, 49:15, and 73:23–24 express belief in an afterlife; if so, the conception is vague.

Some Second Temple nonbiblical texts continue the notion that death leads to a permanent existence in Sheol (Tob. 3:6; Ecclus. 14:16). However, as Isaiah 26 and Daniel 12 attest, the late Persian and early Hellenistic periods mark a significant transition toward the belief that after death God rewards and punishes the righteous and wicked, respectively, according to their deeds. The time, manner, and place of rewards and punishments vary widely, and the conceptions are clarified and worked out gradually over three to four centuries, with no orthodoxy pervading until a century or two into the Common Era. The variety of beliefs in Jewish texts include: resurrection of the body (1 Enoch 1–36, 2 Macc. 7, and perhaps Dan. 12:2); resurrection of the spirit or soul (1 Enoch 102–104); ascent of the spirit to God (Jub. 23:31); immortality of the souls of the righteous (Wisd. of Sol. 1–5); and present participation in eternal life (1QH 3:19–36, 11:3–14). Texts that posit a resurrection of the body envision a renewed earth (and Jerusalem) as the locus of a fabulously long life after death. Where new life takes a spiritual form, heaven is the place of bliss, where one exists eternally in the presence of God and, often, as a member of the angelic entourage. The place of postmortem punishment also varies. Where heaven is the place of blessing, earth may be turned into the locus of punishment (Test. Moses 10). In other texts it is the Valley of Hinnom south of Jerusalem (1 Enoch 27) or Sheol (1 Enoch 103:5–8).

Biblical notions about a uniformly gloomy existence in Sheol stand in contrast to ideas of postmortem judgment (and rewards and punishments) in some of the contemporary ancient world, for example; Egypt (attested in the Book of the Dead) and Greece (Homer's *Odyssey*). While some Jewish texts reflect Greek philosophical speculation about the immortality of the soul, Jewish notions about resurrection, immortality, and eternal life are tied especially to the experience of persecution and oppression and to a persistent faith that the justice of God will prevail in spite of an unrequited life or an unjust death.

Resurrection and eternal life are central to the belief of the early church and are uniformly tied to belief in the resurrection of Jesus. Formulations vary as they do in the Jewish writings. Mark 12:25 and its parallels posit an angellike existence. For Paul, Christians will participate in the glory of the body of the resurrected Christ (1 Cor. 15; Phil. 3:21). In keeping with this, he refers to meeting Christ in the air after the resurrection (1 Thess. 4:14–18); however, Romans 8:18–25 suggests a renewal of creation. The Apocalypse of John envisions eternal life in a new Jerusalem come to earth (Rev. 20–21), which is consonant with the beatitude that envisions the meek inheriting the land (Matt. 5:5). The Fourth Gospel's sharp dualism between heaven and a world darkened by sin and the devil is reflected in Jesus' promise to prepare a place for believers in heaven (John 14:3).

Talmudic writings reveal a wide variety of perspectives on life after death, the soul, resurrection, and the messianic age. While there is agreement on the existence of an afterlife, the absence of thematic, let alone conceptual, unity renders it possible to define only broadly the rabbinic conception of what happens to the soul after death.

For twelve months after death—a period of purgatory for the wicked or, in some views, for the righteous and wicked alike—the soul remains in contact with the disintegrating body (B. Shabbat 152b–153a; see B. Rosh Hashanah 17a). After this, the righteous go to paradise (Gan Eden, the Garden of Eden) and the wicked to hell (Gehinnom). The nature of the soul and the character of death itself are subject to dispute. B. Berakhot 18b–19a and parallels describe the dead as fully conscious and, in some rabbis' views, still able to discern what is happening in the world; they only lack the ability to speak. Other descriptions (e.g., B. Shabbat 152b) have the soul hidden under God's heavenly throne, quite distinct from human existence.

The doctrine of messianic redemption and resurrection of the dead is central to rabbinic thought, although, here again, the exact nature of the resurrection is in dispute. B. Rosh Hashanah 16b–17a holds that on the Day of Judgment, three groups will arise: the thoroughly righteous, the thoroughly wicked, and those in the middle. All authorities agree that the righteous immediately are sealed for eternal life, while the wicked are assigned to hell. The fate of those in the middle is subject to dispute. Some authorities hold that they first are sent to hell, where they scream in prayer and are redeemed; others hold that as a result of God's mercy, they share the fate of the thoroughly righteous. The messianic world itself generally is perceived either as a perfected analog to present times (see B. Berakhot 34b; B. Shabbat 63a) or as a wholly spiritual world in which the righteous sit at God's side (B. Berakhot 17a). *See also* ASSUMPTION; LIFE, ETERNAL; RESURRECTION.

Against Apion English name of the writing by Josephus that is often referred to by its Latin title *Contra Apionem*; the work's title is abbreviated *Ag. Apion* or *C. Apion.* In this work, which is an attack on Apion (who had written an anti-Jewish work), Josephus defends Judaism by quoting various Greek writers who attest to the antiquity and positive values of the Jews and Judaism. *See also* APION.

Against Flaccus *see* IN FLACCUM

Agatharchides of Cnidus Greek grammarian and Peripatetic of the late second century B.C.E. Only some fragments survive of his histories of Asia in ten books and of Europe in forty-nine books. Two passages about the Jews are preserved in quotations by Josephus. Agatharchides stated that the Jews had a custom of abstaining from work every seventh day, at which time they neither bore arms nor did any agricultural or public works, but rather prayed with outstretched hands in the "temples." Because of this custom, he wrote, Ptolemy I was able to take Jerusalem on the Sabbath, since the inhabitants refused to fight on that day.

Agathias (531–580 C.E.) Armenian historian. He was born in Aeolis in Asia Minor and studied law in Alexandria and Constantinople. He compiled a seven-book collection of poetic epigrams written around his time. He intended to write a history that was designed to bring Procopius's *Wars* up to date. However, by the time of his death he had covered only the years 553–559. He treats matters in a rhetorical and moralizing manner. The work contains two excursuses on the history and customs of the Sassanids in which he claims that the Magi have the final say on all matters among the Persians.

age (Heb.: *seiḇah*) old age, commencing at age sixty, and ripe old age, commencing at age seventy. Age is the mark of wisdom: "If the aged say tear down and the youth say build, tear down, for the destruction of age is building, and the building of age is destruction." Death before age sixty is counted as extirpation (Heb.: *karot*), a form of penalty for a sin. Once one reaches age sixty, one knows that penalty has not been incurred for any reason. Age is the acquirement of wisdom and understanding. But the value of age depends on knowledge of the Torah: "When sages grow old, their minds become serene; when the ignorant grow old, their minds become agitated."

age, this (Heb.: *haOlam haZeh*; Gr.: *ho aiōn houtos*) the time period from creation to the judgment that concludes the age and is followed by the age to come. Alternatively, the Hebrew and Greek words may denote the world that exists in the present time. In this scheme, this age (or world) is marked by trouble and evil, which will be eliminated in the age (or world) to come (2 Bar. 15:8, 48:50). The expression is attested in the mid-first century C.E. in the writings of Paul (Rom. 12:2; 1 Cor. 2:6; Gal. 1:4), who shares the notion that the present age or world is under the power of the evil spirits (1 Cor. 2:6, 8). *See also* AGES, TWO; AGE TO COME.

agency (Heb.: *sheliḥut*) the theory that one party may legally act on behalf of another, as though the principal were doing the action. A person's agent is legally equivalent to the person, and one is bound by what one's agent does as though one had done it oneself. But agency does not pertain to transgression, and if the agent does not carry out instructions, the principal is not accountable for the deed. An agent may serve to effect a betrothal or a divorce.

ages, two a theological construct that divides time into two periods, this age, which began at creation, and the age to come, which will begin after the final judgment. Alternatively, one may translate the Hebrew *olam* as "world" and speak of this world and the world to come. The roots of the concept lie in biblical eschatological texts that point toward a future moment when God will create a new heaven and a new earth. Later Jewish eschatological texts tend to posit a multiplicity of periods before the judgment, but the qualitative contrast between the aggregate of these periods and the future is clear. Thus in Daniel 2:36–45 and 7:1–27, the judgment inaugurates the permanent reign of God that replaces the time of the four kingdoms that preceded it. The idea of the two ages (or two worlds) is explicitly attested in the first century C.E. in such texts as Matthew 12:32 and 2 Baruch 15:8 and becomes common fare in rabbinic texts, where "the age to come" is often associated with divine retribution (e.g., M. Sanh. 10:1). *See also* AGE, THIS; AGE TO COME; END OF DAYS, TIMES, AGE; ESCHATOLOGY.

age to come (Heb.: *haOlam haBa*; Gr.: *ho aiōn mellōn/erchomenos*) in the construct of the two ages, the age or world that begins when God's judgment has ended the present age or world. In contrast to the present, which is marked by trouble, evil, and the power of Satan, it will be a time of bliss and the locus of eternal life. In rabbinic literature, the notion is separated from its apocalyptic origins, and the term is a shorthand for the time when the righteous will receive their just reward (M. Sanh. 10:1). *See also* AGE, THIS; AGES, TWO.

aggadah (prerabbinic texts) interpretation of the Hebrew Bible in narrative form. Aggadah in Jewish texts of the Hellenistic and early Roman periods may elaborate biblical narratives or may be new narrative created from nonnarrative biblical texts.

The first kind of aggadah is sometimes called the "rewritten Bible." Texts like Jubilees, the Genesis Apocryphon, the Book of Biblical Antiquities, and Josephus's *Antiquities of the Jews* present running narratives that revise and re-present long sections of biblical narrative. Other texts like 1 Enoch 6–11, the Testament of Job, the Testaments of the Twelve Patriarchs, and Joseph and Asenath elaborate on individual narrative episodes in the Bible. Two complementary principles are operative in both kinds of texts. First, the aggadah is exegetical; narrative is created or reshaped to expound the biblical text. Second, this exposition has a specific function. It may solve a problem in the biblical text, or speak to new times and current concerns, or sometimes just entertain. Joseph and Asenath explains the patriarch's marriage to the daughter of an Egyptian priest and provides a prototype for proselytism. Running narratives have overarching themes and tendencies. The author of Jubilees consistently depicts the pre-Mosaic patriarchs observing the Torah and celebrating festivals according to the solar calendar. Repentance for Israel requires that the people observe the Torah as this author expounds it in a narrative that corresponds to Genesis 1–Exodus 12. The author of the Book of Biblical Antiquities, writing when Israel has a crisis in leadership, retells the narratives from Genesis to 1 Samuel, interpolating incidents that illustrate the successes and failures of Israel's good and bad leaders.

Some aggadic narrative is created from nonnarrative biblical texts. The story of Zebulun the fisherman (Test. Zeb. 5–6) takes its inspiration from the blessing of Jacob (Gen. 49:13). Bel and the Dragon appears, in part, to be a narrativizing exposition of Isaiah 45–46. The legend of the mother and her seven sons (2 Macc. 7) draws details of its narrative from several texts: the song of Hannah (1 Sam. 2), Second Isaiah's passages about the return of the sons of mother Zion, creation and redemption, and the servant of YHWH.

Two factors are operative in aggadic narrative building. Interpretation is a kind of updating of an ancient, and sometimes authoritative, text. The storyteller makes a point not through formal exhortation or explicit teaching (proverbs or halakic exposition), but by creating a story whose characters enact or illustrate the point. Thus one creates fiction in order to present what one considers truth.

The aggadic process is evident in literature that spans many centuries. Although Jubilees (2d c. B.C.E.) is our earliest example of a running narrative exposition of scripture, some of its stories are traditional and may stem from a time when the base text was itself not yet scripture (cf. also the Chronicler's rewriting of the as-yet noncanonical Deuteronomistic history); thus one should use the term "rewritten Scripture" only cautiously and selectively. At the other end of the time span, the Targumim Neofiti 1 and Pseudo-Jonathan contain or allude to narrative episodes that are attested in earlier Jewish literature from the pre-70 C.E. period. Finally, a New Testament text such as Matthew 2 illustrates the aggadic process, recounting a story about Jesus' infancy that mirrors the antagonism between Moses and Pharaoh (2:20; cf. Exod. 4:19) and expounds Hosea 11:1 (Matt. 2:15). *See also* MIDRASH; REWRITTEN BIBLE; SCRIPTURAL INTERPRETATION.

Aggadat Ḥazitah *see* SONG OF SONGS RABBAH

Agnostos theos *see* GOD, UNKNOWN

agoranomos official in charge of a city's market (Gr.: *agora*) who was responsible for regulating buying and selling. He (or they, for there were often several) collected the customs, kept order, regulated the quality of goods, and ensured correct weights and measurements. The post in Tiberias was held by Agrippa I before he became king. The term is also mentioned quite often in rabbinic literature, and Ra<u>b</u> is said to have held the post in Babylonia.

Agr. *see* DE AGRICULTURA

Agrippa I (10 B.C.E.–44 C.E.) son of Aristobolus and Bernice, grandson of Herod the Great; ruled as Roman-appointed king of Judea from 41–44. He was raised in Rome where he became friends with the emperor Tiberius (14–37), the future emperors Gaius Caligula (37–41) and Claudius (41–54), and other members of the aristocracy. In his youth Agrippa was known for his imprudence and extravagance. He fell deeply into debt because he spent lavishly to win imperial patronage and only extricated himself with the help of wealthy friends, after which he left Rome for Judea. His uncle, Antipas, the ruler of Galilee and Perea, made him supervisor of the market in Tiberias, a position he soon found inadequate. He then moved to Antioch to the court of Flaccus, the Roman governor of Syria, but lost favor there when he took a bribe. Returning to Rome, he again ran up large debts in seeking the favor of Gaius. After he spoke loosely about Gaius succeeding Tiberius as emperor, Tiberius jailed him for suspicion of sedition. When Gaius succeeded Tiberius as emperor in 37, he immediately released Agrippa and made him king over the territories north of Galilee. When Antipas lost his tetrarchy in 39, Agrippa was made ruler of his territory, Galilee, and also Perea.

In 41, Agrippa was in Rome when Gaius was murdered. He helped Claudius secure the throne and so received Samaria and Judea as additional parts of his domain. He was an amiable ruler, according to the historian Josephus, and carefully observed the Jewish laws incumbent on a king. At the same time, he erected statues and buildings and supported the athletic games in various Greek cities outside his realm. He attempted to fortify Jerusalem further and coordinate the activities of a number of kings in the area, but the Roman authorities suspected and stopped these activities. According to the Acts of the Apostles, chapter 12, which incorrectly refers to Agrippa as "Herod," he executed James, son of Zebedee, one of Jesus of Nazareth's disciples, and imprisoned another, Peter. He died at Caesarea after a brief illness. After his death, Roman procurators replaced him as the rulers of Judea and Jerusalem.

Agrippa II (28–93, 94, or 100 C.E.) son of Agrippa I and Cypros, daughter of Phasael, raised in Rome during the reign of Claudius. He was too young to succeed his father in 44 but he was active in support of Jewish interests in the imperial court. Around 50, the emperor Claudius appointed him king of Chalcis in Lebanon and gave him the right to appoint the high priest in Jerusalem. In 53, Claudius transferred him to the territories north of Galilee. Nero (54–68) added parts of Galilee and Perea to Agrippa II's territory. He was an active member of the Roman ruling elite and a faithful supporter of the Temple. Amid persistent rumors of an incestuous relationship between them, his sister Berenice lived with him at his court and had great influence on him. According to Acts 25–26, the procurator Festus (60–62) consulted Agrippa and Berenice in Caesarea concerning the case against the apostle Paul.

During the war with Rome (66–70), Agrippa first

tried to reconcile the people of Jerusalem to Rome. When he failed and war broke out, he vigorously supported the Romans with auxiliary troops. After the war his territory was augmented, and his reign endured at least until the time of Domitian (81–96). The date of his death is uncertain, but should probably be placed in the nineties.

agunah *see* ABANDONED WOMAN

Aḥa **1.** second-century C.E. Tannaitic authority, who was a younger contemporary of Simeon b. Yoḥai

2. third-century Palestinian amora referred to as Raba (the Great)

3. third-century Palestinian amora, the brother of Abba

4. fourth-century Palestinian amora, an associate of Jonah and Yose, born in Lydda but active in Tiberias

Aḥa b. Abbuha Savoraic authority active at Pumbedita; died on the Day of Atonement in 510 C.E. He is sometimes referred to as Aḥa b. Raba b. Abbuha; his first name is also given as Aḥai.

ahabah *see* LOVE

Ahabah b. Zera Palestinian amora; son of Zera I; active at Caesaria and known for transmitting his father's teachings and for his scriptural interpretations. His first name is alternatively recorded as Ahabah, Aḥa, and Aḥva.

Aḥa b. Ḥanina Palestinian amora of the late third and early fourth centuries C.E.; active in Daroma, in southern Judea. He is known for his explanations of the ninth and tenth of the Eighteen Benedictions and for his belief that visiting the sick facilitates a cure (B. Nedarim 39b).

Aḥa b. Jacob Babylonian amora of the early fourth century C.E. He was an older contemporary of Abayye and Raba and a student of Ḥuna. Known for his extreme dedication to study (see, e.g., B. Erubin 65a), he was a renowned scholar and legal authority (B. Erubin 63a). He is said to have been a skilled writer of Torah scrolls (see, e.g., B. Baba Batra 14a). Some mystical discussions are attributed to Aḥa b. Jacob (e.g., B. Baba Batra 75a) and he reportedly rid the academy at Pumbedita of a demon (B. Kiddushin 29b).

Aḥa b. Pappa Palestinian amora of the third century C.E.; a contemporary of Abbahu; referred to by the surname Arikha.

Aḥa b. Rab Babylonian rabbi of the end of the fourth and beginning of the fifth century C.E. He was a student of Rabina I and disputed some of Rabina's rules. Mesharshiyah was his grandson.

Aḥa b. Raba Babylonian amora, the son of Raba b. Joseph; a contemporary of Amemar and Ashi; died in 419 C.E. At the end of his life, he was head of the academy at Pumbedita.

Aḥai b. Josiah Tannaitic authority; a contemporary of Judah the Patriarch (late 2d c. C.E.). B. Shabbat 152b reports Aḥai's speaking from his grave to the Babylonian amora Naḥman. The story's setting, on Naḥman's property, and other talmudic traditions regarding Aḥai's activity suggest that he spent considerable time in Babylonia. His name appears exclusively in Babylonian texts.

Aḥa of Lydda *see* AḤA

Aḥa of Shabḥa Babylonian rabbi of the eighth century C.E., who migrated to Israel after being passed over for appointment as gaon of Pumbedita. He is the author of Sheiltot, an influential collection of rabbinic homilies on biblical and rabbinic ethics and values.

Ahawa b. Zera *see* AHABAH B. ZERA

Aḥer *see* ELISHA B. ABUYAH

aḥer, aḥerim *see* OUTSIDER

Ahikar, Story of old Mesopotamian court tale transmitted in Jewish and Christian circles. Although the story is of non-Jewish Mesopotamian origin, its earliest attestation is in a fragmentary fifth-century-B.C.E. Aramaic papyrus discovered in 1907 among the literary remains of the Jewish colony at Elephantine in Egypt. Later and more extensive versions are preserved in manuscripts of Christian origin in languages such as Syriac, Arabic, Armenian, and Slavonic. The oral form of this story must precede the fifth century by some considerable time, making it contemporary at least with the Babylonian exile. Its folkloric roots may be very old indeed.

The heart of this story is a traditional genre about the vindication and exaltation of a persecuted and condemned courtier, attested also in the Joseph story (Gen. 37–45), the story of Mordecai in the Book of Esther, and Daniel 3–6. It is enhanced here through the inclusion of long strings of proverbial material that emphasize Ahikar's role as a court sage. Ahikar, an official of the Assyrian kings Sennacherib and Esarhaddon, falls afoul of a death plot by his own nephew Nadan. Eventually Ahikar is rescued by an old friend and restored to power. Many of his proverbs focus on issues appropriate to the court, family matters, and everyday conduct.

The wide knowledge and influence of the story is evident in the excerpts that appear in the Greek Life of Aesop and in the allusions to details of the story in the Book of Tobit, who is said to be a relative of Ahikar (Tob. 1:21–22, 2:10, 14:10). The story's transmission in Christian circles may reflect the fact that its genre was also used to recount the passion and death of Jesus in the New Testament gospels. The Mesopotamian origins of the story attest the multicultural roots of narrative material like that in Genesis, Esther, and Daniel.

Aila name given to Eilat early in the second century C.E., when the city served as a Nabatean port (Strabo, *Geography* 16:2, 30; Pliny, *Natural History* 5:12). Aila remained a major Roman and then Byzantine commercial and military port, the headquarters of Byzantine defense of the south of Palestine.

aiōn (Gr., age, eternity) When used in reference to God, *aiōn* means "eternity"; but when referring to human matters, its meaning is closer to "age." It is normally the translation of *olam* in the Septuagint. The word is found especially in discussions of eschatology.

aisthēsis (Gr., sense perception) Since philosophers thought that the person should be controlled by the mind (Gr.: *nous*), whereas most people seemed to give themselves over to the senses, the word often had a negative connotation. Among Jewish writers, the term is especially important in the works of Philo of Alexandria.

Aitha Aitha Ashaab, referred to at Tosefta Sheb̲iit 4:11 as demarcating a border area of the Land of Israel

Akab̲iah *see* MAR UKBA II

Akab̲iah b. Mehallel early Tannaitic master, of the late first or early second century C.E. His dictum is recorded at M. Ab̲ot 3:1: "Reflect upon three things and you will not fall into the clutches of transgression: Know from whence you come, where you are going, and before whom you are going to have to give a full account [of yourself]. . . ." M. Eduyyot 5:6–7 reports that he was excommunicated for refusing to retract a legal position.

akedah (Heb., binding) Abraham's binding and (intended) sacrifice of Isaac (Gen. 22). In this central episode of the Abraham cycle, God tests (v. 1) the patriarch's readiness to obey unconditionally. It is a test of Abraham's faith, although this word does not occur in chapter 22. Abraham's faith was mentioned in 15:6 in response to the promise of progeny, and God now asks the old man to give up the son who fulfills that promise.

Early Jewish interpretations emphasize that Abraham had been "found faithful" when put to this test (Jub. 17:15–18:16; Ecclus. 44:20; 1 Macc. 2:52; cf. Neh. 9:8). The version in Jubilees 17–18 enhances the testing motif by framing the story with a heavenly prologue and epilogue reminiscent of Job 1–2. The account of the incident in the Book of Biblical Antiquities 32:1–4 alludes to the prologue and epilogue of the Jubilees version and emphasizes Isaac's willingness to die. The parallel story of the sacrifice of Jephthah's daughter in the Hebrew Bible mentions the same willingness as an essential element in the effectiveness of her sacrifice (LAB 40; cf. Judg. 11). Josephus (*Ant.* 1.13.1–4:222–236) highlights Abraham's faith and Isaac's willingness to die in a father–son dialogue that is reminiscent of the conversation of the mother and her seven sons in 2 Maccabees 7 and 4 Maccabees 8–18. The latter text also cites Abraham's obedience at the *akedah* as a model for the mother's courage (4 Macc. 15:24–30, 16:20, 18:11). Similar elements appear in Philo (*On Abr.* 167–207) and in Targum Neofiti Genesis 22:10.

Explicit New Testament references to the *akedah* describe Abraham's faith as obedient action. In Hebrews 11:17–19, the *akedah* exemplifies the pattern of faith enunciated throughout the chapter. The wording in James 2:21–24 indicates dependence on the tradition attested in Nehemiah, Jubilees, Ecclesiasticus, and 1 Maccabees, and the story reiterates the author's thesis that justifying faith must embody itself in deeds (2:14–26).

The reference to Abraham's faith in the resurrection in Hebrews 11:19 takes up another motif traditional in Jewish texts (Josephus, *Ant.* 1.13.1: 230–231, and its parallels in 2 Macc. and 4 Macc.; LAB 32:3) and suggests the application of the *akedah* story to Jesus (cf. Rom. 4:16–25). Such an analogy between Abraham's sacrifice of Isaac and the God who gives his only, beloved son to die seems implied in several New Testament texts (Rom. 8:32; John 3:16, where the key words "love" and "believe" are displaced to refer to those in whose behalf the son is given; Mark 1:11). The analogy is also suggested in the Testament of Levi 18:6–7 in a portrait of the eschatological high priest reminiscent of the story of Jesus' baptism (Mark 1:9–11). The Isaac-Christ typology takes on increasing importance in Christian patristic discussions of Jesus' sacrifice.

Akhmadiyeh ancient Jewish village site in the northern Golan Heights with architectural fragments of a highly decorated, perhaps third-century C.E. synagogue (Arab. name: Amûdiyee). Carved stones found since 1885 include a lintel stone decorated with a nine-branched menorah having a single bar across the top and a three-pronged base but no lamps or flames. The menorah is flanked to the right by a shofar and to the left by an etrog. A second lintel stone has two seven-branched menorahs, one similar to the nine-branched menorah just described and a second, smaller menorah with arms separated at the ends. One stone was decorated with a relief carving of an eagle with outspread wings standing on a roundel or circular object. Another stone was ornamented with a carved garland attached to a bull's head with a bird to one side and a grape cluster to the other. An architrave or beam was decorated with flowers, amphora, and grapevine and has an enigmatic inscription in Hebrew letters: *tmush mshmr.* A Doric capital is in reuse in the ruined village. These fragments are most easily interpreted as fragments of a synagogue. G. Schumacher visited the ruin in 1885, and an Israeli survey team headed by Clare Epstein and Shmaryahu Gutmann visited the site again after 1968. The site remains unexcavated.

Akiḇa one of the most important Tannaitic authorities, active in the late first and early second centuries C.E. between the two Jewish wars with Rome; his full name is Akiḇa b. Joseph. In the Mishnah and Tosefta, far more legal statements are ascribed to Akiḇa than to any other authority of his generation or to almost any later authority. Mishnaic and toseftan laws cited in Akiḇa's name point to his special concern for the role of human intention in the law. Akiḇa held, for instance, that whether a utensil is susceptible or not susceptible to ritual uncleanness is determined by the intentions of the user rather than by traits intrinsic to it. This interest in the nature and impact of human will and concern for ascertaining the contexts in which a person's actions and intentions affect the law reveal Akiḇa's centrality in the legal program of the Mishnah as a whole. While Akiḇa's concerns were unique in his own age, by the completion of the Mishnah these issues had become a central concern of the document as a whole.

Akiḇa is also known for his unique approach to interpretation of scripture. He maintained that the Bible is derived from God, contains no redundancies, and that every element of the text, including spelling and orthographic characteristics, has meaning and purpose. In line with this thinking, Akiḇa even found meaning in the accusative particle "et," which introduces a direct object but which generally is held to have no semantic significance.

Akiḇa's importance in Tannaitic law is reflected by T. Zaḇim 1:5's statement that he "arranged laws" and by midrashic references to the "great Mishnah-compilation" of Akiḇa (and of several other Tannaitic authorities). Scholars have taken these statements to mean that Akiḇa organized a collection of Tannaitic law that served as a source for the final version of the Mishnah, understood to have been compiled by Judah the Patriarch. This view of Akiḇa's role in Tannaitic law is represented in B. Sanhedrin 86a's statement that all anonymous rules in the Mishnah, Tosefta, Sifra, and Sifre reflect Akiḇa's legal perspective. While reflecting Akiḇa's centrality as a Tannaitic authority, this statement clearly is not in any way literally true.

Early rabbinic sources only preserve Akiḇa's legal pronouncements. Later texts add a great deal of information about his life. Born into a humble family, in his youth Akiḇa reportedly was unlearned and an enemy of scholars (B. Pesaḥim 49b). He worked as a shepherd for Kalḇa Saḇua, the wealthiest man in Jerusalem. Akiḇa's interest in study of Torah began when Kalḇa Saḇua's daughter Rachel, against her father's wishes, agreed to marry him if he would devote himself to study. To fulfill her request, Akiḇa reportedly left Rachel for a total of twenty-four years, eventually returning, according to the talmudic story, with twelve thousand of his own students (B. Ketuḇot 62b).

Akiḇa's early teachers were Joshua b. Ḥananiah, Naḥum of Gamzo, and Eliezer b. Hyrcanus. He also studied at Yaḇneh under Yoḥanan b. Nuri (Sifre 4:9) and with Tarfon (B. Ketuḇot 84b). Akiḇa ultimately headed his own academy in Bene Berak. According to Y. Taanit 4:7, 68d, unlike his rabbinic colleagues, Akiḇa enthusiastically welcomed the Bar Kokhba Revolt and saw in Bar Kokhba the long-awaited messiah. For continuing publicly to teach Torah, Akiḇa was imprisoned by the Romans and was tortured to death after a long stay in prison (B. Berakhot 61b).

Akra Seleucid military citadel or garrison established under Antiochus IV Epiphanes in Jerusalem in 168 B.C.E. Though its precise location has been a matter of great controversy, it was clearly close to the Temple area, according to 1 Maccabees 1:36: "for the citadel became an adversary against the sanctuary." It was staffed by Gentiles (see Dan. 11:39) and supported by some "renegade" Jews (see 1 Macc. 11:21). It is mentioned frequently in 1 Maccabees (1:36; 2:31; 3:45; 4:2, 41; 6:18–21, 26, 32; 7:32; 9:52–53; 10:32; 11:20–21, 41; 12:36; 13:21). Despite the many attempts of the Maccabees to conquer it, it fell to Simon only in 141 B.C.E., thus marking the definitive success of the Maccabean revolt. The name Akra derives from the Greek word *akron* (high point).

Akrabba town located "a day's distance" north of Jerusalem (M. Maaser Sheni 5:2); in manuscripts, alternatively referred to as Akrabbat; probably equivalent to Akrabattene, referred to by Josephus (*War* 3:3, 5). Akrabba is distinct from the biblical

Akrabim (Num. 34:4), on the southeastern border of Judea.

akum abbreviation of the first letters of the words in Hebrew for "worshipers of stars and planets," standing for pagans in general

ala *see* HIPPARCH

alabarch office held by several important individuals of the Jewish community in first-century-C.E. Alexandria, including Alexander, Demetrius, and Tiberius Julius Alexander. The office probably had something to do with the collection of customs duties, originally east of the Nile. The office is also called *arabarches* in some Greek and Latin writings; indeed, this form may be the more original, but Josephus uses the term *alabarches*. Those holding the office were clearly honored by the authorities in being granted the post, showing the esteem in which certain Jews of Alexandria were held.

Albinus, Lucceius Roman procurator of Palestine (62–64 C.E.). According to Josephus's account in *The Jewish War,* he was noted for graft, taking bribes from litigants, opposing political parties and the Sicarii. He stole from public and private funds, freed criminals for a price, and ignored lawlessness. In *Antiquities of the Jews,* Josephus suggests that he was unable to deal effectively with rising unrest. He served as procurator of Mauretania and was executed in 69 C.E. in a power struggle.

Alcimus (Heb. name: Yakim) second-century-B.C.E. leader of the pro-Seleucid party and an opponent of Judas Maccabeus. He was appointed high priest by Demetrius I in 162 B.C.E. and installed by an army led by Bacchides. After a group of Hasideans submitted to him, he executed sixty of them (1 Macc. 7:12–16). Turmoil and conflict required the intervention of the Seleucid general Nicanor, who was defeated, and the intervention of Bacchides again. In 160 B.C.E. Alcimus razed a wall separating the inner court of the Temple from outer areas. It is uncertain whether the wall kept Israelites from areas reserved to priests or Gentiles from sacred areas reserved to Israelites. Alcimus died in 160 B.C.E.

aleinu (Heb., it is incumbent on us) the first words of a prayer. The full prayer reads: "It is incumbent on us to praise Him, Lord over all the world; Let us acclaim Him, Author of all creation. He made our lot unlike that of other peoples; He assigned to us a unique destiny. We bend the knee, worship, and acknowledge the King of kings, the Holy One, praised is He. He unrolled the heavens and established the earth; his throne of glory is in the heavens above; his majestic Presence is in the loftiest heights. He and no other is God and faithful King, even as we are told in his Torah. Remember now and always, that the Lord is God. Remember, no other is Lord of heaven and earth. We, therefore, hope in You, O Lord our God, that we shall soon see the triumph of your might, that idolatry shall be removed from the earth, and false gods shall be utterly destroyed. Then will the world be a true kingdom of God, when all mankind will invoke your name, and all the earth's wicked will return to You. Then all the inhabitants of the world will surely know that to You every knee must bend, every tongue must pledge loyalty. Before You, O Lord, let them bow in worship, let them give honor to your glory. May they all accept the rule of your kingdom. May You reign over them soon through all time. Sovereignty is yours in glory, now and forever. So it is written in your Torah: *The Lord shall reign for ever and ever.*"

Alexander, son of Aristobulus II brother of Antigonus. He was captured by Pompey during the latter's conquest of Jerusalem in 63 B.C.E. He escaped while being transported to Rome. In 57 B.C.E., he raised an army in Palestine, but was defeated and captured by the Roman governor Gabinius. In 49 B.C.E., he was executed in Antioch on Pompey's orders for supporting Julius Caesar.

Alexander, son of Herod son of Herod the Great and Mariamme. He was educated in Rome (23–17 B.C.E.) along with his brother Aristobulus. After Herod brought them back to Jerusalem, intrigues within the Herodian family led Herod to suspect the brothers of plotting against him. On a trip to Rome in 12 B.C.E., Augustus reconciled Herod to his sons. Further discord, slander, and plotting in the Herodian court led to the brothers' arrest, trial in Berytus, and execution by strangulation in Sebaste in 7 B.C.E. A number of their supporters were also executed.

Alexander Balas Seleucid ruler (151–145 B.C.E.). He claimed to be a son of Antiochus IV Epiphanes and was recognized as ruler of Syria, Mesopotamia, and parts of Asia Minor by the Roman Senate in 153 or 152 B.C.E. He gained Jonathan the Hasmonean's support by appointing him high priest in 152 B.C.E. He defeated Demetrius I for the Seleucid throne in 151 B.C.E. and ruled until 145 B.C.E., when he was defeated by Demetrius II and subsequently assassinated.

Alexander Jannaeus (from Heb. Yannai, a shortened form of Jonathan) son of John Hyrcanus; high priest and king of the Jewish kingdom from the death of his brother Aristobulus I in 103 B.C.E. to his own death in 76 B.C.E. He married Aristobulus's wife, Alexandra Salome, and had two sons, Hyrcanus II and Aristobolus II. Early in his reign he killed one of his remaining brothers.

Alexander greatly enlarged his territory through numerous wars. After an early attempt to conquer Ptolemais (Acco) on the Mediterranean coast was repulsed, he gradually conquered all the cities south of it, except for Ascalon. In several campaigns he conquered a number of Transjordanian cities, the Golan and Hauran, and areas north of Galilee.

The middle of Alexander's reign was characterized by internal conflict and external defeat. About 95 B.C.E., when Alexander was presiding in the Temple at the Feast of Tabernacles, a dispute over ritual practice led the people to pelt him with their ritually prescribed citrons (Heb. *etrog*). According to Josephus, Alexander responded by slaughtering six thousand worshipers. Josephus's whole account of Alexander Jannaeus and stories about him in rabbinic literature stress his cruelty and ruthlessness. Popular discontent was so substantial that about 93 B.C.E. a six-year popular rebellion by dissident Jews, including the Pharisees, began when Alexander's army was ambushed and defeated in the Golan by the Nabatean (Arab) king, Obedas I. Alexander fled to Jerusalem. In 88, as the conflict dragged on, Alexander's opponents sought the intervention of Demetrius III, the Seleucid ruler of part of Syria. Demetrius defeated Alexander at Shechem but this Seleucid conquest prompted six thousand Jews to change to Alexander's side. Eventually Demetrius left the country and Alexander besieged and captured the final group of rebels. In a notorious incident recorded in Josephus and alluded to in the Qumran commentary on Nahum, he had eight hundred opponents crucified in Jerusalem and their families slaughtered before their eyes while he caroused with his mistresses.

About 84 B.C.E., the Nabatean king Aretas invaded Judea and imposed terms on Alexander before withdrawing. From 83 to 80 B.C.E. Alexander successfully conquered a number of Transjordanian cities. In his final three years (79–76), he suffered from a painful illness that led to his death. Josephus reports that Alexander was so unpopular that he advised his wife and successor, Queen Alexandra, to form a coalition with the Pharisees so they could win popular support for her rule.

Alexander Polyhistor (c. 105–35 B.C.E.) Greek writer from Miletus. He produced several compilations, that is, works that were mainly excerpts from other writers. One was *Concerning the Jews,* which contained passages from a number of the Fragmentary Hellenistic Jewish writers as well as a few non-Jewish writers who mentioned the Jews. Most of what we know about such writers as Eupolemus, Demetrius, Ezekiel the Tragedian, Artapanus, and Aristobulus the Exegete come ultimately from him, via such writers as Eusebius and Josephus, who quoted him.

Alexander Romance legendary account of Alexander the Great's conquests, which circulated widely in various forms, including Armenian, Latin, and Hebrew. The Romance is apparently based on an actual Hellenistic historical account, but the historical part has been overlaid and spiced up with fantastic and miraculous events. These include a journey to the end of the world. The version under the name of Callisthenes is the product of the third century C.E. Especially interesting is a Jewish story found in some versions in which Alexander visits Jerusalem and bows to the high priest, a story also found in Josephus.

Alexander the Alabarch head of the family of which Philo of Alexandria was a member. Alexander was the brother of Philo and the father of Julius Tiberius Alexander. He was one of the wealthiest individuals of his time, loaning a fortune to Agrippa I before the latter became king (actually to Agrippa's wife, because he knew of Agrippa's profligacy). He was imprisoned by Caligula in a fit of anger but was released by Claudius when the latter came to the throne. The office of alabarch may have been passed down in the family, since it was also held by Alexander's brother, Demetrius, and his son, also named Alexander.

Alexander the Great (356–323 B.C.E.) Alexander III of Macedon, son of Philip II and the Epirote princess Olympias. For three years (c. 342–340), Aristotle was Alexander's tutor. Under Philip II, Macedonia was expanding its power south into Greece and east into the Balkans. When Philip was assassinated in 336 B.C.E., Alexander succeeded as leader and continued Philip's plans to invade Persia. Alexander crossed into Asia in 334 and twice defeated the Persian forces, the first early on at the river Granicus, then at Issus in November 333. Alexander followed up these successes by a long siege of Tyre, the main base for the Persian fleet, and then swiftly moved south through Gaza and entered unopposed into Egypt. A late legend has him visiting Jerusalem during this time, offering sacrifice to God and allowing the Jews to follow their ancestral laws (Josephus, *Ant.* 11, secs. 304–345). In Egypt he laid plans to build Alexandria and was crowned Pharaoh, son of the god Amun-Re.

Alexander defeated the Persian king Darius again in 331 and was proclaimed king of Asia. Alexander gained control of the major cities of the Persian empire, slowly conquered the Persian provinces Bactria and Sogdiana in Afghanistan, crossed into modern-day Pakistan, and was turned back from pushing further into India only by the refusal of his soldiers to go further. Alexander was worshiped as a god by some Greek cities, and he certainly had performed remarkable deeds. He fell ill and died on June 10, 323 B.C.E.

One wonders whether the brilliant soldier could have managed his empire, which stretched from Greece to Afghanistan. Alexander attempted to weld together Macedonians and Persians through marriage and military training, but met with opposition. His lasting legacy would be the great Hellenistic kingdoms, Ptolemaic Egypt and Seleucid Syria, which emerged out of the struggle between Alexander's generals over his inheritance.

Alexandra, Queen Alexandra Salome (Heb.: Shalomtzion), ruler of the Jewish kingdom (76–67 B.C.E.) after the death of her husband, Alexander Jannaeus. Her older son, Hyrcanus II, served as high priest. Alexandra removed many of Alexander's retainers from power and sent them to desert forts. She gave domestic power to the Pharisaic party and took steps to reconcile those who had been estranged by Alexander. Thus, she is remembered as a benign monarch. In international affairs she built up the army, conducted military campaigns, using her other son Aristobulus II as commander, and engaged effectively in foreign negotiations. The divisions that split the kingdom during her husband's reign continued to fester. As she suffered her final illness in 67 B.C.E., Aristobulus II gathered his supporters and took over numerous cities, thus initiating a civil war for supremacy with his brother, Hyrcanus II. The conflict was resolved by the Roman conquest in 63 B.C.E.

Alexandria, Graeco-Roman culture in The Macedonian rulers of Egypt, from the time of Ptolemy I (Soter) on, developed a deliberate policy of patronizing arts and sciences in Alexandria, encouraging the leading scholars and cultural figures to settle there. As a result, Alexandria became the cultural center of the Mediterranean world. The chief symbol of this policy was the establishment of the famous Mouseion (Temple of the Muses) and its Library by Soter, aided by the Peripatetic philosopher Demetrius of Phaleron. There, scholarship and the arts were given a subsidized context in which to flourish.

Alexandrian scientists played leading roles, especially during the Hellenistic period. Medicine achieved a level in Alexandria by the third century B.C.E. that was not exceeded until the seventeenth century C.E. Alexandrian mathematicians and astronomers include such famous figures as Euclid, founder of geometry; Aristarchus, who developed a heliocentric theory of the universe; Eratosthenes, whose calculation of the circumference of the earth was only 200 miles off; and Apollonius, a leader in conic theory. Mechanical engineering was also highly developed in Alexandria. Of course, the "false sciences" of astrology and alchemy were also represented there.

Classical scholarship as we know it developed in Alexandria during the Hellenistic period. This involved the study of Homer and other Greek authors, the development of textual criticism, preparations of new editions of classical works and commentaries thereon, and the development of Greek grammar. Greek philosophy was not so strong in Alexandria in the early period, but Peripatetic (Aristotelian) philosophy is represented in the second century B.C.E. by one Agatharchides and the Jew Aristobulus. Both skeptical and metaphysical branches of Platonism were well represented by the first century B.C.E. One of these philosophers, Eudorus, may have influenced Philo Judaeus, who is also often counted among the (Middle) Platonist philosophers.

Alexandrian literature was a high point of culture in Alexandria. One of the more interesting prose writers was the Egyptian priest Manetho, who wrote, in Greek, a history of Egypt. Much of what survives of his work is preserved in Josephus's *Against Apion*. A number of Alexandrian writers produced geographical works and travel accounts. Alexandrian poetry is especially important. The epigram as an artistic expression was very popular and highly developed. Narrative poetry is best represented by the *Argonautica* of Apollonius. Hymns on traditional themes were important vehicles for poetic expression; the most important of these were composed by Callimachus. Drama, both tragedy and comedy, was also represented, though in this field Alexandria did not succeed in eclipsing Athens.

The arts in Alexandria were also highly developed. Alexandrian craftsmen excelled in work in glass and faience. Alexandrian artists also developed, in paintings and mosaics, themes of a specifically Egyptian character, such as Nile river scenes. The catacombs of Alexandria are particularly rich in examples of Graeco-Egyptian artistic fusion.

It is obvious that the Graeco-Roman culture of Alexandria would have had a major impact on the Jewish population of that city. Alexandrian Greek literature provided models for much of the literature produced by Jewish writers. It is possible that some Jewish scholars were members of the Mouseion, such as Aristobulus, whose allegorical interpretation of Torah was based on contemporary allegories of Homer and who cites Greek writers in his defense of Jewish philosophy. From his time on, there was a strong Jewish philosophical school tradition in Alexandria. Its greatest product was Philo, who, in turn, greatly influenced such Christian theologians as Clement and Origen. It was clearly possible for Jews in Alexandria—Philo is again the best example—both to imbibe the best of Graeco-Roman culture and education and to remain faithful to Torah as observant members of the synagogues. *See also* ALEXANDRIA, JEWS IN.

Alexandria, Jews in Jews settled in Alexandria soon after that city's founding in 331 B.C.E., some of them coming originally as prisoners of war or as military personnel in the service of the rulers of Egypt. Eventually the Alexandrian Jews came to constitute the largest and most important Jewish community of the entire diaspora. They became the predominant population in two of the city's five major neighborhoods, and were present in the others as well. The Alexandrian Jews enjoyed considerable autonomy, and were encouraged by the rulers of Egypt (the Ptolemies, and later the Roman emperors) to live according to their ancestral customs. Their religious life was chiefly concentrated in the synagogues ([houses of] prayer), of which there were many in Alexandria. One of these is described in rabbinic sources as a very large, double-colonnaded basilica, and referred to as "the glory of Israel." It was destroyed in the rebellion of 115–117 C.E.

While the earliest Jewish population was largely Aramaic-speaking, Greek very soon became the dominant language of the Alexandrian Jews. Jewish worship in the synagogues was conducted in Greek, probably from the first half of the third century B.C.E. on. Accordingly, the Hebrew Bible came to be translated into Greek in Alexandria—first the Torah (early 3d c. B.C.E.), and then the Prophets and most of the Writings (by the end of the 2d c. B.C.E.), to which were later added material composed in Greek. The legend of the origin of this translation, the Septuagint, is set forth in the Letter of Aristeas.

The high level of culture and education achieved by Alexandrian Jews is reflected in the literature they produced in Greek: historical writings and prose romances (e.g., Demetrius, Artapanus, 3 Macc., Joseph and Asenath), epic poetry and drama (e.g., Ezekiel the Tragedian), philosophy (e.g., Aristobulus, Philo), poetic compositions attributed to pagan authors (e.g., "Sibylline" oracles), and additions to the Bible (e.g., Wisd. of Sol., 2 [Slavonic] Enoch). The greatest of all of the Alexandrian Jewish writers was Philo, whose numerous writings are dominated by a philosophical interpretation of Torah.

With the Roman conquest of Egypt in 30 B.C.E., resulting in new tax burdens, and the rising hostility of Greek citizens of Alexandria, Jewish life in Alexandria became increasingly difficult. With the acquiescence of the Roman prefect, Flaccus, an Alexandrian mob waged a pogrom against the Jews in 38 C.E., followed by Jewish riots. The situation was stabilized for a time by the new emperor, Claudius, in 41 C.E., but the Jewish community suffered severe losses in another pogrom in 66 C.E., with wholesale bloodshed. Finally, under the emperor Trajan, a Jewish revolt took place in 115–117, which resulted in the virtual destruction of the Jews of Alexandria and had devastating effects in the Egyptian countryside and in Cyrene as well. The Jewish community of Alexandria never recovered from these catastrophic events. *See also* ALEXANDRIA, GRAECO-ROMAN CULTURE IN; EGYPT.

Alexandrian Martyrs, Acts of *see* ACTA ALEXANDRINORUM

Alexandrion (or Alexandrium) fortress built by King Alexander Jannaeus (r. 103–76 B.C.E.) in the territory of the Samaritans about 32 kilometers southeast of biblical Shechem and 26 kilometers north of Jericho (also known as Sartaba). The widow of Alexander Jannaeus hid at Alexandrion with her son Aristobulus, who fought the Roman general Pompey there. Pompey prevailed, captured Aristobulus, and sent him to Rome. Later, in 57 B.C.E., the Romans under Gabinius and Antony razed the fortress to the ground in the war with Alexander, grandson of Alexander Jannaeus. Herod the Great, who rebuilt it as one of his fortresses in 38 B.C.E., buried family members there (including his first wife Mariamme), and used it to guard his treasures.

Excavations at the Alexandrion starting in 1981 disclosed a two-story palace of Herod's day built around a square hall about 20 meters long on each side. The building had been beautifully decorated with frescoes, Corinthian capitals, and mosaics. The remains of an earlier palace, identified by the excavator as that of Alexander Jannaeus, lay beneath the ruins of Herod's palace. Many wine jars imported from Italy were found, smashed, in the levels associated with Alexander Jannaeus. During the First Revolt against Rome, a Roman garrison stayed at Alexandrion.

Ali b. Abutalab (598–661 C.E.) known in Arabic as Ali ibn Abi Talib; Mohammed's cousin, becoming the Prophet's son-in-law upon his marriage to Mohammed's daughter Fatimah. In 656 he was elected the fourth caliph during a period of turmoil. He was assassinated in 661 while preparing to lead prayers at the Mosque of Kufah. Ali was famous as a warrior and general during Islam's early struggles for survival. Sherira states that he conquered Piruz-Shapur in Babylonia in 658. The Jews welcomed the caliph to the city, and he treated them cordially.

aliyah (Heb., ascent) going up, specifically, migration to the Land of Israel, which is held to be higher than all other lands, as Jerusalem is higher than all other cities, and Mount Zion higher than all other mountains

aliyah laregel *see* PILGRIMAGE

allegory from the Greek, meaning "to say something different," the literary device of presenting one subject in the guise of another. Small stories (e.g., 2 Sam. 12:1–6) may have been designed as allegories; no biblical works as a whole are so constructed. While biblical allegories are limited, allegorical interpretation of biblical texts has played a major role in the appropriation of scripture.

In the Hellenistic period (330–31 B.C.E.) allegorical interpretation of Greek mythology became commonplace, and myths were understood as symbols of natural processes. Jewish interpreters, influenced by such cultural currents, adopted allegorical interpretation as a way of preserving the Torah's relevance. In the second century B.C.E. Aristobulus used the method in a limited way to deal with the problem of anthropomorphism in scripture (in Eusebius, *Preparation for the Gospel* 13.13.3–8). The Letter of Aristeas explains biblical regulations as symbols of profound ethical teaching (148–71). One common locus for allegorical ingenuity was the scriptural account of the construction of the tabernacle. This dry bit of priestly lore becomes in the hands of allegorical exegetes a profound cosmic symbol (e.g., Josephus, *Ant.* 3.179–87).

The major exemplar of Hellenistic Jewish allegorical exegesis is Philo of Alexandria, the philosophical interpreter of scripture of the late first century B.C.E. to the early first century C.E. While some of his interpretive work operates on a literal level (*Life of Moses,* bk. 1), much of it seeks deeper meanings hidden in the text (e.g., *Allegory of the Laws*). At the same time, Philo is careful to reject an allegorical interpretation that dispenses with observance of the Torah (*On the Migration of Abraham* 89). Philo's allegorical interpretation features many interesting readings but is dominated by the conviction that scripture is really about the journey of the soul to God. Hence, the patriarchs become symbols of ways to approach God, through teaching (Abraham), natural ability (Isaac), and practice (Jacob).

Evidence of Jewish allegorical interpretation is present among early Christians, particularly Paul (Gal. 4:24). It became even more common among Alexandrian Christian interpreters such as Clement and Origen.

alley (for defining space; Heb.: *mab̲o*) an alley, marked off by a clearcut entryway, that combines all the courtyards opening up into the alley into a single domain for purposes of carrying objects about on the Sabbath. The alley makes the connecting courtyards all one property, so that people may carry things about from courtyard to courtyard throughout the area on the Sabbath. Since on the Sabbath it is forbidden to transport objects from one domain to another, for example, from private domain to public domain, if the alley is not designated as a single space through provision of a crossbeam at the opening into public domain, the alley will be subdivided, and thus on the Sabbath people may not carry objects through it. *See also* ERUB̲.

Alma ancient Jewish village site in northern upper Galilee with architectural fragments of a highly decorated, perhaps third-century synagogue. Carved stones reported since 1880 include fragments of black granite columns, limestone columns, column bases, a stone decorated with a rosette, and a decorated lintel with a Hebrew and Aramaic inscription. Foundations of an ancient building found near the fragments are assumed to be the synagogue. A collapsed cave may be an ancient catacomb.

The lintel is decorated with three rows of leaves, and the bottom row is flanked on both sides with astragali. The three fragments of this lintel were found in 1914, 1949, and 1957 and read as follows: (1) (Heb.) [proper name ending in -nah] of Tiberias R . . . / [donated the l]intel. May the King of the W[orld give his blessing upon . . .]; (2) (Heb.) May there be peace upon this place and upon all the places of his people Israel . . . ; and (3) (Aram.)

Amen Selah, I, Jose bar Levi the Levite, the craftsman who made . . . .

Jose bar Levi is also mentioned in a lintel inscription from Kefar Baram, also in upper Galilee. The scholar who first published the lintel thought that Jose bar Levi the Levite was a Jewish artisan of the third century C.E. who perpetuated his name where he worked. The Aramaic word for "artisan" (*'wn*) appears in Syriac on sixth-century church lintels in Syria.

alms support for the poor, commanded in the law (e.g., Deut. 14:28–29 on tithing) and commended in prophetic and wisdom teaching (Isa. 58:7; Prov. 14:21; Sir. 4:1–6; Matt. 25:31–46). The Sibylline Oracles equates the giving of alms with "lending to God" (2:80), and Pseudo-Phocylides 1:29 insists "of that which God has given you, give of it to the needy." The Vision of Ezra 31–32 describes the torments of the uncharitable (24–26) and the rewards of almsgivers (64–65; cf. Test. Jacob 7:24–25). According to Josephus (*War* 2.8.6), the Essenes offered alms individually rather than through an institutional structure, but the Damascus Document 14:12–16 requires community members to contribute to a charitable fund administered by the Guardian and the judges. Matthew 6:2 suggests that some charitable donations were accompanied by public announcement. Throughout his travels Paul collects money for the poor of the Jerusalem church (Gal. 2:10; 1 Cor. 16:1–4; 2 Cor. 8:1–9:15; Rom. 15:25–33). *See also* POOR, TREATMENT OF.

al-Mundhir *see* MUNDHIR, AL-

altar (Heb.: *mizbeaḥ*) **1.** structure of wood overlaid with bronze plate used for the twice-daily burnt animal offering, but also for grain, wine, and incense offerings in temple worship. Only priests could approach the altar and minister there.

The Jewish altar was "horned" according to Exodus 27:1–8 and 38:1–7 and measured 5 by 5 by 3 cubits or about 7.5 by 7.5 by 4.5 feet. In the First Temple an altar was built by Solomon 20 by 20 by 10 cubits, but it was not called an altar of burnt offering. A nearly complete but dismantled horned altar is known from a seventh-century B.C.E. context at Beer Sheba, though it is made of cut stones and is just over four cubits high. A second early burnt-offering altar measuring 4 by 4 by 4 cubits of unhewn stone is known from Arad near Beer Sheba. Although the altar of burnt offering is mentioned in many Jewish and other texts, we have no archaeological examples. In 1 Maccabees 1:54 the altar was desecrated, which resulted in its dismantlement and in the building of a new altar in 1 Maccabees 4:44–47, though no dimensions are given. In the Second Temple, according to Josephus, the altar of burnt offering would resemble a square 50 by 50 by 15 cubits. It was made of uncut stones and was horned. The altar of burnt offering as described in the M. Middot 3:1–5 would measure 32 by 32 by 9 cubits, and the area for the fire was 24 by 24 cubits, but the whole passage owes more to the Book of Ezekiel than to the Book of Exodus.

2. gold-covered wooden box or a block of stone or masonry used to hold coals with incense as an accoutrement of temple worship. The Jewish altar was "horned." According to Exodus 30:1–10 and 37:25–28, the altar of incense in the Tent of Meeting (Tabernacle) measured 1 by 1 by 2 cubits (about 1.5 by 1.5 by 3 ft.), was made of acacia wood, and was covered with gold plate. This altar was equipped with horns, molding, rings, and poles for carrying by the priests. A simple representation of this or a first-century-C.E. incense altar appears scratched into the wall plaster of a house in Jerusalem destroyed in 70 C.E. This graffito also shows the temple menorah and a third item that could either be the altar of burnt offering or the table of shewbread. Coins of the Jewish king Agrippa II of 85/86 C.E. show an incense altar, but without horns and surely not of the Second Temple, for it has been copied from a coin of the emperor Domitian. Altars—though, for the most part, they are pagan sacrificial ones—appear on third-century C.E. city coins minted at Acco, Caesarea, Neapolis, Aelia Capitolina (Jerusalem), Panias or Caesarea Philippi, and other cities across the Jordan. The incense altar of the Second Temple in Jerusalem is mentioned in Josephus (*War* 5.5.4) and in the New Testament (Luke 1:11), which remarks on Zechariah's priestly service at this altar. In Revelation 9:13 there appears a reference to a gold altar, which is surely the incense altar.

Alypius (4th c. C.E.) native of Antioch and close friend of the emperor Julian. While Julian was in Gaul, Alypius served as his representative in Britain, and he sided with Julian against Constantius. Alypius was also known for his scholarly interests. In 362 C.E., Julian placed him in charge of rebuilding the Jerusalem Temple. In May of 363, an earthquake rocked Jerusalem and caused a fire at the construction site. Julian was in Persia, and it was probably Alypius who called a halt to the building project. Although a pagan, Alypius accepted an important imperial office under the Christian emperor Valens.

Amaduni name of a Jewish family that migrated to Armenia. Moses Xorenazi claims that this family, descended from a certain Manue, came to Armenia in the second century C.E., at the time of Trajan's invasion of the area during Ardashes' reign. Xorenazi states that the family came from the eastern part of the country of the Arik, near Ahmadan (Hamadan), where it was highly regarded, and that it continued to be an important noble family in his day. In Persia the family was known as the Manuyans. It is impossible to know if Xorenazi's report is historically accurate. However, some have seen Manue as the Armenian form of the name Monobases. Thus, the family may be descended from the Adiabenian king Monobazes, whose son, Izates, converted to Judaism in the first century C.E. Monobazes opposed Trajan, and his family could have been forced to flee to Armenia after Trajan invaded Adiabenia. It is also possible that upon the family's leaving Adiabenia, a new royal family came to power, which was favored by those who rejected Izates' conversion to Judaism, and therefore the family could not return to its original home and was forced to move to Armenia. Being the royal family, it is likely that it would have been treated with respect by the Armenians.

Amalek blood enemy of Israel (Exod. 17:8–16), symbolizing implacable foes through all time. He is described as the irreconcilable enemy, ancestor of all later enemies, and is often identified with Rome.

Amanah mountain mentioned in Song of Solomon 4:8 and referred to in rabbinic literature as demarcating a border of the Land of Israel. Apparently situated in southern Syria and distinct from Mount Amanus, further north, it is usually identified with Jabal az-Zevedani, which forms part of the Anti-Lebanon chain, northwest of Damascus.

Ambrose (339–397 C.E.) bishop of Milan. Ambrose was a noted biblical scholar who knew Hebrew as well as Greek and who was familiar with the works of Philo and Plotinus. In 374 he was elected bishop of Milan by both the Arians and the Catholics. He was forced to devote a good deal of his time to fighting Arianism. Ambrose also supported Gratian's removal of the Altar of Victory from the Senate house and the emperor's decrees against paganism that followed. After 388, Ambrose backed the emperor Valentinian, who also enjoyed the emperor Theodosius's support. Theodosius and Ambrose struggled to establish their realms of authority. Ambrose wrote that "civil law must bow before religious devotion," and he believed that Judaism and the Jews were matters of religious concern for the state. In 388 the bishop of Callinicum on the Euphrates incited a mob to torch a synagogue. The governor appealed to Theodosius for advice about what to do. The emperor censured the governor for his inaction and ordered the bishop to rebuild the synagogue. But Ambrose forced Theodosius to rescind his orders so that the synagogue would not be rebuilt. In order to support his authority, Theodosius banished Ambrose from his court and issued a number of decrees that were unfavorable to the church.

Amemar **1.** third-century-C.E. Babylonian amora who was a younger contemporary of Judah b. Ezekiel and Sheshet

2. Babylonian rabbi, an older contemporary of Ashi, who restored and, from 390 to 422 C.E., headed the academy at Nehardea

amen in the Hebrew Bible, a concurring response to a prayer, doxology (Neh. 8:6; 1 Chron. 16:36; Ps. 41:13), command (Jer. 11:5), blessing or curse (Deut. 27:15–26; Num. 5:22). It occasionally occurs in conversation as confirmation of what another has said before (Jer. 28:6; 1 Kings 1:36). It derives from the Hebrew root *'mn* meaning "to support" or "to be true or faithful," or in the *hiphil* "to believe." The Septuagint translates it as "so be it" or "truly" but sometimes leaves it untranslated, attesting to its formulaic nature. Usage in postbiblical Judaism and early Christian literature closely follows that of the Hebrew Bible, except where Jesus uses "amen" not as a response but to introduce a solemn statement. In Revelation 3:14, an angel calls Jesus "the Amen" because of the faithfulness and truth of his witness.

Am haAretz (Heb., people of the land) in rabbinic usage, boor, unlearned, not a disciple of the sages; assumed not to observe certain tithing laws and not to eat home meals in a state of ritual cleanness.

Amidah (Heb., standing) principal part of the fixed liturgy, recited standing and in silence. On weekdays, the Amidah consists of prayers of praise, petition, and gratitude. The prayers conclude with a blessing: "Blessed are You, Lord. . . ." The liturgy also is called the Eighteen Benedictions (Heb.: *shemoneh esre*), though in fact it includes nineteen blessings. In the Mishnah and Talmuds it is called the Prayer (Heb.: *tefillah*). The blessings are as follows: (1) God of the fathers; (2) praise of God's power; (3) holiness; (4) prayer for knowledge; (5) prayer for repentance; (6) prayer for forgiveness; (7) prayer for redemption; (8) prayer for healing the sick; (9) blessing of agricultural produce; (10) prayer for ingathering of dispersed Israel; (11) prayer for righteous judgment; (12) prayer for punishment of the wicked and heretics; (13) prayer for reward of the pious; (14) prayer for rebuilding Jerusalem; (15) prayer for restoration of house of David; (16) prayer for acceptance of prayers; (17) prayer of thanks; (18) prayer for restoration of Temple service; and (19) prayer for peace.

The Amidah includes the following passages. *The founders:* "Praised are You, Lord our God and God of our fathers, God of Abraham, God of Isaac, and God of Jacob [in some contemporary versions of the liturgy: God of Abraham and Sarah . . . Isaac and Rebecca, Jacob and Leah and Rachel], great, mighty, revered God, exalted, who bestows loving kindness and is master of all things, who remembers the acts of loyalty of the founders and who in love will bring a redeemer to their descendants for his great name's sake. King, helper, savior and shield, praised are You, Lord, shield of Abraham." *God's power:* "You are powerful forever, Lord, giving life to the dead. You are great in acts of salvation. You sustain the living in loyalty and bring the dead to life in great mercy, holding up the falling, healing the sick, freeing the prisoners, and keeping faith with those who sleep in the dirt. Who is like You, Almighty, and who is compared to You, King, who kills and gives life and brings salvation to spring up? And You are reliable to give life to the dead. Praised are You, Lord, who gives life to the dead." *God's sanctity:* "We shall sanctify your name in the world just as they sanctify it in the heights of heaven. . . . Holy, holy, holy is the Lord of hosts, the whole earth is full of his glory. . . ." On weekdays, petitionary prayer follows. The concluding blessings, common to all versions of the Prayer, are as follows: "We thank You, O Lord our God and God of our fathers, Defender of our lives, Shield of our safety; through all generations we thank You and praise You. Our lives are in your hands, our souls in your charge. We thank You for the miracles which daily attend us, for your wonders and favor morning, noon, and night. You are beneficent with boundless mercy and love. From of old we have always placed our hope in You. For all these blessings, O our King, we shall ever praise and exalt You. Every living creature thanks You, and praises You in truth. O God, You are our deliverance and our help. Selah! Praised are You, O Lord, for your Goodness and your glory. Grant peace and well-being to the whole house of Israel; give us of your grace, your love, and your mercy. Bless us all, O our Father, with the light of your Presence. It is your light that revealed to us your life-giving Torah, and taught us love and tenderness, justice, mercy, and peace. May it please You to bless your people in every season, to bless them at all times with your light of peace. Praised are You, O Lord, who blesses Israel with peace."

ammah *see* CUBIT

Ammianus Marcellinus (330–395 C.E.) the last major Roman historian. A Greek who was born in Antioch, he settled in Rome after 378 and wrote a Latin history designed as a continuation of Tacitus's work. He wrote thirty-one books covering the period 96–378, but books 1–13 have been lost. Although a pagan, he wrote tolerantly about the Christians and is our most reliable and impartial source concerning Julian's attempt to rebuild the Jerusalem Temple. He did not witness the events, but reports that "balls of fire" suddenly issued from the building's foundations, burning several workers. He states that "the undertaking stopped," without specifying who ordered a cessation of the work.

Ammi b. Abba *see* RAMI B. ABBA

Ammi b. Natan Palestinian amora; student of Yoḥanan and Hoshayah, generally referred to without the patronymic, frequently in conjunction with Assi; active in Tiberias. Ammi was an eminent authority of his day (3d c. C.E.); he and Assi were called "the renowned Palestinian priests" (B. Megillah 22a). A native of Babylonia, he studied there under Ra<u>b</u>. In the Land of Israel, Ammi had close connections with the patriarchate; along with Ḥiyya b. Abba and Assi, he served under Judah II as an inspector of education (Y. Ḥagigah 1:7, 76c).

Ammon a people who emerged from the Syrio-Arabian desert during the second millennium B.C.E. Genesis 19:38 associates them with the incestuous relationship between Lot and his younger daughter. Deuteronomy 23:4 forbids participation by Ammonites (and Moabites) in the Israelite community. Tannaitic authorities narrowed the prohibition to males alone (M. Ye<u>b</u>amot 8:3). Later rabbis totally abrogated the prohibition, holding that contemporary Ammonites and Moabites were not of the same nation as those referred to in scripture (B. Berakhot 28a).

amora rabbinical teacher in Palestine and Babylonia in talmudic times (c. 200–500 C.E.). The term usually refers to a spokesman for a major authority; the teacher spoke and the amora repeated what he said to the audience or translated Hebrew into the Aramaic vernacular.

Amos, Targum to *see* TARGUM TO THE PROPHETS

amphora (pl., amphorae) two-handled ceramic or metal vase, often with a long neck and pointed base or, in depictions on coins, with a stand for a base; used for transportation and storage of wine and other liquids. It can also be a motif in Jewish and other art. Amphorae are portrayed in Jewish art on coins, lamps, gold glass, plates, and on ossuaries. They are also known to have been painted in tombs and carved in relief in synagogue art. Often the amphora is shown with vine tendrils or grape clusters growing out of its neck. The first amphorae on coins appear in year two of the First Revolt (67 C.E.). These specific vessels have two ring handles on the shoulders, open necks without lids, and a stand like an upside down funnel. They are usually interpreted as vessels from the temple cult used to hold water or wine. Amphorae also figure in Jewish epitaphs, sometimes in the center of the stone, sometimes to the side. They also appear in relief in synagogue art, as for example, on lintels or on a frieze, but not commonly with the menorah.

Amram grandson of Levi, son of Kohat, and father of Moses, Aaron, and Miriam (Num. 26:59). Though not prominent in the Bible, he is a hero in the Book of Biblical Antiquities 9, exhorting the Israelite men to disobey Pharaoh by begetting children. The Qumran testament attributed to him legitimates the high priestly line.

Amram, Testament of an Aramaic work in five fragmentary copies (4QAmram^{a-e}) that contains an admonition by Amram—the father of Moses—to his children. The work was discovered in Cave 4, Qumran, in 1952, and published by J. T. Milik in 1972. The oldest of the five copies dates from the early or mid-second century B.C.E., a date that places the work's composition before the foundation of the Qumran Community (c. 150–135 B.C.E.).

The Testament's characters are drawn from the biblical Book of Exodus, but the scene of the Testament is not biblically based. Its genre is uncertain: It contains a testamentary introduction, but the body of the text is a dream vision characteristic of apocalypses. The Testament's importance lies in its testimony to the existence of the dualism found in other Qumran documents (e.g., the Community Rule, the War Scroll) at an early date. The chief characters of Amram's vision are Melchiresha (Prince of Evil)—the angelic leader of the Sons of Darkness—and Melchizedek (Prince of Righteousness; this name has been restored by the editor)—the angelic leader of the Sons of Light. These two are locked in combat over humanity; finally, however, God will give victory to Melchizedek. This dualism of light and darkness is attested in ancient Judaism only in the Qumran scrolls, but it figures prominently in certain strands of early Christianity.

Amram Darah fourth-century-C.E. Samaritan poet, whose poetry forms a base for the Samaritan liturgy and initiates a new poetic style. He lived in Nablus (ancient Flavia Neapolis), a city about forty miles (65 kilometers) north of Jerusalem, in the midst of a brief golden age of Samaritan renaissance. Influenced by the obscure Samaritan leader Baba Rabbah and aided by an unstable political situation, Samaritan culture bloomed.

Amram Darah is the first recorded Samaritan poet. Many feel that his poetry was inspired by the Psalms of the Hebrew Bible. Samaritans refer to his widely imitated poetry as a string of "Pearls" (Durran), and twenty-eight of them appear in the Samaritan prayer book, the Defter. There is no rhyming in his poetry, nor does he have a fixed number of lines in a verse or a set number of words per line. Neither do his poems utilize acrostics, that is, beginning lines or verses with subsequent letters of the alphabet, a frequent feature of biblical and later Samaritan poetry.

From his poems various nuances of fourth-century theology can be deduced, particularly the attributes of God, as well as an early indication of such Samaritan practices as the intercalculation of the calendar to establish the dates of the various feast days. *See also* DURRAN.

amulet portable implement of solid (e.g., earthware, metal) or soft materials (e.g., papyrus or cloth) inscribed with incantations and symbols that are designed to provide protective or coercive power for its owner.

Jewish use of amulets is well documented in the artifactual and literary evidence and extends from at least the Second Temple era to the modern period. Earlier use of amulets is hinted in the biblical text (e.g., Isa. 3:20), but more certain evidence is found beginning in the sixth century B.C.E. A silver amulet tentatively dated to the sixth century and incised with the priestly benediction (Num. 6:24–27) was recovered during excavations of Jerusalem. There are allusions to amulets in the wisdom literature (e.g., Prov. 6:21), and 2 Maccabees has a very clear reference to Jews using amulets (2 Macc. 12:40). The Mishnah and Talmud have several references to amulets and the texts suggest widespread use. The point of the discussion in the rabbinic texts is typically a clarification of the appropriate times and applications of the power carried by the amulet (e.g., M. Sab. 61A) and not an attack on their use. A persistent theme of Christian attacks on Jews from the third century forward is that they are the source of magical devices like amulets (e.g., John Chrysostom, *Against the Jews,* Homily 8), which because of their success continue to seduce the Christian population. The later archaeological evidence also bears witness to the ongoing popularity of amulets among Jews and to the pivotal role of Jews in producing amulets. Late fourth- and fifth-century-C.E. contexts have yielded significant numbers incised in Hebrew, Greek, and Aramaic.

Amulets typically impart their power by way of written or incised magical signs or symbols and incantations. It is not unusual to find amulets associated with Jewish use that invoke powers from across the spectrum of ancient Near Eastern and Mediterranean religions or employ symbols that are not specific to Judaism. The incantations use such things as biblical (I-Am-Who-I-Am) and nonbiblical (Nereg) names for God, angels (Gabriel), biblical verses (Num. 12:13), names (Joseph), places (the four rivers of paradise), magical beings, or powers (Abraxas) to capture the necessary power. The magical signs may be an extension or an addition to the incantation. They may take the form of zodiac signs, letter permutations, or geometric designs or *charaktêres,* but in any case, they are clearly intended as esoteric expressions of magical powers.

The most common use of amulets by Jews was for protection from disease or illness. Illness or disease was frequently considered to be caused by contact with the evil eye. The amulet drew into the sphere of the user the power of divine beings that could deflect the attacks of such evil. Amulets were also used in ways that were not simply protective but rather promoted the welfare of the user in terms of health or fertility. Amulets were employed as well in more coercive ways, for example, to cause another to fall in love with the amulet owner or to bring ill fortune on a business competitor.

Ananias, son of Nedebaeus appointed high priest (c. 47–59 C.E.) by Herod of Chalcis, the grandson of Herod the Great, who had been given this function by the Romans. After a violent clash between Jews and Samaritans, the Roman governor of Syria, Quadratus, sent Ananias and other Jewish leaders to Rome in chains, but they were exonerated through the influence of Agrippa II. Ananias and his family were wealthy and influential in Jerusalem. According to Acts of the Apostles, chapter 23, Paul was brought before the Jerusalem Sanhedrin headed by Ananias in about 58, and Ananias then brought charges against Paul before the Roman procurator Felix in Caesarea.

According to the historian Josephus, Ananias increased his wealth by stealing the tithes destined for other priests and won favor with the people and procurator by giving them gifts. In the sixties, he was active in trying to avoid war with Rome. The Sicarii kidnapped his son and other members of his household and exchanged them for their jailed comrades. His house was burned and he was killed by revolutionaries at the beginning of the war against Rome in 66.

Ananias, son of Onias with his brother, Chelkias, served as a general for Cleopatra III Euergetis in her civil war (107–102 B.C.E.) with her son, Ptolemy VIII Lathyrus. He interceded to keep peace between Alexander Jannaeus and Cleopatra. His father, Onias IV, built the Temple at Leontopolis.

Ananias, son of Tzadok Pharisee and distinguished nonaristocratic leader of the revolutionary party in Jerusalem. In 66 C.E., he was a member of the delegation that promised safe passage to the Roman garrison if it left Jerusalem, a pact not honored. He was also one of the four envoys, all good speakers, sent to Galilee to remove Josephus from command.

Ananus, captain of the Temple son of the high priest Ananias, son of Nedebaeus. After the armed disturbance between Jews and Samaritans, he was one of the Jewish leaders sent to Rome, along with the procurator Cumanus and Samaritan leaders, c. 52 C.E. Through the intercession of Agrippa II, the Jewish leaders were freed.

Ananus, son of Ananus high priest; appointed by King Agrippa II after the death of the Roman procurator Festus in 62 C.E. Because the new procurator, Albinus, had not yet arrived, Ananus convened the Sanhedrin and had his enemies, including James, the brother of Jesus, executed. For this he was deposed after only three months. He was a leading figure in the early stages of the war against Rome (66–70 C.E.). He was put in charge of the defense of Jerusalem and was one of the Jerusalem authorities who sought to remove Josephus from command of Jewish forces in Galilee. When the Zealots, under the leadership of John of Gischala, took over much of Jerusalem, Ananus persuaded the people to oppose them. He closed the gates against the Zealots' allies, the Idumeans, and tried to persuade them to take his side. When the Idumeans finally entered the city, they killed him and his supporters.

Ananus, son of Sethi high priest (6–15 C.E.); appointed by the Roman prefect Quirinius after Archelaus, the son of Herod the Great, was deposed. Five of his sons were appointed high priests at different times during the first century. He appears in the New Testament several times under the shortened name Annas. The Gospel of Luke (3:2) refers vaguely to the high priesthood of Annas and Caiphas as the time when John the Baptist received the word of God, and Acts of the Apostles says that Annas was high priest just after Jesus' death. The Gospel of John correctly identifies Annas as the father-in-law of Caiaphas who was high priest at the time of Jesus' execution (18:13). Though Caiaphas was high priest, Annas retained influence in the governing class.

Anastasius I Byzantine emperor (r. 491–518 C.E.) who improved the economic condition of the empire. He was a supporter of the Monophysites and often used the term "Jew" to abuse his enemies, the supporters of Chalcedonian orthodoxy. He followed a policy of not interfering with the Jews. During the reign of the previous emperor, Leo, a Persian named Amorcessus had occupied the island of Jotaba, expelled the Byzantine custom collectors, levied tolls on ships passing along the gulf, and brought a community of Jewish merchants to the island. In 498, Anastasius occupied the island of Jotaba, leaving the Jews there unmolested.

Anastasius of Sinai abbot of the monastery at Sinai, seventh century C.E. He reports that a monk from his monastery saw a vision in his dreams that caused him to abandon Christianity and convert to Judaism. The convert lived among the Jews of Naaran and Livias in the Jordan Valley.

anathema (Gr.: *anathēma,* translating Heb.: *ḥerem*) something devoted to God, either to be consecrated or cursed (Lev. 27:28; Josh. 7:1–13). The related verb in Greek is used to describe the taking of an oath that will bring a curse upon the person who breaks it. The verb occurs in 1 Enoch 6:4–6 for the watchers' oath and explains the origin of the name of Mount Hermon (cf. Acts 23:14 for a similar oath). Anathema comes eventually to be synonymous with "curse" or "cursed" (Rom. 9:3; 1 Cor. 12:3, 16:22; Gal. 1:8–9).

Ancient Aramaic *see* ARAMAIC, OLD

Ancient of Days title for God in Daniel 7:9. Daniel sees in his vision how "thrones were set and an Ancient of Days took his seat. His clothing was white as snow and his hair like lamb's wool." He is seated on a fiery throne and is surrounded by thousands of attendants. Then "one like a son of man" comes on the clouds and is presented before him. The imagery of this vision has its roots in ancient Canaanite mythology, known now from the texts discovered at Ugarit (modern Ras Shamra in Syria) in 1929. It is unusual in a biblical context in so far as both the Ancient of Days and the "one like a son of man" appear to be divine beings. (In the Hebrew Bible it is YHWH who rides on the clouds.) In the Ugaritic texts, however, the god Baal rides on the clouds, and he is subordinate to the high god El. El is depicted as an aged, gray-bearded god, and is called *ab shanima,* "father of years." In Daniel's vision, the El figure represents YHWH and the Baal figure, the "one like a son of man," most probably represents Michael, the patron angel of Israel.

Andreas leader active in the uprising against the Romans (115–117 C.E.). Dio Cassius reports on the atrocities perpetrated by the Cyrenaican Jews under Andreas's leadership, claiming that the Jews engaged in cannibalism, mutilated the Gentiles, made clothes out of their skins and entrails, and used some in wild beast shows and as gladiators. Dio reports 220,000 Gentiles died.

angel (from Gr.: *angelos*; Heb.: *malakh,* messenger) in modern usage the most common term for a whole range of divine beings to whom biblical and Second Temple texts ascribe a variety of names and functions. The belief that heaven was populated by a multitude of such divine beings was common in the religions of the ancient Near East, and evidence of such belief appears in various strata of the Hebrew Bible. Deuteronomy 32:8 refers to the "sons of God," to whom the Most High apportioned authority over the nations. The Song of Deborah asserts that "the stars" fought against Sisera (Judg. 5:20). Psalm 82 criticizes the *elohim* (gods), the "sons of the Most High" (perhaps the gods of the nations), because they have rebelled against God (*elohim*) by not maintaining justice in the world that had been put into their charge. Other texts refer to a single "messenger (*malakh*) of YHWH," who serves as God's presence among God's people and is difficult to distinguish from God.

Complex "angelologies" developed in the Hellenistic period, especially in apocalyptic literature, paradoxically complementing the notion of God's sovereignty while providing a means of connection with the heavenly throne room. Early texts refer to these divine beings variously as "sons of God," emphasizing their divine nature, "holy ones," focusing on the quality that makes them fit to stand in the presence of the Holy One," and "[holy] watchers," a term of uncertain connotation. A special group, the cherubim, seraphim, and ofanim, are in intimate contact with the divine throne. The holy ones attend the divine King in the heavenly throne room and serve as priests in the heavenly temple. A named group of four or seven holy watchers act as intercessors and advocates and as God's agents in the world, enacting judgment, healing humanity, and interpreting God's activity and bringing messages. In this latter respect they are, properly speaking, "angels." By the turn of the era, this last term is developing into a generic expression for the whole heavenly entourage, gradually replacing "holy ones," "watchers," and "sons of God." The change reflects the fact that many of the texts recount instances of heavenly beings appearing to humans.

Military and governing functions are also ascribed to heavenly beings. The term "host (Heb.: *tzaba*) of heaven" denotes their role as God's army, and the title "prince" (Heb.: *sar*) indicates military and ruling functions (Dan. 10:13, 20; cf. also Dan. 7:13–14, and the enthronement of Israel's patron). On a more cosmic scale, 1 Enoch imagines large numbers of heavenly beings in charge of the heavenly bodies and places of eschatological significance in the world.

If the world of angels, holy ones, and sons of God served to assure a beneficial connection between the heavenly world and the righteous on earth, there was also a dark side to the divine realm. A number of myths developed that ascribed the origin of evil to a revolt by heavenly beings, and thus, as in Daniel 10, human existence and history is perceived as a battleground between warring supernatural powers. *See also* ADVOCATE; ANGELOPHANY; CHERUBIM; DEVIL; EVIL, ORIGINS OF; GABRIEL; HOLY ONES; INTERCESSION; JERAḤMEEL; MICHAEL; OFANIM; PRINCIPALITIES AND POWERS; RAPHAEL; SARIEL; SATAN; SERAPHIM; SPIRITS, TWO; STARS; TEN THOUSAND TIMES TEN THOUSAND; URIEL; WATCHERS.

Angelic Liturgy (Songs of the Sabbath Sacrifice, 4QShirShabb) Hebrew composition found in Cave 4, Qumran, in 1952. There are also eight fragmentary copies from Cave 4 (4Q400–407), one from Cave 11 (11QShirShabb), and one from Masada (MasShirShabb). Since the earliest copy dates from the middle of the first century B.C.E., the work itself was composed no later than the beginning of the first century B.C.E.

The composition, which is most likely sectarian, contains a cycle of songs composed for the first thirteen Sabbaths of the year, according to the solar calendar; each song was evidently meant to accompany the holocaust offering on that Sabbath. The songs emphasize the sect's belief in the simultaneity of heavenly and earthly worship. Each song begins with a heading (e.g., "To the Master. Song of the holocaust of the first Sabbath, on the fourth of the first month."), followed by a call to praise God, addressed to the heavenly court. The body of the songs developed various ideas of angelic praise, the celestial sanctuary, and the divine throne. The songs seem to be intended for communal worship.

The songs, which take their inspiration particularly from the divine-throne vision of the first three chapters of the Book of Ezekiel, are especially important for the light they shed on the historical antecedents of *merkabah* (throne-chariot) mysticism and *hekhalot* (heavenly palace) literature of the rabbinic and postrabbinic eras. The content of the songs, in which angels function as priests in the heavenly temple, indicates a strong priestly identity for the group for whom they were intended; and the large number of copies, and their influence on other compositions from Qumran, show the songs' popularity among the Qumran sect, a group that emphasized the role of the priest. The composition's presence at Masada may be explained by the presence of sectaries there after the destruction of Qumran in 68 C.E., or it may point to a wider distribution of the text outside the Qumran community. In any event, the Angelic Liturgy indicates a wider dissemination (perhaps in a priestly milieu) of the *merkabah* and *hekhalot* literature's mystical and speculative ideas, which the rabbis would later attempt to control and suppress, than was previously thought.

angel of death (Heb.: *malakh haMavet*) in the Talmuds, the divine agent that brings death at the proper time

angelophany appearance of an angel to a human being. The purpose of such appearances is normally to make an announcement or commission the person to a task or role. The stereotyped literary form describing the angelophany parallels the form of other epiphany accounts in the Bible and related literature. *See also* EPIPHANY.

angels, tongues of phrase used by Paul in 1 Corinthians 13:1 to refer to glossolalia, a form of ecstatic speech: "If I speak in the tongues of mortals and of angels, but do not have love, I am a noisy gong or a clanging cymbal." The apparent reference is to sounds that belong to no human language, but are thought to come from the heavenly language of the angels. While the phrase is not found elsewhere, similar ideas are attested in the Testament of Job 46–50 (1st c. B.C.E.–1st c. C.E.): when the three daughters of Job demand a share in their father's inheritance, they are given magical sashes, which allow them to speak ecstatically in the "dialect of angels." The language of their hymns shows that the women have transcended earthly things. Angelic speech is also a subject of reflection in the Songs of the Sabbath Sacrifice (4QShirShabb), a fragmentary text found among the Dead Sea Scrolls. This text describes the songs with which the angels praise God in his heavenly temple. The "wondrous words" of the angels—far superior to any "offering" of "mortal tongue"—reflect their superior knowledge.

angel worship In the Hebrew Bible, angels are God's messengers, lower than God but superior to humans; there is little interest in them as independent entities. During the Second Temple period and afterward, developed angelologies appear showing interest in angels' names and functions; these functions include revelation (Ezek. 43:13–14; Zech. 1:19; Dan. 8:15–17; 1 Enoch 7–8; 4 Ezra 4:1–2; Rev. 1:1), mediation (1 Enoch 15:2), guarding of the heavens (1 Enoch 71:7–8; 3 Enoch), controlling meteorological phenomena (Jub. 2:2; 1 Enoch 7, 60:22), and making war (LAB 61:5). Because of their important roles in the universe, angels are invoked in mystical and magical texts to produce effects such as healing (Test. Sol., Sefer ha-Razim). Colossians 2:18 mentions worship of angels in Colossae, and in Revelation 19:10 and 22:8–9, the seer is rebuked for trying to worship an angel. In the Book of Biblical Antiquities 34:2, Aod gains magical powers through worshiping angels.

aniconism the condition or state of using no images. In the case of the ancient Judaisms of Palestine or the diaspora, this was observed by most populations in the sense that images did not furnish the major matter for the cult. On the other hand, ancient Jewish art after the destruction of the Second Temple developed a huge vocabulary of animal depictions and many human ones. Even some representations of divinities and figures associated with Graeco-Roman religion appear in late Roman and Byzantine synagogue art (Helios, Medusa, Genii, and the like). The absence of images, however, has on occasion been used to argue for the presence of some form of Judaism. For example, in the so-called Hellenistic Jewish Temple of Beer Sheba, the presence in the Phase I floor of images of pagan deities (Demeter and Persephone, a Thoth monkey, a ba-bird, the Nabatean deity Delphinios, a Horus amulet) with cult furniture argues that the temple surely served the interests of a non-Jewish cult. On the other hand, the absence of images or amulets of any kind associated with the later Phase II floor, also provided with cult furniture, argues for an aniconic religion such as some form of ancient Judaism.

In a later context, namely, in the "Cave of Letters" near En Gedi, the Jewish refugees of the Bar Kokhba Revolt hiding in the caves battered the noses or faces of the Roman images on their bronze incense shovels to render them usable. That is, a form of aniconism was at work that required that the Jewish user render the image on the shovel "desecrated" by filing away the nose or face (M. Abod. Zar. 4:5). The interests of aniconism in this context were served by defacing a central element in the image, not by removing the image entirely. From the fourth century C.E., Jewish art was particularly rich in images, especially in mosaic floors in synagogues. Even there, however, aniconism with respect to the deity was observed. Even the hand emerging from the cloud in the binding of Isaac in the floor of the Beth Alpha Synagogue is likely to be understood as that of an angel, not of the deity.

animals, cruelty to (Heb.: *tzaar baalei ḥayim*) inflicting suffering on animals. Cruelty to animals is prohibited by the seven commandments that pertain to all of the offspring of Noah, that is, all of humanity, not only Israel. Its avoidance requires slaughtering animals humanely; not muzzling an ox when it ploughs (Deut. 25:4); allowing animals a Sabbath of rest (Exod. 23:12); feeding animals before eating; not buying animals one cannot properly feed; and showing mercy to animals.

animals, representations of images of mainly fauna, but occasionally of imaginary animals in Jewish art and archaeology both in Palestine and in the diaspora. Animals are well represented in Jewish art and archaeology, but mainly from the fourth century C.E. In the Second Temple, Herod attempted to hang a representation of an eagle above the doorway, but the population took exception to such an addition and tore it down. Josephus records that the palace of Herod Antipas at Tiberias was decorated with sculptures of animals to the displeasure of the local populations. Nevertheless, on everyday objects found in Jerusalem from the time of the Second Temple animals occasionally appear. On the stone handle of a vessel found in a house appears the word *qorban* (sacrifice) engraved with two birds upside down (animals appearing upside down in ancient art are usually understood to be dead). The edge of one table was decorated with a fish. Stucco moldings from the same Jewish houses reveal running stags, lionesses, and boars. Yet hardly two hundred meters away, the enormous architectural presence of the Second Temple was entirely without animal representations. Even at this early period in Jewish funerary art and in the art of everyday objects, animals do appear without apparently offending whatever sense of aniconism prevailed.

In late Roman and Byzantine contexts, animal

representations in synagogue mosaic floors and in other media are very well represented. The synagogue floor at Jerash in the Hashemite Kingdom of Jordan, for example, apparently displays a procession of animals two by two, which is therefore understood by the excavators to be a representation of the Noah's Ark story. Inhabited scrolls in both Byzantine churches and synagogues feature a set of animals within medallions formed by vine scrolls. These include felines, dogs, lions, cocks, ducks, dolphins, fish, peacocks, hares, stags, bulls, goats, sheep, and others. Even in the menorah panel in mosaic floors from ancient synagogues of the Byzantine period birds are found. It even appears that a bull and a red cow are depicted in the late Byzantine synagogue mosaic floor from Sepphoris. In the Jewish funerary art from the catacombs of Beth Shearim in western, Lower Galilee there is an extensive vocabulary in representations of animals. In these catacombs, revealed as Jewish by the names and titles of the deceased and by the many depictions of the menorah, lions, eagles, and birds appear most commonly on the sarcophagi, but also stags and hunting dogs. Engraved on the walls of the burial catacombs appear two horses.

animals, treatment of (in rabbinic Judaism) The rabbis did not approve of hunting for sport and considered it an expression of a base instinct. The prohibition of cruelty to animals is basic to the rabbinic concept of civilization. One of the seven commandments of the children of Noah that governs the conduct of all humans prohibits eating a limb or flesh from a living animal. Some rabbis taught that animal flesh may be eaten only in response to an overpowering need. Others encouraged vegetarianism.

Rabbinic rules generally prohibit inflicting unnecessary pain on all animals. They require that a person feed his animals before he eats and must have feed for his animals before he purchases them. Rabbinic homilies extol kindness to animals as a great virtue. The greatest leaders of Israel, Moses and David, were both compassionate shepherds of flocks before they assumed their positions of greatness. One story tells how Judah the Prince suffered pain for thirteen years because he did not aid a calf that was to be slaughtered. He was relieved of suffering only after showing compassion for kittens. There is little evidence, however, that the rabbis attributed to animals the possession of a soul, subject to reward and punishment or life after death.

The rabbinic attitudes toward domestic animals were generally positive. They considered the sheepdog a reliable pet and they discouraged dwelling in a city that lacked a barking dog. Some, however, considered the dog an unruly and immodest animal. They refer to the contention that is common between cats and dogs and cats and mice and warn of the association of cats with magic. Common folklore about other domesticated animals appears in the literature, including sheep, goats, oxen, swine, horses, and asses.

The fox, wolf, weasel, and lion are wild animals often mentioned in rabbinic legend. The eagle, vulture, and falcon are named from among the birds of prey, while the raven and dove often take on symbolic significance in rabbinic interpretation. The rabbis preached that a person could learn ethical behavior from observing the animal kingdom.

A main concern to rabbis was the identification and preparation of the animals that were permitted for consumption. Humane and hygienic preparation of food were primary factors in many of the regulations legislated by the rabbis. To qualify as kosher an animal, bird, or fish had to belong to an acceptable species and be without disease or defect. Beasts and fowl had to be slaughtered and their blood removed by salting and washing. The rules of kosher slaughter require that a trained *shoḥet* rapidly and without interruption cut through the major portion of the windpipe and esophagus of a beast in order to inflict the least possible pain on the animal and to ensure the efficient drainage of its blood. The Talmud's tractate Ḥullin, which is the major source of information pertaining to these rabbinic issues, includes the following: procedures for slaughtering an animal according to the requirements of rabbinic law; diseases and deficiencies that render an animal *treif,* that is, nonkosher; a talmudic discourse on veterinary pathology; classification of animals, birds, fish, insects, as clean or unclean; a talmudic taxonomy of natural species; laws regarding an animal fetus; fractures in animals and birds; the biblical injunction against killing an animal and its young on the same day; the ritual for covering the blood of an animal after slaughtering; food taboos; forbidden cuts of meat; the injunction against eating an animal's sciatic nerve; mixtures of forbidden meats with permitted cuts; general theoretical discussion of the doubtful status of any item that is subject to rabbinic law; neutralization of a banned food substance in a mixture with permitted substances; the prohibition of mixing milk and meat; meal regulations; preparation of some animal organs for consumption; rules regarding the uncleanness of the carcass of an animal that dies; rules regarding gifts to the priests from animals (taxes); various cuts of meat and shearings of sheep that go to the priests; the biblical law of sending the mother bird away from the nest before taking the young. Interspersed throughout the tractate's discussions and analyses of these subjects are a variety of theological and moral excursuses, biblical exegeses, etiologies of dietary practices, mythic tales, historical legends, and homilies.

Rabbinic sources distinguished domesticated from wild beasts. The latter were not valid for sacrifice, their fats were prohibited, and one was obligated to cover with dust the blood that spurted out at the time of their slaughter. An animal that died was unclean as carrion and prohibited for consumption. A dead reptile was singled out as a generative source of uncleanness.

The rabbinic notion of the messianic age includes the defeat of the mythic beast Leviathan, a banquet served from its flesh, and a sukkah made from its luminescent skin. *See also* RITUAL SLAUGHTERER.

Annas abbreviated form of the Hebrew name Ananus, found several times in the New Testament in reference to the high priest Ananus, son of Sethi (Luke 3:2; John 18:13, 24; Acts 4:6).

Annius Rufus one of the first Roman governors of Judea. A man of equestrian rank, he is the third governor that Josephus names. Scholars usually date his tenure to 12–15 C.E. A Greek fragment from the basilica at Sebaste has the name L. Annius Rufus, and this may be a reference to the governor.

annona Roman tax occasionally imposed upon the provinces in addition to the regular taxes. In the second century, the *annona* signified an imperial order requiring the inhabitants of the provinces to deliver supplies to the Roman troops as they marched through the land. The army paid for the goods, although seldom at their market value. With the increased frequency of troop movements in the third century, the *annona* posed a severe hardship on the civilian populations because it could be demanded at any time and the amount was not set. The Jewish custom of allowing the land to remain fallow every seventh year meant that the *annona* could present unique problems to the Jewish farmers of Palestine, and it may be the basis for some of the rabbinic rules liberalizing the restrictions of the Sabbatical year. By the second half of the third century, it became a mainstay of the Roman economy because severe inflation had forced an almost complete abandonment of a money economy. When Diocletian stabilized the economy, he made the *annona* a regular tax levied on the basis of a property valuation that occurred every fifteen years. The tax affected the peasants and the few town dwellers who owned land.

annual cycle pattern for weekly readings of the Torah (Pentateuch) that takes a year to complete. As early as the first century, Josephus and the New Testament reveal that passages from the Hebrew Bible were regularly read in synagogue worship. By about the sixth century, Jews in Babylonia had established a pattern of reading the whole of the Torah (i.e., the Pentateuch) in one year. This annual cycle divided the Torah into fifty-four divisions (*parshayot*). Over the medieval period, the annual cycle gradually replaced the trienniel cycle among all Jewry, although as late as the twelfth century some synagogues still used the trienniel cycle. Today, the annual cycle is used almost exclusively.

anointed (Heb.: *mashiaḥ* [hence, messiah]; Gr.: Christos) Anointing (with oil) was part of royal and priestly investiture ceremonies (Exod. 29:7 [Aaron]; 1 Kings 1:39 [Solomon]; Sir. 46:19 [David]; 2 Mac. 1:10 [Aristobulus]; 2 Enoch 22 [Enoch]; passages throughout the Testaments of the Twelve Patriarchs [many of which may be Christian additions]). Passages such as 1 Samuel 24:6 and Daniel 9:25, which speak of the "Lord's anointed," contribute to later eschatological speculations: signifying a divine agent, the "anointed one" appears in Psalms of Solomon 17:32 and 18:5; 2 Baruch 29, 30, and 72 and 4 Ezra 12 impart that a future king called "the anointed" is expected. Qumran documents speak of two anointed figures, one royal and one priestly.

Josephus notes that the Essenes reject anointing with oil (*War* 2.8.3). Anointing with spices is a ritual for preparing a corpse, as in Testament of Abraham 20:11; Apocalypse of Moses 40:1; Mark 16:1; and Luke 24:1. The accounts of Jesus' anointing (Mark 14:3–9; Matt. 26:6–13; John 12:1–8) thus foreshadow his death as well as signify divine commission.

Ant. *see* ANTIQUITIES OF THE JEWS

anthropomorphism, targumic treatment of An anthropomorphism is the interpretation of what is not human or personal in terms of human or personal characteristics. In the Bible, anthropomorphic statements frequently attribute human characteristics or activities to God. For example, "God created" (Gen. 1:1), "God spoke" (Gen. 1:3), and "God saw" (Gen. 1:4) speak of God in human terms. The targums have a strong tendency to alter such anthropomorphisms. In Targum Neofiti, these changes are sometimes carried out by assigning an action to an attribute of God; attributes used include God's *memra* (word), *shekhinah* (presence), or "Glory." So instead of God creating, for example, God's *memra* creates. At other times the action is not performed by God but in front of God, or is rendered in the passive voice. In Genesis 1:4, for instance, the statement that "God saw" becomes "it was manifest before the Lord." *See also* ANTHROPOPATHISM, TARGUMIC TREATMENT OF.

anthropopathism, targumic treatment of an anthropopathic statement attributes human emotions or passions to God. The targum translators usually avoid anthropopathisms. When the biblical text has them (e.g., Isaiah 1:10–14), the targumist treats them as it does anthropomorphisms. *See also* ANTHROPOMORPHISM, TARGUMIC TREATMENT OF.

Antichrist the human embodiment of a transcendent eschatological opponent of God. The term, of Christian coinage, occurs in the Epistles of John (1 John 2:18, 22, 4:3; 2 John 1:7) and emphasizes the role of antichrists as deceivers, false teachers who embody the deceit of the devil, the spirit of error. Christian theology cites 2 Thessalonians 2:3–12 as the classic description of *the* Antichrist. This text's portrait of "the man of lawlessness," the opponent of Jesus, may reflect an interpretation of Isaiah 14:4–20 and Ezekiel 28:1–19, which describe the hybris and ultimate judgment of a monarch who strives to be equal or like God. This tradition may also inform descriptions of the death of Antiochus IV (2 Macc. 9) and Pompey the Great (Ps. Sol. 2:24–31), who are seen as human agents of a demonic opponent of God (cf. Acts 12:20–23, of Herod Agrippa I). Reference to the temple of God (2 Thess. 2:4) led some Reformation theologians to identify the central figure as the Roman pope or a personification of the papacy, but the tradition and probably the passage refer to the religious functions or divine aspirations of a royal figure.

anti-Christian prayer *see* BIRKAT HAMINIM

Antigonus, son of Aristobulus II (Heb. name: Mattathias) Hasmonean king of the Jewish kingdom (r. 40–37 B.C.E.). He was captured and paraded in Rome by Pompey after the latter's conquest of Jerusalem in 63 B.C.E. He and his father escaped from Rome and in 56 B.C.E. raised a small army in Palestine, which was defeated by the Romans. The Parthians made him king of Israel and high priest in 40 B.C.E. during their invasion of greater Syria. During 39–37 B.C.E., he fought a series of battles with Herod the Great, who had been appointed king of Israel by the Roman Senate. Finally, he was besieged and captured in Jerusalem in 37 B.C.E. by Herod and the Roman legate Sosius and was subsequently executed in Antioch. With his death, the Hasmonean dynasty ended.

Antigonus, son of John Hyrcanus popular general and talented leader. He served his brother Aristobulus I (104–103 B.C.E.) in the latter's attack on Samaria. He aroused his brother's envy and was murdered by him in Jerusalem.

Antigonus of Sohko Pharisaic scholar, active at the beginning of the third century B.C.E. He is listed at M. Abot 1:3 as the successor of Simeon the Righteous in the chain of transmission of Torah. He is credited with the statement: "Do not be like servants who serve the master on condition of receiving a reward, but like servants who serve the master not on condition of receiving a reward; and let the fear of heaven be upon you."

anti-Judaism, Christian opposition to Judaism on Christian religious grounds. Unique Christian opposition to Judaism arose with the claim that Christianity rather than Judaism was the true embodiment of Israel's religion. Although its origins lie in the first century, this theologically oriented anti-Judaism has flourished in the nineteen-century history of the church.

The results of historical criticism notwithstanding, it seems clear that Jesus of Nazareth criticized persons, practices, and forms of religiosity and social behavior within his native Judaism. This critique, however, was modeled in part on the Israelite prophetic tradition. Jesus spoke as a Jew to Jews.

In the early decades of the church, opposition to Judaism began to emerge that related to one's definition of what truly constituted Jewish religion. Convinced that the God of Israel had raised Jesus from the dead and exalted him in heaven as Lord and Messiah, Christians maintained that history was moving toward a culmination that Israel's prophets had predicted, and they asserted that Jews must affirm Jesus' status as God's unique eschatological agent if they wished to attain the covenantal blessings. Being a true Jew involved being a Christian—having faith in Jesus Christ. The absence of such faith rendered one's Abrahamic descent null and void.

This exclusivism, which had parallels in contemporary sectarian Judaism (e.g., the communities of 1 Enoch and the Qumran Scrolls), was complemented by an inclusivistic strain that drew on impulses in the Bible (e.g., Isa. 40–66) and some pseudepigraphical texts (the Sibylline Oracles, the Letter of Aristeas, and also 1 Enoch). God's new action in Jesus had catalyzed universal salvation for humanity. Thus, with remarkable rapidity, Christian preachers began to develop missions in gentile communities. This raised a crucial question within early Judaism and Christianity: Was obedience to the Torah necessary for Gentile converts? The debate was complex and often heated, but by the end of the first century, a predominantly Gentile church identified faith in Jesus as the mark of a true child of Abraham, while Jews maintained that Torah obedience (however one might construe this), and not faith in Jesus as Messiah, was constitutive of Judaism.

The New Testament attests these developments. Paul argues in Romans and Galatians that both Jews and Gentiles are made right with God through faith in Christ and not through observance of the Torah (especially circumcision and food laws). Nonetheless, as a Jew, Paul anguishes over the "unbelief" of Israel and envisions a day when the Gentile mission will be complete and most Jews will come to faith in Jesus (Rom. 9–11). The gospels present a different picture. The unbelief of the Jews is seen to be permanent, and the people of God is identified with the church. In narrating this state of affairs to their largely Gentile audiences, the evangelists highlight Jesus' critique of aspects of Judaism. Conversely, they depict widespread Jewish opposition to Jesus' ministry, and they lay the blame for his crucifixion on the shoulders of the Jewish hierarchy, in particular, and the Jewish people, in general. Matthew 27:25 describes Pontius Pilate's dramatic declaration of Jesus' innocence, while the Jewish people call down a blood curse on themselves and their children. In Luke 23:13–25, the Roman governor delivers Jesus to the will of the Jewish people, who lead Jesus away to be crucified. Luke's story continues in the Book of Acts with Jewish opposition to the apostolic mission. In Gospel of John, "the Jews" is a veritable synonym for unbelievers. Thus, a picture of the Jews as unbelieving opponents of Jesus, responsible for his crucifixion, is ready for assembly from a selective reading of the texts that are achieving canonical authority in the second and third-century church.

Leaders of the postapostolic church develop the picture. For Ignatius of Antioch, Justin Martyr, and Melito of Sardis, it is the Christians and not the Jews who truly understand the gist and goal of Israel's ancient scriptures and traditions. Justin's *Dialogue with Trypho the Jew* and Melito's *Homily on the Passover* are early examples of a developing genre of anti-Jewish literature.

A crucial turn is taken in the Protestant Reformation, especially in the writings of Martin Luther, where Paul's formulation of law and gospel provides a model for contrasting true Christianity with the legalism of medieval Roman Catholicism. This theological construct has left a deep imprint on nineteenth- and twentieth-century discussions of early Christianity written by Protestant historians; they depict first century Jews as clones of their Roman Catholic opponents. Sometimes employing the philosophical categories of Hegelian idealism, they contrast ethical prophetic religion (thesis) with postexilic legalism (antithesis), which is the foil for the Christian synthesis of Israel's religious tradition. With the coming of Christ at the fullness of time, first-century Judaism is dubbed "late Judaism" by some theologians, a term that characterized it as outmoded and defunct, obsessed with the law, and blind to the fulfillment of the heart of the prophetic message, the coming of the Messiah.

At its center—and true to its origins—this anti-Jewish critique remains theological, based on the conviction that the Jews misunderstand their own religion, and it proves its thesis from elements in Jewish scripture and tradition. Nonetheless, this theological conviction has had wide-ranging and incalculable effects on the social and intellectual history of humanity. At times it has provided a rationale for anti-Semitic agendas and has itself shown an anti-Semitic face.

The Holocaust and its sensitizing of humanity to the long history of anti-Semitism in the West have helped to spur a new, empathic understanding of Judaism at the turn of the era. While the specter of anti-Judaism still hovers over Christian theology, piety, and practice—not least when its scriptures are read in public worship—many Christian individuals and communities are increasingly struggling to redefine their religious self-understanding in ways that are more faithful to first-century history and consonant with a broader range of elements inherited from their mother religion. *See also* ANTI-SEMITISM, PAGAN; LEGALISM.

antinomianism the view that, by grace, Christians are set free from the need to observe any moral law. Although the viewpoint is attributed to the Apostle Paul, his attitude toward the Torah was complex, and he repeatedly emphasized the need to lead a righteous life that was, in effect, often consonant with commandments of the Torah. The use of the Greek expression "do lawlessness" (Matt. 7:23, 13:41) has been cited as evidence that Matthew was combating antinomianism in the early church, but the expression is idiomatic and simply denotes wrongdoing that violates the Torah.

Whether certain Gnostic groups espoused antinomianism on the grounds that matter is evil and, therefore, bodily actions are indifferent, is a point of scholarly dispute because of the polemical character of the ancient documents making the charge. Antinomian teaching, technically speaking, does appear, however, in the Reformation and post-Reformation period. *See also* LAWLESSNESS.

Antiochenes term used in 2 Maccabees 4:9 for the citizens of Jerusalem when it was turned into a polis during the Hellenistic reform under Jason (175 B.C.E.). The exact origin and significance of the name are uncertain, but it is reasonably conjectured that the name derives from that of Antiochus IV, and that Jerusalem may have been renamed Antiochus.

Antioch on the Orontes, Jews in Antioch, located on the coast of northern Syria, was founded in 330 B.C.E. by Seleucus I, one of the successors of Alexander the Great. Seleucus ruled Mesopotamia and Syria. Antioch was a gateway between the Mediterranean and the East and later became one of the three largest and most important cities of the Roman empire. Josephus the historian claims that Jews were recognized there as citizens from the beginning, but the evidence he presents makes it more likely that they were recognized as a legal ethnic community within the city. During the war of Antiochus IV against Jerusalem (167–164 B.C.E.), the community may have suffered some oppression, but it was restored to its former status after his rule. The Roman conquest of Antioch in 64–63 B.C.E. did not change the status of the Jewish community. Any conflicts with the authorities in Antioch were particular and of limited duration, rather than chronic. For example, in 41 C.E. the Antiochene Jewish community protested the expedition of the Roman governor Petronius to place a statue of Gaius Caligula in the Jerusalem Temple on imperial orders. They caused him to delay the expedition until Gaius had died.

During and after the war between Rome and Jerusalem (66–70 C.E.), the Jewish community in Antioch was threatened and persecuted by the rest of the population, but their fundamental legal status was reaffirmed after the war by Titus, the victorious Roman general. Later inscriptions and literary sources show that the Jewish community, which may have numbered twenty thousand or more, was centered in the southern part of the city and ruled by a council of elders (*gerousia*). Among a number of synagogues, there was a prominent one dedicated to the Maccabean martyrs. Jewish leaders were involved in the civic life of the city through the fourth century C.E. and also maintained vital relations with leaders in Palestine. The works of the fourth century rhetorician, Libanius, show that Jewish farmers lived in the rural areas around the city. The Jewish community in Daphne, a suburb south of Antioch, contained a beautiful synagogue.

Antiochus III (the Great) (b. 241 B.C.E.) Seleucid ruler. He succeeded his brother Seleucus III Soter in 223 to a greatly reduced Seleucid kingdom, which he set out to restore and expand. In the Fourth Syrian War against Egypt (221–217 B.C.E.) to regain Palestine and Syria under Ptolemaic control, he was eventually defeated by Ptolemy IV Philopator at Raphia in Gaza (217). Antiochus then turned eastward and conquered Parthia, Armenia, and Bactria (212–205) with forays into India and Arabia, thus earning the title "the Great." Antiochus conspired with Philip V of Macedon against the young Ptolemy V Epiphanes and, by the Battle of Panias (200), gained control of Ptolemaic Syria and Palestine, including Judea. A letter from Antiochus to the Jews allowed them to continue their ancestral laws and granted subsidies to the temple worship (Josephus, *Ant.* 12.138–147). After making peace with Ptolemy in 195, he invaded Europe to recover Thrace, but fell into conflict with Roman interests and was defeated both on land and on sea. The Peace of Apamea (188) ensured that the Seleucid empire was no longer a Mediterranean power, and the high indemnity imposed on the Seleucids kept successive rulers searching for new sources of revenue.

Antiochus IV Epiphanes (c. 215 B.C.E.–164 B.C.E.) Seleucid king (r. 175–164 B.C.E.) regarded as Israel's great enemy before and during the Maccabean revolt; son of Antiochus III. After the Roman defeat of his father at the Battle of Magnesia (190 B.C.E.), Antiochus IV was sent to Rome as a hostage and remained there until 176 B.C.E. Following the assassination of his brother Seleucus IV, Antiochus IV gained control of the Seleucid empire and became king in 175 B.C.E.

Antiochus IV invaded Egypt in 170/169 B.C.E. and again in 168 B.C.E. But the Roman general Popillius Laenas issued an ultimatum that forced Antiochus to withdraw from Egypt or be counted an enemy of Rome. As he returned from Egypt to Antioch, Antiochus IV plundered the Jerusalem Temple (perhaps in both 169 and 168 B.C.E., or perhaps only once). Drawn into political and religious affairs in Judea by a faction of "progressives" (see 1 Macc. 1:11–15), Antiochus IV either promoted or cooperated in a program that brought Greek institutions to Jerusalem (a gymnasium, among others), substituted new laws for the Torah, and changed the order of worship at the Jerusalem Temple.

The Jewish sources describe the Baal altar/stone symbolizing the new order of worship instituted in 167 B.C.E. as the Abomination of Desolation. It involved the worship of the Semitic deity Baal Shamin (Lord of the Heavens), an epithet thought to be the equivalent of ancient Israel's claims about its God as the creator and master of the heavens and earth. Jewish opponents (see Dan. 11:31, 12:11) parodied the divine epithet Baal Shamin as *shikutz meshomem* (a detested thing causing horror, or Abomination of Desolation).

Ancient sources and modern scholarship debate the precise involvement and the motives of Antiochus IV in interfering with Jewish life from 168 to 165 B.C.E. The ancient writings attribute his actions to personal arrogance (1 Macc.) or describe them as divine discipline prior to Israel's vindication (2 Macc.; Dan.). Modern scholars variously view them in terms of religious persecution (though there is little ancient evidence for this), the cultural program of "Hellenization," choosing one side in a Jewish civil war with religious and/or social dimensions, the plan to develop an eastern equivalent to the Roman Empire, or an economic scheme to tap sources of money by giving the Jewish high priesthood to the highest bidder and plundering the Jerusalem Temple and its treasury. A combination of religious, political, social, cultural, and economic motives probably lay behind Antiochus IV's involvement in Jewish affairs. At this point it is not possible to untangle them.

Jewish resistance to the new order centered in the Maccabean movement, led first by the priest Mattathias of Modein and then by his son, Judas. In early 164 B.C.E., Antiochus IV granted conditional amnesty to the rebels and ended the ban on observing the Torah and the persecution. This move coincided with (and was perhaps due to) Antiochus's campaign to stabilize and expand the eastern part of his empire. He died in late 164 B.C.E., around the time of Judas Maccabeus's purification of the Jerusalem Temple. The ancient sources give conflicting accounts of his death. But Antiochus IV most likely died of an unknown disease at Tabae, in ancient Persia (Polybius 31.9; compare Appian 11.66; 2 Macc. 1:13–17, 9:1–28; 1 Macc. 6:1–16; Dan. 11:40–45).

The son and successor of Antiochus IV Epiphanes was surnamed Antiochus V Eupator ("of a good father"), suggesting admiration for Antiochus IV in the Seleucid dynasty. The ancient reports about his character by Polybius suggest that he was both charming and erratic ("mad" [*epimanēs*] rather than "god manifest" [*epiphanēs*]), and that he was a patron (rather than an enemy) of local religious observances—hardly a religious persecutor. Antiochus IV was the first Seleucid king to be named Theos (god) on his coinage—a fact that probably fueled Jewish religious opposition to him. The claim that Alexander Balas was his son was disputed even in antiquity. *See also* MACCABEAN REVOLT.

Antiochus V Eupator (c. 173–162 B.C.E.) son of Antiochus IV, reigned less than two years (164–162 B.C.E.) under the guardianship of Lysias. Both were put to death in Antioch when Demetrius I arrived to claim the throne. During his reign, Antiochus V under Lysias made peace with the Jews and allowed them to resume their ancestral customs (2 Macc. 11:22–26).

Antiochus VI Epiphanes Dionysus (c. 148–142 B.C.E.) son of Alexander Balas and Cleopatra Thea; put forward as a child in 145 as a rival claimant to the Seleucid throne against Demetrius II by the military commander of Apamea, Diodotus, who was later called Tryphon. Jonathan Maccabeus supported him when Demetrius II reneged on his promises to Jonathan; in return, Jonathan's position as high priest and previous concessions were confirmed by Antiochus VI, and Simon Maccabeus was appointed governor from the Ladder of Tyre to the borders of Egypt (1 Macc. 11:54–59). Tryphon later deposed Antiochus VI in 142 and then had him murdered (1 Macc. 13:31–32).

Antiochus VII Euergetes (Sidetēs) (c. 159–129 B.C.E.) second son of Demetrius I, succeeded his brother Demetrius II when Demetrius was captured by the Parthians (139 B.C.E.). Antiochus, able and energetic, hunted down Tryphon and forced him to commit suicide (138). He respected the religion of the Jews but demanded back territory ceded to Jonathan Maccabeus and tribute (1 Macc. 15:26–36). He captured Jerusalem in 131/130, and for a brief period the city was once again under Seleucid rule (Josephus, *Ant.* 13 sec. 236–248). He then set out to reconquer the East from the Parthians (130/129 B.C.E.), supported by a Jewish brigade under John Hyrcanus, but he was defeated and killed.

Antipas *see* HEROD ANTIPAS

Antipater father of Herod the Great; an Idumean by birth. Antipater rose to prominence by reason of his diplomatic skills in dealing with various Roman generals in their efforts to establish Roman rule in Palestine. In 67–63 B.C.E. he supported the legitimate Hasmonean successor, Hyrcanus II, against his brother Aristobulus and acquiesced in Pompey's settlement of the problem despite its reduction of Jewish self-control. He aided Scaurus in reaching terms with his friend Aretas III, the Nabatean king. After the civil war between Caesar and Pompey (49–48 B.C.E.) he was able to win the former's favor by providing him with troops for a campaign into Egypt and was rewarded with Roman citizenship as well as prominent administrative positions for his sons Herod and Phasael. He was murdered in 43 B.C.E.

Antipater, son of Herod son of Herod the Great and Doris, his Idumean first wife. Antipater and his mother were repudiated by Herod, but he was recalled by Herod in 14–13 B.C.E. to counteract the influence of his half-brothers, Alexander and Aristobulus. He plotted their executions (7 B.C.E.) with Herod's brother Pheroras and sister Salome. His intrigues to succeed Herod became known after Pheroras's death in 5 B.C.E., and he was arrested. He was tried before Varus, governor of Syria, and executed days before Herod's death.

Antipatris Roman city in western Judea known as Aphek in the Bible (Josh. 12:18). Antipatris was built or rather built up by Herod the Great in honor of his father, Antipater, as a commercial center at a major crossroad. It had been known as Pegai (springs) in the Hellenistic period, but was of no particular importance aside from protecting the headwaters of the Yarkon River. Antipatris was halfway between Caesarea on the coast and Jerusalem. Travelers could stay overnight at Antipatris on their way to Jerusalem, as in the case of Paul in the New Testament (Acts 23:31). According to Josephus, the emperor Vespasian destroyed Antipatris during the Jewish War, but it was rebuilt again on a grander scale (*War* 4:8.1). Recent excavations have revealed a well-paved and drained street and road, public buildings, graves, and a mausoleum from the Roman period. The mausoleum, evidently used by a local family, was built around 100 C.E. and was destroyed in some major conflagration around 300 C.E.

Antiquitates Judaicae *see* ANTIQUITIES OF THE JEWS

Antiquities of the Jews the English title of the work in twenty books by Josephus that is usually known by its Latin title, *Antiquitates Judaicae,* abbreviated as *Ant.* The work covers the period from the Creation to the eve of the 66–70 C.E. war against Rome. About half the writing parallels the Hebrew Bible and is more or less a paraphrase of it, though it contains many additions, omissions, and reinterpretations. It is usually thought to have been written in the early 90s C.E. *See also* JOSEPHUS.

anti-Semitism, pagan (in the Graeco-Roman period) Pagan attitudes toward Judaism before around 200 B.C.E., as attested in the extant literature, were neutral or positive in nature. The most common characterization of the Jews in this period was as a "nation of philosophers," an image that persisted to some degree throughout the Graeco-Roman era.

The first firm evidence for pagan anti-Semitism occurs in the period following the Maccabean Revolt (167–164 B.C.E.) against Greek (Seleucid) rule; advisers of a Seleucid king are said to have maligned the "misanthropic and impious customs" of the Jews (Diodorus Siculus, *Bibliotheca Historica,* 34.1.1–5). Earlier, Mnaseas of Patara (c. 200 B.C.E.) was the first to report the story, repeated by later authors, that the Jews worshiped the head of a donkey in the Jerusalem Temple.

The official Roman policy toward Judaism, established as early as 150 B.C.E. and continuing until around 400 C.E., granted the Jews full rights to practice their ancestral customs. This does not indicate a special sympathy toward Judaism but reflects characteristic Roman policy toward subject peoples. Among Roman literati during the Republic, divergent attitudes toward Judaism are attested. Varro (c. 50 B.C.E.), for example, praised the Jewish cult, whereas his contemporary Cicero was hostile toward Judaism, attacking Jewish customs as anti-Roman. Criticism of Judaism, where it did occur, was normally directed against the peculiarity of certain Jewish practices, especially circumcision (regarded as unnatural), Sabbath observance (regarded as laziness), and abstention from pork (regarded as superstitious).

Especially significant for a consideration of pagan anti-Semitism in the early Empire are events that took place in Egypt. When Rome annexed Egypt in 31 B.C.E., the large Jewish population of Egypt became pro-Roman, a move that set them at odds with the Greeks and the native Egyptian population. The Romans, in turn, confirmed the rights of the Egyptian Jews, many of whom were attempting to gain citizenship. A number of pagan Egyptian authors of the early first century C.E. include distinctly anti-Semitic material in their writings, indicative of a growing tension between Jews and pagans, especially in Alexandria. Recent studies indicate that much of this anti-Semitism had political causes: the Jews were seen as favorites of the Romans and were hated for that reason, and increasing Jewish ambitions for citizenship were resented.

In 38 C.E. the Roman governor of Egypt, Flaccus,

apparently under pressure from anti-Jewish factions, issued a series of rulings restricting Jewish rights. At the same time, acts of mob violence against Jews broke out in Alexandria. After the violence subsided, representatives from both sides sailed to Rome to plead their case before the emperor. In 41 C.E., Claudius issued a letter instructing the Egyptian Greeks to be more tolerant toward the Jews, but warning the Jews not to be politically overambitious.

These events marked both the end of friendly relations between Rome and Egyptian Jewry, and a rise in military activism among Egyptian Jews. From this point until 117 C.E., Jewish-pagan relations in Egypt were marked by sporadic outbursts of violence. As a result of the Jewish revolt against the Romans in 115–117, the Egyptian Jewish community was decimated.

Attitudes toward Judaism among the Romans themselves in the early empire reflect the same sort of ambivalence as noted earlier. Certain Roman satirists—Martial, Petronius, and Juvenal—direct pointed barbs against Judaism. Especially Juvenal and certain other authors of the late first and early second centuries, such as Tacitus and Quintilian, seem to reflect a growing hostility toward Judaism among Roman literati.

Anti-Semitism in early imperial Roman literary circles can be traced to several causes. One is a general xenophobia among certain Roman conservatives: Jews were seen as representative of undesirable foreign elements in general. Adding fuel to such anti-Semitic attitudes was the fact that Jews seem to have been especially successful in gaining proselytes in Rome in the first century C.E. Thus, Judaism was perceived by some conservative groups as a threat to traditional Roman religion and values.

A second factor contributing to Roman anti-Semitism was the Jewish revolts against the Romans in 66–73 (in Israel) and 115–117 C.E. (in the Diaspora). Negative Roman attitudes toward Judaism seem to have peaked in the late first century C.E. Despite such attitudes, the official Roman policy upholding traditional Jewish rights remained in force.

The other side of the picture is, of course, represented by those Romans to whom Judaism appealed. Admiration for, and conversion to, Judaism seem from the available evidence to have been quite common in Rome during the first two centuries C.E. The appeal of Judaism among Romans of all classes and social strata is attested in many sources. Authors of the early empire who present neutral or positive portrayals of Judaism include the historians and ethnographers Nicolaus of Damascus, Diodorus Siculus, Pompeius Trogus, and Strabo; the philosophers Longinus, Epictetus, and Plutarch; and the natural historian Pliny the Elder. Many of these authors reflect the long-standing tradition that the Jews are a nation of philosophers.

When Judaism ceases to pose a political or social threat to Rome, as after 135 C.E., antipathy toward Judaism largely disappears. Sources from the later empire tend to express a neutral or positive attitude toward Judaism. Several pagan emperors are explicitly portrayed as pro-Jewish. Even the later Christian emperors continue to protect traditional Jewish rights.

It appears, then, that pagan anti-Semitism in the Graeco-Roman period is relatively circumscribed. The anti-Semitism that is attested seems to stem mainly from political and social rather than religious causes. Anti-Semitic sentiments were, on the whole, expressed among discrete and identifiable groups that were reacting against specific political and social issues concerning Jews and Judaism. Pagan attacks on particular Jewish practices were generally not invective directed against Judaism per se but pretexts for an antagonism arising from Jewish involvement in concrete political or social circumstances. *See also* ANTI-JUDAISM, CHRISTIAN.

Antonia Fortress, archaeology of the excavation and reconstruction on paper of the Roman fortress adjacent to the northwest corner of the Second Temple Mount in Jerusalem. In the nineteenth century, builders of the Sisters of Zion Convent in the Old City of Jerusalem unearthed nearly 40 by 90 meters of a fine stone pavement formed of large limestone blocks. The blocks were well worn from use, and some of them were scored with multiple, shallow grooves to prevent slippage of pack animals and horses. The pavement was also well drained. The pavement was bordered on the west by the remains of a triple-arched Roman triumphal arch. The central arch measured 5.2 meters wide and 6.25 meters high. (This arch spans the Via Dolorosa today and is termed the Ecce Homo Arch. See John 18:33). The two side arches were 2.36 meters wide and 5.2 meters high. The two side arches were for pedestrian traffic, and the central arch was for carts, horses, and the like. This triumphal arch is beautifully decorated with carved stone moldings and niches, which once held statues. On the eastern side of pavement, a row of stones was laid to form a stylobate, an architectural feature that supports a row of columns such as those found around a courtyard, beside a street, or around a forum.

Beneath the pavement is a vaulted pool of apparent Roman construction, which the excavators identified with the Strouthion Pool mentioned in Josephus (*War* 5.467). A narrow, rock-cut staircase ascends from the pool to the pavement. The excavators identified this pavement with the lithostrotos, the stone pavement where the Roman governor Pontius Pilate condemned Jesus (John 19:13). In other words, the pavement was understood to comprise the courtyard inside the Antonia Fortress, which was itself identified with the praetorium of John 18:33, the place where Jesus' trial took place. Since renewed excavation in 1972 and after renovation since 1980, the pavement and triumphal arch are identified as the remains of the eastern forum of the city of Hadrian, which was built after 135 C.E. The pool is understood to have been originally an open pool from the time of Herod the Great and is probably the Strouthion Pool. The sole trace of the Antonia Fortress is the rock-cut platform or plinth at the northwest corner of the Temple Mount. This plinth is about 40 by 120 meters in extent. The Strouthion Pool lay outside the boundaries of the Antonia Fortress to the northwest.

Antonines and the Jews (138–193 C.E.) After the Bar Kosiba War (132–135) the Romans evidenced a healthy respect for the Jews' military abilities. The Antonines' policy of common sense and moderation was the result of many factors: the threat of another Jewish uprising; the ties between the Palestinian Jewish community and the Jews living under Persian domination; and the large number of Gentiles who were attracted to Judaism. In Palestine, Antonius Pius relaxed Hadrian's ban on circumcision among the Jews, but left it in force for non-Jews. Jews were prohibited from circumcising Gentile slaves, and the policy may have functioned to restrict converts to Judaism. However, Judaism was again viewed as a legitimate religion; its rites were practiced openly, and the Jews expressed a generally favorable opinion of the Romans. The period of relative peace in Palestine allowed the restoration of normal life within the province; however, there had been major changes. As a result of the Bar Kosiba War, the Jewish population in Palestine moved north into the Galilee, while Judea and Jerusalem became primarily Gentile. Sepphoris, Tiberias, Beth Shearim, and Usha became the centers of rabbinic culture and the Jewish government. The Sanhedrin was reestablished, and the position of the *nasi* was again filled. Simeon III, the *nasi,* raised the dignity and prestige of the office so that it could act as the supreme leader of the worldwide Jewish community. His son, Judah, established control over the totality of Jewish civil and religious life within Palestine, and his authority was recognized by the Jewish communities throughout the world. Babylonian sages traveled to Palestine to study in Judah's schools, and they recognized him as the supreme Jewish authority. The patriarch sent emissaries throughout the diaspora to supervise the organization of individual communities and to collect an annual tax for the support of the patriarch, which replaced the annual Temple tax. The Romans recognized the patriarch's authority, supplying him with bodyguards from Gaul. Nevertheless, Antonius maintained the pagan character of Jerusalem, and he placed a statue of himself next to the one of Hadrian on the Temple Mount. Antonius also maintained the size of the Roman garrison at its postwar level, approximately one-fifteenth of Rome's troops. He selected governors of high rank and ability. Even though Palestine's economy had been devastated, Antonius kept the high tax rates established by Hadrian as punishment for the revolt. As a result of the Parthian War of 162–166, the Romans greatly improved the Palestinian system of roads. In 175 the legate of Syria, Avidius Cassius, revolted against Marcus Aurelius and was accepted as emperor by the eastern provinces. While the troops supported Avidius, there is no evidence of a Palestinian revolt against Marcus Aurelius, who seems to have visited Palestine to secure its loyalty. This visit may be the basis of the rabbinic stories that speak of cordial meetings between Judah I and the Roman emperor, Antonius.

Antoninus, Marcus Aurelius *see* CARACALLA

Antonius Julianus *see* JULIANUS, MARCUS ANTONIUS

Antonius, Marcus *see* MARK ANTONY

Antonius Pius Roman emperor (r. 138–161 C.E.) He was born in 86 into a consular family at Lanuvium in the Alban Hills in northern Italy. He was consular in Etruria and Umbria, and between 133 and 136 he was proconsul of Asia. As emperor he centralized the general administration of the empire, altered many of Hadrian's anti-Jewish policies, and inaugurated a period of good relations between the Palestinian Jews and the Roman government. Although Jerusalem remained Aelia, a pagan city in which Jews could not reside, he relaxed the ban on circumcision among Jews. However, a non-Jew who had himself or his slave circumcised was exiled, his property was confiscated, and the doctor who performed the circumcision was executed. Any Jew who circumcised his Gentile slaves was deported or executed. Papyri indicate that Antonius also allowed circumcision for the Egyptian priestly caste, for whom the rite was also a religious ritual. However, each operation had to be individually approved by the civil and religious authorities after the inquiries concerning the candidates priestly qualifications. Although Palestine's agricultural economy had suffered as a result of the Bar Kosiba War, Antonius maintained Hadrian's high rate of taxation for the country.

Apamea **1.** capital of Apamene, Syria, south of Antioch. According to Josephus (*War* 2.18, 5), at the outbreak of the Jewish War, its citizens protected the city's Jewish inhabitants.

2. Phrygian city to which Antiochus transplanted many Jews (Josephus, *Ant*. 12.3, 4). It is referred to at B. Berakhot 62a, in connection with witchcraft; B. Niddah 30b; and possibly B. Yeḇamot 115b.

3. town at the division of the Tigris. At B. Kiddushin 71b, the genealogical purity of its residents is questioned.

Apamea, Peace of After losing to Rome at the Battle of Magnesia, Antiochus III (the Great) was forced to accept Roman peace terms at Apamea, on the southern shore of the Black Sea, in 188 B.C.E. Antiochus gave up all claims to Thrace and Greece, withdrew to eastern Asia Minor, and was burdened with a huge, yearly indemnity payment to Rome. These terms weakened the Seleucid kingdom over the next few decades by cutting it off from its source of Greek manpower and its mines in Asia Minor and by imposing a huge financial burden. *See also* MAGNESIA, BATTLE OF.

Apamea, synagogue in located in the Orontes Valley south of Antioch. Apamea yielded a late-fourth-century synagogue with an elaborate mosaic floor built according to the style of the Antiochene school. A mosaic menorah at the sourthern end of the synagogue is in front of a Torah niche in the wall facing Jerusalem. The nineteen inscriptions in the synagogue indicate that the synagogue officials included three *archisynagogi* (leaders of the synagogue), a leader of the council of elders, and at least four elders. In the fifth century a church was built over the synagogue.

Apellaios name of a Macedonian month; appears in a number of Jewish sources, such as the writings of Josephus. Unfortunately, there was not a uniform usage; sometimes it corresponded to the Hebrew month of Ḥeshvan (October/November) and sometimes to the month Kislev (November/December).

Aphek *see* ANTIPATRIS

Apheka ancient Jewish village site in the northern Golan Heights with architectural fragments of a highly decorated, perhaps third-century synagogue (Arab.: Afiq, Fiq). Carved stones reported since 1885 include a fragment of a lintel with a circle enclosing a seven-branched menorah with a shofar to the right and a bound palm branch (lulab) to the left, another fragment with a five-branched menorah, an Ionic capital, and a column fragment with a seven-branched menorah and an Aramaic inscription. The inscription reads: "I, Judah, the *ḥazan* . . ." The word *ḥazan* (*khz'nh*) appears only once more in synagogue inscriptions for a synagogue functionary, at Khirbet Ammudim.

apikoros *see* EPIKOROS

Apion Greek writer of Alexandria in the early first century C.E. He represented the Greek citizens of Alexandria before Caligula in their dispute with the Jews over the question of citizenship. He wrote a history of Egypt in which he discussed the Jews in several passages. According to him, the Jews originated from a diseased people expelled from Egypt, while Moses was himself an Egyptian. He also stated that Antiochus IV found a Greek kept captive in the temple, awaiting sacrifice by the Jews at one of their festivals. Apion was later attacked by Josephus in *Against Apion*. *See also* AGAINST APION.

apocalypse genre of revelatory literature popular in the period 200 B.C.E.–100 C.E., (and much later in Christianity). The main biblical examples are the Book of Daniel in the Hebrew Bible and the Book of Revelation in the New Testament. The oldest Jewish apocalypses, however, are found in the Book of Enoch, some parts of which date from the the third century B.C.E. Apocalypses claim a supernatural character, which is highlighted by the role of a mediating angel, who interprets visions or serves as guide on an otherworldly tour. The Jewish apocalypses are always pseudepigraphic, that is, they are attributed to venerable figures from the past, such as Enoch, Daniel, Ezra, or Baruch. The content of the apocalypses always involves eschatology, and differs from the older prophetic revelations in the prominence attached to the judgment of the dead. Some parallels can be found in the neighboring cultures, from Greece and Rome on the one hand to Persia on the other, but the sources are not sufficient to permit a full reconstruction of the development of the genre.

Apocalypses are of two types. One type, which may be called "historical" apocalypses, typically takes the form of a symbolic vision, followed by an interpretation. Daniel chapter 7 is a classic example. The revelation in this kind of apocalypse concerns the course of history, much of which is "predicted" after the fact. Often history is divided into a set number of periods, ten generations, four kingdoms, or the like. The revelation concludes with a real prediction of the climax of history. First there will be a period of great distress. Then there will be a decisive divine intervention, sometimes mediated by an angel or by the messiah. Then there will be a judgment, which includes a judgment of the dead; in the historical apocalypses it is cosmic in scope. A new, utopian state results, sometimes involving a new creation. This kind of apocalypse is found in Daniel and some sections of 1 Enoch (the Animal Apocalypse in chaps. 83–90, the Apocalypse of Weeks in chaps. 93 and 91) from the early second century B.C.E., and in several apocalypses from the late first century C.E. (Revelation, 4 Ezra, 2 Baruch). These apocalypses are clustered around two great, traumatic events in Jewish history, the persecution under Antiochus Epiphanes in 167–164 B.C.E. and the destruction of Jerusalem by the Romans in 70 C.E.

The second type of apocalypse is characterized by an otherworldly journey, in which the visionary ascends to heaven or descends to the netherworld. The oldest apocalypse of this type is the Book of the Watchers in 1 Enoch 1–36, which dates from the late third or early second century B.C.E. Enoch has a vision of God on his throne, which has a close parallel in the "historical" apocalypse of Daniel 7. He is then taken on a tour to the ends of the earth, guided by an angel. The places he sees include the abodes of the dead and the place that is prepared for the final judgment. Later apocalypses often have the visionary ascend through seven heavens. Some of these apocalypses show relatively little interest in history, but all include some element of eschatology, in so far as they describe the judgment of the dead and subsequent rewards and punishments. Other apocalypses of this type include 3 Baruch and 2 (Slavonic) Enoch, both of which are thought to have been composed in Egypt in the first century C.E. These apocalypses represent an early stage in the tradition of Jewish mysticism.

The apocalypses functioned as a means of consolation in time of distress and of exhortation. They claimed that there was more to the world than meets the eye. Human destiny is shaped by the actions of angelic and demonic forces, and the course of history is predetermined. Ultimate success is not achieved in the temporal realm, but depends on the final judgment. The apocalypses, then, provided a way of framing human actions against the backdrop of a heavenly world of angels and demons and the prospect of a definitive judgment to come. They offered an imaginative view of the world which had great influence in some strands of Judaism and especially in Christianity.

apocalypticism The noun apocalypticism (and the adjective apocalyptic) derive from the term "apocalypse" and refer to a worldview that is similar to what we find in that genre. Because there are different degrees of similarity, there is some variation in what scholars call apocalyptic. Key elements in the world view of the apocalypses include lively eschatological expectation, on the one hand, and interest in the heavenly, angelic world on the other.

Apocalyptic eschatology has its roots in the later books of the Hebrew prophets, and is marked by colorful mythic imagery. Isaiah 24–27, a late passage sometimes called "the apocalypse of Isaiah," envisages a time when God "will swallow death forever" (25:8) and will slay Leviathan and the dragon that is in the sea (27:1). According to Isaiah 65:17, God is about to create new heavens and a new earth. Some of these passages date from a time shortly after the return from exile in the late sixth century B.C.E., but many eschatological passages in the prophetic books are difficult to date. This line of tradition is taken up in the Book of Daniel at the time of the Maccabean revolt. Daniel envisages the Gentile kingdoms as beasts that come up out of the sea, which will be destroyed by divine judgment. Daniel, however, introduces an element not found in earlier biblical books in the resurrection of individuals for judgment (12:1–3). Several apocalypses of the late first century C.E. (Revelation, 4 Ezra, 2 Baruch) are heavily dependent on the imagery of Daniel.

Another apocalyptic tradition is found in 1 Enoch, which is really a collection of five apocalyptic books. In this tradition, the basic myth is provided by the fall of the angelic "sons of God" in Genesis 6. This myth is taken up in the Book of the Watchers (1 Enoch 1–36), as an allegory for the spread of evil on earth. Again there is the promise of a judgment to cleanse the earth. The Book of the Watchers goes on to describe the ascent and otherworldly tour of Enoch, with the result that earthly upheavals are seen against the backdrop of cosmic order.

The sectarian community of the Dead Sea Scrolls may reasonably be described as an apocalyptic movement. The books of Enoch and Daniel were popular and influential in the Dead Sea sect. The sect, however, developed a distinctive mythology of its own, which was probably indebted to Persian dualism. According to the Qumran Community Rule, the world is divided between the Spirits of Light and Darkness, and humanity is divided according to its share in each. The War Scroll anticipates a final battle between the Sons of Light, led by the archangel Michael, and the Sons of Darkness, led by Belial. The Kittim, or Romans, figure prominently among the Sons of Darkness. Important roles in the final transformation will be played by messianic figures, a warlike messiah of Israel and a priestly messiah of Aaron. The Scrolls are also characterized by a strong interest in the heavenly world. Several passages in the Thanksgiving Hymns (Hodayot) indicate that the sectarians thought they were already joined in community with the angelic host. A document called The Songs of Sabbath Sacrifice describes the heavenly liturgy and represents an early example of the Jewish mystical tradition. Unlike the apocalypses, the Scrolls contain few references to the resurrection of the dead, but there are eternal rewards and punishments for the followers of the two Spirits in the Community Rule. It may be that resurrection was less urgent for the sect because of the belief that they were already mingling with the angels.

Early Christianity also had its origin in a Jewish apocalyptic movement. While the Book of Revelation is the only full-blown apocalypse in the New Testament, much of early Christianity is informed by a view of the world similar to what we find in the historical apocalypses. Paul taught that the resurrection of Jesus was the first fruits of a general resurrection, which could not be far away (1 Cor. 15). The Gospels of Matthew, Mark, and Luke all promise that Jesus would come back on the clouds of heaven as the Son of Man foretold by Daniel. Apocalypticism continued to flourish in Christianity down to the Middle Ages. In contrast, Tannaitic Judaism seems to have repudiated apocalypticism, probably because of the disappointment of eschatological hopes in the great revolts of 66–70, 115–118, and 132 C.E. Apocalyptic motifs do reappear, however, in the later midrashim, and the tradition of apocalyptic ascents to heaven was taken up in Jewish mysticism.

Apocrypha a collection of Jewish writings composed between about 250 B.C.E. and 100 C.E. The origin of the designation (from Gr., meaning hidden things) is uncertain. Most of the writings were included in major manuscripts of the Greek translation of the Hebrew Bible, but excluded from the rabbinic canon. The Apocrypha consists of 1 Esdras, Tobit, Judith, Rest of Esther, the Wisdom of Solomon, Ecclesiasticus, Additions to Jeremiah (Baruch, the Letter of Jeremiah), Additions to Daniel (the Prayer of Azariah, the Song of the Three Children, Susanna, Bel and the Dragon), the Prayer of Manasseh, and 1 and 2 Maccabees. Most editions also include the apocalypse 2 Esdras (4 Ezra), which is not found in extant manuscripts of the Septuagint. There is some indication that the Apocrypha continued to circulate in Jewish circles even after they had been excluded from the rabbinic canon; however, they have been preserved because Christian scribes included them in their Greek manuscripts of the Bible.

The development of the Apocrypha as a collection was the work of Jerome, the fourth-century Christian translator, exegete, and theologian, who included them in his new Latin translation (the Vulgate), but gathered them separately at the end, emphasizing that the Jewish community did not consider them canonical. The Council of Trent (1546), called by Pope Paul III, decreed that all of the Apocrypha except 1 and 2 Esdras and the Prayer of Manasseh were part of the Old Testament, although the Roman Catholic Church subsequently distinguished between protocanonical works (the Hebrew canon) and deuterocanonical books (the Apocrypha). The latter appear in Roman Catholic Bibles roughly in the sequence in which they appear in the Greek codices. The Eastern Orthodox churches follow the same practice and also include 1 Esdras, Psalm 151, the Prayer of Manasseh, and 3 and 4 Maccabees. Although the Protestant Reformers showed respect for some of the Apocrypha—though not according them canonical status—subsequent English-speaking Protestant practice deleted them from editions of authorized translations. Thanks to the renewed study of Judaism in the past decades, the Apocrypha are regularly included in editions of the Bible, where they provide a valuable resource for the study of early Christianity and its Jewish context.

Apollonia city on the coast of Palestine, 9 miles north of Jaffa, referred to twice in antiquity, both times by Josephus. In *Antiquities of the Jews* 13.395, he says that Apollonia belonged to Jewish territory during the reign of Alexander Yannai (102–76 B.C.E.). In *The Jewish War* i. 166, Josephus says that Apollonia had been restored by Gabinius, in the time of Alexander the Great. Some scholars hold that Apollonia was founded by the early Seleucids, at the beginning of the third century B.C.E. This is improbable, since they did not control the coast of Palestine.

Apollonis military magistrate of Apollinopolis-Heptacomis in Upper Egypt (113–120 C.E.). A major owner of property in and around Hermoupolis in Middle Egypt, he served in the campaigns against the Jews (115–117). Jewish forces invaded Hermoupolis and plundered Apollonis's estate. Two minor officials in Lycopolis were reprimanded for failing to supply Apollonis with agricultural goods he was expecting. They claimed that the "Jewish commotions" had prevented them from fulfilling their obligations. In the autumn of 117, after returning home, he requested sixty days' leave from the prefect, arguing that his property in the villages and the metropolis of Hermoupolis needed his attention as a result of the Jewish attacks.

Apollonius Molon Greek rhetor who taught at Rhodes and Rome in the first century B.C.E. Among his pupils were Cicero and Julius Caesar. He seems to have written a work about the Jews in which, according to Josephus, he made a variety of slanderous charges, including the accusation that the Jews sacrificed and ate a Greek each year. Other quotes from him, however, seem to be only descriptive rather than defamatory and to show considerable knowledge of Jewish tradition. He included references to the migration of Abraham, Abraham's son "Laughter" (the meaning of Isaac in Hebrew), and Abraham's sons by Keturah.

apologetic literature genre that developed significantly during the Hellenistic period. After the conquest of Alexander the Great, Jews came into intimate contact with Hellenic culture, both in such centers as Alexandria and in the Land of Israel itself. The dominance of Greek philosophy, literature, and science challenged Jews and other eastern peoples to defend their contributions to civilization. Greek rationalism called into question the meaning of Torah observances. Tension between Jews and Gentiles elicited more specific and threatening charges. Jews, said their enemies, were misanthropes, offspring of Egyptian lepers, and worshipers of an ass's head in Jerusalem. Jewish apologists responded.

An early apologetic work from the Hellenistic period is the Letter of Aristeas. Written in Alexandria in the second or first century B.C.E., this work recounts the legend of the origin of the Septuagint, the translation of the Torah into Greek by seventy sages. It further recounts a banquet given by the Greek king Ptolemy II, where the translators responded to questions about Jewish observances, demonstrating that apparently irrational practices had a profound ethical meaning.

Other early apologetic works survive in fragments preserved by Christian writers such as Eusebius, particularly in his *Preparation for the Gospel.* In the second century B.C.E. Aristobulus, who apparently had some philosophical training, defended the antiquity of Israelite culture and argued that it was the source of Greek culture. Aristobulus also explained biblical anthropomorphisms as acceptable metaphorical language. Further cultural polemics appear in the fragments of Pseudo-Eupolemus, who claimed that Abraham taught Egyptian priests astrology, and in Artapanus, who credits Moses with the invention of most significant Egyptian institutions.

As relations between Jews and Greeks worsened during the later Hellenistic period more serious apologetics became necessary. Throughout the writings of Philo, in the early first century C.E., there are numerous apologetic touches, and several works with an explicit apologetic focus. The most important are the *Embassy to Gaius* and *Against Flaccus,* both occasioned by disturbances in Alexandria in 38 C.E. In these works, Philo, a member of an official delegation to the emperor, presents the Jewish side of the affair and attacks the Roman governor Flaccus as biased. His smaller apologetic treatise, the *Hypothetica,* preserved in Eusebius (*Prep. Gos.* 8.5.11–8.7.20; 8.11.1–18), explains such Jewish practices as Sabbath observance and defends the excellence of the morality taught by the Torah.

The final major work of Jewish apologetics of the Hellenistic-Roman period is *Against Apion,* written by the historian Josephus in the last decade of the first century C.E. This two-volume work records the slanders leveled against the Jews during the Hellenistic period by Egyptian polemicists such as Apion, Apollonius Molon, and others. Like his apologetic predecessors, Josephus defends the antiquity of the nation and the humanity and reasonableness of the Torah.

Apologia pro Iudaeis *see* HYPOTHETICA

apostasy rebellion against authority; specifically, rebelling against kings (1 Esd. 1:48; 2:23.27; cf. Jdt. 7:15). Israel's covenantal relationship with God meant that acting against the laws of God was seen as a rebellion (Josh. 22:22; Jer. 2:19). So Daniel 9:9–10 is a prayer for forgiveness from God to his people, who have rebelled against Him and not followed his law; see also Prayer of Azariah 3–10 and the Wisdom of Solomon 3:10. A more precise definition of apostasy, however, is given in Exodus 22:19, where one who sacrifices to another god is to be utterly destroyed. In Deuteronomy 13 those who incite their fellow Israelites to follow other gods are to be put to death. This law is restated in the Temple Scroll found at Qumran and is echoed particularly in the description of those whom the author of 1 Maccabees accuses of wanting to destroy Israel's traditions: "In those days lawless men came forth from Israel and misled many saying, Let us go and make a covenant with the Gentiles round about us" (1 Macc. 1:11). The leaders of this movement, the high priests Jason and Menelaus, are called apostates (2 Macc. 5:8, 15). Similarly, in 3 Maccabees, some Jews are said to have committed apostasy under the threat of persecution (3 Macc. 2:25–30). In the dream vision of the history of the world in 1 Enoch, the sheep of Israel are often blinded and go astray, that is, are guilty of apostasy (apostasy and return to belief, 89:32–33, 41, 51–54, 74; 90:8). The same view is found in 1 Enoch 93:4, 8, 9, and 91:11. The motif of apostasy is also used to characterize primordial events: the angelic watchers deliberately rebel against God (1 Enoch 6). Apostasy is also part of the description of eschatological evil (Jub. 23:16f.; cf. Dan. 12:3). Since the members of the Qumran Community also entered into a covenantal relationship with God, one finds rules governing those who committed apostasy and left the community (1QS8). Within the early Christian writings, Paul is described in Acts of the Apostles 21:21 as one who has allegedly rejected Moses. Paul himself, in the opening chapters of Romans, describes the history of humans as one of progressive movement away from God. In Hebrews 6:6, those who have once entered the Christian community and then left are said to crucify the Son of God and hold him up to contempt. In the Book of Revelation, the primordial rebellion is that of the dragon (Rev. 12:7), while 2 Thessalonions 2:3 predicts that the coming of the Lord will take place only after the rebellion and the appearance of the man of lawlessness.

apotropos (Gr., guardian) court-appointed custodian of affairs of another person, for example, an adult unable to take care of his or her own property. *See also* BAILEE.

Appian Greek writer from Alexandria in the early second century C.E. who worked in Rome. An admirer of Roman imperialism, he wrote a history of Rome during the Republican period and the early Empire to the time of Trajan. Not all of his work survives, but the section called the *Civil Wars* is extremely valuable for events during this period of time, from the death of Julius Caesar to the eventual triumph of Augustus. This period was very important for Judea, extending from the end of Hasmonean rule to the rise of Herod the Great. Appian also mentions other Roman interactions with Judea in a number of passages, especially in his work *On Syria*. He mentions the conquest of Jerusalem by Pompey, Pompey's procession in a chariot studded with gems, and the imprisonment of Aristobulus II. He knows of the special tribute required of Judea and other eastern countries under Mark Antony. He mentions the same oracle of a ruler from the East that Josephus recorded. He refers to a special tax on the Jews of his own time, though the exact significance of this is disputed. He himself had to flee for his life during the Jewish revolt in Egypt under Trajan.

Aquila translator of the Hebrew Bible into Greek, probably in the second century C.E., alleged to have been a convert to Judaism. His translation, a replacement for the Septuagint (which had gone out of favor with the Jews) is characterized by its extreme literalness and faithfulness to the then-current Hebrew text. *See also* ONKELOS.

Araba city referred to by Josephus as one of the three leading cities of the Galilee, alongside Tiberias and Sepphoris. Yoḥanan b. Zakkai and Ḥanina b. Dosa taught there. *See also* GABARA.

Arabia the region of the Arab tribes, who are usually understood to originate in the northwestern corner of the Arabian peninsula in modern Saudi Arabia. The location of a place called "Arabia" is not always the same from period to period. The Fourth Satrapy of the Persian empire was named Arabia. It occupied the area between Athura, the Fifth Satrapy (Syria-Palestine) and Babylon, the Third Satrapy. During this same period, notably during Nehemiah's struggles to rebuild Jerusalem in mid-fifth century B.C.E., one of the groups opposing Nehemiah was Geshem the Arab (Neh. 4:7, 6:1). This Geshem is usually identified as a member of an Arab group south of Judea, perhaps the king of Qedar named Geshmu in sources outside the Bible. During the Maccabean period, Zabdiel the Arab is mentioned from Arabia, which seems to be east and south of Damascus. The "Arabs who are called Zabadeans" in 1 Maccabees 12:11 also appear to have lived in the vicinity of Damascus. In 2 Maccabees 12:10–12, Judas Maccabeus defeated a force of five thousand Arabs with five hundred cavalry at Dathema east of the Sea of Galilee. These Arabs are sometimes identified with Itureans, since the Nabateans, who were also ethnically Arabs, sympathized with the Jews. In the New Testament, Paul mentions that he went away into Arabia, which is usually understood to be in Transjordan or Nabatea. In fact it appears that in the Roman period Arabia referred to a general area south and east of Judea with no firm boundaries. Part of this was the Arab kingdom of Nabatea.

In 106 C.E., the Roman emperor Trajan annexed this kingdom and the wider area occupied by Arab tribes as Provincia Arabia. By 107 C.E. Claudius Severus was the new governor with one Roman legion, the III Cyrenaica, brought in from Egypt. From a scrap of papyrus, a soldier's letter to his father in March of 107 C.E., we know that the main cities of Arabia were Petra, southwest of the Dead Sea, and Bostra to the north of the province. The letter mentions that merchants have taken advantage of the annexation of Arabia to pour into the new province from Pelusium, the commercial city between Palestine and Egypt. A new highway was built from Ailia at the head of the Red Sea northward to Petra and Bostra. Other Roman army units spent time in Arabia as attested by Greek graffiti left by soldiers. These include the Ala veterana, an auxiliary from Italy, the Cohors I Hispanorum from Egypt, and the Cohors I Thebaeorum, also from Egypt. Three former cities of the Decapolis found themselves in the new province: Aderaa, Gerasa, and Philadelphia. Furthermore, the people of Oboda in the Negeb began to date their inscriptions by the founding of the new province, which suggests that Arabia extended perhaps to the eastern Negeb. Indeed, since Roman outposts are known in the Sinai, it is likely that informally at least, parts of the Sinai were considered to be Arabia. Emperor Trajan elevated several towns of Arabia to the status of cities: Rabbath-Moab (later called Aeropolis), Characmoba (later Kerak), and Heshbon, now called Aurelia Esbus. Nabateans entered the Roman army in numbers now, as did other Arabs in the new province. Since discharged veterans were usually granted Roman citizenship, from this point onward Arabs will be Roman citizens. There was a census in Arabia, likely in 107 and another in 117, and we have mention of the census of 127 in a court document of a woman named Babatha. During the reign of Valerianus (253–260), the town of Edrei or Adraene was elevated to a city.

Arabia underwent some changes with the accession of Emperor Diocletian in 284 C.E. Diocletian split the civil and military command. The army was under the command of the Dux Arabiae. It may have been Diocletian who transferred the southern part of Arabia from the Arnon River southward from Arabia to Palestine. The Tenth Legion was transferred from Jerusalem to Ailia at the head of the Red Sea. The Dux Arabiae commanded all garrisons in the line of forts across the Negeb and in Transjordan from Aelia to Bostra.

In about 324 C.E. the Christian emperor Constantine solidified civil and ecclesiastical controls. Major cities became the seat of a bishop. We find episcopal sees in Augustopolis, Elusa, Mampsis, Petra, and other cities. By about 358 C.E. Palestine was divided north and south at the Limes Palaestinae, or the line of forts just mentioned. The southern half was no longer Arabia, but Palaestina Salutaris. Its lead city and bishopric was Petra. Other changes took place in Palestine about 400 C.E., so that Palestina Salutaris was now named Palestina Tertia.

Arabianus, Marcus Ulpius governor of Syria Palaestina, 196 C.E. His governorship is mentioned in an inscription in his honor at Amatris, Paphlagonia, most likely the place of his birth. Later he served as a proconsul of Africa.

Arabs The first literary evidence for the Arabs occurs in the Assyrian records of Shalmaneser III, which lists one of their leaders as part of a military coalition against the Assyrians. They are subsequently mentioned in various extrabiblical records (Assyrian, Babylonian, and Persian). However, in the Graeco-Roman period they become much better known and various regional groups come to be distinguished in the literature. Their origins are obscure, but they were certainly nomadic tribes that operated on the fringes of the Arabian Desert, and various opinions prevail as to whether they originated in the southern or northern part of the peninsula. Throughout the first millennium B.C.E. their livelihood was based on providing the settled communities with livestock and in controlling the caravan routes that transported luxury goods through the desert. It was the campaign of Alexander the Great that opened up the Arabian peninsula to the Greek world. Both the Seleucids and Ptolemies colonized various parts of the region and entered into trading alliances with various local kingdoms. The continuing interest was due to the geographical location and the importance of the trade routes, both on land and by sea. Rome's policy of absorbing local kingdoms and territories into its provincial system was only partially successful with the Arabs. Pompey's campaign resulted in the emergence of the Roman province of Syria and also in the recognition of the Iturean Arab principality in northern Transjordan, which was only gradually dissolved under Augustus by being parceled out to various city-states, as well as to the enlarged kingdom of Herod the Great in 20 B.C.E. In the south, the Nabatean Arabs held out as client kings until 106 C.E.

arakin *see* VALUATION

Arakin Mishnah tractate on Leviticus 27:1–8, vows of the value of a person (chaps. 1–6); Leviticus 27:16–25, dedication to the Temple and redemption from the Temple of a field one has inherited (chaps. 7–8); Leviticus 27:28–29, the devoted thing (chap. 8); and Leviticus 25:25–34, the sale of a house in a walled city and how it is redeemed (chap. 9). All may pledge the value of another or have their own value pledged by others; there is a difference between pledging a valuation, which is fixed, and pledging the worth or price, which is determined by the market; pledges are collected from those who promise a valuation. A field that one has inherited reverts at the Jubilee; if its value is pledged to the Temple, one redeems it proportionate to the years the Temple will hold it; if the field is not redeemed when the Jubilee comes, the priests take it and pay for it. The tractate is ignored by both Talmuds.

Aramaic an important Semitic language of the ancient Middle East. Even though it was the lingua franca of the Fertile Crescent during the middle of the first millennium B.C.E., Aramaic is now best known as the language of the targums, the Peshita, and large sections of the Talmuds and the midrashim.

The Aramaic language was brought into the Middle East by the invading Aramaean tribes during the last centuries of the second millennium B.C.E. By the ninth century, the Aramaeans had settled in the region of Syria, after they were stopped in their southern movement by the newly formed Israelite kingdom in Palestine. From this period, Aramaeans gradually entered and became influential in the Assyrian Empire. By serving as scribes and political advisers, Aramaeans made their language widely used in official business throughout the empire. This is the period of Old Aramaic, also called Early or Ancient Aramaic.

With the rise of the Neo-Babylonian Empire in 612 B.C.E., Aramaic became the official language of government, at least in its dealings with the scattered parts of the empire. This official status of Aramaic continued during the Persian Empire and into the third century B.C.E. A single, dominant dialect was used across the whole empire, from the Indus valley in the east to Egypt in the west, although there were regional variations caused by interaction with local dialects. Scholars call this official dialect by several names, including Imperial Aramaic, Official Aramaic, and Standard Aramaic. Alongside Imperial Aramaic, a literary version of the dialect developed, now called Standard Literary Aramaic. The Aramaic portions of Ezra and Daniel, for example, were written in this dialect.

When Alexander the Great conquered Persia in 330 B.C.E., Greek replaced Aramaic as the official language of state. This inaugurated the period of Middle Aramaic, which had two dominant characteristics. First, Imperial Aramaic, although no longer in use, continued its influence through its offspring Standard Literary Aramaic. Second, the dominance of Greek as the language of state led to the isolation of Aramaic in different regions across the territory of the former Persian Empire. This brought about the development of independent dialects, such as Jewish Literary Aramaic, Nabatean, Palmyrene, and Hatran. Historically important works such as the Aramaic texts from Qumran and Bar Kokhba, as well as the original versions of Targums Onkelos and Jonathan, were composed in Jewish Literary Aramaic.

By the third century C.E., the development of different dialects hit its peak, while the influence of Standard Literary Aramaic had largely disappeared. This begins the period scholars designate as Late Aramaic. It lasted well into the Middle Ages, despite the impact of Islam and Arabic that began in the seventh century. The plethora of dialects in this period can be divided into two groups, Eastern and Western. Eastern Aramaic consists primarily of dialects originating in Syria and Mesopotamia. Western Aramaic consists of dialects based in Palestine.

There are three main Eastern Aramaic dialects. First, Syriac was written and spoken by Christians in the Eastern church. It is the best documented dialect, with translations of the Old and New Testament as well as theological, philosophical, and scientific literature. There was also a wide range of poetic and prose literature composed in Syriac. Second, Babylonian Aramaic was used by Jews in the Aramaic sections of the Babylonian Talmud and was the language of the later gaonic writings. Third, Mandaic Aramaic was used by the non-Christian gnostic sect of the Mandaeans.

The three main Western dialects known to modern scholarship are from Palestine. Palestinian Jewish Aramaic is the best evidenced and can be divided into two subdialects. The first is Palestinian Targumic Aramaic and appears in the Palestinian Targums to the Pentateuch. The second is Galilean Aramaic and appears in the Palestinian Talmud, early aggadic midrashim, such as Genesis Rabbah and Leviticus Rabbah, inscriptions, and later gaonic writings. The other two Western Aramaic dialects are Samaritan Aramaic, used by the Samaritans, and Christian Palestinian Aramaic, possibly centered in Judea.

Only one dialect straddled the division of Late Aramaic into Eastern and Western dialects, namely, Late Jewish Literary Aramaic, which combined aspects of earlier Eastern and Western Aramaic. It contains elements from Biblical Aramaic, Jewish Literary Aramaic, Jewish Palestinian Aramaic, and Babylonian Aramaic. Its vocabulary shows similarities to Syriac as well. Late Jewish Literary Aramaic was used in Targum Pseudo-Jonathan, the Targum to Psalms, and other targums to books of the Writings.

In the modern period, Aramaic survives only in isolated pockets. A Western Aramaic dialect is spoken in the region of the Syrian village of Malula. A descendant of Syriac is still used by some Christians in eastern Turkey. A few Mandaeans in southern Iraq and Iran, until recently at least, still used Aramaic.

Aramaic, Babylonian an Eastern dialect of the Late Aramaic period, used primarily by Babylonian Jews. It appears extensively in the Babylonian Talmud (completed around the sixth century C.E.) and in the later writings of the Babylonian geonim.

Aramaic, Biblical the Aramaic used in the books of Ezra (4:8-6:18, 7:12-26), Daniel (2:4-7:28), and a verse in Jeremiah (10:11). Scholars consider it to be a form of Literary Aramaic or its offshoot, Standard Literary Aramaic.

Aramaic, Christian Palestinian a Western dialect of Late Aramaic. It was probably used by Jewish Christians living in Judea. Unlike other Western dialects, it was written in a Syriac script.

Aramaic, Eastern a group of dialects of the Late Aramaic period from the eastern Fertile Cresent, that is, from Syria and Mesopotamia. The three main dialects are Syriac, Babylonian Aramaic, and Mandaic—the language of a non-Christian sect of Gnostics.

Aramaic, Galilean a form of Jewish Palestinian Aramaic, used by Galilean Jews from the late third century C.E. into the seventh century and perhaps later. Most Aramaic inscriptions from Galilean synagogues were composed in this dialect, as were the Aramaic portions of the Palestinian Talmud and the earlier aggadic midrashim—Genesis Rabbah and Exodus Rabbah. After 600 C.E., it was also used by the Palestinian geonim.

Aramaic, Imperial the empirewide Aramaic dialect used by the Neo-Babylonian and Persian Empires as their official language of state as early as 625 B.C.E. It survived the fall of the Persian Empire (in 330 B.C.E.) by about a century. It had a remarkably stable orthography, despite minor local variations, and was used from the Indus Valley to Egypt.

Aramiac, Jewish Literary Middle Aramaic dialect used in Palestine, probably centered in Judea. The Genesis Apocryphon, the Testament of Levi, the Targum to Job, and other Qumran Aramaic texts were written in this language. It was probably also the language of the earliest versions of Targum Onkelos and Targum Jonathan to the Prophets. The dialect has much in common with Standard Literary Aramaic.

Aramaic, Jewish Palestinian a Western form of Late Aramaic, based primarily in Palestine. It appears in two subdialects: Galilean, which we know from the Palestinian Talmud, the midrashim of Genesis and Leviticus Rabbah, and synagogue inscriptions; and Targumic Aramaic, which is the sole dialect of all but one of the Palestinian Targums to the Pentateuch (Targum Neofiti, the Fragmentary Targums, and the targum fragments from the Cairo Geniza). Targum Pseudo-Jonathan contains some passages written in this dialect, but other passages are in Late Jewish Literary Aramaic.

Aramaic, Late the period of the Aramaic language beginning in the third century C.E. and lasting into the Middle Ages. Most Aramaic texts are from this period, including the targums, the Peshita, and other Syriac literature, as well as the two talmuds and some midrashim.

Aramaic, Late Jewish Literary a composite, literary dialect of Late Aramaic, probably used in the general region of Syria. It combines elements of Biblical Aramaic, Jewish Literary Aramaic, Palestinian Jewish Aramaic (especially targumic Aramaic), and Babylonian Aramaic. Portions of Targum Pseudo-Jonathan were written in it, as well as the Targum to Psalms and other Writings targums.

Aramaic, Middle a period of the Aramaic language lasting from the mid-third century B.C.E. to the third century C.E. It follows the period of Imperial Aramaic. With the breakdown of Imperial Aramaic, regional and local dialects came to prominence, with only Standard Literary Aramaic providing any semblance of the language's former international character.

Aramaic, Modern a few dialects of Aramaic used by peoples that have long been separated from each other. The most numerous are Jacobite Christians in eastern Turkey. Mandaic speakers in southern Iran and Iraq, and the villages of Malula and Jubbadin in Syria.

Aramaic, Old the earliest period of recorded Aramaic language lasting from the initial appearance of the Aramaeans in the Middle East to Aramaic's standardization as the Imperial dialect at the end of the seventh century B.C.E. The few inscriptions from across the Middle East suggest regional differences. The *beit David* inscription from Tell Dan was composed in this dialect.

Aramaic, Samaritan a Western dialect of the Late Aramaic period, used by Samaritans living in and around the Palestinian city of Shechem. The Samaritans translated their Pentateuch into this language, as well as composing liturgical, exegetical, and poetical works in it.

Aramaic, Standard Literary a literary form of Imperial Aramaic that survived the disappearance of Imperial Aramaic during the third century B.C.E. It remained influential throughout most of the Middle Aramaic period, appearing as late as the second century C.E. Jewish texts written in it include the Aramaic portions of Ezra and Daniel as well as the Aramaic texts as Qumran and the Aramaic Bar Kokhba letters.

Aramaic, Western a group of Late Aramaic dialects, primarily from Palestine. They include Palestinian Jewish Aramaic, Samaritan Aramaic, and Christian Palestinian Aramaic. Scholars generally consider Palestinian Jewish Aramaic to be centered in the northern part of the country, that is, in Galilee. Samaritan Aramaic, used by the Samaritans, comes from the area around Shechem, while Christian Palestinian Aramaic was probably used by Jewish Christians in Judea.

Araq el-Emir the modern name for Cave of the Prince, an ancient Jewish village or town across the Jordan in today's Hashemite Kingdom of Jordan. Josephus explained (*Ant.* 12.4.11) that Joseph ben Tobiah ben Hyrcanus settled across the Jordan early in the second century B.C.E. Joseph built a strong fortress in Arab territory, decorated it with animals carved to a great size, and otherwise built it into a fortified village or town that he called Tyre. Thus this settlement is important for understanding the significance of the Hellenistic Tobiads, who are also known in Ezra 2:60, Nehemiah 2–4, 6–8, 2 Chronicles 17:8, and Zechariah 6:8–15. They are also known in the Zenon papyri as a politically powerful family in Transjordan in the late Hellenistic period. Excavations and surveys at the site have revealed an aqueduct bringing water from the wadi to the north, a large square building, a fortified castle or a fortress with great lionesses in relief, many caves, and a monumental gateway. The castle appears never to have been finished but was destroyed with its builder about 175 B.C.E. This two-storied, fortified building was reused during the Byzantine period. The monumental gateway east of the castle was also destroyed about the same date in an unfinished state. It was never reused. The site was quite rich in finds, including jewelry, coins, glass, pottery, stamped Rhodian jar handles (amphorae for wine imported from Rhodes), and stucco decoration. A stone weight was inscribed in Aramaic with the name of its owner, Raham-Ner, perhaps an Ammonite name.

arbah kosot *see* FOUR CUPS

Arbela location in the Galilee, northwest of Tiberias, where the remains of a third-century-C.E. synagogue and fortified caves, connected by stairs, have been found; possibly equated with Beth-Arbel, mentioned at Hosea 10:14. Josephus (*Ant.* 12:421) reports that in the campaign against Judah Maccabee, the Seleucids captured the "steps at Arbel." In 39 B.C.E., Zealots sought refuge from Herod the Great in these caves; in 66–70 C.E., Josephus fortified the area (*Vita,* 188); after 70 C.E., priests of the house of Jeshua settled in the area, known for its fertility. *See also* ARBEL SYNAGOGUE.

Arbela, Chronicle of Syriac history of the Nestorian Christian community of Arbil, capital of the Hedayab (Adiabene) region of northern Mesopotamia (present-day Iraq), covering a period from the beginning of the second century C.E. to the middle of the sixth century C.E. It survives in a single tenth-century manuscript, which is full of anachronisms and chronological impossibilities and must be used with caution.

Arbel Synagogue ancient Roman and Byzantine synagogue north of Tiberias and west of the lake. There is an ancient Jewish village there, evidently of the same name, but only the synagogue has been investigated archaeologically. In Maccabees 9:2 the Hasmoneans fought a battle with Bacchides in the plain of Arbel. At the beginning of his reign, Herod the Great killed the last of the rebels against his reign in the cliffs of Arbel just north of the ancient settlement. The ancient synagogue of the town had its major facade pointed south toward Jerusalem. The interior space was divided by columns into a nave and two side aisles, with a series of benches between the walls and the columns. The stonework is highly decorated with moldings, Corinthian capitals, engaged columns, triglyphs, dentilation, and pieces ascribed to windows, though they may be pieces of a synagogue ark. It is possible that this is the building seen by Samuel bar Simson in 1210 and by Rabbi Isaak Chelo in 1333. They both ascribed the synagogue to Rabbi Nitai of Arbel, though the locality was known as the ruin of Irbid.

arbit *see* EVENING PRAYER

Arcadius emperor of the Eastern Roman Empire (r. 395–408 C.E.). Some of his court officials favored Hellenism, and he hesitated to persecute any community that regularly paid its taxes. In 400 he prevented the bishop of Gaza from destroying a pagan temple because the pagan citizens were loyal taxpayers. He also respected the Jews' loyalty and their regular tax payments. In 396 Arcadius, along with the western emperor Honorius, issued a decree stating that no outsider should pass judgment on Jewish religious or secular activities. Their decree was eventually incorporated into the Theodosian Code.

Archelaus son of Herod the Great and his wife Malthace. Herod had designated Archelaus as his principal successor in his final will, to be ratified by the emperor Augustus. Archelaus badly mishandled the protests of the Jewish people on the death of Herod (4 B.C.E.), leading to a massacre of many Jews. Though Augustus confirmed him as ruler of Judea and Samaria in accordance with the terms of Herod's will, thus thwarting the ambitions of his brother Antipas, he refused him the title king until he should prove worthy of it. While these matters were being debated in Rome a serious revolt broke out in Jerusalem and all over Palestine against the Herods. On his return Archelaus was never able to win acceptance from either the Jews or the Samaritans. He continued many of the oppressive policies of his father, but without his astuteness. In 6 C.E. Augustus summoned him to Rome to answer charges against him emanating from Palestine, banished him to Vienna in Gallia Narbonensis, and imposed direct Roman rule in Judea for the first time. His cruelty is referred to in the Gospel of Matthew 2:22, which gives it as the reason for the parents of Jesus migrating to Galilee on their return from Egypt after the death of Herod the Great.

archiereus (Gr., high priest) often used in Jewish writings in Greek to refer to the Jewish high priest in Jerusalem. In the writings of Josephus and in the New Testament, however, it sometimes seems to mean not the high priest in office but a former high priest or even only an immediate member of his family.

archisynagogos (Gr., head of the synagogue) Although a number of assumptions are often made about the office and its duties, neither Josephus nor Philo of Alexandria uses the term. However, it occurs in inscriptions from the first century C.E.

archon a Greek term for an official, especially of a Greek city. Whatever the precise government of the city, its decrees were usually carried out by these elected or appointed officials. Leaders of the Jewish communities in various places often bore this title as well. The term is also used of demonic powers in Gnosticism.

Ardashir I (c. 180–241 C.E.) first ruler of Sassanid Babylonia. He was a Persian, the son of Papak and the grandson of Sasan, who later Sassanids claimed were heirs of the Achaemenids, descended from Darius. Sasan, the eponymous ancestor of the new dynasty, was a Zoroastrian priest in Persis, and his son Papak, born in about 150 C.E., achieved no higher post. Ardashir, by contrast, became commandant of the garrison and fortress of the town. By about 208, he began a struggle for supremacy in the district.

Ardashir's reign came about when, in response to Ardashir's attempt to extend his power, the Parthian king Artabanus V engaged him in battle. Artabanus's defeat, coupled with his death in 227, ended four and a half centuries of Arsacid control of the lands of present-day Iran. When Ardashir finally defeated a coalition of Parthians, Armenians, and Kushans, who may have had Roman support, he firmly placed the Sassanid dynasty in control of the lands once ruled by the Parthians. During his reign, he extended the Sassanid territory by constantly waging campaigns on the Roman frontiers, particularly intent upon capturing Armenia and Mesopotamia. Ardashir died in 241 and was succeeded by Shapur I.

Ardashir legitimated his reign through marriage to an Arsacid, a daughter or cousin of Ardavan. He was crowned in September 226 at Istakar, where four centuries of his Sassanid successors were to be invested. His capital was across the river from Ctesiphon, at Seleucia-on-the-Tigris, renamed Veh-Ardashir. Babylonia was the center of his interest, and he engaged in an expansive program of construction of new towns, buildings, canals, temples, and other public works. At his death, the frontiers of the empire stretched from the Euphrates to Merv, Herat, and Seistan; this territory would be further extended by Shapur I.

Jews had enjoyed a long period of peace and political autonomy under the Arsacids and did not welcome the change in dynasty. Worse, the Sassanids immediately determined to unify their disparate empire through cultural and religious reforms, establishing a state church and intervening as they wished in the affairs of their subjects in the Mesopotamian valley. B. A<u>b</u>odah Zarah 10b–11a reports Ra<u>b</u>'s dismay over the death of Ardavan; B. Ye<u>b</u>amot 63b reports Yoḥanan's concern over the arrival in Babylonia of Zoroastrian Magi. After centuries of religious freedom, under Ardashir, Jews confronted the Mazdean state church's repression of all practices that offended the Zoroastrian Mobads' sensibilities. Prohibited acts included ritual slaughter of meat, the use of ritual baths, and burial of the dead (B. Yeb̲amot 63b). The Persians undoubtedly also enacted decrees to protect the sanctity of fire (see, e.g., B. Sanhedrin 45a). In light of these developments, the Jews turned to Rome, under whose rule third-century Palestinian Jews lived in relative freedom, and who, despite its destruction of the Second Temple, was viewed as a likely savior from Persian oppression (B. Yoma 10a). Only with the coronation of Shapur I do Jews appear to have been conciliated with the new state.

Ardashir II Sassanid ruler (r. 379–383 C.E.). Some Arabic sources incorrectly claim that he was Shapur II's brother. He supposedly did not collect taxes, which made him a popular ruler. Some Armenians, led by Manuel, revolted against the pro-Roman Moushegh and acknowledged Ardashir as their ruler. Ardashir exchanged Iranian protection for Armenian tribute, effectively establishing a short-lived joint suzerainty with Manuel over Armenia. Ardashir was a follower of Ohrmazd. He opposed the appointment of Christian bishops in his territory, often martyring those who assumed the post. The nobility deposed him after less than four years, complaining of his tyranny.

Ardavan III Parthian ruler (r. 12–36 C.E.), originally king of Atropatene. After defeating Vonoes, he was declared king in Ctesiphon. He probably had close ties with the Jewish rulers surrounding his domain. He recognized the legitimacy of the Babylonian Jewish satraps Anileus and Asineus. When the Romans attempted to put Mithradates of Iberia on the Armenian throne, Ardavan was unable to remove him. He was forced to flee to Adiabene, and he made a treaty with Izates, who had recently converted to Judaism. Eventually he was able to regain his throne.

Ardavan V (also known as Artabanus V) the last Parthian ruler (r. 213–227 C.E.). The Roman emperor Caracalla sought to marry Ardavan's daughter after failing to achieve a military success over the Parthians. Ardavan agreed to the marriage, probably hoping to pit Rome against his rebellious brother, Vologases V. But Caracalla allegedly slew the wedding guests, except for Ardavan, who fled. Caracalla's successor, Macrinus, also failed to defeat Ardavan and was forced to pay a humiliating ransom before Ardavan agreed to the peace of Nisibis in 218. Ardavan's constant dynastic struggles with his brother Vologases V diverted his attention from the threat posed by Ardashir, his rebellious satrap in Persia. Ardavan fell in battle against the Persians in 227. A Jewish story maintains that Ardavan sent a priceless gem to Judah the Patriarch, who sent him a mezuzah. This exchange of gifts may reflect the attempt to form an alliance between Rome and the Parthians during the reign of either Caracalla or Macrinus. Another Jewish source depicts a close relationship between Rab̲ and Ardavan, paralleling the one between Rabbi in Palestine and the Roman emperor Antoninus. Just as Rabbi lamented Antoninus's death, so Rab̲ lamented Ardavan's passing.

aretalogy a hymn or story of praise; from the Greek *aretai,* meaning virtues or manifestations of divine power. An aretalogy was usually written in honor of a god or goddess, though some were written in honor of heroic or semidivine human figures (e.g., Jesus). Some of the best-preserved examples of hymnlike aretalogies are those to the goddess Isis.

Aretas III king of the Nabateans in the first century B.C.E. He was quite successful in resisting Seleucid power in its final days and Roman expansionism in the East under Pompey. According to Josephus he gained possession of Damascus about 85 B.C.E. following the death of Antiochus XII of Syria. On the basis of numismatic evidence, he held Damascus from about 85 until 72 B.C.E. He was not able, however, to hold the city against the incursions of the Armenian king, Tigranes, who in turn had to cede it to Pompey in 66. Aretas also encountered the expansionist policies of Alexander Jannaeus (r. 103–76 B.C.E.) in the Transjordan region of Moab and Galaaditis. This led to a foray into Judea by Aretas, where he defeated Alexander at the battle of Adida, not far from Lydda on the coast, about 84 B.C.E. He withdrew in obscure circumstances, however, only to become embroiled again in Jewish affairs by siding with Hyrcanus in the struggle for succession with Aristobulus II. He actually besieged the latter in Jerusalem, withdrawing only on the order of Scaurus, the Roman general, in 65 B.C.E. Pompey intended to march against Petra, but had to return because of trouble in Judea. In 62 B.C.E., Scaurus exacted the payment of three hundred talents from Aretas through the good offices of Antipater the Idumean. Aretas died soon after.

Aretas IV king of the Nabateans (r. 9 B.C.E.–40 C.E.). A certain Aeneas seized the Nabatean throne on the death of Obodas III in 9 B.C.E., adopted the royal name of Aretas (IV), and ruled successfully in

the Nabatean kingdom until 40 C.E. Augustus was reluctant to recognize him initially, prompted by the powerful administrator of the previous king, Syllaeus. Eventually Aretas, aided by Nicholas of Damascus, Herod's envoy in Rome, was able to win the imperial favor leading to Syllaeus's execution as well as his own acceptance by Rome as king of the Nabateans. On the death of Herod the Great in 4 B.C.E., Aretas sent aid to the Roman governor of Syria, Varus, who was engaged in putting down the disturbances that occurred in Judea. The enmity of the Nabateans for the Jews was expressed in the pillaging and murder that occurred in two villages, Arus in Samaria and Sappho in Judea. The emperor Tiberius ordered Vitellius, the Roman governor in Syria, to punish Aretas for an unwarranted violation of the *Pax Romana* after Herod Antipas had divorced his daughter, but before the order could be carried out Tiberius died and Vitellius ignored the command. This skirmish with Roman imperial power does not seem to have damaged Aretas's standing unduly. The account of Paul's escape from Damascus mentions a governor of King Aretas in that city (2 Cor. 11:32). It is possible that Gaius Caligula had given the city to Aretas as a gift, a fact that would seem to be confirmed by the city coins of Damascus that lack any image of the emperors Gaius and Claudius.

arete *see* VIRTUES AND VICES

Argarizin Greek transliteration of the name of the mountain Har Gerizim (Mount Gerizim), located near ancient Shechem (modern Nablus). The term is found in a number of Greek writings, which were probably written by Samaritans, whereas Jewish writers usually referred to *horos* (Gr., mountain) Garizin. *See also* GERIZIM, MOUNT.

Arianism a fourth-century doctrine about God and Christ condemned as a heresy in Alexandria around 320 and by the Ecumenical Council of Nicaea in 325. Named after its first proponent, the priest Arius of Alexandria (d. 336), Arianism in its earliest stage was also taught by the Cappadocian sophist Asterius, whose work is only known through its refutation by Marcellus of Ancyra. In a later stage a strict form of Neo-Arianism was presented in the late 350s by the rhetor Aetius from Antioch (d. 370) and the Cappadocian Eunomius who became bishop of Cyzicus in 360 for a few years. A coalition of Oriental bishops, initially headed by Eusebius of Nicomedia, ignored the anti-Arian decision of Nicaea by keeping a doctrinal line close to Arius's teaching. Ulfilas, a Cappadocian living among the Goths, was consecrated bishop by the same Eusebius in 341. Ulfilas translated the Bible into Gothic and preached the Arian creed to the German tribes, giving Arianism a chance to prevail among the Visigoths and the Vandals who settled in the West in the later part of the fourth century.

Arianism focuses on the Christian notion of deity in reinforcing the transcendent unity of the godhead against any Gnostic attempt to introduce multiple beings. A century earlier, Origen of Alexandria had also opposed Gnosticism, mainly that of the Alexandrian Gnostic Christian Valentinus. In a pioneering theory of divine Trinity, Origen had stressed the peculiar nature of deity understood by church tradition. In his work *On First Principles,* he affirmed the complete divinity of the Son of God and the Holy Spirit, both *uncreated* as revealed in the New Testament, and insisted on the *created* nature of all the heavenly powers constituting the so-called noetic cosmos that transcends the material world. Arius followed some of Origen's insights but failed to keep a trinitarian notion of deity. He reduced the Son and the Spirit to the level of created being originating from the Father. A rationalistic approach to scripture and a proximity to Neoplatonic metaphysics characterize the Arian exegesis of the New Testament: Jesus in his human limitations was understood as witnessing to the inferior and created nature of the divine Logos; in his religious dedication, his virtues, and his suffering, Jesus was seen as a model for personal salvation. In response to the Arian challenge, Athanasius of Alexandria, Gregory Nazianzus, Gregory of Nyssa, Hilary of Poitiers, and other intellectual leaders of the fourth century improved the doctrine of divine Trinity in line with Origen's founding intuition. *See also* ARIUS.

Aristeas, Letter of a pseudonymous Jewish account of the Torah's translation into Greek. Composed in a not very elegant Greek, this document of 322 verses purports to have been written by Aristeas, a courtier of Ptolemy II (r. 285–247 B.C.E.), to his brother Philocrates. Elements of the letter style are largely missing, although the second-person address appears at various points in the text, which is mainly a first-person narrative that employs a variety of traditional Hellenistic genres. Most scholars place its composition in Alexandria between 150 and 100 B.C.E. It is preserved in twenty Greek manuscripts copied between the eleventh and sixteenth centuries.

The first major section of Aristeas describes Ptolemy's alleged request that Eleazar the high priest at Jerusalem send a committee of translators to Alexandria (vv. 1–82). In the second section (vv.

83–171), Aristeas describes how he and other members of an Egyptian delegation were awestruck by the Temple of Jerusalem and its cult and were greatly impressed by Eleazar's learned disquisition on the Torah. The longest and most significant section recounts Ptolemy's reception of the Jewish translators and the table talk during the banqueting that preceded the translation work (vv. 172–300). A brief account of the translation and the positive gentile response to it concludes the body of the document (vv. 301–21).

Aristeas is held together by three themes. Basic is the repeated assertion of the universal sovereignty of the one God, who is the Creator, the God of Israel, and the one who guides and moves gentile kings in the ways of justice. Second is the emphasis on the impressive character of Jewish institutions—the Temple, its furnishings and its cult, the Torah and its interpreters. Aristeas's idealized description of Judea employs utopian elements typical of travelogues in classical and Hellenistic literature. The Torah is recommended as "most philosophical," and the allegorical meaning of its commandments is applicable to Gentiles as well as Jews. This connects with the author's third theme. Gentiles need not obey the letter of the Torah to find God's favor; however, they are required to eschew idols and idolatry, avoid promiscuous sexual unions, and act justly to other human beings. In a section that imitates Hellenistic treatises on kingship, the sages enjoin Ptolemy to show justice, munificence, gentleness, mercy, and patience, and to avoid arrogance, cruelty, and tyranny. Although it presents the Torah as divine revelation and the criterion for human conduct, Aristeas also offers a very positive estimate of Greeks and Greek culture and urges peaceful and mutually beneficial coexistence and interaction between Jews and Gentiles.

The account of the Torah's translation has the marks of legend: seventy-two scholars work separately for seventy-two days and then compare and harmonize their translations, which are ratified by the Alexandrian Jewish community and admired by the king, who had instigated the project in the first place. Subsequent Jewish and Christian authors in antiquity progressively embellished the legend into a highly miraculous account, which underscored the character of the Greek Bible as an inspired and authoritative text (Philo, *Life of Moses* 2.25–44; Ps.-Justin, *Exhortation to the Greeks* 13; Irenaeus, *Against the Heresies* 3.21.2; Epiphanius, *On Weights and Measures* 3–11; B. Meg. 9a).

Aristeas the Historian (or Exegete) Jewish writer, probably from the second century B.C.E., known only from one fragment of his work *On the Jews*. This concerns Job, who is said to be a son of Esau and is identified with the Jobab of Genesis 36:33. The three friends who come to comfort him are all said to be kings.

Aristobulus, son of Herod son of Herod the Great and Mariamme. He was educated in Rome (23–17 B.C.E.) along with his brother Alexander. After Herod brought Aristobulus and Alexander back to Jerusalem, Aristobulus married Berenice, the daughter of Herod's sister, Salome. Competition and intrigues within the Herodian family led Herod to suspect the brothers of plotting against him. On a trip to Rome in 12 B.C.E., Augustus reconciled Herod to his sons. Further conflict, slander, and intrigue in the Herodian court led to the brothers' arrest, trial in Berytus, and execution by strangulation in Sebaste in 7 B.C.E. A number of their supporters were also executed.

Aristobulus I son and successor of John Hyrcanus to the high priesthood (104–103 B.C.E.). He imprisoned his mother, who had been bequeathed the rule of the kingdom, and starved her to death. He imprisoned three of his four brothers and eventually had the fourth, Antigonus, assassinated. He also adopted the title of king for the first time. Before his death from disease, he extended Jewish rule to Ituraean territory north of Galilee. He was succeeded by his brother, Alexander Jannaeus, who married Aristobulus's wife, Alexandra.

Aristobulus II (Heb. name: Judas) Hasmonean king of the Jewish kingdom (r. 67–63 B.C.E.); son of Alexander Jannaeus and Alexandra. During the reign of his mother, 76–67 B.C.E., he plotted to seize power from her and his older brother, Hyrcanus, who was high priest. After her death, he forced his brother to resign, after which he ruled from 67 to 63 B.C.E. Antipater of Idumea recruited Aretas, the Nabatean king, to support Hyrcanus. Hyrcanus prevailed until Aristobulus recruited Roman support from Pompey. Civil war continued for several years. In 63 B.C.E. an embassy from Israel to Pompey in Syria sought to have both Hyrcanus and Aristobulus removed. When Aristobulus fled from Pompey, Pompey pursued him, conquered Judea, and finally besieged the Temple Mount, where Aristobulus's supporters were overcome with great slaughter. Aristobulus was transported to Rome for Pompey's triumph; he later escaped to Judea, but was captured again and sent back to Rome (c. 56 B.C.E.). Julius Caesar released him from jail (49 B.C.E.) and sent him to oppose Pompey in Syria. He was poisoned by Pompey's adherents.

Aristobulus the Exegete a Jewish biblical interpreter, probably from Alexandria in the second century B.C.E. Unfortunately, his work is preserved only in a few fragments, quoted by Eusebius. Aristobulus is the first Jewish writer known to use allegory as a major interpretative device. He puts the Passover in cosmological perspective by discussing the placement of both sun and moon at the time. In a treatise addressed to the Ptolemaic king, he deals with the question of why Moses seems to describe God in human terms. He argues that Pythagoras, Socrates, and Plato all borrowed from Moses. This was possible because at least some of the Pentateuch had been translated into Greek even before the conquests of Alexander, though he acknowledges that all of it was translated only at the time of Ptolemy II in the Septuagint version. He puts the Sabbath into cosmological terms, makes use of an arithmology on the number seven, and gives the correct etymology of "sabbath" (Gr.: *sabbaton*) as "rest." However, he also quotes verses of Homer and Hesiod to support his argument, even though these are almost certainly spurious.

aristocracy literally, government by the best; historically, a small, privileged class. In ancient bureaucratic societies and empires, 2–3 percent of the population controlled most of the power, land, and wealth, assisted by a small number of specialist retainers (officials, priests, scribes, military, merchants, etc.). About 90 percent of the population lived at a subsistance level from farming or crafts.

Aristotelians *see* PERIPATETICS

arithmology the use of numbers in exegesis. The practice might also be termed "number symbolism" since those who make use of it see significance in the use of certain numbers, especially such numbers as seven, twelve, and forty. "Number mysticism" as found in some Kabbalistic writings is not necessarily implied, however.

Arius Alexandrian priest, born in Libya, declared a heretic about 320 C.E. by the local synod of Bishop Alexander of Alexandria. The Council of Nicaea confirmed the excommunication in 325, but a conservative opposition to Nicaea continued to support Arian doctrine until Theodosius I established Nicaean orthodoxy as official religion in 381. Arius himself died in 336. A few of his letters and fragments of a pamphlet entitled *Thalia* are the only literary remains handed down as documentary evidence by his staunchest adversary, Athanasius of Alexandria, who succeeded Alexander in 328. *Orations Against the Arians* and voluminous apologies witness to Athanasius's opposition to Arian ideas. *See also* ARIANISM.

ark (Heb.: *aron*) place for holding Torah scrolls in the synagogue; generally the visual focus of a synagogue prayer hall

ark, representation of a major motif in ancient synagogue art during the Roman and Byzantine periods, namely, representations of the Ark of the Scrolls in mosaic floors and other media. The motif is also called a synagogue ark. The ark is a chest or standing cabinet with double doors decorated with several square or rectangular panels, and on later arks there is elaborate decoration on the panels. The ark stood on legs and is surmounted by a gable or pediment with a shell. In the diaspora the ark is rendered with doors open showing scrolls on shelves, but ordinarily within ancient Palestine the doors are executed as though shut. Often a curtain hangs in front of the ark. In the mosaic floor from Tiberias the curtain is tied in a knot to reveal the ark. The ark often stands within a Torah shrine or aedicula, which was built of stone, but some arks are depicted as free standing cabinets. The Torah shrine is a stone edifice holding the ark. The Torah shrine contains two columns in front, a pediment with shell motif in the center, and a roof. The Byzantine Torah shrine from Nabratein was even covered with roof tiles, while the pediment found at the same site had two lions sculpted in relief on top of the pediment and a shell in the recessed triangle of the pediment.

Ark of the Covenant boxlike piece of cultic paraphernalia associated with YHWH's presence (Exod. 25:10–22; Deut. 10:1–5). Housed first in the tabernacle and then in Solomon's temple, the ark appears to have been considered the footstool of the invisible deity. According to the accounts in Exodus and Deuteronomy, it contained the "testimony" or the tablets of the ten commandments. Hebrews 9:4 adds to these a pot of manna and Aaron's blossoming staff (cf. Exod. 16:32–34; Num. 17:8–10). At some indeterminate time in the monarchical period, the ark disappeared, and it is not mentioned among the booty that Nebuchadnezzar took to Babylon (2 Kings 25:13–17). A Jewish legend datable to the early second century B.C.E. claimed that Jeremiah hid the ark and other temple furnishings before Nebuchadnezzar pillaged Jerusalem (2 Macc. 2:4–8; 2 Bar. 6, cf. M. Shekal. 6:1–2; B. Yoma 53b–54a). Hebrews 9:11–14 contrasts Jesus' presentation of his own blood in the heavenly holy place with the priestly sprinkling of blood on the "mercy seat" (Heb.: *kapporet*) of the ark (Lev. 16:1–14). According to Revelation 11:19, the ark stands in the heavenly temple and emanates the stormy signs of God's presence.

Armageddon mysterious location of the eschatological battle (Rev. 16:16). It is traditionally thought to be a transliteration of Hebrew *har-megiddon,* "Mount of Megiddo," either the hill city in the Plain of Esdraelon, or nearby Mount Carmel or Tabor, the site of important battles in Judges 5:19 and 2 Kings 23:29. Identification of the location remains disputed.

Armenia, Jews of Although we cannot date the origins of the Jews in Armenia, we know that in 83 B.C.E. the Armenian ruler Tigranes I invaded Syria and northern Palestine. As part of his effort to develop Armenia's economy, the king transported a number of Jews from Syria-Palaestina to Armenia in order to increase the population of Armenia's commercial centers: Armavir, Vaharsabat, Van, Artashat, and Van-Dosp. It also seems likely that in the early second century Ardashar removed the Jews settled in Yerevan to Artashat. It is also plausible that around 365 C.E. Shapur II deported thousands of Jewish families from Armenia and resettled them at Isfahan as part of his policy to destroy Armenia's economy and increase its dependency on Persia. For a few years during the first century C.E., Armenia was ruled by a dynasty of Jewish descent, which was imposed upon the country by the Romans. For a time, Armenia was ruled by Tigranes IV (10–26 C.E.), son of Herod's son Alexander. Tigranes V (60 C.E.) and Aristobulus (60 C.E.), both Herodians, were placed on the throne by Nero.

Josephus did not regard these rulers as good Jews and implies that they had left Judaism. In any case, they had no discernible effect on the history of the Jews or of Judaism in Armenia. There is no reliable information on the religion of Armenian Jewry. The Palestinian Talmud mentions Rabbi Armenia and R. Jacob of Armenia, but we have no way of knowing if they actually were from Armenia. It is reasonable to assume that Judaism must have influenced those areas of Armenia in which Jews settled. We have stories that some of the leading families of these regions were Jewish. Cities such as Vagharshabat had a large Jewish population, and it is probably no coincidence that Gregor Lusavoric, who is credited with having brought Christianity to Armenia, was born in this city. Edessa was the chief center from which Christianity reached Armenia, and its church had a significant number of Jewish converts and was heavily influenced by Judaism. Although Armenia bordered on Babylonia and was close to centers of Babylonian Jewry, Armenian Jewry had no known impact on Babylonian Judaism, and it appears that Babylonian Jewry did not influence the Armenian Jewish community.

There are a number of legends that were created after Armenia had become Christianized, entirely without historical foundation, which attempt to establish a direct connection between Armenia and the narratives of the Hebrew Bible. The most famous of these legends concerns a Jew by the name of Sambat who allegedly settled in Armenia at the time of the Judean exile in 586 B.C.E. Sambat is the ancestor of the Bagartuni family, who were consistently willing to compromise with paganism. Other stories connect the Bagartuni with the Herodian high priest Hyrcanus. In this story the Bagartuni, named Enanus, was forced to reject Judaism, adore the sun, and pay homage to idols.

ARN *see* FATHERS ACCORDING TO RABBI NATHAN, THE

aron, aron haKodesh *see* ARK

Artapanus one of the Fragmentary Hellenistic Jewish writers in Greek. His work entitled *On the Jews* has survived only in fragments, taken from Alexander Polyhistor by Eusebius. Artapanus probably wrote in the second century B.C.E., most likely in Egypt. He is especially important as an example of a Jew who was willing to interpret Jewish tradition by reference to Greek culture, in which he seems at home. His writings have the quality of Graeco-Roman romance and also function as apologetic literature on behalf of the Jews. Like Pseudo-Eupolemus, he claims that Abraham taught astrology to the Egyptians. His story of Joseph differs in a number of ways from the Genesis account: Joseph flees to Egypt of his own accord, becomes finance minister to Pharaoh, is the first to divide off the plots of land, and makes much of the waste land tillable. Artapanus gives a long account of the life of Moses, which seems to be preserved more or less complete. In it Moses is presented as an inventor and the first to divide Egypt into nomes. Artapanus also states that Moses then became an Egyptian general and led in the conquest of Ethiopia before having to flee for his life because the Pharaoh was jealous of him.

Artaxerxes I Longimanus Persian emperor (r. 465–425 B.C.E.) following the murder of his father, Xerxes. Ezra arrived in Jerusalem in the "seventh year of Artaxerxes," probably Artaxerxes I (Ezra 7:7–8), and Nehemiah's mission took place in the twentieth year of the same reign, which would be 445 or 444 B.C.E. (Neh. 2:1).

Artemion leader of the Jewish revolt in Cyprus. Dio Cassius is the only ancient author who mentions that Artemion was the leader of the revolt of Jews on Cyprus (115–117 C.E.). After mentioning the Jewish atrocities in Cyrenaica, Dio states that the Jews did similar things in Egypt "and also in Cyprus under the leadership of a certain Artemion." Dio claims that 240,000 people were killed on Cyprus during the revolt. Because of the revolt, Dio claims, no Jews may land on Cyprus and even those who end up there as a result of a shipwreck are executed.

Artemisios name of a Macedonian month; appears in a number of Jewish sources, such as the writings of Josephus. Unfortunately, there was not a uniform usage; sometimes it corresponded to the Hebrew month of Nisan (March/April) and sometimes to the month Iyyar (April/May).

Asael (Heb., God has made) one of the two chieftains of the rebellious watchers (angels) in 1 Enoch 6–16. He brings evil to earth by revealing forbidden secrets about metallurgy and mining, which enable humans to forge weapons and armor and fabricate seductive jewelry and cosmetics. Raphael the angel casts him into the Abyss until the final judgment (1 Enoch 10:4–6). His portrait may reflect stories about Prometheus in Greek mythology, and it has influenced Revelation 20:1–3. Early in Jewish tradition he is identified with Azazel. *See also* NEFILIM.

asarah batlanim (Heb., full-time, perpetual students) ten men free of all other obligations, available for the study of the Torah and recitation of prayers in a quorum. A large town had ten such persons, assigned to the permanent work of learning and prayer.

asarah beTebet (Heb., tenth of Tebet) fast day on the tenth of Tebet, mourning for the beginning of Nebuchadnezzar's siege of Jerusalem in 587 B.C.E.

Asatir a Samaritan chronicle in Aramaic extending from Adam to Moses. It is parallel to the Pentateuch but with many differences, including the addition of aggadic elements. In this it resembles Jewish works sometimes referred to as "rewritten Bible." It has been variously dated but is probably medieval.

ascent journey to the heavenly throne room. The earliest account of such a journey is recorded in 1 Enoch 12–16, from the first half of the third century B.C.E. The text recounts a prophetic call in the tradition of Ezekiel 1–2, although the seer ascends to heaven rather than the chariot throne descending to earth (but cf. Ezekiel 40–48, where the prophet travels in the spirit from Babylon to Jerusalem). Other pseudonymous accounts of ascents occur in Daniel 7, the Apocalypse of Abraham 9–20, and the Life of Adam and Eve 25–29. Among identifiable persons, the Apostle Paul refers to a trip to paradise (2 Cor. 12:1–4), John of Patmos ascends in the spirit to see heavenly mysteries (the Book of Revelation), and a talmudic tradition in B. Hagigah 14b refers to four who entered the Garden: Ben Azzai, Ben Zoma, Aher (Elisha ben Abuyah), and Akiba, all of them from early second century C.E. Subsequently, a massive Hekhalot and Merkabah literature develops in Judaism. Thus, accounts of ascents appear to have begun in an Ezekiel-related tradition that is marked by a prophetic consciousness. Increasingly, though not exclusively (cf. Rev. 1:11, 22:6–20), ascents (or descents as they are often described) focus on the throne vision in its own right without any notion of bringing a divine message to earth. *See also* CALL; MYSTICISM.

asceticism abstaining from pleasures of this world. Asceticism is common in Judaism in the form of fasting, for example, in time of crisis, along with prayers for rain and divine grace, and may also involve abstaining from wine and/or sexual relations. It expresses fear of sin or penance for sin. *See also* NAZIRITE.

asebeia, asebēs *see* ATHEISM

Ashdod coastal city of ancient Palestine north of Gaza, south of Joppa and about 4 kilometers from the Mediterranean. Ashdod was one of the main Philistine cities in the Bible (Josh. 11:22). During the Persian period Ashdod was capital of the Persian satrapy of Yehud (Neh. 13:23–24). Residents of Ashdod opposed Nehemiah's rebuilding efforts in Jerusalem (Neh. 4:1ff). With the reestablishment of Israel under the Hasmonean kings, Ashdod was reconquered and destroyed by John Hyrcanus (Josephus, *Ant.*, 13.4.5). During this period the city was known as Azotus (Acts 8:40). The Roman general Gabinius rebuilt Azotus as a prosperous city, which it remained during the reign of Herod the Great. Herod was awarded Azotus as a royal estate by Augustus, and he in turn left it to his sister Salome. Salome willed it to Livia, the wife of Augustus, whereupon it became an imperial estate. This was a city of both Jewish and gentile population. Excavations at Ashdod have found John Hyrcanus's destruction of the well-planned Hellenistic city. It was also possible to show from the excavations that Gabinius's rebuilding followed the lines of the Hellenistic city. This showplace was destroyed in 67 C.E. during the First Revolt. The city continued to be occupied, probably because of the major north-south highway upon which it rested and because of its anchorage, Azotus Paralius. Finds of the Byzantine period indicate that both Jews and Samaritans lived in a small town or village closer to the shore.

Ashi (d. 427 C.E.) Babylonian amora, known by the honorific title Rabbana. The most celebrated authority of his day, for over fifty years he headed the academy at Sura. Tradition holds that he was responsible for the major part of the redacting of the Babylonian Talmud, editing and organizing material that had been collected in the Babylonian academies for over 200 years.

Ashkelon coastal city of ancient Palestine (also known as Askelon and Ascalon) north of Gaza, south of Ashdod (Azotus), and situated directly on the coast of the Mediterranean. Ashkelon is one of the oldest biblical cities of Palestine and one of the cities of the Philistines (Josh. 13:32). Sometime after its conquest by Nebuchadnezzar, perhaps during the sixth century B.C.E., it became a commercial satellite of Tyre. Under the Ptolemies it became a free port and an autonomous city with connections to Egypt. The Hasmonean kings of Israel never succeeded in defeating Ashkelon. It minted its own coins from 111 B.C.E., and seven years later became independent and dated its coins from its own independence. Herod the Great was a native of Ashkelon and adorned the city with a large stoa, temples, and a palace. During the Roman period the city was a flourishing port with a large gentile population and a significant Jewish population. Many Graeco-Roman deities were worshipped at Ashkelon, such as Isis, Atargatis (a local goddess with the face of a woman but the tail of a fish), Heracles, and Apollo. Graeco-Roman institutions flourished at Ashkelon, including schools of Graeco-Roman rhetoric and philosophy. During the Byzantine period a Jewish population thrived at Ashkelon, and the rabbis knew of the gardens of Ashkelon and the city market. Archaeological investigations in the Roman phase have disclosed a city wall with towers and a gate, a bouleuterion or civic meeting hall attached to a huge basilica, including a small temple to Apollo, many examples of Roman sculpture and architecture, and a magnificent painted tomb of fine Graeco-Roman decoration. Byzantine Ashkelon has yielded remains of two basilica churches and a synagogue with a *bimah* and a chancel screen decorated with finely engraved menorahs, shofars, and lulabs.

Ashkenaz at Genesis 10:3 (= 1 Chron. 1:6), a people traced through Gomer to Japheth, Noah's third son; at Jeremiah 51:27, a nation called to oppose Babylon. In the talmudic literature, the Ashkenaz of Genesis 10:3 is identified with areas in the Roman province of Asia Minor, particularly Lydia, Phrygia, and Caria. The Jerusalem Targum and Targum Onkelos, by contrast, identify it with Riphath (Riphas), elsewhere associated with Adiabene. By the medieval period, Jews identified Ashkenaz with Germany, an identification earlier found in Eusebius's correlation of Ashkenaz with the Teutons.

ashrei (Heb., happy are they) Psalm 145, read during morning and afternoon worship

Ashur Assyria, in the northern part of Mesopotamia; referring in the talmudic literature to Seleucia (e.g., B. Ketubot 10b) or Parthia (e.g., B. Sanhedrin 106a)

Asia Minor, Jews in Ancient authors and inscriptions testify to the presence of Jewish communities in many cities of Asia Minor. Josephus reports that Antiochus III (r. 223–187 B.C.E.) settled two thousand Jewish families from Mesopotamia in western and central Asia Minor. 1 Maccabees (15:23–24) contains a letter with a list of places where Jews lived, which included most of Asia Minor. Numerous cities on the west coast and its hinterland had Jewish communities, including Pergamum, Thyatira, Smyrna, Sardis, Philadelphia, Ephesus, Priene, and Halicarnassus. Farther inland cities, such as Aphrodisias, Laodicea, Apamea, Antioch in Pisidia and the territory of Acmonia, had a strong Jewish presence. Many cities along the south coast and Tarsus, the gateway to the interior, are mentioned. Less is known about a Jewish presence in Galatia and Cappadocia in the interior and on the north coast of Asia Minor. *See also* EPHESUS, JEWS IN; SARDIS, JEWS IN.

Askelon *see* ASHKELON

asmakta (Aram., support) an agreement in rabbinic law buttressed by an extravagant penalty or dependent on the fulfillment of a condition that is not binding unless supported by more definite indicators. In rabbinic Bible interpretation, it is a verse that buttresses a legal rule without serving as an integral basis for its authority.

Asmodeus demon in love with Sarah, the heroine of the Book of Tobit. Seven times Asmodeus kills Sarah's husbands on their wedding nights, before Raphael the healing angel exorcizes him, binds him, and banishes him to Egypt. The angelic-demonic opposition recalls 1 Enoch 10:4 and the story may be known in Mark 12:18–23.

ass, slander of Jews worshiping A widespread belief in the Graeco-Roman world was that the Jews worshiped an ass or an ass's head. It probably originated in Egypt, where Judaism was sometimes associated with worship of the god Tryphon, or Seth, who was represented by an ass. We find this repeated by, among others, Apion.

Assalieh ancient Jewish village in the Golan Heights about 3 kilometers west of Qatsrin. Here a building was found with an entrance through the south wall, which indicates that the building's facade was oriented to Jerusalem. On the lintel of the main entrance appears an outline in relief of what may be a Torah shrine with two columns in front and a niche above that may represent a shell. To the right and left of this possible Torah shrine stand incised two seven-branched menorahs, each with two large knobs affixed in relief. The interior space is divided into a central nave and two side aisles by two rows of Ionic columns. This building is usually dated from the fifth century C.E.

Assi **1.** Babylonian amora of the early third century C.E.; a contemporary of Raḇ. He lived in Ḥuzal, near Nehardea and reportedly was wealthy (B. Ḥullin 105a).

2. Palestinian amora of the late third and early fourth centuries C.E.; also cited as Issi. A student of Samuel, he emigrated to the Land of Israel, where he was taught by Yoḥanan. He is frequently cited in both Talmuds, often with Ammi, also a student of Samuel.

assimilation accommodation to the surrounding culture. The term is often used, especially in modern times, in a negative sense to imply accommodation to the point that Jews abandon their Judaism. The expression can also be used as a matter of degree, however, without necessarily meaning loss of Jewish identity.

Jews have always adapted to their local environment, especially when living in the diaspora. It was common in antiquity, as now, to adopt the language, clothing, and many other aspects of the lifestyle of those among whom they lived. Typically, Jews dressed as those around them. The mode of dress varied, depending on one's wealth and social status, but the descriptions preserved do not generally indicate a differentiation between the Jews and others in clothing. Indeed, the mode of dress that sets some Jewish groups (e.g., Hasidic Jews) apart today was worn as normal clothing by their ancestors at another time and place (such as in Eastern Europe).

In language, Jews took on the dominant speech of their habitation. During the later Assyrian, Persian, and Parthian periods, the Jews of the Syrian and Mesopotamian areas spoke Aramaic in its various forms. This was true even when Hebrew may have been known to a lesser or greater extent (Palestine, for example, was a multilingual society). In the Graeco-Roman part of the Mediterranean, Greek was the primary language (despite the prominence of Latin in Italy), and the Jews were linguistically a part of this world, with the vast majority of Jews speaking Greek as their first, and often only, language.

Much of the Jewish writing known from this period is in Greek. Although in some cases the literary conventions followed have most in common with the biblical tradition, the bulk of Jewish literature shows a greater or lesser acquaintance with Greek literary practices, and even in some cases considerable training in rhetoric and literary style. Perhaps the pinnacle of this is reached in the works of Philo of Alexandria, but others such as Josephus and some of the fragmentary Hellenistic Jewish writers also show a high level of skill in Greek literary style even when interpreting the biblical or other Jewish traditions.

Despite embracing much of the surrounding culture, most Jews of the time accepted that certain aspects of their neighbors' lifestyle could not be taken on without compromising their religion. For example, some dietary habits would violate *kashrut,* and most Jews regarded this as unacceptable. Even such "assimilated" Jews as Philo were totally opposed to abandoning those areas of Judaism regarded as essential, including dietary laws, circumcision, the Sabbath, and holy days. Indeed, we know of very few Jews who are alleged to have abandoned their Judaism (such as Julius Tiberius Alexander). Thus, the extreme form of assimilation seems to have been rare.

associations *see* COLLEGIA

assumption (Heb.: *lakaḥ*; Gr.: *analēmpsis*) the taking of the soul, spirit, or body to God. Although a few later biblical texts (Isa. 26:19; Dan. 12:2) indicate belief in a resurrection, Psalms 49:15 and 73:24 may refer to an assumption to God's presence. Extraordinary assumption is attributed to Enoch (Gen. 5:24), Elijah, in the body (2 Kings 2), and Moses (Assumption of Moses). Jubilees 23:31 contrasts the spirit's joy in God's presence and one's bones resting in the earth, and Wisdom of Solomon 2–5 presumes that the immortal souls of the righteous are taken to God's presence at death. Resurrection of the body is the predominant notion in the New Testament, and Acts 1 describes Jesus' visible bodily ascent to heaven. A few texts suggest a nonbodily assumption to God or paradise (Luke 16:19–31, 23:43; Phil. 1:21–23). The farewell discourses in the Gospel of John assert that Jesus' death is at the same time his exaltation to God (John 14–17). *See also* AFTERLIFE.

astral immortality Daniel 12:3 states that the reward of the righteous person is to be transported to heaven as a star or starlike being at death. It was a widespread belief in Judaism in the postexilic period that the stars were angels (e.g., in 1 Enoch), suggesting that the righteous became angels.

astrology belief in influence of stars and planets on human life and prognostication based on stars and planets; widely affirmed by sages of Judaism, but denied as a force in Israel's history or in individual Jews' lives. The word for a guiding star is "mazal" (lit.: planet), and the blessing "mazal tob" means "under a propitious star."

astronomy the study of the movements of the sun, moon, stars, and planets. Although the Bible mentions that God created the sun, moon, and stars on the fourth day and assigned them calendrical tasks (Gen. 1:14–18), it devotes little space to further details about them and their functions. An exception is Psalms 104:19, which says that the moon designates the seasons and the sun knows when to set (see also Isa. 30:26, 47:13; Amos 5:8). The third-century-B.C.E. Greek writer Theophrastus reports that the Jews were known for observing the stars. As it happens, the earliest Jewish text that deals explicitly and in detail with astronomical topics is the Astronomical Book of Enoch (1 Enoch 72–82), which was written in the Aramaic language, also in the third century B.C.E. It shows that observation of or speculation on the heavenly bodies served primarily a calendrical purpose. The booklet is not scientific in the modern sense of the term; rather, it is a heavily theological presentation in which an angel reveals information about the sun, moon, and stars to Enoch and tells him that angels guide the various heavenly bodies. Moreover, it contains a warning about the days of the sinners, when the year will be shortened and other such disasters will occur. Enoch, the recipient of these revelations, had lived to the suggestive age of 365 years, according to Genesis 5:21–24, and as an anonymous second-century-B.C.E. writer (called Pseudo-Eupolemus) says, he was considered the discoverer of astrology. In the Astronomical Book, the angel Uriel discloses to Enoch that a solar year has 364 days and a lunar one has 354 days. The solar year consists of twelve thirty-day months, with four extra days. A major concern in the section about the moon is the amount of the lunar surface that is light or dark on the different days of the twenty-nine- or thirty-day months. The astronomical theories in 1 Enoch 72–82 were probably influenced by Babylonian astronomy and astrology. One indication of this is that in both, the fraction of the day that is light or dark at the two solstices and two equinoxes is identical. Several of the Dead Sea Scrolls deal with similar topics: they describe a solar year of 364 days and use the same fractions (fourteenths) to indicate the increase or decrease of the lighted portion of the moon throughout a month.

The data of astronomy could be used for calendrical ends, such as close observation of when, after the lunar surface became completely dark, the first crescent of the moon became visible, thus marking the beginning of a month and fixing the date of festivals that might occur in it. It was also possible, however, to appeal to the data for astrological purposes—to predict on the basis of celestial patterns. The Bible contains warnings against the divinatory procedures that were practiced widely in the ancient Near East (see Deut. 18). The Wise Men who visited the infant Jesus in Bethlehem were apparently astrologers; they had followed a special star, which they had interpreted as announcing the birth of a king.

ataraxia (Gr., calmness or indifference) a technical philosophical term among Epicureans, used with reference to their view of an untroubled mental attitude as one of the forms of pleasure. The Skeptics also sought this state of mind by denying certainty of knowledge.

atheism literally, the belief that there is no God. It was unusual in antiquity to find a true atheist, since almost all acknowledged the existence of gods, even those following Epicureanism, who thought that the gods were not concerned with humans. However, those who differed from conventional beliefs might be accused of atheism, as Socrates was. Because Jews refused to honor other gods or to participate in sacrifices and ceremonies in their honor, they are represented as impious (*asebeia/asebēs*) or atheists (*atheotēs*) by some writers, such as Apion and Apollonius Molon.

atheotēs *see* ATHEISM

athletes, athletic imagery During the Hellenistic period the imagery derived from athletic competitions became common in Jewish sources.

In the Hellenization movement of the early second century B.C.E. the establishment of a gymnasium, where even priests would exercise, offended traditionalists (1 Macc. 1:14; 2 Macc. 4:12–17). Despite rejection of Greek athletics in the Maccabean revolt, support of athletic contests resumed under later rulers. Herod endowed the Olympic games (Josephus, *War* 1.426–28) and athletic contests took place in the Greek cities in and around the Land of Israel: Caesarea, Scythopolis, and Caesarea Philippi.

Hellenized Jews utilized athletic imagery in two major contexts. Most common was the notion that life is a contest of virtue, in which the moral athlete engaged in training (*askesis*) prepares for the struggle against vice. This image, familiar in Greek moralists, appears in Jewish texts (Testament of Job 4:6 and 27:3–4; Wisdom of Solomon 4:2; Josephus, *Antiquities* 3.15) and with particular force in Philo of Alexandria (*On Agriculture* 110–23; *On Rewards and Punishments* 4–6; *On the Migration of Abraham* 133). Based on Genesis 32:24, Jacob becomes the model of the athlete of virtue (*Allegory of the Laws* 3.190; *On the Sacrifices of Abel and Cain* 17). Those who would imitate him must exercise the soul (*On the Virtues* 18). Successful competitors in life's contest will win a final crown (*Allegory of the Laws* 2.108).

Another application of athletic imagery appears in martyrologies. An influential example of the genre, 4 Maccabees, a reflection on the story of the Maccabean martyrs (cf. 2 Macc. 7), argues that reason informed by piety overcomes all obstacles. The story of the martyred mother and her seven sons is portrayed as a contest in which they win the prize of incorruption (4 Macc. 17:12). They war against a tyrannical adversary with the world as an audience (17:14). In their victory they receive the champion's crown (17:15). Christian texts continue both metaphorical applications, life as a contest (1 Tim. 6:12; 2 Tim. 4:7) and the contest of martyrdom (Heb. 12:1–3).

Athronges (or Athrongaeus) a shepherd who was remarkable for his great size and strength. During the social disorder that followed Herod the Great's death (4 B.C.E.), Athronges and his four brothers led bands of brigands, presumably in Judea, in raids against Romans, Herodians, and their countrypeople. According to Josephus, Athronges claimed to be king, wore a crown, and rendered judgment. After several years two of the brothers were killed and others were captured or surrendered.

Atilianus, Publius Calpurnius governor of Palestine, 139 C.E. There is some evidence that his name should read Atticus Rufus instead of Atilianus. He was consul in 135. We know nothing else about his career, and it is not certain that this was his first postconsul post.

atonement (Heb.: *kippur/kippurim*) atoning for sin and reconciliation with God, effected through animal offerings while the Temple stood (to 70 C.E.) and through prayer, repentance, and acts of selflessness, afterward; or through suffering and exile; and always through death. Repentance must be accompanied by reconciliation with one who has been injured.

atonement for the land a purpose that the Qumran community set for itself in its foundation document (1QS8–9). The idea of atoning for the land may be based on the difficult final words of the Song of Moses (Deut. 32:43). The founders of the Qumran community judged that the majority in Israel were sinful and unfaithful to the biblical covenant and laws and that the priests had polluted the Temple. Thus they founded a community that was to be just and upright, seeking truth and atoning for sin "by the practice of justice and by suffering the sorrows of affliction" (1QS8:3). The community was to be a house of perfection and truth in order to establish the covenant. In addition, it would be expepted to atone for the land (1QS8:10), to expiate the guilt of transgression and the infidelity of sin and obtain favor for the land without sacrifices (1QS9:4). While the idea of defilement of the land is not absent, the context indicates that the Qumran community wished primarily to renew society and its institutions. Similarly, 1 Enoch 10 envisions the destruction of the wicked, the renewal of the earth, and the rule of the just, but this cleansing comes about as a result of God's intervention through the Flood. *See also* ATONEMENT; EXPIATION.

attendant of synagogue (Gr.: *hyperetes*) a functionary who assisted the synagogue's president (Gr.: *archisynagogos*) in carrying out various liturgical duties. Josephus uses the term *hyperetes,* which simply means "assistant" or "servant," for Levites who assist priests in the sanctuary. In the explicit context of synagogue worship, the Greek term occurs only once, in Luke 4:20, where Jesus, after reading aloud from the scroll of Isaiah in a synagogue service at Nazareth, hands the book back to the *hyperetes.* The office of *hyperetes* is sometimes associated with the Hebrew *ḥazan* and may also be related to the later Christian office of deacon.

Atticus, Tiberius Claudius Herodes legate of Judea (c. 99/100–102/103 C.E.). Eusebius reports Hegesippus's claims that Simeon, son of Cleopas, second bishop of the Jerusalem church and Jesus' cousin, was executed by the governor Atticus under Trajan's reign. This reference could well be to this official. He was the father of a second-century sophist of the same name.

Atticus Rufus *see* ATILIANUS, PUBLIUS CALPURNIUS

Attius Suburanus Aemilianus *see* AEMILIANUS, SEXTUS ATTIUS SUBURANUS

Audynaios name of a Macedonian month; used by a number of Jewish writers, such as Josephus. Unfortunately, there was not a uniform usage; sometimes it corresponded to the Hebrew month of Kislev (November/December) and sometimes to the month Tebet (December/January).

Augoustesioi name applied to the Jewish community in Rome by Josephus. He does not explain the meaning of the term, but the community was apparently named after Augustus Caesar. Perhaps the community itself took the name to honor the emperor, or even petitioned him for it, since he seems to have respected Jewish rights.

Augustine, Aurelius (354–430 C.E.) Christian church father. He was born in Thagaste in the Roman African province of Numidia, the son of a devout Christian mother. Classically educated locally and in Carthage, he rose to a prominent rhetorical appointment in Milan. Through Neoplatonism and Bishop Ambrose, he made a commitment to Christianity. Shortly after returning to Africa, he became presbyter and then bishop of Hippo Regius, on the coast of Numidia, where he served until his death. His controversial writings are directed against the Manichaean sect, to which he had belonged for a decade; against Donatism, a separatist form of Christianity; against the Pelagian view of human potential; and, in *On the City of God,* against Roman paganism. His scriptural commentaries include extensive treatments of the initial chapters of Genesis, the Psalms, the Gospel of John, and those sections of Paul's letter to the Romans dealing with the status of Israel. *The Confessions* provides a spiritual autobiography through the first half of his life. *On the Trinity* made his major contribution to the development of the Christian interpretation of the scriptures and the doctrine of God. His doctrinal innovations included the theory of inherited guilt and of predestination without regard for human merits.

Augustus Caesar (63 B.C.E.–14 C.E.) grand-nephew of Julius Caesar and first Roman emperor. Named Gaius Octavius at birth, he was adopted into Caesar's household as a young man. He was of a serious disposition, was not particularly robust, and showed an interest in literature and philosophy. Under Caesar's tutelage he became acquainted with the ways of Roman politics. In his will Caesar named him his heir. On hearing of his patron's assassination in 44 B.C.E., Octavius returned to Rome, won the respect of the legions and the Senate, and joined Mark Antony and Lepidus in a triumvirate to avenge Caesar's murder. He changed his name to Gaius Julius Caesar Octavianus. After the Battle of Philippi he won the support of the western provinces and Italy with his conservatism and respect for the ways of ancient Rome, which he shared with his wife Livia. While Octavian was already being celebrated by the poets Virgil and Horace, Antony's fascination with Cleopatra had lost him favor in Rome and Italy. In 32 B.C.E. Octavian did not renew the pact with him and, receiving the support of the legions, declared war on Cleopatra, which led to the defeat of Actium in 31 and the subsequent death of Antony. Octavian was virtually sole ruler of Rome. He adopted the title *princeps,* first citizen, and was hailed as the bringer of peace after the bitter conflicts of the previous civil wars. He respected the institutions of the state and allowed the Senate to confer on him the title Augustus, with its quasi-religious associations, in 27 B.C.E. Later he was designated High Priest (Pontifex Maximus) and Father of the Fatherland (Pater Patriae). His achievements included bringing peace to Rome, the reorganization of the administration of the city and the provinces, and the restoration of Roman moral standards by enacting legislation supporting the family. He thus laid the foundation for imperial rule for centuries. His friend and adviser, Marcus Agrippa, was seen as his likely heir after he had married Augustus's daughter Julia, but his untimely death, as well as that of their two sons, resulted in Tiberius being adopted as coregent and heir. When Augustus died in 14 C.E. the Senate decreed that he should be accepted among the gods, a fitting tribute for one who had been seen as *divi filius* (son of God) since 42 B.C.E. with the deification of Julius Caesar, his patron.

Aurelius, Marcus *see* MARCUS AURELIUS

Aureliaurum coronarium crown tax. Gold crowns were offered to the rulers and conquerors in the ancient Near East and in the Hellenistic world. From the early second century B.C.E., similar gifts were presented to Roman generals, who eventually required that they be given to them. Under the Roman Empire, the emperor alone received the crowns, which were required so frequently that they emerged as a new form of taxation. The term also refers to a tax that the patriarch's messengers collected for his benefit and that replaced the half-sheqel temple tax, so that the references in the Talmuds to the tax are unclear.

Avidius Cassius, Gaius (d. 175 C.E.) Roman official. In 165–166 he captured Seleucia and Ctesiphon in Parthia. In 168 he became governor of Syria and supreme commander over the eastern provinces, including Egypt. In 175 he had himself declared emperor. However, the Jews did not support Avidius's claim to power. Avidius was assassinated before civil war broke out. In response to these events, Marcus Aurelius visited Syria, Palestine, and Egypt in late 175–176.

Avot *see* A̲BOT

aylonit *see* BARREN WOMAN

Azael (Uziel) according to Targum Pseudo-Jonathan to Genesis 6:4, one of the fallen angels who came to earth with Shamḥazai. Azael may be linked with Azazel of 1 Enoch who, as the leader of the fallen angels, corrupted humanity by teaching the arts of making weapons and jewelry as well as teaching women how to use cosmetics. He was punished by Raphael.

Azariah, Prayer of a traditional prayer of confession ascribed to Azariah (Abednego) and inserted into the Greek version of Daniel 3 between verses 23 and 24. Based on Israelite covenantal theology, it acknowledges the righteousness of God's judgments on Israel and appeals for restoration that responds to the people's repentance. Its closest parallels are Baruch 1:15–3:8 and Daniel 9:4–19. *See also* SONG OF THE THREE CHILDREN.

Azaryah Palestinian amora of the fourth century C.E., often cited in conjunction with Aḥa, Yudan, and Judah b. Simon. He is mentioned primarily in midrashic settings.

Azazel place or person to which the scapegoat is dispatched (Lev. 16:8–10). The term comes to be identified with Azael, who is one of the two chieftains of the rebellious watchers (angels) in 1 Enoch 6–16. Azazel appears as a name for the chief demon in the Apocalypse of Abraham. *See also* ABRAHAM, APOCALYPSE OF.

Azotus Mesogaeus the Greek name of the inland city of Ashdod, also known as Azotus Hippenus by one ancient author, or Ashdod of the Cavalrymen. The latter name implies that cavalry veterans were settled there, perhaps at the behest of Herod the Great. The city was called Azotus Mesogaeus to distinguish it from its main harbor city of Azotus Paralius. The city territory of Azotus Mesogaeus extended north about five kilometers to the River of Azotus south of Jamnia. The south boundary was with Ashkelon, and its eastern boundary extended perhaps 16 kilometers to the east. In the fourth century, Eusebius called Azotus "a famous townlet in Palestine" (*Onomasticon* 20:18). In the Byzantine era, the harbor city of Azotus Paralius was larger. Some 3 kilometers north of Azotus Paralius stood the small, secondary harbor of Cariathmaus. *See also* ASHDOD.

Ba *see* ABBA B. ZABDAI

baal habayit (Heb.) householder; *see also* GENDER ROLES, IN RABBINIC JUDAISM

Baal Shamem Phoenician divine name meaning "lord of heaven." It seems to be a title given to the chief deity in various Syro-Phoenician cults but was also used (in its Aramaic form) of the Jewish God in Ezra. It has been proposed that this name lies behind the Hebrew Abomination of Desolation in the Book of Daniel. *See also* ABOMINATION OF DESOLATION.

Baba Batra (Heb., the last gate) Mishnah tractate on civil law; *see also* BABA KAMMA

Baba b. Buta teacher at the time of Herod, perhaps related to the "sons of Baba," who, during the siege of Jerusalem (37 B.C.E.), resisted its surrender and later were executed by Herod the Great (Josephus, *Ant.* 15.7, 10). B. Baba Batra 3b states that Herod put out Baba b. Buta's eyes, but that he was the only teacher whom Herod spared from death.

Baba Kamma (Heb., the first gate) Mishnah tractate on civil law. The three Babas—Baba Kamma, the first gate; Baba Metzia, the middle gate; and Baba Batra, the last gate—comprise thirty Mishnah chapters devoted to torts and damages. Baba Kamma addresses torts, specifically, damages done by chattels (1:1–6:6) and damages done by persons (7:1–10:10). The chapters on damages done by chattels (that is, damages caused by one's property, animate or inanimate) distinguish damages done in the public domain from those done in private property, set forth the ransom and the death penalty for the ox, and cover damages done by a pit, by a crop-destroying beast, and by fire. The chapters on damages done by persons encompass penalties for theft (e.g., of an ox or a sheep, in line with Exod. 33:1–4), penalties for assault and personal injury, penalties for damages to property, and restoring stolen goods. Baba Metzia proceeds to the disposition of disputed property (1:1–3:12), covering conflicting claims to lost objects and returning an object to the original owner, rules concerning bailment (3:1–12), and illicit commercial transactions (4:1–5:11), such as overcharging, false advertising, and usury, which is strictly forbidden. After fifteen chapters on torts and damages, the exposition shifts to normal relationships, such as hiring of works, mutual obligations of worker and employer, and rentals and bailments in which no tort is involved (6:1–8:3). Rules on real estate run from Baba Metzia 8:4–10:6 through Baba Batra 1:1–5:5. The subject includes landlord-tenant relationships and landlord relations with tenant farmers and sharecroppers; prompt payment of workers; rules governing joint holders of a common property; infringement upon the property rights of others; establishing title to a field through usucaptions (squatter's rights); and transferring real estate and movables through sale of real estate. Baba Batra then turns to licit commercial transactions (5:6–7:4), covering conditions for the irrevocable transfer of goods, the point at which a sale is final, and unstated stipulations in commercial transactions. Finally, Baba Batra addresses inheritances, wills, and other commercial and legal documents (8:1–10:8), dealing with rules of inheritance, preparation and confirmation of commercial documents, such as writs of debt, and the like. The plan of the whole thus covers torts, damages, labor, real estate, and commercial transactions, with the opening part dealing with the restoration of the status quo in cases of torts and damages and the second part dealing with normal, or licit, transactions. Both Talmuds devote important and lengthy expositions to these three tractates.

Baba Metzia (Heb., the middle gate) Mishnah tractate on civil law; *see also* BABA KAMMA

Baba Rabbah Samaritan high priest (332–372 C.E.). He maintained a standing army to protect Samaritan territory. He divided the country into twelve administrative districts, each administered by a priest and a layperson, and created a legislative body of priests and laypersons to teach Torah and decide legal matters throughout the country. He reopened many schools and synagogues closed by the Romans and directed the collection and preservation of old legal and religious manuscripts. The Byzantine emperor invited him to Constantinople to sign a peace treaty in 372; however, he was imprisoned and died a captive.

Babata a woman whose personal records were found among the Bar Kokhba manuscripts. A bag containing her personal archive of documents in Greek, Aramaic, and Nabatean was found in one of the caves of Nahal Hever. These form a record of her legal endeavors and give a window into the life of ordinary Jews at that time.

Babel, Tower of the building intended to reach the heavens (Gen. 11:1–9). In the Book of Biblical Antiquities 6–7, Abraham opposes the idolatrous construction project and is thrown into a fiery furnace (cf. Dan. 3), the *ur* (Heb., fire) from which God rescues him, having chosen him for his faithfulness. A related interpretation of Genesis 11 appears in 3 Baruch 2–3.

Babli the Talmud of Babylonia, produced in the Persian satrapy of Babylonia as a commentary to the second, third, fourth, and fifth divisions of the Mishnah. Most of the work of writing the compositions and compiling the composites was done between 500 and 600 C.E. The Babli generally inquires into the scriptural sources of rules in the Mishnah and the authorities behind unattributed laws of the Mishnah; it harmonizes passages of the Mishnah that appear to conflict. It also contains extensive commentaries to extended passages of scripture, essays on theoretical problems, and inquiries into modes and principles of scriptural exegesis that yield details of law, not necessarily in the context of Mishnah exegesis. While drawing on a variety of sources, including scripture, the Mishnah, the Tosefta, and materials given final form as authoritative statements of the law in the names of Tannaitic figures, the framers of the document reworked the materials they used into a cogent, orderly, and well-crafted piece of writing.

The purpose of the Talmud of Babylonia is to clarify and amplify selected passages of the Mishnah. It may be said that the Mishnah is about life, and the Talmud is about the Mishnah; that is, while the Mishnah records rules governing the conduct of the holy life of Israel, the Talmud concerns itself with the details of the Mishnah. The one is descriptive and freestanding; the other, analytical and contingent. Were there no Mishnah, there would be no Talmud. But the Talmud of Babylonia—which is what people mean when they speak of "the Talmud"—in fact vastly transcends the Mishnah and forms an eloquent statement of its own. Exactly how a vast and dense writing turns out to say some few things (and to say them with such power as to impose its judgment upon an entire prior writing and on the intellect of an entire religious world to come) requires attention—for in the Judaism of the dual Torah, the faithful meet God in the Torah, and the Talmud of Babylonia forms the centerpiece of the Torah. Together with its associated Midrash compilations, the Babli's compilers and the writers of its compositions found the way to form the mind and define the intellect of the faithful. They did this not through statements of doctrine or law, but through the public display of "right reasoning," the exposition of argument; if you can show people how to think, then, in the context of a revealed Torah, you can also guide them to what to think: right thoughts, right deeds, right attitudes.

The Babli is a uniform document from beginning to end. Different from and much more than a haphazard compilation of traditions, this Talmud shows itself upon examination to be a cogent and purposive writing in which, through a single determinate set of rhetoric devices, a single program of inquiry is brought to bear on many and diverse passages of two inherited documents, the Mishnah and scripture. The voice is one and single because it is a voice that everywhere expresses the same limited set of sounds; these notes are arranged in one and the same way throughout. The Babli's one voice, sounding through all tractates, is the voice of exegetes of the Mishnah. The document is organized around the Mishnah, and that ordering is not merely formal, but conveys substantive meaning. At every point, if the framers have chosen a passage of Mishnah exegesis, that passage will stand at the head of all further discussion. Every turning point in every sustained composition and even in a large composite of compositions brings the editors back to the Mishnah, always read in its own order and invariably arranged in its own sequence.

It follows that well-crafted and orderly rules govern the character of the sustained discourse that the writing in the Bab̲li sets forth. All framers of composites and editors of sequences of composites found guidance in the same limited repertoire of rules of analytical rhetoric: some few questions or procedures, directed always toward one and the same prior writing. Moreover, a fixed order of discourse dictated that a composition of one sort, A, always come prior to a composite of another type, B. A simple logic instructed framers of composites, who sometimes also were authors of compositions, and who sometimes drew upon available compositions in the making of their cogent composites. Thus we must see the Bab̲li as entirely of a piece, cogent and coherent, made up of well-composed, large-scale constructions.

We are able to classify all composites in three principal categories: (1) exegesis and amplification of the law of the Mishnah; (2) exegesis and exposition of verses of or topics in scripture; (3) freestanding composites devoted to topics other than those defined by the Mishnah or scripture. These classifications were not forced or subtle; the grounds for making them were consistent; appeal throughout was to gross and merely formal characteristics, not to subjective judgments of what unstipulated consideration might underlie or define the intention of the framer of a passage. With that classification in place, it is a matter of simple fact that much more than four-fifths of all composites of the Bab̲li address the Mishnah and systematically expound that document. These composites are subject to subclassification in two ways: Mishnah exegesis and speculation and abstract theorizing about the implications of the Mishnah's statements. The exegetical composites, further, can be classified in a few simple taxa, for example as composites organized around (1) clarification of the statements of the Mishnah, (2) identification of the authority behind an anonymous statement in the Mishnah, (3) scriptural foundation for the Mishnah's rules, or (4) citation and often systematic exposition of the Tosefta's amplification of the Mishnah. That means that most of the Bab̲li is a systematic exposition of the Mishnah. The abstract that you read will conform to this description in the proportion and order of its comments on the Mishnah. The other fifth (or still less) of a given tractate will comprise composites that take shape either around scripture or around themes or topics of a generally theological or moral character. Distinguishing the latter from the former, of course, is merely formal; very often a scriptural topic will be set forth in a theological or moral framework, and very seldom does a composite on a topic omit all reference to the amplification of a verse or topic of scripture. The proportion of a given tractate devoted to exegesis and amplification of authorities other than the Mishnah is generally not more than 10 percent.

The Bab̲li speaks about the Mishnah in essentially a single voice, about fundamentally few things. Its mode of speech, as much as of thought, is uniform throughout. Diverse topics produce slight differentiation in modes of analysis. The same sorts of questions phrased in the same rhetoric—a moving, or dialectical, argument, composed of questions and answers—turn out to pertain equally well to every subject and problem. The Talmud's discourse forms a closed system, in which people say the same thing about everything. The fact that the Talmud speaks in a single voice supplies striking evidence that the Talmud does speak in particular for the age in which its units of discourse took shape, and that that work was done toward the end of the long period of Mishnah reception that began at the end of the second century and came to an end at the conclusion of the sixth century.

Five hermeneutical rules yielding theological facts govern throughout the Talmud of Babylonia:

(1) *Defining the Torah and the context for meaning*. The Torah consists of freestanding statements, sentences that are sometimes formed into paragraphs, but more often not; and we are to read these sentences both on their own—for what they say—and also in the context created by the entirety of the Torah, oral and written. Therefore the task is to set discrete sentences side by side and show their compatibility; documents mean nothing, the Torah being one. The entirety of the Torah defines the context of meaning. All sentences of the Torah, equally, jointly, and severally, form the facts out of which meaning is to be constructed.

(2) *Specifying the rules of making sense of the Torah*. Several premises govern in our reading of the sentences of the Torah, and these dictate the rules of reading. The first is that the Torah is perfect and flawless. The second is that the wording

of the Torah yields meaning. The third is that the Torah contains, and can contain, nothing contradictory, incoherent, or otherwise contrary to common sense. The fourth is that the Torah can contain no statement that is redundant, banal, silly, or stupid. The fifth is that our sages of blessed memory when they state teachings of the Torah stand for these same traits of language and intellect: sound purpose, sound reasoning, and sound result, in neat sentences. The task of the reader (in secular language) or the master of the Torah (in theological language—in context the two are one and the same), then, is to identify the problems of the Torah, whether written or oral, and to solve those problems. Knowing what will raise a difficulty, we also know how to resolve it.

(3) *Identifying dialectics as the correct medium of Torah discourse.* Since our principal affirmation is that the Torah is perfect and the primary challenge to that affirmation derives from the named classifications of imperfection, the proper mode of analytical speech is argument. This is because if we seek flaws, we come in a combative spirit: proof and conflict, not truth and consequence. Only by challenging the Torah sentence by sentence, at every plausible point of imperfection, are we going to demonstrate the governing fact of perfection. We discover right thinking by finding the flaws in wrong thinking, the logical emerging from the failings of illogic.

(4) *The harmony of what is subject to dispute; the unity and integrity of truth; finding what is rational and coherent.* The final principle of hermeneutics is to uncover the rationality of dispute. Once commitment is to sustained conflict of intellect, it must follow that our goal can only be the demonstration of three propositions, everywhere meant to govern: first, that disputes give evidence of rationality, meaning that each party has a valid, established principle in mind; second, that disputes are subject to resolution; and third, that truth wins out. The first proposition is most important. If we can demonstrate that reasonable sages can differ about equally valid propositions, for instance, which principle governs in a particular case, then schism affords evidence not of imperfection but of profound coherence. The principles are affirmed, their application subjected to conflict. So, too, if disputes worked out in extended, moving arguments, covering much ground, can be brought to resolution, as is frequently the case in either a declared decision or an agreement to disagree, then the perfection of the Torah once more comes to detailed articulation.

(5) *Knowing God through the theology expressed in hermeneutics.* In a protracted quest for the unity of the truth, what is always required through detailed demonstration is that beneath the laws is law; a few wholly coherent principles are inherent in the many and diverse rules and their cases. In that sustained quest, which defines the premise and the goal of all talmudic discourse, Israel meets God; in mind, in intellect, that meeting takes place.

Babylon one of the most magnificent cities of the ancient world and capital of the empire that sent the Jews into exile in the sixth century B.C.E. The impact of the Babylonian exile on the worldview of later Jews was so dramatic that early Jewish literature alludes often to the historical memory of the event; see, for example, Baruch 1:9–12; 1 Esdras 1:40–56; Additions to Esther 2:6, 11:14; Sibylline Oracles 3:265–287. Following the Deuteronomistic pattern, the exile is usually interpreted as punishment for Israel's sins (Bar. 2:21–24, 4:6–20; Ep. Jer. 6:1–3; cf. Acts 7:43); the restoration is seen as a sign of God's forgiveness (Bar. 4:21–5:9; 1 Esd. 3:1–5:6).

Several important pieces of early Jewish literature are set in Babylon during the exile. Probably the most familiar is the cycle of stories in Daniel 1–6; others are the books of Baruch, Susanna, Bel and the Dragon, the Song of the Three Young Men, and 4 Ezra. The Letter of Jeremiah presents itself as having been written to Jews about to be exiled to Babylon, whereas 2 Baruch (77:12–19) mentions (but does not preserve) a letter of Baruch to Jewish exiles in Babylonia. The Book of Judith depicts the Jews as successfully resisting the advances of Babylonian forces in central Israel.

Several sources connect the Babylonians with idolatry (Ep. Jer. [esp. 6:4]; Bel and Dragon; cf. Jub. 11–12). Others preserve woes, oracles, or prophecies against Babylon of a type familiar from the Hebrew Bible (2 Bar. 39:3, 67:7; Sib. Or. 3:300–313; 5:434–446; 11:201–209; cf. Tobit 14:4; Sus. 1:5). The Jewish Sibylline Oracles attest the idea that one of the sibyls, or prophetesses, is from Babylon (3:809–810; cf. the Christian prologue to the collected Sibylline Oracles).

In certain early Jewish writings the name "Babylon" is used symbolically to designate Rome (Sib. Or. 5:143, 159; 4 Ezra 3:1–2, 28, 31; often in rabbinic literature). This identification, which became current after 70 C.E., arose primarily from the fact that both of these world empires had destroyed Jewish temples in Jerusalem.

Babylon appears infrequently in early Christian sources. Acts 7:43 was mentioned above. In the genealogy of Jesus in Matthew 1:1–17, the Babylonian exile is one of the two central events between Abraham and the Messiah. Three other sources—1 Peter 5:13; Revelation 14:8, 16:19, 17:5–6, 18:2, 10, 21–22; and 6 Ezra 15:43, 46, 60, 16:1—use Babylon as a symbolic name for Rome. In the later Apocalypse of Daniel, "Babylon" becomes a cipher for the city of Byzantium (7:2, 5, 11).

Babylonia remained an important Jewish settlement long after the exile, supplanting the land of Israel as the intellectual center of Judaism after the second century C.E. and producing around 600 C.E. what is today considered the authoritative version of the Talmud.

Babylon, Jews in (450 B.C.E.–135 C.E.) Babylon in a narrow sense refers to the area of central Mesopotamia around the ancient cities of Babylon, Ctesiphon, Seleucia, and contemporary Baghdad. In 597 and 586 B.C.E., Nebuchadnezzar and the Babylonians exiled the Judean leadership to this area, along canals such as the Chebar and Tel-Aviv (Ezek. 1:1, 3:15). In a wider sense to be used here, Babylon in Jewish literature refers to all of Mesopotamia, including the north around Nisibis, where northern exiles had been settled by the Assyrians in the eighth century B.C.E. and all the areas where Jews spread in Mesopotamia. Evidence concerning Babylonian Jews during the Persian and Parthian periods is sparse and scattered. Jews were settled in many places, including Nisibis, Adiabene, Armenia in the north, Seleucia, Babylon, and Nehardea in the south, and Charax Spasinu at the mouth of the gulf. For the most part we have only isolated stories and anecdotes about them.

The most highly placed Jew of the mid-fifth century, Nehemiah, the cupbearer to the Persian king Artaxerxes I, was given authority to restore and govern Jerusalem. His memoirs are contained in the biblical Book of Nehemiah. In the late fifth century in Nisibis, the Murashu family engaged in complex loans, contracts, and commercial ventures. Their archives contain thousands of names, some of which contain the Jewish theophoric element *Ya-*, and so are probably Jewish. According to the Murashi tablets, these Jews came from many towns around Nisibis, were engaged in a variety of occupations and, in many cases, had given their children Babylonian names. In the mid-fourth century, Artaxerxes III Ochus transported Jewish captives from Egypt to Hyrcania, at the southern end of the Caspian Sea. When Alexander the Great conquered Mesopotamia, he continued the privileges the Persians had granted the Jews. His successor, Seleucus I, consolidated his rule in Mesopotamia by founding the city of Seleucia north of Babylon. He moved a large Semitic population there, including a substantial number of Jews. Jews served in the Greek armies and helped drive off a Galatian invasion in 220 B.C.E. (2 Macc. 8:20). A decade later, Antiochus III sent two thousand Jewish families to Asia Minor as settlers in order to dampen unrest there. Mesopotamian Jews remained loyal to the Seleucid government and did not rise up to help the Hasmoneans in their war against Antiochus IV in 167–164 B.C.E.

During the second century B.C.E., the Parthians near the Caspian Sea gradually gained control of Mesopotamia by taking advantage of Seleucid weakness. By 120 B.C.E., the Parthian king, Mithridates I, had conquered Babylon. The Parthians left Greek and local laws and customs in place, including those of the Jews. Thus, the transition from Seleucid to Parthian rule was smooth for Babylonian Jews. Parthian conflicts with the Seleucids served the interests of Jews in Judea as well, since during this time, the Hasmoneans established their independence from the weakened and distracted Seleucid Empire.

The Parthians had a direct impact on Jews in Palestine in the first century B.C.E. The Parthians had come into conflict with the Romans, who were spreading their rule throughout the Near East. In 40 B.C.E., the Parthians capped a series of campaigns against Rome by conquering Syria and Palestine. They captured Hyrcanus II, the son of Alexander Jannaeus, who had been ruling as high priest, supported by Herod the Great and his brother Phasael, and installed Antigonus, Hyrcanus's brother, who had been removed from office by the Romans over twenty years earlier. In 38 B.C.E., however, the Parthians were driven out, and Herod the Great, who had by then been appointed king by the Roman Senate, took over the government of the country. Communication and migration among Babylonian and Palestinian Jews was not stopped by conflict between Rome and Parthia. Herod appointed a Babylonian Jewish priest as high priest in Jerusalem, probably to avoid giving a political base to a local rivals and to improve relations with the Babylonian community. He brought Hyrcanus II back from exile in Parthia, though he soon assassinated him. He also recruited a Parthian Jewish cavalry commander, Zamaris (Zimri), and five hundred horsemen to settle at Bathyra in Trachonitis (east of the Sea of Galilee) as a defensive force at the edges of his kingdom.

Rabbinic literature claims that Hillel and other sages came from Babylon and that one sage, Judah ben Bathyra, lived in Nisibis.

We know almost nothing about the ordinary life of Jews in Babylon. A few stories have been preserved by the historian Josephus. In the first century C.E., Jewish brothers Anileus and Asineus ran away from their employer in Nehardea and gathered flocks and a strong force of the poor in an outlying area of Babylonia. They built a citadel, protected the inhabitants of the area and collected taxes from them. After they had defeated a Parthian armed force, the king, Artabanus III, recruited them as governors. They ruled part of Mesopotamia for about fifteen years (21–36 or 36–51 C.E.). Another story speaks of Jews being persecuted in Babylon and fleeing to Seleucia and then to the royal city of Ctesiphon, only to be persecuted there. Finally, they fled to Nehardea and Nisibis, fortified cities where Jews collected the taxes for Jerusalem. Though Nehardea and Nisibis later became centers of rabbinic study, we do not know how the Jewish community was organized in the first century or whether they had a ethnarch (an official appointed by the government to rule the Jewish communities). When Vologases (51–80 C.E.) reorganized the Parthian kingdom about 70 C.E., he must have made some provision to recognize and rule the numerous Jews in his kingdom.

Another series of stories concerns the conversion of the ruling house of Adiabene in Northern Mesopotamia to Judaism and their devotion to Jerusalem and the Temple. Izates, the favorite son and heir of King Monobazus of Adiabene and Helene, was sent to Charax Spasinu in far southern Mesopotamia to avoid the hostile envy of his other brothers. There he was taught to worship God in the Jewish tradition by a merchant, Ananias (Hananiah). His mother meanwhile had been instructed in Judaism at home. When Izates returned to inherit the kingdom, he was circumcised following a dispute between two Jewish teachers over whether this was a prudent course of action for a king. Later, the rest of his family converted to Judaism as well. The cycle of stories about Izates' reign show him as an important vassal of the king of Parthia and one who survives various plots and battles. These stories, like those in Daniel 1–6, teach that the practice of Judaism is consistent with life in the diaspora, even for the most powerful, because God protects those who are faithful. They also teach a proper attitude toward Judea and Jerusalem. Helene was generous and contributed to the material welfare of Judeans. She and Izates were buried near Jerusalem. Though the historical reliability of the stories is difficult to assess, their social setting shows the significant and varied presence of Jews in Mesopotamia. That Izates could become a Jew and survive as ruler implies that Jews were a significant social force in northern Mesopotamia with whom he could form alliances.

Jews in Mesopotamia helped resist the Roman invasion of Parthia in 115–117 C.E. The Roman Emperor, Trajan, initially conquered most of Mesopotamia and organized it into provinces. In 116, however, a Parthian counteroffensive led to a general uprising against the Romans among the indigenous population, including Jews. Probably the Jews of Mesopotamia, along with other ethnic groups, hoped to throw off Roman rule with the help of the Parthians, under whom they had more intracommunal freedom. Since this revolt threatened a sensitive border region of the Roman Empire, Trajan ordered his general, Lucius Quietus, later governor of Israel, to put down the revolt. In the course of the campaign, thousands were massacred. At the same time, Jews in Egypt, Cyrene, and Cyprus, responding to Trajan's absence in Parthia, had risen against the Roman government and attacked their fellow countrymen. In the end, Trajan's successor Hadrian (r. 117–138) abandoned the Parthian conquests as too costly to defend and Babylonian Jewish communities escaped Roman rule. *See also* TRAJAN, WAR OF.

Babylonia province of the Persian Empire, corresponding to the central part of present-day Iraq, where Jews in the time of the fall of the First Temple in 586 B.C.E. were settled and remained through biblical times. The Talmud of Babylonia was produced in this area, where large Jewish communities flourished under Iranian (Zoroastrian) rule until the rise of Islam in the seventh century. *See also* BABYLON; BABYLON, JEWS IN.

Babylonian Aramaic *see* ARAMAIC, BABYLONIAN

Babylonian Talmud *see* BA*B*LI

Babylonian Targum *see* ONKELOS, TARGUM

Ba b. Za*b*dai *see* ABBA B. ZA*B*DAI

Bacchides Seleucid general who supported Demetrius I in 162–150 B.C.E. He led a strong Syrian force to Judea, which installed Alcimus as high priest and reestablished Seleucid rule in late 162 and early 161 B.C.E. After Judas Maccabeus defeated a Syrian force under Nicanor, Bacchides returned in 161 B.C.E. and defeated Judas's forces, killing him in battle in 160 B.C.E.

Bacchus *see* DIONYSUS WORSHIP, JUDAISM ASSOCIATED WITH

Badan a location in Samaria, known for its pomegranates (e.g., M. Orlah 3:7)

Baghdad capital of the Abasid dynasty and home of the largest Jewish community in the Abasid Empire; seat of the exilarchate. By the ninth century C.E., Baghdad was home to the academies of Sura and Pumbedita and to many prominent gaonic scholars and poets, including the important academy heads Isaac b. Israel and Eleazar b. Jacob haBabli.

Bagoas **1.** Persian general under Artaxerxes II (r. 404–358 B.C.E.) who, according to Josephus (*Ant.* 11.297–301), defiled the Temple and imposed tribute on the Jews; sometimes identified with the Bagohi (= Bagoas), governor of Judah, to whom the Jews of Elephantine wrote for support in rebuilding their Temple

2. the eunuch of Holofernes, who discovered the decapitated body (Jdt. 12:11, 14:14–18)

Bahram I Sassanid ruler (r. 273–276 C.E.). He suppressed the Manichaeans, the Christians, and probably the Jews. He may have supported Zenobia of Palmyra in the building of his empire. When Zenobia was defeated in 273, the Roman emperor's triumph included Persian envoys bearing rich gifts. Bahram supported Katir's attempt to create the Sassanid Mazdayasnian state church, perhaps because Katir had supported Bahram's rise to power. Therefore, it is likely that under Bahram the Persian Jewish community suffered at Katir's hands. While Katir's inscription mentions the persecution and expulsion of foreign religions, including the Jews, Jewish sources do not mention these problems. Only one passage in the Talmud, which mentions the removal of a lamp by a certain Magus, probably on a Zoroastrian festival, hints at troubles during Bahram's reign.

Bahram II Sassanid ruler (r. 276–292 C.E.). His reign was disastrous, for he was unable to maintain the frontiers established by Shapur. He seems to have been goaded into fighting mostly defensive campaigns. He fought a Scythic people in Seistan and in Afghanistan. The Roman emperor Carus defeated him and took Seleuci-Ctesiphon. When the war ended in 284, Rome held Mesopotamia. In 286, the Roman emperor Diocletian undertook an aggressive policy against the weak Bahram. In 288, the Sassanid ruler relinquished all claims to Mesopotamia and acknowledged Trdat II as king of Armenia and client of Rome. The loss of Armenia meant that the Sassanid Empire's enemies had an easy invasion route into the heart of the western territories of present-day Iran. Katir continued to hold power under Bahram II, and it is likely that the persecution of the Jews continued during his reign.

Bahram V Gor Sassanid ruler (r. 420–438 C.E.); called "the wild ass." Apparently he was raised and educated among the Arab tribes of Mesopotamia. Bahram persecuted the Christians, and many fled to Roman territory. A war with Rome followed, but in 422, he concluded a peace with the Romans, allowing the Christians to remain in the Roman territories and ending the persecution of Christians in the Sassanid Empire. Bahram defeated an Hephtahlite invasion in 427 at Merv. He probably continued the favorable policies of his father, Yazdagird I, toward the Jews. He supposedly knew Hebrew, Greek, and Arabic.

Bahram VI Chobin Sassanid ruler (r. 590–591 C.E.). As Hormizd II's general, Bahram defeated the Turks and the Huns, but failed to take the province of Lazica. After a public insult by Hormizd, he openly revolted. In 590, Hormizd was deposed, but Bahram refused to recognize his successor, Khusro II, whom he eventually defeated. Khusro fled to Circesium, seeking Byzantine support. Bahram took Ctesiphon, discovering that Armenia and Mesopotamia favored Khusro. In 591, Khusro took Seleucia, received the surrender of Ctesiphon, and was proclaimed emperor. Bahram fled to the Turks. During the war, the Jews supported Bahram against Khusro because the latter had closed Jewish schools. Furthermore, Khusro favored the Christians and received support from Byzantium. Khusro's severe persecution of Jews was probably related to their support of Bahram, whom they considered a benevolent protector and to whose army they may have provided subsidies.

bailee a custodian of the property or affairs of another, usually of a minor or mentally defective adult. The Hebrew term *apotropos* derives from the Greek, meaning "father of minors." Women generally were excluded from appointment as a bailee, although their designation by a father during his lifetime was deemed valid (T. Baba Batra 8:17).

Rabbinic law permits the bailee to take all actions necessary to provide for his ward. However, he is responsible for maintaining the ward's estate, for example, by not selling landed property or freeing slaves (T. Baba Batra 8:14). The bailee is subject to supervision by the court (B. Gittin 52a), although the extent to which he needed to provide an accounting of his activities was subject to dispute (T. Baba Batra 8:13, 15). Even though the bailee has no right to the property (or usufruct of the property) under his care, the bailment is created through an act of *meshikhah* (Heb., pulling) of the subject property, the same procedure used for the acquisition of property (*kinyan*).

Balaam non-Israelite seer who was summoned by Balak, king of Moab, to curse Israel, but was forced by YHWH to utter oracles of blessing (Num. 22–24). Balaam receives mainly negative notices in Jewish literature (Philo, *Life Mos.* 1.263–304, *On Migr. Abr.* 113–17; Josephus, *Ant.* 4.6.3–6: 107–30; LAB 18) and the New Testament (2 Pet. 2:15–16; Jude 11; Rev. 2:14). However, his star oracle (Num. 24:17) is featured in 4Q Testimonia 9–13, was the source for Simon Bar Kosiba's nickname Bar Kokhba (Aram., son of the star), and may be alluded to in Matthew 2:1–12. Anomalous is 1 Enoch 1:2–3, 93:1–3, where Enoch the pre-Israelite seer speaks in the idiom of Balaam's oracles (Num. 24:15–17).

balance, judgment a device by which judgment is decided in the divine court. The Testament of Abraham 12–13 (A) depicts an elaborate heavenly judgment scene in which the angel Dokiel weighs human souls and counterbalances sins and righteous deeds. The scene and the detail have been influenced by illustrations in the Egyptian Book of the Dead, where souls are weighed in a scale balanced by the feather of *maat* (truth). Daniel 5:27, Job 31:6, and 1 Enoch 41:1 allude to the motif, and the image stands behind a number of rabbinic sayings about reward and punishment after death.

Balas *see* ALEXANDER BALAS

balsam a perfume derived from a tropical spice referred to as *aparsemon* in rabbinic sources; used also in medicinal applications. The oil of the balsam orchards in the Dead Sea region had significant commercial value.

Banaah Palestinian rabbi active in the early third century C.E.; a contemporary of Bar Kappara. His teachings are transmitted primarily by Yoḥanan b. Nappaḥa. He is known primarily for his exegetical interpretations. Later rabbinic tradition preserves many legends about his saintliness.

banaim a term found at M. Mikvaot 9:6, referring to construction workers (from the Hebrew root *bnh*) or, possibly, to bathhouse attendants. In light of the Mishnah's question of the conditions under which mud on these individuals' clothing prevents their purification from ritual uncleanness, scholars have asserted that the reference is to an Essene sect. There is no evidence, however, that the term refers to a sect or is in any way associated with the Essenes in particular. The claimed association is purely conjectural.

bandits (Heb.: *listim*) people involved in prepolitical social protest and disruption that occurs in most traditional agrarian societies. Upper-class writers of antiquity often use the term "bandits" as a pejorative epithet in reference to guerrilla fighters and other rebels, such as the Zealots in Jerusalem in 67–70 C.E. Social disruption such as intermittent warfare, economic hardship, and lax political control or sharp political repression can bring endemic banditry to epidemic proportions, as happened in Palestine before Herod the Great and again as social order disintegrated in the mid-first century C.E. (*War* 2.14.1–2, no. 271–278). Hezekiah in Galilee and Eleazar ben Dinai are among the more famous of the bandit leaders (*War* 1.10.5, no. 204; 2.13.2, no. 253). Biblical stories of the young David, son of Jesse, suggest that he got his start as a bandit chieftain.

banquet, eschatological (or messianic banquet) image used to portray the joys of the end-time, especially in apocalyptic literature and the New Testament. In the ancient Near East the banquet symbolizes joy, often as a celebration of victory; for example, in the Babylonian story of creation, the divine warrior Marduk hosts a great feast to celebrate his victory over the chaos monster Tiamat (Enuma elish 6.69–94). Stories of religious and victory feasts are common in the Hebrew Bible (Exod. 12:43–47, 1 Sam. 9:12–13, 1 Chron. 12:38–40). In Isaiah 54:1–55:2, a prediction of return from exile in Babylon, the imagery of divine marriage (God will take back his rejected wife Israel) is combined with the promise of abundant food. In postexilic prophecy and Jewish apocalyptic texts, the banquet comes to symbolize the blessings expected in the end-time: the restoration of Jerusalem, pilgrimage of the Gentiles, victory over human and suprahuman enemies (including death), resurrection of the dead, final judgment, absence of need, unending joy (Isa. 25:6–8, 1 Enoch 60:7–10, 2 Bar. 29–30). According to 2 Baruch 29 the banquet food will include bountiful fruit, manna, and the two monsters, Leviathan and Behemoth, who were made on the first day of creation. In some apocalyptic texts the eschatological feast is presided over by the messiah (1 Enoch 62:12–14, 2 Bar. 29). Sectarian texts included among the Dead Sea Scrolls look forward to the time when the ordered ranks of the community will sit at table with the royal messiah and the priestly messiah (1QSa 2:11–22); the pure meals of the community in the present time are an anticipation of this great feast (cf. 1QS 6:3–5).

In the New Testament, sayings attributed to Jesus compare the "kingdom of God" (God's eschatological reign) to a wedding banquet (Matt. 22:1–12) and foretell the gathering together of Gentiles with the patriarchs of Israel at the eschatological feast: "I tell you, many will come from east and west and will eat with Abraham and Isaac and Jacob in the kingdom of heaven" (Matt. 8:11). At the Last Supper, Jesus tells his disciples: "I have eagerly desired to eat this passover meal with you before I suffer; for I tell you, I will not eat it again until it is fulfilled in the kingdom of God" (Luke 22:15–16, cf. 22:30, 1 Cor. 11:26). In Revelation 19:6–21, the eschatological banquet is depicted as the wedding feast of Jesus, the Lamb, which will celebrate his victory over all the evil kings of the earth.

Banyas *see* CAESAREA-PHILIPPI

baptism ritual act of religious initiation in which the initiate is immersed in water. The earliest certain example of such initiatory immersion appears to be that associated with John the Baptist. Working in the "wilderness of Judea," John cut the figure of an eschatological prophet who called people to repentance in the face of the imminent divine judgment (Matt. 3:1–12; Mark 1:2–8; Luke 3:1–17; John 1:19–28). The precise function(s) and symbolism of John's baptism are difficult to ascertain, since the New Testament accounts may have been influenced by Christian concerns and viewpoints. Nonetheless, the words ascribed to John in Matthew 3:8–10 and Luke 3:8–9 suggest that he believed that both his baptism and the repentance associated with it were essential to one's identity as an Israelite. Whether his baptism in the Jordan near the wilderness symbolized a new Exodus and new crossing of the Sea or of the Jordan is uncertain. That it symbolized a purification seems likely.

The precise relationship between John's baptism and the purificatory rites alluded to in the Qumran Community Rule (1QS 5:13) is unclear. This passage provides a striking parallel to gospel material about John because it describes a radical conversion associated with one's entry into the "Covenant of God" (1QS 5:7–15), and it emphasizes the need to dissociate oneself from the mass of wicked humanity and to live as God demands. John's call to "bear fruits that are appropriate to repentance" is paralleled by the Qumranic requirement to obey the Torah. It is unclear what the precise relationship is between this complex of ideas and the testimony of Josephus that the Essenes bathed daily before their meals (*War* 2.8.5 sec. 129).

Like John's baptism, the Christian baptism attested in the New Testament is a one-time act that accompanies one's entrance into the religious community. For the apostle Paul, it symbolized and effected participation in the life-giving effects of Jesus' death and resurrection and was closely associated with the imperative to live a righteous life (Rom. 6). Other texts, such as John 3:1–6, Titus 3:5, and 1 Peter 1:22–2:2, associate baptism with rebirth imagery. A connection between baptism and the Holy Spirit runs through the New Testament texts about John's baptism and Christian baptism.

The possible relationship between Qumranic practice, John's baptism, Christian baptism, and Jewish proselyte baptism is disputed. At the very least, proselyte baptism is a one-time initiatory rite by which a non-Israelite "is deemed to be an Israelite in all respects" (B. Yeb̲am. 47b). *See also* BAPTISMAL SECTS; PROSELYTIZATION.

baptismal sects generic term applied to various Jewish and other groups before 70 C.E. who practiced baptism in one form or another. The reasons may have differed considerably from group to group. Thus, one group may have done it mainly as an initiation rite, while others may have practiced it regularly for purification purposes. A number of them seem to have lived in or around the Jordan Valley, where running water was freely available. One of the prime examples seems to have been John the Baptist, who called on all Jews to be baptised as a sign of repentence. This was not clearly an initiation, but more probably purificatory. The Mandaeans claimed John the Baptist as their ancestor, though it is debated whether their origin actually goes back to John. Another baptismal group seems to lie behind the Fourth Sibylline Oracle. The best-known group, however, is the Essenes, who, according to the sources, practiced daily baptism. It is debated whether they are to be identified with the Qumran community or whether the cisterns at Qumran were ritual baths or simply water sources for normal domestic use.

bar *see* BEN

Barabbas (Aram., son of the father; or, in a name, son of Abba) In the gospel stories of Jesus' death, Barabbas is a prisoner jailed for insurrection and for murder (Mark 15:6–14; Matt. 27:15–23; Luke 23:17–23) or a bandit (John 18:40; cf. Mark 14:48) whom the people of Jerusalem chose for release at Passover rather than Jesus of Nazareth. Barabbas fits the profile of social bandits who proliferated in Israel because of dissatisfaction with Roman rule. No other evidence exists for Barabbas or the custom of releasing a prisoner.

baraita a teaching formulated as a Tannaitic rule but not included in the Mishnah, hence "external" to the Mishnah but authoritative

Baraita deSifrei *see* SIFREI ZUTTA

Baris Fortress Jerusalem fortress of Nehemiah's era built near the (then) northwest corner of the Temple Mount. It is mentioned in the Letter of Aristeas in vivid language, so evidently its size and grandeur at the eve of the Hasmonean era impressed the author of that letter. Josephus says, however, that the Baris Fortress was built by the Hasmoneans (*Ant.* 15.11.4, p. 403). In a later passage Josephus says that John Hyrcanus, the high priest, lived at the Baris for a while, so some scholars conclude that the place was also a palace. Herod demolished the Hasmonean Baris and rebuilt it as his own fortress, the Antonia. The only vestige remaining of Herod's building is a water canal cut out of the rock at the northwest corner of the present-day Temple Mount.

Bar Jonah (Aram., son of Jonah) patronymic of Simon, the disciple whom Jesus nicknames "Peter," the "rock" on whom the church is built (Matt. 16:17–18).

Bar Kappara common abbreviation for Eleazar b. Eleazar HaKappar, a Palestinian rabbi active at the beginning of the third century C.E., at the nexus of the Tannaitic and Amoraic periods. A student of Judah the Patriarch, Bar Kappara established the academy at Caesaria, where, along with others, he taught Hoshaya and Joshua b. Levi.

Bar Katra family Jerusalem family of the Second Temple era known from the Talmud and from an archaeological find in Jerusalem. On a stone weight found in the Burnt House in the Jewish Quarter of Jerusalem there appears an Aramaic inscription, "[of] Bar Katros" or "[of] Bar Qatros." The find electrified the excavators, as the name House of Katros is known as one of the aristocratic, high priestly families who aided Rome in their rule of Judea. In the Babylonian Talmud a saying ascribed to Abba Saul b. Batnit in the name of Abba Joseph b. Ḥanin relates the corruption of the house of Katros (Qatros): ". . . woe is me because of the house of Qatros, woe is me because of their libel. . . ." (B. Pesaḥim 57A, IV.7B). The house in question evidently belonged to members of this family in a part of Jerusalem inhabited by aristocrats. Since the house included a workshop of some sort, the excavators concluded that the family manufactured something used in the Temple, perhaps spices, incense, or the like. The large stone vessels found in the house may have been used for ritually pure water for the manufacture of the product.

Bar Kokhba *see* BAR KOSIBA, SIMON

Bar Kokhba Revolt *see* BAR KOSIBA WAR

Bar Kosiba, Simon leader of the Judean Jews who declared their independence from the Roman Empire and fought the Roman forces from 132 to 135 C.E. In Greek and early Christian literature his name is recorded as Bar Kokhba, literally, "son of a star," a messianic nickname based on Numbers 24:17. In rabbinic literature he is called Bar or Ben Kosiba, literally, "son of a lie." This pejorative epithet reflects the rabbinic rejection of Bar Kosiba as the messiah. In documents found in the Judean desert this leader's real name appears in Hebrew, Aramaic, and Greek as Simon Bar (or Ben) Kosiba (spelled variously as *kwsbh, kws'bh,* or *ksbh*). The vowels are given in the Greek transliteration. Nothing is known about Bar Kosiba's origin or life before the revolt.

The place names from documents found in caves in the desert indicate that Bar Kosiba's forces were scattered at various sites adjacent to and in the Judean Desert south of Jerusalem. A number of fortified caves containing living and storage areas have been found in the desert. The coins from this period identify Simon and Eleazar as the leaders of the revolt against Rome. They assign to Simon the title *nasi* (prince, leader) and to Eleazar the title "the priest." The Bar Kosiba coins are dated according to the four years of the Freedom or Redemption of Israel or Jerusalem. They are mostly older coins that have been overstruck. According to the documents from the Judean Desert, Bar Kosiba supervised district officials, ordered the provision and moving of supplies, made preparations for the observance of festivals, rebuked leaders for not fighting, and saw to the collecting of taxes. This information suggests that Bar Kosiba was the leader of a guerrilla-like insurrection against the Romans.

In the Palestinian rabbinic literature, Bar Kosiba is an ambiguous figure who is both admired and condemned. According to the Palestinian Talmud, Rabbi Akiba proclaimed him messiah on the basis of the star from Jacob in Numbers 24:17, but other sages rejected this identification. The historical accuracy of this singular tradition is hard to evaluate. Other Palestinian stories about Bar Kosiba in the Talmud and Midrash Lamentations are clearly legendary and built on the pattern of the biblical hero (*gibbor*). In these legendary stories, Bar Kosiba has suprahuman strength, bravery, and appeal. His soldiers number in the hundreds of thousands and share his bravery. His battles with the Romans take on apocalyptic proportions. At the same time, Palestinian rabbinic literature articulates serious reservations about Bar Kosiba. He is pictured as overconfident in his own powers, arrogant in rejecting divine help, and misled in killing

Eleazar of Modiin. These defects bring about his defeat. The sages subtly imply that they, and not a messianic hero, are the proper leaders of Israel.

The Babylonian Talmud is more negative than Palestinian sources. The Bar Kosiba materials are merged with other stories about war, so that the connection of the Bar Kosiba stories with concrete historical events is lost. Bar Kosiba is consistently treated as a false messiah who misled Israel, and his stature as a hero is undermined. *See also* BAR KOSIBA WAR; ELEAZAR THE PRIEST.

Bar Kosiba War insurrection against Roman rule in Judea in 132–135 C.E., led by Simon Bar Kosiba. Roman, Christian, and rabbinic sources, along with archaeological finds and documents from the Judean desert, provide meager evidence for this conflict and often contradict one another. The rabbinic stories about Bar Kosiba and the war are exaggerated, heroic legends. Attitudes toward the war and its leader range from grudging admiration to critical rejection of Bar Kosiba as a false messiah. The Roman historian Dio Cassius has the most reliable account of the war, but his work needs careful interpretation as well. The later Historia Augusta is generally unreliable. Brief notices by Christian writers, especially Eusebius, contain some information that is hard to evaluate. Archaeological remains, coins of the revolt, some inscriptions, and the documents recently discovered in Judean caves provide reliable but sparse evidence about Bar Kosiba and his period.

The social and political context and causes of the war are much disputed and uncertain. One historical stimulus for popular unrest stands out. When Roman emperor Hadrian (r. 117–138 C.E.) toured the eastern Roman Empire in 129–131 C.E., he decreed the foundation or restoration of many cities, temples, and other civic institutions. Thus in 130, he probably announced the foundation of the city Aelia Capitolina and a temple to Jupiter Capitolinus to be built on the ruins of Jerusalem. (The story that Hadrian gave and then withdrew permission for the rebuilding of the Jewish Temple is almost certainly legendary.) Since he did not fund the restoration, building was probably not begun until after the war. Just the promise of Hadrian's grand scheme of restoration probably aroused opposition and resentment in Judea. A second imperial decree may have aggravated Jewish–Roman relations. At some point during his rule Hadrian strengthened the Roman laws against castration and included circumcision under the ban. This law was directed against a variety of peoples and groups in the East who practiced circumcision, such as Nabatean Arabs and Egyptian priests, not against Jews specifically. If this decree preceded the war, it might have been perceived as a hostile act. The date of this decree, however, is uncertain; it may have followed the war. In general a decades-long undercurrent of political and social unrest, and perhaps apocalyptic expectation, probably provided energy for an armed protest against Roman rule. The assignment of a second Roman legion to the area after 120 and extensive Roman road building in 120–130 suggest that the Romans anticipated trouble.

Traditional stories about the war have stressed its duration, wide scope, and ferocity. Myriads of troops are pictured in apocalyptic battles. In reality, Simon Bar Kosiba commanded a scattered guerrilla-like force based in towns and hidden, fortified caves in the Judean desert south of Jerusalem. Though nothing is known about his origin or personal history before the war, he was probably a local charismatic leader who mobilized built-up resentments and led his followers into the traditional refuge of dissidents, the Judean desert. Caves and lookouts found in the hills above the Dead Sea at Wadi Murabbaat, Nahal Hever, and elsewhere contained documents, coins, clothing, personal items, pottery, and weapons. Complexes of caves with interconnected rooms, ventilation shafts, alcoves for lamps and storage areas have been found in the hills west of Hebron. These finds suggest that small groups, sometimes including women and children, hid from the Romans and lived daily life in the desert. The places found in the Bar Kosiba documents are located in Judea. Later claims that Galilee and the rest of the country were involved in the revolt are ill founded.

Letters indicate that Simon Bar Kosiba appointed and supervised regional officials, maintained order and gathered supplies and taxes. Rebukes of various people for not sending fighters or supplies testify to less than total support for Bar Kosiba's struggle. He seems to have controlled some towns at the edge of the desert but not major population centers. Bar Kosiba minted his own coins by overstriking older ones. The coins depict the facade of the Temple, the lulab and etrog, palm branch, grapes, trumpets, and harp. They are dated by the four years of the war and refer to either the redemption or the liberation of Israel or Jerusalem. Whether Bar Kosiba captured Jerusalem is debatable. The coin inscriptions which refer to Jerusalem mostly say, "For the freedom of Jerusalem," perhaps voicing a hope rather than a reality. The tenth legion of the Roman army garrisoned the ruins of Jerusalem, defended by Herod's three towers and some of the western city walls. A siege of the Roman camp would probably have taken more time and forces than Bar Kosiba had available. Even if captured, the devastated site of Jerusalem would have been militarily indefensible and unimportant even though it was of great symbolic importance.

The coins and documents found in the desert caves name two leaders of the revolt: Simon who was called *nasi,* a biblical title meaning tribal chief, popularly accepted leader, or something like prince, and Eleazar, "the priest." Eleazar's title suggests priestly leadership analogous to that of the high priest while the Temple stood. Nothing else is known about him and the sources contain no explicit claim that he was high priest. Suggested identifications of this figure with Eleazar of Modiin or Eleazar ben Azariah are unlikely. Simon's title is a biblical designation for a tribal chief or royal leader. The Palestinian Talmud Taanit (4:8, p. 68d) claims that Rabbi Akiba declared Bar Kosiba to be Bar Kokhba, that is, son of a star. This expression is found in Balaam's blessing of Israel in Numbers 24:17 and was later given messianic meaning. Akiba's view was opposed by Rabbi Joḥanan ben Torta and by subsequent Talmudic tradition. Despite this testimony, there is no other evidence that Bar Kosiba claimed to be or was looked upon as the messiah. Hypotheses that Akiba was a leader for the revolt and that his earlier travels aimed to gather support for it have no support in the sources.

The surviving evidence does not give a detailed account of the war. When the war broke out, Tineius Rufus was the Roman governor of Judea. Since he and his two legions were initially unable to suppress the hostilities, reinforcements, probably consisting of parts of other legions and auxilliary units, were brought in from surrounding jurisdictions. Rufus fought a large number of small military actions against scattered groups of Jewish fighters over a long period. The hypothesis that the twenty-second legion was wiped out in the war is based on a misunderstanding of the Roman sources. It had probably been disbanded by 123 C.E. At some point Julius Severus, an experienced and successful Hadrianic general, was reassigned from Britain to Palestine. Though he is usually thought to have come early in the war to deal with a crisis Rufus could not handle, a newly discovered inscription suggests that he arrived to take over the governorship only in 135 C.E. when the war was ending. This would be consistent with rabbinic sources that refer to Rufus as the Roman general in the war.

The Roman historian Dio Cassius claims that 580,000 Jews were slain in battle, more died of starvation and disease, and that over a thousand villages and outposts were destroyed. Rabbinic sources put 200,000 Jewish defenders in the final battle for Betar along with hundreds of children from the five hundred schools of Betar. These numbers are highly exaggerated and the stories are legendary. Lamentations Rabbah 2:2 collects Bar Kosiba stories with a number of others, all of which contain very large, unrealistic numbers. Decriptions of rivers of blood and numerous corpses are drawn from apocalyptic imagery. These stories attempt to give the conflict heroic proportions.

Though Dio may be correct that the Romans suffered many losses, they did so little by little. Bar Kosiba's followers were dispersed and, as Roman writings testify, difficult to find and dislodge. A Roman camp on the ledge above a cave under attack and the forty skeletons found in the so-called Cave of Horrors, all near the Dead Sea, suggest that siege and starvation of small groups rather than great battles characterized the three-and-a-half years of the war. Bar Kosiba and his followers were finally flushed out of the desert and killed in a siege of the hilltop town of Betar (Khirbet el-Yahud), six or seven miles southwest of Jerusalem, in 135. The outline of the walls and towers of the town can still be seen, though the site has not been excavated.

After the war the Hadrianic city, Aelia Capitolina, was built on the ruins of Jerusalem and Jews were forbidden to live there. Rabbinic literature reports that the Jewish practices of circumcision, Sabbath observance, and teaching of Torah were forbidden until the reign of Hadrian's successor, Antoninus Pius (138–161). The name Judea was eliminated in order to suppress the Jews' connection with the land. The Roman province was named Syria Palestina. Palestine was derived from the Greek Palaistina, which was in turn derived from the Hebrew Pleshet, meaning Philistia or Land of the Philistines. Archeological surveys and digs show that Judea was not totally devastated or depopulated of Jews, contrary to reports in some Roman and rabbinic literature. The rabbis, however, who emerged as community leaders in the third through fifth centuries, had their center in Galilee. After the Bar Kosiba War, the Jewish people as a whole did not again rise up in political revolt against the Roman Empire.

Rabbinic literature speaks admiringly of the martyrdoms of Rabbi Akiba and other sages during the Bar Kosiba War. In the Palestinian Talmud and Lamentations, however, Rabbah Bar Kosiba and the war are treated ambiguously. Bar Kosiba is called Bar Koziba, the Liar, because he is judged a false messiah. Yet heroic stories paint him and his men as larger than life and similar to biblical heroes. The rabbis grudgingly acknowledge Bar Kosiba but are quick to criticize his arrogance and failure to assert their authority as community leaders. The authors of the Babylonian Talmud, removed from the historical context, mingled the stories about Bar Kosiba with those of other conflicts and with reflections concerning the end of the world. The Babylonian Talmud's attitude toward Bar Kosiba and the war is universally negative. *See also* BAR KOSIBA, SIMON; BETAR, SIEGE OF.

bar mitzvah (Heb., responsible adult) one who is competent to carry out religious duties; later, a ceremony at which a thirteen-year-old boy becomes an adult member of the Jewish community; an adult male Jew who is obligated to carry out the commandments (Heb.: *mitzvah/mitzvot*)

Barnabas, Letter of pseudonymous anti-Jewish treatise written by a Christian in the late first or early second century C.E., either in Alexandria or Syria. It is attributed to the apostle Barnabas (Acts 4:36) and thus is collected with the writings known as the Apostolic Fathers. The text of the Letter of Barnabas is copied in Codex Sinaiticus right after the New Testament books and was treated as canonical by Origen and some other early authors. Barnabas claims that Israel lost the covenant permanently when they worshiped the golden calf (Exod. 32) and that the covenant properly belongs to Christians. He teaches that the biblical laws were never meant to be taken literally and gives them symbolic interpretations. Washings are connected with baptism, circumcision and the Temple with the heart, dietary rules with ethics, and sacrifices with salvation through Jesus' death. Many of the themes of Barnabas were taken up in later Christian polemics against Judaism.

Bar Nappaḥa *see* YOḤANAN B. NAPPAḤA

Bar Pedayah *see* JUDAH B. PEDAIAH

barrenness Occasionally viewed as divine punishment (Gen. 20:18), the inability to conceive may be cured through prayer and divine favor. In such cases, the children are often destined for greatness. Women depicted as initially infertile, but not because of any explicit wrongdoing on their part or by their husbands, include: Sarah; Rebecca; Rachel; Samson's mother; Hannah; the Great Woman of Shunem (2 Kings 4:8–37); and Elizabeth, the mother of John the Baptist (Luke 1). Less frequent are considerations of male infertility (the discussion between Manoah and Eluma in LAB 42; perhaps Gen. 15:2). *See also* FERTILITY.

barren woman (Heb.: *aylonit*) woman incapable of conceiving a child. M. Niddah 5:9 gives as evidence of this status the fact that the woman has reached the age of twenty without producing a minimum of two pubic hairs. Such a woman is not subject to levirate marriage, intended solely to produce a child to carry on her deceased husband's name. The term *aylonit* derives from the Hebrew *ayil* and means "ram-like."

Bar-Sanidora Kilat Nimrod, at the foot of Mount Hermon, referred to at T. Shebiit 4:11 as demarcating a border area of the Land of Israel

Bar Sauma (c. 415–496 C.E.) bishop in the city of Nisibis in the Sassanid (Neo-Persian) Empire (in present-day eastern Turkey). He was educated at a Nestorian Christian school in nearby Edessa and became bishop of Nisibis when driven out of Edessa in 457. He engaged in extensive and effective missionary activity on behalf of Nestorian Christianity and gained a reputation as a persuasive and brutal advocate. He persuaded the Sassanid king Peroz to banish the opposing Monophysite Christians. His writings were mainly liturgical, but in reports of his missionary journeys he reflects some of the interfaith tensions among Jews, Samaritans, and the relatively few Christians. Although Byzantine leaders had forbidden anti-Semitism, Bar Sauma witnessed some of the continuing clashes. He claimed that Christians, rather than Jews or Samaritans, were persecuted.

Bar Timaeus (Aram.: son of Timaeus) patronymic of the blind man of Jericho healed by Jesus (Mark 10:46)

Baruch scribe in Jerusalem at the time of the Babylonian destruction of the city; friend of Jeremiah. Jeremiah dictated a scroll to him, which King Jehoiakim burned (Jer. 36) and Baruch subsequently rewrote. Scholars attribute at least the beginnings of the historical accounts in Jeremiah to Baruch.

Four later books were ascribed to Baruch, all of which reflect on the loss of Jerusalem and the Temple. The apocryphal Baruch claims to have been read by Baruch to the Babylonian exiles (1:1–14). It includes a penitential prayer, a wisdom poem, and a Zion poem. The other three books actually concern the loss of the Second Temple, but use the fictive setting of the Babylonian destruction. Baruch is the main character in 2

Baruch, where he engages in a dialogue with God about the problems of theodicy raised by the destruction. In 3 Baruch, he is a seer who tours the heavens to receive revelation. In 4 Baruch (Paraleipomena of Jeremiah) he plays a role subordinate to that of Jeremiah. *See also* 1 BARUCH; 2 BARUCH; 3 BARUCH; JEREMIAH, PARALEIPOMENA OF.

1 Baruch (Book of Baruch, Apocryphal Baruch) the first of several literary works attributed to the secretary of Jeremiah. This composite text of mixed genre (narrative, prayer, and exhortative discourse) and style (prose and poetry) was compiled from traditional materials, some of which may have been composed in Hebrew. A date after the persecution by Antiochus IV Epiphanes (c. 164 B.C.E.) may be indicated by the emphasis on repentance and restoration and by similarities to texts from this time which focus on the exile and the capture of the Temple vessels. Baruch came to be included in the Greek Bible, where it stands before the Book of Jeremiah.

The four sections of Baruch are bound together by the theme of exile and return, which is embodied in biblical idiom and imagery. The narrative begins with the people in Babylonian exile and concludes with a strong affirmation that they will return. The narrative introduction (1:1–14) leads to a pair of penitential prayers in which the people in Jerusalem and Babylon respectively confess their sins and ask God to withdraw the divine wrath that sent them into exile (1:15–2:5, 2:6–3:8). The logic of the prayers follows the scheme of Deuteronomy 28–30 and 32, and the influence of Deuteronomic and Jeremianic language is immediately evident. Verbal parallels between the first prayer and Daniel 9:4–19 indicate a close relationship between these two exemplars of a traditional liturgical genre. The prayers lead into a poem about the finding of wisdom, which is identified with the Torah (Bar. 3:9–4:4). Human searches for wisdom have been fruitless (cf. Job 28), but adherence to the "book of God's commandments" will deliver Israel from the death of exile (cf. Ezek. 37). A close connection with Ecclesiasticus 24 is evident, although the present texts lacks Ben Sira's explicit personification of wisdom. The book concludes with a poetic section in the idiom of Second and Third Isaiah (Bar. 4:5–5:9). Mother Zion appeals to her children to take heart because their return to the land is a certain consequence of their repentance, and the author addresses Jerusalem in a set of strophes that closely parallel the poem in Psalms of Solomon 11.

The Book of Baruch is a remarkable example of how, in the second century B.C.E., Deuteronomic and prophetic texts that had already been reshaped and embodied in anonymous traditions, such as prayers and poems, were compiled and recast into texts that spoke to new situations in the pseudonymous voice of an ancient Israelite scribe.

2 Baruch apocalypse written in response to the destruction of the Second Temple by the Romans in 70 C.E.; also called the Syriac Apocalypse of Baruch. It is eighty-seven chapters long, and makes extensive use of traditional materials, which it adapts to its own purposes. The main witness to the work is a single Syriac manuscript dating from the sixth or seventh century. The Syriac was translated from a Greek version (two short passages are preserved in P. Oxy. 403). The Greek is probably a translation of a Hebrew original. An Arabic version has been discovered recently, but it is a free translation from another Syriac manuscript and is influenced by Islam. The apocalypse dates from around the turn of the second century B.C.E. and is from Palestine.

Baruch was secretary to the prophet Jeremiah, who flourished just before the destruction of the Jerusalem Temple by the Babylonians in 587 B.C.E. That event became a paradigm through which to interpret the destruction of the Second Temple (as in 4 Ezra; see also Rev., in which Babylon is a cipher for Rome). Remarkably, Baruch is the main character and Jeremiah plays a minor role in 2 Baruch.

The book consists of seven sections. In the first section (chaps. 1–9), God tells Baruch that Jerusalem is to be destroyed because of Israel's sins and instructs Baruch and Jeremiah to leave the city because their deeds and prayers protect it. Baruch, distressed at God's revelation, asks whether the impending destruction means the end of Israel, forgetfulness of God's deeds, the annihilation of the universe, the passing of humanity, and the annulment of God's promises to Israel. God explains that Israel's punishment is temporary. God says that the earthly Jerusalem is but a shadow of the heavenly one. Baruch objects that the Gentiles will boast about their destruction of the city but is told that God will destroy it. Angels destroy the city after the sacred objects are removed, and God departs. The first section ends with the lamentation of Baruch and Jeremiah.

Sections 2 through 6 (comprising chaps. 10–20, 21–34, 35:1–47:1, 47:2–52:7, and 53:1–77:17, respectively) contain prayers of Baruch, visions, dialogues, revelations, and Baruch's addresses to the people, through which he conveys the essence of what he learns from God. The content of the sections is as follows. Israel has lost everything except God and Torah. Israel's distress is a chastisement for its sins, but the future age will see the righteous elevated to the heavenly realms, and the Gentiles will receive their punishment. Although Israel has lost its leaders, the Torah itself will engender leaders. The concept of free will is defended. The present world is corruptible and full of evils, but the future world is incorruptible. The end is near, but cannot come before its time. History is periodized and consists of alternating good and bad periods. A messianic age, in which Israel's enemies are conquered and judged, will precede the future world. The middle sections end with Baruch's exhortation to obey Torah, an exhortation reminiscent of Moses' speeches in Deuteronomy.

Section 7 (77:18–87:1) is Baruch's letter to the nine and a half tribes exiled by the Assyrians. It repeats much of what is found earlier in the apocalypse. The letter exists in multiple copies apart from the apocalypse, and some have suggested that it was not an original part of 2 Baruch. However, most scholars see it as integral to the work.

2 Baruch addresses Jews living after the destruction of Jerusalem in 70 C.E. It defends God's righteousness in the face of Jerusalem's destruction, consoles Israel with the thought of a future judgment, and encourages obedience to Torah. It advocates rebuilding Judaism on the basis of the Torah.

3 Baruch (Greek Apocalypse of Baruch) a pseudonymous text in which Jeremiah's secretary recounts his journey through the five heavens. Although it claims to be set in the time of the Babylonian exile, 3 Baruch was composed toward the end of the first century C.E., in response to the Roman destruction of Jerusalem. Egypt was very possibly the place of its composition, and it is preserved in Greek, the language of its composition, and in a Slavonic version.

Paralleling the "story line" in both 1 Baruch and 2 Baruch, the text begins with the seer's grief over Israel's defeat by the Babylonians, and it concludes as he gives praise to God. This change in attitude is facilitated by the assurance of God's justice, which is conveyed to the reader in traditional apocalyptic form, as "Baruch" recounts in the first person how an angel guided him to places of eschatological import and explained the workings of God's justice. Of special importance is a long description of the mediatorial activity of the angel Michael, who gathers the virtues of the righteous in a gigantic vessel and brings them to God's throne in the fifth heaven.

Baruch's cosmology differs from that in 1 Enoch and agrees with 2 Enoch in that it locates the places of punishment and reward in the various levels of the five heavens rather than at the outer edges of the earth's disk. Similarly, his eschatology is not oriented to a future cosmic resolution of present evils, but envisions individuals receiving their reward or punishment immediately after death.

Although the author's authority is asserted in the claim of revelation inherent in the apocalyptic genre, the text also deals with the problem of divine justice by reference to scripture, specifically Deuteronomy 32:21, 30. In 1:2, Baruch asks God, "Why have you not requited us with another punishment, but rather delivered us to nations such as these?" The answer in 16:2–4—in a virtual quotation of Deuteronomy 32:21—is that the destruction of Jerusalem and the scattering of the people are punishment for their sins.

At many points 3 Baruch reflects concerns and traditions that also appear in contemporary Jewish texts such as 2 Baruch, 2 Esdras, and the Book of Biblical Antiquities. On the other hand, at some point in its transmission, the apocalypse acquired a clear Christian interpolation at 4:15. The cursed vine that caused Adam's sin will be turned to blessing when its fruit becomes "the blood of God . . . Jesus Christ Emmanuel."

4 Baruch *see* JEREMIAH, PARALEIPOMENA OF

Bassus, Gaius Julius Quadratus legate of Judaea (102/3–104/5 C.E.). An inscription from his native Pergamum indicates that he held a post in Crete and Cyrenaica before he was governor of Judaea. He fought in the Second Dacian War and was legate of Galatia-Cappadocia, Syria, in 114–116, and then in Dacia.

Bassus, Marcus Aemilius procurator of Judea. His exact dates are unknown, but a date in the middle of Hadrian's reign as emperor (117–139 C.E.) seems likely. Bassus was procurator in Bithynia and in Egypt before he was assigned to Judaea. The name "Judaea" implies that he served before 135 C.E.

Bassus, Sextus Lucilius legate of Palestine (71–72/73 C.E.). During the revolt against Rome, Bassus captured the Jewish strongholds of Herodian and Machaeros. To conquer the latter, Bassus's men filled in a large ravine to gain access to its lower slope. He eventually captured those who fled Machaeros in "the forest of Jardes," as yet unidentified.

bastard *see* MAMZER

bath unit of fluid measure in ancient Israel, from the Hebrew word *bat* (the resemblance to the English word "bath" is sheer coincidence). As with most weights and measures of the time, it was not standardized; however, archaeological findings indicate that it would have been roughly 5½ gallons, or about 20 liters.

bat kol (Heb.) in rabbinic literature, a heavenly or divine voice that conveys God's judgment or will to individuals or groups; literally, "daughter of a voice," usually in the sense of a small voice or sound. The term frequently is translated as "echo"; Exodus Rabbah 39, however, states that, unlike a person's voice, the voice that proceeds from God has no *bat kol,* suggesting that this rendering is not accurate.

In scripture and the rabbinical literature, heavenly speech occurs frequently and often is designated simply by the term *kol* (voice). Daniel 4:28 is paradigmatic, referring to a voice that "fell from heaven." This and similar explicit references to a voice from heaven apparently stand behind the historically later, concise usage of *bat kol,* which always refers to a voice the heavenly origin of which is assumed but not explicitly stated.

The *bat kol* derives from an invisible source and is characterized by its remarkable tonal quality. It sometimes is portrayed as powerful—a *bat kol* reportedly rang throughout the Israelite camp to proclaim Moses' death (B. Sotah 13b)—but generally is perceived as a quiet sound. After praying along the road in a ruin, the Tannaitic authority Yose reportedly was confronted by Elijah, who asked what sound Yose had heard. Yose reports that he heard a *bat kol* that "murmured like a dove" (B. Berakhot 3a). Similarly, Elisha b. Abuyah heard a chirping voice behind the Temple (Eccles. Rabbah 7:8).

In rabbinic history, the heavenly voice served an important political function, proclaiming, for instance, that the law follows the views of the House of Hillel (Y. Yebamot 6:6) and reporting that, among their entire generations, Hillel and his student Samuel the Small were worthy to receive the Holy Spirit (T. Sotah 13:3–4). In these passages, the *bat kol* indicates God's concurrence with the emerging rabbinic power structure.

At the same time, the rabbis explicitly deny God's right to use the *bat kol* or other methods to intervene in earthly deliberations and legislative activities. When God attempts to intercede in a dispute between Eliezer and Joshua, first by disrupting the natural order and then by stating through a *bat kol* that the law follows Eliezer (Baba Metzia 59a–b), Joshua responds that such decisions are in the hands of the rabbis alone, a position that God is reported to accept. Accordingly, despite the understanding that God could speak in human terms, the rabbis assigned to themselves complete control over determination of proper Israelite practice and behavior.

batlan (Heb., idle person) The term may connote a loafer, but it is most often used as an honorific title for one employed only in the service of the community and the synagogue.

Batra a probable synagogue site and ancient village in the Golan Heights, 4 kilometers east of Bethsaida-Julias. A modern village stands here on the foundations of an ancient village located on a steep slope with the synagogue at the top of the site, virtually on a cliff. The synagogue was about 10 by 12.9 meters in size and faced roughly southwest. Many of the architectural fragments of the synagogue were in reuse in the houses of the modern village. For example, there were fragments of cornices, a Doric capital, an Ionic capital, as well as fragments of a lintel stone depicting a wreath in the center with a Hercules knot (square knot) at its base. The ends of the knot evolve into vines with rosettes and leaves. An additional capital depicts an amphora in low relief with a vine branch emerging from it. This capital also depicts acanthus leaves and a bird. It is possible that the building dates to the third century C.E.

Bavli *see* BABLI

B.C. abbreviation for "Before Christ," used in the Christian calendar to designate the years before the nominal year of Jesus Christ's birth; *see also* B.C.E.

B.C.E. abbreviation for "Before the Common Era." This alternative terminology is often used instead of "B.C." in non-Christian contexts.

beard and shaving The rabbis considered one's beard a symbol of manhood. Leviticus prohibits removing the side locks and shaving the beard. Rabbinic authorities prohibited close shaving with a straight edge under all circumstances and any shaving during the periods of mourning after the death of a close relative, between Passover and Shebuot, or during the three weeks preceding the Ninth of Ab.

beatitude literary form that declares a person to be blessed or fortunate. Attested forty-three times in the Hebrew Bible, mainly in the wisdom literature, beatitudes begin with a stereotyped formula, "Blessed is the man (*or* those, *or* you) who . . . ," that is followed by a description of the conduct, quality, or situation that is cause for the beatitude: "Blessed is he whose transgression is forgiven, whose sin is covered" (Ps. 32:1). Second Temple Jewish literature and the New Testament reflect a tendency to declare persons blessed or fortunate because their quality, actions, or situation will effect something good in the future: "Then blessed will be all who listen to the words of the wise, and learn to do the commandments of the Most High . . . , for they will be saved" (1 Enoch 99:10). Often these beatitudes have an eschatological tone; those who are pious and righteous now will be blessed when God acts in the near future. Some of these beatitudes paradoxically declare those who are presently deprived to be fortunate because their situation will be reversed: "Blessed are you poor, for yours is the kingdom of God; Blessed are you who hunger now, for you shall be satisfied" (Luke 6:20, 21). Matthew's version of some of Jesus' beatitudes spiritualizes the more original version in Luke: "Blessed are the poor *in spirit,* for theirs is the kingdom of God; Blessed are those who hunger and thirst *for righteousness,* for they shall be satisfied (Matt. 5:3, 6). *See also* ESCHATOLOGY; WOES.

Bebai **1.** Palestinian amora of the third century C.E. He studied under Yoḥanan, Resh Lakish, and others, and was a close associate of Ammi and Assi. He spoke of his own poverty.

2. Babylonian amora of the fourth century C.E. He studied under Naḥman. Joseph placed him in charge of religious affairs in his city (B. Kiddushin 76b).

Bebai b. Abayye **1.** Babylonian amora of the fourth century C.E. He studied under his father, head of the academy at Pumbedita, and Joseph. He was a successful farmer (B. Ba<u>b</u>a Metzia 109a). B. Ḥagigah 4b–5a relates that he was visited frequently by the angel of death, who disclosed to him the secrets of the other world.

2. Palestinian amora of the mid-fourth century C.E.; a contemporary of Naḥman b. Isaac, Pappai, and Ḥuna b. Joshua. As a descendant of the house of Eli, Bebai b. Abayye was assumed to be short-lived (B. Rosh Hashanah 18a). Pappai taunted him about this, claiming that, like his health, Bebai's teachings were frail (B. Eru<u>b</u>in 25b).

Be-Dura *see* DORA

Beelzebul "the prince of the demons," according to Matthew 12:24–27, Mark 3:22–26, and Luke 11:15–19. The derivation is disputed. The manuscript variant, Greek *beelzebub,* suggests an identification with *baal zebub* (Heb., lord of flies), the deity of the Philistine city of Ekron (2 Kings 1:2, 3, 6, 16). More likely, Beelzebul reflects the Semitic *zbl* (lord/exalted one; or [exalted] abode, i.e., heaven). The latter option may reflect an identification of the chief of the evil spirits with Baal Shamayim, whose worship was installed in the Temple by Antiochus IV. Such a meaning is suggested in Matthew 10:25, where "master of the house" (Gr.: *oikodespotēs*) seems to be a translation of Beelzebul. The references to "house" in Mark 3:22–27, Matthew 12:22–45, and Luke 11:15–26 could indicate a wordplay on this meaning.

Beer Sheba known as Barsaba in the Roman period; lies east of the modern city in the northern Negeb. In the early seventh century B.C.E., there were attempts to rebuild the destroyed biblical city, but it lay unoccupied until about 400 B.C.E. when a Persian period fortress appeared at the site. Forty-five ostraca, that is, potsherds with texts written on them in ink, were found in pits around the fortress. The ostraca were apparently records of wheat and barley storage. They contain dates that correspond to the years from 359 to 338 B.C.E. The names on the ostraca are Jewish, Edomite, and Arab. The pits are likely for grain storage and attest to the general fertility of the region. The Persian fortress went out of use in the fourth century B.C.E. and was succeeded by a Hellenistic fortress and a temple. The temple is rectangular, about 11.5 by 24.9 meters in extent. It is comprised of a large, unroofed courtyard with one large room across the width of the building at its east end and with three small rooms at the southwest corner of the courtyard. A stone block about 2.1 meters square stands near the center of the courtyard and evidently forms an altar. The excavator interprets the whole as a sanctuary originally used for the worship of several minor deities (such as the Egyptian Thoth, the Nabatean Delphinos, the Greek Demeter and Persephone, and others). Seven small incense altars were found from this period. During the religious reforms of King John Hyrcanus I of Israel (135–104 B.C.E.) the sanctuary was converted to the worship of Yahweh. During this time no figurines were to be found, as they were buried in pits beneath the floor. In this renovation the central altar was erected. By the 60s B.C.E. the temple was abandoned. Shortly afterward, in the Roman period, Barsaba was the site of a Roman fort that was in use until the third century C.E. The excavators found no remains of the Byzantine period.

begging not acknowledged in most of the Tanakh on the assumption that its welfare system made such poverty unlikely. Rabbinic sources encourage itinerants to seek aid from a centralized village fund or kitchen rather than door-to-door. Poor women were the first to receive assistance to avoid the humiliation of seeking aid in the street.

Behemoth (from Heb.: *behemah,* beast) mythological land monster, often paired with the sea monster Leviathan. Behemoth and Leviathan originated in ancient Near Eastern myths, where creation resulted from the conquest of monsters of chaos. In Job 40:15–24 the might of Behemoth, which God created, is used to emphasize God's greatness. Leviathan is used similarly in Job 41. 2 Baruch 29:4 and 4 Ezra 6:49–51 attest to a tradition that the two beasts were created on the fifth day when water creatures were made (Gen. 1:20–23) and that they will be eaten at the eschatological banquet. 1 Enoch 60:7–10 adds that Leviathan is female and Behemoth is male. Revelation 13 uses the two monsters, without naming them, to represent cosmic evil forces supporting the Roman Empire.

beit am (Heb.) house of the people; early word for synagogue

beit din *see* COURT

beit haMikdash (Heb.) house of the sanctuary; *see also* SANCTUARY

Beit Hillel *see* HILLEL AND SHAMMAI, HOUSES OF

beit kenesset (Heb.) house of assembly; sometimes, synagogue; *see also* SYNAGOGUE

beit midrash *see* SCHOOL

Beit Shammai *see* HILLEL AND SHAMMAI, HOUSES OF

bekor *see* FIRSTBORN

Bekorot Mishnah tractate devoted to rules on the firstborn. The firstborn son of a man is to be redeemed for five shekels (Num. 18:16); the firstborn of a clean beast, for example, of a flock or herd, is to be given to the priest; and the firstborn of an unclean beast, for example, of an ass (Exod. 13:13), is to be redeemed in exchange for a lamb or destroyed. The firstborn of an ass is discussed in chapter 1; the firstborn of clean cattle is discussed in chapters 2 through 7; and the firstborn of a man is discussed in chapter 8.

Issues raised are secondary to the scriptural laws on the same subject, for example, the status of an unborn offspring of the ass of a Gentile that was purchased by an Israelite, a cow that bore an offspring resembling an ass, and other matters that are subject to doubt. Since a firstling beast may be slaughtered when it is blemished, the process of examining the firstling, the blemishes taken into account, and the like, are set forth. The firstborn son of a man may or may not receive the inheritance of the firstborn. The rules on tithing cattle are set forth in chapter 9, stipulating that the tithe is given both in the Holy Land and abroad and prescribing the extent of the herd that is tithed and how the tithing is carried out. The Talmud of Babylonia (Bab̲li) provides a commentary to this tractate.

Bel and the Dragon an entertaining tale about Daniel's battle with idolatry in Babylon, which is one of several expansions in the Greek version of the Book of Daniel that form part of the Apocrypha. The original language of the story is uncertain. As to its date, it appears to be typologically later than the tales in Daniel 1–6, whose style and general theme it imitates. Pointing in this direction are the complexity of its plot, the identification of Daniel's opponents as Babylonians rather than the courtiers typical in such stories, the additional legendary features in the episode about the lion's den, and the explicit conversion of the monarch ("the king has become a Jew," v. 28). The story may have been composed to supplement the tales about the kings Nebuchadnezzar, Belshazzar, and Darius, by describing the conversion of Cyrus, the last of Daniel's overlords (cf. Dan. 6:28, 10:1). Bel and the Dragon is inserted in manuscripts of the Greek Bible at the end of the Book of Daniel and is counted as chapter 13.

The story comprises two related episodes about Daniel. In the first he exposes the fraud of the priests of Bel, who eat the food they say the god consumes. In the second Daniel feeds a sacred dragon (or snake) cakes made of pitch, fat, and hair, which cause the beast to explode. The two stories are interwoven into a single plot that reaches its climax with Cyrus's conversion from idolatry and the destruction of Daniel's Babylonian enemies. Different from the other Daniel stories, Bel and the Dragon focuses exclusively on the antagonism between the living God (with his protagonist Daniel) and the idols and their Babylonian advocates, the priests, the king at first, and the people in general.

The story as a whole, with its reference to the destruction of Bel and Cyrus's acclamation of the God of Israel as the only God, appears to be a narrativizing interpretation of Isaiah 45–46. There YHWH addresses Cyrus his anointed, who does not know him but will come to know him (45:1, 3). The polemic against idols in Isaiah 46 begins with the words, "Bel has fallen" (v. 1, LXX). The story's mocking, satirical tone is typical of biblical and early Jewish critiques of idolatry (Isa. 44:9–20; Letter of Jeremiah; Apoc. Abr. 1–8), and the author's humorous contrast between the idolaters' stupidity and Daniel's wisdom parallels the theological juxtaposition of Torah as wisdom and idolatry as folly.

Belial (Gr.: Beliar) common name for the chief of the evil spirits. The word *beliyaal* in the Hebrew Bible has usually been derived from *beli* (without) and *yaal* (worth). The rabbis applied it to those who cast off the yoke of the Torah (*beli yol,* without the yoke, B. Sanh. 111b). Most likely, however, it comes from *bl* (swallow) and reflects the notion of Death (the god Mot) or Sheol as the Swallower (Isa. 25:8; cf. Psalm 18:4–5) and the parallelism of death, Belial, and Sheol.

This mythic background reemerges in the Graeco-Roman period; the old god, Death, becomes the chief evil spirit, who leads people to destruction. The name occurs primarily in the Qumran literature (1QS, 1QH, 1QM, CD), the Testaments of the Twelve Patriarchs, the Ascension of Isaiah, and occasionally Jubilees, where Mastema predominates. Belial stands in opposition to God or God's chief angel, rules over a horde of spirits, and specializes in prompting humans to sin.

Beliar *see* BELIAL

bemah *see* BIMAH

ben (Heb.) son of; equivalent to the Aramaic *bar*

Ben Azzai *see* SIMEON B. AZZAI

Ben Bag Bag rabbinic authority of the first century C.E. He is known for the dictum (referring to the Torah): "Turn it and turn it, for everything is in it, and reflect upon it and grow gray and worn over it, and do not leave it, for you have no better lot than this" (M. Abot 5:22). Some identify him with Yoḥanan b. Bag Bag, mentioned at T. Ketubot 5:1.

Ben Bukri Tannaitic authority of the period of Yavneh (1st c. C.E.). He is referred to at M. Shekalim 1:4 as in dispute with Yoḥanan b. Zakkai over whether or not a priest validly may pay the annual shekel due to the sanctuary.

Ben Drosa individual known in talmudic times for consuming partially cooked food (B. Shabbat 20a; Y. Shabbat 1:5, 4a); also referred to as Ben Drosai. Food cooked sufficiently for Ben Drosa to eat became the standard for what was deemed fully cooked under talmudic law. Such food, if left in the oven after the beginning of the Sabbath, was not prohibited as having been cooked on the holy day. Comparably, if such food was cooked additionally by Gentiles, it did not become prohibited under the law that forbids Israelite consumption of foods prepared by Gentiles.

Ben Ezra Synagogue *see* CAIRO GENIZA

Ben Ḥakinai *see* ḤANANIAH B. ḤAKINAI

Ben Ḥakola *see* ISAAC B. ELEAZAR

Ben Hanila *see* TANḤUM B. HANILAI

Ben He He rabbinic authority of the first century C.E., known for the dictum: "In accord with the effort is the reward" (M. Abot 5:23). B. Ḥagigah 9b suggests that he was a student of Hillel. Later authorities claimed he was a convert, whose name marked him as the son of Abraham and Sarah, to each of whose names the Hebrew letter "he" was added (Gen. 17:5, 15).

Benjamin b. Levi Palestinian amora of the fourth century C.E.; a younger contemporary of Ammi and Isaac. He is most often associated with biblical interpretation.

Ben Koziba *see* BAR KOSIBA, SIMON

Ben Nanas *see* SIMEON B. NANAS

Ben Patzuri Tannaitic authority of the late first and early second centuries C.E.

Ben Sirah, Book of *see* SIRACH, WISDOM OF

Ben Torta *see* YOḤANAN B. TORTA

Ben Yasyan *see* YOSE B. YASYAN

Ben Zakkai, Yohanan *see* YOHANAN B. ZAKKAI

Ben Zoma *see* SIMEON B. ZOMA

beRab place of learning; household where a school was conducted by a major authority. The same word may stand for "son of Rab," or "son of a master," but it ordinarily refers to a household academy.

berakhah (Heb.) benediction, blessing, or praise

Berakhot (Heb., blessings) Mishnah tractate setting forth the liturgy governing everyday life at home. The tractate encompasses reciting the Shema (chaps. 1–3); reciting the Prayer Amidah (chaps. 4–5); the various blessings recited before eating different kinds of food, and the grace after meals and its protocol (chaps. 6–8); and blessings recited on occasions other than eating, as well as personal prayers (chap. 9). Both the Talmud of the Land of Israel and the Talmud of Babylonia provide commentaries to this tractate.

Berekiah Palestinian amoraic authority of the fourth century C.E., sometimes referred to as Berekiah haKohen. A student of Ḥelbo, he is known primarily for exegetical comments found in midrashic compilations and in the Talmud of the Land of Israel.

Berenice Israelite queen (r. 41–44 C.E.), daughter of Agrippa I. She married her uncle, Herod of Chalchis, and after his death in 48 became the consort of her brother, Agrippa II (r. c. 50–92/96), as rumors of incest circulated. She and Agrippa II tried to prevent the Jewish war against Rome (66–70) and supported Rome throughout. During the war, she started a love affair with Titus and continued it in Rome in 75. When Titus became emperor in 79, he sent her back to Palestine.

Bereshit *see* GENESIS

berit milah (Heb.) covenant of circumcision; *see also* CIRCUMCISION; COVENANT

Berossus Babylonian priest who flourished in the early third century B.C.E. He wrote a work entitled

Babyloniaca (Babylonian matters). It was a summary of Babylonian tradition, history, and mythology. Where it can be compared with cuneiform sources, it has been shown to be very accurate (though sometimes it gives only one tradition when there was more than one). Berossus wrote in Greek, evidently with "apologetic historiography" in mind; that is, he was trying to present the Babylonians in a good light to the Greeks, who had only recently conquered the ancient Near East under Alexander, but also to counter inaccurate Greek accounts, such as that of Ctesias. His work is known mainly in fragments from quotations in Josephus and Eusebius. He mentioned the Jews a couple of times. For example, he provided valuable information relating to the campaigns of Nebuchadnezzar in the West in the years before the taking of Jerusalem by the Babylonian king in 597 B.C.E. However, in some cases, Josephus seems to read his own interpretation into Berossus; for example, Josephus says that that Berossus confirms the flood story, though Berossus gave the Babylonian version, not the Hebrew one.

bet *for words beginning with* BET, *see also under* BEIT

Betar city in southern Palestine, seat of the Sanhedrin, and a base of Bar Kokhba's operations during the Revolt against Rome. In the summer of 135 C.E., Bar Kokhba's army was forced to withdraw from Jerusalem and to take refuge in Betar. For several months, it was under Roman siege. According to Jewish tradition, the siege ended on the Ninth of Ab, when the Romans gained access to and conquered the city through the use of a rampart. T. Yebamot 14:8 refers to sixty men who "went down to the camp of the besiegers at Betar," possibly a reference to the Jewish defense of the city at this time. Elsewhere the talmudic literature refers to individuals who were killed in the fighting at Betar, whom Hadrian would not allow to be buried. Lurid descriptions in rabbinic literature of the slaughter of hundreds of thousands of defenders contradict the small size of the site. *See also* BAR KOSIBA WAR.

beth *for words beginning with* BETH, *see also under* BEIT

Beth Alpha Synagogue ancient synagogue near the east end of the Beth Shean valley and west of Mount Gilboa. The synagogue was found by accident in 1928 and excavated in 1929. The building proved to be 29.4 by 19 meters. The entire edifice was built of black basalt blocks carefully cut and dressed. A large atrium with a porch at one end and paved in white mosaics led through three entrances into the worship area. This prayer hall was divided by columns into a nave and two side aisles on the basilica in plan. At the entrance to the nave an inscription in Aramaic names the donors and gives the date of the construction during the reign of the emperor Justinian (early sixth century C.E.). A second dedicatory inscription in Greek mentions the two artisans, Marinos and Haninah, who made the mosaic. On either side of the inscriptions stand a buffalo and a lion in the mosaic. The next panel represents the binding of Isaac with two servants and a pack animal to the left, the ram with horns hung in the bush in the center, and Abraham, knife in hand, prepared to place the bound Isaac on the flaming altar to the right. At the center top, a hand emerges from a cloud and says in Hebrew, "Do not extend [your hand]!" The ram, Abraham, and Isaac are labeled in Hebrew. The second panel is of a zodiac with a representation of the sun god Helios driving his four-horse chariot (a quadriga) directly toward the viewer. The zodiac has each sign labeled in Hebrew. The circle of the zodiac is inscribed in a square. Each corner of the square has a season of the year represented as a woman with wings, which the excavator interpreted as a variation on a cherub. Each season is labeled in Hebrew. The final panel before the apse at the focus of interest shows a synagogue ark flanked by two menorahs, each with shofar, etrog, lulab, and incense shovel. Two lions with mouths open stand on either side of the ark. In the mosaic, a curtain has been drawn back on both sides to reveal the scene. The entire style is simple, with figures rendered frontally and with no shadows. Presumably a Torah shrine stood in the apse of the synagogue. The colored mosaics in the west side aisle represent geometric figures and carpets.

Beth Guvrin ancient synagogue site and town about 37 kilometers southwest of Jerusalem in the Judean Shephelah. Alternate names for the town are Beth Jibrin in Arabic or Beth Govrin in Hebrew. Its name is preserved as Betogabris in the earliest Greek texts, but the emperor Septimus Severus renamed the city Eleutheropolis (city of freedmen) around 200 C.E.

A Corinthian capital of the synagogue has been found. This capital depicts a seven-branched menorah with tripod base. A small pillar, perhaps from a window or even from a Torah shrine, was decorated with a double, braided grapevine growing out of an amphora. The vine outlines three medallions or scrolls with grapes and grape leaves within. A very small marble column is probably part of a chancel screen. Two almost identical Aramaic inscriptions carved within circles on columns honor a donor: "Be remembered for good Kyrios bar Shai, peace upon him, bar Auxentios, who donated this column in honor of the synagogue. Peace." That is, the donor's full name is Kyrios bar Shai bar Auxentios. He has a Greek name, his father has a Hebrew name, and his grandfather has a Greek name. On the marble colonette the fragmentary Aramaic inscription reads: "Be remembered for good Severus bar Jonathan bar. . . ." The excavators postulate that the inscriptions date from the fourth to the sixth centuries C.E.

Excavations have also disclosed an impressive amphitheater, used as an area for Roman period games, and a Roman inn. The Roman inn contains a magnificently carved facade with naked winged children, called erotes, in hunting postures. The inn appears to have been built in the fourth century C.E. In the same period, a Roman villa was built about 200 meters north of Eleutheropolis; a second villa has been found on the next hill southeast of the city. Extensive cemetery remains of the Roman and Byzantine periods have been located to the south and east.

Beth Haram town in Transjordan, north of the Dead Sea, in the area of the tribe of Gad (Num. 32:36; Josh. 13:27); in scripture alternately called Beth Haran. Y. Shebiit 9:2 (38d) associates it with Beth Ha-Ramta, which Herod Antipas had fortified and renamed Livias, in honor of the Roman empress. After Augustus's death in 14 C.E., he named the town Julias, after the name the deceased emperor's wife had taken according to the terms of Augustus's will. Up to the Byzantine period, Beth Haram was the administrative headquarters of its region.

Beth Ha-Ramta *see* BETH HARAM

Beth Haran *see* BETH HARAM

Beth Horon two cities, referred to at Joshua 16:5 (Upper Beth Horon) and Joshua 16:3 and 18:13 (Lower Beth Horon); located at the western end of the Ephraimite Mountains, on the road from Gibeon to the coastal plain. Syrian attempts to attack the Land of Israel through Beth Horon were repulsed by Judas Maccabeus (1 Macc. 3:13ff; 2 Macc. 15:35f.). Several talmudic scholars are said to have come from Beth Horon.

Beth Horon, Battle of battle in which Judas Maccabeus defeated a Seleucid force under the command of Seron, which had been sent to suppress his rebellion at Beth Horon, 12 miles northwest of Jerusalem. The road between Lydda and the coast went through a narrow, steep ascent at the villages of Lower Beth Horon and Upper Beth Horon. Thus, Judas's small force was able to rout the larger Syrian force by using guerrilla tactics (1 Macc. 3:13–24).

Beth Kerem in the First Temple and Second Temple periods, a village near Jerusalem; in Jeremiah 6:1, referred to as a fortress on the road to Tekoa, where beacons were lit in times of danger. M. Middot 3:4 reports that the stones for the building of the Temple altar came from the valley of Beth Kerem. The Dead Sea writings comparably refer to a valley of Beth Kerem, including, in the Copper Scroll, the mention of this valley in a list of places where treasure is hidden.

Beth Laban the present-day Beth Rima and Lubban, about 20 miles northwest of Jerusalem, referred to at M. Menaḥot 8:6 as one of the locations in which wine used in Temple rites was produced. The name is also given as Beth Luban.

Bethlehem (North) village of Lower Galilee in the territory of Sepphoris during the Second Temple period. This may be biblical Bethlehem of the tribal territory of Zebulun in Joshua 19:15. After the destruction of the Second Temple it is listed as the seat of the priestly course of Malchiah. In the Jerusalem Talmud it was called Bethlehem Soraiya or Tyrian Bethlehem (Y. Megillah 70a), which suggests that it once belonged to Acco-Ptolemais rather than Sepphoris. The modern village of Beit Lahm now occupies the site in Lower Galilee. The ancient village remains have not yet been excavated.

Bethlehem (South) city in the territory of Judah about 10 kilometers south of Jerusalem; the city of David (1 Sam. 17:12) and the birthplace of Jesus (Matt. 2:1–12; Luke 2:1–7). Although Bethlehem was mentioned in the Egyptian Amarna letters of the fourteenth century B.C.E., it was as the birthplace of David that it emerged from relative obscurity (1 Sam. 16). When David was involved in a campaign against the Philistines, who had placed a garrison in the town, he pined for a drink from the well of Bethlehem (2 Sam. 23:5). Despite the fact that it was a walled city, David did not make it his capital, choosing instead Jerusalem because he wished to break with all tribal affiliations. Subsequently, the town was a border fortress of the southern kingdom (2 Chron. 11:6). Its continued prominence in the literature was based on the promise to David that the Messiah would be from his house. It thus became associated with the birthplace of the Messiah.

According to Ezra 2:21, only a small contingent of people returned to Bethlehem from Babylon. At

Herod the Great's building of the fortress of Herodium, Bethlehem grew in importance, since it overlooked both the roads to Herodium and to Masada. Herod built the aqueduct of Jerusalem from Bethlehem, which stands on a hill higher than the Temple Mount.

According to both Matthew and Luke, Jesus was born in Bethlehem, though only the latter evangelist mentions the census of Quirinius as the reason for his parents being there at the time of the birth. The place is not mentioned again in the New Testament.

Bethlehem plays little role in Jewish or Christian history in the Roman period, and c. 200 C.E., Christian authors note that no Jews lived in Bethlehem in that day. About 246 C.E., Origen, the Christian writer, mentions those who show the cave where Jesus was born, probably to Christian pilgrims. In the fourth century the emperor Constantine built an imperial church in Bethlehem, namely, the Church of the Nativity, begun in 326 C.E. He may also have stabilized the tradition of the location of David's tomb, which is lost today.

From the fourth century, Christian pilgrimage to Bethlehem was so much a fact of economic life that a large contingent of Christian monks and clergy lived in the vicinity to care for travelers. The Church of the Nativity, according to archaeological reconstruction, was organized in three or four architectural units. One approached the nave through a forecourt with a porch on four sides. The nave featured double rows of columns on either side and opened directly onto the octagon on the east, which was built directly above the cave. The octagon was decorated in fine mosaics with birds, geometric figures, and grapes. At the end of the fourth century, St. Jerome (Hieronymus) settled in Bethlehem with a company of matrons and founded two monasteries. Since Jerome learned Hebrew from the rabbis, evidently Jews again lived in the vicinity. The Church of the Nativity was destroyed in the Samaritan Revolt of 529 C.E. and was rebuilt by the emperor Justinian. A cloverleaf triple apse was built in place of the octagon and can be seen today. Justinian's architect enlarged the church but used columns and other elements from Constantine's church. Today's entrance is from the south transept, but otherwise one views mainly the church of Justinian.

Beth Netopha *see* NETOPHA

Beth Nimra town in the territory of Gad, on land taken from the Amorite king Sihon (Num. 32:36; Josh. 13:27). In rabbinic sources, Beth Nimra is designated as a valley in the Galilee, an important consideration in the application of the law of the Sabbatical year (T. Shebiit 7:11).

Beth Phage walled village on the Mount of Olives, in Second Temple times deemed to mark the eastern limit of Jerusalem (see M. Menaḥot 11:2). Beth Phage is the city in which Jesus found the ass on which he rode into Jerusalem (Matt. 21:1–2; Mark 11:1–2).

Beth Ramah town in the Galilee, referred to by Abot deRabbi Natan B, chapter 27 (version A: Ramat Bene-Anat), where Yoḥanan's student Joshua investigated a ḥasid who is said not to have known the rules regarding the uncleanness of stoves and ovens. The site may be the same as Rum Beth Anat, referred to at T. Mikvaot 6:3.

Bethsaida-Julias city built by Herod Philip on the northeastern shore of the Sea of Galilee, near the entrance of the Jordan River into the lake. Bethsaida (Aram., house of fishermen) was already a Jewish village before Herod Philip's building activities. Herod built the city in grand style, granted it the status of a city, and called it Julias in honor of Augustus's daughter, though after Julias's disgrace the honor referred to Augustus's wife, Livia. Although Herod Philip built his capital north of Bethsaida at Paneas (Caesarea-Philippi), he decreed that he was to be buried at Bethsaida. In the New Testament Bethsaida is the home of three of Jesus' disciples: Philip, Andrew, and Peter (John 1:44, 12:21). Later Bethsaida was transferred to the kingdom of Agrippa I. Bethsaida seems to have had an anchorage on the lake. The later rabbinic literature confuses the name of Sidon (Besidon) with Bethsaida, which makes research difficult regarding the role the city played in later Jewish history. Today the tell, called simply *et-tell* in Arabic, is usually identified with Julias, while the villages on the shore would be regarded as parts of the original settlements. More recent geological analysis implies that the lake shore has changed considerably in the past two millennia, probably because of seismic activity. In antiquity it is likely that the lake extended inland to et-Tell (Julias), which makes its identification as Bethsaida-Julias more credible. Recent archaeological exploration has unearthed the biblical city at the tell, but little remains of Herod Philip's constructions. More of Herod Philip's city may lie beneath the alluvium formed by the Jordan over the past two millennia.

Beth Shean city of the Persian period to the Arab Conquest, identical with the biblical city (1 Sam. 31:10) and located at the east end of the Jezreel Plain near the Jordan Valley. After the destruction of the biblical city at the hands of Tiglath Pileser

III, only scant occupation was to be found on the ancient city mound, including finds of Persian period figurines. However, the city gained new life in the Hellenistic period, when it surrendered to Antiochus III (the Great) upon his invasion of Palestine in 218 B.C.E. Beth Shean already controlled an extensive territory, for it was observed then that the city could support Antiochus's entire army. The city had already become known as Scythopolis or city of the Scythians, though no satisfactory reason for this name has been discovered. The city was also known as Nysa or Nysa Scythopolis, probably originally named for a Seleucid princess. Nysa is also the name of the mythological nymph who is reported to have raised the Greek god Dionysus. This is the most common name found on the coins of Beth Shean, which indicates that the city adopted veneration of Nysa (and Dionysus) as its official worship. Evidently, the city was virtually wholly gentile in this period (2 Macc. 12:29–31). The city figured in the confrontation of Judas Maccabeus with Seleucid Greek forces after the rededication of the Temple (I Macc. 5:52). Excavations of Hellenistic Scythopolis or Nysa have revealed houses with handles of wine jars imported from Rhodes and Cnidos, 65 kilometers northwest of Rhodes. Scythopolis therefore participated in trade in the eastern Mediterranean network. Hellenistic Scythopolis passed into the power of the Jewish king Alexander Jannaeus about 106 B.C.E. In 63 B.C.E., however, the Roman general Pompey separated Scythopolis from Jewish rule. The earliest coins of the city seem to mention Gabinius, the Roman governor. Beth Shean-Scythopolis joined the Decapolis, or league of (ordinarily) ten Hellenistic cities, all of which except Scythopolis were located across the Jordan. Soon Beth Shean-Scythopolis became the leading city of the Decapolis.

Beth Shean-Scythopolis became a prominent and busy metropolis that dominated the north–south road in the Jordan Valley and its crossing with the west–east road from the coastal, Hellenistic cities. This road led inland to markets such as the Decapolis and Damascus. A large Jewish population developed in the city, for by the time of the First Revolt 13,000 Jews were killed at Beth Shean. By the third century C.E., the city territory of Beth Shean-Scythopolis included about 30 Roman miles of the Jordan Valley to the east of the city. The city territory extended nearly 30 miles westward into the Beth Shean valley.

The excavations at Beth Shean have uncovered an extensive Roman and Byzantine city finally destroyed in the earthquake of 749 C.E. The theater of Beth Shean has been excavated for some time and is usually dated to the second century C.E. Its stage is 54.6 meters long. A colonnaded street, called the Palladius Street after a governor whose name appears in a Greek inscription in the sidewalk, ran northeast from the theater to a central temple and its plaza. Shops stood on either side of the colonnade, and a large bath complex of the sixth century C.E. occupied nearly 6,000 square meters on the north side of the street. A semicircular structure recently identified as a brothel also stood on the north side of the street. The street may have been built in the fourth century and refurbished in the sixth century. It seems likely that it followed the course of an earlier street.

The Roman temple contained an inscription in Greek mentioning the Emperor Marcus Aurelius Antoninus (161–180 C.E.) which reads in part, "the people of Nysa also [called] the people of Scythopolis . . . one of Coele Syria's Greek cities. . . ." East of the Roman temple stood a second century C.E. Nymphaeum or public fountain watered by an aqueduct. At the Roman temple, a second Roman and Byzantine, colonnaded street intersected the Palladius Street and led southeast past the Nymphaeum and past a Roman-period monument, both of which stood on the south side of this second street. A third street led northeast away from the monument. A public basilica or a roofed Roman structure with rows of columns on the interior stood southwest of the monument. It dates to the first century C.E. and contained, probably not in its original place, a hexagonal altar of Dionysus. The altar contains a Greek dedicatory inscription with a date that corresponds to 12 C.E. Elsewhere an altar dedicated to the Egyptian-Greek god Serapus was found. Both these altars were donated by a certain Seleucos, son of Ariston.

A large amphitheater stood some 270 meters south of the theater. A large street paved with black basalt blocks connected the two. The amphitheater, used for games and gladiatorial contests, measures 102 by 67 meters on the outside with an arena that measures 83 by 48 meters. The excavators believe that it was first erected in the second century C.E. A Byzantine street and residential quarter stood on the north side of the amphitheater. That is, it appears that the amphitheater was first built in an area where no houses stood, but eventually, certainly by the fifth century C.E., a residential quarter developed beside this public building. One of the lamps found in this quarter bore a relief of a menorah. A cloth bag was also found that contained a hoard of bronze coins of the mid-sixth century C.E. From the Roman period it is clear that Beth Shean-Scythopolis supported a vigorous population of Greek-speaking Jews, Christians, and pagans. The structures dedicated to Greek gods were only destroyed from the fourth century onward with the Christianization of the empire.

Beth Shean Synagogue synagogue site east of the city gate of the Roman/Byzantine city of Beth Shean, which lies in the Beth Shean valley, east of the Jezreel plain. The building, called the House of Kyrios Leontis (Lord Leontis) after a Greek inscription in one of its floors, was only partially excavated. The building proved to be several rooms built around a central courtyard paved with mosaics, but the courtyard was not square with the external walls of the building. On the north side were three rooms; a mosaic floor in the western room depicts scenes from the Odyssey. In the center was a Greek dedicatory inscription that mentions a certain Jonathan and his brother Kyrios Leontis, who donated the mosaic. A five-branched menorah accompanies the inscription. In the lower half of the mosaic there is a Nile scene, complete with a depiction of a nilometer, a device to measure the flooding of the Nile. There is also a depiction of a city marked "Alexandria" in Greek. On the south side of the courtyard and opposite the House of Kyrios Leontis stood a single door, which opened into an interior space (7 m × 7 m) that proved to be worship space for a synagogue. Low benches were built against the walls of the prayer space; the walls had been plastered and painted red. Entrance and egress was through the north door and a second door on the east.

The floor of the prayer space was paved with a mosaic, the border of which is a wide vine-trellis pattern with repeated birds, baskets, etrogs, and other motifs. The center of the mosaic depicts a seven-branched menorah with an etrog to the left and an incense censer hanging from three chains to the right. Originally, there was probably also a shofar to the right, now destroyed. The menorah is unusual in that it is fairly elaborate: its stem and branches form buds. The branches end in a horizontal strip upon which sit seven cups. Within the seven cups there stand seven green glass lamps bearing single flames. The word "shalom" is written in Hebrew letters above the menorah. A square panel surrounds the menorah. This panel is divided by a meandering vine emerging from an amphora into nine medallions; the central medallion contains the menorah. The other medallions originally contained two facing bulls, two facing goats, and two facing pheasants pecking grapes. In the central top medallion stood a facing peacock. The surrounding border between the central square panel and the outside vine trellis contains an amphora at each corner from which a vine sprouts. In and among the vine tendrils one sees two lion cubs, while a fox chases a hare on the north side and a dog chases a deer on the opposite side. On the east one sees a bear, a stag, and an elephant. On the west side a long Aramaic inscription honors "all the members of the holy congregation who endeavored to repair the holy place." A shorter Aramaic inscription beneath a vase flanked by two guinea hens reads, "Be remembered for good the artisan who made this work." To the east of the outer border of the mosaic is a fragment of a Greek inscription between two facing pheasants. The inscription was added after the mosaic was in place, perhaps replacing an earlier dedication. It reads, "The gift of those whom the Lord knows the names. He shall guard them in times. . . ." The date of the mosaic floor is given as sixth century C.E., though it may have been built slightly earlier. The building went out of use as a synagogue at the end of the Byzantine period, or early seventh century C.E. It is possible that the whole complex is an inn, used for hospitality to travelers, with an appropriate prayer space.

Beth Shearim ancient Jewish town site in western Galilee, famous for its synagogue and Jewish catacombs of the Roman and Byzantine periods. Josephus mentions Beth Shearim under the name Besara and describes it as a village in southern Galilee on the border with Acco-Ptolemais. According to rabbinic literature, famous rabbis lived and were often buried at Beth Shearim, such as Rabbi Johanan ben Nuri of the second century C.E., but above all Judah the Patriarch (the Prince) of the third century C.E. Rabbi Judah moved to Sepphoris for his health, but after his death was brought to Beth Shearim for burial. Excavations at Beth Shearim reveal a village or town that begins in the Herodian period. This town expanded considerably from about 200 C.E. and includes a fine public basilica and the beginnings of the necropolis. The period of the synagogue is from about 250 C.E. until its destruction during the Gallus Revolt in 351 C.E. This building measured about 15 by 35 meters in extent, with interior columnation dividing the space into a nave and two side aisles.

Marble slabs were fixed to the walls on the interior with inscriptions honoring donors in Greek. In one of the small rooms annexed to the northwest side of the synagogue, there appeared two Greek inscriptions, one of which mentions a Rabbi Samuel who prepared the dead, and the second of which mentions Jacob of Caesarea, head of the synagogue of Pamphylia (then in Hebrew Shalom). Near the raised platform or *bimah* at the far end of the synagogue was found a marble slab that mentions a Rabbi Thietetos. The necropolis contains a series of catacombs or interconnecting, underground chambers for burial. It is clear that Jews from many communities outside the land of Israel were reburied here, including Jews from Tyre, Sidon, Beirut, Antioch, Palmyra, and Nahardea in Mesopotamia. Tomb architecture varied with the period. Many have courtyards or exterior corridors leading to stone doors that swing on hinges and open into burial halls. Several have spendid rock-cut facades with elaborate portals. The graves within are sometimes pit graves, sometimes arcosolia or arches above rock-cut sarcophagi, or free-standing sarcophagi. Some burials were in stone or lead coffins, but most were in special slots (*kokhim,* or loculi) cut into the walls. Catacomb 1, which was quite elaborate, included 400 burial places in sixteen halls.

Beth Shearim is famous as a huge repository of Jewish funeral art. In many catacombs one might see in relief on the walls such motifs as a horse and rider, menorahs in relief or incised into the stone, a Torah ark, or a man carrying a menorah on his head. The art on the sarcophagi repeated some of these motifs and used others as well: the Torah ark, Leda and the swan, two lions on either side of a bull's head, an eagle with outstretched wings, and two lions on either side of an object. Numerous fragments of marble sculpture in the round were found, ordinarily understood to be from sarcophagi. Other finds included lamps, a few glass vessels, coins, and some jewelry. Almost all the catacombs had been broken into and looted.

Beth Zur, Battles of battles between Judas Maccabeus and Seleucid forces. Beth Zur, at the top of a mountain ridge 15 miles south of Jerusalem, guarded the southern approach to Jerusalem. Lysias, the Seleucid general, encamped there in 165 B.C.E. before his defeat by Judas Maccabeus and their subsequent truce. Judas then fortified Beth Zur. In 165 B.C.E. Lysias and Antiochus V besieged Beth Zur and then defeated Judas Maccabeus in battle at Beth Zechariah, a few miles north on the road to Jerusalem. This resulted eventually in a truce and a Syrian garrison in Beth Zur (1 Macc. 6:28–50).

betrothal legal relationship between two partners who will later consummate their union with a wedding (see Jos. Asen. 21). Betrothals could be contracted between the suitor and the woman's parents (Tob., Jos. Asen.) or between two fathers. Tobit records the first mention of a *ketubah,* or marriage contract (7:13). According to Josephus (*War* 2.18.3), Essene men test their wives for three years prior to marriage, but the Dead Sea Scrolls do not mention this practice. According to Matthew 1:18 (see also Luke 2:5), Mary became pregnant while betrothed to Joseph but before they had had intercourse. *See also* ERUSIN; KIDDUSHIN.

Betulia setting of the Book of Judith (4:6), in what may be Samaria. The name is otherwise unattested, is similar to the Hebrew for "virgin" (*betulah*), and enhances Judith's identification with her ancestor Simeon, who had protected his (virgin) sister from foreign defilement (Gen. 34); thus the site may be fictional like the rest of Judith's narrative.

betzah *see* EGG'S BULK; LOG

Betzah Mishnah tractate, also called Yom Tob (festival), on preparing food on a festival day. Scripture permits preparing food on a festival day, though not on the Sabbath (Exod. 12:16). Food for use on the festival must be designated for that purpose, in fact or at least potentially, prior to the festival day; the preparation must be done in some manner different from the way in which food is prepared on secular days. A distinction is drawn between actually preparing food and acts of labor not directly pertaining to the actual preparation but relevant thereto. Both Talmuds provide commentaries to this tractate.

Biblical Antiquities, Book of a rewriting of the biblical story from Adam to Saul's death. It is sixty-five chapters long. There are twenty-one extant manuscripts, eighteen complete and three fragmentary, dating from the eleventh to the fifteenth centuries C.E. All manuscripts are in Latin, but it is likely that the original work was in Hebrew and was translated into Greek and later into Latin. The work was written in Palestine, probably around the middle of the first century C.E. The English title is a translation of the Latin Liber Antiquitatum Biblicarum (LAB), a title first found in a manuscript from the sixteenth century. The work was transmitted among Latin translations of the works of Philo of Alexandria, but it is not by Philo.

The genre of the Biblical Antiquities is rewritten Bible. It rewrites the Bible very freely. It omits large portions of the biblical text, adds much material, and alters biblical stories liberally. The additions consist of names, hymns, visions, speeches, narratives, and so on. The author shows a pronounced interest in major characters, especially leaders. God's direct role in Israel's history is emphasized.

Although the Biblical Antiquities contains apocalyptic elements, such as descriptions of the end of time, judgment, visions, and angels, it is not an apocalypse, nor do the apocalyptic elements determine the tone of the whole. Creation and eschaton provide a frame that stresses God's control of history and the moral structure of the universe. The most prominent theme is the indestructibility of God's covenant with Israel. Israel is frequently unfaithful and is punished, but God never cancels the divine relationship with Israel. The Deuteronomistic pattern of sin, punishment, and salvation occurs repeatedly throughout the book. A related theme is that every sin is punished, and that the punishment fits the crime. The Biblical Antiquities is strongly against intermarriage with Gentiles. Idolatry is of special concern, and the role of women is remarkably important.

The Biblical Antiquities is an important example of the retelling of the Bible that probably took place in first-century Palestinian synagogues. Since it cannot be traced to a specific Jewish group and since attempts to assign it a polemical purpose have been unsuccessful, it represents a mainstream, scribal adaptation of the Bible to first-century conditions. It affords the earliest attestation for many traditions known from later documents, and supplies details and traditions not found in other texts.

Biblical Aramaic *see* ARAMAIC, BIBLICAL

biblical interpretation *see* SCRIPTURAL INTERPRETATION

biblical scenes scenes in Jewish art taken from the Hebrew Bible. In general, the representations of biblical figures and events conform to the conventions of art in the times and places where they were produced, with few exceptions. Most biblical scenes appear in wall frescoes and in mosaics. One of the most famous is in a late synagogue mosaic floor at Beth Alpha in the east end of the Jezreel Plain near Beth Shean. The first panel at the entrance to the worship space depicts the binding of Isaac (the *akedah*) in a simple, even primitive style. We see two pack animals to the left with two servants waiting patiently. Abraham is standing to the right, knife in hand, in front of a blazing altar to the right. Isaac is about to be laid on the altar, but a hand reaches out from a cloud at top center with the injunction in Hebrew "Do not extend [your hand]!" To the left of the hand of the angel a ram waits, its horns tangled in the bush. A Hebrew inscription reads, "Behold the ram." The artists have thoughtfully labeled the two main characters in Hebrew. Other biblical scenes known in synagogue floors include King David playing the harp in a floor from Gaza and David as a boy with Goliath's arms stacked beside him in the mosaic floor from Marous, likely ancient Meroth. A parade of animals from the synagogue at Gerasa is usually interpreted as a scene from Noah's ark. The mosaic floor at Naaran may depict Daniel in the lion's den. On the other hand, the biblical scenes painted in fresco on the walls of the third-century synagogue at Dura-Europos in ancient Syria are breathtaking. In these fifty-eight scenes, one can see Abraham (also in the *akedah*), Moses, Aaron, Jacob, Samuel, David, Solomon, Elijah, and Ezekiel. All are dressed in the fashion of the mid-third century C.E.

Bikurim Mishnah tractate devoted to the laws governing the presentation of firstfruits in the Temple in Jerusalem, in line with Deuteronomy 26:1–11 and Leviticus 23:9–21, and the appropriate declaration on that occasion. At issue are the classes of persons who present firstfruits and make that declaration, those who present the firstfruits but make no declaration, and those exempt from presenting firstfruits. The tractate further compares the rules that govern firstfruits, heave-offering, second tithe, and similar matters. Chapter 3 describes the disposition of firstfruits from when they are designated as such until they reach the hands of the priest in the Jerusalem Temple. The Talmud of the Land of Israel provides a commentary to this tractate.

bimah (Heb.) platform from which worship is led in synagogue

binding of Isaac *see* AKEDAH

birds excluding eagles, a minor motif in Jewish art. Birds figure in mosaic floors, especially in inhabited scrolls, which are multiple circles formed of vines. In these contexts, birds are sometimes so accurately portrayed the species can be identified. Birds also appear in some surprising contexts, as for example on either side of the Torah shrine, or *aedicula,* in the mosaic floor at Beth Alpha. The "bird in a cage" motif is used, borrowed from Graeco-Roman art. Birds are the primary decorative element in certain Byzantine mosaic panels, as for example in the floor of the En-Gedi synagogue. The peacock may receive special place, but this is likely due to the magnificence of its plumage rather than any symbolic value. Birds often appear in relief in stone plaques or as part of Nile scenes in more or less bucolic representations in houses. "Birds pecking grapes" also appears as a minor motif in certain synagogue floors.

Birkat A<u>b</u>elim (Heb., blessing of mourners) mourners' blessing. It was known in Tannaitic times, but it is no longer extant.

Birkat A<u>b</u>odah (Heb., blessing of worship) the seventeenth benediction of the daily Amidah and the first of the final section known as "Thanksgiving." The blessing praises God for accepting worship. After 70 C.E. it included a prayer for the restoration of the sacrificial cult. Liberal Jews generally omit the petition for restoration.

Birkat A<u>b</u>ot (Heb., blessing of the fathers) the first benediction of the Amidah. It asks God to deal graciously with those who offer prayer, not because they deserve it, but because of the merit they inherit from the patriarchs. *See also* ZEKHUT A<u>B</u>OT.

Birkat Binah (Heb., blessing of discernment) the fourth benediction of the daily Amidah (and the first of the intermediary petitionary blessings). The prayer requests wisdom from God.

Birkat David (Heb., blessing of David) the fifteenth paragraph of the standardized rabbinic daily prayer of originally eighteen blessings. The benediction asks for the restoration of the house of David and messianic salvation and alludes to the phrasing of Jeremiah 33:15: "I will cause a righteous branch to spring up for David; and he shall execute justice and righteousness in the land." The Talmud of the Land of Israel supposes that this paragraph in the liturgy was part of the preceding one, which makes reference to the rebuilding of Jerusalem (cf. Tos. Ber. 3:25). Some scholars see in it an anti-Christian polemic. *See also* AMIDAH.

Birkat Erusin (Heb., blessing of betrothal) blessing that marks *erusin,* the first of the two stages constituting rabbinic marriage. It is recited at the bride's home prior to the interlude separating betrothal from marriage proper (i.e., the second stage that occurs later, at which time the bride takes up residence with the groom). The prayer affirms the couple's intention to live apart until the second stage of marriage takes place.

Birkat Ge<u>b</u>urot (Heb., blessing of god's might) the second benediction of the Amidah, praising God for divine saving power, and stipulating specifically the resurrection of the dead and rain (the means by which the world of nature is revived and a symbol for human resurrection).

Birkat Geulah (Heb., blessing of redemption) the seventh paragraph of the standardized rabbinic daily prayer of originally eighteen blessings. The benediction concludes with the prayer "Blessed art thou, Lord, who redeems Israel," which was understood as a reference to future salvation. The label Birkat Geulah may also refer to the liturgy that follows the Shema and precedes the prayer of eighteen blessings, which makes reference to the past redemption from Egypt. *See also* AMIDAH.

Birkat haAretz (Heb., blessing of the land) the second paragraph in the standard rabbinic blessings of the meal, ascribed by tradition to Joshua at the conquest of the Land of Israel (Ber. 48b). The prayer invokes major mythic and symbolic themes of Israel (the Exodus, circumcision, the Torah and its laws) and cites Deuteronomy 8:10, "And you shall eat and you shall be satisfied and you shall bless the Lord your God," as the scriptural basis for the meal blessings. *See also* BIRKAT HAMAZON.

Birkat haḪodesh (Heb., blessing of the month) This benediction is recited in the synagogue on the Sabbath after the reading of the Torah to announce and pray for good fortune in the new month that begins during the following week.

Birkat haMazon (Heb., blessing for food) grace after meals, recited after eating a meal that has included bread; made up of four principal blessings. The first blessing praises God for nourishing all creatures ("blessed . . . who nourishes all things"); the second gives thanks for the Land of Israel, redemption from Egypt, the covenant of circumcision, and the revelation of the Torah; the third asks mercy on Israel, the rebuilding of the Temple, and the restoration of Davidic rule; and the fourth gives thanks for God's goodness.

The principal liturgy is as follows: "Blessed art Thou, Lord our God, King of the Universe, who nourishes all the world by his goodness, in grace, in mercy, and in compassion: He gives bread to all flesh, for his mercy is everlasting. And because of his great goodness we have never lacked, and so may we never lack, sustenance—for the sake of his great Name. For He nourishes and feeds everyone, is good to all, and provides food for each one of the creatures He created. Blessed art Thou, O Lord, who feeds everyone. We thank Thee, Lord our God, for having given our fathers as a heritage a pleasant, a good and spacious land; for having taken us out of the land of Egypt, for having redeemed us from the house of bondage; for thy covenant, which Thou hast set as a seal in our flesh, for thy Torah which Thou has taught us, for thy statutes which Thou hast made known to us, for the life of grace and mercy Thou hast graciously bestowed upon us, and for the nourishment with which Thou dost nourish us and feed us always, every day, in every season, and every hour. For all these things, Lord our God, we thank and praise Thee; may thy praises continually be in the mouth of every living thing, as it is written,

And thou shalt eat and be satisfied, and bless the Lord thy God for the good land which He hath given thee. Blessed art Thou, O Lord, for the land and its food. O Lord our God, have pity on thy people Israel, on thy city Jerusalem, on Zion the place of thy glory, on the royal house of David thy Messiah, and on the great and holy house which is called by thy Name. Our God, our Father, feed us and speed us, nourish us and make us flourish, unstintingly, O Lord our God, speedily free us from all distress. And let us not, O Lord our God, find ourselves in need of gifts from flesh and blood, or of a loan from anyone save from thy full, generous, abundant, wide-open hand; so we may never be humiliated, or put to shame. O rebuild Jerusalem, the holy city, speedily in our day. Blessed art Thou, Lord, who in mercy will rebuild Jerusalem. Amen. Blessed art Thou, Lord our God, King of the Universe, Thou God, who art our Father, our powerful king, our creator and redeemer, who made us, our holy one, the holy one of Jacob, our shepherd, shepherd of Israel, the good king, who visits his goodness upon all; for every single day He has brought good, He does bring good, He will bring good upon us; He has rewarded us, does regard, and will always reward us, with grace, mercy and compassion, amplitude, deliverance and prosperity, blessing and salvation, comfort, and a living, sustenance, pity and peace, and all good—let us not want any manner of good whatever."

Birkat haMinim (Heb., blessing for the heretics) the twelfth paragraph of the standardized rabbinic daily prayer of originally eighteen blessings. Also called the "Blessing for the Sadducees" and the "Curse of the Slanderers," it asks for the destruction of the enemies, traitors, and apostates. The Talmud attributes it to Samuel the Younger (c. 100 C.E.) on behalf of Gamaliel II and his court at Yavneh. The wording was modified to mollify medieval religious authorities who thought it was an anti-Christian polemic. It should be viewed as an imprecation against dissenters within Judaism. *See also* AMIDAH.

Birkat haMishpat (Heb., blessing of justice) the eleventh paragraph in the standardized rabbinic daily prayer of originally eighteen blessings. It is also known as Birkat haDin, the "blessing of judgment." The concluding formula, "Blessed are you, Lord, the King who loves righteousness and justice," is changed to "the just King" between New Year and the Day of Atonement to reflect the solemnity of the season. *See also* AMIDAH.

Birkat haNehenim (Heb., blessing for benefits) recited before partaking of food, drink, fragrances, and pleasant vistas. The standard rabbinic formulary usually praises God for creating the material from which one is to benefit. The recitation does not bestow any blessing upon the substance or change its status in any way.

Birkat haShanim (Heb., blessing of the years) the ninth paragraph of the standardized rabbinic daily prayer of originally eighteen blessings. The benediction asks for material prosperity and during the winter, the words "grant us dew and rain for a blessing" are added. *See also* AMIDAH.

Birkat haShir (Heb., blessing of the song) also known as Nishmat. It is commonly recited at the Passover Seder for the fourth cup of wine and in the morning service for sabbaths and festivals. More a poem than a formal blessing, it thanks God for sustenance and salvation.

Birkat Ḥatanim (Heb., blessing of the bridegrooms) the seven blessings recited at a rabbinic marriage ceremony and at the meals of the first week of celebrations thereafter, provided there are new guests at each meal as specified by the Talmud (B. Ketub. 7b–8a). They make reference to creation, the joy of Zion and Jerusalem in the messianic age, and to the joy of a bridegroom and bride. The substance of the texts of the blessings after (1) the blessing for the wine is as follows: (2) "Blessed art thou, O Lord our God, King of the Universe, who created all things for his glory"; (3) "Blessed art thou . . . who creates humans"; (4) "Blessed art thou . . . who created humans in his image, according to his likeness, and established from them an everlasting paradigm. Blessed art thou, O Lord, who creates humans"; (5) "The barren one will surely be glad and rejoice when her children are gathered into her with happiness. Blessed art thou . . . who brings joy to Zion through her children"; (6) "The loving companions will surely rejoice just as your creatures rejoiced in Eden of old. Blessed art thou . . . who makes the groom and bride rejoice"; (7) "Blessed art thou . . . who created joy and gladness, groom and bride, mirth and exultation, pleasure and delight, love, brotherhood, peace, and companionship. Soon, O Lord our God, may there be heard in the towns of Judah and the streets of Jerusalem the voice of joy and gladness, the voice of the groom and bride, the jubilant voice of grooms from their marriage canopies and of youths from their feasts of song. Blessed art thou . . . who makes the groom rejoice with the bride."

Birkat haTob Vehametib (Heb., blessing of the good one who does good) the fourth section in the standard rabbinic blessing of the meal. The Talmud considers this the latest addition to that liturgy, added as an affirmation of faith after the Jews buried the martyrs who died in the Bar Kokhba rebellion (Ber. 48b). *See also* BIRKAT HAMAZON.

Birkat haTorah (Heb., blessing of the Torah) blessing recited before and after reading verses of the Torah: "who has chosen us from all nations and has given us your Torah" or "who has given us the true Torah and planted in our midst eternal life."

Birkat haTzadikim (Heb., blessing of the righteous) the thirteenth paragraph of the standardized rabbinic daily prayer of originally eighteen blessings. The benediction asks for mercy for the pious, the elders, the scribes, and the true proselytes. Scholars consider it to have originated in the time of the Maccabees; based on their interpretation of "the remnants of their scribes" included in the blessing. *See also* AMIDAH.

Birkat haZan (Heb., blessing of the provider) the first paragraph in the standard rabbinic blessing of the meal. The benediction expresses gratitude for providing food for all creatures. The Talmud suggests that Moses formulated this blessing when the manna came down for Israel (Ber. 48b). *See also* BIRKAT HAMAZON.

Birkat haZeman (Heb., blessing of the season) a blessing (known less technically as Sheheḥiyanu) said at numerous occasions throughout the year such as the onset of holidays and the first harvest. The prayer thanks God "for giving us life, for sustaining us, and for bringing us to this season."

Birkat hoDayah (Heb., blessing of thanksgiving) the eighteenth benediction of the daily Amidah, and the second of the final section known as "Thanksgiving." The prayer offers gratitude to God.

Birkat Kibbutz Geluyot (Heb., blessing of the exiles' return) the tenth benediction of the daily Amidah (and the seventh of the intermediary petitionary blessings). The prayer requests the messianic return of all Jews from wherever they may dwell to the Land of Israel.

Birkat Kohanim *see* PRIESTLY BENEDICTION

Birkat Refuah (Heb., blessing of healing) the eighth benediction of the daily Amidah (and the fifth of the intermediary petitionary blessings). The prayer requests the healing of the sick.

Birkat Seliḥah (Heb., blessing of forgiveness) the sixth benediction of the daily Amidah (and the third of the intermediary petitionary blessings). The prayer requests God's forgiveness.

Birkat Shalom (Heb., blessing of peace) a late term used to refer to the final blessing of the Amidah. It is a prayer for peace that includes the Priestly Benediction.

Birkat Shomea Tefilah (Heb., blessing of [the one] who hears prayer) the sixteenth benediction of the daily Amidah (and the last of the intermediary petitionary blessings). The prayer praises God for hearing prayer and implicitly asks that the petitions just offered as part of the Amidah be accepted.

Birkat Teshubah (Heb., blessing of repentance) the fifth benediction of the daily Amidah (and the second of the intermediary petitionary blessings). The prayer praises God for renewing the covenantal relationship with those who abandon their sinful ways and return to God in repentance.

Birkat Yerushalaim (Heb., blessing for Jerusalem) the third section in the standard rabbinic blessing of the meal. The benediction appeals for mercy on Israel, Jerusalem, the house of David, and for sustenance. *See also* BIRKAT HAMAZON.

birth, miraculous a birth resulting from a conception directly initiated by God. Three major figures in the Hebrew Bible are conceived after God "opened the womb" of a barren woman: Isaac, Samson, and Samuel. Each person advances God's purposes. Isaac fulfills God's promises that Abraham will engender the covenant people (Gen. 12:1–3, 15:1–6, 17:1–21). Samson will "begin to deliver" (Heb.: *yasha,* save) Israel (Judg. 13). Samuel was judge and prophet (1 Sam. 1:1–2:11). Less explicit is the case of Immanuel (Isa. 7:10–17); however, the announcement formula in 7:14 recalls Judges 13:3, and the child's function as a sign suggests divine intervention with the unnamed young woman (*almah*). Two prophetic call texts also fit this category; the servant of YHWH (Isa. 49:1) and Jeremiah (Jer. 1:5) trace their commissioning to the womb.

The story of the seven brothers and their mother in 2 Maccabees 7 interprets the old traditions. Although the mother's comment about the mystery of their conception could be a commonplace about God's creative power (vv. 22–23, 27), the number seven is reminiscent of Hannah's song (1 Sam. 2:5), and the story's allusions to Deutero-Isaianic servant theology recall Isaiah 49:1, especially given the sons' role as God's spokesmen (Isa. 50:4–8). Thus the story hints at God's intervention in the conception of the young men whose deaths initiate the return of God's favor to Israel (2 Macc. 7:37–38, 8:5). In the story of Noah's birth (1 Enoch 106–107; 1QapGen 2), Lamech misunderstands the child's radiant appearance at birth as evidence that he had been conceived through intercourse with a watcher. In fact, it signals his role in preserving humanity from the flood's destruction. Lamech's misperception is set against the background of 1 Enoch 6–11, where the watchers mate with women and produce malevolent giants. This tradition, which reflects Greek notions and may be a parody on the Hellenistic kings' claims of divine parentage, offers an etiology for destruction and violence and thus inverts the notion that God initiates the conception of savior figures.

Stories about Jesus' conception in Matthew 1 and Luke 1 draw heavily on biblical and Second Temple Jewish traditions. Matthew 1 is beholden to Judges 13, employs the Noah story's motif of the husband's suspicion, and quotes Isaiah 7:14, following the Septuagint translation of *almah* as *parthenos,* "virgin." Luke 1–2, with its focus on Mary, draws motifs and language from 1 Samuel 1–2. Although the stories share the biblical notion that God intervenes in the conception of savior figures, the virginal conception differs qualitatively from its prototypes since contemporary physiology required male seed to effect conception in the barren field of the womb.

Paul affirms the importance of his mission by alluding to Isaiah 49 and Jeremiah 1 and attributing his call to God's choice before his birth (Gal. 1:15). His reference to himself as an "abortion" plays on this image by seeing his persecution of the church as a rejection of his prenatal divine call (1 Cor. 15:7–9).

birth, monstrous the birth of deformed animals or human beings, of creatures of mixed species, or of one species by another. Religious texts ranging from ancient Mesopotamia to the classical Mediterranean world attest the belief that such births are omens of bad things to come, and a whole science developed to interpret their meaning. The descriptions of the beasts in Daniel 7:4–8 and the eagle in 2 Esdras 11 reflect such a tradition. 2 Esdras 5:8 lists the human birth of monsters as one of a plethora of signs that reflect the confusion of creation as the world nears the end time.

biur ḥametz (Heb.) the burning of leaven on the morning preceding the Passover seder. Since Israelites leaving Egypt had no time to wait for bread to rise, the Bible (Exod. 13:3) bans leavened food throughout Passover. After all such foodstuffs are removed, the last crumbs are sought out at night, usually with a feather as scoop and a candle for light, and burned ceremoniously the next morning.

B.J. *see* WAR OF THE JEWS

blameless translation of Greek *amemptos* used by Paul in Philippians 3:6 to describe his pre-Christian life as a pious Pharisee: "As to righteousness according to the law [I was] blameless." The same term describes the parents of John the Baptist in Luke 1:6: "Both of them were righteous before God, being blameless in their observance of the commandments." Paul's claim in Philippians 3:6, which seems at odds with his assertion elsewhere that it is impossible for anyone to keep the law (Gal. 3:10–11), is to be understood on the basis of the use of *amemptos* and of such Hebrew terms as *tam, tamim* (blameless), and *tzadik* (righteous) in the Tanakh (Old Testament) and other Jewish texts: these terms designate not perfect fulfillment of the law but sincere devotion to God and his law (Job 1:1; Wisd. of Sol. 10:5, of Abraham; Wisd. of Sol. 18:21, of Aaron). Psalm 119 begins with the statement: "Happy are those whose way is blameless (Heb.: *tamim*), who walk in the law of the Lord" (v. 1). "Blameless" designates one who seeks God with his "whole heart" (v. 2), whose delight is in the decrees of the Lord (v. 111). The Psalm makes clear that the "blameless" can neither understand (v. 125) nor observe the Torah (v. 133) without divine help. In the Psalms of Solomon 2–4, the "righteous one" (Gr.: *dikaios*) or "the innocent one" (*akakos*) is the man who lives by the judgment and the mercy of God; in contrast to the "sinner," he does not heap up "sin upon sin" (3:5–10) but seeks constantly to observe the commandments. When he stumbles, he repents and atones for his sins (3:5–8). In the Sectarian texts of the Dead Sea Scrolls, the adjective *tam* describes those who enter the monastic community; they are to "walk perfectly" in the ways of God, a task for which they require the assistance of the gracious mercy of God (1QS 2:1–3).

blaspheme (Gr.: *blasphēmia,* corresponding to a number of Hebrew and Aramaic words) to act or, more specifically, to speak contemptuously against God. Leviticus 24:10–23 describes the stoning of a man who "blasphemed the name of YHWH" (Heb.: *yaqav* equated with *killel,* to curse). The story of the Rabshakeh, who denied YHWH's power to deliver Jerusalem (2 Kings 19:8–28, *gadaf,* v. 22) is recalled in 2 Maccabees 15, where Nicanor's threat against the Temple and his claim that his sovereignty rivals God's is referred to as "blasphemy" (*blasphēmia,* vv. 22–24). In 1 Maccabees 2:6 and 2 Maccabees 8:4 "blasphemy (against the name," 2 Macc. 8:4) denotes the Hellenizing activities in Israel, including the defiling of the Temple and the killing of the martyrs. In Daniel 3:29, Nebuchadnezzar threatens with death anyone who speaks blasphemy (*yemar shalvaḥ*) against the God who delivered Daniel (cf. 3:15, where he had challenged that God's power).

Two New Testament construals of blasphemy are significant. In the trial of Jesus, the high priest condemns Jesus for blasphemy (Mark 14:64) and tears his garments (cf. 2 Kgs. 18:37). The culpable act would not have been Jesus' claim to be the Messiah, but his acceptance of the title "Son of the Blessed" (v. 61) interpreted as a claim to divine status. Conversely, because the church understood Jesus as God's agent, the people who mocked him at his crucifixion are said to blaspheme him (Matt. 27:39; Mark 15:29; Luke 23:39), and blasphemy against the Holy Spirit, as the one who is operative in the activity of the early church, is considered an unforgivable sin (Mark 3:29; Luke 12:10).

blessing A blessing is frequently spoken in forms of the Hebrew root *brk,* while the term *asre* denotes an existing state of happiness. Corresponding to *brk* in the Septuagint, intertestamental literature, and the New Testament is the Greek *eulogein* and its derivatives.

Blessing has to do with relationships of power. Despite the Letter to the Hebrews 7:7, an inferior can bless a superior as well as a superior bless an inferior. When one of inferior status blesses someone of higher status, he/she is extolling the benefits conferred, as, for example, when Judith is blessed (Jdt. 14:7, 15:9, 12) for delivering the people. When God is blessed by humans, God is extolled for benefits He has or will bestow. At meals, for example, a blessing is said over the bread and wine to thank God for the food provided, as at the Qumran covenanters' meal (1QSa 2:17–21) and at the meal Jesus provides (Mark 6:41; 14:22). In Jubilees 19:17, Jacob is called a blessing from God in the midst of humans.

As in the biblical traditions, a father blesses his children (Sir. 3:8–9) and a priest pronounces a blessing from the Lord on the people (Sir. 50:20–21). In Jubilees, Rebekah, as well as the patriarchs, blesses her child (25:11–23). At Qumran, the Master (*maskil*) also pronounces blessings on the covenanters, the priests, and the prince of the congregation (1QSb). Jesus blesses his disciples as he departs for heaven in the Gospel of Luke (24:50). The blessings of God are most often found within the covenantal pattern—"If you obey me, I will bless you; if you do not, I will curse you"—as articulated in Deuteronomy 28. Such a covenantal pattern is explicitly found in the initiation ceremony of the Qumran covenanters (1QS 1:16–2:18; cf. 1QM 13). The story of the persecuted righteous one in the Wisdom of Solomon (1:16–3:9) refutes the idea that God does not bless the righteous. The righteous only seem to die, but in reality they attain the blessing of immortality. The barren woman and the eunuch are blessed if they lead righteous lives (Wisd. of Sol. 3:13–14). *See also under* BIRKAT.

Blessing against Enemies *see* BIRKAT HAMINIM

Blessing for Economic Prosperity *see* BIRKAT HASHANIM

Blessing for Redemption *see* BIRKAT GEULAH

Blessing for the Coming of the Messiah *see* BIRKAT DAVID

Blessing for the Restoration of Justice *see* BIRKAT HAMISHPAT

Blessing for the Righteous *see* BIRKAT HATZADIKIM

Blessing of Enjoyment *see* BIRKAT HANEHENIM

Blessing of Food *see* BIRKAT HAZAN

Blessing of Goodness *see* BIRKAT HATOB̲ VEHAMETIB̲

Blessing of Jerusalem *see* BIRKAT YERUSHALAIM

Blessing of Song *see* BIRKAT HASHIR

Blessing of Thanksgiving *see* BIRKAT HODAYAH

Blessing of the Bridegrooms *see* BIRKAT ḤATANIM

Blessing of the Land *see* BIRKAT HAARETZ

Blessing of the Month *see* BIRKAT HAḤODESH

Blessing of the Torah *see* BIRKAT HATORAH

Blind Man and Lame, Story of parable found in Epiphanius of Salamis, *Panarion* 64.70, 5–17, and in B. Sanhedrin 91a–b (with other rabbinic parallels). Two men, one blind and one lame, angry at being excluded from the wedding feast of the king's son, decide to ravage the royal garden in retribution, the lame man sitting on the blind man's shoulders and acting as his eyes. Afterward, each denies involvement by claiming his respective disability. The king, who perceives what happened, places the lame man on the shoulders of the blind one, thus forcing them to admit their common guilt. So will God judge body and soul together at the Resurrection.

blindness the inability to see. The loss of sight is seen in the Bible as the direct result of God's action. Moses is told in Exodus 4:11: "Who makes mortals mute or deaf? Is it not I, the Lord?" Special warning is given against taking advantage of those who are blind (Lev. 19:14; Deut. 27:18). It is a horrible act to blind anyone, whether a powerful figure such as Samson (Judg. 16:21) or a humble slave (Exod. 21:16).

The ability to see, or the lack of it, is also used symbolically to describe how well God's people understand his purpose. Lack of vision among them is compared with blindness (Deut. 28:28–29). God will also punish his disobedient people by closing their eyes so that they walk like the blind (Isa. 29:10); their refusal to seek justice will result in their groping like the blind (Isa. 59:9–10). Yet

God will enable them to regain their insight, to be filled with hope (Isa. 42:18, 43:8), to have their eyes opened (Isa. 35:5), and to enable others to see God's saving purpose in the world. This vision is not only for Israel but also for all the nations (Isa. 42:6–7).

The Dead Sea community believed that the Teacher of Righteousness had been sent by God to free his people from their blindness so that they could see and understand God's purpose for them (CD2). As for the physically blind, the Temple Scroll from Qumran excludes the blind from even entering Jerusalem when it is renewed in the new age (45:13–14). But for Philo of Alexandria in the first century C.E., blindness is a figure of speech for the failure of those concerned with wealth and power to see God and his way for his people. In the Gospel of Luke, Jesus is described as quoting from Isaiah 61 to declare that the coming of Messiah will bring recovery of sight by the blind (Luke 4:18). Jesus' answer to John the Baptist about who he is declares that through him "the blind receive their sight" (Luke 7:22, quoting Isa. 35:5–6). Several stories about Jesus report his restoring sight to the blind (Matt. 9:27–31; Mark 8:22–26; Luke 18:35–43; John 9:1–12). The importance across cultures of this belief in recovery from blindness as a sign of divine favor is evident in the report of Roman historians that the emperor Vespasian (69–79 C.E.) restored sight to a blind man.

blood The life force of all living beings, blood was forbidden for human consumption by Genesis 9:4–5; this legislation is repeated in the Book of Biblical Antiquities (Liber Antiquitatum Biblicarum) 3:11–12 and Pseudo-Phocylides 31 (probably a Christian addition) and strongly emphasized throughout Jubilees. Blood sacrifices were particularly potent (Lev. 16; Heb. 9–10), blood was employed in purification rituals, and it had an apotropaic function (Exod. 12, 29; Lev. 8). While the Qumran community did not participate in the Temple sacrifices, they did expect blood offerings in the new age (11Q Temple, cols. 11–12).

Mark 14:23–24 identifies the cup of the Last Supper as "blood of the covenant" (also 1 Cor. 11:25); the idea of actually drinking blood, however, would likely have been scandalous to most Jews (John 6:52–65). Following Genesis 9:4, the Apostolic Decree (Acts 15:29) forbids Gentile Christians to consume blood.

Boanerges (Gr.: Boanērges) nickname of James and John, sons of Zebedee, according to Mark 3:17, which interprets it "sons of thunder." The Semitic expression behind the Greek is debated, but the origin of the name is usually related to the incident in Luke 9:54.

Boethus, house of a high priestly house. Most of the post-Hasmonean high priests were appointed from several families. Simon, son of Boethus, an Alexandrian priest, was appointed high priest in 24 B.C.E. by Herod the Great, when Herod married Simon's daughter, Mariamme. Josephus's account of the relationships among the members of this family is confused. Simon's sons or brothers, Joazar, Eleazar, and perhaps Matthias, served near the end of Herod's reign and just after. Simon Cantheras, son of Boethus, was appointed by Agrippa I (r. 41–44 C.E.) in 41 C.E., as was his grandson Elionaeus, son of Cantheras, a few years later.

Boethusians a Jewish sect related philosophically to the Sadducees and in conflict with the Pharisees. According to a late rabbinic story, the sect is named for Boethus, a student of Antigonos of Sohko, who reported his teacher's statement that one should be like a servant who serves his master without thought of receiving wages. Interpreting this to mean that there is no future world nor resurrection, either Boethus himself or, in some versions, his students rejected the Pharisaic concept of divine reward. According to this same story, the Sadducees were created when Zadok, another of Antigonos of Sokho's students, reached the same conclusion (Abot deR. Natan 5).

The Boethusians disagree with Pharisaic authorities on a number of legal issues. These include determination of the day on which the omer is to be offered and whether on the Day of Atonement the high priest should prepare the incense within or outside of the holy of holies. It is unclear how late in rabbinic history the Boethusians existed. B. Shabbat 108a refers to a Boethusian's participation in a dispute with Akiba, but in the passage, the term seems to refer simply to a heretic. While no later references to Boethusians are extant, there is no particular evidence indicating the period of or reason for the demise of the sect.

bomolatry a type of worship, found especially in some Syrian cults of the Graeco-Roman period, in which the deity was represented by a stone or altar (*bomos*) rather than by a carved image. The term is from the Greek word *bōmos* (altar), which may derive from the Northwest Semitic word meaning "high place" (Heb.: *bamah*). The pagan cult imposed at the time of the Maccabean revolt has been alleged to have been a *bomos* cult. The reason is that the early sources mention a pagan altar placed on the altar of God before the Temple, but do not mention any sort of statue of a pagan god (only some much later sources refer to a statue of Zeus Olympius).

Bonosus commander of the Byzantine garrison in Antioch, early seventh century C.E. At the end of the sixth and the beginning of the seventh centuries, the Persian army moved westward into the Byzantine Empire. The Christian population, for the most part, did not become involved in the invasion. The Jews outside of Palestine, however, were anxious to rid themselves of Byzantine domination as a result of the policies of Justinian and his successors. In September 610, Khusro II approached Antioch with his army. The Jews of the city revolted, and Bonosus put down the revolt and ruthlessly punished the Jews.

Book of Deeds heavenly record of human deeds. Fundamental is the notion that God sees all that humans do and judges them on the basis of these deeds (Gen. 6:5–8). In Hellenistic times, the function of witnessing is delegated to angels (1 Enoch 9), who preserve knowledge of these deeds in the concrete form of books that will serve as evidence at the final judgment. The record is conceived of variously: a ledger containing all the deeds of humanity since creation; individual books for each person; separate books containing good and unrighteous deeds. Examples appear in Daniel 7:10; 1 Enoch 81:2, 89:70, 90:27, 97–104; Testament of Abraham 12–13 (A); and Revelation 20:12. *See also* BOOKS, HEAVENLY.

Book of Life heavenly register of the righteous who will survive the final judgment and obtain eternal life. In Psalm 69:28, the author asks that God the vindicator destroy his enemies, erasing them from the book of the living. Malachi 3:16–18, Isaiah 4:2–6, and Words of the Heavenly Lights 6:14 imagine a register of citizens for the earthly Jerusalem, the latter two connecting it with the return from the dispersion. Daniel 12:1 associates it with the eschatological judicial activity of Michael, Israel's angelic patron. According to 1 Enoch 104:1, it is located in God's throne room. The scenario of the final judgment in Revelation 20:12 mentions the books of human deeds and the book of life. *See also* BOOKS, HEAVENLY.

books, heavenly books or tablets of various sorts believed to exist in heaven. Texts from Mesopotamian antiquity are replete with references to books of wisdom and records of primordial history, as well as to heavenly tablets containing the details of human destiny and recording human deeds and misdeeds. These ideas have left their mark in biblical texts (Isa. 4:2–6; Mal. 3:16–18; Ps. 69:28), in the literature of Jewish apocalypticism and its Christian successors, and in rabbinic literature. In the apocalyptic world view, heavenly tablets or scrolls are important because their contents have special reality and permanent implications. According to Jubilees 1:27–29, an angel of the presence dictated the history of the world up to that time from a set of heavenly tablets. In addition, the Torah as revealed in Jubilees was engraved from eternity on heavenly tablets and dictated to Moses by angels (Jub. 3:31, 15:25). In 1 Enoch 81:1–4 the record of all human deeds exists already in prediluvian times (cf. also 93:2). One Qumran text mentions tablets standing in God's presence that schematize the periods of human history (4Q180). Both conceptions suggest a powerful determinism. Conversely, books of human deeds, with new entries written daily by angelic scribes, emphasize human responsibility and God's knowledge of the good deeds of the righteous and the wicked conduct of sinners, especially their oppression of the righteous. These books of deeds are guarantors of the judgment, where they will serve as evidence for reward or punishment. In general, the conception of heavenly books is integral to the dualistic world view of apocalypticism in which the hidden realm of heaven already contains the mechanisms and personnel that will effect the coming judgment. This world view is expressed in Christian form in Revelation 5–10, where the account of imminent historical events is revealed through the progressive unrolling of the seven-sealed scroll, which is one of many events in heaven that John witnesses as he learns of the imminent judgment and new creation. Paul is more selective, alluding on the one hand to a heavenly book of life (Phil. 4:3), but citing the angelic transmission of the Torah as an indication that it was second hand (Gal. 3:19–20) rather than as a guarantee that it reflected heavenly reality. The literature of rabbinic Judaism, while not apocalyptic in its world view, allows for the existence of heavenly books containing human deeds and the names of the righteous and the wicked (M. Abot 3:10; B. Ros. Has. 16b; B. Arak. 10b). *See also* BOOK OF DEEDS; BOOK OF LIFE.

books, hidden books considered secret, usually because they contain esoteric knowledge. There is a long tradition of "hidden" or "secret" books in antiquity, most claiming to contain esoteric teaching revealed by a supernatural figure.

In ancient Judaism, the tradition of hidden books is most strongly attested in the Graeco-Roman period (300 B.C.E. to 400 C.E.). Many Jewish apocalypses and other works belonging to the so-called pseudepigrapha claim either to be hidden books themselves or to have knowledge of such books (examples include 1 Enoch 74:2, 82:1–3; Jub. 4:19, 23:32; Dan. 12:4 and 9–10; 2 Enoch 23:1–6, 33:3–12; Life of Adam and Eve 50:1–2; Assumption of Moses 1:16–18; and 4 Ezra 12:36–38, 14:37–48). The apocalyptic genre, which many of these works represent, is an especially apt context for hidden books because apocalypses, by definition, claim to contain secrets revealed to a human seer by a divine agent.

The tradition of hidden books remains strong in early Christianity, especially within the apocalyptic genre, and is also widely attested in Gnosticism and Manichaeism.

books and scrolls Scrolls are rolls of papyrus or leather (parchment) made by gluing together into a single, long sheet up to about fifteen short sheets of papyrus. The whole is then wound around a wooden rod to form a scroll. Papyrus was made from the stem of the papyrus plant, which has a stem that is triangular in cross-section. The stems were first cut into pieces about 30 centimeters long, and then each stem was peeled and sliced lengthwise into strips. One layer of strips was placed on a flat surface so that all the fibers ran in one direction. A second layer was added at right angles to the first and the whole double layer was pressed and dried. The resulting sheet was polished and trimmed before being glued into long sheets for a scroll. Parchment or vellum was made from the skins of young goats, sheep, cattle, or antelopes. The leather was specially prepared by washing, polishing with pumice, and dressing with chalk. Technically speaking, vellum was a high-quality parchment. In the Byzantine period some vellums were died purple and written on with gold or silver inks.

Books were a feature mainly of the Graeco-Roman world from the second century C.E. The ancient book was really the codex, a sheaf of parchment or papyrus sheets sewn together at one edge like the Roman *pinax*. The latter consists of two wooden tablets with wax in their recessed faces held together at their edges with leather thongs. A codex was most often made by folding a stack of papyrus sheets together across the middle and sewing them together at the fold. There was an advantage in using parchment sheets for the codex, as one could write on both sides of a sheet with ease, and under constant use parchment lasted longer than papyrus. On the other hand, it is a bit easier to read papyrus with a highly contrasting ink.

Scribes wrote on either scroll or codex in black ink with a reed pen. Normally the scribe prepared for writing by scoring horizontal lines in double columns on each sheet of the scroll or codex. The Hebrew and Aramaic letters of the Dead Sea Scrolls, for example, hang from clearly scored lines, which are often easily seen, even in photographs. Most scrolls are written in a formal book hand rather than in an informal hand. The formal hand used the square letters derived from Aramaic, which supplanted the Old Hebrew forms of the letters by about 200 B.C.E. The informal hand is most often seen on receipts, deeds, and the like. Occasionally, because of the high cost of properly prepared parchment, scribes would reuse an old scroll. In this case, they simply scraped off the ink of the previous text and wrote a new text on the reused parchment. There is no recorded case where this was done with the Hebrew Bible, although such renditions are known for portions of the Greek Bible.

Booths, Feast of *see* TABERNACLE, FESTIVAL OF

borrowing the receipt at one's own request of the property of another, for free use, with the understanding that the property will be returned to its owner. In rabbinic law, the borrower of property is distinguished from the borrower of money (Heb.: *loveh*), since while the former must return exactly that which is borrowed, the latter may repay the lender in kind. Like scripture (Exod. 22:14), the Talmud holds the borrower to the strictest responsibility toward the borrowed goods. At the same time, rabbinic law is clear that since the object was borrowed for use, the borrower is not responsible for loss in value or depreciation resulting from normal operation. This extends even to a case in which the use of a borrowed animal leads to its death (B. Baba Metzia 96b). The responsibility of the borrower begins upon receipt of the object, marked by the same rite of drawing near (Heb.: *meshikha*) that finalizes a sale. A borrower who misuses and thereby damages the property is liable for the difference in value between the broken parts and the object as it was received (B. Baba Metzia 97a). The borrower need not entirely replace the borrowed item.

boulē *see* COUNCIL, CITY

bread an important food staple in ancient Israel, a "staff" supporting life (Lev. 26:26). In biblical Judaism, the word carries both literal and figurative significance since, in the Hebrew Bible, bread is commonly used as an image of nourishment and sustenance—the basic material support to maintain life. The word often occurs in an extended sense to mean "food" in general.

Three important biblical references to bread are (1) as a ritual offering to God, in the form of either a burnt sacrifice or the "Bread of the Presence"; (2) the unleavened bread that was eaten during Passover; and (3) the manna that the Israelites ate in the wilderness, which is often referred to as "bread from heaven" (e.g., Exod. 16:3–32).

In intertestamental Jewish literature, these basic meanings are both continued and extended. Several sources stress the importance of giving bread to the needy (Tob. 4:16–17; Sir. 12:5). Ben Sira states that Wisdom will feed the wise with "the bread of understanding" (Sir. 15:3). A noteworthy description of the Exodus manna appears in the Wisdom of Solomon 16:20–21: "Thou [God] didst supply them from heaven with bread ready to eat . . . and the bread, ministering to the desire of the one who took it, was changed to suit everyone's liking." In rabbinic literature, manna is referred to as bread eaten by ministering angels (B. Yoma 75b).

An important formulaic usage occurs in Joseph and Asenath, which describes a Jew as one who "eats bread of life and drinks a cup of immortality and anoints oneself with ointment of incorruptibility" (8:5 and pass.).

Bread is significant in a number of contexts in early Christian literature. Stories of Jesus' multiplication of the loaves in all four canonical Gospels are probably intended in part to evoke Moses' miracle of the manna. It is noteworthy that descriptions of this miracle and accounts of the synoptic eucharistic meal both list the same sequence of events: Jesus "took" bread, "blessed" and "broke" it, and "gave" it to his companions. These are actions that occurred at the beginning of a traditional Jewish meal. In the synoptic accounts of the eucharistic meal, Jesus identifies the bread as his "body" (Mark 14:22 and parallels).

The most extended early Christian treatment of bread occurs in John 6, where, after multiplying the loaves, Jesus identifies himself as the "bread of life" (6:35) and as "the living bread which came down from heaven," which, "if anyone eats . . . , he will live forever" (6:51).

bread of the presence *see* SHOWBREAD

Breshit Rabbah *see* GENESIS RABBAH

bride *see* MARRIAGE; VIRGIN; WOMEN, POSITION OF

bridegroom A symbol of rejoicing, the bridegroom may be crowned (Song of Sol. 3:11) or garlanded (Isa. 61:10), and accompanied by musicians (1 Macc. 9:37–39) and friends (Matt. 25:1–10). The bridegroom's new status grants him exemption from army service (Deut. 24:5, and see Luke 14:20). As metaphor, the bridegroom is God and the bride is Israel (Hos.; Isa. 54); similarly, Paul describes the Church as a bride of Christ (2 Cor. 11:2; Eph. 5:26–27; Rev. 21:2). Calling Jesus a bridegroom thus suggests his association with heaven, the new relationships his followers engage in, and the joy his presence brings (Matt. 9:15).

brigands *see* BANDITS; LĒSTĒS

brit milah *see* BERIT MILAH

building traditional Jewish and early Christian metaphor for the righteous and faithful community. Isaiah 28 (especially, vv. 14–22), with its critique of the religious and political leadership in Jerusalem, provided an exegetical basis for the image, which sometimes contrasts the righteous and their opponents as the true and the false Israel. Two passages in the Qumran literature combine the metaphor with the image of the community as God's "everlasting planting" (cf. CD 1:7). In the Community Rule 8:1–10, the building metaphor governs the description of the founding and functions of the Qumran community. Line 7 quotes Isaiah 28:16, and the passage expands the metaphor by depicting the community as a temple and priesthood offering atonement for the Land of Israel and meting out God's recompense on the wicked. An explicit contrast between two communities is also evident in Hodayot 6, which mixes several metaphors. The author's new religious home is, at once, a tree that is "an everlasting planting" (lines 14–17) and a fortified city into which the author has fled for shelter from the chaotic waters of death (cf. 1QH 6:25–27 and Isa. 28:16–17). Although the language of Isaiah 28 is not explicit, the Apocalypse of Weeks (1 Enoch 93:1–10, 91:11–17), which antedates the two Qumran texts, also combines the images of plant (93:2, 5, 10) and building (91:11). The former refers to Abraham (93:5a, also its root, 93:8), Israel (93:5b), and the eschatological community of the chosen (93:10). The building metaphor describes the activity and teaching of the wicked as "the foundations of violence" and "the structure of deceit," whom the righteous, the executors of God's judgment, will "uproot" (91:10–11; cf. 1QS 8:6–7). The metaphor is striking in the absence of any reference to construction of the Second Temple and in contrast to the promise that God will build a glorious eschatological temple (91:13).

The building metaphor, sometimes with allusion to Isaiah 28, appears with some frequency in the New Testament, notably in connection with the figure of the apostle Peter, whose Aramaic and Greek names mean "rock." In Matthew 16:17–19, Jesus commissions Simon the son of Jonah to be the rock on whom the church will be built, which will withstand the powers of Sheol (cf. Isa. 28:16–18; 1QH 6:22–17), and in 1 Peter 2:4–8, the apostle (alleged to be the author of this text), describes the church as building and priesthood, combining rock language from Isaiah 28:16, Psalm 118:22, and Isaiah 8:14–15. A related use of the image appears in Ephesians 2:19–22, where the church is the household of God, built on the apostolic foundation and functioning as God's temple. The images of building and planting are combined in Paul's discussion of the founding of the church at Corinth (1 Cor. 3), which also refers to Cephas (Peter, v. 22; cf. 1:12). *See also* CORNERSTONE; FOUNDATION; PILLARS IN JERUSALEM; ROCK.

bull a minor motif in Jewish art, usually in funerary art and in synagogue mosaic floors. The bull's head (bucranium), borrowed directly from Graeco-Roman heraldic art, appears in relief on two sarcophagi in the Jewish catacombs of Beth Shearim. Bulls also appear in the middle register of the great painted frescoes of the synagogue at Dura in Iraq. The bull also appears in relief on lintels from the synagogues of Ahmadieh, Kasabieh, Tiberias, and Horvat Ammudim. In mosaic floors there is more variation in the depiction of the bull. For example, a bull and a lion flank the Greek and Aramaic inscriptions at Beth Alpha, though both the bull and the lion are upside down with reference to the inscriptions. The bull appears with the red cow in the Sepphoris mosaic. Bulls are part of the art of the zodiac panels at Beth Alpha, Naaran, and Hammath Tiberias. Considering the frequent use of the bull motif in Graeco-Roman art and its antecedents in the ancient Near East, one might be surprised that the bull does not appear more commonly in Jewish art of the period. On the other hand, it is a strong symbol for divinity in pagan religions, which may explain a reluctance to permit it a greater role in Jewish art.

Bun a shortened form of the names A<u>b</u>in, A<u>b</u>un, and Ra<u>b</u>in, appearing exclusively in Palestinian sources; *see also* A<u>B</u>IN

Bürger-Tempel-Gemeinde German phrase meaning "civic-temple community." It was coined by modern scholars as a way of describing the type of temple state in which the citizens (as opposed to slaves and free noncitizens) governed. Several examples are known from antiquity. It has also been proposed that Judah after the return from exile was organized in this way under Persian rule: the *golah* (diaspora), or those returning from Babylonia, were citizens, while those Jews who had not gone into captivity (and their descendants) were excluded from the privileges of citizenship and worship.

burial Providing for proper burial of the dead was treated in ancient Israel as a paramount responsibility of the surviving family or other kin. Biblical depictions of the importance of the purchase of a burial site (e.g., the story of the cave purchased by Abraham, Gen. 23) and the Bible's use of the image of unburied corpses to depict the worst possible fate (e.g., Deut. 28:26) suggest the importance attributed to proper treatment of the corpse in general and to burial in particular.

The Bible commonly refers to burial in family tombs. To be buried with one's family or, at least, in one's ancestral homeland was a significant concern of those who had moved away from their kin. In light of this attitude, death often is referred to as being "gathered to one's kin" (Gen. 25:8) or "sleeping with one's fathers" (I Kings 11:23). Since scripture does not depict an afterlife, such references appear to refer literally to entombment in a family burial place.

The Israelites did not practice cremation or embalming (cf. Jacob and Joseph, Gen. 50:2, 26, who were embalmed following Egyptian practice). Coffins were not normally used, the body instead being dressed in shrouds and carried to the burial place on a bier (2 Sam. 3:31; cf. Gen. 50:26, which refers to the customary Egyptian use of a coffin). Since contact with corpses caused ritual impurity, tombs were marked with whitewash, and priests' participation in funerary rites was limited (Lev. 21:1–4; Num. 19:11–22; Ezek. 44:25–27).

Most of our knowledge of Israelite and early Jewish burial practices derives from the Second Temple period and later. In the majority of Palestinian sites that have been excavated, corpses were left in tombs until the flesh decayed, at which time the remaining bones were placed in ossuaries. Individual burial, however, is also evidenced. The cemetery at Qumran, for instance, reveals over a thousand individual burials. Literary evidence for this period indicates that burial practices included washing and anointing the body and wrapping it in a shroud (John 11:44, on Lazarus, mentions linen strips of cloth). Interment is the major ritual present in the Book of Tobit and is of concern in the Testament of Job.

Talmudic law requires that burial occur as soon as possible after death, usually on the same or following day. This requirement is derived from Deuteronomy 21:22–23, which states that the body of one executed by hanging must be buried on the same day. As signs of respect and honor, prior to burial, the corpse was watched over (*shemirah*) and washed (*taharah*). This washing was not out of concern for cultic cleanness (a corpse is intrinsically unclean and renders unclean all who touch or are shadowed by it) but was viewed as a continuation of the hygiene that applied when the individual lived. Prior to burial, the body was dressed in shrouds made of plain linen.

In Talmudic times, as in the Bible, burial generally was in a cave, to which the corpse was carried on a bier in a funeral procession (M. Berakhot 3:1). In posttalmudic Jewish practice, burial is in the ground in a wooden casket with no metal, to assure complete disintegration to dust. In light of the requirement that the body return to dust, embalming to prevent decay or improve the corpse's appearance is forbidden. Embalming is permitted only if it is a requirement of the non-Jewish government. Cremation is prohibited as an act of desecration of the corpse. *See also* BURIAL SITES; CATACOMBS, ITALIAN; COFFIN; OSSUARY; SARCOPHAGUS.

burial sites Jewish burials during the Persian period continued the traditions of the Iron Age, with family tombs predominating. In rectangular underground chambers, the dead were laid out on benches cut from the rock. Reburial took place in special chambers cut out below the benches. In the Hellenistic period burial slots or recesses (loculi) were cut into the sides of the tomb chambers, and occasionally the walls of the tomb bore paintings of vine motifs and birds or even hunting scenes. In the Roman period, the family tomb continued with loculus burial the rule, then reburial in ossuaries (see below). Roman tombs often have an unroofed forecourt opening onto several tombs. Beginning in the Hellenistic period, but continuing in the Roman period, great burial monuments are known, for example, the Tomb of Absalom in Jerusalem. In the Byzantine period, tombs generally reverted to the bench type, or sometimes two or three sarcophagi were cut into the bedrock. Individual sarcophagi burials and an occasional coffin are also known from the Roman period onward, as noted in the following survey.

Persian period burials are well represented in ancient Judea or Persian Yehud. For example, at Tell el-Farah (South) the typical tomb was a rock-cut rectangular chamber with a wide door. The dead were laid out on benches to the left and right of the central standing area. Grave goods are well known, most commonly pottery and an occasional tool or weapon.

Hellenistic period cemeteries of impressive size are associated with sites such as Marissa (biblical Maresha). A typical family tomb at Marissa was cut from the soft chalklike limestone of the area. Steps led into a low, flat-roofed antechamber. Straight ahead stood a long, rectangular burial chamber with a flat roof. To the left and right stood rectangular burial chambers with barrel-vault roofs. In each rectangular chamber one stood in a room with thirteen to sixteen burial slots cut into three walls. Each slot had a pitched roof, while the walls of the burial chamber were painted in an animal frieze. After the family placed the body in its loculus, they placed a stone over the door that was sealed with clay. Above the burial recess or loculus someone wrote the name of the deceased in charcoal or clay. The surprise is that several languages appear in the same tomb: Aramaic, Greek, and Nabatean. For example one such inscription reads, "In the second year in the month of Dystros [grave of] Sabo, the daughter of Kosnatanos." Kosnatanos is an Idumean name, the descendants of the ancient Edomites. The Tomb of Absalom (also known as the Pillar of Absalom) in Jerusalem is a series of burial chambers cut into a limestone cliff with a monolith cut from the bedrock about 6 by 6.5 meters in dimension. It was decorated with pilasters of Ionic columns. The superstructure was built of masonry and resembles a conical tower. The total height of the monument, also known as a *nephesh* (the Hebrew word for person or soul), comes to 16.5 meters.

Roman cemeteries are well represented in ancient Palestine around any village, town, or city. A typical cemetery would have many open courtyards or forecourts cut down into the bedrock. A flight of steps led into the interior forecourt where one could approach the blocked entrances to the three or four tombs that were cut into the bedrock. Rolling stones, and sometimes large cut stones, blocked the entrances. The so-called Sanhedriyya tombs in Jerusalem furnish an important example of a wealthy family's tomb (with no necessary connection with the Sanhedrin). In this case, several tombs, evidently cut at the same time, face a common forecourt. The entrances to the tombs were cut to resemble the facades of buildings. The facade is decorated with acanthus leaves, citrons, and pomegranates carved in low relief. The first room is an internal vestibule about 9.9 by 9 meters with low benches around three sides. From the vestibule one entered the square burial chamber by walking down a set of stairs. A series of loculi opened off the main chamber, and four secondary burial chambers were cut into the south and east walls. The burial chambers were furnished with smaller chambers, evidently for reburial of the bones one year after interment. This is secondary burial, also known from the biblical period. Fragments of ossuaries and sarcophagi were found in the tombs.

The only excavated Jewish catacomb in ancient Palestine is at Beth Shearim in western Galilee, though there may be another at Alma near the border with Lebanon. These catacombs are of the Roman and Byzantine periods and were sometimes furnished with imposing masonry facades with three entrances. In general one entered each catacomb from an open courtyard cut into the hill. Sometimes there are entrances to catacombs on three sides of the courtyard, each supplied with stone, hinged doors, cut to resemble wooden doors. Long halls with side niches provide room for the burials, which may be in sarcophagi, loculi, or arcosolia (flat benches with a rock-cut arch over the burial spot). These catacombs are a rich repository of inscriptions in Greek, Hebrew, and Aramaic, and also of Jewish art.

Jewish catacombs are also known in Rome. For example the catacomb of Monteverde has produced many Jewish epitaphs in Greek, Aramaic, and Latin. Some of these epitaphs show, in addition to the epitaph proper, menorahs, grape or ivy vines, but also shofar, etrog, lulab, and incense shovel. One such epitaph in Aramaic reads, "Annia, wife of Bar Calabria."

Sarcophagi and ossuaries are cut stone coffins and reburial containers, respectively. They are best known from the Roman period. Coffins, often of lead, but also of wood, are known from a few Jewish burials. The lead coffins were decorated with generic motifs, copied from the general culture, or featured Jewish motifs well known in other contexts. For example, one lead coffin from Beth Shearim shows a Menorah with shofar, incense shovel, lulab, and etrog at its end. Its cover is decorated with vines, birds, human heads, and small menorahs. *See also* CATACOMBS, ITALIAN.

burnt offering *see* ALTAR; OLAH

Butmiyyah ancient Jewish village and synagogue site in the northern Golan Heights. The evidence for the synagogue's presence is a set of highly decorated black basalt stones in reuse in the modern village. A carved basalt lintel bears a nine- or ten-branched menorah, which displays a circle on either side and several Greek letters. A doorpost elsewhere on the site presents a ten-branched menorah flanked by etrogs. A second lintel bears no distinctive Jewish art, only a design that looks like a four-leaf clover and a second design that looks like a spoked wheel and has parts of a Greek inscription. There may have been a Christian presence in the village, as a third lintel has crosses carved on it. The village was watered by a perennial spring using an aqueduct. The usual date assigned to the architectural fragments is the third or fourth century C.E.

buying and selling transfer of property from one individual to another. In talmudic law, such transfer is dependent upon the establishment of explicit terms of the transfer and evidence that the parties involved agree upon these terms. Prima facie evidence for this agreement is *kinyan,* that is, a physical act of acquisition appropriate to the object involved, movable or immovable. In the absence of *kinyan,* a party to the agreement may withdraw, even if all other terms of the purchase were fixed.

Following *kinyan,* a purchaser or seller may withdraw if in similar circumstances most people would have rejected the agreement, for example, in cases of duress or an error regarding price. Certain sales are intrinsically void, including those involving a person who lacks the capacity to formulate intention (e.g., a deaf-mute, idiot, or minor) or, according to some talmudic sources, in a case in which the object being purchased does not yet exist. Sales may, however, be made subject to specific terms and are not valid until those terms are met. M. Ba<u>b</u>a Batra 4:8ff. lists conditions that automatically apply to the sale of specific types of property. *See also* ACQUISITION OF PROPERTY.

Byzantine period roughly the mid-fourth to the mid-seventh centuries C.E., representing one of the greatest flowerings of Jewish material, cultural, and intellectual life in the long history of Jews in the Land of Israel. This fact has been obscured until scholarship began to focus on the late centuries of Jewish life and the Islamic takeover of the region from 638–643 C.E. It has also been difficult to gauge the success of Jews in Israel until massive archaeological evidence was published in the last three decades. This material began to offset the literary picture that had been heavily determined by the rule of Christian emperors beginning with Constantine the Great, who took control of the area in 324, and the establishment of Palestine as a Christian Holy Land during the same period. Although Jewish rule over Jews of Palestine was officially ended when the patriarchate was abolished (c. 425), the communities continued to flourish as wealthy, creative, and intellectually vibrant entities up to and well into the first century of Islamic rule. The great synagogues of Capernaum and Naburiya in the Galilee and Kazrin in the Golan Heights are evidence of this continued activity. Thus, it is no accident that one of the greatest Jewish intellectual achievements of antiquity, the Palestinian (or Jerusalem) Talmud was codified around 400 C.E. by this first generation of Byzantine Jews.

M. Broshi's estimate that the total population of the country was around a million people in this period is probably correct. Great ethnic, religious, and linguistic diversity, however, characterize the peoples of the Holy Land. By the end of the period, Greek was the dominant language in the heavily gentile areas of the country, like the Kinneret region, Judea, the southern Golan Heights, and the northern Negeb. It was also the official governmental language of the country, having replaced Latin sometime in the fifth century. Many of the inscriptions by the Jewish populace in these regions appear in Greek, as the donor inscriptions from the fourth-century synagogue at Hammath Tiberias or the fifth-century Homeric scenes and quotation on the mosaic floor of the home of Leontius in Beth Shean (Sythopolis) indicate.

Most families in the more exclusively Jewish areas (such as Upper Galilee, Hebron Hills, and northern Golan) spoke and wrote Late Palestinian Aramaic, the language of the Palestinian Talmud. Hebrew had become the language of scripture and of holy dedicatory synagogue inscriptions.

The Samaritans, clustered in small groups in cities such as Caesarea Maritima and concentrated in Samaria, continued to use their own language. After Greek, the most important gentile Christian language was Syriac, as indicated by the Syriac version of Eusebius of Caesarea's *Martyrs of Palestine,* as well as the importance of having a Syriac translator participate in the Christian liturgy. In the southern part of the Negeb and the northeastern corner of the Golan, the pre-Islamic period tribes spoke Arabic. Groups of resident foreigners, mostly from Egypt, Asia Minor, Greece, and Syria, also inhabited the land.

The very small number of cemetery and tomb excavations that have been carried out and published leave scant information about what the various peoples looked like and whom they married. What we do know from the two numerically largest groups, Jews and Christians, from skeletal and literary evidence is that they tended to marry into their own separate groups and to minimize contact between themselves and outsiders.

Such limited evidence as we now have makes excavations being currently carried on at sites like Beth Shean in the Jordan Valley, Caesarea Maritima, and Sepphoris all the more important for information they may yield on the interaction of Jew and Christian. The late fourth-century date of the beautiful limestone synagogue at Capernaum and its continuance throughout this period, just a few meters from the Church of the House of St. Peter, also shows continued Jewish determination to stake out its turf, as Christians began to move into completely or predominantly Jewish areas.

The most dramatic shift in the religious orientation of the country since the tenth century B.C.E. occurred during the Byzantine period as Christian pilgrims flocked to Palestine to visit and settle. The long march to establish Christian reverence for and ownership of the Holy Land by the sixth century C.E. has been recently studied and detailed by R. L. Wilken. The building program carried on in Jerusalem by Christian emperors beginning with Constantine best underscores Christianity's designs on the Holy Land. Such designs reach their apogee with the building project carried out by Justinian (527–565), who extended the main *cardo* (north/south street) of Jerusalem to the south and built a huge church called the Nea in the Jewish Quarter. Best known previously only by the depiction of the *cardo* and the church on the sixth century Madeba mosaic map, N. Avigad's excavations in the Jewish Quarter recently located both sites.

The newly powerful Christian presence in the land also settled the deserts of Judaea and the northern Negeb and Sinai to an extent unknown in previous history. The Christian monks who settled the Judaean Desert originally came themselves as pilgrims and stayed to service the needs of other pilgrims coming to and through the deserts. By the late fifth and early sixth centuries, a whole system of roads and footpaths with access to the fifty-five monasteries were established by the three thousand inhabitants of the Judaean Desert, as Y. Hirshfeld has recently shown.

In the northern Negeb, where almost no Jews resided, the Byzantine Christians brought about a revival of city culture and a blooming of the desert. Superb advancements in the use of dams, channels, and terracing made possible the irrigation of the desert from runoff rainwater. So competent and extensive was the cultivation of the arid land that by the sixth century the boundary of the uncultivated "inner desert" had receded from the north to some ten miles south of Nessana Village (Tel Nessana). The northern Negeb cities were adorned with multiple churches, serving both the pilgrims passing through to Jerusalem and as pilgrimage spots for the local inhabitants. The first conversions of the Arab tribes to Christianity were carried out by these Christian descendants of the Nabateans.

In spite of more recent indications that the Jewish population declined in numbers in selected regions like Galilee and Golan, the fifth and sixth centuries inaugurated a period of extensive building of basilical (interior columned) synagogues in a variety of styles, including the Galilean style (three-doored building, oriented by the narrow end or facade towards Jerusalem) and the basilical building with an interior or exterior apse on the wall facing Jerusalem (either the long or "broadhouse" wall or the short or narrow wall of the hall).

There are indications, however, that the elaborate synagogues of the Byzantine period functioned for a Jewish populace that had raised its personal piety towards scripture and individual prayer to new heights. The numerous rebuilds of the *bimah* to raise the height of the platform from which scripture was read indicates this, as does the appearance of a separate building for the study of scripture directly adjacent to the synagogue, the *beit midrash* or "house of study." The discovery of such a complex at Meroth in Galilee illustrates this new trend. Similarly, the recent work by Dan Urman demonstrating that the synagogue building within Israel (as opposed to the diaspora nomenclature) is not referred to as a "house of prayer" until the Byzantine period further underscores the new personal piety of the Jews, perhaps in response to the newly pious Christians around them. Conversely, the takeover by Christians of long-practiced Jewish observances, such as ossuary burial, resulted in their abandonment by Jews.

What makes the Byzantine period so very difficult to characterize is the fact that two completely opposite trends are accelerating throughout these centuries. On the one hand, by the late fifth century Israel is an international province with religious links to the entire empire and trade links to Britain, North Africa, and the entire eastern Mediterranean, as witnessed by both the presence of pilgrims and ceramic evidence. On the other hand, as the various groups withdrew into themselves, most peoples in the Holy Land lived, shopped, and traded locally. Hence, most archaeological surveys and excavations carried out these days are careful to set their findings within a regional picture, making regionalism of paramount importance in scholarly discussions.

Sometime around 350 C.E. the country was divided politically into north and south districts, and then, around 400, it was separated into three separate provinces: Palestina prima (the north coastal plain, Judaea, Idumaea, Samaria, Peraea) with its capital at Caesarea Maritima; Palestina secunda (Galilee, the Palestinian Decapolis, the Golan) with its capital at Sythopolis (Beth Shean); and Palestiana tertia (formerly Palestina salutaris) whose capital has not yet been determined. Working archaeologists have known for a long time that the political divisions of the country had very little to do with the divisions of the country as measured by material remains of the peoples. Looked at archaeologically, the three regions of the country have always been divided by material differences into the North, Samaria, and Judaea and the South. These three subdivisions, nonetheless, have given way to new regions and subregions in a series of studies by Eric M. Meyers and James F. Strange on Galilean regionalism, Dan Urman on the Golan, and Kenneth Gutwein on the Negeb.

By the Byzantine period, each region or subregion of the country had its preferred market towns, and each region seems to have had its own pottery factories that produced the kitchen or crude-ware pottery used for daily life and the commercial amphorae in which local products were packaged and shipped.

The end of Jewish and Christian Palestine in the most recent research has come to resemble the picture of the founding of the Jewish nation in the tenth century B.C.E. The incursion of the Arab peoples of the southern and eastern deserts in the late 630s and early 640s C.E. resembles not so much a conquest as a melding with and takeover from the resident peoples of ancient Palestine.

When the Islamic rulers appeared out of the inner desert and entered the cultivated lands, they found groups of people somewhat fragmented into regional enclaves and not particularly fond of each other. They entered into a land where defense had become quite a local and irregular matter since the subsidies sent from Constantinople to pay the frontier army had been terminated in the reign of the Byzantine emperor Justinian. Indications from the Nessana Papyri and from the building boom suggest that lowered taxes at first produced some new wealth among the inhabitants. The long-term result was that the Moslem invaders found a badly divided and badly defended populace. Within the first one hundred years of Islamic rule, the attention, economies, and political accountabilities of all the residents of formerly Byzantine Israel will have been turned away from Jerusalem and the West towards Damascus and the East for the first time in over a millennium.

caduceus *see* COIN SYMBOLS

Caesar cognomen (additional third personal name) common in the gens (clan or group of families) named Julia. Gaius Julius Caesar was the family's most famous member. C. Octavius, the son of Julius Caesar's niece, was adopted by Julius Caesar and took the adoptive name Gaius Julius Caesar Octavianus. Because of the family's prominence at the beginning of the imperial period, later emperors also took that cognomen, and Caesar came to be a title for the Roman emperor. *See also* AUGUSTUS CAESAR; GAIUS CAESAR; JULIUS CAESAR.

Caesarea coastal city of ancient Palestine and its capital, built by Herod the Great and named in honor of Caesar Augustus. Its port, named Sebastos (Greek for Augustus), was built by Herod's engineers of huge blocks of stone and of concrete poured in forms under water. These formed huge breakwaters with an entrance on the north. According to Josephus the port featured a lighthouse and three colossal statues (*War* 1.21.6–7 or 411–414). The port could hold the entire Roman fleet at anchor. A series of Roman vaults on the shore formed magazines for off-loading freighters that plied its port. At least one of these vaults was converted into an underground worship center for the god Mithra, who was popular among Roman soldiers. There is also archaeological evidence for an inner harbor.

Herod built a palace at Caesarea, a theater near the palace, a temple to Augustus, an impressive aqueduct bringing water from Mount Carmel, and other Roman structures. The theater seats about four thousand and has been rebuilt for modern productions. In one of its later renovations, a Latin inscription was found in reuse simply as a stone. The inscription mentions a Tiberium or temple to Tiberius built by Pontius Pilate, the Roman governor (procurator) from 26–36 C.E. His rank is given as prefect, which was not known before this inscription was found. Originally the floor of the theater was plastered, and the plaster was then painted in brilliant colors. The podium of the Temple of Augustus stood fifty Roman feet above the surrounding terrain and was built on enormous Roman vaults. Other pagan temples undoubtedly were erected but have not yet been found. The city coins of Caesarea show other deities, such as Tyche (Fortuna), Artemis, and Serapis. A sixth-century-C.E. inscription mentions a temple to Hadrian.

The aqueducts of Caesarea are a marvel of Roman engineering. The high-level aqueduct brought drinking water, sometimes in a tunnel, sometimes in a pipe on stone arches, from springs more than twelve kilometers to the north. Later a second, low-level aqueduct brought water from the Crocodile River (or Zerqa River) five kilometers to the north. This aqueduct evidently served for irrigation of the many fields around Caesarea. Latin inscriptions affixed to the aqueducts attest to their repairs by Roman auxiliary legions in the second century C.E. and later. The city wall of the Herodian period cannot be identified with certainty, but two round towers and a polygonal tower in a wall on the north side of the city appear to be part of Herod's gate.

Most of the archaeological evidences of Caesarea date to the Byzantine and later periods. For example, most of the paved streets of Caesarea are Byzantine in date. Also a hippodrome, or horse-racing arena, turned out to be Byzantine when excavated. This structure stood near the Byzantine city wall east of the center of the city. The *spina* down the center of the hippodrome has been identified, as well as some of its red granite stones, including the base of an obelisk. A possible amphitheater, supposedly used for Herod's dedicatory games and later for bloody spectacles held by Titus to dispose of Jewish insurrectionists, has been identified by aerial photography. Excavation shows only that its stones were used by later builders in other structures. A synagogue of the fourth century was excavated next to the shore measuring about 18 by 9 meters. In its vicinity were found many architectural fragments, including one capital with a menorah in relief. A fragment of marble gave the traditional list of localities in Galilee where the twenty-four priestly courses from Jerusalem settled after the destruction of the Second Temple. A Greek inscription of the Byzantine period reads, "Beryllos, the head of the synagogue and administrator, the son of Justus, made the mosaics of the dining room [triclinium] at his own expense." Near the synagogue was found a hoard of 3,700 Byzantine coins, the last of which dated to 356 C.E. A bath of the Byzantine period is also known. From the fourth century C.E. the Christian population of the city increased dramatically, so that Christian churches were eventually built at Caesarea in the fourth century. One such church has been excavated east of the city. A building just south of the crusader city contained a mosaic with a quotation from the New Testament. The excavator has suggested that this was the Christian library or archive of great notoriety mentioned in many ancient sources. Many sarcophagi and funerary inscriptions have been found north, northeast, east, and south of the city. One large tomb with a colonnaded forecourt has been excavated south of the city, suggesting that a large cemetery is yet to be investigated around the city. *See also* CAESAREA SYNAGOGUE.

Caesarea in Cappadocia capital of Cappadocia; prior to becoming a Roman province under Tiberius in 17 C.E., known as Mazaca. In the Talmud it is referred to as Mezigah of Cappadocia, Megizah of Cappadocia, and Mazaca-Caesarea. B. Moed Katan 26a reports that during the war between Shapur I and the Romans, Shapur killed twelve thousand Jews in Mazaca-Caesarea.

Caesarea-Philippi city on the southern slope of Mount Hermon, built at a major spring that serves as a source of the Jordan River. The city is known under the name of Panion or Paneas in Hellenistic sources, an indication of a local sanctuary dedicated to Pan. Augustus Caesar gave the city to Herod the Great (Josephus, *Ant.* 18.2.1). Herod is credited with building a sanctuary to Augustus and with building his palace at Caesarea-Paneas. The city, however, was not a political center until it passed into the hands of his son Herod Philip in 4 B.C.E., the era of its founding used on its coins. The city minted its own coins from the time of Augustus until the early third century C.E. Philip made the city the capital of his tetrarchy and called it Caesarea in honor of Augustus Caesar or Tiberius Caesar. Later, King Agrippa II used the city as his capital but renamed it Neronias in honor of Nero, his patron. Today it is called Caesarea-Philippi to distinguish it from another Caesarea, namely, Caesarea Maritima on the Mediterranean coast. A large cave, evidently the cave of Pan, is associated with rock-cut niches outside the cave to the left. One of the Greek inscriptions mentions Pan and Echo, a mountain nymph. Evidently a spring arose in the cave in antiquity. Its course was covered and altered by Roman engineers, probably of Herod Philip, who had it emerge outside the cave directly from a round lagoon. The coins minted at Caesarea-Philippi feature Pan playing his pipes or, on smaller denominations, his pipes alone. Recent excavations have revealed a huge Roman period building, perhaps a palace. The location of the palace of Herod the Great has been recognized for years because of the remains of walls with stonework unique to his reign. The city may be mentioned in the Talmud under the name Kisariyon.

Caesarea Synagogue fourth- and fifth-century synagogue excavated near the Mediterranean Sea at Caesarea, capital of ancient Palestine. The earliest remains identified by the excavator as a synagogue are those of a nearly square, Herodian-period building only about nine meters each side, built directly on top of foundations of houses from the late Hellenistic period. It is impossible to determine what the building was used for in this period, but it may have been a small gathering room for the Jewish community. In the third century a long, narrow prayer hall was built on top the ruins of the square building and paved with mosaics. It is in poor condition. This building was refurbished in the late fourth century and paved with a new mosaic. It remained in use until it was destroyed by fire in the sixth century. When founded its mosaic floors contained Greek inscriptions honoring donors: Theodorus the son of Olympus and Beryllos the son of Justus, the head of the synagogue. Other remains with Jewish art or symbols include a fragment of a Hebrew inscription mentioning the list of the priestly courses in Jerusalem and the localities to which they fled in 70 C.E., lamps decorated with menorahs, capitals with menorahs incised or in relief, and fragments of a chancel screen decorated with a menorah. A certain Patricius was honored as counsul on an additional capital. It is known that Patricius was consul at Caesarea in 459.

Caiaphas, Joseph high priest (18–36 C.E.), appointed by the Roman prefect Valerius Gratus. According to the Gospel of John 18:13, Caiaphas was the son-in-law of Annas (Ananus, son of Sethi). When Vitellius, the Roman consular legate of Syria, removed Pilate from office, he also replaced Caiaphas with Jonathan, son of Ananus. According to the Gospel of Matthew (26:3, 57) and the Gospel of John (11:49; 18:13–14, 24, 28), Caiaphas was the high priest instrumental in sending Jesus of Nazareth to the Roman prefect Pilate for execution.

Cain son of Adam and Eve; father of Enoch; the first city-builder. He was ancestor of Jubal, the first musician, and Tubal-cain, worker in bronze and iron (Gen. 4). Cain became angry when God rejected his sacrifice but accepted that of his brother, Abel, so he killed Abel, becoming the first murderer.

Cain is remembered primarily as Abel's murderer and as a negative moral example (Jub. 4; 4 Macc. 18:11; Life of Adam and Eve 23). The Apocalypse of Abraham 24:5 says that the "crafty adversary" made Cain kill Abel; 1 John 3:12 blames it on the "evil one"; and Testament of Benjamin 7:1–4 blames Beliar. Testament of Adam 3:3 says that Cain killed Abel out of passion for their sister. Wisdom of Solomon 10:3 says that when Cain killed the righteous Abel out of anger, he departed from wisdom. Josephus considers Cain the embodiment of greed (*Ant.* 1.2.1–2, secs. 52–66).

Cain's descendants also attract attention. Testament of Adam 3:3 says Cain's daughters caused the Flood. 1 Enoch 22:7 says that Abel's spirit will petition God until Cain's seed is eliminated from the earth. Testament of Benjamin 7:5 and Jude 11 liken all immoral people to Cain.

Cairo Damascus Document *see* DAMASCUS DOCUMENT

Cairo Geniza The word *geniza* denotes a repository for Jewish sacred manuscripts (especially those that include the name of God) that were no longer suitable for use but could not be destroyed. In 1896 this particular *geniza* was discovered in Old Cairo in the Ben Ezra Synagogue (a building still standing today) by Solomon Schechter of Cambridge University. The *geniza* contained a store of medieval manuscripts belonging to the Karaites, a Jewish sect that flourished in the Middle Ages and that rejected the rabbinic tradition of the Talmud and confined itself to the study of scriptures alone.

The most famous document discovered in the Cairo Geniza is the Damascus Document, which was first published by Schechter in 1910 under the title Zadokite Fragments. Two partial manuscripts of this work were found: Manuscript A, which dates from the tenth century C.E., and Manuscript B, from the twelfth century C.E. The text is a rule book from a then unknown Jewish sect; when fragments of the same work were found among the Dead Sea Scrolls in the 1950s, the identification of the text with the Essenes at Qumran seemed assured. However, because of this overlap between the Geniza material and the scrolls, Solomon Zeitlin identified the scrolls with the Karaites, an identification that overlooks the antiquity of the scrolls and that is rejected by most scholars today. *See also* CAIRO GENIZA, TARGUM FRAGMENTS FROM; DAMASCUS DOCUMENT.

Cairo Geniza, targum fragments from Since approximately the ninth century C.E., the Ben Ezra Synagogue in Cairo, Egypt, placed its old documents in a storeroom called a *geniza.* In the late nineteenth century, the decaying documents were taken to libraries in Europe and the United States. Many of the fragments constitute the remains of targums—translations of the Hebrew Bible into Aramaic. Many fragments were originally continuous targums; there are remains of Targum Onkelos, the Targums to the Prophets, and the Palestinian Targums to the Pentateuch. The *geniza* also contained targum festival collections (with special readings for religious festivals such as Passover, Purim, and Sha<u>b</u>uot, fragmentary targums, and Tosefta targums.

calendar systematic arrangement of time into set units, such as days, weeks, months, and years. The different parts of the Hebrew Bible provide evidence for three systems of naming months: by old Canaanite names, such as Abib and Ethanim; by ordinal numbers (first, second, etc.); and by Babylonian names (Nisan, Adar, etc.). At times these systems are used together for greater clarity. Exodus 12:2 says that the year was to begin in the spring, and the dates for the festivals presuppose a vernal inception (see Lev. 23). The dated documents from the Jewish military colony at Elephantine in Egypt (4th–5th cs. B.C.E.) show that these Jews also used the Babylonian or Persian month names; the same appears to be true in the fourth-century B.C.E. Samaritan texts from the Wadi ed-Daliyeh. 1 Enoch 72–82, a third-century B.C.E. text, describes in full a solar calendar of 364 days (beginning in the spring) and a lunar system of 354 days (with alternating 29- and 30-day months). It gives no specific indication of how the two might have been brought into harmony with each other through intercalation of extra days. This same solar calendar of 364 days is strongly defended in the Book of Jubilees, which was written in Hebrew in about 150 B.C.E. The author alludes to people who observe the moon in making calendrical calculations and strongly criticizes them (chap. 6). It is not clear what the standard Jewish calendar might have been at this time, although a lunar calendar, which was harmonized with the solar year by adding a thirteenth month approximately every third year, was widely accepted in the Hellenistic world.

The Book of Daniel (about 165 B.C.E.) hints that Antiochus IV (r. 175–164 B.C.E.), the Seleucid monarch who banned the practice of Judaism, may have introduced calendar changes in Jerusalem (Dan. 7:25). There may have been debates about the proper calendar in the following years, and the disagreement involved may have been one reason why a group left Jerusalem to settle near the Dead Sea, where they wrote and copied their scrolls. These Dead Sea Scrolls supply a rather large amount of calendrical information. They show that the group adhered to the 364-day solar calendar but also had a 354-day lunar scheme, to which 30 days may have been added every third year. The people who wrote the scrolls (they date from about 150 B.C.E. to 68 C.E.) dated their festivals by the solar calendar and therefore celebrated them at a different time than other Jews did. Nevertheless, they did attempt to correlate their solar calendar with their peculiar lunar one. If intercalation of the solar calendar was practiced, it probably involved seven-day units, since the week, with its Sabbath, is a basic principle of the calendar.

The familiar Jewish calendar of twelve lunar months, augmented seven times in nineteen years by a second Adar, is first attested in rabbinic and later sources, although it, or something like it, was undoubtedly practiced at an earlier time. This calendar ensures that the festival of Passover, which falls at the full moon of the lunar month of Nisan (the fifteenth of Nisan), always coincides with the first full moon after the vernal equinox (Mar. 21), and that the festival of Tabernacles (Sukkot), which falls at the full moon of the lunar month of Tishri, always coincides with the first full moon after the autumnal equinox (Sept. 21). By periodically adding a month following Adar (late winter), called Adar Sheni, or the Second Adar, the lunar and solar calendars are synchronized.

Caligula *see* GAIUS

call the act by which God appoints a person to a particular role, status, or task. In the Hebrew Bible, such a commissioning is usually directed toward one whom God has designated as a prophet (Exod. 3, Isa. 6, 49:1–3; Jer. 1; Ezek. 1–2). Elsewhere in the Hebrew Bible and later literature, the literary form of an epiphany, traditionally used to describe a call, can also shape a story in which the birth of one who will serve God's purposes is announced (Judg. 13:2–20; cf. Luke 1:5–23, 26–38).

The stereotyped literary form employed to recount the story of a prophetic call includes all or most of the following narrative elements, with some variation in the order: circumstances; appearance of the Deity or the audition of God's voice; the prophet's fearful reaction and God's response, "fear not"; commission to serve as a prophet; a protest that one is not fit for the office; divine reassurances such as "I am with you" or, again, "fear not, do not be dismayed"; the prophet's acquiescence to the call. In their present settings, these stories assert the prophet's credentials and thus authenticate the book's message,

Among the nonbiblical literature of Second Temple Judaism, 1 Enoch is remarkable for its use of the prophetic commissioning form. According to chapters 12–16, the ancient patriarch was taken to heaven, where the enthroned Deity commissioned him to announce doom to the fallen watchers. In context, this pseudonymous account authenticates the divinely sent message of judgment that runs through the literary collection (cf. 1:2–3, 93:2). A somewhat different use of the call form appears in Daniel 10–12, where an angel reveals the future, which the sage is to write in a book that is to be sealed until the time of its imminent fulfillment.

The prophetic call form and allusions to it appear in New Testament accounts of apostolic commissioning. The post-Resurrection appearances of Jesus in Matthew 28:16–20, Luke 24:36–53, John 20:19–29, 21:1–19 are commissioning stories. The accounts of Jesus' appearance to Saul of Tarsus in Acts 9:1–9, 22:6–22, 26:4–18 are also call stories, which have been influenced by Isaiah 49 and Jeremiah 2, as has Paul's own reference to the event (Gal. 1:12–17). The Book of Revelation as a whole imitates Daniel 10–12 as an account of eschatological revelations that the seer is commanded to write in a book (1:11, 22:8–10). *See also* BIRTH, MIRACULOUS; EPIPHANY.

Callistus bishop of Rome (c. 217–c. 222 C.E.). According to Hippolytus, Callistus sought martyrdom by creating a disturbance in a Jewish synagogue, purportedly as a way to cover up a crime. When he embezzled a large amount of money, his employer, a Christian belonging to the imperial household, had him arrested and put to the treadmill. Entreaties by friends, however, secured his release. Pretending to meet his creditors, he went instead to the synagogue on the Sabbath. When he disrupted the service, the Jews roughed him up and dragged him before the Roman prefect Rusticus. Although his former employer tried to secure his release, the prefect sentenced him to a mine in Sardinia for violating laws protecting Jewish worship.

Calpurnius Atilianus *see* ATILIANUS, PUBLIUS CALPURNIUS

Campanus, Sextus Hermetidius governor of Syria-Palaestina, 93 C.E. A wooden diptych from Egypt refers to Domitian's edict granting favors to veterans. In addition, it refers to soldiers of the Tenth Legion serving in Jerusalem while Campanus was legate. We do not know anything else certain about his career.

Canaanite an inhabitant of the Land of Canaan; the biblical designation for the indigenous inhabitants of Israel in the pre-Israelite and Israelite periods (Gen. 12:5–6). In the Gospel of Matthew (15:22), the term is used for a woman from the coastal territory of Tyre and Sidon, northwest of Galilee. (In Mark she is referred to as a Greek, a Syrophoenician by birth.) Josephus uses the term only of biblical times, and it is likely that Matthew is making a biblical allusion.

Cananaean epithet of Jesus' disciple Simon (Mark 3:18; Matt. 10:4). "Cananaean" derives from the Aramaic for "zealot" or "enthusiast" and signifies an individual opposed to the Roman occupation of Palestine (see also Luke 6:15; Acts 1:13).

candlestick, seven-branched *see* MENORAH

cannibalism, Jews accused of This comes from a slander that in 168 B.C.E., when Antiochus IV suppressed Judaism, he found a Greek imprisoned in the temple who claimed he was being fattened up for a cannibalistic feast. This is mentioned by several Graeco-Roman writers, including Apion. The origin of the tale is difficult to pin down. There may be folklore elements that have nothing to do with the Jews, but it has been suggested that it was also official Seleucid propaganda to excuse the Seleucids' attack on Judaism. Whatever its exact origins, the story was evidently widely circulated in first-century B.C.E. Egypt at a time of tremendous rivalry between Greeks and Jews.

canon (Lat., rule or guide) term that came to be applied to the list of books that were considered a part of authoritative scripture. The fixing of the canon of the Hebrew Bible was a long process about which we know little. The Pentateuch was probably the first of the works to be canonized, since it is accepted in all traditions. After that, the Prophets seem to have been agreed on by several traditions some time before the common era, but they were not accepted by everyone (e.g., the Samaritans). The Writings were probably the last to receive assent: their content as found in the present Hebrew Bible is not known before 100 C.E., and it is clear that certain books not in the present list were accepted by some communities; also, some in the present canon were evidently not universally accepted. For example, Esther is not known at Qumran, while 1 Enoch seems to have been accepted not only at Qumran but also by the writer of the New Testament epistle of Jude and the Ethiopic Church. When the canon became fixed in the Jewish community generally is not known, but the idea that it was done at the Council of Jamnia is not supported by evidence; however, Jewish sources after 70 C.E. list no other books as canonical.

The canon of the New Testament also had a long period of growth. Some early lists of books include such writings as the Epistle of Barnabas but leave out others (e.g., 2 and 3 John, Jude, and the Book of Revelation). Even by the time of the Christianization of the Roman Empire, the church historian Eusebius still indicates some debate about certain books. By about a century later, however, the present canon appears to have been accepted by all areas of Christendom. Thus, the contents of the Old Testament canon vary among the Christian churches, but the New Testament canon is the same for all.

Capernaum major Jewish town on the northwest shore of the Sea of Galilee dating mainly from the late Hellenistic period to the Arab conquest. Capernaum means "village of Nahum," likely after its otherwise unknown owner from some early period in its history. Capernaum is mentioned often in the gospels as the headquarters of Jesus' ministry.

According to Luke 7:2–5 a Roman centurion was the patron of the local synagogue, a situation paralleled often in Syrian sources where centurions patronize local deities and build their sanctuaries. Jesus taught in the local synagogue, and several of his miracles are located at Capernaum (Matt. 8:5; Mark 1:21–28, 2:1–12; Luke 7:1–10). According to Matthew 8:14, Jesus was staying at the house of his chief disciple, Peter (or of Peter and his brother Andrew in Mark 1:29). Peter's mother-in-law also lived there. In his autobiography Josephus tells how he was injured in a fall during his activities as general of Galilee during the Jewish War and was taken to "Capharnaoum" for first aid (*Life* 72). A village of Kefar Tanhoum, Kefar Tanhoumin, or Kefar Tehoumin is known in rabbinic sources (Midrash Shir ha-Shirim 3.18; Y. Terumot 11.7).

Archaeology began at Capernaum in 1905 and has continued intermittently to the present. It appears that people lived at Capernaum in the thirteenth century B.C.E. and even earlier, but occupation began in earnest only during the Persian period. From the late Hellenistic period onward, the town was laid out in regular blocks or *insulae,* which are composed of cluster houses. The houses are organized as rooms around central, unroofed courtyards, sometimes with other, smaller courtyards elsewhere in the dwelling. The houses are built of the local black basalt. One of these houses is identified by recent excavators as the house of Simon Peter. This identification is based upon the transformation of the house into a church early in the fourth century, perhaps at the instigation of Count Joseph of Tiberias. Christian visitors to the house scratched prayers on the walls in Greek and Syriac, quotations from the Hebrew Bible in Hebrew, and something fragmentary in a few Latin words. This church ultimately was destroyed in the fifth century to make room for an elaborate octagonal church. One block away to the north, in the first century C.E., stood a prayer hall or synagogue built of black basalt for the local Jewish population. This was large by ancient standards. During the fourth century, this building was torn down to make way for the elaborately decorated white limestone synagogue so well known in Jewish archaeology and history. This synagogue contains a prayer hall oriented to the south toward Jerusalem and an elaborate courtyard building on the east. This latter building may be a hospice for visitors, though it may also have been used for civic purposes by the townspeople. Some of the most arresting examples of Jewish art are known from the late synagogue at Capernaum. The center of town seems to have moved to the east after the Arab conquest of 640 C.E. Capernaum remained an Arab town until about 1030 C.E., though both the synagogue and the church fell into disrepair. This suggests that the Jewish and Christian populations either left or were in no position to maintain their worship edifices. *See also* CAPERNAUM SYNAGOGUES.

Capernaum synagogues At the ancient village site of Capernaum are remains of a spectacular white limestone synagogue of the fourth century C.E., beneath which may lie a synagogue, built of black basalt, of the first century C.E. The fourth-century synagogue was often misdated in reports before the 1970s as being from the second or even first century C.E. It stood facing south toward Jerusalem on an elevated platform with carefully finished exterior walls and decorated stucco interior walls. The exterior was extensively decorated with some of the most striking Jewish art of the period. A courtyard to the east, surrounded by a roofed portico, was accessed from the synagogue's east aisle. At nearly 25 by 19 meters, this is one of the largest synagogues known. The synagogue's interior space was divided into nave and two side aisles and an aisle in the rear by columns with Corinthian capitals. Three doorways in the facade gave entry to worship space. To the left and right of the central portal stood small platforms upon which likely stood a menorah on one and a Torah shrine on the other. A donor's inscription in Greek on a column in the back honors Herod, the son of Monimos. Another column displays a donor's inscription in Aramaic that honors Halphai bar Zebedee bar Yoḥanan. The floor was paved with large flagstones.

The exterior decoration includes an eagle with outstretched wings above the central entrance. Six genii carried five garlands above the eagle. Date palms stood on the fronts of consoles. Another stone features a brace of eagles, back to back, holding a garland in their beaks. To their right stands a Capricorn in harness. On yet another stone a portable Torah shrine is carved in perspective in relief. It has spoked wheels, columns, and, in front, a double door topped by a shell. One of the site's Corinthian capitals features a seven-branched menorah, a shofar, and an incense shovel. One of the synagogue lintels bears a carving of a double-leaf door with gable that perhaps is a Torah shrine. Other motifs carved in relief include griffins, flowers, an amphora, a five-pointed star, and a six-pointed star. A small stone fragment bears a five-branched menorah topped by a shell in relief. Lions sculpted in the round are known from Capernaum, but it is not known if they are from the synagogue. Thousands of coins of the fourth century C.E. found in the fill beneath the synagogue floor confirms the synagogue's date of construction. It appears to have been destroyed about 638 C.E.

Beneath the fourth-century C.E. synagogue stood an earlier building of the first century B.C.E. This earlier building also had two aisles and a central nave precisely beneath the aisles and nave of the later synagogue. The nave was paved in the first century C.E. to cover earlier structures. It had used black granite columns to hold up the roof. Its stones were carefully cut and fitted, unlike a private dwelling. The stones beneath the gabled roof had been carved with egg-and-dart molding. This building had not been simply removed to build the upper synagogue, but rather its walls had been pushed inward so that the stubs of its walls stood nearly three feet high and retained the rubble within. Dirt with thousands of bronze coins (perhaps a symbolic offering?) of the fourth century was poured into the interstices of the stones to consolidate the debris and form the elevated platform for the fourth-century synagogue. All these clues conspire to suggest that this had been a first-century prayer hall or synagogue partially retained by the community even as they destroyed it to build the later synagogue.

C. Apion *see* AGAINST APION

capital punishment execution, inflicted for sins or crimes specified in the Torah. Four modes of execution were inflicted by the earthly court (in order of severity): stoning, burning, decapitation, and strangulation.

captives, ransoming of (Heb.: *pidyon shabuim*) religious duty to ransom an Israelite captured by slave traders or kidnappers. The community as a whole was responsible for ransoming captives.

Caracalla (188–217 C.E.) nickname of Marcus Aurelius Antoninus, Roman emperor. He was the eldest son of Lucius Septimius Severus. In 199 he was coregent with his father. In 212, he arranged for the murder of his brother Geta and became the sole ruler of the empire. He saw himself as a second Alexander and hoped for vast conquests to the east. In 215 he enlarged the province of Osroene to include Edessa, but failed to take Armenia. He invaded Media in 216, but was assassinated in Carrhae in 217 before he could continue his conquests.

In 212 Caracalla had issued the *Constitutio Antoniniana,* an edict granting citizenship to all communities inside the empire. Although the text states that Caracalla promulgated the edict to enhance the prestige of the Roman gods who had preserved him from some danger, many scholars suggest that he increased the number of Roman citizens in order to collect more revenue from the inheritance tax. The edict placed the Jews on the same level as all other Roman citizens. Jerome notes that Severus and his son Antoninus greatly favored the Jews. One Roman tradition records that Caracalla refused to speak with his father because he held the latter responsible for flogging his friend "for his Jewish religion." The story is one of many designed to draw a sharp contrast between Caracalla, the kind-hearted young boy, and Caracalla, the wicked adult. He visited Palestine in 199 with his father and again in 215 on his way from Asia to Egypt. Like his father, Caracalla permitted Jews to become lawful trustees and guardians. Severus and Caracalla also issued edicts that recognized the rights of Jews to serve on municipal councils. Several scholars believe that the "Antoninus" to whom the rabbinic traditions attribute a friendship with Judah the Patriarch was Caracalla.

carpenter Jesus' occupation, according to Mark 6:3; Matthew 13:55, perhaps to increase Jesus' stature, makes him the son of the carpenter Joseph. The Greek *tekton* may also be translated as woodworker or builder. The Infancy Gospel of Thomas depicts the child Jesus helping Joseph by stretching boards in the carpentry shop.

carrion beasts that have died of natural causes or through means other than proper, ritual slaughter

Carus, Marcus Aurelius Roman emperor (r. 282–283 C.E.), born in Narbo, Gaul. In 282, after Probus was murdered by his troops, Carus announced to the Senate that he was the new emperor. In 282–283 he led an army into Persia. Upon crossing the Euphrates, he defeated Bahram II, captured Seleucia-Ctesiphon, and assumed the title of "Parthicus Maximus." He was mysteriously killed before he could move further east. When the war ended in 284, Rome had possession of Mesopotamia. This invasion by Rome into Persia is echoed in a few passages in the Babylonian Talmud, which mentions that the Romans proclaimed pagan festivals in Jewish towns.

Cassius, Avidius *see* AVIDIUS CASSIUS, GAUIS

Cassius, Dio *see* DIO CASSIUS

castration Already in Neolithic times, pastoralists had learned to castrate male animals to make them more docile and to make sure that only selected animals were able to breed. According to Josephus and rabbinic literature, however, Jews did not practice this common custom. Neither did they make men into eunuchs, as was the custom in some Near Eastern countries, especially where bodyguards were needed for harems. In the eyes of some Graeco-Romans, however, circumcision was interpreted as castration and had to be specifically excluded from a general ban on the castration of humans in Roman law.

catacombs, Italian deep burial tunnels used for Jewish burials in Rome. From paleographical analysis of their inscriptions, it appears that these catacombs date primarily from the first through the fourth centuries C.E. Catacombs with Roman and Christian burials are also known.

Most catacombs have burial chambers leading off winding subterranean tunnels, while others merely contain niches in the tunnels for the depositing of the dead. In Rome, Christian catacombs are known to contain large rooms that were used for meetings, because Christianity was not a lawful religion until the fourth century C.E. Though Jewish catacombs do contain some rooms, they lack these large rooms, probably because Judaism was a permitted religion in Roman society. The term "catacomb" comes from a late Latin word, *catacumba,* whose etymology is uncertain. The word seems to have originally referred solely to one particular burial tunnel—"ad Catacumbas"—located on the outskirts of Rome. Since at least the ninth century C.E., the word has been used to refer to burial caves in general.

Unfortunately, half of the Jewish catacombs in Rome have been unavailable for modern research and viewing. Two discovered in the late nineteenth century (Vigna Cimarra and Via Labicana) have been lost in modern times. Another, the Via Appia Pignatelli Catacomb, is very small and almost inaccessible.

The other three Jewish catacombs (Monteverde, Vigna Randanini, and Torlonia), however, provide much information about Jewish burial practices during this period. The Catacomb Monteverde was the first Jewish catacomb discovered in Rome during modern times. It was first discovered in 1602 and then rediscovered in 1904. It contained hundreds of important Greek, Latin, and Hebrew inscriptions as well as several sarcophagi. Today the catacomb has collapsed and is inaccessible. The dedicatory inscriptions are commonly accompanied by symbols, mainly the the menorah. Several symbols of a Graeco-Roman origin are also found: the four seasons, a heavenly banquet with a child, birds, a dog, dolphins, a bull, and birds with grapes.

The Catacomb Vigna Randanini (Via Appia) was discovered in the late nineteenth century, and it too points to the adaptation of traditional Graeco-Roman symbols into Jewish life. Several painted rooms contain various Graeco-Roman symbols. One depicts a winged Victory crowning a nude youth, and another shows the crowned goddess Fortuna holding a cornucopia in her left hand and pouring a libation with her right hand. Despite these images, the catacomb is identified as Jewish because of the presence of several menorahs and several hundred Jewish inscriptions.

The Catacomb Torlonia (Nomentana), discovered in 1920, is the largest Jewish catacomb. In this catacomb Graeco-Roman art motifs are inextricably mixed with Jewish art. For instance, one ceiling depicts a menorah with a wreath, peacocks eating grapes, a grapevine, a lion, a dolphin, astral symbols, rosettes, sun, pomegranates, and birds. The integration of Graeco-Roman symbols with traditional Jewish symbols is also known from numerous sarcophagi from this catacomb. Thus, it seems clear that Graeco-Roman symbols were incorporated into Jewish depictions of the afterlife by the Jews of Rome during the first through the fourth centuries C.E.

catenae (Lat., chains) commonly used as a literary term to refer to the genre of a series of quotations used in support of a theological argument or exegesis. A good example is the series of quotations from the Hebrew Bible in Romans 3:10–18.

Catullus governor of the province of Cyrenaica (Josephus, *War* 7:439–450), the most fertile part of which comprised five Greek cities known as the Pentapolis. Josephus reports that in 73 C.E., Catullus encouraged Jonathan, a member of the Sicarii, to bring false charges of sedition against wealthy Jews of the area. Catullus then arranged the murder of three thousand of them. He subsequently encouraged Jonathan to similarly accuse respected Jews in Alexandria and Rome. According to Josephus, Catullus's plan failed when Vespasian—whom Josephus views favorably—recognized Jonathan and Catullus's treachery. The former was executed. The later, though treated leniently under the law, succumbed to psychological and physical illness and was said to have died tormented by the ghosts of those he had murdered.

caution *see* EULABEIA

CD *see* DAMASCUS DOCUMENT

C.E. abbreviation for "Common Era." This alternative terminology is often used instead of "A.D." in non-Christian contexts. *See also* A.D.

celibacy refraining from sexual relationships in the interest of religious purity and devotion.

Celibacy is relatively uncommon among Jews, since procreation is enjoined by Genesis 1:28. Josephus (*War* 2.8.2; *Ant.* 18.1.5; but contrast with mention of married Essenes in *War* 2.8.12), Philo (*Hyp.* 11, 14–17), and Pliny (*Nat. Hist.* 5.73) insist that Essenes did not marry; the two Jewish writers attribute this practice to the Essenes' view of women's natural infidelity. However, the Qumran Scrolls do not prohibit marriage, and both Rule of the Congregation (1QSa 1:4) and the Damascus Document 7:6–7 (see also 1QM 7:4–5) mention it. Judith explicitly forgoes remarriage, and Philo's Therapeutae were celibates: the men adopted the practice after leaving their family life; the women were "elderly virgins" (*Vit. Cont.*). The History of the Rechabites/Apocalypse of Zosimus depicts a miraculous community in which parents have intercourse once, conceive two children of which one will continue the family and the other will remain virgin, and then forget the pleasure of the experience (11:6–9).

Jesus' comment on eunuchs (Matt. 19:12) indicates an ascetic preference. Paul advocated celibacy as an alternative to the distractions caused by families (1 Cor. 7:7–8). While the pastoral Epistles favor marriage and, by implication, procreation (1 Tim. 2:15, 5:14, etc.), New Testament apocryphal works such as the Acts of Paul and Thecla stress celibacy. Revelation 14:4 describes the number saved as 144,000 male virgins. Celibacy is not endorsed by rabbinic Judaism. *See also* MARRIAGE; VIRGIN.

Celsus philosophical writer of uncertain origin and affiliation from the second century C.E. His only known work, *The True Doctrine,* was primarily an attack against Christianity, which he regarded as a serious threat to Graeco-Roman civilization. The work is known only from the extensive quotations in Origen who wrote a refutation in *Contra Celsum.* In order to refute Christianity, Celsus also had to attack the basis of Christianity in Judaism. Although his arguments against the Jews do not draw on the gross slanders found in some writers, such as Apion, he shows no sympathy for them or their religion. He regarded the Christian belief in Christ as merely an extension of the Jewish belief in a Messiah, with the differences being of no account. He attacks the anthropomorphism found in the writings of both religions. He is one of the few Graeco-Roman writers to show a knowledge of the Hebrew Bible, though he spends a good deal of space trying to denigrate the Genesis creation account, as well as that of the flood and the Tower of Babel. Of interest is his manner of criticizing Christianity by putting objections to it in the mouth of a Jew.

centaur fabulous half-man, half-horse monster in Greek mythology, whose origins were in ancient Thessaly. The centaur was a very minor motif in ancient Jewish art, especially in synagogue art. The centaur is difficult to identify with certainty, as it has suffered at the hand of the iconoclasts of later generations. Badly damaged figures of leaping centaurs, alternatively interpreted as panthers or lions, appear on a lintel from the later synagogue of Capernaum. A damaged depiction of a galloping centaur (or horse and rider) is known from the synagogue of Chorazin.

centurion *see* CHILIARCH

Cerialis, Sextus Vettulens Roman general. He was a trusted commander whose troops had destroyed Hebron and who was commander of the Fifth legion during its siege of Jerusalem. After Titus had conquered the city, he left Cerialis in command of the Tenth legion and the detachment that had been associated with it in holding the city.

Cestius Gallus, Gaius legate of Syria (63–67 C.E.). Gallus visited Jerusalem during Passover in 66. The Jews approached him and denounced the procurator Gessius Florus, who in turn demeaned the Jews. In the summer of 66, Florus's demand for seventeen talents from the Temple treasury was met with ridicule by the population of Jerusalem. Florus took a cohort to Jerusalem, sacked the upper city, and crucified those who were taken prisoners. Florus, the Sanhedrin, and Berenice immediately sent reports to Gallus concerning these events. Gallus sent a member of his staff to investigate the situation in Jerusalem; he reported back that the Jews were loyal to Rome and hostile only to Florus. But by September of 66 Gallus had assembled an army of over thirty thousand, which easily marched through the Galilee, establishing its base at Caesarea. By mid-October he led his troops toward Jerusalem. Believing he could take advantage of the disorder among the Jews in the city, Gallus encamped his troops on Mount Scopus, one mile north of the city. After five days of attacking the city, Gallus suddenly withdrew his troops. His retreat on the verge of victory remains a mystery, for had he continued, he could have put down the revolt at that time.

Chaeremon Egyptian priest and Stoic of the first century C.E. who wrote a history of Egypt. His single reference to the Jews is an account of the Exodus. It has many similarities to that of Manetho but also shows knowledge of traditions independent of Manetho. According to Chaeremon, the Israelites arose as a group of afflicted persons banished by Amenophis on the instructions of the goddess Isis. Under Moses and Joseph, in this account, they joined up with refugees on the border of Egypt who had been refused entry and were then able to attack Amenophis, who fled; when Amenophis's son Rameses grew up, he drove the Jews out.

Chair of Moses modern name of stone chairs found in several ancient synagogues: Delos in the Greek islands, Dura-Europos in ancient Syria, Hammath-Tiberias on the west shore of the Sea of Galilee, Chorazin in Lower Galilee, and En Gedi on the west shores of the Dead Sea. These chairs were placed to the side of the Torah shrine, with their backs against the wall that the congregation faced, though at Delos the stone chair formed part of the congregational seating. The example from Chorazin has decorated hand rests, one arm with a lion and the other with an eagle. Recent study has emphasized that the Delos stone chair is for a synagogue official, but that the others are for a fourth-century ritual of enthronement of the Torah during worship. The "Chair of Moses" or "Throne of Moses" is mentioned in Matthew 23:2, where it is described in terms of prestige seating, apparently in the synagogue or *beit midrash*. This would accord well with the situation at Delos, where the marble "Chair of Moses" is in the center of the other seating, rather like a patriarch seated with his elders to the right and left. With regard to the stone chairs in ancient Palestine, they do not appear to have been designed for actual seating. Instead, they resemble honorific "empty thrones" known in both Roman and Byzantine non-Jewish art in the eastern Mediterranean, which were supposed to represent the deity.

Chalcedon, Council of (451 C.E.) the fourth ecumenical council. The council of five hundred bishops began their meeting at Nicea, but they were moved to Chalcedon at the request of the emperor Marcian (r. 450–457). The major issue before the council was the spread of Monophysitism. The council accepted the formula that proclaimed the unity of Christ "in two natures," while the Monophysites preferred the phrase "one nature." The Chalcedonian creed maintained that in Christ the divine and human natures coexist, entirely and completely, without mixture, transformation, separation, or division. This means that Christ is consubstantial with the Father according to his divinity and consubstantial with humans according to his humanity. Juvenal, the bishop of Jerusalem, dropped his support of the Monophysites and accepted the doctrine proposed at Chalcedon. In recognition of his support, the council elevated him to the rank of patriarch and gave him full authority over the churches in Palestine and Arabia, abolishing the authority of the bishop of Antioch over the Palestinian churches. When he returned to Jerusalem, Juvenal found that the Monophysites had declared another priest the bishop of Jerusalem. It took Juvenal over a year and a half to regain his authority. The anti-Monophysitism of Chalcedon created a division among the Christians in Syria-Palestine. The Monophysites often termed the supporters of Chalcedon as "Jews" because the latter claimed that a human had been crucified.

Chaldeans tribal people of southern Mesopotamia; Nebuchadnezzar and other Neo-Babylonian rulers (612–539 B.C.E.) were Chaldeans. In the Graeco-Roman world, the term became applied to experts in astrology and other esoteric arts. "Chaldee" is also (incorrectly) applied to the Aramaic language in some older modern works.

chambers of souls repositories for the souls of the dead, sometimes called "treasuries." 1 Enoch 22 describes a mountain in the far west with caves containing spirits or souls sorted according to their character or lot in life. 2 Baruch 24:1 and 30:2 posit the existence of such chambers, allotted to the righteous and the wicked. 2 Esdras 7:75–101 contrasts the torment of the wandering souls of the wicked with the repose in the quiet chambers of the righteous. Revelation 6:9–11 places the martyrs' souls under the heavenly altar. Presumed in all cases is the separate conscious existence of the disembodied soul or spirit, which awaits the judgment and, for the righteous, a new resurrection body.

Charax Spasinu city built by Characene, who, in the early second century B.C.E., broke away from the Parthian ruler Phraates II and established an independent kingdom under the satrap Hyspaosines. He quickly enlarged his realm, for a time controlling all of Babylonia and founding Charax Spasinu. Soon after, a Parthian campaign restored Babylonia, and with it Charax Spasinu, to Parthian control. A commercial center on the Persian Gulf, the city had a largely Hellenized population and was home to a Jewish community.

charisma (Gr., favor or gift) in common usage, the ability to inspire others with devotion and enthusiasm. In scholarly study, "charisma" has a somewhat different connotation, which varies according to its two technical meanings: First, it may be used in a sense taken from sociological study to mean the power residing in an office like that of king or prophet; second, it can refer to a divine gift of special powers, such as those of healing, casting out demons, or performing miracles. We know of a number of charismatics in Jewish history, such as Honi the Circle Maker and Ḥanina b. Dosa. *See also* CHARISMATIC JUDAISM.

charismatic Judaism modern scholarly term for a putative type of Second Temple Judaism in the Land of Israel. The term refers to Second Temple figures who, following the model of the early Israelite prophets Elijah and Elisha, were known for miracles, primarily healing and control over weather. Two figures in rabbinic literature, Honi the Circle Maker and Ḥanina ben Dosa, as well as Jesus of Nazareth, are used to illustrate the charismatic type. Charismatic Judaism is judged to stand in contrast to the halakhic Judaism of the Pharisees and other levitical groups and to derive from Galilee.

Widespread in the 1970s and 1980s, the category became less popular in the 1990s. Close analysis of the rabbinic sources about Honi and Ḥanina showed these figures to resemble Jesus less than previously had been assumed and weakened the connection to Galilee as well. Though still in use, the category charismatic Judaism has lost most of its analytical force.

chastisement *see* DISCIPLINE

Chelkias a general for Cleopatra III Euergetis in her civil war (107–102 B.C.E.) with her son, Ptolemy VIII Lathyrus. Chelkias died in Coele Syria while pursuing Ptolemy toward Egypt. His father, Onias IV, built the Temple at Leontopolis. His brother Ananias also served as a general for Cleopatra.

Cher. *see* DE CHERUBIM

cherubim winged creatures of composite animal and sometimes human form associated with God's presence. Two- and three-dimensional depictions of these creatures were placed in the tabernacle and the Jerusalem Temple, and in the Holy of Holies two massive statues of cherubim spread their wings over the ark (1 Kings 6:23–28, 8:6–7). These depictions, which drew their inspiration from the ancient Near Eastern environment, suggest the existence of such wondrous creatures in the divine throne room. According to 1 Enoch 14:18, they flank the heavenly throne (cf. Ezek. 1:4–14). 1 Enoch 61:10 and 71:7 list them with other classes of heavenly beings. *See also* ANGELS; DE CHERUBIM; OFANIM; SERAPHIM.

child sacrifice or exposure, Jewish laws on Although human sacrifice was still sporadically practiced by the Carthaginians, it was generally abhorred in the Graeco-Roman world; however, the exposure of unwanted children was widely accepted. The Jews were unusual in forbidding it, and writers comment on their rearing of all their children.

chiliarch (Gr., ruler over a thousand) generally used as the military title of a commander over a unit of one thousand troops, though sometimes it could be applied to more administrative offices. It is the equivalent of a Roman military tribune or a Persian *hazarapatish*.

Chionites central Asian people, probably related to the Hunas and the Hephthalites. They were allies of Shapur II at Amida in 359 C.E. During the reign of Bahram V in the early fifth century C.E., they crossed the Oxus, ravaged Merv, crossed the Elburz into Khorasan, and reached Rey. They made peace with Bahram at Oxus.

chōra (Gr., countryside) sometimes used to designate a district or even a country. More often, however, it was used generically to refer to the rural and village population as opposed to those in the cities. Thus, it took on the connotation of "peasant" or "unsophisticated."

Chorazin (Arab.: Korazin, Khirbet Kerazeh) ancient village and synagogue site in the mountainous area north of the Sea of Galilee, west of the Jordan, and only 4 kilometers from Capernaum. The site is mentioned in the Ba<u>b</u>li at least twice (B. Men. 85a and 85b). The synagogue is quite large, measuring nearly 23 by 17 meters. It stood facing south toward Jerusalem with carefully finished and decorated exterior walls on an elevated terrace virtually in the center of the ancient village. A grand staircase on its north facade led up to a triple-portal entrance from the street or square in front of the building. Chorazin's exterior was extensively decorated with some of the most striking Jewish art of the period; the interior was also decorated. The interior space of the synagogue was divided into two side aisles and a rear aisle by columns with Ionic capitals. Three doorways in the facade gave entry to worship space. A narrow courtyard to the west was accessed from the synagogue's front portico. A small room at the north end of the courtyard was accessed from the west aisle of the synagogue.

External decorations in relief include immense shells, presumably above the portals; lions sculpted in the round on the cornice of the pediment; and a frieze of lions and acanthus leaves crowned by an eagle. Interior decoration includes a menorah (?), two lions carved in the round, relief carvings of a centaur, a lion attacking a centaur, a lioness suckling her young, and a lion devouring its prey. One stone fragment displays a Torah shrine within a wreath, but also a Medusa or head of Helios inside a wreath. A frieze on one wall displayed viticultural motifs, including two men treading out grapes and human figures reaching for or holding grape clusters. One of the most famous finds is a "Chair of Moses" carved from a single block of basalt and having an Aramaic inscription carved on its front: "Remembered be for good Judah bar Ishmael who made this stoa and its steps. For his work may he have a share with the righteous."

A hoard of coins was found beneath the synagogue's threshold. Since the majority date from the end of the fourth to the end of the fifth century C.E., the building cannot have been built later than the fifth century, assuming that the hoard was concealed while the building was in use. Some have argued for the third or fourth century C.E. as its earliest date, finding it analogous with Capernaum. Artifacts found within the building suggest that it was in use until the seventh or eighth century C.E.

chosen one (Heb.: *baḥir*; Gr.: *eklektos*) one chosen by God for a specific purpose. The earliest certain use of the term with reference to an individual appears to be in Second Isaiah, where it is a synonym for the servant of YHWH (Isa. 42:1). Postexilic texts apply the term to Abraham (Neh. 9:7), Moses (Ps. 106:23), David and the future Davidic king (Ps. 89:3, 19, both parallel to "my servant"), and Zerubbabel the Davidite (Hag. 2:23). In the Parables of Enoch (1 Enoch 37–71), it is the preeminent title of the exalted judicial figure also known as "righteous one" and "son of man" (e.g., 49:2; 51:3; 52:6; 61:8, 10; 62:1). Its source is Second Isaiah, whose portraits of the servant are among the origins of Enoch's visions of the exalted one (cf. 1 Enoch 48 and Isa. 49; 1 Enoch 49:4 and Isa. 42:1). The title, moreover, parallels Enoch's use of "chosen ones" as a major title for the righteous, whose cause "the chosen one" champions (1 Enoch 62:1–8). Elsewhere in Second Temple non-biblical texts, the term is used of an individual only in the Paraleipomena of Jeremiah with reference to Jeremiah the prophet (Par. Jer. 1:1, 4, 7; 3:4, 5).

In the New Testament the singular is applied once, and possibly twice, to Jesus. In his rewriting of Mark's story of Jesus' crucifixion, Luke changes "the Christ, the king of Israel" to "the Christ of God, the chosen one" (Luke 23:35), and some manuscripts of John's version of the story of Jesus' baptism ascribe to John the Baptist the confession that Jesus is "the chosen one of God" (John 1:34). The latter usage fits with the baptism stories in Mark 1:11 and Matthew 3:17, where "my son in whom I am pleased" is a conflation of Psalm 2:7 and Isaiah 42:1. This combination of servant and messiah language can be traced back through 1 Enoch to Second Isaiah, where the servant combines features of the prophet and king. *See also* CHOSEN ONES; SERVANT OF THE LORD.

chosen ones the segment of Israel on whom God's favor is bestowed. In Third Isaiah (Isa. 56–66) it parallels the plural "servants" (Isa. 65:9–15) because, unlike Second Isaiah (Isa. 44:1–2, 45:4), this prophet does not believe that all of Israel is God's servant and chosen one. Among Second Temple nonbiblical texts, the term is prominent in 1 Enoch (1–5, 37–71, and 93) and in some of the Qumran scrolls (1QS 8:6; 1QH 14:15), where it reflects a clear sense that only certain Israelites are true Israelites. At Qumran, and perhaps in 1 Enoch, the authors have a particular group in mind. In the New Testament, "the chosen" refers to those who accept Jesus as Messiah (Mark 13:20, 27; Rom. 8:33; 1 Pet. 1:1–2; cf. 2:9). *See also* CHOSEN ONE; ELECTION.

chosen people Israel; refers to the belief that the people of Israel were elected by God and covenanted with Him through the Torah. The belief is stated throughout the Hebrew scriptures: for example, "For you did separate them from among all the peoples of the earth to be your heritage" (Deut. 7:6); "For they are your people and your inheritance" (1 Kings 8:51). The election of Israel is expressed in terms of the Torah; God wished to show Israel grace; He therefore gave it the Torah and the commandments. In the words of the sage, R. Ḥananiah b. Akashiah, "The Holy One, blessed be He, wanted to show grace to Israel. Therefore He gave them abundant Torah and numerous commandments, as it is said, 'It pleased the Lord for his righteousness' sake to magnify the Torah and give honor to it'" (Isa. 42:21). *See also* ELECTION.

Chosroes *see* KHUSRO I; KHUSRO II

Christ (Gr.: *christos,* one who is anointed; Heb. *mashiaḥ*) In the Hebrew Bible, the "anointed" were the king and the high priest. In later Jewish writings in Greek, "Christos" could mean the messiah (however conceived). The term comes into wide currency as the New Testament designation for Jesus. It is used with the definite article to refer to an expected eschatological figure (Matt. 2:4) or to refer to Jesus as Messiah (e.g., Matt. 16:16). It also occurs in combination with the name Jesus (Acts 5:42). Most often "Christ" occurs without the article as a proper name, alone or in combination with "Jesus." Paul employs the expression "in Christ" to designate the church as the extended body of the risen Jesus. As a proper name, Christ seems to have been used widely and very early to reflect the belief that Jesus fulfilled Jewish messianic expectations. *See also* MESSIAH.

Christian Palestinian Aramaic *see* ARAMAIC, CHRISTIAN PALESTINIAN

Chronicle 2 one of the Samaritan Chronicles, apparently extending from the death of Moses to medieval times (though not yet fully published). The early part of it ascribes the origins of the Samaritan sect to a dispute over the high priesthood in the time of Eli. There is controversy over how early and original it is.

Chronicles, Targum to This targum exists in two related versions—one dating from the eighth century, the other from the ninth—each of which seems to derive from an earlier targum. Both are quite eclectic, combining materials from the Palestinian Targums to the Pentateuch, the Targum to Kings found in the Targum to the Prophets, and the Babylonian Talmud. It also has similarities to the Peshita version of Chronicles. It is not surprising, then, that linguistically the targum is quite mixed, revealing evidence of Western and Eastern Aramaic.

chronography This term refers broadly to the science of writing chronicles. In antiquity, however, the object of determining chronology had more than just a scientific or historical function. It was believed by many that the world and history had a finite number of years, at the end of which they would come to an end, or at least a climax. Thus, calculating how much time had elapsed since the beginning of the world was the key to determining how much time was left. A number of Jewish writings show evidence of such calculations, or provide figures that could be used for them. One of the early ones was the seventy weeks of years in Daniel 9, itself a reinterpretation of the seventy years in Jeremiah 25. Eupolemus calculated the age of the world to his own time as being just over five thousand years, as did Josephus, while many Christian chronographers worked on the assumption that Jesus was born in the year of the world 5500. Behind such calculations was often the view that there was a world week; that is, just as the week had seven days, the world had seven millennia to exist. *See also* ESCHATOLOGY.

church customary New Testament translation of the Greek *ekklēsia*. In the Septuagint, *ekklēsia* translates both the Hebrew *kehal* and *edah,* terms frequently rendered in English by "congregation." In classical Greek and Hellenistic literature, *ekklēsia* became a technical term for the assembly of the people, a meaning found in Acts 19:32–39, where it is translated "assembly." The earliest Christian usage is in the phrase "church of God" (1 Cor. 1:2, 10;32, 11:22, 15:9; 2 Cor 1:1; Gal 1:13; plural of "church" in 1 Cor. 11:16; 1 Thess. 2:14), which may reflect *kehalel* found in apocalyptic Judaism to designate the eschatological assembly of God (1QM 4:10; 1QSa 2:4) and which would envision early Christian self-understanding as the eschatological community of God. Paul also speaks of the churches of Christ (Rom. 16:16; Gal. 1:22) whereby God's action in Christ founds the Christian community. Most occurrences of "church" in the New Testament refer to local groupings, whether a single household (Rom. 16:5; Philem. 2), a single city (Rom 16:1; 1 Cor. 1:2; 2 Cor. 1:1; 1 Thess. 1:1; Rev. 2:1) or a single province (Gal. 1:2, 22; 1 Thess. 2:14; 2 Cor. 8:1). Paul can also speak of the churches of the Gentiles (Rom. 16:4). Paul does not see local groupings as completely autonomous, however, for he teaches the same in every church (1 Cor. 4:17) and expects the Corinthians to adopt the rule found in the churches of God (1 Cor. 11:16). In his development of the metaphor of the community as a body, Paul says that "God has appointed in the church first apostles, second prophets, third teachers. . . ." (1 Cor. 12:28). Thus, in the notion of church, there is interaction between the idea of a specific body of Christians at a particular place and a more universal body that includes all of God's eschatological people. The universal meaning is particularly present in the hymn in Colossians where Christ is the head of the body, the Church (Col. 1:18). Here the metaphor of 1 Corinthians 12 and Romans 12 has been transformed into a hierarchical organization with Christ as head. The same development is also found in Ephesians (1:22–23, 2:11–22, 5:23–24). In Ephesians 2:19–22, the church is the household of God built on the foundation of the apostles and prophets. Such an image is also present in Matthew 16:17–19—where Jesus says he will build his church on the rock of Peter—as play on the Aramaic word for rock, *kepa,* and Peter's name, Cephas.

As regards the organization of the church, Paul speaks in Philippians of "overseers and deacons" (1:1) and provides lists of various ministries in 1 Corinthians 12:28 and Romans 12:6–8. In the post-Pauline letters, the offices of deacons (1 Tim. 3:8–13), elders (1 Tim. 5:17–22; Titus 1:5–6), and bishop (1 Tim. 3:1–7; Titus 1:7) are described in more detail, whereas the Johannine literature, where the church seems to be designated by "the elect lady" (2 John 1), guards against such organization (3 John 9–10).

Cicero (c. 106–43 B.C.E.) Roman rhetorician, politician, and author. He personally does not seem to have had much interest in Jews or Judaism. He makes no mention of either in his philosophical writings, unlike his contemporary Varro; neither does he mention Jews in his published letters. Only in two of his published speeches does he refer to Judaism, attacking it as a barbaric religion; however, as these are trial speeches for the defense, they cannot be taken at face value. In fact, he attacks other ethnic groups just as ferociously when it suits his purpose.

circumcision the act of cutting off the foreskin of the male genital. Practiced in many ancient cultures (cf. Jer. 9:25–26), circumcision was seen by the Israelites as a sign given to Abraham of their covenant with God (Gen. 17:10–14). This customary ritual act became particularly significant in Judaism when its practice was forbidden by Antiochus IV Epiphanes in 167 B.C.E. (1 Macc. 1:48). Circumcision came to be seen more and more as a distinguishing mark of Judaism. Judith and Esther insist on the circumcision of proselytes (Jdt. 14:10; Esther 8:17 [LXX]). Mattathias, leader of the Hasmonean revolt, forcibly circumcised all uncircumcised boys found within the borders of Israel (1 Macc. 2:44–46). King Josiah is praised in 2 Baruch 66:5 for leaving no one uncircumcised. Philo of Alexandria defended the law of circumcision for hygienic and allegorical reasons (*Spec. Leg.* I.1–11). Josephus relates an account of a Jewish merchant who converts Izates, the prince of Adiabene, then tries to dissuade him from being circumcised; the narrative ends with another, more learned Jew arguing that Izates should be circumcised (*Ant.* 20 secs. 38–48). The circumcised Jew is even seen as imitating the holy angels, who were created circumcised (Jub. 15:27), and Moses, who was born circumcised (LAB 9:13).

Thus, to become a Jew normally required circumcision. But what of the situation at the eschatological end times? Often the destruction of the Gentiles or their subjugation is described, but sometimes Gentiles are said at the end times to turn from idolatry with no mention of their undergoing circumcision (Isa. 2:2–4; Sib. Or. 3:710–731; 1 Enoch 90:30–36). For early Christians who believed they were living in the last days (1 Thess. 4:15), a major debate erupted about twenty years after Jesus' death over whether Gentiles entering the movement should be circumcised. At first, they did not demand the circumcision of Gentiles (Acts 15:19–20) but, as time passed and the end did not come, the question arose as to whether one should enforce the normal rules for admission to Judaism, namely, circumcision, onto Gentile converts to the Christian movement. Paul vehemently denied this in his letter to the Galatians. In Colossians, the entrance into the Christian community is described as a circumcision made without hands (Col. 2:11).

The rabbis explain circumcision's importance by describing the foreskin as a disgusting imperfection, the removal of which renders the body perfect (M. Nedarim 3:11). In line with this, only after circumcision did God tell Abraham, "Walk before me and be perfect" (Gen. 17:1; see also Gen. Rabbah 46). In this same passage, circumcision is described as the primary purpose for which God created the world in the first place, the embodiment of the covenant that made creation worthwhile.

The rabbis attributed to circumcision protective powers similar to those they credited to phylacteries or other amulets. Circumcision saves Jews from the tortures of Gehenna, to which the uncircumcised are subject. Even Moses' considerable merit could not protect him from the dangers he faced prior to circumcision (M. Nedarim 3:11). Failure to observe the covenant of circumcision was one of the reasons for the destruction of the Temple (B. Menaḥot 53b). *See also* BERIT MILAH; COVENANT.

citizenship In English, as in Greek (*politeia,* from *polis,* city), this term means membership of a city, though it has been extended to mean membership of a nation. Nevertheless, the concept of citizenship in the Graeco-Roman world was different from that of modern times. One was not normally referred to as a citizen of a country; citizenship was confined to a city. Even when the idea of Roman citizenship was developed to embrace all Italians and even others within the empire, the term still carried the idea of being a citizen of Rome, the city. The concept of citizenship goes back to the Greek city-states, in which citizens were those with civic rights in the government. The model often used in the Graeco-Roman world was that of Athens, in which all citizens were members of the gymnasium and the popular assembly, which voted on many issues. This model was to some extent a fiction, since above all the cities was an empire (e.g., the Seleucid or the Roman Empire) that restricted its autonomy to certain areas only. Nevertheless, most rulers respected the rights of cities within their autonomous spheres, so that cities were self-governing up to a certain point. The citizens would thus be able to determine to a large extent the city's governing and administration.

To be a citizen, one would usually have to be

born to parents who were both citizens (i.e., a citizen by birth) or one would have to be made a citizen (usually as an honor for some major service to the city). Simply being born in the city did not make one a citizen. Indeed, most of the inhabitants of a city were usually not citizens, though most cities had ethnic communities that were to some extent autonomous (*politeuma*) but did not enjoy the privileges of citizenship. The Jews were no different from other ethnic communities in most Graeco-Roman cities, since they formed their own *politeuma,* which applied Jewish law within its own sphere of authority.

The question of citizenship came to a head in the first century C.E. in several cities, especially in Alexandria. Generally, a few Jews (e.g., Philo of Alexandria) were citizens because of wealth or the deeds of ancestors. It was therefore natural that others also desired this privilege and agitated for it. The result was civil disorder, riots, and, in some cases, severe persecutions. Eventually, the emperor Claudius issued an edict that restricted citizenship to those who already possessed it by birth. *See also* GYMNASIUM.

citron (Heb.: *etrog*) a citrus fruit; one of four species carried in synagogue on Sukkot; from Leviticus 23:40, "fruit of a goodly tree." *See also* ETROG.

city of refuge a place where a man who has incurred blood guilt by unintentionally killing another may find sanctuary until he is brought to trial. He must remain there until he is proved innocent and the high priest has died. Should he leave the city of refuge before this, he may be slain because he has shed blood, no matter how innocently—a prerogative of YHWH alone. The cities of refuge were not intended to afford sanctuary to one who killed intentionally, that is, committed murder. In such a case, it was the obligation of the elders of the city in which he was born to extradite him and to hand him over to the proper avenger. Although there is general agreement that there are six cities of refuge, their disposition is not agreed upon. The Chronicler treats them as Levitical, but he only mentions two by name: Hebron and Shechem.

Clarus, Gaius Erucius *see* ERUCIUS CLARUS, GAIUS SEXTUS

Claudius (10 B.C.E.–54 C.E.) Roman emperor. Claudius's proclamation as emperor in 41 was virtually an accident. He was hiding in the palace when the emperor Gaius was murdered, and upon being discovered, he was taken to the Praetorian camp and saluted as emperor by the Praetorian Guard. His rule was less authoritarian than his predecessors. He constantly urged the senators to take their responsibilities more seriously. Even though he lacked military experience, he participated in the invasion of Britain in 43. His administration is noted for the rise in power of rich and powerful freed slaves.

Dio claims that in 41 Claudius deprived the Jews in Rome of the right of assembly because they were too numerous to expel. Suetonius says that Claudius expelled the Jews because of the constant riots instigated by Chrestus. Orosius claims that Josephus reported Claudius's expulsion of the Jews from Rome in 49, but there is no reference to this in our versions of Josephus. In 41 Claudius sent an edict to the city of Alexandria reestablishing the position of its Jewish community after the attacks it had experienced there during Gaius's reign. There is speculation that his Jewish friends Agrippa I and Herod of Chalcis encouraged him to investigate the matter. Claudius seems to have heard from Alexandrian delegations representing both sides of the dispute before he issued his edict confirming the rights of the Jews to follow their own customs. Shortly after this, he issued a similar edict affecting the whole empire that also confirmed the rights of the Jews to follow their own traditions, but also reminding them not to be disrespectful to the cults of other peoples. However, the situation in Alexandria was still unstable, and Claudius was forced to send a letter to Alexandria in November 41. He writes that both sides must give up their mutual and stubborn hostility. He reaffirms that the Jews, long-time residents of Alexandria, should continue to enjoy the privileges granted them by Augustus. Furthermore, the Jews must not seek to gain more rights; they must refrain from sending more delegations to Rome; they must not invite Jews from Syria or Egypt to Alexandria; and they must not intrude into the events at the gymnasium.

A papyrus known as the Acts of the Alexandrian Martyrs refers to Claudius's punishment of Isidorus and Lampo for their attempt to defame Agrippa before the emperor. Unfortunately, the state of the text is so poor that it is difficult to ascertain the details of the event or even to ascertain whether the text refers to Agrippa I or II. In 45 Fadus sought to strengthen his control over Judea by placing the high priest's vestments under Roman control. Fadus was forced to send an embassy along with one from the Sanhedrin to Claudius to resolve the matter. Josephus claims that the presence of Agrippa II at the imperial court was the reason that the emperor supported the Jews' position. At this same time, Claudius granted the nomination of the high priests to Herod of Chalcis.

Claudius Paternus Clementianus procurator of Judea and Syria of uncertain date. The province is called "Judea" and not "Syria-Palaestina," suggesting a date before 135 when Hadrian renamed the province. Claudius is identified as the "procurator of the dead or recalled governor," but there is no indiction to whom this refers.

Clearchus of Soli Peripatetic writer who flourished c. 300 B.C.E. He spent time in Asia Minor, where he probably came in contact with Jews. In a quotation from Josephus, he relates a supposed meeting between Aristotle and a Jew of Syria, who "not only spoke Greek but had the soul of a Greek." It is unlikely that such a meeting took place, but, like similar stories, it served as a vehicle for Greeks of this time to idealize Oriental wisdom. The same story claims that the Jews descended from Indian philosophers. A number of early Greek writers spoke positively of the Jews.

Clemens procurator of Syria-Palestine under Diocletian. We find only one reference to him on the side of an inscription of the legate L. Valerius Valerianus. The inscription merely mentions his name and the emperor under whom he served.

Clementianus, Claudius Paternus *see* CLAUDIUS PATERNUS CLEMENTIANUS

Clement of Alexandria (c. 150–c. 215) theologian. He may have been born in Athens and seems to have become a Christian as an adult. He headed a school in Alexandria that introduced Christian ideals of life in philosophical terms. Although popular in the early church, he fell out of favor beginning in the eighth century, when he was presumed to be one of Origen's teachers. Only three of his works survive. His *Protrepticus,* like Aristotle's lost work of the same name, is presented in the form of a proclamation addressed to educated people. He is familiar with Jewish Hellenistic authors, especially Philo, and the philosophical principles of Clement's thought come from Jewish-Alexandrian philosophy. He follows Philo's method of allegory in interpreting scripture and believes that Moses' legislation is natural law. Clement praises the Bible's dietary laws, restrictions on dress, and sexual mores, for they help humans achieve a modified asceticism that is necessary for a true Christian life. Several times he refers to Jewish customs, such as washing, and sometimes he supports his own views by stating that "a Jew told me so." However, he does not seem to have extensive knowledge of Judaism. While he has some sympathy toward Judaism, he did write a tract against the Jews.

Cleodemus Malchus writer, quoted by Josephus and Eusebius, about whom little is known. He is called a prophet, but the significance of this is uncertain. Only one fragment survives of his writing, which seems to have been about Libya. This quotation came through Alexander Polyhistor, showing that Cleodemus lived earlier than that writer, but his date is otherwise uncertain (perhaps the second century B.C.E.). We also do not know his nationality. Some have identified him as a pagan because he combines Jewish with Greek tradition; however, we find similar practice in some writers who are certainly Jewish or Samaritan, such as Artapanus or Pseudo-Eupolemus. Thus, the suggestion that he was Jewish or Samaritan seems the best guess. According to Cleodemus, Abraham had many sons by Keturah. Assyria was named after one called Assouri, and Africa was named after one called Iapheras (actually a grandson in Gen. 25:4). Iapheras and another son, Iaphras or Aphranes, joined with Heracles in fighting against Libya. Afterward, Heracles married a daughter of Iaphras or Aphranes, thus joining in the line of Abraham.

Cleopatra III Euergetes (Kokke) daughter of Ptolemy VI and Cleopatra II. She was married to her uncle Ptolemy VIII Euergetes in 142 B.C.E., while her mother was also his wife. After his death in 116 she was made co-regent with one of her sons, Ptolemy IX Philometor (Lathyros), whom she disliked intensely. She incited rebellions against Lathyros, and she finally drove him out in 107; a second son, Ptolemy X Alexander, was installed. Alexander Jannaeus in Judea tried to take advantage of this split in Ptolemaic power to expand his kingdom, without success. Eventually, Cleopatra quarreled with Ptolemy X, and in 101 she was assassinated by him.

Cleopatra VII Thea Philopator (69–30 B.C.E.) daughter of Ptolemy XII; ruled Egypt along with Ptolemy XIII in 51 B.C.E. The last of the pharaohs, Cleopatra tried desperately to revive the fortunes of Egypt and to provide for her subjects. She ruled during a time of transition in the Roman Empire; intelligent and quick-witted, she allied herself with Julius Caesar and bore him a son, Caesarion. After Caesar's assassination, she joined with Mark Antony, bearing him twin children. Antony returned to Cleopatra former portions of the old Ptolemaic Empire, as well as parts of the Phoenician seacoast and the spice-bearing areas around Jericho and in Arabia, and she supplied money and stores to aid Antony after his failed expedition against Parthia. In 34 B.C.E. Cleopatra and Antony staged a triumphal scene at Alexandria, whereby all the lands once ruled by Alexander the Great, from Greece to the Indus, were divided between

Cleopatra and her children, even though much of the area remained unconquered or was held by client kings. This vision died with the defeat of Antony at Actium in 31 B.C.E. by Octavian. Cleopatra committed suicide soon after, on 10 August 30 B.C.E.

cleruchy (from Gr.: *klēruchia,* inheritance) The term became generally applied to a military colony in the Graeco-Roman world. It derives from the Greek *klēros* (part, or share), in reference to the allotments of land that settlers were given. A ruler would often found such a colony in a border or other area of potential trouble. The settlers were responsible for police work and border defense and could be conscripted into the army in time of war. It was an effective way of keeping order in the area, as well as having reserves ready to fight at short notice.

client kingdom kingdom under Roman domination but not administered directly by Rome; also known as a "friendly kingdom." During the period of Roman expansion, many states were turned into Roman provinces with Roman governors. Nevertheless, a few native kings were able to retain their thrones and maintain their own internal governments. Such a kingdom was usually in a border area. The king had to be approved by Rome; he had restictions placed on his activity, especially with regard to other kingdoms, but he otherwise often functioned as a virtual autocrat in his own country. Herod the Great is a major example. He was appointed king of Judea during the late Republic, held on to his throne during the Roman Civil War, and was confirmed in it by Octavian in 31 B.C.E. During his long reign, Herod generally had good relations with Augustus, but he consulted him about any matters relating to the succession. When Herod evidently accused some of his sons of plotting against him, the trial was presided over by the Romans. Herod was once admonished for attacking the Nabateans, a neighboring kingdom, and had to endure humiliating raids from them until Augustus changed his mind.

clothing any of the apparel used in antiquity by Jewish communities in Palestine and in the diaspora. Our sources for reconstructing dress stem mainly from ancient Jewish and non-Jewish art, especially in wall murals, mosaic floors, and in wall mosaics of the Byzantine period. There is a small amount of evidence from coins, relief sculpture, and finds of clothing at Masada and En Gedi in Israel. Clothing in general consisted of an outer garment, perhaps a cloak, a main garment, and sandals or boots. In general Jews wore garments that reflect the culture in which they lived. We have no details of dress from the Persian period, but it seems likely that local styles persisted except where one dressed like the Persians for reasons of status or political expedience. In the Hellenistic period the major form of dress was the rectangular mantle (Gr.: *himation*; Heb.: *talit*) over a tunic (Gr.: *chiton*; Heb.: *haluk*), the main garment. The tunic was simply two rectangular sheets sewn together with holes at the edges for the head and arms. Two broad stripes in a dark color ran from top to bottom in front and in back. The mantle could then be removed by men working in the fields. The main garment for a woman was longer than a man's, short-sleeved, and may have been pleated with many small pleats. Women generally wore a belt or sash, while a virgin could wear two belts, one at the waist and one below the breasts. Both sexes wore sandals that do not appear to have been distinctive for the sexes. Both sexes also had the option of wearing an outer cloak (Gr.: *chlamys*). This was fastened at the neck and wrapped around the body in inclement weather. In the Roman period, men wore the toga over the tunic and added an outer cloak during bad weather. The outer cloak in purple was also a sign of status and authority for Roman officers. Some Jewish soldiers depicted on the special Roman issue coins called "Judaea Capta" (71–79 C.E.) depict a Jewish soldier wearing the outer cloak. According to the finds in the Cave of Letters near En Gedi (135 C.E.), Jewish men wore white or pale yellow outer garments with notched, straight bands woven into the corners of the rectangular cloth. Women wore colored outer garments with a notched band in the form of a capital gamma woven into the corners. Some of the men's clothing found in the Cave of Letters was striped in the area around the neck. Both men and women wore similar sandals, and both wore the tunic as a main garment. A linen cloth worn like a loincloth, called the *sindon* in Greek, was an occasional undergarment. Wealth and status were easy to display in clothing, as one could buy outer garments in cotton, linen, or even silk, in addition to the most widely worn fiber, wool. Dyed linen clothing with woven gold threads could be made to order, and one could purchase ersatz purple or true purple as a sign of status. Dense weaving and weaving of garments in various patterns were also telling in matters of wealth and status.

clover, four-petal very minor motif in ancient Jewish art, especially in synagogue art. The design is somewhat enigmatic, since the four-leaf clover is not part of the flora of ancient Israel. On the other hand it could simply be a four-leafed plant. One low-relief example on basalt stone is known from the ancient synagogue site of Butmiyyah in the Golan Heights.

clubs *see* COLLEGIA

Codex Reuchlinianus *see* REUCHLINIANUS, CODEX

Coele Syria (Lat., from Gr., Hollow Syria) geographical designation with varied meaning. During the third century B.C.E., the name was used unofficially for Ptolemaic possessions in Asia, that is, for South Syria, Phoenicia, and Palestine. When the Seleucids acquired these Ptolemaic possessions, they referred to them as Coele Syria and Phoenicia. In a more restricted sense, the term Coele Syria refers to the valley between the Lebanon and Anti-Lebanon mountains. Under Septimius Severus (r. 193–211 C.E.), the name Coele Syria referred to a province comprising northern and inland Syria with its capital at Antioch on the Orontes (in contrast to the southern Syrian area called Phoenicia).

coffin wooden, lead, stone, or clay box for the burial of the dead. Stone coffins are ordinarily termed sarcophagi. Coffins were not common in Jewish burials, but they are known. For example, an intact, undecorated clay coffin is known from catacomb 14 at the Jewish necropolis at Beth Shearim. This coffin was 1.87 meters long and 0.22 centimeters high by 0.54 meters wide. This is shallower than modern coffins. Clay coffins have broad rims for installation of clay tiles as a cover. Clay coffins are mainly associated with Phoenician burials of the Iron 2 and Persian period on the Mediterranean coast, and clay coffins of later periods are often associated with that geographic area. On the other hand, lead coffins are more widely known. For example, five lead coffins are known from the same necropolis at Beth Shearim. These ranged in length from 1.84 to 2.07 meters long, and all were decorated in low relief with stereotypical designs: bands of vine scrolls, bead and reel patterns, triangles, eight-petaled flowers, grape clusters, an arch on two columns, running animals, and two menorahs, which establish the Jewish character of the burials. The menorah on lead coffins is modeled somewhat realistically in relief, sometimes with shofar, etrog, and incense shovel. It is often hypothesized that lead coffins originated in Hellenized Phoenicia, and specifically in Tyre, Sidon, and Beirut. They are most commonly dated to the third and fourth centuries C.E. They are known as far east as the Jordan Valley, but have been found mainly in Judea and western Galilee.

Wooden coffins are known from Roman Jericho, where they were decorated with geometric and stereotypical inlays. Sarcophagi are known everywhere in Roman Palestine, and many of them were imported. They could be purchased decorated or plain, and at Beth Shearim many of them were apparently decorated by the families that used them. Sarcophagi are generally more massive than wood, lead, or clay coffins because of their greater width and the thickness of their lids, which may approach 60 centimeters. For example, sarcophagus 87 from catacomb 20 (in which no less than 125 sarcophagi were found) was 2.05 meters by 0.87 meters by 0.61 meters, not counting the lid. This would require a 2.6 ton limestone block for carving just the receptacle. Even larger sarcophagi are known at Beth Shearim and elsewhere, some of them approaching seven tons in weight. Lids of sarcophagi are typically carved to resemble a roof with *acroteria* or rounded projections on each corner. Sometimes families inscribed the name of the deceased on the side of the sarcophagus, presumably so that family members who entered the tomb at a later date for a new burial could locate family members. In catacomb 20 at Beth Shearim, twenty of the sarcophagi are inscribed with a family member's name. Other sarcophagi in fine marble feature carvings in high relief of war scenes and other popular motifs. The white marble sarcophagi with such scenes have been traced to Attica in Greece and to the island of Marmara in the Dardanelles. One of the most popular themes depicted on these sarcophagi of the first to the third centuries C.E. is the war of the Amazons with the Greeks. These are found in both Jewish and non-Jewish contexts.

cohen *see* PRIEST

coin symbols emblems, designs, or figures found on coins of ancient Judea, either minted directly by Jewish rulers or by other rulers who sometimes allowed Jewish sensitivities. The earliest minted coins in Judea after the return to Zion were minted by the Persian rulers and therefore reflect Persian motifs. The earliest of these coins is a small silver obol bearing a head facing forward. On the reverse an owl stands right, and around one reads a Hebrew inscription: "Yohanan the Priest." This coin is dated to the mid-fourth century B.C.E. Yohanan is Yohanan II, who is mentioned in the Elephantine Papyri. Another small silver coin shows the head of Athena facing right on the obverse (front), while the reverse (back) depicts an owl and the Greek abbreviation for Athens. An Aramaic inscription reads "Yadua," who has been provisionally identified with the high priest Yadua II (about 390–323 B.C.E.). Other coins of this type were struck by the alien rulers and therefore reflect their motifs. These silver coins are known in about a dozen varieties. Symbols on the coins include birds (a bird looking backward, owl, and falcon), lily, rosette, a human head, and a bust of a male or female. After 312 B.C.E. these coins show a head of Ptolemy, a horse, a bird looking backwards, and an eagle with spread wings. An Aramaic inscription reads "Yehudah" (the Persian province of Judah) or "Yehezkiyah the Priest" and apparently these coins are to be dated to about 330 B.C.E.

From the time of John Hyrcanus I (135 B.C.E.) a new type of Jewish coin enters history. This tiny bronze coin (Heb.: *prutah*; Gr.: *lepton*) features a wreath with a long Hebrew inscription on one side, for example, "Yehohanan the High Priest and Council of the Jews." On the other side one sees double cornucopias with a pomegranate between horns. Other issues of the Hasmonean rulers may show two parallel cornucopias on one side and a crested helmet on the other, an anchor on one side and a lily on the other, or an anchor on one side and a star on the other (always Alexander Jannaeus, who reigned from 106–76 B.C.E., or Judah Aristobulus II, who reigned from 67–63 B.C.E.). A few lead coins of Alexander Jannaeus show an anchor surrounded by a circle (a diadem) with a Greek inscription "Alexander the King," and on the other side an Aramaic inscription in three lines, "King Alexander." The star and diadem are clearly a symbol for kingship. The anchor may be associated with Jannaeus's annexation of the coastal cities from 95 B.C.E. The cornucopias clearly are symbols for plenty, and the pomegranate is normally associated with fertility. The wreath is known from all parts of the Graeco-Roman world as a symbol of authority and leadership, a symbol fit for a king. The helmet likely serves a similar function. In the Hasmonean issues depictions of living things, humans, or angelic beings are scrupulously avoided.

Mattathias Antigonus reigned only from 40–37 B.C.E. and engaged in continual warfare with Herod the Great in the struggle for power. On his largest denominations he depicted a wreath on one side with the inscription "Of Antigonus the King" in Greek. On the other side he struck the double cornucopias and a Hebrew inscription, "Matityah the High Priest and Council of the Jews." On the smaller denomination, which was evidently half the value of the larger, there appears only one cornucopia. The third and smallest denomination, the *lepton* or *prutah,* mainly has the wreath and Hebrew inscription on one side and a head of wheat on the other, though some show the double cornucopia as on the earlier Hasmonean coins. On a few of these smallest denominations, which he minted in bronze only, he depicted the menorah and the table of showbread or the table for the bread of the presence. This is normally understood to be a bid for support from the Jewish population of Palestine. The menorah would never again appear on a Jewish coin, but the table of showbread will appear on coins of the second Jewish Revolt against Rome.

Herod the Great (37 to 4 B.C.E.) was the first Jewish ruler to use symbols from Roman republican issues. The coins therefore sometimes depict instruments of Roman cult, but were likely used to show the source of his power and not to advocate Roman religion. The symbols he used on dated coins include the apex (crested helmut), tripod, shield, winged caduceus, fruit, aphlaston or curved stem of a ship, and palm branch. On undated coins he used a table (sometimes with bowl), diadem, wreath, double or crossed palm branches, the vine, anchor, galley, and eagle. The table may commemorate the silver table that Herod gave to the Temple as part of its grand reconstruction. Likewise the vine could commemorate his gift of a gold vine to the Temple, just as the eagle probably represents the eagle Herod attempted to have installed in the Temple in honor of Rome. The galley is usually understood to commemorate his construction of the harbor at Caesarea, and the anchor may have served the same purpose. The caduceus is a surprise, although scholars usually think this has become a generic symbol for health and recovery and therefore a political symbol.

The sons of Herod the Great, each of whom inherited a portion of their father's kingdom, continued to use Hasmonean coin symbols and those introduced by Herod the Great. They also introduced their own symbols. For example, the eldest son, Herod Archelaus, Ethnarch of Judea, continued to use the galley, anchor, double cornucopias with caduceus between the horns, and diadem. Archelaus also used the crested helmet.

Herod Antipas, who was tetrarch of Galilee and Peraea (Trans-Jordan), introduced the reed on his coins, probably to symbolize his founding of the city of Tiberias. He also used the palm branch on coins of Tiberias and introduced the palm tree on a coin minted at Tiberias. This motif became a specifically Jewish symbol on several issues by later Jewish rulers.

Herod Philip, who reigned as tetrarch of Gaulanitis and other northeastern territories, used wholly Roman symbols on his coins, including busts of himself and the emperor Augustus. His coins are not distinctively Jewish. On the reverse of his coins, he even depicted the temple to Augustus, the Augusteum, which he built at Caesarea-Philippi.

From this point forward in history coins of the Jewish rulers often borrow their symbols freely from Roman issues. Herod Agrippa I (37–44 C.E.) copied Roman issues in honor of the emperor Caligula, complete with Caligula as charioteer. On the other hand, he seems to have softened his approach in certain coins, using a canopy as a symbol of authority on one type and three heads of wheat on another. The wheat is one of the seven "kinds" that are to be found in the land. Likewise coins of Herod Agrippa II (56–97 C.E.) are virtually indistinguishable from Roman coins.

With the outbreak of the Great Revolt in 66 C.E. a new silver Jewish coin appears. On the obverse or front of the coin there is the omer, a silver vessel from the Second Temple. There is a Hebrew inscription around the edge of the coin: "Shekel of Israel." The Hebrew letter *aleph* above the omer indicates that it is the first year of the revolt. On the reverse one sees within the inscription "Jerusalem the Holy" (or "Jerusalem Is Holy") and three pomegranates on one branch. The half-shekels use the same symbols for the first year.

The same design continues in the second year of the revolt (67 C.E.), but a new shekel appears with an amphora on one side and a vine leaf, small branch, and tendril on the other side. There is also a new inscription: "Freedom of Zion." Now coins begin to be struck in bronze also.

On the coins of the third year (68 C.E.), the amphora sometimes has a conical lid. On coins of the fourth year (69 C.E.), a few of the coins identical to the second-year shekels are struck in bronze. A new type appears with three palm branches tied together by the stems on one side and a wreath of palm branches on the other side. A second new type depicts a palm tree with seven or nine branches flanked by two baskets of dates. The inscription reads "For the Redemption of Israel." Another type depicts the omer on one side with the Hebrew inscription "For the Redemption of Zion." On the reverse there is a lulab flanked by two etrogs.

On a few surviving coins of the fifth year of the revolt (70 C.E.), the same design as on the first year shekels appears. It is interesting to see that wheat, barley, figs, and olives play no role as symbols on these new coins. In fact, it is clear that these coins are making a nationalistic and religious statement about the Jewish festival of Sukkot (Tabernacles). This festival commemorates the dwelling in tents in the wilderness (Lev. 23:42–43). The palm branches are mentioned in a Hellenistic historical text that reasserts the importance of the feast in II Maccabees 10:6–8. Therefore, it is of no surprise that temple objects (the omer) and images associated with festivals appear on these new coins.

On Roman coins, called "Judea Capta" by scholars, issued after the collapse of the First Revolt, Rome uses the palm tree as the operative symbol for Israel. On one side of the palm tree sits a mourning female captive. On the other side of the palm tree stands a captive male wrapped in a cloak with his hands tied behind his back. These coins are inscribed "Judea," "Judaea Capta," "Judaea Devicta" (conquered).

The next occasion of the minting of Jewish coins is during the Bar Kosiba Revolt of 132–135 C.E. All these coins are overstrikes on contemporary Roman or other coins. Overstriking in itself makes a political and religious statement.

The symbols on coins of the Bar Kosiba Revolt include the images associated with Tabernacles, such as the lulab, but other symbols are from the previous vocabulary of Jewish symbols: a cluster of grapes, the vine leaf, the palm tree, and the wreath. The new symbols are the facade of the Temple, a jug (surely a vessel from the Temple cult), a harp (used in Temple worship), a lyre (also from Temple worship), and two trumpets, presumably those used in the Temple cult to announce the daily offerings and other events.

The largest silver coins (the tetradrachms) of the first and second years of the Bar Kosiba Revolt show the Temple facade in Jerusalem and an object within the facade that is usually interpreted as the Holy Ark. The facade has four columns with a pediment above, a star or other device within the pediment, and sometimes a low barrier in front of the columns. On the reverse of this coin is a detailed representation of a lulab, a bundle formed of the palm branch bound with myrtle and willow branches, with an etrog on the left. On the reverse appears the Hebrew inscription "Year One of the Redemption of Israel." A second, smaller silver coin (a denarius) shows a golden jug or flagon with handle, a lulab on the right, and a Hebrew inscription: "Eleazar the Priest."

The large bronzes show grape leaves and an amphora, probably also understood to be a vessel of the Temple. The small bronzes have a palm tree with seven branches and two clusters of dates on one side and a grape leaf on the other. Other small bronzes depict the harp (nebel) with four, five, or six strings. A large, undated silver coin shows a two-column facade of the Temple with an architrave above the two columns and a podium with two steps beneath the columns. The table of showbread stands between the two columns. On the reverse stands a bundled lulab and a Hebrew inscription: "For the Freedom of Jerusalem." Silver denarii of year two show the harp or the lyre (*kinor*), while others depict two temple trumpets with the Hebrew inscription "For the Freedom of Jerusalem." Many of the coins of this revolt were also inscribed in Hebrew: "Simon, Prince of Israel," (Simon Bar Kosiba). This surprisingly rich vocabulary of coin symbols gives expression to the desires of the Jewish people in the revolt, namely, to gain freedom and redemption for Israel and to recover the Temple and its cult.

collegia (Lat., association, club) used in reference to political and religious associations or clubs common in the Graeco-Roman world (known in Greek as *hetaireiai*). Usually organized around a deity or religious cult, with drinking and socializing, some had a serious political purpose and could be subversive. Thus at various times they were banned, especially from Rome, as potentially seditious against the government of the day. Since synagogues came under the strict definition, they had to be and were generally exempted from bans under the Roman emperors.

commandment *see* MITZVAH

commissioning *see* CALL

Commodus, Lucius Ceionius legate of Judea, 75 or 76 C.E. An inscription from Gerasa mentions Commodus. The nature of the inscription leaves some questions about Commodus's authority, and the subsequent course of his career in relationship to that of his predecessor, Bassus, is unclear.

community (Heb.: *yaḥad*; Gr.: *koinōnia*) The Hebrew root of the word "community" denotes a sense of unity and common purpose, and this notion persists during the many changes through which the "community" of Israel went throughout its history. In the period of the tribal league (c. 1200–1000 B.C.E.), Israel's community was a loose confederation of tribes united by common worship of the god YHWH. Membership in this community was determined by birth into a clan, part of the larger unit of the tribe. Tribes came together periodically for festivals and for holy war and also began to unite around a tradition of common law that defined the obligations of members both to fellow members and to outsiders. The autonomy of the tribes, however, threatened the very existence of the community Israel, and, in the face of outside threat, a monarchy was established. The institution of monarchy disrupted the tribal community and conferred on Israel the status of nation-state. However, the office of prophecy kept alive the traditions of the tribal league throughout the period of the monarchy. During the exile, the Jews struggled to reclaim themselves as a community. Two competing definitions emerged: one, a universal Yahwism embracing all nations (the Isianic corpus); and the other, a radical separation from other nations through adherence to the Torah (Ezra, Nehemiah, etc.).

In the Second Temple period, several groups emerged that may fit the sociological definition of "community" (Pharisees, Sadducees, etc.), but one group in this period actually named itself the Community, or *yaḥad,* and that is the group living at Qumran, usually identified with the Essenes. In fact, in the Qumran library there were found two rule books: one, the Damascus Document, was written for Essenes living in "camps" among the towns of Judah; while the other, the Community Rule, was written for the *yaḥad* par excellence, the Community at Qumran.

The Community Rule envisages a group living in radical separation from the rest of Judaism (and, of course, from Gentiles). The Community is divided into priests and laity, with a strict hierarchical structure by rank. The leadership of the Community is given to the priests and Levites, governed by a Master. Members hold property in common. Part of the archaeological evidence (a large dining hall) from Qumran supports an injunction to eat in common. Infractions of the Community's rules caused severe punishment, including expulsion. This points to a less attractive aspect of the Community at Qumran: while the sectarians were called upon to love their fellow members, they were also called upon to hate outsiders.

This radical disjunction between "us" and "them" seems to have been rejected by the early Christian community, which was united by their belief in Jesus of Nazareth as Messiah and their eschatological hope in the coming of the Kingdom of God. Therefore, the community theoretically welcomed all comers and had an organization of leadership that was charismatic and nonhierarchical, including women. However, as the Christian movement expanded in the second and third centuries C.E., the community moved to a more hierarchical structure, with organized statements of belief (creeds).

Judaism, after the fall of the Second Temple in

70 C.E., followed the path begun by the Pharisees, characterized by a community bound together by adherence to the Torah, both written and oral, that comes together for worship and study. Observance of the Torah, as interpreted by the Beit Din (which replaced the Sanhedrin as the chief governing body of the Jews), was the main indication of membership in the community. In Palestine the Jewish community was headed by the patriarch and in Babylon by the exilarch, each being unofficially responsible for the internal governance of the community. A radical separation from non-Jews was not necessarily sought, but a focus on the Jewish community, particularly in the face of persecution, became natural. This type of Judaism, rabbinic Judaism, continues as the norm in the Western world today. *See also* COMMUNITY RULE.

Community Rule a collection of rules and hortatory material governing community life (presumably the life of the Community at Qumran); alternative titles are the Manual of Discipline and the Serekh haYaḥad. The major manuscript of the Community Rule (1QS) was discovered in 1947 in Cave 1 at Qumran and published by M. Burrows in 1951. This manuscript is a complete (although damaged) Hebrew scroll consisting of eleven text columns; its handwriting dates from c. 100 B.C.E. The text exists also in ten copies from Cave 4 (unpublished) and one copy from Cave 5 (published by J. T. Milik, DJD III). Since the oldest copy we possess (4QS[e]) has already undergone editing, the text itself must have been composed no later than the second half of the second century B.C.E.

The Rule, as it now exists, is a composite document; that is, it is composed of units that were originally independent. As it now stands, it can be easily divided into six sections: (1) 1:1–15, a statement of the Community's aims; (2) 1:16–3:12, the entry into the covenant; (3) 3:13–4:26, a treatise on the two spirits; (4) 5:1–9:11, regulations for the Community; (5) 9:12–26, rules for the Master; and (6) 10:1–11:22, the Master's hymn.

The regulations describe a community that shares a common life and keeps its property in common (sect. 4). The Community is headed by priests and Levites and governed by a *maskil,* or Master; the members evidently do not mingle with people outside the Community, including their fellow Jews (sect. 4). Within the Community, they adhere to a strict hierarchy of priests, Levites, and others, and within those divisions, to a further ranking based on age and standing in the Community. Regulation of daily life is strict, and punishments for such offenses as lying, spitting, anger against a fellow member, speaking out of turn, and swearing range from complete expulsion from the Community to exclusion from the common meal for a fixed period of time. The precepts for the Master remind him of his duty to love and instruct in the "Way"—the doctrines of the sect—those who are members of the covenant, but to reject absolutely those outside of the covenant.

This dichotomy between those inside and those outside the covenant is illustrated most strongly in the Treatise of the Two Spirits (sect. 3). According to this piece, which probably existed as a separate document before its incorporation in the Rule, all of humanity is divided into two groups or lots: the lot of truth, or light, and the lot of falsehood, or darkness. Each of these lots is governed by an angel (the angel of light and the angel of darkness, or Belial), and there is an absolute distinction between the two. There is a strong flavor of predestination in this section, for it is God who has appointed the lots and each individual's place in them. Those who belong to the lot of light will choose entry into the covenant (sect. 2), thereby rejecting the lot of darkness and the people in it. This doctrine has important repercussions for the study of early Christianity (e.g., the dualism of the Gospel of John).

The Community Rule is very important for reconstructing the beliefs and practices of the Community at Qumran, which illustrate the variety of Judaism in the Second Temple period.

conch *see* SHELL

Conf. *see* DE CONFUSIONE LINGUARUM

confession the explicit acknowledgment and confession of human sinfulness, which is found in many prayers in Second Temple Judaism. The same Hebrew verb (*yadah*), "to confess, to acknowledge," is used both for a declaration of human sinfulness and for a declaration of God's attributes and works of deliverance. Thus, confession and praise are more closely bound together than in our modern English understanding of these terms.

Of particular interest are a group of extended prose prayers (Ezra 9:6–15; Neh. 1:5–11, 9:6–37; Dan. 9:4b–19; Prayer of Azariah; Bar. 1:15–3:8; and Words of the Heavenly Lights [4Q504]), which share certain distinctive features. All draw upon a common vocabulary, very much influenced by the Deuteronomistic tradition (note esp. 1 Kings 8:47). The same confession formula reoccurs with slight variations: "We have sinned, we have done wrong, we have acted wickedly and rebelled" (Dan. 9:4, 9, 15; Bar. 1:17–18; Prayer of Azariah 1:6–7). Often there is an explicit acknowledgment of God's justice and righteousness, a doxology of judgment: "You have been just in all that has come upon us" (Neh. 9:33); "Yours is righteousness, O Lord, for it is You who have done all this" (4Q504 vi. 1; cf. Prayer of Azariah 1:4, 8). The confession itself is set within a context of praise (e.g., Prayer of Azariah 1:3: "Blessed are you, O Lord, God of our ancestors, and worthy of praise") and an extended explicit recalling of God's acts of deliverance and convenantal fidelity in Israel's past history. All of these features point to a common origin for these prayers, probably in a postexilic liturgical setting.

Other prayers of confession share many of the same features. From the Dead Sea Scrolls, we have the text of the confession to be recited in a liturgical ceremony by those entering the covenant: "We have strayed. We have [disobeyed]. We and our ancestors before us have sinned and done wickedly" (1QS i. 25–26). In Greek, the Prayer of Manasseh is an extended poetic confession of sinfulness, "I have sinned, O Lord, I have sinned, and I acknowledge my transgressions" (v. 12), which culminates in praise and doxology, "and I will praise you continually all the days of my life" (v. 15).

confession of sin (Heb.: *vidui*) On the Day of Atonement, in line with Leviticus 16, the high priest and the people confessed their sins and asked for divine forgiveness.

Congr. *see* DE CONGRESSU QUAERENDAE ERUDITIONIS GRATIA

congregation most frequently a translation of the Hebrew *edah* and *kehal*. The word *edah* can be applied to any gathering, group or company (Ps. 22:16: "company of evil-doers") but in Exodus, Leviticus, and Numbers, it frequently designates the congregation of the Israelites encamped around the tent of meeting in the wilderness (Exod. 12:3, 16:1–2; Num. 10:2–3), that is, the national, legal, and cultic community. *Kehal* is used especially in Deuteronomy, Ezra, Nehemiah, and Chronicles. However, there is no essential distinction between the two. In the Septuagint, *synagōgē* and *ekklēsia* could be used for both Hebrew words, with *edah* most often rendered by *synagōgē*. In 1 Maccabees 2:42 and 7:42, *synagōgē* has the meaning of a company or group of Hasidim and of scribes, while in 2:42 it refers to a national gathering. The Qumran covenanters thought of themselves as the "holy congregation" (1QSa 1:12), as the congregation of Israel in the last days" (1QSa 1:1), and the "congregation of God" (1QM 4:9) opposed to the "congregation of Belial" (1QH 7:34). The Septuagint translates Numbers 16:24 as: "Tell the congregation, "Separate . . . from the congregation of Korah."

The more restricted sense of a local congregation can be found in Susannah 41.52.60, that is, the congregation at Babylon, and Psalms of Solomon 10:7 speaks of the congregations of Israel or the congregations of the pious (17:16). Inscriptional evidence, particularly from Rome, also documents this shift toward *synagōgē* as referring to the local congregation.

Within the New Testament, *ekklēsia* is the preferred form and is normally translated "church." *Synagōgē* does refer to a Christian congregation in James 2:2, but usually the term is translated by "synagogue" and can refer either to the Jewish congregation or to the building itself. Thus a clear distinction is drawn between the two terms, which originally were not distinct.

conscience a concept of Greek moral philosophy. During the late Second Temple period it became increasingly significant among Jews affected by Hellenistic culture.

The Greek word for conscience, *syneidesis,* developed out of classical expressions for "awareness" or "consciousness," and one could be conscious or aware of many kinds of things, moral and nonmoral. Prominent among those things was the consciousness of guilt for past transgressions. During the late Hellenistic and early Roman periods the understanding of consciousness developed into the notion of a mental faculty that embodied norms of conduct. Seneca, the Roman Stoic of the first century C.E., understood conscience as a "spirit within us . . . an observer and guard of our evil and good deeds" (*Moral Epistles* 41.1), and he prized a "good conscience" (*Moral Epistles* 28.9–10; 43.5; 105.79; *On the Happy Life* 19.1; 20.5). Among some moralists, especially neo-Pythagoreans who influenced Seneca, there arose the discipline of examining the conscience daily to determine whether one had committed any faults (Seneca, *On Anger* 3.36). In the late first century C.E. Epictetus (*Discourses* 3.22.94) speaks of conscience as an awareness of what is right, enabling one to do it.

The Hebrew Bible does not know any term for conscience. The Septuagint rarely uses the Greek *syneidesis* and does so simply in the sense of consciousness (Kohelet 10:20).

Appropriation of the concept of conscience as a moral faculty of awareness of past deeds appears in Alexandrian Jewish literature. The Wisdom of Solomon (17:10) personifies wickedness, "distressed by conscience." A liturgical use appears in the prayer, possibly based on a synagogue liturgy, in the Apostolic Constitutions 7.33.3. Philo develops extensive reflections on conscience. It is knowledge of misdeeds (*On the Virtues* 124; *On the Special Laws* 2.49; *That the Worse Attacks the Better* 146; *On Rewards and Punishments* 84). It is a faculty that functions as an accuser, judge, and monitor (*On the Special Laws* 1.235; *On Flight* 118; *On the Virtues* 206; *Against Flaccus* 180; *On the Decalogue* 87). Some of Philo's formulations suggest an understanding of conscience as a moral guide (*That the Worse Attacks the Better* 23; *On Flight* 130–31), but this notion is not fully developed. Philo also suggests that the conscience is a device used by God to lead people to confess sin (*On Rewards and Punishments* 163; *On the Immutability of God* 126). Josephus uses the notion to refer to the consciousness of guilt, but can also refer to "good conscience" (*War* 2.582; *Antiquities* 2.52; 13.316; 16.100).

Early Christian sources follow the use of the term in Hellenistic Judaism. Paul refers to conscience as a faculty that will confirm the divine verdict on the day of judgment (Rom. 2:15). It embodies knowledge of what is right (Rom. 13:5) and the individual's conscientious judgment about moral matters needs to be respected (1 Cor. 8:1–11:1). Hebrews refers to conscience as a faculty whereby one is aware of guilt that stands in need of cleansing (9:9, 14; 10:2, 22). According to 1 Timothy 1:19–20, the person who leads a righteous life has a "good conscience."

consolation of Israel comforting of Israel. This term occurs literally only once, in Luke 2:25. Here the devout Simeon, who comes to the Jerusalem Temple to see the baby Jesus, is characterized as one "looking forward to the consolation of Israel." The following verse implies that this aspiration is now fulfilled by his seeing "the Messiah of the Lord." In Luke 2:38, a parallel passage describes the prophetess Anna's audience as "looking for the redemption of Jerusalem."

The phrases "consolation of Israel" and "redemption of Jerusalem" both refer to Jewish hopes for God's eschatological restoration of the sovereignty of Israel (or Jerusalem). This event is conceived and described in terms drawn from Deutero-Isaiah (Isa. 40–55), often called "The Book of the Consolation of Israel," wherein the prophet promises the imminent restoration of their homeland to the exiled Judahites in Babylon. Deutero-Isaiah throughout extends a message of hope and consolation; it begins, "Comfort, O comfort my people, says your God" (40:1). Again, Isaiah 52:9 states, "For the Lord has comforted his people, he has redeemed Jerusalem."

The Lukan usage extends this idea of consolation to those living in the "exile" of the present age who look forward to "deliverance" at the eschaton. This concept also occurs in later rabbinic Judaism.

Constantine (c. 280–337 C.E.) Roman emperor. Born in the Balkan city of Naissus (modern Niš), he was the son of the emperor of the West, Constantius Chlorus, and his concubine, Helena. He fought against the Persians in the army of the emperor of the East, Galerius. Constantine remained at Galerius's court until 306 when his father requested that he join him in Britain. Upon Constantius's death that year, his troops proclaimed Constantine Augustus. Constantine remained in Europe, mostly in Gaul, until 312 when he invaded Italy. He defeated the Roman princeps, Maxentius, at the Milvian Bridge and was honored by the Senate for his victory. In 313 he and his brother-in-law Licinius, the ruler of the East, issued the Edict of Milan, which recognized freedom of worship for Christians and ordered the restitution of goods and property previously confiscated from the Christian communities. By 324 Constantine succeeded in reuniting the Roman Empire and ruled as sole emperor. He completed Diocletian's administrative reforms, separating the civil and military commands of the army. A large field army was created with a new command structure. He reorganized the central government, creating new corps of guards, couriers, and agents. His founding of Constantinople on the site of Byzantium, on the Bosporus, gave him an imperial headquarters near the eastern frontier and the Danube. Major work was begun on the city in 326, and dedication ceremonies with both Christian and Roman religious rites were held in 330.

Constantine became a follower of Christianity, although he did not persecute the followers of the old Roman religions. He favored Christians for administrative posts in his government, for he believed that Christianity could serve as a unifying force for his empire. He declared Christianity a legal religion, which gave the church the same status within the empire as Judaism. The Church could hold property, Christians were excused from pagan sacrifices, and their leaders could head courts and judge cases if the litigants agreed. Although he failed in his attempts to solve the Donatist schism in North Africa, he did call the first general council of the Church in Nicea in 325 to deal with the Arian controversy.

Constantine's policy toward the Jews followed

the bishops' desires to separate Jews from Christians. In 335 Constantine decreed that any slave circumcised by a Jewish master had to be freed. In 337 the emperor issued a law prohibiting Jews from bothering or causing any damage to Jews who converted to Christianity. The punishment for one who harassed a convert to Christianity varied according to the severity of the harassment. Like Hadrian, Constantine prohibited the Jews from living in Jerusalem or passing through the city. Constantine and his mother undertook the construction of a number of churches in Jerusalem and Bethlehem, and he actively supported the spread of Christianity throughout Palestine. In 321 Constantine ordered that the Jews should be nominated to serve in the municipal courts, called curia, which meant that they had to share the financial burden of administrating the cities. Constantine notes that this is a change of ancient custom, and he declared that only two or three Jews should be exempted from this responsibility. This was part of Constantine's general policy of increasing the number of those who had to serve in municipal posts.

Constantius II (317–361 C.E.) Roman emperor. He became ruler of the East upon his father Constantine's death in 337. After a series of wars with his brothers, he became ruler of the whole empire in 350. He spent most of his reign repelling Persian attacks and fighting usurpers for his throne. He appointed his cousin Gallus as caesar in Antioch in the hopes of establishing a stable ruler to ward off the Persian invasions. In 336, the Persian king Shapur II began his wars against the Romans, and these struggles continued into 351. These Persian incursions may have been a factor in the Jews' revolt against Gallus, which broke out in Sepphoris in 351. Constantius deposed and executed Gallus in 354. In 355 he appointed Julian as caesar in Gaul to respond to the military threat posed by the Franks and the Alamanni. After Julian's military successes against the barbarians, his troops declared him Augustus in Paris in 360. Constantius died in 361 while marching to quell Julian's revolt.

While his father Constantine's personal animosity toward Jews and Judaism did not lead him to enact laws that ran counter to previous Roman policy, Constantius's legislation does move in new directions. To Constantius, Judaism is a "savage" and "abominable" sect, which is a "disgrace and an infamy." The Jews are "sacriligious" and "blasphemers." The Theodosian Code includes three laws that were decreed in 339. One ruling forbids Jews under penalty of death to marry or to convert Christian women. Also, marriages between Jews and women who had been part of the imperial *gynecaeum* were annulled. (The *gynecaeum* were factories that manufactured cloth products. The women who left these establishments to marry Jews brought their skills to the Jewish factories, which then could compete with the imperial manufacturers.) Another law threatens death by burning to any Jew or non-Jew who throws stones at converts to Christianity or attacks them in any other way. Finally, the Jews were prohibited from holding slaves of all religions or nations except for Jewish slaves. Christian slaves owned by Jews were set free immediately. The imperial treasury confiscated the non-Christian slaves owned by Jews. If a Jew was discovered holding a Christian slave, all of his property was confiscated by the government. If a Jew circumcised a non-Jewish slave, the Jew was executed. These rulings had far-reaching economic significance, because all artisans and manufacturers were dependent on slave labor. By removing this labor force from the Jews, Constantius put them at a severe economic disadvantage. In 353 Constantius II prohibited Christians from converting to Judaism. Upon conversion, the proselyte's property was confiscated by the government. A Roman statute at the end of the third century had decreed that those who converted to Judaism would lose their property and would be sent into exile. Constantius's ruling does not mention exile, and it refers only to Christians who converted to Judaism. Non-Christian converts were not punished.

Constitutio Antoniniana decree issued by Emperor Caracalla in 212 C.E. granting Roman citizenship to all free inhabitants of the empire. A badly damaged papyrus contains a Greek translation of the text and excludes the *dediticii* from some of its provisions. The *dediticii* were individuals, communities, or nations that had made a formal and unconditional surrender of all of their property to Rome; this status was normally only temporary. The scholarly consensus is that the *dediticii* were granted citizenship but were excluded from other provisions of the law. Unfortunately, the damaged state of the papyrus does not allow scholars to discover the nature of those provisions. Under the terms of the Constitutio, virtually all Jews in the empire would have become Roman citizens. Dio claims that Caracalla enacted the law in order to increase the number of citizens from whom he could collect the taxes needed to support his extravagant style of life. The Greek text, however, claims that the edict sought to enhance the prestige of the Roman gods by increasing the number of their worshipers. Caracalla issued the decree to express his appreciation to the gods for having protected him from some danger. The text is damaged at this point and we cannot determine the event to which Caracalla responds. Dio's discussion of the Jews at this time indicates that they were granted full citizenship even though their religious sensitivities prevented them from fully participating in Roman civic life, which was permeated by Roman religious practices and rituals. Nor did this in any way limit the Jews' religious liberty. Given the fact that the Jews clearly were not added to the number of the worshipers of the Roman deities, Dio's explanation of Caracalla's motives seems closer to the truth than the one that appears in the Constitutio itself.

consul title given to the two chief magistrates of Rome. They were originally elected for one-year terms, though reappointment was possible. Since only ex-consuls were eligible for certain offices, it became customary for the consuls to resign halfway through their terms and thus allow two extra candidates to serve each year.

contract legally binding agreement between two or more parties. Rabbinic law lacks a single, generic term to describe such agreements, which in the Roman system commonly took the form of a document (*contractus*). Instead, rabbinic law recognizes a number of distinctive ways in which parties create binding ties in particular legal circumstance.

The absence of a general term meaning "contract" is a reflection of rabbinic law's insistence that a physical act mark the transfer of a right. Just as actual or symbolic transfer of the subject property completes the process of acquisition, so rabbinic law understands an agreement to become binding only upon the transfer from one party to the other of the consideration, for example, the borrower's receipt of the loan money, or, in the case of the creation of a partnership, each partner's receipt from the other of a portion of the partnership's property. In the same way, a contract for work to be performed is valid only when the work begins, that being the consideration for which the agreement is established.

The requirement of physical transfer of the subject consideration presented a significant impediment to the creation of contracts. Accordingly, in the talmudic period, *kinyan sudar* (acquisition by kerchief), used to acquire property, also became an accepted and widely used method of creating contracts. The promisee gave the promisor some object he owned, in return for which the promisor agreed to undertake the obligation. The procedure was symbolic only, requiring no correspondence between the value of the object and that of the obligation (indeed, upon completion of the procedure, the object could be returned to its original owner). As a symbolic act, *kinyan sudar* served as a convenient way to easily create a wide range of contractual agreements.

conversion From the Latin for "to turn around," conversion generally indicates a shift in religious-group affiliation, but its forms and functions vary across times, locations, and groups. Sojourners, if the men submitted to circumcision, could participate in some rituals (Exod. 12:48), and intermarry (Ruth). Esther 8:17 (*mityehudim*: declared themselves Jews) is the first textual example of conversion to a new belief system, as opposed to ethnic affiliation. According to Josephus, John Hyrcanus I converted the Idumaeans; Aristobolus I, the Itureans; and Alexander Jannaeus, Pella. Among the more famous Jewish converts or proselytes are: the Ammonite Achior (Jdt.); the royal house of Adiabene; Aquila (Onkelos?), the Greek translator; Flavius Clemens, Vespasian's nephew; Fulvia, the wife of the senator Saturninus; and Nicolaus the Deacon (Acts 6:5). Conversion to Judaism was not an uncommon phenomenon in antiquity, as sources as diverse as Juvenal, Josephus, Joseph and Asenath, and early Christian documents attest. Jewish rituals of conversion included circumcision for males, the donation of money to the Temple, and, eventually, ritual immersion; the Church required baptism. Some scholars claim on the basis of such passages as Isaiah 2:2–4, 66:18–21 and Zechariah 14:16–17 that Jews anticipated the eschatological conversion of Gentiles. But the term must be nuanced: while the Gentiles turn from their idols, they do not become "Jews" (i.e., they do not participate in Jewish initiation rites). Debate continues over whether Jewish affiliation with the Jesus movement should be seen as a conversion to a new religious group or as a shift within the Jewish community. The problem is less with the sources than with the imprecise term "conversion." *See also* GER.

Coponius Roman of equestrian rank who was the first prefect (governor) of the new Roman province of Judea, which included the seacoast and Samaria. He served under the emperor Augustus and the consular legate of Syria, Quirinius, from about 6 to about 9 C.E., after the removal of Herod the Great's son Archelaus, who had served from 4 B.C.E. to 6 C.E.

Copper Scroll (3Q15) one of the most curious manuscripts among the Dead Sea Scrolls; found in

1952 in Cave 3, Qumran. This manuscript consisted of two rolls, which originally came from one sheet of a copper-based metal (hence the manuscript's name). Because of the metal's heavy oxidation, the manuscript could not be opened, so it was eventually sent to the University of Manchester, where it was divided into strips and subsequently published by J. T. Milik in 1951.

Written in postbiblical (mishnaic) Hebrew, the manuscript consists of a list of sixty-four hiding places in and around Jerusalem and Palestine where an enormous treasure of gold, silver, spices, and manuscripts would be found. The treasure's weight, calculated in modern measurements, would have totaled over ninety-one tons. Milik, because of these large amounts, considers the work a fiction that was composed about 100 C.E. and is therefore unrelated to the rest of the Qumran documents (the settlement at Qumran was destroyed in 68 C.E.). Other scholars (e.g., Allegro, Golb) view the treasure as real, deposited either by the Essenes from Qumran or by the Temple authorities in Jerusalem prior to the destruction of the city in 70 C.E. (F. M. Cross dates the scroll's handwriting as 25–75 C.E., so the scroll may have been written before the end of the Qumran settlement.)

The arguments supporting Milik's theory are the treasure's vast quantity and the fact that there is no record, either from antiquity or modern times, of any such treasure (or part of it) being found. However, Milik's argument is undermined by two of the document's most striking characteristics: the dry realism of its style ("At Horebbeh which is in the Vale of Akhor, under the steps that go eastwards, [at] forty cubits: a box of silver totaling 17 talents" [1:1–4]) and the fact that it is engraved on a sheet of expensive copper, rather than inscribed on the more common writing materials of leather or papyrus. The question becomes: why would someone go to such trouble and expense for a fairy tale? Objections may equally well be raised against those who argue for the document's reality. If the treasure did belong to the Essenes, how did they own such an enormous amount of silver and gold, and why did they hide it? Further, while it is conceivable that the Temple in Jerusalem contained such a treasure, it is not clear why the Temple authorities would hide it prior to the Temple's destruction in 70 (which they could not have foreseen), and why they concealed the record in a cave in the Judean Desert. The arguments from either side are not completely satisfactory, and thus the mystery of the Copper Scroll remains unresolved.

cornerstone part of a complex metaphor that describes the religious community as a building. The Community Rule 8:7–8 mentions it in connection with the foundations of the community, but does not specifically identify it. Ephesians 2:19–22 identifies Christ as this stone and the apostles and prophets as the foundation of the church. *See also* BUILDING.

corporal punishment in Rabbinic law, punishment by whipping, applied for a wide variety of offenses, civil, criminal, and cultic. Thirty-nine lashes were imposed, that is, the maximum number permitted by scripture (Deut. 25:3) less one. This assured that, even if there were a mistake in the count, more than the maximum permitted number would not be inflicted (B. Makkot 22a; cf. M. Makkot 3:10).

Flogging was carried out with a cowhide strap, with the offender tied by his hands around a pillar. He received two-thirds of the lashes on his back and the rest on his breast. During the flogging, a reader read admonitions and consolatory verses from scripture (M. Makkot 3:12–14).

Flogging was inflicted for crimes punished by divine extirpation (*karet*) and for overt violation of negative commandments. The Talmud also refers to punishment by lashes in cases of behaviors deemed inappropriate by the rabbis themselves, for example, for taking unreasonable vows (Y. Sukkot 5:2, 55b) or for having marital relations in public (B. Yeḇamot 90b).

corpse, treatment of Out of respect for the dead, talmudic law strictly prohibits mutilating, deriving any use or benefit from, or delaying the interment of any part of a corpse. These duties, including the requirement that burial occur as soon as possible after death, are derived from Deuteronomy 21:22–23, which states that the body of one executed by hanging must be buried on the same day, so as not to defile the land.

As signs of respect and honor, prior to burial, the corpse is watched over (*shemirah*) and is washed (*taharah*). This washing is not out of concern for cultic cleanness (a corpse is intrinsically unclean and renders unclean all who touch or are shadowed by it), but is viewed as a continuation of the hygiene that applied during life. The body is dressed in shrouds made of plain linen. This is in line with the premise that in death all people are equal. In biblical through talmudic times, the body generally was entombed in a cave. In posttalmudic practice, the corpse is buried in the ground in a wooden casket with no metal, to ensure a complete return to dust. Cremation is prohibited.

In light of the requirement that the body return to dust, embalming to prevent decay or improve the corpse's appearance is forbidden. Embalming is permitted only if it is a requirement of a non-Jewish government.

Despite these severe restrictions on treatment of a corpse, several talmudic passages permit autopsies, for example, in a case of murder when it must be determined that the victim in fact died as a result of the attack (B. Ḥullin 11b). The Talmuds also refer to dissection for anatomical research, but apparently contemplate the use of corpses of non-Jews (B. Bekhorot 45a).

corruption (Gr.: *diaphthora, phthora*) decay of the body due to death. Acts 2:27–31 and 13:34–37 present Jesus' resurrection from the dead as the fulfillment of Psalm 16:10, where the Septuagint has mistranslated "the pit" (Heb.: *shaḥat*) as "corruption" (*diaphthora*); Jesus has survived the decay of death. Working with a traditional Jewish eschatological scheme (2 Bar. 74:2), Paul sees the present age as characterized by a propensity to decay, which will be overcome when the resurrection transforms "the corruptible" to "incorruption" (Rom. 8:21; 1 Cor. 15:42, 50). *See also* DEATH; IMMORTALITY, INCORRUPTION.

cosmetics, cosmetic tools pigments and small implements used by women, as far as we know, for adornment of the eyes, lips, and face. These are not known in any distinctive Jewish forms, as these are to be associated with the broader Persian culture or the later Graeco-Roman culture in which Jews participated. Nevertheless, various items for personal beautification, especially cosmetic tools, are well known, though mainly from tombs. One of the most commonly found cosmetic tools is the kohl stick or cosmetic applicator. This device is made of bronze and resembles a modern eye pencil at its narrow end. This narrow end was dipped into the oily or wet mixture of black, green, or red eye makeup (kohl) for application. The other end might be formed into the shape of a small spoon for mixing the kohl. Small bronze or ivory spatulas and spoons for mixing eye cosmetics are also known. Small glass vessels for holding the cosmetics play a role. Dipping rods were used to extract oil-based perfumes and unguents from the narrow-necked glass or pottery vessels in which they were kept. In the early Roman period, the latter take the form of a double-tubed flask with glass threads wound around the top in decoration. Small palettes for mixing eye makeup are also well known, as are hand-held mirrors of polished bronze in wooden cases and with wooden handles. Lotions and therefore lotion bottles of glass appear everywhere in Roman contexts, attesting to their wide usage.

council, city (Gr.: *boulē*) judicial and/or legislative assembly. Numerous cities around Israel were organized as Hellenistic cities with councils composed of up to several hundred members, who were elected or chosen by lot annually by full citizens. This model was based on the Athenian Council of Five Hundred created by Cleisthenes in the late sixth century B.C.E. In the Graeco-Roman period, three Greek words are used for ruling assemblies in areas under Jewish rule: *gerousia,* an aristocratic council of elders; *boulē,* used less often; and *synedrion,* a word that enters Mishnaic Hebrew as Sanhedrin. Up until the Hellenistic period and subsequently in the mishnaic period, the traditional governing group in Jewish cities and towns was the elders, who exercised legislative and judicial roles. During Maccabean times Jerusalem was ruled by an aristocratic council of elders (*gerousia*), which probably consisted of prominent leaders of aristocratic families, both priestly and nonpriestly. In the Roman period, the more general term *synedrion* (assembly or council) became most common. In the first century B.C.E., the Roman governor Gabinius divided the country into five *synedria* that met in major cities. Local councils (*synedria*) and the council or Sanhedrin in Jerusalem are mentioned in the Gospels (e.g., Matt. 5:22; Mark 13:9, 14:53; Luke 7:3) and in Mishnah Sanhedrin. In these cases, judicial function is emphasized. Some hypothesize the existence of two or three councils in Jerusalem before 70 C.E., but the evidence for this is far from certain.

counselor *see* ADVOCATE

court (Heb.: *beit din,* house of judgment) According to the Mishnah, a court of three judges had jurisdiction in civil matters, including divorce, conversion, and absolution from vows, and was empowered to penalize a defendant through fines, flogging, and even enslavement. Courts of twenty-three judges adjudicated in criminal matters, including capital cases. A court of seventy-one judges had essentially unlimited legislative, administrative, and judicial power, including the authority to elect a king or high priest. Since, in rabbinic times and thereafter, the Jewish government had only limited autonomy, its courts could not exercise many of the functions described here. This was particularly so in capital cases, in matters involving a Jew and a non-Jew, and in cases in which Jews chose of their own volition to resort to a non-Jewish court.

courtyard The Mishnah describes smaller houses as grouped around an open courtyard (*ḥatzer*) served by a single covered entrance way (*maḇui*). While generally deemed to be public areas, for the purpose of transporting objects between domains on the Sabbath, these courtyards could take on the status of a continuous domain with the houses they served (see M. Eruḇin 1 and 2). This depended upon certain design elements (e.g., a maximum allowable height of the entranceway) as well as all inhabitants' preparing of a common meal (*shituf*), which symbolically joined their private domain to that of the shared courtyard.

covenant a treaty. Although there are different types of covenants, all covenants between YHWH and the children of Israel are suzerainty treaties, that is, treaties between unequal parties. There are both conditional and unconditional suzerainty treaties. In both types of treaties, it is YHWH, the superior party, who grants the Israelites, the inferior party, the covenant and he does so of his own volition. YHWH's responsibilities are primarily protection, succession, and land, although not necessarily all in the same covenant. Those of the sons of Israel vary in accordance with the type of covenant. In an unconditional covenant, there are no stipulations laid upon them. In a conditional one, there are various stipulations to which the sons of Israel are subject.

It is YHWH who makes the unconditional covenant irrevocable. In a conditional treaty, the superior party grants the covenant to and lays conditions on the inferior party, to which the latter is required to swear under oath. So in a conditional covenant between YHWH and Israel, if Israel violates its oath, the covenant will no longer be binding on YHWH. For this reason, the Jew prefers death to a violation of the Mosaic covenant, which promises him eternal life; and at the same time, he acknowledges that all men violate the covenant. This means that everybody, even members of the covenant community, sins. But precisely because a violation of the Mosaic covenant is a sin, Jews believe that the Most High can, if He wills, grant mercy and not exact the requisite punishment whereby the Jews are to be scattered among the nations.

The supreme covenant is the Mosaic covenant: that is, the covenant mediated by Moses, who saw the Deity face to face. In the pre-exilic and exilic portions of the Hebrew scriptures, the Mosaic type of covenant is patterned on ancient near eastern, and particularly Hittite treaty formulary. During the Second Temple period, various interpretations of the Mosaic covenant altered the preexilic and exilic scriptural traditions in such a way that the Hittite treaty formulary was almost completely eliminated. This is also true of the rabbinical interpretation of this covenant although the rabbis claimed to hold to the Sinai covenant as depicted in scripture.

From the early Second Temple period onward, the Mosaic covenant is deemed the conditional treaty that YHWH, the Most High God, granted the Israelites at Sinai/Horeb and that He again granted them after the Babylonian exile. The Mosaic covenant is generally certified by a ritually performed circumcision—connected with the covenant with Abraham in the Pentateuch—that an Israelite/Jewish male must undergo when he is eight days old. By the postmishnaic rabbinic period, circumcision and the Mosaic covenant were treated as one and the same thing.

Within the Qumran Community, for whom the covenant was reformulated to reflect its own teachings, more than mere circumcision is required for covenant compliance. The Community had its own covenant, but it is not clear whether it considered its covenant as different from the Mosaic one. In any case, those who join the Qumran Community are considered converts who are entering the covenant of the Community. After a probation period, those who wish to become members of the Qumran Community take part in a ritual ceremony of entry, which seems to have been part of the larger (annual) rite of covenant renewal. They view those in Judah and Jerusalem or elsewhere who scoff as violators of the Mosaic covenant, wherefore they bring God's curses on themselves.

From the perspective of Judah and Jerusalem, the Mosaic covenant was the law of both life and of knowledge, that is wisdom, that Moses was to teach Israel and Jacob. It is actually the inheritance of Jacob's congregations. The Jews themselves are sometimes equated with the eternal covenant as well as the Temple and Mount Zion. That a covenant is eternal, however, does not mean it is unconditional. Precisely because of the prior exilic experience, there is a sense that the covenant could be revoked. Significantly, then, the Mosaic covenant also has ethical dimensions, particularly in regard to the treatment of others, and it must be defended with one's life if necessary.

The laws of the covenant are said to have been handed down in a Book of the Covenant. There is no reason to presume that this is either the Covenant Code of Exodus, Josiah's Law Code, or even the entire Torah, although the latter is the more likely in Judah and Jerusalem. The community's own rules are more likely in Qumran. In Second Temple Judaism, there is a distinct relationship between the divine commandments and the Mosaic covenant, just as there is between wisdom and the Mosaic covenant. The law need not coincide with what is in the Pentateuch. Moreover, for Ben Sira, neither the law nor wisdom is identical with the Mosaic covenant to which they are related. Possibly in response to the Hellenistic practice of epispasm by certain Jews, Ben Sira stresses that people must not be ashamed of the law of the Most High or the covenant.

Covenant is also the treaty to which Abraham gave witness by circumcision, which Yahweh gave to Abraham unconditionally. Notably, Ben Sira indicates that YHWH took an oath reassuring Abraham in regard to the stipulations of this unconditional treaty. In addition to the promises in Genesis, YHWH promised Abraham he would exalt his descendants like stars, and that their inheritance would extend from one sea to another as well as from the Euphrates River to the earth's ends. This covenant was transferred to Jacob.

The covenant with Abraham is sometimes treated as unconditional. Baruch, like others of the Second Temple period, thought it had been revoked during the Babylonian exile, but it was reoffered to the children of Israel provided they follow the Deity's stipulations. The covenant with Abraham seems to have been so confused with the Mosaic covenant that it was believed that should the Jews keep it, they would be given a (new) everlasting covenant whereby the Most High would be their God and they would be his people. As part of this covenant with Abraham conjoined with the Mosaic covenant, God stipulated that He would never again remove the children of Israel from the land that he will have given them under the terms of the covenant.

Covenant is the unconditional treaty given to Noah that never again would the Deity destroy mankind by a flood. Convenant is also the seemingly unconditional treaty that the Most High gave to Aaron, which established him as a priest for however long the heavens continue. The apocalyptic expectation of a new heaven and a new earth that was expected during the Second Temple era gives the covenant with Aaron a sense of the conditional. On the other hand, the covenant with Aaron resembles the unconditional Davidic covenant establishing David's succession, which was restricted to his male descendants. Only Aaron's sons are to inherit the priesthood just as David's sons are to inherit kingship.

Another such covenant was granted to Phinehas, son of Eleazar. He was to have charge of both the sanctuary and the Jewish people, and his descendants should hold the priesthood eternally. This is specifically called a friendship covenant.

covenant renewal the act of reaffirming an existing agreement. The fundamental covenant in the Hebrew Bible is the one made between God and Israel at Mount Sinai. There are several episodes in which the provisions of that agreement are renewed or reinstated; examples are the Book of Deuteronomy, perhaps Joshua 24, and the covenant of King Josiah in 1 Kings 22–23. However, the prophets Jeremiah and Ezekiel provided a somewhat different perspective by speaking of a "new" covenant (Jer. 31; Ezek. 36). Both do make clear that, while the pact can be called a new one, it is really an improved version of the old, and the same law will be integral to it (Jer. 31:33). Later, Ezra and Nehemiah presided at a ceremony in which the Judeans took upon themselves to uphold the ancient covenantal law.

The Qumran Community renewed the covenant annually, apparently on the Festival of Weeks. They pledged to obey and recited blessings and curses to reinforce the agreement (Manual of Discipline 1–2). They, too, spoke of a new covenant made with their community. New Testament writers used the prophetic language of the new covenant (New Testament means new covenant). Luke's Gospel speaks of the wine at the last supper as a new covenant in Jesus' blood (Luke 22:21). Paul draws a sharper contrast between the ancient covenant and the new one that comes with Christ—a covenant, not of the letter but of the spirit (2 Cor. 3:4–11). In drawing this contrast, Paul was followed by the author of Hebrews, who called Jesus the mediator of a better covenant (Heb. 8:1–9:22).

Crassus, Marcus Licinius first-century-B.C.E. Roman consul. He escaped to Spain after the victory of Marius and Cinna in the Roman social war (87 B.C.E.). He subsequently supported Sulla, was consul with Pompey in 70 B.C.E., and later supported Julius Caesar. As a member of the first Triumvirate with Caesar and Pompey, he was given command of an army in Syria as consul (55 B.C.E.). He was defeated and killed by the Parthians at Carrhae (biblical Haran) in eastern Syria in 53 B.C.E.

creation fundamental affirmation of heirs of the biblical tradition. That God created all things is a forceful expression of divine sovereignty and is frequently repeated in Jewish sources addressed to the Hellenistic world (Sibylline Oracles 1:5–60; 3:20; Philo, *On the Eternity of the World*). Josephus

(*Antiquities* 1.21) emphasizes the fact that the Jewish "constitution" begins with cosmology, claiming that such an approach leads readers' thoughts to God and wins their obedience to the dictates of piety.

The radical quality of the act of creation found expression in the notion that creation was "from the invisible to the visible" (2 Enoch 48.5; Heb. 11:3) or "from nothing" (Joseph and Asenath 12:1–2; Wisdom of Solomon 11:25). Philo of Alexandria insists on this point as a way of distinguishing the true creative act from the formation of preexistent matter (*On Dreams* 1.76; *On the Special Laws* 4.187).

The details of the six days of creation could serve as the subject for lengthy exposition (2 Enoch 24–33; 4 Ezra 6:38–54). Philo gives special attention to the interpretation of the biblical accounts. His treatise *On the Creation of the World* combines various elements of his philosophical background—Platonic, Stoic, and Pythagorean—into an exposition of Genesis. The *Allegory of the Laws* pays more attention to the problem of the two accounts of creation, finding in the first a reference to the ideal creation and in the second an exposition of the creation of the physical.

creia moral anecdote. The term derives from the Greek word for "useful." A literary form in Greek education and rhetoric, the *creia* was used to illustrate an ethical or moral point. It was one of the exercises in the *progymnasmata* (prerhetoric stage of Greek schooling), where it served to teach students proper grammar as well as forms that would later be useful in rhetoric.

criminals, in rabbinic Judaism Rabbinic law does not distinguish between a criminal, who violates human law and is punished by human authority alone, and a sinner, who commits a crime against and is punished by God. Rather, the rabbinic system understands civil, criminal, and religious law all to derive from God, through the processes of revelation. In rabbinic parlance, therefore, the Hebrew term that best defines a criminal in general—*poshea*—describes a willful transgressor or even an apostate. Terms for those who commit specific crimes—e.g., *ganaḇ,* a thief, or *ratzḥan,* a murderer—appear. But no general term signifying one who violates human law alone is available. It follows from this fact that while rabbinic law details the procedures through which human courts try and sanction wrong doers, these courts are seen as acting on religious authority, on behalf of God.

At the foundation of the rabbinic trial system is Hebrew scripture, which holds that an individual's guilt or innocence is evaluated through the testimony of witnesses (see esp. Deut. 19:15; Num. 35:30; and Deut. 19:16–19), and which specifies punishments for specific crimes: a fine or monetary compensation for larceny, robbery, and even rape (Deut. 22:28–29) as well as for certain instances of manslaughter (Exod. 21:29–32); flogging (Deut. 25:1–3) for violation of religious dicta; and the death penalty for murder. The rabbinic system develops scripture's approach by carefully distinguishing crimes against persons, which are in the hands of the human court, from crimes against God, which are punished by the Divine hand, through extirpation. Additionally, unlike scripture, the rabbinic system accepts monetary compensation as a generally appropriate sanction, in most cases replacing flogging or other forms of physical punishment.

According to rabbinic law, most cases were brought before a two- or three-judge panel (M. Sanhedrin 1:1), while capital cases were heard by a court of twenty-three (M. Sanhedrin 1:4). The rabbis offered especially detailed guidelines for how these capital cases were to be heard, including how witnesses were to be questioned, the types of responses that would disqualify them, and other matters of procedure. Imposition of the death penalty was made almost impossible. The argument for acquittal came first, and acquittal required a majority of only one judge. While the decision to acquit could be made on the day of the trial, a determination to convict had to be made on the following day. A judgment for acquittal was deemed not reversible, and a witness who at any point argued for acquittal was not allowed to change his mind and argue for conviction.

Such rules assured that the accused had ample opportunity to defend himself and that he received every benefit of the doubt. At the same time, certain aspects of the biblical system, which placed justice in the hands of an avenger (Num. 35:21) or of witnesses, who were obligated to help in carrying out the sentence (Deut. 13:6–11, 17:2–7), still appear (see M. Sanhedrin 9:6). Despite the development of a sophisticated criminal procedure, rabbinic law still imagines imposing special punishments upon individuals deemed to deserve harsher treatment than that normally applied. In cases of recidivism, when the punishment of flogging appeared insufficient, the individual was to be put in prison and fed barley until his belly explodes (M. Sanhedrin 9:5). Similarly, someone who is known to have killed but, because of the absence of witnesses, cannot be tried, is put in prison and fed the bread of adversity and the water of affliction (Isa. 30:20), understood to cause the death of the guilty (M. Sanhedrin 9:5).

Since the court acted on behalf of God, the punishment it imposed was understood to provide full atonement, so that the convicted person again stood in proper relationship to God and could receive a place in the world to come. The death penalty coupled with confession (M. Sanhedrin 6:2) or the infliction of stripes (M. Makkot 3:15) constituted full atonement for the sin. Atonement for crimes punished by monetary damages depended further upon the individual's seeking pardon from the one he injured.

crooked generation (Heb.: *dor ikesh, dor tapukhot*; Gr.: *genea skolia*) the idolatrous "generation" that brought God's wrath against Israel according to Deuteronomy 32:5, 20. The image of crookedness, twisting, and turning emphasizes that the people have turned from God or perverted God's commandments and thus renounced faithfulness to the covenant. 1 Enoch 93:9 applies the image to the postexilic generation, at the end of which a remnant is chosen to receive the "sevenfold wisdom" that will deliver them from divine judgment (v. 10). A similar assessment of the postexilic generation appears in 1 Enoch 89:72–74 and the Damascus Document 1:1–12. In these Jewish texts, crookedness describes the perversion of or apostasy from the Torah (cf. 1 Enoch 99:2, 104:10; cf. 5:4). The image recurs in Acts 2:40 and Philippians 2:15, where the Christian proclamation is seen as the eschatological revelation that will save people from the crooked generation.

cross *see* CRUCIFIXION

crown symbol of the eternal reward of the righteous. Drawing on Isaiah 62:3, the author of Wisdom of Solomon 5:15–16 concretizes the eternal life which is the reward of the righteous as "a glorious royal crown" (Gr.: *basileion*) and "a beautiful diadem" from the Lord. Second and Third Isaiah (Isa. 40–55, 56–66) played down the importance of the Davidic dynasty and assigned royal attributes to the servant of YHWH, and Wisdom follows in this tradition, interpreting the servant figure as the suffering and exalted righteous one who will judge his persecutors. This notion of exaltation reappears in the Book of Revelation, where the martyrs are raised from the dead to "rule" with Christ for a thousand years (20:4–6). Thus, Revelation 2:10 promises "a crown of life" to those who endure tribulation and are faithful unto death. A similar notion appears to lie behind James 1:12 and 1 Peter 5:4, where trial and suffering are part of the context of these writings. However, 1 Corinthians 9:24–25 indicates another possible context for such reward, namely, the athletic contest in which the victor is crowned with a garland. Since much Jewish and Christian exhortative literature of this period, whether it is apocalyptic or written in a wisdom or philosophic mode, describes the virtuous life as an athletic contest, it is difficult to know whether a particular passage reflects the one set of images or the other, or both. *See also* SERVANT OF THE LORD.

crucifixion a cruel and torturous form of execution by binding or nailing a person to a stake or cross. The particular forms of crucifixion, usually preceded by flogging, depended on the sadistic imagination of the executioners. The Persians, the Greeks, and especially the Romans used crucifixion extensively to punish with gruesome cruelty the peoples they conquered, rebels against the Pax Romana, brigands, and even ordinary criminals. Crucifixion thus also served to terrorize the rest of the subject populations. The Romans used crucifixion above all as a painful punishment for disobedient slaves. Crassus had six thousand slaves crucified along a well-traveled route to Rome following the slave rebellion led by Spartacus in 71 B.C.E. In a unique event in Judean history, high priest–king Alexander Jannaeus (103–76 B.C.E.) crucified eight hundred of his opponents (perhaps Pharisees) and had their wives and children slaughtered before them as they were slowly dying (*War* 1.4.1, no. 97; *Ant.* 13.14.2, no. 380). Roman officials and their troops used crucifixion extensively in their conquests and reconquests of Judea and other districts of Palestine. In the suppression of the rebellions in 4 B.C.E., for example, Varus crucified two thousand in Judea (*War* 2.5.1, no. 75; *Ant.* 17.10.10, no. 295). In the first century, Roman governors ordered both brigands and their sympathizers crucified in their periodic repressive measures to maintain social order. Archaeological evidence for crucifixion in the first century has come from a tomb at Gib at haMibtar just northeast of Jerusalem, in which a man's skeleton was found with the lower legs broken and the heels pierced by an iron nail. According to the Christian Gospels, Jesus of Nazareth was crucified between two brigands after being condemned to death by Pontius Pilate (Mark 15:22–27; Matt. 27:33–38; Luke 23:33–34). Thousands of Judean rebels were crucified as both punishment and as a terrorizing spectacle for the remaining defenders of Jerusalem in 70 (*War* 5.11.1, no. 446–51).

Ctesiphon city on the west bank of the Tigris, 25 miles southeast of modern Baghdad. Ctesiphon had a large Jewish community and was a commercial center for Jews in the area. In 41 B.C.E., Jews of Seleucia took refuge there (Josephus, *Ant.* 18:374ff.). B. Yoma 10a identifies Ctesiphon with Resen (Gen. 10:12). The Amoraic authorities Ḥiyya b. Abba and Rabba b. Ḥiyya resided there. The city quickly declined after the founding of Baghdad in 762 C.E.

cubit measure of length in the ancient Near East generally, as well as in ancient Israel. It was usually defined as the distance between the elbow and the tips of the outstretched hand, making it roughly 17–18 inches (45 cm), though it varied from region to region. The great cubit was a cubit plus a handbreadth (c. 50 cm).

cult set of ceremonies and practices through which people offer worship to their god(s); in Judaism, primarily the acts of worship performed at the Temple in Jerusalem. The religious practices of ancient Israel, which centered on sacrifices, resembled those of their neighbors in many respects. While there seems to have been a time when anyone, not just priests, was permitted to offer sacrifices, later, especially when temples became important, the role of officiating at the altar fell to priests alone. The priests traced their ancestry to Aaron, the brother of Moses; all of them are supposed to have belonged to the larger tribe of Levi. The Bible presents detailed legislation about worship. There were daily sacrifices, offered in the morning and evening; sacrifices that fit individual cases (sin offerings, thank offerings, peace offerings); and many prescribed sacrifices for the different festivals of the sacred calendar. These are enumerated in Numbers 28–29. Numbers 16 specifies the ritual acts involving two symbolic goats on the Day of Atonement. When King Solomon dedicated his temple, the ceremony included a procession of the ark to the temple, the slaughter of many sacrificial animals, and a lengthy prayer. It is also very likely that some psalms were used in temple worship. The Books of Chronicles attribute to David the project of organizing temple personnel—priests, Levites, singers, gatekeepers. When the nation of Israel split into a northern and a southern state (around 930 or 920 B.C.E.), other state temples were constructed at Dan and Bethel. The prophets at times were critical of the kind of worship offered in the temples. Amos, for example, expressed the Lord's contempt for cultic acts done by people who violated the fundamental stipulations of the covenant to care for the poor and to do justice. The prophets and the historical books also report that cults of other gods were conducted in the Jerusalem temple.

The First Temple at Jerusalem was destroyed in 587 or 586 B.C.E.; the Second Temple, which was completed in 515 B.C.E., stood until the Romans burned it in 70 C.E. (a long-lived remodeling project, begun by King Herod in 20 B.C.E., had been completed just before this date). There, the sacrificial cult was reinstated, under the control of the priests. It appears to have been during the time of the Second Temple that the types of Temple personnel described in Chronicles assumed their roles. The Temple in Jerusalem was the most famous one and was regarded by many Jews as the only legitimate one, but the Jewish military colony in Elephantine, Egypt, also had a temple, where they worshiped Yahu (YHWH) and, for a time at least, engaged in animal sacrifice. The Wisdom of Jesus ben Sira (c. 180–175 B.C.E.) describes the ceremonies that the high priest Simon led at the temple on a festival that is often identified as the Day of Atonement (chap. 50). In the Books of Maccabees, one reads about the celebration of the festival of Hanukkah which was instituted as an annual eight-day holiday to celebrate the rededication of the Jerusalem Temple to the service of God; the cult had been suppressed a few years earlier (in 167 B.C.E.) by decree of the Seleucid king Antiochus IV (for this festival, see also John 10). The Dead Sea Scrolls provide information about the group's worship and understanding of it. They had removed themselves from the temple-centered cult in Jerusalem, and it appears almost certain that they did not have an altar for animal sacrifice at Qumran. However, they did worship in other ways. Numerous psalms and hymns have been found there; in them it is clear that the group worshiped through them and that the worshipers understood that their actions were done in harmony and fellowship with the angels or with the liturgy that is conducted in heaven. The festivals (with some new ones, such as a festival for bringing wood to the temple and more firstfruits holidays) also occupy a prominent place in their writings.

cult, ruler a cult established in honor of kings and emperors in the Graeco-Roman world, similar to cults for the gods. The origin of the ruler cult is most directly associated with Alexander (though there were some pre-Alexandrian Greek precedents). The peoples of the East would often honor Alexander by obeisance (*proskynesis*) and with rites accorded to Persian kings that were unusual for Macedonian rulers. In Egypt it had long been customary to regard the pharaoh as the son of the sun god. Alexander accepted these honors, despite criticisms from his fellow Macedonians. In the next decades and centuries, the practice became standard for the Hellenistic rulers and, later, the Roman emperor. This dynastic cult was adopted by most rulers, who established regular sacrifices and sometimes appointed their own priests, though some simply added their own celebrations to preexisting cults and temples. Although the cult was parallel to that for deities, the living (or dead) ruler was not necessarily regarded as actually divine, though different people may have interpreted it in different ways. A regular festival might be established as well, though this varied from a monthly festival to one observed every four years.

Cumanus Ventidius Roman procurator of Palestine (48–52 C.E.). During his term of office, a number of inflammatory incidents exacerbated relations with the Jewish population. An armed conflict between Jews and Samaritans led to his recall to Rome and banishment by the emperor Claudius.

cumin aromatic herb. Its seeds were mixed in bread flour and its oil used as a disinfectant. As part of his broadside against Pharisaic "hypocrisy," Matthew contrasts their tithing of cumin seed with their alleged ignoring of "the weightier matters of the law" (23:23).

cup In about half of its occurrences in the Hebrew Bible, the word "cup" is a symbol of God's blessing (Ps. 23:5, 116:13; cf. Ps. 16:5) or, more frequently, of God's wrath (Ps. 11:6; Jer. 49:12) poured out on humans. The other occurrences are divided between literal uses and a symbol of one's fate. The cup of God's wrath is the cup of divine judgment (Ps. 75:7–8), which can cause one to reel as if drunk (Isa. 51:17, 22; Jer. 25:15–16; Ezek. 23:31–33; Hab. 2:15–16). In Revelation, both Babylon and the worshipers of the beast will drink the cup of God's wrath, equivalent to eternal damnation (14:10, 16:19; cf. 18:6). Revelation transforms Jeremiah's image of Babylon as the cup of God's wrath (Jer. 51:7) into one of Babylon holding a golden cup (Rev. 17:4; cf. 14:8, 17:2, 18:3) full of abominations and fornication.

In the Gospels, the cup symbolizes Jesus' suffering (Mark 10:38–39), which he prays to avoid (14:36). "Cup" is also used of the eucharistic cup (Mark 14:23; 1 Cor. 11:25–26). Paul's contrast of the eucharistic "cup of blessing" with the "cup of demons" (1 Cor. 10:16, 21), through which he insists that one cannot engage in both idolatrous ceremonies and Christian Eucharist, uses language reflecting the Jewish "cup of blessing" offered at meals. Similar language is used in Joseph and Asenath 8:5 when Joseph compares Judaism—characterized as drinking "a blessed cup of immortality"—to the worship of idols, where one drinks "from their libation a cup of insidiousness."

curse expression of a wish that evil may befall someone. The English word "curse" encompasses a variety of Hebrew and Greek words that express a wide range of meanings (Heb.: primarily *alah, arar, kalah,* and *ḥerem*; Gr.: principally *kataraomai* and *anathematizo*). A curse can predict or wish trouble for another, someone or something can be said to be accursed (i.e., banned and off-limits), or a curse can be used to back up a statement. Curses, in these traditional cultures, have a visceral and a mutually acknowledged power to bring about misfortune on the person who is cursed. In the Hellenistic as in earlier biblical literature, curses can be used in any situation in which one party feels aggrieved, as, for example, a borrower against his creditor (Ecclus. 29:6). To be effective, a curse must be backed up with power, and a curse invoking the divine power is especially effective. Thus, a foreigner would curse by his gods (Ps. 151:6). Ben Sira warns his readers not to give anyone a reason to curse them (Ecclus. 4:5), for God could bring about the desired evil. Curses by prophets (2 Kings 2:24; Mark 11:21) and mothers (Ecclus. 3:9) are particularly effective. However, one should not be too ready to curse (Ps. 109:17; Ecclus. 27:14; 1 En 95:4), for a curse might be invoked against a curser. As in other Near Eastern treaties, the covenant between Israel and God was framed in terms of stipulations which, if broken, would bring down evil upon the people (Deut. 11:26–28; Dan. 9:11). The covenantal setting for blessings and curses is seen clearly in the initiation ceremony of the Qumran covenanters (1 QS 1:16–2:18) whereby those who enter the Qumran covenant bind themselves to be faithful to God's demands.

Whoever attacks the covenantal relationship between God and Israel is accursed (11QTemple 64:9–12). Tobit predicts the restoration of the sanctuary at Jerusalem, and nations who try to harm Jerusalem shall be accursed (Tob. 13:10–12). For the author of Revelation, when the new Jerusalem descends, all accursed things shall disappear (Rev. 22:3). The belief in the power of the covenantal curse is so strong that one can predict that judgment and disaster will fall on those who attack Israel and its faithful people. Such predictions find expression in what is called a woe oracle, which can be against nations, against classes of people, and against individuals. 2 Esdras contains woes against Assyria (2:8), and Babylon, Asia, Egypt, and Syria (16:1). The Sibylline Oracles contain woes against Babylonia, Ethiopia, and Libya (3:295–334), against Phoenicia, Crete, and Thrace (3:492–511), against Lycia (5:126), and against Greece (11:183–184). Woes are pronounced against the rich who oppress the poor and sinners in general in 1 Enoch 94:6–95:7 and also in Luke 6:24–26. In both Matthew (23:13–33) and Luke (11:42–48), woes are spoken against the Pharisees and against Judas, Jesus' betrayer (Matt. 26:24). Paul held that anyone who preached a gospel different from Paul was accursed (Gal. 1:8)

One special case within this frame of curses and blessings is when someone within the covenant would wish evil on him/herself so that blessings might come on others. So, in Paul's view, Jesus became accursed at his crucifixion, but God changed that curse into a blessing (Gal. 3:13–15). Paul could even pray to become an outcast, accursed of God's covenant, if it would result in his natural kinsfolk, the Jews, being blessed by believing in Jesus (Rom. 9:3).

curtain, ark a minor motif in ancient Jewish art. In the mosaic from Beth Alpha, the panel that shows the Torah shrine or ark flanked by two seven-branched menorahs displays a curtain to the right and to the left. There is sufficient detail to indicate that they hung from rings attached to a curtain rod that extended across the entire scene. These specific curtains or "veils" (*parokhet*), decorated with flowers, were pulled back to reveal the entire space in which the shrine stood. The same scene in the mosaic floor of the synagogue at Hammath-Tiberias shows a single curtain hanging from three rings attached to a rod. The curtain is rolled and tied in a single knot in front of the Torah shrine or ark. The mosaic floor in the first synagogue found at Beth Shean shows a Torah shrine with a decorated curtain hanging from rings on a rod between the two pillars in front, completely concealing the ark behind.

curtain, temple one of two drapes or curtains that hung in the sanctuary of the First and Second Temples, according to Josephus (*War* 5.5.4–5). The main curtain in front of the inner door (not the Holy of Holies), according to tradition, was sewn or woven by eighty-two young virgins who were paid from the Temple treasury (Y. Berakot 2:5, 4d). Upon this curtain they embroidered lions and eagles, which may explain how these two symbols entered Jewish art. Josephus insists that the first curtain was a "Babylonian" curtain with mystical symbols on it, including zodiacal signs, though no animals. He does not describe the inner curtain.

Cynics Graeco-Roman philosophical school (though perhaps more a broad movement than a unified school of thought), characterized by independence from material possessions and refusal to accept conventional sexual morality. Cynics lived off the charity of those who would give them gifts, often bedding down in the public baths or buildings. The founder is usually regarded as Diogenes of Sinope (c. 400–325 B.C.E.), who rejected accepted societal conventions and lived without wife, home, or possessions; hence, he was given the nickname "Kynos" (dog), which gave rise to the popular etymology of "Cynic." Behind the Cynic lifestyle lay a radical critique of conventional morality and civilization. In preaching about the evils of society—delivering moral sermons known as diatribes—Cynics clearly had many characteristics of a religious movement in which adherents live in poverty as wandering preachers. Since they also became associated with the Stoics, some of their institutions are labeled Cynic-Stoic. Among the Jewish groups they might be compared most closely to the Essenes.

Cyprian, Pseudo- Several Latin writings in the name of the patristic writer Cyprian (c. 200–258 C.E.) are thought not to be written by him and thus carry the attribution "Pseudo-Cyprian." One such work is the *Adversus Iudaeos* (Against the Jews), dating from around 200 C.E.; some think this work is aimed at Jewish-Christians rather than Jews. By yet a different author is *De montibus Sina et Sion,* which compares Mount Sinai to the Old Testament and Mount Zion to the New Testament. It also probably dates from around 200 C.E. and may have been written by a converted Jew, since it shows knowledge of various Jewish traditions. The work includes etymologies of Hebrew names.

Cyprian of Carthage (c. 200–258 C.E.) rhetorician who became a Christian in 246 and bishop of Carthage in North Africa about 250. His letters and treatises mostly concern the treatment of Christians who had lapsed during persecutions. In his collection of biblical testimonies entitled *To Quirinus* (c. 248), the first book contains twenty-four theses against the Jews with scriptural verses offered as proofs. His arguments are similar to those of Tertullian's second-century treatise against the Jews and to those found in a sermon against the Jews incorrectly attributed to him.

Cyprus, Jews in A Jewish community on the island of Cyprus is referred to in a letter said to have been sent in the mid-second century B.C.E. (1

Macc. 15:23), in Philo's writings (*Leg.* 282), and in Acts of the Apostles (11:19; late first century C.E.). During the uprisings of diaspora Jews against Trajan from 115 to 117 C.E., the Jews on Cyprus, led by Artemion, massacred almost a quarter-million Gentile inhabitants and destroyed the capital, Salamis, according to the exaggerated account of the Greek historian Dio. When Roman control was restored, many Jews were killed, and all Jews were banned from the island. A couple of inscriptions suggest that Jews were back on the island in the third and fourth centuries. *See also* TRAJAN, WAR OF.

Cyrean Jews, revolt of (115–117 C.E.) a revolt that seems to have been the culmination of a long period of tense relationships between the Jewish and non-Jewish communities in North Africa, which probably began as a local struggle. During the last years of Trajan's reign, while he was occupied with his wars against Parthia, the emperor faced Jewish revolts in Cyrene (the capital of Cyrenaica on the coast of North Africa), Egypt, and Cyprus. Eusebius contains the fullest account of the uprisings in North Africa. He states that in 115 the Jews in Alexandria, Egypt, and Cyrenaica revolted against the Greeks and initially were successful. The Greeks returned to Alexandria where they were able to defeat the Jews, killing some and imprisoning others. At this point the Jews of Egypt and Cyrenaica joined forces and plundered the rest of the country. Eusebius claims that in 116 the situation developed into a war with Rome, and he describes the Jewish leader, Lucus, as a "king" (*Ecclesiastical History* 4.1–2). Whether or not this is meant to imply that the uprising had taken on a messianic tone is unclear. Marcius Turbo, who had been serving in Parthia under Trajan, was sent to quell the rebellion. That Trajan would send one of his most able generals underscores the extent and gravity of the revolt. After a significant amount of time and many military encounters, Turbo prevailed. Turbo must have been totally successful in Cyrenaica by the time of Trajan's death in 117 because the new emperor, Hadrian, sent Turbo to Maurentania to put down another revolt.

The Greek historian Dio Cassius views the situation as a Jewish uprising against their non-Jewish neighbors, not as a political revolt against Roman rule. Dio goes into gory detail about the atrocities that the Jews perpetrated against the Greeks and Romans in Cyrenaica. He records that the Jews ate their victims' flesh, made clothes and belts from their victims' skin and entrails, painted their own bodies with their victims' blood, sawed some in half lengthwise, and fed some to wild animals. He claims that 220,000 were massacred by the Jews. With regard to the situation in Egypt, Dio merely states that the Jews did similar things there. Dio identifies Andreas as the leader of the Jews. Orosius, writing in the fifth century, agrees with Dio that this was not an uprising against Roman authority but a war in which the Jews sought to destroy their non-Jewish neighbors. Orosius claims that Cyrenaica was almost totally depopulated because the Jews murdered so many farmers. The archaeological evidence indicates that the center of the city of Cyrene was destroyed. Many public buildings were burned, the Caesareum (the complex that was dedicated to the worship of the emperor) was destroyed, and the temples of Zeus, Apollo, Demeter, Artemis, and Isis, among others, were destroyed or damaged. Milestones on the road between Cyrene and the port of Apollonia indicate that the road was destroyed during the Jewish disturbance, perhaps in an effort to slow the advancing Roman forces.

Cyrenaica North African coastal area and later Roman province in modern Libya. Cyrenaica was settled by Greek colonists from Thera in the course of the seventh century B.C.E., but peopled by Jews as early as Ptolemy I Soter, son of Lagus. In his role as expansionist ruler of Egypt in about 323 B.C.E., Ptolemy Soter sent Jews from Egypt to inhabit Cyrene, the leading city, and to other cities of Cyrenaica. The major coastal cities included Berenice, Arsinoe, Barca and its port city of Ptolemais, Cyrene (the capital) and its port city of Apollonia, Darnis, Antipyrgus, and Teucheira. According to a Roman letter quoted in 1 Maccabees 15:23, Jews were in Cyrene in 140–139 B.C.E. According to Greek inscriptions from Cyrene there was a Jewish presence in all levels of government and commerce during the Roman period. For example, according to one Greek inscription, a body of free Jewish citizens existed in the city of Berenice in Cyrenaica in the first century C.E. In the inscription of 55 C.E. the Jewish congregation voted to list the names of those who repaired the local synagogue on a marble inscription attached to the building. Ten of the donors listed bear the title archon, an honorary municipal title, and one bears the title priest, therefore a Cohen. Epitaphs in Greek from Teucheira in Cyrenaica also contain a substantial number of Jewish names, including their appearance on two seven-branched menorahs carved above the entrance to tombs. Jewish names also occur in similar epitaphs from Apollonia and Ptolemais. In Ptolemais, in a list of youths who reached manhood about 3 or 4 C.E., there are a few clearly Jewish names, such as Barthubra (Bar Thubra), Iulios Iesoutos (Julios son of Ieshu or Joshua), and Elaszar Elazaros (Elazar son of Elazar). A list of Cyrenean city officials from 60–61 C.E. mentions Elazar son of Jason (perhaps Joshua). According to Josephus, Augustus issued a decree favorable to the Jews of Cyrene (*Ant.* 16.161).

According to the New Testament, Jews of Cyrene were present in Jerusalem on certain occasions. For example, in Acts 2:10, Cyrenean Jews were present in Jerusalem at Passover. According to Acts 6:9, there were enough Cyrenean Jews in Jerusalem to build their own synagogue. At the time of the first revolt against Rome, several thousand Cyrenean Jews were killed because of their sympathies with the rebellion in Palestine. By 74 C.E., Rome had annexed Cyrenaica as one of its North African provinces. Rome ruled Cyrene and Crete as a single province until the third century C.E. From 115 to 117 C.E., there was a general rebellion in Cyrenaica against Rome by the Jewish population. This rebellion was put down at great cost to both parties to the conflict. *See also* CYREAN JEWS, REVOLT OF.

Cyril of Alexandria born in Alexandria between 370 and 380 C.E.; nephew of the Alexandrian Patriarch Theophilus (385–412) who had destroyed the most important Alexandrian sanctuary, the Serapeion, and its library in 391, persecuted Origen's admirers from 399 on, and deposed John Chrysostom in 403. As a monk, Cyril was trained as the successor to his uncle, whose harsh, ambitious character he inherited to the point of being depicted by modern critics as a "Christian pharaoh." Elected bishop of Alexandria in October 412, he encouraged violent campaigns against local minorities, pagan and heretic. One of these riots resulted in the death of the Platonist philosopher Hypathia, murdered by a gang of fanatical monks. When Nestorius, a monk of the rival see of Antioch, became patriarch of Constantinople in 428, Cyril hastened to respond to protests in the imperial capital against the preaching of the new bishop. Within the year Cyril had engaged an offensive action with a series of letters to Nestorius in which he accused the latter of destroying the unity of Christ by separating the humanity from the divinity. Both parties appealed to Pope Celestine whose advisers favored Cyril's report, more immediately accessible to them because it was written in Latin. Hence in August 430, the Roman council asked Nestorius to confess his errors and nominated Cyril to execute its verdict. Only in November did Cyril transmit to Nestorius the Roman decree, in adding to it twelve anathemata that pretended to impose as common faith the most extreme peculiarities of Alexandrian Christology. The latter centered on the notion of the physical unity of the divine and the human in Christ. Termed as such, the statement was unacceptable in Antioch or in Constantinople. In the meantime, Nestorius had asked the emperor to call a council, which convened in Ephesus on 22 June 431. Cyril and his delegation hastily condemned and deposed Nestorius before the arrival of the Oriental bishops united under the Antiochenes and favorable to Nestorius. Soon after their arrival these bishops condemned and deposed Cyril. The Emperor Theodosius II approved the decision of both parties. Nestorius retired into a monastery and was replaced by Atticus, and Cyril recuperated his episcopal throne. He negotiated with the Oriental bishops and in April 433 convinced them to ratify the condemnation of Nestorius. In return he agreed to withdraw the twelve anathemata.

Cyril's doctrine laid a one-sided stress on the divinity of Christ, absorbing the human subject into the divine, even while maintaining the traditional distinction between the man and God in Jesus. The eloquent and zealous leader buttressed his position by attacking the memory of the two most famous Antiochene exegetes, Diodore, bishop of Tarsus (378–c. 394), and Theodore, bishop of Mopsuestia (392–428), both of whom he accused of having inspired Nestorius. He died 27 June 444.

Cyril wrote commentaries on the Pentateuch, Isaiah, the minor prophets, the Gospels of Matthew, Luke, and John, the Letter to the Romans, Hebrews, and others. Before the controversy with Nestorius he established himself as a theologian in benefiting from Athanasius' literary legacy. His *Thesaurus de Trinitate* and the dialogues *De Trinitate* are based on Athanasius's *Orations Against the Arians*. In the last decade of his life, Cyril refuted Julian the Apostate's pamphlet *Against the Galileans*.

Cyrus founder of the Persian Empire after the defeat of the Medes, the conquest of the kingdom of Lydia, and the occupation of Babylon in 539 B.C.E. His early successes brought hope of repatriation to Jewish deportees in Babylon (Isa. 44:28–45:7, where he is described as "YHWH's anointed"). The Cyrus cylinder, inscribed in 538 B.C.E., announced a magnanimous policy of repatriation for ethnic groups, including Jews, deported by the Babylonians; and the same policy is reflected in the imperial decrees quoted in Ezra 1:1–4 and 6:1–5. Cyrus died fighting the Massagetai tribe in the summer of 530 B.C.E.

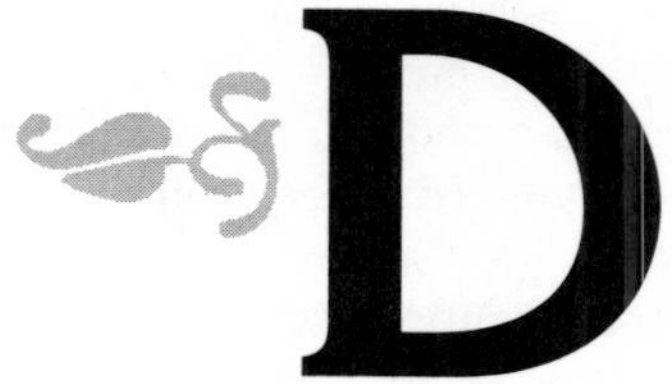

Dabar haLamed meIniano a principle of exegesis of scripture that holds that the meaning of a verse of scripture may be established by the context in which the verse occurs; *see also* MIDRASH

Dabbura (Heb.: Dabura) ancient village and synagogue site in the northern Golan Heights. The site has been identified with ancient Seleucia, but this is uncertain. Many carved basalt stones, six with inscriptions, and now reused in the abandoned village, have long suggested the presence of an ancient synagogue, though its exact location is unknown. A broken lintel stone displays an eagle holding a wreath in its beak. Below one wing are two fish, which may represent Pisces. In a narrow band above the eagle, the remains of an Aramaic inscription—". . . made this gate"—are visible. A second, larger lintel bears two eagles with outstretched wings who are holding snakes in their beaks. The snakes intertwine and form a plaited wreath tied in a Hercules knot at the bottom. The lintel bears a Hebrew inscription: "Eliezer haQappar. This is the school (beit midrash) of the rabbi." An architrave bears an Aramaic inscription: "Elazar bar Eliezer the Great made the columns above the arches and beams." Then in Greek: "Rusticus built [it]." Yet another fragmentary Aramaic inscription reads, "They made the house of . . . . May he be blessed." Rabbi Eliezer haQappar was a sage of the fifth generation of Tannaim mentioned in the Mishnah, but he is from ancient Lydda (Lod or Diospolis) in Judah (M. Abot 4, 21). He is also called Rabbi Elazar bar Rabbi Eliezer haKapar (T. Betza 1,7; y Betza 1,3).

Dabiyye ancient Jewish village and synagogue site in the eastern Golan Heights. The evidence for the presence of the synagogue here are the remains of a rectangular building, entered from the south and paved with large basalt slabs. A second doorway let through the western wall. Inside the building, which had been reused in the modern period, were architectural fragments such as column bases, capitals, and lintels. A lintel stone decorated with two incised seven-branched menorahs and a second stone with a Hercules knot and a rosette were found elsewhere on the site. In general, the cutting of the building stones and architectural members and the carving of the menoroth resemble the cutting of stones and carvings in synagogues of the third or fourth centuries C.E.

Dabyra Synagogue *see* DABBURA

Dagobert I king of the Franks (r. 628–638 C.E.) Sometime between 631 and 639, following the lead of the kings of Neustria and of Byzantium and reflecting the general anti-Jewish atmosphere of the region, Dagobert decreed that the Jews under his control were to be baptized or expelled.

daimōn (Gr., spirit, minor deity, or demon) The term had a wide variety of meanings, though they all center around the idea of spiritual power. The word could refer to the mind, to the spirit of a dead person, or to angelic or demonic beings (the term *daimonion* is often used for the latter).

Daisios name of a Macedonian month; appears in a number of Jewish sources, such as the writings of Josephus. Unfortunately, there was not a uniform usage; sometimes it corresponded to the Hebrew month of Iyyar (April/May) and sometimes to the month of Sivan (May/June).

Dalmanutha village or other locality mentioned in the Gospel of Mark 7:31; it remains as yet without a secure identification. The parallel text in Matthew 15:39 is Magdala, so either Dalmanutha is another name for Magdala or it is an unknown place name. It seems to be a genuine Aramaic place name ending in *-tha,* as Canatha in the territory of Tyre. The noun appears in y Kil 32d meaning "wall," so it is linguistically possible that this is a real place name. There is an anchorage visible when the waters are low on the northwest shores of the sea of Galilee west of Capernaum. Dalmanutha may have been simply an anchorage with no attached village, or Mark did not understand the tradition he was using and coined a place name from an Aramaic phrase meaning "which belongs to the territory of. . . ."

Dalton (Arab.: Kafr Dallata) ancient village site in Upper Galilee that has traces of an ancient synagogue. There is architectural evidence of a large building that faces south and lies beneath the modern mosque. Architectural elements from the earlier, possibly third- or fourth-century-C.E. building include a double "heart-shaped" column (often used at the corner of two lines of columns joining at a right angle), a capital, and a threshold. A stone inscribed with a sixteen-line Hebrew inscription on one side and five lines on the other has been judged to be early medieval. Parts of the inscription read "Mercy," "Seat," "His memory for good" (twice), and "Blessing, Amen, Selah [shalom?]."

damages money recoverable as compensation for a wrong or injury suffered through another individual's own negligence or through acts of his chattels. In the latter category, damages can be sought for losses suffered under four principal types of negligence: (1) leaving an open pit into which an animal falls and dies (Exod. 21:33–34); (2) igniting a fire that spreads to a neighbor's fields (Exod. 22:5); (3) possession of an ox that causes harm through goring (Exod. 21:28–32, 35–36); and (4) ownership of an animal that causes damage by trespassing on another's fields (Exod. 22:4). In rabbinic law, these primary categories yield derivative types of negligence for which damages also may be demanded. A knife or rock left where someone can be injured, for instance, yields liability under the category of the open pit; an animal's kicking, biting, or butting yields liability under the category of goring.

Under talmudic law, an individual is liable for damages only if the result of his actions could have been foreseen, for example, if he knew that his ox was a gorer or that he had left an open pit in an accessible area. But if an ordinary person would not have anticipated the damage, for example, if the ox had never before caused harm or if a properly covered pit had somehow been unsealed, the occurrence is treated not as negligence (*peshi ah*) but as a mishap or accident (*ones*). In such a case, no liability is incurred. Under this same theory, minors and people who are deaf, mute, or mentally incompetent are exempted from payment of damages under the laws of negligence, for they are deemed incapable of foreseeing the consequences of their actions.

In most instances, rabbinic law treats an agent as equivalent to the one who appoints him. The case of an agent commissioned to commit a tort is different, since, while the agent could foresee the damage to be caused by his actions, the one who commissioned him could not know that the agent actually would carry out the wrongful deed. Accordingly, an agent alone is liable for damage he causes; the one who appointed him is exempt. This applies unless the agent, for instance, a minor, could not himself know the implications of his actions. Then the one who commissioned him is liable for damages, the agent's having been nothing more than a tool in his hand.

The amount of damages to be paid is determined on the basis of (1) the permanent loss caused by the injury (*nezek*); (2) the temporary loss due to recovery time (*she<u>b</u>et*); (3) the amount of pain and suffering caused by the injury (*zaar*); (4) the cost of restoring health, for example, medical expenses (*ripui*); and (5) the degree of embarrassment felt by the injured (*boshet*). In establishing appropriate compensation, rabbinic law rejects the literal meaning of Leviticus 24:19, which states: "When a man harms his neighbor, as he has done, so shall it be done to him." Talmudic law holds that the verse refers only to monetary compensation, not to mutilation of the body of the offender.

Damascus Document The only document from Qumran considered to be sectarian that was known before the discoveries at Qumran, the Damascus Document (also called Damascus Covenant or Zadokite Fragments; abbreviated CD) was first discovered in the late nineteenth century in the *geniza* (storeroom) of an old Karaite synagogue in Cairo by Solomon Schechter and subsequently published by him (1910). The *geniza* fragments consisted of two Hebrew manuscripts: Manuscript A, dating from the tenth century C.E., contains sixteen text columns, while Manuscript B, dating from the twelfth century C.E., contains two text columns (numbered by Schechter as XIX and XX) that partially overlap columns VII and VIII of Manuscript A. The text consists of a hortatory introduction and conclusion and contains rules and regulations governing the life of a Jewish sect in the Second Temple period. It takes its name, Damascus Document, from the fact that the name Damascus, as a place of exile (not yet satisfactorily identified), is mentioned several times throughout the text.

Scholars wrestled with the question of the origins and purpose of the Damascus Document, some considering it to be Sadducaic in origin; others, Pharisaic; still others, Essene. This problem appeared to be resolved by the discovery in 1952 at Qumran of Caves 4, 5, and 6, all of which contained fragments of the Damascus Document ($4QD^{a-e}$, 5QD, 6QD). The text as a product of, or at least belonging to, the Qumran community seems assured.

The document itself is important for illuminating the history of the group that produced it and for recounting some of their legal precepts. Since the text is considered by most scholars to be a product of the group at Qumran or its ancestors, the discussion of the text is usually carried on in the light of other texts from Qumran. The document begins with a history of the sect's origins (col. 1), claiming that the sect arose 390 years (Ezek. 4:5) after the exile to Babylon, and that after twenty years of groping, God raised up for the sect a "Teacher of Righteousness" (a title that recurs in several Qumran texts), who instructed it in the true way. If these figures are taken more or less literally, it places the sect's origins in the first half of the second century B.C.E. Since the oldest manuscript from Cave 4 dates from c. 100 B.C.E., this places the composition of the Damascus Document sometime in the second half of the second century B.C.E., around the period of the first settlement at Qumran (150–135 B.C.E.).

The introduction (cols. 2–8 [19–20]) goes on to emphasize the need for repentance and entry into the New Covenant (the sect). The sect names its members both "the Repenters of Israel" and "those who enter the New Covenant," so the two activities go hand in hand. The sect believes, according to the document, that they are living in the time of the reign of Satan, and that Israel at large is sinful, caught in "the three nets of Belial" (4:5). Therefore, contact with nonsectarians is to be avoided. In order to maintain their purity and righteousness, the group had special laws, derived from a strict interpretation of the Torah, that were designed to keep the sectaries from transgression and impurity. So, for example, the laws concerning Sabbath observance (cols. 10–11), are particularly strict, with a man forbidden to draw water for a drink on the Sabbath.

An important problem not yet satisfactorily resolved is the relation of the Damascus Document to other rule books found at Qumran, particularly the Community Rule. The similarities are strong: adherence to a special (and strict) set of rules, a strong sense of difference vis-à-vis the rest of the Jews, and the following of a special leader or leaders within a hierarchical community. However, differences also exist: women and children are mentioned in the Damascus Document, but not in the Community Rule; the sectaries in the Damascus Document appear to be living in "camps" throughout Judah, where they hold private property, unlike the participants in communal life in one location envisioned in the Community Rule; and there is much more interest in the Damascus Document in laws pertaining to nonsectaries, while the Community Rule emphasizes rules for the common life of the members. These differences are usually explained by supposing that the Community Rule was written specifically for the group of sectaries living in relative isolation in the desert community at Qumran, while the Damascus Document was written for that larger group of sectaries living within the towns and settlements of Judah. *See also* CAIRO GENIZA; COMMUNITY RULE; DEAD SEA SCROLLS; MASKIL; QUMRAN.

damnation (Gr.: *katakrisis, krisis*) condemnation, a negative decision by God the judge; the opposite of vindication. In eschatologically oriented Jewish and Christian literature, one is condemned to eternal punishment. In John 3:16–19, eternal life and condemnation are present realities based on one's faith in, or rejection of Jesus. *See also* JUDGMENT, DIVINE; VINDICATION.

Dan city in Upper Galilee, at the foot of Mount Hermon, modern Tel Dan. Previously named Laish, it became the territorial center for the tribe of Dan. Judges 17–18 suggests it was a sacred site from the time of the judges. In the tenth century B.C.E., Jeroboam selected Dan (along with Bethel) as the location for one of his golden calves (1 Kings 12:30). 1 Enoch 13:7 mentions "the waters of Dan," one of the headwaters of the Jordan River that rises near and on Tel Dan, as the site of Enoch's heavenly revelation about the fallen watchers' condemnation and probably implies a wordplay on "Dan" (Aram., for he has judged).

Daniel hero of the biblical book that bears his name. He is described as an exile from Judah who rose to prominence at the Babylonian court because of his ability to interpret dreams. Despite his position, he does not compromise his fidelity to Judaism. Consequently, he is thrown into the lions' den but is miraculously preserved. The second half of the book recounts revelations Daniel received. The apocryphal additions to the Book of Daniel contain further, in part contradictory, traditions. According to Bel and the Dragon, Daniel is a priest who is thrown into the lions' den because he destroyed the idols of the Babylonians. In Susanna, he is an unknown young man among the exiles in Babylon.

It is the consensus of modern scholarship that this Daniel never existed. The earliest allusion to him, outside the Book of Daniel, is in 1 Maccabees 2:60 (c. 100 B.C.E.). There is mention of a priest named Daniel in Ezra 8:2, but this individual lived a century after the exile. Two passages in the Book of Ezekiel suggest that Daniel was already a legendary figure at the time of the exile. Ezekiel 14:14 says that when a land sins, "even if these three, Noah, Daniel, and Job, were in it, they would deliver but their own lives by their righteousness." Ezekiel 28:3 taunts the king of Tyre: "Are you wiser than Daniel?" In fact the name Daniel occurs in a text from Ugarit (modern Ros Shamra in Syria) in the second millenium B.C.E. There, a king named Daniel appears as the father of Aqhat, a young man who is killed by the goddess Anat. In that story, Daniel is a righteous man who supplicates the gods and, as king, gives judgment for widows and orphans. He is not portrayed as exceptionally wise and even his righteousness is incidental to the story. The Ugaritic Daniel can not have been the model for the biblical Daniel. It seems, however, that Daniel was the name of a legendary wise man, and that new stories were attached to this name in the Second Temple period. The name Daniel means "my judge is God," but judgment appears as a motif only in the story of Susanna.

A number of fragmentary texts related to the Daniel traditions have been found in the Dead Sea Scrolls. The Prayer of Nabonidus is closely related to the story of Nebuchadnezzar's madness in Daniel 4, but the name Daniel does not occur in the extant fragments of the Prayer. The name is found in a fragmentary pseudo-Daniel text, which apparently reports a prophecy by Daniel in the presence of a king. This text is very fragmentary, and it is not clear whether it is dependent on the biblical book of Daniel.

Daniel was regarded as a prophet in the Dead Sea Scrolls (in the Florilegium [4Q174]), and in the New Testament. Josephus regarded him as the greatest of the prophets, because he not only prophesied future things but fixed the time at which they would come to pass (*Ant.* 10.266–267). According to Josephus, Daniel had built a fortress at Ecbatana in Media, in which the kings of Media, Persia, and Parthia were buried and which was entrusted to a Jewish priest "to this very day" (*Ant.* 10.264–265). There is no other corroboration for this story, however.

Daniel, Book of found among the Writings in the Hebrew Bible but placed with the Prophets in the versions and in modern Christian editions. As found in the Hebrew Bible, it is a book of twelve chapters. Chapters 1:1–2:4a, and chapters 8–12 are in Hebrew. Chapters 2:4b–7:28 are in Aramaic. While no fully satisfactory explanation of the two languages has been found, it probably reflects the fact that the book was not composed all at once but grew over a period of time. Eight manuscripts of Daniel have been identified in the Dead Sea Scrolls. All twelve chapters are represented, including the two points of transition between Hebrew and Aramaic. (Chap. 12 is only represented in quotations in the Florilegium [4Q174]). The Greek and other versions have a significantly larger text. Two long liturgical pieces, the Prayer of Azariah and the Song of the Three Children, are inserted in chapter 3, and there are two additional stories, Bel and the Dragon and Susanna. Besides, there are two Greek forms of chapters 4–6. The Old Greek translation of these chapters is significantly different from the Aramaic text. The translation attributed to Theodotion, which is a faithful rendering of the Aramaic and Hebrew text, became the standard translation of Daniel in the Greek Bible.

The first six chapters purport to describe the adventures of Daniel and three companions at the Babylonian court after they had been taken into exile. These chapters bristle with historical problems. They refer to a nonexistent king, Darius the Mede. Belshazzar, who did exist, is wrongly given the rank of king and said to be the son of Nebuchadnezzar (though he was actually the son of Nabonidus, the last Neo-Babylonian king). The stories are obviously legendary in character. Nebuchadnezzar is transformed into a beast in chapter 4. The three young men are unharmed in the fiery furnace and Daniel emerges unscathed from the lions' den. Nonetheless, the stories contain occasional historical reminiscences. Before the discovery of the Dead Sea Scrolls, scholars suspected that the story of Nebuchadnezzar's madness had its origin in a story about Nabonidus, who was absent from Babylon for ten years and lived in Teima in Arabia. This suspicion was confirmed by the discovery of the Prayer of Nabonidus at Qumran, which is obviously related to Daniel 4. The stories in Daniel, however, are not historical accounts, but legends that took shape over time and reached their present form in the late third or early second century B.C.E. They provide a model of Jewish life under Gentile rule. Daniel and his friends serve the kings faithfully, but they never compromise their Jewish religion.

Chapters 7–12 are quite different. They consist of apocalyptic visions, and clearly reflect the persecution of the Jewish people by Antiochus Epiphanes in 167–164 B.C.E. Daniel describes this persecution in vivid imagery. The Gentile kings are beasts that come up out of the sea, but they will be overcome by divine judgment, and the kingdom will be given to "one like a son of man" and the holy ones of the Most High. The "son of man" and the holy ones are often taken to be symbols of the Jewish people. They are better identified as the archangel Michael, patron angel of Israel, and the heavenly host. The logic of Daniel's vision is that the earthly conflict is only a reflection of a struggle between the angelic powers that represent the various peoples. In the end, Michael will arise in victory (12:1) and the dead will be raised for judgment. Then the wise people who have withstood the persecution will shine like the stars, which means that they will be exalted to the angelic host. The Book of Daniel was presumably put together by one of these "wise" people.

Not all the writings associated with Daniel found a place in the Hebrew Bible. Besides the additions in the Greek Bible, we now have two apocalyptic compositions in the Dead Sea Scrolls that are related to Daniel. One, the pseudo-Daniel text, mentions Daniel explicitly. The other, the Son of God text (4Q246) envisages some figure who falls before a throne and utters a prophecy that draws some of its language from Daniel. The Book of Daniel had broad influence on the Scrolls and on other Jewish writings of the period (notably the Similitudes of Enoch in 1 Enoch 37–71). It also had profound influence on the New Testament, especially in the Gospels of Matthew, Mark, and Luke (in the image of the Son of Man who will come on the clouds of heaven) and in the Book of Revelation.

Danqalle (Arab.: ad-Danqalla, ed-Danqale, Qadiriya, 'Edriya, Khan Bandak; Heb.: Dannikleh) ancient village and synagogue site in the northern Golan Heights. The evidence for the synagogue's presence is a set of decorated black basalt stones in reuse in a nearby village. A carved basalt lintel in secondary use bears two seven-branched menorahs. One menorah has a tripod base, but the other's base is missing. A fragment of a second lintel also displays a menorah. Further artistic motifs include a wreath tied in a Hercules knot, ivy leaves, and a spoked wheel or circle. A brief Aramaic inscription was discovered on a lintel fragment, perhaps part of one of the above lintels. It reads, "Blessed be . . . Halfo bar . . . bar . . ." Some assign these architectural fragments to the remains of what may have been a synagogue: two walls of an ancient building, oriented north-south, which measured about 14 by 19 meters and was built of finely cut basalt masonry. The architectural fragments are most reasonably assigned a date in the third century C.E.

Darius III Codommanus the last king of Persia (r. 336–331 B.C.E.). He was defeated by Alexander the Great at Issus, in northwestern Syria, in 333 B.C.E. Alexander's victory led to his conquest of the province of Judah and the satrapy of Egypt. Darius was defeated again at Gaugamela, in northern Mesopotamia, in 331 B.C.E. and assassinated by his own troops in 330 B.C.E. His death and the end of the Persian Empire began the Hellenistic rule in Israel and Babylon.

darkhei haAmori *see* WAYS OF THE AMORITES

darkhei noam (Heb.) ways of pleasantness

darkhei shalom (Heb.) ways of peace

Daroma (Aram., south; also Darom, Daromas). During the period immediately following the Bar Kokhba Revolt, the term Daroma referred to an area just south of Hebron in Judea, where many Jews who were fleeing from Roman persecution and forced desegregation resettled. The area is also often called Darom (Heb., south) or Daromas (Gr., south).

The area of Daroma needs to be understood historically as well as archaeologically. It developed as a phenomenon of the failed Bar Kokhba Revolt. The revolt lasted over three and a half years (132–135 C.E.), during which time the Jewish rebels succeeded in temporarily overthrowing Roman rule in many places, including Jerusalem. After the Romans regained control and defeated the rebels, the Roman emperor Hadrian undertook steps to wipe out major Jewish settlements and Jewish customs in Israel. Those Jews who survived the battle and ensuing slaughter in the Jerusalem area were expelled. The expulsion area included the Judean Hills to the south and north of Jerusalem. Over seventy-five Jewish settlements have been identified archaeologically from the period before the Bar Kokhba Revolt, but there is no evidence of Jewish occupation in any of them in the period following the suppression of the Bar Kokhba rebels. Hadrian also decreed that circumcision, the teaching of the Torah, and ordination of rabbis would be punishable by death. The Jews who were not expelled from Palestine were forced to resettle among Gentiles (mainly Syrians and Arabs), making any hope of a revitalization of a Jewish state even more remote. Fortunately, the plans for resettlement of the Jews and the implementation of these repressive laws were not enforced systematically. Thus, when Hadrian died in 137 C.E., there was still hope in a few isolated areas of Israel for a Jewish community. Though a few communities were able to preserve their Jewish heritage, the resettlement and desegregation had been carried out to such an extent that there was no hope of reestablishing a Jewish state in the immediate future.

Daroma is one of these isolated pockets of Jewish settlement that remained following Hadrian's death in 137 C.E. The area was a actually a very thin slice of what was formally Judea. It stretched about 60 kilometers from En Gedi at the edge of the Dead Sea to the west at the edge of the Shephelah region. In most places, the dense settlement in Daroma was only about 10 kilometers wide from north to south. Several towns that contain archaeological remains include Horvat Susiya (probably Carmel during this period), Horvat Tilla (Thalla), Horvat Rimmon (En Rimmon), and Eshtemoa.

Horvat Susiya was in the heart of ancient Daroma. The name Susiya is actually an Arabic one, and it does not give any clue to the town's ancient identity. Most scholars believe that the site should be identified with Carmel of Daroma. There is another site identified with biblical Carmel a few kilometers away, but this site seems to have moved to Horvat Susiya during the period of Daroma.

The archaeological remains reveal that the town was able to construct a defensive building with a tower in the period following the Bar Kokhba defeat. The tower is 6 by 9 meters, and three courses are still intact. The defensive building functioned in place of a wall (which the Romans would not have permitted) and was used as a defensive installation. There are also remains of two caves and a synagogue that give clues to the extent and culture of the Jewish settlement in Daroma.

One cave is known as the Menorah Cave. The entrance to the cave contains a large lintel and doorposts that are hewn out of natural rock. A menorah figure is carved into the lintel. The function of this cave is uncertain, but it might have served as a storage place for the synagogue treasures. The second cave is known as the Wine Cellar Cave. It is larger, and its function is evident from its name. The synagogue at the site attests to the survival of Jewish culture and religion in Daroma. The remains attest to an elaborate building, and impressive mosaics are still preserved. Several of these mosaics contain complete and fragmentary Hebrew and Aramaic inscriptions.

Horvat Tilla is located adjacent to Tel Halif and the modern settlement of Kibbutz Lahav. The site preserves eight caves from the late Roman period. These caves seem to be part of an ancient community in Daroma identified by Eusebius as Thalla. The town of Thalla seems to be located on part of Tel Halif where there were extensive signs of occupation during the late Roman period.

Horvat Rimmon is another site that exhibits extensive remains from the late Roman period. It is identified as an important site in Daroma by Jerome's Latin translation of Eusebius, where it is called En Rimmon. Most of the town's remains from the second century have been destroyed by later settlements, but there are archaeological clues of settlement during the period following the Bar Kokhba Revolt and extensive remains, including a synagogue from the third and fourth centuries C.E.

Eshtemoa is located about 14 kilometers south of Hebron in the heart of Daroma. Eusebius states that it was "a very large Jewish village," and it remained settled until some time during the fourth century C.E. Like the other sites in Daroma, Eshtemoa also contains ruins from a synagogue, attesting to the survival of Jewish culture and religion in the days following the persecution by Hadrian. The synagogue contains remains of several mosaics with typical Jewish images and an Aramaic inscription mentioning Lazar the priest.

date's bulk (Heb.: *kotebet*) the bulk of a certain species of date; a measure of food volume. If one eats food on the Day of Atonement, when fasting is required, and the bulk is that of a date, one incurs liability; if one eats leaven (leavened grain) on Passover, which is forbidden, and the bulk is that of a date, one incurs liability.

David second king of Israel; son of Jesse of the tribe of Judah. After being anointed by Samuel (c. 1000 B.C.E.), he reigned over Israel in Hebron for either seven years (1 Kings 2:11) or seven years and six months (2 Sam. 2:11) and then in Israel for thirty-three years. According to Deuteronomic history, David united the Israelite tribes into a centralized kingdom with Jerusalem as its capital, brought the ark to Jerusalem, and received an eternal covenant (2 Sam. 7; Ps. 89:4). He was succeeded by Solomon, his son by Bathsheba.

By the Hellenistic era, David, YHWH's special chosen one, was thought of as set apart from other Israelites. David was known for his mercy; because of this quality, YHWH had established a covenant with him whereby David inherited the throne of the kingdom of the Israelites forever. The royal patrimony would pass from son to son without deviation. The family line would never be destroyed, and at the end-time, the Messiah will be from David's house. Consequently, even when there were only a few Israelites, their ruler was from David's house. As a result, David became an eschatological figure.

David was considered the psalmist par excellence, and the Qumran Psalms Scroll (11QPs[a]) attributes 4,050 psalms to him. The Apocalypse of Zephaniah accords David special status along with Enoch, Elijah, and the patriarchs in heaven (9:5); he appears exonerated in 4 Ezra 3:23–24 and 2 Baruch 61. *See also* DAVID, KEY OF; DAVID, SON OF.

David, key of Isaiah 22:22 states that he who possesses the "key of the house of David . . . shall open, and none shall shut; and he shall shut, and none shall open." Revelation 3:7 applies Isaiah's words to Jesus; here they clearly refer to messianic authority. The "keys of the kingdom" (Matt. 16:19) entrust this authority to church leaders (see also Matt. 18:18).

David, son of According to 2 Samuel 7 and Psalms 89:4, David received an eternal covenant; such statements contributed to speculation on the political and eschatological roles of David's descendants, especially following the end of Davidic rule under Zerubbabel and the subsequent confusion, if not loss, of Davidic genealogies. The Psalms of Solomon 17 explicitly predicts a Davidic savior, as does Patriarchal Blessings; 4 Ezra 12:32; Targ. Jon. on Isaiah 11:1 and Hosea 3:5. In the Gospels, Jesus does not unequivocally claim Davidic descent (Mark 12:35–37 and parallels; see also John 7:41–42). As a title for Jesus used by some in Jerusalem (Matt. 21:9), "son of David" may hold political connotations: Jesus is the new king who would replace Roman rule. According to Hegesippus, Davidic descendants were executed by Vespasian, Domitian, and Trajan, but such claims may well be apologetic fictions. *See also* DAVID; GENEALOGY.

David's Tomb Synagogue building on modern Mount Zion in Jerusalem that today is called David's Tomb; the medieval room that in the Christian tradition is called the Cenacle is on top of this building. This lower room may have been a synagogue of the fourth century C.E. The building's main hall is rectangular in plan with a large, high apse, or niche, in the north wall, positioned to point directly at the Temple Mount, or 10 degrees east of north. Two other niches on either side of the large niche remind one of the niches in the north wall of the Eshtemoa synagogue. Beneath the modern pavement of David's Tomb lies a colored mosaic pavement in geometric patterns. Beneath this pavement is perhaps another, earlier pavement. Some of the plaster fragments from the walls of the first phase of the building have traces of Greek letters. It has been suggested that this structure was built during the reign of Julian the Apostate (361–363 C.E.).

Day of Atonement *see* YOM KIPPUR

day of the Lord phrase common in the prophets to refer to the anticipated time of judgment and redemption; also "that day" and "day of YHWH." The major events expected on the day of the Lord are judgment of the nations and of the superhuman powers of evil, punishment of Israel (or Judah), and restoration of God's chastised people. The prophets predict that God will punish his people by subjecting them to foreign nations (Isa. 5:26–30) or through disasters such as a locust plague (Joel 2:1–11). The prophet Amos corrects his contemporaries' expectation: "Alas for you who desire the day of the Lord! . . . It is darkness and not light" (Amos 5:18). While his hearers look forward to the "day" as the time when God will punish their enemies, Amos predicts that the day will bring punishment on the inhabitants of Judah for their lack of justice.

The apocalypses speak of the "day of judgment" when the righteous will be rewarded and the sinners punished (1 Enoch 94:9, 96:2–8, 98:8–10; cf. "that day" and "this fated day" in Sib. Or. 3:55, 741). In 2 Esdras (4 Ezra) 7:26–44, the "day of judgment" follows the four-hundred-year kingdom of the messiah. On this day the dead will be raised and assigned to the places of reward and punishment (paradise and Gehenna); sun and moon, times and seasons will cease to exist (cf. Gen. 8:22).

The expectation of the day of the Lord plays a key role in the eschatological teaching of the New Testament (1 Cor. 5:5, Acts 2:20, 2 Pet. 3:10), where it is usually identified with the expectation of the parousia, or second coming of Jesus. This identification is possible because the Greek word for "Lord" (*kyrios*) can refer either to YHWH (as in the Septuagint) or to Jesus. The final day is called by a variety of names: the "day of judgment" (Matt. 10:15, 1 John 4:17); the "day of wrath" (Rom. 2:5, Rev. 6:17); the "day of Christ" (Phil. 1:10); the "day of our Lord Jesus Christ" (1 Cor. 1:8); the "last day" (John 6:39); the "day of God" (2 Pet. 3:12); and the "day" (Rom. 2:16, 1 Cor. 3:13). The day is pictured primarily as the last judgment, when all people will be tested (1 Cor. 3:13) and either rewarded (1 Cor. 1:8) or punished (Rom 2:16). Paul describes the day as imminent: "the day of the Lord will come like a thief in the night" (1 Thess. 5:2). Other New Testament authors reckon with a longer period before the end (cf. 2 Pet. 3, where the author responds to "scoffers" who complain of God's slowness in bringing the "day").

Days of Awe (Heb.: Yamim Noraim) ten-day period beginning on Rosh Hashanah (the New Year) and extending through Yom Kippur (the Day of Atonement). On these days, God judges all humanity, individuals and nations, for the coming year. On the New Year, the first of Tishrei, the decree is written; on the Day of Atonement, the tenth of Tishrei, the decree is sealed. It is a season of repentance, remembrance, and acts of contrition.

dayyan judge in a Jewish court

De Abrahamo the tractate *On Abraham* by Philo of Alexandria; its title is abbreviated as *Abr.* This work is one of two tractates on Abraham and allegorizes various events in Abraham's life. The tractate's main image is the soul's journey from godless astrology to self-knowledge and, finally, to knowledge of God. *See also* DE MIGRATIONE ABRAHAMI.

Dead Sea Caves specifically, the eleven caves near Qumran, at the northwest shores of the Dead Sea, where the Dead Sea Scrolls were found. Four other caves are included under this rubric near En Gedi, where other ancient documents were found. Qumran Cave 1 (designated 1Q in the standard terminology) was really a simple cleft or crevice in the cliff high above the plateau of the ruins of Qumran, about one kilometer north of Qumran. It is about eight meters deep, four meters high, and varies in width from 75 centimeters to about two meters. This cave contained a large quantity of scrolls that were removed by their Bedouin discoverers. About forty-five scrolls from this cave have been published. Other finds included many scraps of linen cloth, fragments of a wooden comb, olive and date stones, palm fiber, leather phylactery cases, and quantities of pottery sherds. The pottery, when mended, proved to be three cylindrical jars of Qumran, lids, bowls, a cooking pot, a juglet, two Hellenistic lamps, and two early Roman lamps. The two types of lamps correspond to the occupation of Qumran from the second century B.C.E. to 68 C.E., when Qumran was destroyed in the Great Revolt. A carbon 14 date on the cloth yielded the date 33 C.E., plus or minus two hundred years.

Cave 2 (2Q) lies about 100 meters south of Cave 1. It contained only fragments of scrolls rather than any intact scrolls, and its robbers left behind eight cylindrical jars, one lid, and three bowls. This cave was very uneven and was formed in two levels. About thirty-six fragments of scrolls have been published from this cave.

Cave 3 (3Q) lies about two kilometers north of Qumran. In it were found the famous copper scroll and also about fourteen fragments of leather and papyrus. A huge quantity of pottery was found: thirty-five cylindrical jars, twenty-six lids, two jugs, and a lamp.

Cave 4 (4Q) lies just west of Qumran in the finger of a marl terrace that, like Qumran itself, extends southward. Marl is a dense calcinate desert soil; this cave was cut wholly by hand in a marl layer that proved to be hard and suited to such cutting. Originally access was from a narrow entrance cut high above the floor, though later excavation revealed clues that there may have been yet another entrance near the floor level. This cave yielded parts of several jars, several lids and bowls, two jugs, a cooking pot, a juglet, and a lamp. Simply thousands of manuscript fragments were recovered from Cave 4. So far about three hundred titles are known from Cave 4.

Cave 5 (5Q) is about 15 meters immediately north of Cave 4 and cut into the same marl terrace. This cave was a simple chamber with rounded corners. It contained scraps of manuscripts but not artifacts. About twenty-five fragments from this cave have been published.

Cave 6 (6Q) is a natural cavity 300 meters west of Cave 4 at Qumran. It contained one cylindrical jar and a bowl in addition to fragments of manuscripts. About thirty-one scroll fragments from 6Q have been published.

Caves 7, 8, and 9 (7Q, 8Q, 9Q) lie at the end of the finger of the marl terrace and extend southward from Qumran. There are only traces of caves today, as massive slides and erosion have carried away most of the remains. In the erosion in Wadi Qumran, however, were found manuscript fragments, phylactery cases, date stones, scraps of ropes and leather, and some pottery. The pottery consisted of eight cylindrical jars, six lids, one bowl and two large bowls, one goblet, and two lamps. About nineteen tiny fragments of scroll material are known from 7Q, five from 8Q, and one papyrus fragment from 9Q.

Cave 10 (10Q) was cut into the west side of the finger of the marl terrace into which Cave 4 had been cut. Only half of cave 10 survived erosion, and its floor had been covered with a mat. Its interior proved to contain a Hebrew ostracon, date stones, desiccated dates, fragments of a lamp, and fragments of two jars. No scroll fragments are known from this cave.

Cave 11 (11Q) is a low natural cave in the bedrock about 1.8 kilometers north of Qumran. Its entrance was blocked by erosion, but it contained two pottery lids and a juglet and several artifacts, including fragments of cord and basketry, an iron knife, a pair of iron shears, and an iron adze or pick. Twenty-one major scrolls are known from this cave.

Five caves in Wadi Murabbaat 18 kilometers south of Qumran delivered up a cache of documents of the early second century C.E. The main cave, Cave 2, was high up in a cliff face where apparently Jews had fled to hide from the Romans during the Bar Kokhba Revolt, about 135 C.E. Nearly ninety manuscripts in Greek, Hebrew, Aramaic, and Nabatean were found by Taamireh tribesmen in Cave 2, including actual letters of Bar Kokhba to his lieutenants at En Gedi. Two documents were found in Cave 1, and one was found in Cave 5. These finds inspired more searches on the Israeli side of the armistice line, which resulted in the find of fourteen documents in Greek, Hebrew, Aramaic, and Nabatean in a cave in the Naḥal Heb̲er (Wadi Khabra). One group of documents evidently formed the personal archive of a woman named Babathra. The cave, called the Cave of Letters by the excavators, had two entrances high up on a cliff of the wadi, but it was accessible only from above by rope. The cave was some 150 meters deep and was divided naturally into three chambers. During the same search of caves in the vicinity, three documents were found in a cave in Naḥal Seelim (Wadi Seiyal). All of these finds were to be associated with the Bar Kokhba Revolt. All the inhabitants of the Cave of Horror on the south side of the Nahal Hever died in the cave, evidently by their own hand. Their remains were found, along with their clothing and belongings, such as knives, wooden bowls, spindle whorls, door keys, glass vessels, coins, leather water bags, pottery storage jars and lamps, and food and grain remains. *See also* DEAD SEA SCROLLS.

Dead Sea Scrolls name given to deposits of ancient texts found in caves along the western shore of the Dead Sea, written in Hebrew, Aramaic, and Greek. The Dead Sea Scrolls are without doubt the most famous archaeological discovery of the twentieth century and are also one of the most important finds relating to biblical studies in the modern period. The broadest sense of the term encompasses all the scrolls found at Qumran, Masada, Wadi Murabbaat, Naḥal Ḥeb̲er, Naḥal Seelim, and Naḥal Mishmar. In the narrow sense it refers only to those documents found in eleven caves near Khirbet Qumran; this is the definition we will use in the following discussion.

The discovery of the scrolls began in 1947, when a Taamireh Bedouin shepherd, tending his flock near the shores of the Dead Sea near the Wadi Qumran, discovered in a cave several old leather scrolls wrapped in linen and stored in jars. The news of the discovery of these seven scrolls electrified the scholarly community, leading to further discoveries in ten more caves in the vicinity of Khirbet Qumran. The largest cache of manuscripts, in Cave 4, was discovered in 1952, yielding thousands of fragments from more than five hundred manuscripts. The final cave, Cave 11, was discovered in 1956. The larger, more intact scrolls were published relatively quickly, and the fragments from the minor caves (2–3, 5–10) have also been published in the series Discoveries in the Judean Desert (DJD). The Cave 4 material was assigned to an international team of scholars, but their slow pace of decipherment and publication prompted the addition of more members to the team in the late 1980s, and as of this writing, final publication of all the fragments is anticipated in the year 2000.

The Dead Sea Scrolls are considered by most scholars to be the library of a Jewish community (usually identified with the Essenes) that inhabited the settlement at Qumran from the mid-second century B.C.E. until its destruction by the Romans in 68 C.E. The settlement's date was fixed according to archaeological criteria by the excavator, Roland de Vaux; the scrolls can be dated paleographically from the middle of the third century B.C.E. to the middle of the first century C.E., thus overlapping with the dates of the settlement. Further evidence also points to a relationship between the scrolls and the settlement: the same type of pottery was used in the caves and at the site, and inkwells and scraps of leather were found at the site that match the material of the scrolls in the caves. Therefore, most scholars accept a common community in the caves and at the settlement.

For modern readers, the scrolls can be conveniently divided into three categories: biblical texts, previously known nonbiblical texts, and not previously known nonbiblical texts (although it must be understood that these are not categories used by the Essenes of Qumran themselves). In the first category, fragments of every book of the Hebrew Bible were found, with the exception of the Book of Esther (which may exist in an Aramaic prototype). The question of what canon, if any, existed at Qumran, however, is more difficult. The five books of the Pentateuch were without doubt authoritative; they form the backbone of the halakhic teaching of the sect. The prophets also must have been considered authoritative; several commentaries on their books were found (Isaiah, Nahum, Habakkuk, Micah, and Zephaniah) as well as one on the Psalms. Many of the biblical books are cited in the sectarian documents with the formulas "it is written" or "it is said," indicating authority. Therefore, the canon at Qumran appears to be generally the same as that of the later Hebrew Bible, but a few qualifications are in order. First, other books, such as Jubilees, are cited as authoritative in sectarian documents, indicating a larger canon. Second, some texts, such as Enoch, appear in multiple copies, indicating at least a great deal of study. Finally, books such as Chronicles and Song of Songs do not seem to have played much of a role in the sect's ideology at all, calling these books' authoritative status at Qumran into question.

In a subcategory of the biblical material are those texts that rewrite, comment on, or otherwise use the canonical Bible. The genre "rewritten Bible" occurs most frequently in the Pentateuch, in compositions such as the Genesis Apocryphon, an Aramaic expansion of the Abraham story in the Book of Genesis; the Book of Jubilees, a retelling of Genesis 1:1–Exodus 15:22 with a particular halakhic point of view (a composition previously known in Ethiopic but now preserved in Hebrew at Qumran); the Temple Scroll, a representation of the Torah purportedly given by God speaking in the first person; and 4Q Reworked Pentateuch, a full Pentateuchal text with additions and rearrangements of material. It is difficult to ascertain when and by whom these texts were composed; there is nothing overtly sectarian about them, but many of their ideas reappear in compositions labeled sectarian.

A particular form of biblical interpretation, the *pesher,* is found among the Dead Sea Scrolls. The *pesher* takes the following form: citation of a biblical verse, followed by some form of the word *pesher* (its interpretation is), finishing with an interpretation involving characters or events associated with the Qumran Community. A *pesher* can be a whole commentary on a biblical book (continuous *pesher*), for example, the Habakkuk Commentary or the Nahum Commentary; a collection of biblical texts gathered around a common theme (thematic *pesher*), for example, the Florilegium or the Pesher on Melchizedek; or an isolated interpretation of a biblical verse within a larger composition (isolated *pesharim*), for example, the pesher on Amos 5:26–27 in the Damascus Document. These *pesharim* are products of the Qumran Community, being replete with sectarian ideas and language.

A final group of texts closely related to the biblical texts might be labeled "biblical paraphrases," since they are related to a particular biblical book, but are not necessarily bound to it. Examples are the Prayer of Nabonidus, related to the Book of Daniel; 4Q Pseudo Ezekiel, related to the Book of Ezekiel; and 4Q Proto Esther, which may be an Aramaic precursor to the canonical Book of Esther.

Growing out of the Qumran Community's interest in the biblical text and its interpretation are the halakhic works and rule books found among the scrolls. One of these halakhic works, 4QMMT, may give the clue for the reasons for the founding of the Qumran Community. Identified by its editors as "a letter from a leader of the Qumran sect (possibly the Teacher of Righteousness himself) to the leader of its opponents," 4QMMT sets out the legal issues concerning which the sect differs from its opponents. These include the calendar, ritual purity, and laws on marital status, which are all stated as the reasons for the sect's separation from the rest of Judaism.

The Damascus Document and the Community Rule are the two major rule books found among the scrolls. The Damascus Document was known before the discovery of the scrolls, having been found in the Cairo Geniza in the late nineteenth century. It is aimed at a sectarian group of Jews, probably the Essenes, who live in camps in the towns and villages of Judah. It falls into two parts: an Admonition, which outlines the history of the sect in figurative language and discusses the nature of membership in the group; and the Laws, which give the specific sectarian rules. These are severe, involving a strict interpretation of the halakhah, designed to enforce a strict separation from "the sons of the Pit" (all other Jews and Gentiles).

The Community Rule, on the other hand, is a rule book for the life of the Community at Qumran. It presupposes a fairly large, isolated community, sharing meals, pooling their property, and governing themselves under the leadership of priests and certain lay officials. The Rule, a composite text, contains the procedure for admission into the sect, as well as a special set of precepts for the *maskil,* the chief lay official of the Community, and the Treatise on the Two Spirits, an exemplar of the sect's dualistic doctrine. The halakhah of the Rule, like the Damascus Document, imposes strict rules of purity and conduct, and makes it virtually impossible for members of the sect to mix with outsiders.

Many liturgical works exist among the Dead Sea Scrolls, some sectarian, others of uncertain provenance. One, the Psalms Scroll from Cave 11, contains most of the last third of the biblical Psalter, but in a different order, plus several noncanonical psalms, all of which are attributed to David. None are specifically sectarian. Other liturgical works lacking distinctive sectarian traits are a collection of noncanonical psalms (4Q380–381) and the Words of the Heavenly Lights, a prayer for deliverance based on the covenant relationship. Other liturgical texts also occur, too fragmentary to enumerate.

There are also liturgical compositions that are clearly sectarian in nature, using language of community and separation, dualism, and covenant, in addition to embracing a strict halakhah. The best known of these is the Hodayot, of which copies were found in Caves 1 and 4. The majority of these hymns begin with the formula "I give thanks to thee, O Lord," and continue with thanks for deliverance from sin and knowledge of the way of the sect. Several hymns may have been composed by the Teacher of Righteousness himself. Other sectarian liturgical works include the Songs of the Sabbath Sacrifice (4QShirShabb), the Benedictions ($1QS^b$), and several other fragmentary works. We do not know how or if any of these compositions were used by the Community.

Many of the works from the Qumran library, both sectarian and nonsectarian, have strong eschatological overtones. It is clear that the sect believed itself to be living at the end of days and, further, believed itself to be at the center of events leading up to the end. This eschatological orientation is most strikingly illustrated by the War Scroll, a composition that relates the events to take place in the final battle between the armies of God, which include the members of the sect under their sobriquet "the Sons of Light," and the armies of Belial, including "the Sons of Darkness," all those outside the sect. The War Scroll envisions a conflict in which the forces of Light and Darkness alternately prevail, with the final victory being wrought by God. Another eschatological text concerned with the conflict between good and evil is the Aramaic Testament of Amram (4QAmram), in which the good and evil archangels battle for possession of humanity.

Several nonsectarian apocalyptic works were also found among the documents at Qumran. The best known, 1 Enoch, was found in eleven (Aramaic) copies in Cave 4 (with the exception of chaps. 37–71), along with the related Book of the Giants. Also among these discoveries, fragmentary texts relating to Noah and Lamech may be apocalyptic, and several testamentary texts (Testament of Naphtali, Apocryphon of Levi) are apocalyptic in nature. However, no apocalypses that were previously unknown and certainly composed by the sect have been discovered.

Despite occasional arguments to the contrary, the identification of the manuscripts found in the eleven caves in the vicinity of Khirbet Qumran as the library of a community of Essenes who lived at Qumran (with roots going back to a larger group or movement in the 4th and 3rd cs. B.C.E.) is well established. This library is not merely a collection of miscellaneous religious texts, but is a fairly coherent collection with common themes: a reverence for the biblical text supported by interpretation (which took a written form) and reading of related texts, a strict interpretation of the law leading to a separation from the rest of Judaism (bolstered by a strong dualism and sense of predestination), and a strong eschatological hope in which their cause would be vindicated by God. Far from being vindicated, these Essenes, as far as we know, perished in the Roman attack on Qumran. However, the accidental discovery of their library causes them to live again by offering us a unique chance to discover the ideology of a particular strand of Judaism from the late Second Temple period, and to follow that strand into rabbinic Judaism and early Christianity. *See also* COMMUNITY RULE; DAMASCUS DOCUMENT; HABAKKUK COMMENTARY; HODAYOT; NABONIDUS, PRAYER OF; NAHUM COMMENTARY; TEMPLE SCROLL; WAR SCROLL; WORDS OF THE HEAVENLY LIGHTS.

De Aeternitate Mundi the tractate *On the Eternity of the World,* generally thought to be by Philo of Alexandria, though there is not complete agreement on this attribution; its title is abbreviated as *Aet.* This work discusses the questions of whether the cosmos was created and whether it is indestructible and presents detailed arguments of various philosophers.

deaf-mute In the Mishnah and Talmuds, the deaf-mute is classified together with the imbecile and the minor and is deemed to have no independent will. Accordingly, the deaf-mute is unable to perform religious obligations requiring the formulation of intention, for example, the designation of agricultural offerings (M. Terumot 1:1) or the preparing of foods in a state of cultic cleanness (T. Terumot 1:1). Those known to be of sound mind who become deaf and mute, or who are either deaf or mute alone, are exempt from these restrictions.

De Agricultura the tractate *On Husbandry* by Philo of Alexandria; its title is abbreviated as *Agr.* This work gives an allegorical exegesis of Genesis 9:20, in which Noah is said to be a "husbandman," an identification that is interpreted as a symbol of the cultivation of the soul to produce the fruit of virtue. Noah the husbandman is contrasted with Cain, who is a mere "worker of the earth" (i.e., one who serves pleasure).

death Views of death in the Hebrew Bible, Second Temple Jewish texts, and the New Testament vary widely. Death is seen as both natural and a result of sin. The tension appears already in Genesis 2–3. God warns the first humans that if they transgress the commandment they will die (2:17). Nonetheless, their exclusion from the immortality that the tree of life could give them indicates that they were mortal at the time they sinned (3:22–24). However one resolves that tension, the Hebrew Bible as a whole accepts death as a fact of life from which only Enoch and Elijah were exempted (Gen. 5:24; 2 Kings 2:1–12). Nonetheless, certain kinds of death were viewed as evil. If one died at a young age, as a result of illness or violence, or if one died without a good number of children, this was interpreted as an evil occurrence that might even be evidence of divine punishment for one's sins.

The term "death" developed a moral dimension, particularly in the wisdom literature in the concept of the two ways of life and death. To sin was to walk in the way of death, in two senses. One's sins could lead to premature death. The person who lived an unrighteous life, apart from God, was already walking in the realm of death.

In time, reflection on the problem of unjust death, especially the violent death of the righteous in times of persecution, led to beliefs in resurrection, immorality, and eternal life. The earliest attestations of these beliefs are in Isaiah 26:19 and Daniel 12:2, although Psalms 16:10–11, 49:15, and 73:24 may intimate some such belief. As these beliefs develop and postmortem retribution is seen not just as the vindication of those who die unjustly but as reward and punishment for everyone, death itself is perceived to be a wrong that must be righted. The wicked, of course, will perish eternally, and words like "death" and "destruction," which previously referred to physical death and its result, describe the fate of the wicked. However, the righteous will inherit eternal life, or at least an extraordinarily long life like that of the patriarchs (1 Enoch 25:4–6).

In the New Testament death is generally seen to be unnatural and the ultimate enemy. For Paul the sin of the first humans brought death into the world, and the righteous life, the unjust death, and the resurrection of Jesus reverse that situation and bring life to all who believe (Rom. 5; cf. 6:23). Death, the last enemy, is overcome through the resurrection of Jesus, whose appearance will transform mortality to immortality and corruptibility to incorruptibility (1 Cor. 15).

Conservative sectors in Judaism (e.g., the Sadducees) rejected a belief in resurrection, following the biblical notion that a good and full life was ample reward for one's deeds. However, the development of a belief in resurrection and eternal life changed for many the valuation of this life and the understanding of death as its end.

Among the 903 forms of death that the rabbis of the Talmuds enumerated, some were more favorable predictors than others of one's future in the world to come; death from bowel disorders, for example, was a favorable omen. In the early rabbinic period, death was considered inevitable, a part of the natural order from the time of creation; a person's sins might hasten death but did not cause it; sinlessness enabled one to live out one's allotted years or to prolong one's lifespan. According to another view, without sin there would be no death; if the truly righteous did not request their own deaths, they would live forever. Some of the many rabbinic statements about death include assertions that it serves as an atoning process; that Adam brought it into the world by eating the forbidden fruit; that the Israelites had the opportunity to overcome the power of death by receiving the Torah but lost it by sinning with the golden calf; and that the wicked are considered dead even during life, while the righteous are considered living even after death. *See also* CORRUPTION; DESTRUCTION; IMMORTALITY, INCORRUPTION; LIFE, ETERNAL.

death, personified In the Testament of Abraham, when the patriarch refuses to surrender his soul to

Michael, God sends Death, a horrifying, many-faced creature (chaps. 16–17 [A]). The personification of death is attested in the Canaanite god Mot and is hinted at in Isaiah 25:8. The conception in the Testament of Abraham appears, however, to reflect contemporary Egyptian ideas, and the association of Death with a cup of poison suggests an identification of Death with Sammael, the poisoning angel of death. The text exemplifies the religious syncretism typical of Jewish texts in the Graeco-Roman period.

debt (Aram.: *ḥob̲;* Gr.: *opheilēma*) metaphor for sin. The idea that sin incurs a debt with God is attested as early as the third or second century B.C.E. in 1 Enoch 6:3, and the noun is employed in the targums as a translation for "sin" (Heb.: *ḥatah*). This is sometimes seen as evidence of an increasing "legalism" in Jewish religion; however, the image occurs in the prayer of Jesus (Matt. 6:12), and the parable in Matthew 18:23–35 plays out in detail the notion of debt and forgiveness. The common notion that good deeds constitute a treasure at the time of judgment may be a reverse of this metaphor.

In light of the prohibition against loaning on interest, in rabbinic law the central concern regarding loans and other debts is the conditions under which repayment is to be made or can be demanded. A loan or credit sale is assumed to come due in thirty day (T. Bab̲a Metzia 10:1). Where other terms for repayment have been established either orally or in a bond, the creditor cannot demand repayment prior to the set day. After the due date, the creditor may demand payment at any time, although he must leave the debtor with sufficient resources to return home. On the other hand, should the debtor offer repayment in an inconvenient setting, for example, a wilderness (M. Bab̲a Kamma 10:6), the creditor may refuse it.

During the talmudic period, debts of decedents, including the sum owed a widow under the terms of her marriage contract (*ketub̲ah*), were collectable only from immovables, that is, slaves and real estate, viewed as the only property that could secure a loan. In medieval times, when the majority of Jews became landless, it became necessary to alter this rule in order to allow collection of debts from goods, chattels, and money due the estate as well. *See also* SIN; TREASURE.

Decal. *see* DE DECALOGO

Decalogue term derived from the Greek words *deka logoi,* meaning "ten sayings." It is used as a synonym for the Ten Commandments, which are so important in the laws God gives to Moses on Mount Sinai in the biblical account. Different stories in Exodus and Deuteronomy, probably from different times and traditions, describe God's communicating these commandments to his people, Israel. In Exodus 20:1–17, when Moses returns from the mountain after God appeared there in the sight of all the people and they agreed to do "everything that the Lord has spoken" (Exod. 19:8), Moses reports to them what "God spoke": the Ten Commandments. Later in Exodus, when Moses returns to the mountain, it is these rules for the life of the covenant people that are written by God on the stone tablets and that Moses brings back from the mountaintop to the people below, "written upon both sides, front and back" (Exod. 32:15–16). On returning and finding the people of Israel engaged in worship of a golden calf, Moses becomes furious and smashes the stone tablets (Exod. 32:19).

After the people accept the Lord's rebuke of them and after Moses' plea to the Lord in their behalf, he returns with newly cut stone tablets to meet God again on the mountain (Exod. 34:1–9). Moses receives from God the summary of the law in ten parts, and is told to write them on the stone tablets during the forty days and nights he is alone with the Lord on the mountain. They are referred to as "the words of the covenant: the ten commandments" (34:28). The powerful acts of God in driving out the inhabitants of the land promised to Israel should serve as proof of the enduring quality of his covenant with his people (34:10–14). But they must obey these laws, or they will forfeit the covenant relationship with God. Later, as the people prepare to enter the promised land from east of the Jordan River, Moses convenes them and once more repeats the Ten Commandments to them (Deut. 5:1–21). He tells them that they are to hear "all the commandments, statutes and ordinances" that God has given them through Him, to teach these to their children after they settle in the land, and above all to obey them, doing exactly as the Lord commanded them if they are to live and prosper in their new land (5:28–33). When the Israelites began to settle in the land at Shechem, Joshua set up a large stone that was to be a constant reminder of the law given on the tablets of stone (Josh. 24:24–27).

Central to each report of God's laws for his people are the Ten Commandments. The wider implications of these mostly brief rules are spelled out in some detail in other parts of the Mosaic law. The basic thrust of these laws, which God's people are to obey, may be summarized as follows: (1) They are to honor and reverence no other god more than ("before") Yahweh, the Lord (Exod. 20:3; Deut. 6:5). This commandment must have been formulated before Israel became strictly monotheistic and while the people still recognized the existence of other deities who were considered inferior to the Lord. (2) They were not to worship any idols or images of any deity, since nothing that humans can make can represent the creator of all that is (Exod. 20:4; Deut. 5:8–10). (3) They are not to use the power that is inherent in the very name of God by uttering an oath they do not intend to carry out, or by using God's name to curse someone (Exod. 20:7; Deut. 5:11). (4) They are to observe the Sabbath as the day of rest by abstaining from any work on the seventh day, and by avoiding any requirement that slaves, livestock, or visitors work on that sacred day of rest (Exod. 24:8–11; Deut. 5:12–15). (5) They are to honor their parents; not merely children obeying father and mother, but adults honoring and treating their elderly parents properly. By doing so, they will see their own lives extended as they live in the land (Exod. 20:12; Deut. 5:16). (6) They are not to commit murder, although killing enemies in warfare and executing convicted criminals are not prohibited (Exod. 20:13; Deut. 5:17). (7) They are not to commit adultery, which is to have sexual relationships with a partner other than one's spouse, or to violate a woman sexually who is part of another family. Men could have multiple wives and concubines, but were not to have sex with other women (Exod. 20:14; Deut. 5:18). (8) The commandment against stealing included not only taking someone else's property but "stealing" a person by selling them into slavery (Exod. 20:15; Deut. 5:19). (9) They are to give truthful testimony concerning their neighbors, both Israelite and Gentile (Exod. 20:16; Deut. 5:20). (10) They are not to covet anything that belongs to a neighbor, either property or spouse, slave or domestic animal (Exod. 20:17; Deut. 5:21).

These moral demands are all placed in the context of reminders that God set Israel free from slavery in Egypt (Exod. 20:2; Deut. 5:15), that God has made a covenant with Israel (Exod. 34:10, 27), that punishment is certain for those who disobey and loving support is sure for those who show their love of God by keeping these commandments (Exod. 20:5–6). They are called to love and obey God, to instruct their children in these laws, and to keep a copy of the commandments in a small container (phylactery) on their foreheads as a sign to others and as a reminder to themselves (Deut. 6:1–9). The enduring power of these laws is evident in the teachings of the prophets of Israel (Hos. 4:1; Jer. 7:9) and in the discovery of such phylacteries among the remains of the Dead Sea community at Qumran.

Decapolis refers to a group of ten cities in Transjordan. These cities may have formed a loose confederacy after the restoration of their autonomy by Pompey, after his intervention in Jewish affairs in 67 B.C. Alternatively, the name is applied loosely to the whole territory east of the Jordan and opposite Galilee, as in Mark 5:20; 7:31. The region had previously been incorporated into the Hasmonean kingdom by Alexander Jannaeus. Pliny is our most reliable authority on the names of the cities, but even he notes that not everybody agreed on which cities were included among the ten (*Natural History V,* 15:22–23). He notes that most include Damascus, Philadelphia, Raphia, Scythopolis, Gadara, Hippos, Dion, Pella, Galasa (Gerasa), and Canatha. Of this list only Scythopolis (Beth Shean) was located west of the Jordan, but the inclusion of Damascus and Philadelphia shows that the territory covered a large area. These cities, which date from the Ptolemaic and Seleucid periods, were centers of Greek culture and commerce in the region, but this did not preclude Jewish inhabitants even after Pompey's liberation. Christian communities with episcopal sees were found in many of these cities during the Byzantine period.

De Cherubim the tractate *On the Cherubim* by Philo of Alexandria; its title is abbreviated as *Cher.* This treatise is an allegorical explanation of Genesis 3:24 and 4:1; the first citation describes the cherubim set at the entrance of the Garden of Eden, and the second passage relates the birth of Cain. The cherubim represent the "powers" of God, and the sword of the cherubim represents the Logos.

Decius, Trajan (c. 201–251 C.E.) Roman emperor (r. 249–251); born in Pannonia. He was a firm upholder of the old Roman traditions and supported the Senate. In 250, he demanded that his subjects offer sacrifices to the emperor under pain of death for refusal. This led to persecution of Christians. There is no record that the demand was pressed on the Jews or that they were persecuted for refusing to worship the emperor. He is the last emperor under whom the coins of Aleia Capitolina, Jerusalem, were especially plentiful. Coins from Caesarea also were minted under his reign.

De Confusione Linguarum the treatise *On the Confusion of Tongues* by Philo of Alexandria; its title is abbreviated as *Conf.* This treatise is an allegorical commentary on Genesis 11:1–9, the story of the Tower of Babel. The "one speech and one tongue" of the biblical text are interpreted as a symphony of evils, which especially include the passions that attack the soul.

De Congressu quaerendae Eruditionis gratia the treatise *On the Preliminary Studies* by Philo of Alexandria; its title is abbreviated as *Congr.* This work is an allegorical commentary on Genesis 16:1–6, in which Sarah gives Hagar to Abraham to have a child. Hagar represents the *encyclia,* or lower school of instruction, whereas Sarah stands for philosophy.

De Decalogo the treatise *On the Decalogue* by Philo of Alexandria; its title is abbreviated as *Decal.* The work is an allegorical discourse on the giving of the Decalogue. After discussing why the Ten Commandments were given in the desert and why there are ten of them, Philo devotes much of his treatise to an examination of the Commandments themselves, in two groups of five.

Dedication, Feast of *see* HANUKKAH

De Ebrietate the treatise *On Drunkenness* (abbreviated as *Ebr.*) by Philo of Alexandria that together with *On Agriculture* and *On Planting* forms an allegorical commentary on Genesis 9:20–29. *De Ebrietate* focuses on Noah's becoming drunk and considers the various qualities that wine symbolizes, such as foolish talk, stupor, and greed.

deeds, works translates several Hebrew words and the Greek *erga,* a term of broad application that has assumed a special sense in Christian theology because of Paul's polemical use of the phrase "works of the law." In the Tanakh (Old Testament), "work(s)" refers to God's action in creation (Gen. 2:2, 3; Ps. 8:3) and in the history of Israel (Exod. 34:10, Deut. 3:24). It also describes human labor in a general sense (Exod. 20:9), as well as moral or immoral action (Ps. 62:12: "For you repay all according to their works"; cf. Ps. 28:3–4).

The contrast between the "works" of the righteous and those of the sinners is frequent in the literature of early Judaism (2d c. B.C.E.–2d c. C.E.): "Our works are in the choice and power of our souls, to do right and wrong" (Ps. Sol. 9:4). God is a righteous judge, who will repay each person according to his works (2 Bar. 48:38–40). The identification of righteous works with the actions required by the law—a point generally presupposed in the Tanakh—is made explicit: "the Lord is just in all the works that he has commanded us to do." (Bar. 2:9; cf. Test. Naph. 2:6, 2 Bar. 48:38–40). A recently published fragmentary letter found among the Dead Sea Scrolls (4Q394–99; sometimes referred to as 4QMMT) contains the phrase "works of the law" (Heb.: *ma aseh haTorah*). The "works" in question here have to do with specific understandings of the laws about the purity of the Temple and the Temple offerings. The author promises his reader that, in the impending "end of days," his return to the law "will be reckoned to you for righteousness" (for this phrase, cf. Ps. 106:31, referring to the priest Phineas, and Gen. 15:6: "And Abraham believed God, and it was reckoned to him for righteousness"). David is presented as a model: a man of pious works (Heb.: *ḥasadim*) whose sins were forgiven when he sought the Torah.

Paul gives a very different evaluation of "works of the law": "We hold that a person is not justified by works of the law but by faith" (Rom. 3:28, cf. Gal. 2:16). In Romans 4, he argues on the basis of Gen. 15:6 that Abraham was "justified" before God by his faith, before he observed any of the "works of the law." The contrast between "faith" and "works of the law" is part of Paul's argument that God has acted in Jesus Christ to save all people, Jew and Gentile, and that salvation is offered as a free gift, which cannot be earned by any human "work." Although Paul's letters make clear the importance of "works" in the general sense of merciful and virtuous deeds (cf. Rom. 2:6, where he says that God will judge each person "according to his works"), his words were open to antinomian misinterpretation (cf. Rom. 6:1). The discussion in James 2:14–26 is probably directed against such misuse of Paul. Addressing Christians who are neglecting good works such as care for the poor, the author of this late-first-century text asserts: "faith without works is barren" (2:20). He, too, appeals to the example of Abraham: Abraham's willingness to sacrifice his son shows that "his faith was perfected by his works" (2:22).

The debate about "faith" and "works" figures in later Christianity, for example in second-century debates between Gnostic and "orthodox" Christians and in disputes between Protestants and Roman Catholics. In addition, Paul's discussions of "works of the law" in Romans 3–4 and Galatians 2–3 have influenced Christian perception of Judaism. These texts have given rise to a one-sided view of Jewish religion at the time of Paul as a legalistic religion of "works righteousness," which attributed salvation to human effort and gave no place to divine grace. The Dead Sea Scrolls, among other texts, challenge this view. While they emphasize "works of the law," the Scrolls also exhibit an acute awareness of the need for divine grace (1QH11:29–31; cf. 4Q394–399). *See also* GRACE.

defile mouth expression that describes the consequences of eating forbidden food and, perhaps, of speaking blasphemy: one is in a state of cultic impurity. The early occurrence of this notion in Isaiah 6:5 is difficult to interpret, though it is related to Isaiah's inability to function as God's spokesman (cf. v. 7 with Jer. 1:9). Joseph and Asenath makes repeated reference to Asenath's impure mouth, which results from her consumption of food sacrificed to idols (8:5; 11:8–9, 16; 12:5), but the text also describes her blasphemous words against Joseph, "the son of God" (6:2–3, 7; 12:4; 13:13).

The use of the term in 1 Enoch 5:4 is ambiguous and is open to three interpretations. The sinners' mouths are impure because they have spoken arrogant words against God's majesty. The revisionist teaching about the Torah, implied throughout chapters 2–4 in the repeated reference to changing things, is tantamount to idolatry (cf. 98:9–99:9). The sinners are guilty of consuming blood or forbidden food (cf. 98:11).

Defter "The Book," written in Samaritan Aramaic, was the main Samaritan prayerbook until the fourteenth century C.E. and continues to be their common book of prayer. A series of *katafim* form the earliest part of the prayerbook; these are brief quotations, in biblical order, from each book of the Torah. Ninety-three liturgical poems were gradually added and are interspersed among the hymns and *katafim*. A majority of these poems are the work of the fourth-century poets Amram Darah, Markah, and Markah's son, Noneh. Several more poems were added in the tenth and eleventh centuries, particularly those of Abul Hassan of Tyre and his son Ab Geluga. After the rise of Islam, Muslim religious devices, particularly the phrases "There is no God, but God" and "In the Name of God" find their way into the liturgy. The order in various manuscripts differs considerably. In the fourteenth century, many special services were developed for such times as Passover, Pentecost, the Day of Atonement, Sukkot, and other special celebrations, and the Defter became the prayerbook for weekly and Sabbath services. It encompasses almost a hundred pages of A. E. Cowley's work, *The Samaritan Liturgy* (1909), based on the manuscript Vatican 3. Earlier manuscripts are fragmentary.

De Fuga et Inventione the treatise *On Flight and Finding* by Philo of Alexandria; its title is abbreviated as *Fuga*. This work continues an allegorical treatment (begun by *De Congressu*) of Genesis 16:1–9, about the eviction of Hagar from Abraham's household. Genesis 16:1–9 serves as the focal point in a discussion that moves on to other passages where "flight" and "discovery" are mentioned.

De Gigantibus the treatise *On the Giants* by Philo of Alexandria; its title is abbreviated as *Gig*. This work is an allegorical exegesis of Genesis 6:1–4, which mentions the intercourse of the "angels of God" with women, and the resultant offspring who were giants. Much of the discussion concerns the "spirit of God" in verse 3.

De Iosepho the treatise *On Joseph* by Philo of Alexandria; its title is abbreviated as *Ios*. This work allegorizes the story of Joseph (Gen. 37, 39–50), who here represents the ideal of the statesman. Joseph's dream in prison serves as a meditation on the fact that life is a dream and that the statesman must find and set forth the dream's underlying truths.

deisidaimonia (Gr., pious respect, or superstition) In a negative or critical sense it was used to label those things one considered "superstition"; however, it could also convey the more positive sense of something deserving serious religious respect. Only the context clarified which meaning was intended.

delatio (Lat., denunciation, accusation) It came especially to be used as a technical term to refer to an accusation of treason against the Roman emperor. Those who engaged in *delatio* might do so out of genuine loyalty, but it was often a way to gain political advantage, settle old scores, or protect oneself.

De Legatione ad Gaium the treatise *On the Embassy to Gaius* by Philo of Alexandria; its title is abbreviated as *Leg.* or *Gaium*. This treatise describes the Jewish mission of 39–41 C.E., led by Philo, to present the Jews' case before the emperor Gaius, also known as Caligula. A mission from the Greek citizens had also gone to Rome to complain about the Jews before the emperor.

Delos Synagogue Roman period synagogue built by and for the local Jewish population on the Greek island of Delos in the Aegean Sea. Josephus mentions the Jewish community of Delos, and it is interesting to note that there was also a Samaritan community at Delos. The building identified as a synagogue is simply a hall in a house. The hall measures about 14.4 by 16.9 meters with three entrances on the east. The entrance was through a square courtyard with a covered portico or colonnaded porch in front of the three entrances. Inside the hall stood beautifully cut marble benches on the north half of the western wall opposite the entrances. Centered in these benches stood a finely cut marble throne, recalling the stone seats found at Chorazin and Hammath-Tiberias. There is no niche for a Torah shrine, nor is there any sign of Jewish decorative art. On the other hand, four votive inscriptions in Greek give thanks to the "most high God" for healings. This is a common phrase for God among diaspora Jews. A fifth inscription indicates that something is done "for prayer," and the sixth evidently gives thanks for freedom from a freedman. On the other hand the spareness of the hall suggests that only one of its uses may have been prayer. The throne suggests that an Archisynagogos (head of a synagogue) sat with the elders in formal meetings.

Delta the predominantly Jewish district of Alexandria. The city was divided into five districts referred to by the first letters of the Greek alphabet. As Jews spread into other districts, friction with the Greek citizens increased; after a pogrom in 38 C.E., the Jews were temporarily restricted to that district.

demai (Heb.) doubtfully tithed produce

Demai Mishnah tractate on doubtfully tithed produce. The tractate discusses items subject to tithing as doubtfully tithed produce, how doubtfully tithed produce is handled and used, commercial and commensal relations between those who are trustworthy in tithing and outsiders, details of the tithing procedure, the rule that tithes must not be separated in behalf of produce liable to tithing out of produce that is exempt, and the extent to which, in a case of shared ownership of produce, one owner is responsible for tithing the portion that he gives to the other owner.

Demetrius I Soter of Syria (187–150 B.C.E.), Seleucid king (r. 162–150 B.C.E.); second son of Seleucus IV, sent as a hostage to Rome in 176/175. He escaped in 162, perhaps with the help of the historian Polybius, and had his cousin Antiochus V and Lysias executed. Alcimus, the Jerusalem high priest, instigated Demetrius against Judas Maccabeus, and the king sent first Bacchides, who recaptured Jerusalem, and then Nicanor against Judas. On Nicanor's defeat, Bacchides was again sent, Judas died in battle, and Judea was retaken. When Egypt and Pergamum conspired to send Alexander Balas as a rival claimant to the Seleucid throne, Jonathan Maccabeus (Judas's brother and successor) skillfully played Balas and Demetrius against each other to gain more power, eventually siding with Alexander Balas. Demetrius died in 150.

Demetrius II Nicator (161–126 B.C.E.) Seleucid king; son of Demetrius I. He succeeded with Egyptian help in defeating Alexander Balas (151–145 B.C.E.) and occupying the Seleucid throne his father had lost, ruling from 145 to 140 or 139 and from 129 to 126 B.C.E. In the dynastic struggle with the general Tryphon and Alexander Balas's minor son, Antiochus VI, Simon, son of Mattathias, sided with Demetrius II, who made him high priest and freed him from tribute (143/142 B.C.E.). Demetrius was captured by the Parthians in 138 B.C.E. He was released by them, and regained the throne from his brother, Antiochus VII Sidetes in 129 B.C.E. He was subsequently defeated by a son of Alexander Balas and Egyptian forces and was assassinated in 126 B.C.E.

Demetrius III Eukairos Seleucid ruler, son of Antiochus VIII; vied with his three brothers for the Seleucid throne. Demetrius was asked in 88 B.C.E. by a Jewish party for aid in deposing Alexander Jannaeus. He defeated Jannaeus but then withdrew. Later, Demetrius was blockaded by a force that included Arabs and Parthians, was forced to surrender, and was sent to Mithridates, king of Parthia, who held him in honorable captivity. Meanwhile, back in Jerusalem, Jannaeus regained control and had eight hundred of his enemies crucified alive while their wives and children were slaughtered before them. This incident and Demetrius's role are referred to in the Commentary on Nahum (4Q169) from the Dead Sea Scrolls.

Demetrius the Alabarch Egyptian Jew of a prominent family of Alexandria in the first century C.E. Whether he was related to the family of Philo is not known. He held the office of alabarch from about 50 to 60 C.E. He married Mariamme, the daughter of Agrippa I, by whom he had a daughter named Agrippinus.

Demetrius the Chronographer one of the Fragmentary Hellenistic Jewish writers in the late third century B.C.E. His work, preserved only in quotations in Eusebius and Clement of Alexandria, was apparently called *On the Kings of Judah,* though the extant fragments relate mainly to Jacob and the time of the Exodus. From what we know of his writing, it focused on reconciling interpretative difficulties in the text and it emphasized chronographic matters. For example, he gives exact dates for the births of each of Jacob's children; he makes Zipporah, the wife of Moses, a descendant of Abraham through Keturah and thus not a Gentile. In the same way, he tries to resolve the problem of how Moses, who was the seventh generation after Abraham, could have married Zipporah, who was only the sixth. She is also identified as the "Ethiopian" woman whom Moses had married (Num. 12:1). Demetrius is important for the translation of the Pentateuch into Greek. He used only the Septuagint text and was one of the earliest writers to do so, thus indicating that the translation was already in existence in the latter half of the third century B.C.E.

De Migratione Abrahami the treatise *On the Migration of Abraham* by Philo of Alexandria; its title is abbreviated as *Migr.* This work is an allegorical exegesis of Genesis 12:1–6, and a considerable portion of the tractate discusses the five gifts or promises to Abraham, including land and descendants, that these verses in Genesis imply. *See also* DE ABRAHAMO.

demiurge (Gr., creator) The term is often used in Greek writings (e.g., by Plato) to describe a fashioner of the universe who is not necessarily the supreme deity and is often viewed as an artisan. In Jewish writings in Greek, such as those of Philo of Alexandria, the term is naturally used of the supreme and only God himself. In Gnosticism, the demiurge is the ignorant creator of the material world and is identified with the Jewish God, but is not the supreme God.

demons (Gr.: *daimonia*) incorporeal beings of various sorts. In Greek literature they are minor deities or divinities. In Jewish and Christian literature, the term has pejorative connotations. 1 Enoch 19:1 identifies demons as the spirit powers revered as the gods of the nations. Thus here, in 1 Enoch 99:7, and in 1 Corinthians 10:19–21 (cf. 8:4–5), they are associated with idols and idolatry. The word, however, is not a generic designation for spirits who tempt people to sin. Often it is applied to evil spirits who cause sickness, especially mental disorder (cf. Josephus, *Ant.* 6.8.2:166; Luke 8:27). Josephus suggests that demons are the malevolent ghosts of wicked people (*War* 7.6.3:185).

The rabbinic literature offers a number of theories regarding the origin of demons: that they were created directly by God; that they are the offspring of Adam through Lilith or the children of Eve through male spirits; or that they are angels whom Satan led to rebel against God. Demons are seen primarily as workers of harm and are held responsible for diseases ranging from blindness to fever. Talmudic rabbis hold that the best protection against demons is observance of the law (B. Berakhot 5a) and, additionally, suggest as protection the wearing of phylacteries and fringes (*tzitzit*), affixing of a mezuzah to one's doorpost, and recitation of the daily prayers. In talmudic times, the common people used other talismans, in particular, pottery bowls on which were written magical formulas and which were buried in the corners or by the doorposts of homes.

De Mutatione Nominum the treatise *On the Change of Names* by Philo of Alexandria; its title is abbreviated as *Mut.* This work is an allegorical exegesis of Genesis 17:1–5 and 15–22. In this episode, Abram's and Sarai's names are changed; this account serves as the focus for a discussion of other name changes and their significance.

De Opificio Mundi the treatise *On the Creation of the World* by Philo of Alexandria; its title is abbreviated as *Opf.* This work is a version of Genesis 1–3, and especially of its creation accounts, but in Hellenistic terms. There are many parallels between Philo's treatise and the *Timaeus* of Plato.

De Plantatione the treatise *On Noah's Work as a Planter* by Philo of Alexandria; its title is abbreviated as *Plant.* The work's first part is a discussion of "planting" in a broad sense, including God's planting and mankind's imitation of it. The second part, relating to Noah's planting of a vineyard, looks at drunkenness as discussed by various philosophical schools.

De Posteritate Caini the treatise *On the Posterity and Exile of Cain* by Philo of Alexandria; its title is abbreviated as *Post.* This work provides an allegorical explanation of Genesis 4:16–25—the genealogy of Cain's descendants. The Hebrew etymology of the names is a key element in Philo's interpretation.

De Praemiis et Poenis the treatise *On Rewards and Punishments* by Philo of Alexandria; its title is abbreviated as *Praem.* Philo discusses his subject under the rubrics of individuals, houses, cities, countries, and larger regions. He also discourses on blessings and curses, following mainly those in Leviticus and Deuteronomy.

De Providentia the treatise *On Providence* by Philo of Alexandria; its title is abbreviated as *Prov.* This work is laid out as a dialogue between Philo and his nephew Julius Tiberius Alexander. Answering his nephew's objections and doubts, Philo argues that the world is governed by providence.

derash amplification or exegesis; *see also* MIDRASH

derekh eretz *see* WAY OF THE LAND

Derekh Eretz Rabbah (Heb., moral conduct, major [version]) a minor tractate included in editions of the Babylonian Talmud. Its eleven chapters begin with a discussion of forbidden marriages, including some maxims on marriage in general. This material is late, distinct from what follows and, as Elijah Gaon suggested, may belong with the tractate Kallah, on marriage, which precedes it. Chapter 2 purports to contain Tannaitic material, describing twelve classes of good and twelve classes of bad people, and then listing misdeeds that cause misfortune. It ends with mystical reflections on God and the 390 heavens. In the medieval period, chapter 3, concerning the origin and destiny of humankind, may have comprised the beginning of Derekh Eretz Rabbah, referred to under the title Perek Ben Azzai (see, e.g., Rashi on B. Berakhot 22a). Only in chapters 4 through 11, which cite only Tannaitic names, does the tractate turn exclusively to the theme of conduct. Chapters 4 and 5 contain rules of conduct for sages and their students, illustrated by events of the biblical and Tannaitic periods. Chapters 6 and 7 prove through several stories that one should never act differently from the people one is with. The same theme, focusing upon the individual's place in society, appears in chapters 8 and 9. Chapter 10 sets forth correct behavior for the bathhouse, and chapter 11 lists practices that are dangerous to human life and to the soul.

Derekh Eretz Zuta (Heb., moral conduct, minor [version]) a minor talmudic tractate, to be distinguished from Derekh Eretz Rabbah, comprising ethical teachings. The tractate contains nine chapters and a supplement, Perek haShalom (Section on peace). A different version appears in Halakhot Gedolot, in which the same material is divided into two sections, entitled Derekh Eretz Zuta (chaps. 5–8) and Derekh Eretz Rabbah (chaps. 1–4, 9). One of two manuscripts with the latter division designates chapters 1–4 as Yirat Ḥet (Fear of sin). A third division appears in the Maḥor Vitry, in which the first part of chapter 8 and all of chapter 9 have the title Darkan Shel Talmidei Ḥakhamim (the conduct of sages).

The text contains short maxims giving rules of conduct and exhortations to self-examination, piety, patience, and meekness. The organization appears to have been determined by the initial word of each maxim and by the number of maxims in each category. As a result, unrelated maxims often appear together, making it difficult to isolate the theme of each chapter. In general, the tractate begins with rules for the conduct of students of sages, continues with a series of admonitions directed at students, and concludes with diverse rules for the behavior of people in a range of professions. While the tractate may contain some old materials, especially in chapters 1–4, the work as a whole is clearly posttalmudic, probably deriving from the ninth century C.E.

De Sacrificiis Abelis et Caini the treatise *On the Sacrifices of Abel and Cain* by Philo of Alexandria; its title is abbreviated as *Sacr.* This work is an allegorical explanation of Genesis 4:2–4, which tells of the birth of Abel and the sacrifices of Cain and Abel.

De Sobrietate the treatise *On Sobriety* by Philo of Alexandria; its title is abbreviated as *Sobr.* This work is an allegorical exegesis of Genesis 9:24–27, in which Noah awakens from his drunkenness and curses Canaan. In Philo's interpretation, Ham represents potential evil; Canaan, evil in action; and Shem, generic good.

Desolating Sacrilege *see* ABOMINATION OF DESOLATION

De Somniis the treatise *On Dreams* by Philo of Alexandria; its title is abbreviated as *Somn.* This work is the second of Philo's two allegorical treatises on dreams, although the first work has evidently been lost. Philo discusses two dreams of Jacob and the many dreams in the Joseph story, including those of Joseph, the chief butler and baker, and Pharaoh.

De Specialibus Legibus the treatise *On the Special Laws* by Philo of Alexandria; its title is abbreviated as *Spec. Leg.* or *S.L.* In this treatise's four books Philo surveys much of the legal material of the Pentateuch in a somewhat systematic way. Because he also treats the Ten Commandments here, this work overlaps with his *De Decalogo.* Book 1 mentions the First and Second Commandments but is mainly about the Temple, its cult, and regulations concerning proper worship. Book 2 covers the Third, Fourth, and Fifth Commandments, and devotes much space to a discussion of the Fourth Commandment and its subsidiary topics—annual festivals and the Sabbath. Book 3 studies the Sixth and Seventh Commandments, which in the Septuagint concern adultery and murder, respectively. Under "adultery" Philo discusses a range of forbidden sexual acts, and under "murder" he considers such topics as the death penalty for particular sins, manslaughter, the cities of refuge, and violence in general. The first part of Book 4 covers the Eighth, Ninth, and Tenth Commandments, but then goes on to relate the four cardinal virtues to all of the commandments. The last part of Book 4 deals with the system of administering justice and, especially, with the appointment of judges. *See also* DE DECALOGO.

destruction (Heb. and Aram.: *a̱bad, e̱bad*; Gr.: *apollymi*) the destruction of the body at death or the punishment of the wicked after death. As Jewish beliefs in postmortem retribution developed, words that had described the disintegration of the human when the body died were applied to the ultimate destruction of the wicked. Thus, the term appears frequently in combination and contrast with "eternal life," a common expression for the ongoing reward of the righteous immediately after death, after the resurrection, or even beginning in this life (Ps. Sol. 3:11–12, 13:11, 14:9–10, 15:12–13; cf. Gal. 6:8). In effect, the expression means damnation. In texts that see eternal life as the present possession of the righteous, the normal term to describe the present state of the wicked is "death" rather than "destruction." Thus in John 5:24 the believer has passed from death to life, while in John 3:16, to perish is the future fate of those who do not believe and have eternal life.

The translations "destruction, destroy, perish" are perhaps deceptive because they suggest annihilation of the person. Such a notion is present in the Wisdom of Solomon 2:1–5, 5:9–14, but other texts envision ongoing torment in the fires of hell (1 En. 103:7–8). *See also* CORRUPTION; DEATH; IMMORTALITY, INCORRUPTION; LIFE, ETERNAL.

Deutero-Canonical Books *see* APOCRYPHA

Deuteronomistic History *see* FORMER PROPHETS

Deuteronomy Rabbah a homiletical midrash on Deuteronomy, comprising twenty-seven sections corresponding to the divisions of the Book of Deuteronomy found in the Palestinian triennial lectionary cycle. Despite the compilation's underlying literary structure, in printed editions, it is divided according to the eleven sections of Deuteronomy found in the yearly system of pentateuchal readings. The text's twenty-seven sections mostly follow the pattern of the typical Tanḥuma-Yelammedenu midrash, beginning with a legal question, introduced by: "[What is] the correct practice for a person of Israel . . . ? Thus our rabbis taught. . . ." In the ensuing exposition, the legal inquiry ultimately leads into a homily, normally introduced by: "This [previous point reflects] that which Scripture said." As is common in this type of composition, the homilies generally end with a message of consolation or statement of hope for the future messianic redemption.

In the medieval period, Deuteronomy Rabbah was alternatively known as Haggadat Eleh haDeḇarim Rabbah and Deḇarim Rabbati, in which names the terms "Eleh haDeḇarim" and "Deḇarim" are the Hebrew equivalents of "Deuteronomy." In later usage, the designation Rabbah (great) distinguishes the compilation from Deuteronomy Zuta (a "minor," or "small," midrashic treatment of Deuteronomy).

Two different versions of Deuteronomy Rabbah exist, apparently deriving from distinct versions of Tanḥuma-Yelamedenu Midrashim. One, represented in Deuteronomy Rabbah's printed edition, was known to scholars in France and Germany. This text is homogeneous in structure and language. The other version, of a less homogeneous character, was known in the Middle Ages to Spanish scholars. It is extant in the truncated Munich manuscript of Deuteronomy Rabbah (written in 1295 and published by S. Buber in 1895), in the complete manuscript of A. Epstein, and in the Oxford manuscript (published by S. Lieberman in 1940). The textual situation is additionally confused by considerable divergences among these manuscripts and by the existence of medieval quotations purporting to cite Deuteronomy Rabbah but containing materials absent from any existing version. Further, some medieval citations in the name of Tanḥuma or Yelamedenu contain materials found in one or another of the texts of Deuteronomy Rabbah.

Deuteronomy Rabbah cites the Tannaitic literature, the Talmud of the Land of Israel, Genesis Rabbah, Leviticus Rabbah, and, in the printed edition, Lamentations Rabbah. While the text exclusively cites authorities who lived earlier than the fifth century C.E., it appears to contain anti-Karaite polemics and, in the printed edition, homilies typical of the period after the Muslim conquest. Redaction accordingly should be dated to the ninth century C.E.

Deuteronomy, Targum to *see* PALESTINIAN TARGUMS; ONKELOS, TARGUM

Devarim Rabbah *see* DEUTERONOMY RABBAH

devil the chief evil spirit. This generic English designation derives from the old German equivalent of the Greek *diabolos* and usually translates that word in the New Testament and modern translations of the Pseudepigrapha. *Diabolos* is the normal translation of *satan* in the Greek translation of the Hebrew Bible and carries the connotations of both adversarial activity and (false) accusation. In the Apocalypse of Moses and the related Life of Adam and Eve, the opponent and tempter of the first parents is identified as the *diabolos* (Lat.: *diabolus*), and in the fragments of the Assumption of Moses, this figure strives with Michael for the body of Moses, accusing Moses of his sins. In the New Testament he is the tempter of Jesus (Matt. 4:1–11; Luke 4:1–13) and the accuser of the righteous (Rev. 12:7–12), and some passages define him with terms that emphasize his enmity and antagonism (Matt. 13:39; 1 Pet. 5:8–9). Remarkably, the Semitic *satan* occurs in the New Testament as often as *diabolos*.

Although common modern usage employs "the devil" as the normal term for the chief evil spirit, Jewish texts from the Graeco-Roman period employ a variety of expressions, which express different aspects of this figure, although in general they highlight his opposition to God or God's high angel and his malevolence to human beings. Among these terms are the following, in addition to *satan* and *diabolos*: Asael; Azazel; Beelzebul; Belial (death, the swallower); the Prince of Mastema (hostility); Melchiresha (king of wickedness; opposed to Melchizedek, king of righteousness); the Ruler of this World; Sammael (the deceitful angel who blinds, or the angel of death who poisons); Satanael; Shemiḥazah; the Spirit of Error (opposed to the spirit of truth). *See also* DEATH, PERSONIFIED; DEMONS; DUALISM; EVIL, ORIGINS OF; *and various figures mentioned herein*.

De Virtutibus the treatise *On the Virtues* by Philo of Alexandria; its title is abbreviated as *Virt.* This work is organized around four main headings: courage; humanity (*philanthropia*), which is the twin of piety; repentence (*metanoia*); and nobility.

De Vita Contemplativa the treatise *On the Contemplative Life* by Philo of Alexandria; its title is abbreviated as *Vita Con.* A portion of this treatise is devoted to a group known as the Therapeutai and is our only source of knowledge about that community. *See also* THERAPEUTAI.

De Vita Mosis the treatise *On the Life of Moses* by Philo of Alexandria; its title is abbreviated as *Vita Mos.* This work is an allegorical presentation of the life of Moses. Its first book focuses on Moses' life and deeds, and the second looks at his character under the rubrics of legislator, high priest, and prophet.

Dhu-Nawas Jewish king of Himyar, and the last independent king of Himyar, located in South Arabia and controlling the Straits of Aden. He was converted to Judaism sometime after 516 C.E. One source claims that he executed Byzantine merchants, responding to Byzantium's persecuting Jews. The Christian stories of his extermination of the Christian community of Najran may be exaggerated, for they seem to have served as a pretext for the Ethiopian invasion of Himyar. His attack on Najran most likely occurred after 523, between the two Ethiopian invasions. It appears that the Christian communities in Zafar and Najran, Yemen, acted as an Ethiopian fifth column. In the 520s, Dhu-Nawas sought help from al-Mundhir of Persia against the Ethiopians, who were supporting Byzantium. The Persians refused to help, and this led to Dhu-Nawas's defeat. When Dhu-Nawas was defeated in battle in 525, Ethiopia gained control of the country.

diaspora (Gr., scattered abroad) term designating Babylonian Jewry and its areas of settlement from the period of the Babylonian exile of 586 B.C.E. and on (see, e.g., Jer. 28:6; 2 Chron. 36:20). The meaning expanded to include all places outside of Palestine in which Jews lived. In the period following the destruction of the Second Temple (70 C.E.)—which marked the cessation of the sacrificial cult—and the failed Bar Kokhba Revolt (133–135 C.E.)—which marked the end of any Jewish hope for renewed political control over the promised land—rabbinic authorities grappled with the fact that Judaism in the foreseeable future would be a diaspora religion. The term *galut* (exiles) took on theological meaning. In the face of the devastating wars caused by attempts to regain Jewish political control, rabbinic leaders rejected the use of military means to effectuate a return to the promised land. At the same time, they continued to dream of an end to the exile, to be marked by the return of Israelite sovereignty over the Land of Israel, the rebuilding of the Temple, and the reinstitution of animal sacrifice. Unlike the prior political approach to these occurrences, seen, for instance, in the Bar Kokhba revolt, the rabbis increasingly envisioned these events in messianic terms, as brought about directly by God in response to the Jewish people's proving themselves worthy of redemption.

In line with this approach, the rabbis firmly expressed their larger view that the existence of the diaspora was undesirable, the result of the people's sin (see, e.g., Numb. Rabbah 7:10; M. Aḇot 5:9) and that the return of all Jews to the Land of Israel was the ultimate goal of Judaism (Gen. Rabbah 98:9). The Rabbis hold that the destruction of the First Temple and the Babylonian exile resulted from the people's engaging in idolatry, sexual licentiousness, and shedding innocent blood; the Second Temple was destroyed as a punishment for the people's increasing love of money and groundless hatred toward each other (B. Yoma 9b). Just as the diaspora was created as a divine punishment for the people's sins, so life in exile of itself constitutes an act of repentance (B. Berakhot 56a). In keeping with this negative attitude, the rabbis describe the suffering of life in exile as tantamount to all of the other suffering the people have endured combined (Sifrei Deut. 43). This suffering is so great that even God is understood to lament having had to respond to his people's sins by destroying the Temple and sending them into exile (B. Berakhot 3a).

The rabbis' negative attitude toward the diaspora is balanced by the creation of modes of piety and attitudes to allow the diaspora community to find meaning and closeness to God in their current life. Indeed, a central focus of the rabbinic movement is the creation of a Judaism that can be carried out independently of priestly activities and nationalistic aspirations. Additionally, even as the rabbis defined ritual and communal practices appropriate to a diaspora religion, they legitimated diaspora life by arguing that the Temple had never been the only place in which God could be found. God, rather, was everywhere (see, e.g., Lev. Rabbah 4:8 and B. Berakhot 10a). Even the question of whether God's presence had dwelled in the Second Temple at all was subject to debate (Pesikta Rabbati 160a). In keeping with an approach that lessened the centrality of the Temple in Jewish life, the rabbis imputed to a wide range of human activities the power previously granted only to sacrifice. Along with daily prayers corresponding to the prior sacrificial worship, the rabbis saw in acts of loving kindness and study of Torah direct replacements for animal offerings (see, e.g., Deut. Rabbah 5:3; M. A̱bot 3:2; and B. Shabbat 127a).

The Rabbis accordingly assured that, even in the diaspora, the people could enjoy fulfilling and productive lives. They rejected the ascetic response to the destruction of the Temple, which reduced people to a continual state of mourning, abstaining from meat, wine, and even from procreation (B. Ba̱ba Batra 60b). Instead, the rabbis encouraged a moderate path of limited mourning, to recognize what was lost but also to allow enjoyment of all that life in the diaspora offered. The rabbis went so far as to identify positive reasons for and consequences of exile, for example, in increasing the number of converts to Judaism (B. Pesaḥim 87b) and in making the name of the people of Israel great throughout the world (Song of Songs Rabbah 1:4).

Rabbinic Judaism thus provided a multifaceted response to the condition of exile. On the one hand, as a punishment for the people's sin, exile was viewed as temporary and a source of great suffering and degradation. On the other hand, the rabbis saw in the Diaspora the likely home of the majority of Jews and of Jewish life for the foreseeable future. Accordingly, they defined modes of Jewish existence and established a theological foundation that allowed diaspora Jews to make sense of and find meaning in productive and happy lives far from the promised land. *See also* EXILE.

Diasporanovelle German expression coined by modern scholars meaning "novel/romance of the diaspora [Jews]." A number of biblical and Jewish writings fall into this category. The theme is usually of a Jew in a Gentile environment, often with a high position in government, who falls into adversity but succeeds by faithfulness to God's law and divine help. Daniel is a classical example of this pattern. The Joseph story follows a somewhat different sequence of events, but the themes of obedience in an alien environment, adversity, and success are also there.

diatribe technical name of a rhetorical form (it became a loanword into English with a somewhat different meaning) derived originally from the Cynics. A diatribe was essentially a moral sermon, the aim of which was to convince its hearers to the point of changing their behavior. It was essentially dialogical in form, and it included such characteristics as rhetorical questions as well as answers to the objections of imaginary opponents. The oral form influenced some literary compositions, allegedly including those of Philo of Alexandria.

dictator (Lat., chief magistrate, leader [hence the English "dictator"]) In the Roman Republic the office of dictator was given to a leader in time of crisis. Originally, only a temporary authority was given to the dictator until the crisis was past; however, Julius Caesar was voted dictator for life.

dietary laws rules about food one may or may not eat and how certain foods are to be prepared. These derive from the Torah, which permits only fish that have fins and scales and animals that part the hoof and chew the cud (e.g., sheep and cows, but not camels or pigs). Animals must be ritually slaughtered (Heb.: *shehitah*), which involves a humane method of slaughter accompanied by a blessing of thanks. The Torah prohibits the eating of shellfish, worms, snails, flesh torn from a living animal, and certain other foods. Blood must be drained from meat before the meat may be eaten. Any mixture of meat and milk is forbidden; after eating meat, one may not eat dairy products for a period of time (one to six hours, depending on custom). Fish are neutral (Heb.: *pareve*). *See also* FOOD TABOOS; KOSHER.

dikaiosynē (Gr., righteousness, or justice) term widely used in religious literature. In the Graeco-Roman world, it was one of the four cardinal virtues. In Jewish compositions and translations in Greek, *dikaiosynē* was frequently the Greek equivalent of Hebrew and Aramaic *tzdk*.

Dikke (Arab.: ed-Dikke) ancient Jewish village and synagogue site just east of the Jordan and 4 kilometers north of the Sea of Galilee. A synagogue building made of fine limestone masonry once stood on a platform or raised terrace (the meaning of the site's name). The building faces west rather than south toward Jerusalem, which is explained by its location across the Jordan. It measured about 16 by 12 meters and was carefully finished and decorated on the exterior. A narrow porch stood in front. The interior space of the synagogue was divided into two side aisles and a rear aisle by six columns with debased Corinthian and Ionic capitals. Three doorways in the facade—a large central portal and two smaller doors on either side—gave entry to the worship space. One could also exit to the outside through a doorway in the synagogue's south wall. Five engaged pillars decorated the inner side of the facade and could support arches between the wall and columns or intercolumnar arches. Two tiers of benches were found on three walls of the interior space (the two sides and the back wall). External decorations in relief include vine motifs, but the central portal was surmounted by a pair of genii or victories holding a wreath. There also appears a second wreath behind the genii. Other patterns include egg and dart, grapevines, and meanders, especially on window fragments. The usual suggested date for the building is third century C.E.

Dimi Palestinian amora of the fourth century C.E., known as "the traveler to Babylonia." He ultimately settled in Babylonia, where, at Pumbedita, he transmitted Palestinian traditions. He is known also as Abudimi and Abdimi.

Dimi of Nehardea frequently cited Babylonian amora of the fourth century C.E.; head of the academy at Pumbedita in 385–388. Besides his status as a scholar, he appears to have been a produce merchant (B. Ba<u>b</u>a Batra 22a).

din (Heb.) a law or a lawsuit

dina de-malkuta dina (Aram., the law of the state is the law) legal edict attributed to the talmudic rabbi Samuel in the third century C.E., requiring that Jews accept the law of their Persian host nation at points where Persian law conflicts with Jewish civil or criminal practice (but not religious duties). In the Babylonian Talmud, Samuel's pronouncement is applied in particular to real estate law. Rabbah (Ba<u>b</u>li Ba<u>b</u>a Batra 55a) reports that, in line with Samuel's dictum, land may be acquired only through a deed; the rabbinic practice of gaining ownership through tenancy is deemed inoperative since, following Persian law, such acquisition would be complete only after forty years.

Dinah daughter of Jacob and Leah, raped by Shechem (Gen. 34). In the Book of Judith she symbolizes Israel ravaged by Assyria. The Testament of Job has her married to Job. According to several midrashim, Asenath, the Egyptian priest's daughter who married Joseph (Gen. 41:45), is identified as Dinah's daughter by Shechem, but a Jew by virtue of her maternal lineage.

Diocaesarea *see* SEPPHORIS

Dio Cassius (c. 160–230 C.E.) Roman writer (in Greek); wrote a *History of Rome* from its beginnings to 229 C.E. Although not of the first rank among ancient historians, his work is nonetheless valuable in that he made use of such authors as Tacitus, whose writings have been partially lost; however, Dio's own work survives only in part or in a medieval epitome (summary). He is especially important for events of the first century B.C.E. and first century C.E. His references to Jewish history and religion are an important supplement to Josephus. He shows no particular hostility to the Jews or their customs, even though he sometimes finds their actions inexplicable (e.g., allowing Jerusalem to be captured because of refusal to fight on the Sabbath). He does not accuse the Jews of misanthropy, which many writers do, even though he sees their customs as the opposite of those of most other peoples. He tells us that Archelaus had the name Herod, as coins confirm. Jewish attempts at proselytization in Rome during the reign of Tiberius are mentioned. His account of the siege of Jerusalem notes that some Roman soldiers actually deserted to the Jewish side. Many other details of value for Jewish history are also given by him.

Diocletian Roman emperor (r. 284–305 C.E.). While serving as the commander of Emperor Numerian's bodyguards, he was chosen by the army to be emperor upon Numerian's death. Diocletian devoted a good deal of his time leading battles on the empire's frontiers and putting down revolts. In 293 he established the tetrarchy by which he ruled in the East, with Galerius's help, and Maximian was emperor in the West with the aid of Constantius Chlorus. The tetrarchy provided both parts of the empire with a strong ruler and created a system of nonhereditary succession. To enhance the emperor's stature, Diocletian adopted many of the trappings of the eastern rulers. In order to create a better mechanism for managing the empire, Diocletian divided many of the provinces into smaller administrative units. Also, he separated the military from the civil authorities by removing control of the army from the civil rulers. He introduced a new system of taxation, based on a unit of land and a human unit, which was revised every fifteen years. Diocletian supported the old Roman religion and traditions, and he worked hard to ensure that Roman law was followed in the provinces. He oversaw a persecution of the Christians in 303.

Unlike many of the other provinces, Palestine was enlarged, rather than divided. The area between Idumea and the Red Sea and Moab south of the Arnon River were removed from Arabia and joined to Palestine. This change allowed the defense of the southern border to be under the jurisdiction of one province instead of two. While we have little information about the civil administration of Palestine, we do know more about Diocletian's fiscal policies in the province. Boundary stones of a number of villages in the Galilee indicate that a land survey was carried out. It was necessitated by Diocletian's reform, which converted the *annona* into a regularly collected tax in kind. Diocletian visited Palestine at least twice while he was emperor, the first to do so since Caracalla. In 286 he stayed in Tiberias long enough to issue several decrees, and this visit may be the basis for stories in the Palestinian Talmud about the emperor. One story claims that late one Friday, Diocletian sent a message ordering the patriarch and another rabbi to appear before him early on Sunday. The rabbis were miraculously transported before the emperor, so that they avoided desecrating the Sabbath or angering the ruler. While he was oppressing Paneas, according to another rabbinic account, the people threatened to leave the province, but their threat was discounted by one of the emperor's advisers. In another passage Yoḥanan fails to condemn a member of a priestly family who was so anxious to see the emperor that he took a short cut and knowingly became ritually impure. Finally, one reference in the Palestinian Talmud, reflecting on Diocletian's persecution of the Christians, claims that the Jews were the only nation that the emperor did not force to pour out libations to the Roman deities.

Diodorus Siculus Greek historian and compiler of the first century B.C.E. (fl. c. 60–30 B.C.E.). He wrote a universal history to the time of Caesar's Gallic wars. Although he was more of a compiler than a critical historian, his work is sometimes the main source for the history of certain periods. The quality varies considerably, of course, depending on his source at any one time. His work is especially important as general background for history in the Persian and Hellenistic periods. He makes a number of references to Jews and Judaism, especially in Hasmonean times and at the time of Pompey's conquest. Unfortunately, it is often not possible to identify the source of his statements about the Jews. Some of them come from Hecataeus of Abdera, but others are unidentified. He ascribes the origins of the Jews to colonizing by the Egyptians (pointing to the common practice of circumcision). Moses took his laws from the god known as Iao. The wonders of the Dead Sea are described. He also relates that when Antiochus IV entered the Temple, he found a statue of a man seated on an ass with a book in his arms, a story that recurs in other writers.

dioikētēs (Gr., governor, administrator) Under the Ptolemies, the term was especially used to refer to the finance minister, who was the overall financial director of the entire Ptolemaic Empire. Very well known from the Zenon Papyri is Apollonius, who was *dioikētēs* about the middle of the third century B.C.E.; Zenon was one of his agents.

Dionysus worship, Judaism associated with Dionysus was a Greek god of emotion and fertility, as well as wine; his Roman equivalent was Bacchus. Dionysus was worshiped with orgiastic rituals, including uncontrolled and lawless behavior. This is vividly described in *The Bacchae,* a play by Euripides in which a man is torn apart alive by a frenzied group of female worshipers. Judaism is described as Dionysus worship by several Graeco-Roman writers. The exact reason is unclear but seems to be connected to Jupiter Sabazios, who was identified with Dionysus. Perhaps the name Sabazios was associated with the epithet Sabaoth, which was associated with God; possibly it was even associated with the word "sabbath." Especially important is the discussion by Plutarch in his *Convivial Questions,* where he describes the procession at the Feast of Tabernacles as a celebration in honor of Dionysus. He points especially to the parading with the *thyrsus,* to the dress of the high priest, and to the blowing of small trumpets. Plutarch also connects "sabbath" with the name Sabi, which referred to worshipers of Dionysus and points to the use of wine on the Sabbath. Tacitus, however, denies rather indignantly any connection. *See also* THYRSUS.

Dios name of a Macedonian month; appears in a number of Jewish sources, such as the writings of Josephus. Unfortunately, there was not a uniform usage; sometimes it corresponded to the Hebrew month of Tishri (September/October) and sometimes to Ḥeshvan (October/November).

Diospolis *see* LOD

disciple of a sage (Heb.: *talmid ḥakham*) member of the rabbinical aristocracy, characterized by comprehensive knowledge of the Bible and all of rabbinic law, by proper deportment learned by serving under a sage (B. Berakhot 47b), and by piety in all behaviors (B. Yoma 72b). The *talmid ḥakham* was exempt from taxation and received preferential treatment in the allocation of communal benefits, for example, having precedence in being redeemed should he be taken captive. So long as the *talmid ḥakham* devoted himself to study, the community held him in the highest respect and provided for his personal needs.

disciples of Jesus those who follow Jesus; the broad category includes such figures as the women who supported him (Luke 8:1–3) and even crowds (Luke 6:17). Luke distinguishes from these many twelve "apostles," who witnessed Jesus' activities from the beginning of his ministry. Matthew 10:2–4, Mark 3:16–19, Luke 6:13–16, and Acts 1:13 list twelve special disciples, but the names vary. Among these are Galilean fishermen (Peter, Andrew, James, John), a tax collector (Matthew in the First Gospel; Levi in Mark); a Zealot (Simon the Cananaean); and Judas Iscariot. The number twelve recollects the twelve tribes of Israel. Mark's disciples frequently misunderstand Jesus; rehabilitated in the other Synoptics, they become models of higher righteousness and the expediters of the Gentile mission. Only John includes the "beloved disciple" (variously identified as the evangelist; a composite; ideal follower; or, less likely, Lazarus) and Nathanael. Jesus' disciples in all the Gospels serve as foils to other groups of disciples: of John the Baptist, of the Pharisees, and even of Moses (Matthew 9:14, 11:2; Luke 11:1; John 1:35). Paul indicates that Peter and John, along with Jesus' brother James, became pillars of the Jerusalem church (Gal. 2:9); the Acts of the Apostles offers some details on these figures as well as on the death of James, the son of Zebedee (Acts 12:2). Fanciful accounts in the Apocryphal Acts portray the fates of the other disciples.

discipline to reprove someone for the purpose of correcting them. Jewish literature, especially texts in the wisdom tradition, describes that activity by which God afflicts Israel or individuals in order to get them to change their ways that they may receive God's blessing. The two principle verbs in the Hebrew Bible are *yasar* and *nakkah* (smite), which are generally translated in the Septuagint by Greek *paideuō* (teach, hence discipline) and *mastigoō* (to scourge). The verbs "chasten" and "chastise," which derive from the Latin meaning to cleanse or correct, appear in some English versions.

Proverbs 3:11 likens God's chastening to the action of a father, who reproves the child in whom he delights; the Septuagint employs both Greek verbs. The Book of Tobit pairs the verbs "scourge" and "have mercy" to explain how and why God smites Tobit, the righteous one (who, however, is not perfect) and afflicts Israel, whose sin has resulted in exile (3:9; 11:15; 13:2, 5, 9). The Psalms of Solomon convey the same idea by means of the Greek noun *paideia* (7:9, 10:2, 13:9, 14:1) but also uses the verb "cleanse" (Gr.: *katharizō*), a term with cultic connotations, to describe the chastening function of God's scourging of the righteous (10:1–2).

The notion of divine discipline and chastisement is also used to distinguish between the divine Judge's dealings with Israel (or the righteous) and the nations. God disciplines so that Israel or the righteous will not pile up sins, but seek forgiveness. Conversely, God withholds punishment from the nations so that they increase the measure of their sins and hence earn terrible and final punishment (Ps. Sol. 13:7; 2 Macc. 6:12–16; 2 Bar. 13:10–12).

A number of New Testament passages employ the notion of divine discipline or chastisement (1 Cor. 11:32; 2 Cor. 6:9; Titus 2:12; Heb. 12:5–7, quoting Prov. 3:11–12).

disease and sickness In the law, historical books, and Prophets, disease and sickness are regarded as being sent by God on those of his people who are guilty of moral failure or ritual impurity and on those non-Israelites who seek to thwart God's purpose for his people. Disobedience on the part of Israel will result in their being afflicted with incurable "boils, ulcers, scurvy, itch," in "madness, blindness, and confusion of mind." Their exposed corpses will serve as food for vultures and wild animals (Deut. 28:15–29). Any members of the covenant community who rebel against God and his rules for his people are warned to "end their complaints, or else they will die" (Num. 17:10–13).

The prophet Zechariah sees the coming day of judgment that is to fall on disobedient Jerusalem as including panic that will overtake horses and madness that will seize the riders (Zech. 12:3–5). The day of doom that Ezekiel foretells will fall on Israel "because of their iniquity" (Ezek. 13–16) will result in military attack from without ("the sword is outside") and "famine and pestilence" for those within the city of Jerusalem. A similar warning about death of the disobedient through "sword, famine, and pestilence" is given in Jeremiah 21:1–7, although now the prediction of exile in Babylonia is also included as part of God's judgment on disobedient Israel.

On the other hand, if God's people are fully obedient to his will and laws, then God will remove from them "every illness." The diseases will be laid instead "on all who hate" his people (Deut. 7:15). In the story in Exodus of Israel's escape from slavery in Egypt, one of the ten plagues that God sends on the Egyptians for their refusal to free the people of Israel is "festering boils on humans and animals" (Exod. 9:10). A prime example of this divine punitive action against the enemies of Israel or those who violate Israel's special relationship with God appears in 1 Samuel 5:6–6:19, where the account is given of the Philistines' capture of the ark of God and their placing it at Ashdod in the shrine of one of their local deities, Dagon. God's action was to smite the people of Ashdod with tumors, as well as the people of the other Philistine cities where the ark was taken. Only when they sent the ark back into Israelite territory, complete with golden images of the tumors as a guilt offering, was the plague relieved.

The fullest presentation of the links between moral failure, ritual impurity, and disease is offered in Leviticus 13–15. There the disease and its symptoms, described in detail in Leviticus 13–14, indicate some kind of skin ailment—inaccurately identified in most translations as leprosy. Whatever the disease is, the priests who examine its victims look for various symptoms by which they can pronounce whether the afflicted person is "clean" or "unclean" (13:13–14). For example, if the color of the hair changes or if baldness occurs, these are signs of uncleanness, but if black hair has grown back, then the individual is clean (13:30–42). The bodily discharges described in Leviticus 15 are sex-related and may be symptoms of gonorrhea or some other venereal disease. In any case, the link between moral behavior and punishment in the form of bodily affliction is clear.

The jealousy toward Moses on the part of his brother, Aaron, and his sister, Miriam, is punished by God's sending a skin disease (leprosy?) on her (Num. 12:1–10). A similar catastrophe falls on King Azariah of Judah (2 Kings 15), who is punished by God for his failure to remove the high places where Israelites are worshiping other gods and to prohibit the people from sacrificing to these false deities. Because he did not stop these idolatrous practices, Azariah is stricken with some kind of skin disease and must live "in a separate house" in order to avoid polluting the royal residence and those who would have contact with him there. 2 Chronicles 26:16–21 gives an even more vivid report of God's striking Uzziah (Azariah) with this dread skin disease as a consequence of his having entered the temple of Yahweh and made an offering there—a role that only priests should carry out. During the reign of an unnamed king of Israel, the king of Aram (Syria) sends the commander of his army, Naaman, to the king of Israel so that he might be cured of his "leprosy" (2 Kings 5:1–19). The king is shocked at the suggestion that he could perform the cure, since he believes only God can "give death or life." However, Elisha the prophet instructs Naaman to wash in the Jordan, which he does with great reluctance, and he is indeed cured.

The one who suffers from sickness and death sent by God is not always the one who committed the wicked act. After David committed adultery with Bathsheba and she was pregnant with his child, he arranged for her husband, Uriah the Hittite, to be killed (2 Sam. 11) and then took her as one of his wives. Denounced by the prophet Nathan for what he had done, David confessed his sin, but when the child was born to Bathsheba, it was gravely ill. The child died within a week despite David's contrition and petitions to God to spare his son (2 Sam. 12).

In Israel's prophetic tradition, especially in Jeremiah, sickness is used as a metaphor for the people's failure to maintain a right relationship with God through full obedience to the law. The perverse nation looks for "healing, but there is terror instead" (Jer. 8:15, 14:19). The coming of the exile to Babylon evokes the cry, "My wound is severe" (Jer. 10:19); "my pain is unceasing, my wound incurable, refusing to be healed" (15:18). "Your hurt is incurable; there is no medicine for your wound, no healing for you" (30:12–13, 46:11). While there is hope for the healing of God's people through an agent whom he will send (Mal. 4:2), Babylon is beyond healing (Jer. 51:9). The prophet Hosea (5:13) tells his people that the vain attempt of the northern tribes of Israel to strengthen their position ("sickness") by an alliance with the Assyrians had shown that the Assyrian king "was not able to cure you or heal your wound." Likewise, the prophet Nahum informs Nineveh, the capital of Assyria, that "there is no assuaging your hurt: your wound is mortal" (Nah. 3:19).

In 1 Samuel 15–16, God punishes the disobedience of Israel's first king, Saul, who had encouraged the people to offer sacrifices to him rather than to God alone; God sends an "evil spirit" that seizes and torments him (16:14). When David plays his lyre in Saul's hearing, the king is temporarily relieved and the evil spirit departs for a time (16:23). In the Book of Job, however, YHWH allows Satan to afflict Job with "loathsome sores from the sole of his foot to the crown of his head" (2:1–8) in order to test Job's integrity and the firmness of his trust in God. The disease is not identified, but its symptoms are described. They include "flesh clothed with worms and dirt, skin that hardens and breaks out again" (Job 7:5). But Job also has terrifying visions (7:14), and his skin turns black and he is overcome by burning heat (30:30). Once Job has passed the test, however, his health is restored and he lives 120 more years (42:16–17).

The role of Satan as the one who actually causes the illnesses of humans, which is probably Iranian in origin, develops more fully in the Jewish literature of the second and first centuries B.C.E. as a major feature in accounting for ailments and in dealing with them. In Jubilees, where the story of Noah is being retold (10:1–6), it is the demons who are not only leading astray his children, but also blinding and killing them. Noah is taught how to heal these illnesses by the use of herbs. Similarly, when in 1 Enoch 6–11 the angels take wives from among earthly women, one of their first efforts is to teach these women "magical medicine, incantations, the cutting of roots, and . . . about plants" (7:1). These are the techniques through which diseases and sickness are to be overcome.

In the Dead Sea Scrolls, it is evil spirits sent by God that cause human sickness. A prime example of this occurs when Pharaoh takes Sarai from Abraham and wants to kill him (1QapGen 20). In response to Abraham's prayer to God, "the Most High God sent an evil spirit to scourge" Pharaoh and "all his household." All the magicians and all the healers of Egypt are called in to remedy Pharaoh's ailment, but none of them can cure him. Instead, they also fall under the scourge and flee. Pharaoh is told that if he restores Sarai to Abraham, "this scourge and this spirit of festering will vanish from you." So Abraham prayed for him, laid his hands on Pharaoh's head, and the evil spirit departed from him and he regained his life and health. Similarly, in the Prayer of Nabonidus (4QPrNab), the king reports how, when he was stricken with an ulcer, an exorcist pardoned his sins and effected a cure.

In Philo's treatise *On the Contemplative Life* (chap. 2), he notes that the Essenes were famed for the cures of "souls oppressed with grievous and well-nigh incurable diseases, inflicted by pleasures and desires and griefs and fears, by acts of covetousness, folly injustice and the countless host of other passions and vices." Josephus, in his *Antiquities* (8.136), notes that the Essenes combine several modes of cures for human diseases: "They display an extraordinary interest in the writings of the ancients, singling out in a particular way those which make for the welfare of the soul and the body; with the help of these, and with a view to the treatment of diseases, they make investigation into medical roots and the properties of stones." Thus important features of medicine are present in the Essene methods of treating diseases.

It suits well the other evidence from Jewish sources that when Jesus performs healings and exorcisms in the Gospel accounts, he is accused by his critics of being in league with Beelzebul, one of the names for Satan or the prince of evil powers (Mark 3:22). To this accusation, Jesus responds by claiming that he expels demons "by the finger of God" (Luke 11:20), or that it is by the power of the Holy Spirit of God that he accomplishes his cures (Matt. 12:22–32). Sickness has become a metaphor not only for the disobedience of God's people and their alienation from God, but for the hidden yet powerful presence of the forces of evil in the life of humanity.

In some texts, the Talmudic rabbis follow the approach to sickness and disease familiar from the Hebrew scriptures and Hellenistic Judaism, holding that sickness represents divine punishment for sin. The Talmud states that a sick person cannot recover until all of his or her sins have been forgiven. Such recovery is a greater miracle than Hananiah, Mishael, and Azariah being saved from the furnace (Dan. 3), since, while they were saved from a human fire, illness is a fire made by God (B. Nedarim 41a). God brings suffering on those who can study Torah but do not (B. Berakhot 5a); observance of the law and study of Torah, by contrast, lead to health (Mekhilta Vayassa 1; B. Ketubot 103a).

Alongside these theological explanations for disease, rabbinic texts much more frequently view illness as the consequence of natural processes or the result of people's failure to take proper care of themselves. The rabbis hold that, on account of communicable diseases, one should not share a drinking cup or take a bite from a piece of bread and return it to the serving plate (T. Berakhot 5:8–9). Similarly, numerous rabbinic texts list folk remedies appropriate for specific ailments (see, e.g., B. Shabbat 109b; Pesikta deRab Kahana 18:4; B. Baba Metzia 107b). In line with this understanding of disease, the rabbis insist upon the importance of visiting the sick (B. Gittin 61a; B. Nedarim 41a), which God himself is understood to have done when he appeared to Abraham at the oaks of

Mamre (Gen. 18:1; B. Sotah 14a). Rather than being condemned as sinners, those who are ill require and deserve the sympathy and comfort that will help relieve their suffering.

Diskarta Babylonian town on the river Diala, northeast of Baghdad. The city was home to two rabbis, Judah and Ḥuna of Diskarta, suggesting that a fair-sized Jewish community existed there in Sassanid times. The name Diskarta is from the Persian *das* (district) and the Aramaic *karta* (town). In the Talmud the term sometimes means a town in general. In nontalmudic sources, the place-name is given as Daskara.

dispersion *see* DIASPORA

dissimulation the use of lying or deception as a means of protecting oneself from religious persecution. When their Judaism has been persecuted, often the only worthwhile defense for Jews has been to practice dissimulation. For example, under extreme duress some Jewish communities converted to Christianity outwardly but continued to carry on their Judaism secretly. The justification for religious dissimulation can already be found in the Hebrew Bible (e.g., 1 Sam. 16:1–2). Because Judaism was normally tolerated in the Graeco-Roman period, there are few, if any, examples of Jewish dissimulation before the Christian dominance of the Roman Empire. The only early true persecution of Judaism took place briefly under Antiochus IV, but the stories preserved emphasize the Jews' faithfulness to God even to death, and not their dissimulation. Under Christianity, we know of examples of Jews who converted or denied their Judaism publicly but maintained it privately; the Marranos of Spain and Portugal are a well-known example of this behavior (beginning in the fourteenth century).

divination the attempt to gain knowledge of the future by the use of certain mechanical and often secret techniques. It was widely practiced in the ancient Near East and in the Graeco-Roman world. In Mesopotamia a major form of divination was the inspection of the internal organs generally (*ectispicy*) or the liver particularly (*hepatoscopy*) of a sacrificial animal. Despite official opposition to divination in Judaism in such passages as Deuteronomy 18, various forms of it were found. The one recognized form was the priestly manipulation of the Urim and Thummim. Although the precise form of these is nowhere defined, they seem to have functioned as some sort of casting of lots. On the popular level, other forms of divination seem to have been widespread. Although Saul had theoretically rid the country of witches, he had no problem finding one when required (1 Sam. 28). David consulted the ephod, which also seems to have given a "yes" or "no" answer to questions. The long list of practices prohibited in Deuteronomy 18 suggests that most or all of these types of divination were in fact used. Even Joseph was said to have used his cup for divination purposes (Gen. 44:5).

divorce Deuteronomy 24:1–4 states that a man can divorce his wife for "something shameful" (see Josephus, *Ant.* 4.253 and *Life* 76, on his own divorce). The Elephantine Papyri include women's right to sue for divorce (see also Mark 10:12). Limiting these various rights, the Qumran scrolls (e.g., CD 13.17; 4QDb18.2.5) appear to eliminate remarriage after divorce. Mark 10:2–12 (followed by Luke 16:18) records Jesus' forbidding divorce on the basis of Genesis 2:22–24 and in contradistinction to Deuteronomy. Matthew 5:31–32 and 19:3–9 permit divorce only in cases of *porneia* (indecent acts or, more likely, Gentile marriages that would under Jewish law be considered incestuous). The Gospels add that a divorced individual could not remarry. The effect of the Gospel legislation remains debated: some argue that it prevented the abuse of women; others that it trapped women in abusive relationships; still others that it was originally meant to be a temporary condition ended by the eschaton. Paul permits separation only if both partners agree (1 Cor. 7:10–11, 15, 17).

In rabbinic Judaism divorce is effected through a writ, called a *get,* which the husband transmits to his wife. Both husband and wife must be of sound mind for the transaction to be valid and must act of their own free will. In cases where there is not mutual consent to the divorce, a rabbinic court may recommend or compel one in response to a demand by either the wife or husband. Grounds for divorce typically include physical problems that prevent a conjugal life, the claim that one party or the other is the cause of childlessness, either party's failure to engage in sexual relations, infidelity, or conduct against the commandments. *See also* GITTIN; INCEST; MARRIAGE.

dog As a metaphor, "dog" is a humiliating label for those apart from or enemies of the covenant community (1 Sam. 17:43; Ps. 22:16; Prov. 26:11, cited by 2 Pet. 2:33; Matt. 7:6; 15:26; Mark 7:27). However, dogs are portrayed positively in the Book of Tobit (6:2; 11:4); in Joseph and Asenath 10:13 (Asenath is concerned that her pets also eat kosher food); and in the domestic analogy presented in Matthew 15:27 and Mark 7:28.

dolphin minor motif in Roman and Byzantine Jewish art. Generally the dolphin is depicted with a beak, so it is not confused with other sea creatures. More than two dozen dolphins are depicted on ceiling tiles in the Dura Europas synagogue in Mesopotamia, and both pairs of dolphins and individual dolphins appear in Palestinian Jewish art of the Roman period. For example, in the Jewish catacombs of Beth Shearim two dolphins flank a wreath and shell on two sarcophagi. In the mosaic floor at Beth Shearim catacomb 11, four dolphins are used to fill the corners of a square. Since the dolphin is so popular a motif in Graeco-Roman art, including coins of Caesarea Maritima, it is no surprise that it appears in Jewish art of the period.

domain, public or private publicly or privately owned areas. The distinction between these types of property is important in rabbinic law, which, on the Sabbath, prohibits carrying anything except the clothing one wears between private and public domains or from one person's domain into that of another (T. Shabbat 1:3). The distinction also has importance under the laws of damages, since one's actions on his own private property in many instances are shielded from claims of negligence. For instance, unless his property is open to public domain, an individual is not liable for damage caused by a pit he digs on it.

Domitian (51–96 C.E.) Roman emperor (r. 81–96 C.E.). Vespasian's younger son, he became emperor upon the death of his elder brother Titus, whom some claimed he had poisoned. For the first eight years of his reign, he was a firm but fair ruler; however, from Lucius Antonius Saturninus's rebellion in 88, Domitian progressively became more harsh and ruthless. Domitian gathered sufficient power to eventually determine the composition of the Senate. He rarely sought the advice of the Senate, preferring instead to consult with his body of advisers composed of both senators and wealthy non-senators, *equites*. He was an able administrator of the empire, selecting competent governors and dismissing bad ones. His system of taxation was harsh, but fair. He worked diligently to improve the level of public morality by strictly enforcing the laws against immorality. However, Domitian received a good deal of criticism during his reign for his licentious lifestyle, his suppression of the Senate, his attempt to impose Greek standards on the Romans, and his virtual assumption of divine honors by accepting the trappings of the oriental monarch for himself. By the end of his rule Domitian had instituted a reign of terror, which culminated in his murder; the conspirators included his wife and seem to have had the tacit approval of Nerva, his successor.

Suetonius states that Domitian rigorously administered the Jewish tax, prosecuting those who followed the Jewish way of life without formally converting or those who concealed their Judaism in order to avoid paying the levy. It appears that while Vespasian had taxed only practicing Jews and converts, Domitian extended the tax to those who practiced Judaism without being circumcised or otherwise converting, perhaps a reference to Jewish Christians. Dio reports that in 95 Domitian executed his cousin Flavius Clemens and in 91 his consul Glabrio, both for atheism, a charge that Dio claims was made against those of the Roman nobility who favored Judaism. If we accept Dio's comment, it seems that by the end of Domitian's reign atheism was equivalent to treason, and converting to Judaism was a form of atheism. Any rejection of the state religion was regarded as treason because it challenged Domitian's claim to be a deity. While the Jews were still allowed to practice their own customs and were not forced into the state cult, converts were a different matter. The matter is unclear, however, because Suetonius refers to the executions of Clemens and Glabrio without referring to atheism or Judaism. Some later Christian writers have claimed that there was an organized Jewish disturbance in Palestine during Domitian's reign, but there is virtually no evidence to support this. According to Christian sources, Domitian's desire to limit the spread of Judaism led to his resentment of Christianity. According to Christian sources, Domitian is compared to Nero in his persecutions of the early Church. However, contemporary Christian sources provide little evidence for persecutions under Domitian.

Domitianus bishop of Melitene (582–602 C.E.) and brother of the Byzantine emperor Mauricius. He forcibly baptized the Jews and Samaritans in his diocese from 590 to 592. John of Nikiu, the Egyptian who informs us of this event, complained that these Jews were only Christian hypocrites. Nevertheless, Domitianus continued to force the clergy under his control to admit them to ecclesiastical functions. Domitianus's activity may be part of Mauricius's general policy toward the Jews. An ancient source reports that a Jew of Antioch insulted an image of the Virgin, whereupon Mauricius expelled all the Jews from the city.

Domitilla, Flavia niece of the Roman emperor Domitian and wife of Flavius Clemens, the emperor's cousin. In 95 C.E., Domitian executed Clemens and exiled Domitilla to Pandateria on charges of atheism. Dio Cassius claims that the charge against both of them was related to their adoption of Judaism, implying that conversion to Judaism was a criminal offense, for which the penalty was death or confiscation of property. He also pictures Domitilla and Clemens as two of many who were condemned for practicing Judaism. Some fourth-century Christian writers claim that Domitilla converted to Christianity, but these assertions are unfounded.

Dor biblical city on the coast of Israel and south of Mount Carmel, also known as Dora. During the Persian period, a Phoenician inscription attests to Phoenician rule at Dor. The Greek writers thought Dor was founded by Sidonians, but there may indeed have been a Greek colony at Dor, a Greek trading center. Dor was a strong city in the Hellenistic period, since it withstood an attack of the Seleucid army under the command of Antiochus III (the Great). It was also a major commercial center, as excavations reveal a shopping strip or emporium at the sea shore. In the archaeological remains there are many pieces of Attic red-figured wares, indicating that Dor was a major entry point for such wares into Palestine. The Jewish king Alexander Jannaeus took Dor near the beginning of his reign about 103 B.C.E. At the arrival of Rome in 63 B.C.E., Dor was awarded autonomy and the right to mint its own coins. Portions of a major Roman theater have been excavated in the northern part of the city. A strong Jewish community was present at Dor in the second half of the first century C.E. In the Byzantine period at least one church was built at Dor, which has been excavated, but no synagogue ruins are yet known. The city declined until the Arab conquest of Palestine in 640 C.E.

Dor, Cliff of location on the Mediterranean coast, north of Kisrin, referred to at T. Shebiit 4:11 as demarcating a border area of the Land of Israel

Dora site referred to at B. Berakhot 31a: "R. Mordecai accompanied R. Shimi b. Ashi from Hageronia to Be-Kipi, and some say, to Dora" (some manuscripts read Be-Dura). The town's location is unknown. *For the coastal city of Dora, see* DOR.

Dosa Palestinian amora, also known as Dosai, apparently of the fourth century C.E. He is infrequently cited in the Jerusalem Talmud and midrashic literature.

Dositheans group of separatists within Samaritanism beginning in the first century B.C.E. and continuing until the fourteenth century C.E. Jewish, Samaritan, and Christian sources speak of the Dositheans in very contradictory ways, creating confusion in the dating of their origins, raising the possibility of more than one Dositheus, and describing alternative beliefs and practices.

The destruction of the Samaritan holy place on Mount Gerizim in 128 B.C.E. created conditions favorable to separatism, particularly a schism between a lay oriented and a priestly oriented Samaritanism that some liken to the split between the Pharisees and the Sadducees within Judaism. The lay movement was focused in the first century C.E. by Dositheus. There are no clear details of his life. Many traditions decribe him as an associate of Simon Magus who appears in Acts 8 in the New Testament. Some traditions affirm that Dositheus did not die, but went directly to heaven, and most groups of Dositheans affirmed resurrection earlier than other forms of Samaritanism. The Dositheans used water extensively in their worship, both for ritual immersion and as a significant place to pray. They modified the dietary laws, and later Dositheans were vegetarians. They accepted the same calendar as the Qumran sect, with twelve thirty-day months to restore the "original" solar calendar, so their feast dates differed from orthodox Samaritanism. Removed from Mount Gerizim, the Dositheans discontinued blood sacrifices. They resisted the orthodox move to avoid pronouncing the divine name, YHWH. Periodic serious quarrels broke out between Dositheans and orthodox Samaritans.

Shared adversity worked toward the healing of the schism between the Dositheans and the orthodox Samaritans. In the fourth century C.E., when the Samaritan community was in serious decline both in numbers and in spirit, Baba Rabbah (whom many regard as a Dosithean) arose to fire the will of the community, mend its fractures and inspire the writing of its liturgy and theology. The work of Amram Darah and Markah ensued. A parallel movement took place in the fourteenth century when the community was dwindling in the wake of the Crusader onslaughts. The high priest, Pinḥas, healed the schism between the orthodox Samaritans and the Dositheans, thus inspiring a new surge in liturgical writing and a recording of Samaritan history represented in the work of Abul Fath.

Dositheus b. Judah *see* DOSTAI B. JUDAH

Dositheus b. Yannai *see* DOSTAI B. YANNAI

Dositheus of Kefar Yatma *see* DOSTAI OF KEFAR YATMA

Dostai b. Judah Tannaitic authority; a contemporary of Judah the Patriarch in the late second century C.E. He transmitted statements of Simeon b. Yoḥai.

Dostai b. Yannai Tannaitic authority of the second half of the second century C.E.; a contemporary of Judah the Patriarch. He transmitted statements of Meir, Yose b. Ḥalafta, and Eleazar. The Talmud reports on a mission to Babylonia that he took with Yose b. Kiper (see, e.g., B. Gittin 14a–b).

Dostai of Kefar Yatma Tannaitic authority, referred to at M. Orlah 2:5 as a student of the House of Shammai who had heard a ruling directly from Shammai himself. Nothing else is known about him.

dough offering (Heb.: *ḥallah*) an offering from dough while it is being prepared for baking, consisting of one twenty-fourth part given to the priest. *See also* HALLAH (*Mishnah tractate*).

dove a small species of pigeon. Doves are mentioned in literal and figurative senses in the Hebrew Bible and in early Jewish and Christian literature. In the Hebrew Bible, the dove stands for various attributes: mourning (Isa. 59:11; Ezek. 7:16); freedom through flight (Ps. 55:6); and endearment (Cant. 2:14, 5:2). The dove was also used in the Jewish sacrificial cult (Lev. 1:14; cf. Luke 2:24).

Early Jewish literature (e.g., 4 Ezra 5:26; Pseudo-Philo 39:5) uses the dove as a figure for Israel. In early Christian literature, the dove symbolizes the Holy Spirit at the baptism of Jesus (Mark 1:10 and parallels; cf. Odes of Sol. 24:1–4). Matthew 10:16 employs the dove as a figure for innocence.

dowry (Heb.: *nedunyah*) property brought by a wife to husband at marriage

doxology statement ascribing praise, honor, and glory to God. The term is sometimes used in a very general sense to designate any statement of praise of God. More precisely, it is restricted to statements that specifically mention God's glory (Gr.: *doxa*). A doxology explicitly fulfills the injunction of Psalm 29:2 "Give to the Lord the glory of his name." Often mention is made of God's eternity with such expressions as "forever and ever" or "from everlasting to everlasting." In contrast to other types of praise of God for specific acts of deliverance and beneficence, a doxology is more general, more concerned with God's being and qualities. In the final arrangement of the Psalter, a doxological verse is appended at the end of each section (Ps. 41:13, 72:19, 89:52, 106:48), and the book as a whole ends with Psalm 150, which functions as a final statement of praise.

In most of the earlier prayers of the Hebrew Bible, praise and petition were kept distinct as two separate forms of prayer. However, in the postexilic period, extended doxological statements came to form the introduction to petition, for example, the praise of David in 1 Chronicles 29:10–19: "To you, Lord, is the greatness, and the power, and the glory, and the victory, and the majesty" (v. 11). Often the doxology takes the specific form of a blessing, for example, 1 Enoch 84:2: "Blessed are you, O Great King" (cf. Genesis Apocryphon 20:12; Tobit 3:11). Sometimes a doxological statement serves to conclude a prayer (e.g., Prayer of Manasseh, v. 15: "And yours is the glory forever"). This Jewish practice is probably reflected in the doxology that came to be added to the Lord's Prayer in certain Christian circles: "For the kingdom and the power and the glory are yours, forever. Amen" (see the Didache and some manuscripts of Matt. 6:13c). Occasionally doxological-type statements are added at the conclusion of narratives (3 Macc. 7:23; 4 Macc. 18:24; Tob. 14:15).

dragon sea monster representing forces of chaos, common in ancient Near Eastern myths. In Enuma Elish, the Babylonian creation myth, Marduk defeats the dragon Tiamat to bring about creation and become head of the pantheon. In Canaanite mythology, Baal fights Yam, the sea god, and becomes king. Traces of such myths appear in the Bible, where the dragon is called Leviathan or Rahab. In Psalms 74:12–14, God's kingly victory over the sea is synonymous with breaking the dragons' heads and crushing Leviathan's heads and is seen in the context of creation. God gives the dragon to the animals to eat (cf. 4 Ezra 6:52; 2 Bar. 29:4; Test. Asher 7:3 for eschatological versions of this banquet). God's victory over sea, dragon, and Leviathan illustrates creative power and control over creation (e.g., Job 7:12, 9:5–14, 26:5–14, 38:8–11, 41; Ps. 65:6–7, 89:10–15, 104:1–9; Nah. 1:4). Isaiah 51:9–11 unites themes of creation and exodus, juxtaposing God's piercing of the dragon with drying the sea for Israel. The dragon also represents historical entities such as Pharaoh (Ezek. 29:3, 32:2), Egypt (Isa. 30:7; Ps. 87:4), or Babylon (Jer. 51:34). Isaiah 27:1 looks forward to the day when God will kill the dragon.

Revelation focuses on the dragon's eschatological aspects. The dragon is Satan, God's enemy, who is thrown out of heaven by Michael and, using the Roman Empire as an instrument (Rev. 12–13; 16:13), makes war on Christians. In Revelation 20:2, an angel imprisons the dragon for a thousand years, at the end of which he is thrown into the fiery lake.

Dream of Mordecai the first of the aprocryphal, Greek additions to the biblical Book of Esther. This addition describes a dream in which Israel is seen undergoing terrible calamities and evils. At the end, the Israelites are saved from disaster. The text probably dates from the late second or early first century B.C.E. Neither Jews nor Protestants consider it part of the canonical Bible, but Catholics do accept it.

drunkenness Since the planting of the first vineyard by Noah (Gen. 9:18–25), drinking too much wine is pictured in the Bible as a sign of wicked self-indulgence. In ancient Israel, parents with a rebellious and stubborn son who refuses to obey them are told in Deuteronomy 21:18–21 to turn him over to the town authorities for execution. He is to be identified publicly as "a glutton and drunkard" and to be put to death by stoning at the hands of the whole community. Proverbs 23:20–21 warns all heavy drinkers of wine that they will end up in poverty, dressed in rags.

In both the wisdom literature and the writings of Israel's prophets, drunkenness is a common image for those who are interested only in personal gain and in sexual satisfaction. They will find themselves in a hopeless condition within society and under the judgment of God. God causes the fools of this earth to "wander in a pathless waste" and to "stagger like a drunkard" (Job 12:24–25). Those who find themselves in such a condition should "cry to the Lord in their trouble," so that they may be "brought out from their distress" (Ps. 108:27–28). The earth itself, as it awaits the final judgment of God, "will be utterly broken" and "stagger like a drunkard" (Isa. 24:19–20). Those who claim to be prophets but do not understand God's purpose for his people become so involved with their own foolish, misguided notions that they are compared with drunkards: "Stupefy yourselves and be in a stupor; blind yourselves and be blind. Be drunk, but not from wine; stagger, but not from strong drink! For the Lord has poured out upon you a spirit of deep sleep; he has closed your eyes, you prophets, and covered your heads, you seers" (Isa. 29:9–10).

The prophet Jeremiah is discouraged by the self-serving religious leaders among his own people and is so certain of their being punished by God that he has "become like a drunkard, like one overcome with wine" (Jer. 23:9). In a similar way, the destruction of the leaders of the nations that have oppressed Israel is described in Jeremiah's prophecy to them from "the Lord of Hosts, the God of Israel: Drink, get drunk and vomit; fall and rise no more" (Jer. 25:17–27). When God's punishment has fallen on these "oppressors of Israel," the slaughter of them will be so extensive that they will become "drunk with their own blood as with wine." Similarly, in Ezekiel 39:17–20 Israel is told that, as a result of the slaughter of the great enemy of God's people, Gog, they will "eat the flesh of the mighty and drink the blood of the princes of the earth . . . until they are drunk." The prophet Nahum foretells that the enemies of Israel will become "entangled with thorns" and "drunk like drunkards." The uncontrolled excess of drunkenness is thus a common image for the fate of those who oppose God's purpose for his people.

The use of wine in moderation, however, was an important aspect of religious practice in Israel, as in the wine offering (Exod. 29:40; Lev. 23:3; Num. 15:7). In the Dead Sea community, a shared cup of wine was a central feature of the expectation of the two Messiahs who were to bring in the new age (1 QSa2), as the early Christians' cup of wine was "the symbol of the new covenant in [Jesus'] blood" (1 Cor. 11:25–26). The abundance of wine, water, and milk was a sign of the new relationship between God and his people, "the everlasting covenant" (Isa. 55:1–3).

Drusilla (c. 38–79 C.E.) daughter of King Agrippa I. She was married to Azizus, king of Emesa, by her brother, Agrippa II. Soon after this marriage, Antoninus Felix, procurator of Judea (52–60), persuaded her to leave Azizus and marry him (in 55?). Acts of the Apostles (24:24–26) reports that Drusilla and Felix met with Paul the Apostle to discuss virtue and the judgment (58 C.E.).

dualism a construct that divides reality into two opposing principles. One major form of dualism is cosmic in scope and pits gods against one another. Canaanite religion describes the conflicts of Baal with Yam (sea) and Mot (death), and some biblical texts reflect this mythic tradition, as well as a battle between Leviathan and an unnamed deity (YHWH in the Bible), perhaps to be associated with El's creation of the world. Iranian Zoroastrian texts present a more severe cosmic/ethical dualism, which posits the existence of an Evil Being coordinate and coeternal with primal Good. Although this religious tradition was put into written form only in the early centuries of the Common Era, it is of great antiquity, and it may have influenced Israelite thought from the exile onward.

However one solves this historical question, Jewish texts written after the exile in Babylon increasingly depict a cosmic conflict between God and the personified forces of evil, or God's angelic chieftain and his forces and a chief evil spirit and his forces. The former is often identified as Michael, while the evil spirit is called by a variety of names. The nature of the conflict varies from text to text. One set of myths focuses on a heavenly revolt. According to 1 Enoch 6–16, Shemihazah and his hosts confound the distinction between heaven and earth by mating with women and spawning malevolent offspring, and Asael and other spirits reveal heavenly secrets. In Isaiah 14, Day Star (Heb.: *helel*), the son of Dawn, strives to sit on God's throne. Daniel 8–12 applies this myth to the battle between Michael and his hosts and the spirit powers behind Antiochus IV. Both 1 Enoch and Daniel employ primarily a military metaphor; generals and their armies clash on heavenly battlefields. The military conflict also has a judicial aspect. God's high angel executes judgment against the arrogant oppressive activity of Israel's enemies. The opposition of an accusing and a defending angel also appears in many texts apart from revolt myths and warfare imagery.

The Qumran Community Rule (1QS3–4) presents perhaps the starkest form of dualism in Jewish texts, maintaining that God has appointed two spirits, the Prince of Light and the Angel of Darkness, to rule over humans by influencing them for good or evil. Although God is the sovereign creator and judge, aspects of the text and its imagery suggest influence from Iranian dualism, something not unambiguously evident in other Jewish texts, except perhaps 1 Enoch 108.

Thus many texts of the period explain the origins of evil and the causes of sin by positing a spirit realm that corresponds to the earthly realm. Battle between nations are functions of heavenly clashes; indeed, in the Qumran War Scroll, the two realms collapse as the Children of Light intermingle with Michael and his hosts in the eschatological battle against the Kittim and Belial and his hosts. In other cases, oppression, devastation, sickness, and sin are functions of evil spirits. Whatever the specific origins of the worldview, it reflects a deepened sense that the world is not right and that humans are victimized by forces they cannot see and cannot conquer with their own resources.

The principal locus for this dualism is in the apocalyptic literature of the Graeco-Roman period. Its thoroughgoing dualism also has spacial and temporal dimensions. Heaven is where God's will is done, while earth is the locus of devastation and injustice. The present unjust and evil time is contrasted with a future age on the other side of a final judgment that will make all things right. Although the seeds of these ideas are present in the exilic and postexilic prophets, the converging and highlighting of these dualisms of space and time emerge in the apocalyptic literature, which resolves the problems of the here-and-now present by positing the seer's revelations of the heavenly world and the future judgment and new age.

An anthropological dualism begins to emerge in some early Jewish texts. For the most part, the Hebrew Bible views human beings as holistic entities. Flesh, spirit, and nefesh (soul) denote what people are in one aspect or another but do not refer to separate components of their make-up. The beginnings of an anthropological dualism are evident in texts that posit a significant postmortem existence. Early texts are vague and do not indicate a sharp dualism, but some depict the continued existence and reward and punishment of the spirit or soul after death and apart from the body. Some later texts envision a restoration of the body-spirit/soul unity through a resurrection of the body, while others, influenced by some Greek thought and its dichotomy between the material and the spiritual, speak of the immortality of the souls of the righteous. None of these Jewish texts, however, make a distinction between a material world that is essentially inferior to the heavenly or spiritual realm. What is wrong with this world and human life is not due to defects in creation, but results from the activity of spirit powers gone awry and from human sin that results from this.

Although some Jewish and Christian texts describe the chief evil spirit as the ruler of this present age and the one who presides over a world that has been plunged into darkness (Gospel of John), they stop short of depicting the creation as evil. Gnosticism, however, deviates from Jewish and Christian tendency to resist an absolute dualism. Creation itself is the result of the heavenly revolt, the creator is identified as the evil spirit Sammael, and the created world is essentially evil. Salvation comes through revealed knowledge that facilitates the release of the divine element from its material embodiment and its return to its heavenly place of origin. This system synthesizes a radicalized apocalyptic world view with the sharp dualism typical of late Platonism, and justifies itself through an inverted exegesis of the Genesis creation accounts. Its creative matrix must have been an exceedingly dismal experience of the world and human existence. *See also* DEVIL; EVIL, ORIGINS OF; LIGHT AND DARKNESS.

dukhan *see* PLATFORM

Dukhenen medieval term for the synagogue priestly benediction. It is derived from the Hebrew term *dukhan,* the temple platform from which the benediction of the people is said to have been pronounced.

Dura Europos city in ancient Syria founded by Seleucus I c. 300 B.C.E. and destroyed in a Sassanid siege in 256 C.E. The Parthians, inheritors of the Persian realms, captured Dura in the middle of the second century B.C.E. It remained a successful Parthian commercial center and dominated east-west trade. Rome captured Dura during the course of the second century C.E. It remained in Roman hands until its destruction. Dura had many ethnic and religious groups within the city, as indicated by the sanctuaries unearthed there. Sanctuaries honoring the traditional Greek and Roman gods abounded, as did sanctuaries to lesser known deities. A church contemporaneous with the synagogue was also destroyed in 256 C.E. The synagogue was found in the west side of the city about a block from the city wall. It was a house converted to public use. In its first phase an entryway opened from the street on the west into a long hall that led to an open courtyard with porches on two sides. From the courtyard one could enter four rooms of the five in the building. The long hall against the west wall was the prayer hall. It contained benches on four walls which sat about forty people and had two doors in its east wall and a niche or Torah shrine in its west wall. The prayer hall was nearly 11 by 5 meters, which is not so large as a sanctuary, but understandable as part of a house. In its second phase, dedicated as a synagogue in 245 C.E., the next house to the east was incorporated into the synagogue complex. The main entrance was also relocated in the east. This purchase of new space gives an idea of the relative prosperity of the Jewish community in the middle of the third century. Two of the rooms off the open courtyard were incorporated into the enlarged courtyard with colonnaded porches on three sides.

The prayer hall was built to fit within the architecture so that worship focused on the shrine in the long, west wall. This is a broadhouse in terms of its architecture. The benches on all four walls give no hint that there was provision for separate seating for women. The prayer hall was expanded to extend the entire width of the building or about 13 meters internally. Now about sixty-seven could sit on the benches around the four walls. Next to the Torah shrine was an elder's seat.

The main importance of the Dura Synagogue is, however, its art. All four walls and the ceiling were covered with narrative art drawn from the Bible. These paintings depict biblical characters in Persian costume that was contemporary with those who came to worship: the Exodus, Solomon and the Queen of Sheba, the return of the ark from Philistia, Jerusalem and Solomon's Temple, the dedication of the tabernacle with Aaron and his sons, the Israelite camp in the Sinai, Pharaoh and the infancy of Moses, Mordecai and Esther, Elijah raises the widow's son, consecration of the Tabernacle, the prophets of Baal on Mount Carmel, Elijah and the widow of Sarepta, Jacob at Bethel, Hannah and Samuel at Shiloh, the battle of Ebenezer, Ezekiel's vision of the dry bones, David and Saul in the wilderness, and Belshazzar's Feast. Three of the panels elude identification. A total of six of these panels were destroyed in the siege.

The area above and around the Torah shrine, which is an aedicula crafted to extend into the prayer hall, is provided with more paintings of a more symbolic character. Here on the arch above the entry into the shrine one sees a depiction of the facade of the temple with a Torah shrine or Holy of Holies of the temple within the facade. To the left stands a menorah with lulab and etrog. To the right is the binding of Isaac. Above and behind this painting is possibly a tree of life, a table with a cushion, and two lions beside a stand. Biblical scenes were above and to the right and left of this symbolic set. Evidently these symbolic paintings were important to the Dura worshipers, but we no longer know their meaning. In any case, this is the most heavily decorated synagogue in either the diaspora or in Palestine. The painters copied neither Parthian narrative art nor Roman portraiture but developed compositions of their own style.

Dura Europos, Jews in The archaeological finds at a synagogue in Dura Europos allow some inferences to be made concerning a diaspora community otherwise unknown. The synagogue began in a small house in the late first century C.E., and then was enlarged with the renovation of a larger house in the third century, indicating that the Jewish community had grown. (The benches could seat about sixty-five worshipers.) Like Christian, Mithraic, and Graeco-Semitic installations, the synagogue was on a residential street and lacking in prominence. The synagogue paintings suggest acquaintance with complex Jewish traditions. An inscription mentions a synagogue member, Samuel the Priest. The presence of local gods in the paintings in place of the biblical Dagon testifies to attempts to preserve Jewish identity. The costumes of figures reflect Parthian and other local influences. This community in a fortress and trading post at the edge of the Roman Empire was open to multiple influences from East and West and represents one of the many local adaptations made by Jewish communities in Mesopotamia and the Mediterranean region.

Durran a style of poetry named after Amram Darah, whose poetry is the earliest found in the Samaritan prayer book, the Defter. A regular feature of the common Samaritan liturgy is a reading of a Durran amid biblical readings and hymns.

Like free verse, these poems base their artistry and craft in the imagery and power of the words, rather than any set structure. Some consider Amram Darah's work as prose rather than poetry. It has been called less sophisticated than later Samaritan poetry because of the lack of formulae and the complete absence of acrostic poetry found in the Hebrew Bible and later Samaritan poetry.

The fervor of these poems reflects the intensity its author saw infused into the world by the Creator: "Praised be the One who lit for all the world a torch that never dies; it passes over the firmament and lights all the world . . . He lit for the world a torch that is never extinguished."

Other theological ideas are present in the Durran. For example, it offers glimpses into the Rautah, or Day of God's Favor: "Peace comes," "His mercies are spread forth," "misfortune is removed," "wickedness is withdrawn," and "protection is upon them." Belief in the coming end of the era of Divine Disfavor (Fanutah) and the inauguration of the Day of Favor (Rautah) and belief in an expected "messiah" (Taheb), a prophet like Moses, are found very early in Samaritan thought. The idea of the two eras could have its antecedent at Qumran or in general apocalyptic thought. Messianic notions are found in the Hebrew Bible, the New Testament, and at Qumran. The Durran witnesses the fusion of these two ideas in a single eschatological event: "Happy is the Taheb and happy are his disciples who are like him, and happy is the world when he, who brings his peace with him, comes and reveals the Divine favor and purifies Mount Gerizim."

dwelling, God's *see* SHEKHINAH

dynameis (Gr., powers) term frequently used in reference to the attributes of God in Jewish writers in Greek, such as Philo of Alexandria. In Philo's writings, God's attributes are often treated as *hypostases*; that is, they are discussed and viewed as if they were separate divinities in their own right, alongside God. God's powers include his creative power and his ruling power, which Philo finds allegorized in a variety of biblical imagery. One graphic biblical model interprets the cherubim guarding the Garden of Eden as the two powers, while the sword is the Logos, their superior.

Dystros name of a Macedonian month; appears in a number of Jewish sources, such as the writings of Josephus. Unfortunately, there was not a uniform usage; sometimes it corresponded to the Hebrew month of Shebat (January/February) and sometimes to the month Adar (February/March).

eagle **1.** motif that occurs frequently, largely in a metaphorical sense, in early Jewish and Christian literature. The eagle is noted mainly for its size, strength, majesty, and ability to fly at high altitudes. In the Hebrew Bible it is a predator (Deut. 28:49), a soaring flier (Prov. 23:5), and a symbol of kingship (Ezek. 17:3, 7). In the visions of Ezekiel (1:10) and John of Patmos (Rev. 4:7), it is connected with divinity. Revelation 8:13 cites the high-flying eagle as a messenger or agent of God, as do 2 Baruch 77:17–26, 4 Baruch 7:1–21, and Pseudo-Philo 48:1. In 4 Ezra 11–12, the eagle is a symbol of the evil Roman Empire.

2. important figurative motif in ancient Jewish art that is especially notable in synagogue art. The eagle is usually represented in the "Oriental" or "Syrian" tradition: wings outstretched, body rounded, legs stout, and head turned to one side. Feathers are usually not depicted realistically but resemble petals of flowers. Eagles sometimes have garlands in their beaks, but the eagles in the synagogue art of the Golan Heights often attack snakes or have snakes in their beaks, which may be a bow in the direction of "realism," since, in fact, the short-toed eagle in the Golan Heights feeds on snakes. Most eagles appear on the fronts of lintels in the main entrance, but they also appear on capitals and building stones. At least one eagle was "tucked away" on the bottom of the lintel of the major entrance at Gush Halav. An eagle with folded wings also appears on coins of Herod the Great, which may reflect Herod's attempt to erect a great golden eagle over the Temple's main gate. Eagles also appear in mosaic floors of synagogues and on lamps. We have at least eighteen eagles in Jewish synagogue art from the third to the sixth century, perhaps reflecting the statement in Midrash Rabbah Exodus 23:14, where the eagle is identified as the most exalted of the birds.

Early Judaism phrase coined by scholars to refer to the period from around 200 B.C.E. to 200 C.E., the time after the last books of the Tanakh (Old Testament) were written and before the composition of the Mishnah, the earliest rabbinic writing. (The dates assigned to this period vary. Some scholars begin it in 300 B.C.E., or end it in 100 C.E.; there is an overlap between Early Judaism and the Second Temple period from around 520 B.C.E. to 70 C.E.) The phrase "literature of Early Judaism" is used to designate the books of the Apocrypha and Pseudepigrapha, the Dead Sea Scrolls, and the writings of Josephus and Philo (but not the New Testament). Early Judaism replaces the previous designation of this period as Late Judaism (Spätjudentum), with its implication that this period represented a decline compared with the pure Judaism of the Bible and that Judaism effectively ended with the destruction of the Temple in 70 C.E. Scholars now use the term Early Judaism for the period because it was during this time that the terms "Jews" (to designate the people of Israel) and "Judaism" (to designate their religion) first became current. *See also* ISRAEL.

earth, inherit the expression that describes the earthly eschatological blessing that awaits the righteous. Psalm 37, a formative text for the use of this expression, emphasizes that the righteous, who have suffered oppression from the wicked, will "possess the land" (vv. 3, 9, 11, 22, 29, 34). "Land" (Heb.: *aretz*) in this context refers not to the earth, as opposed to heaven, but to the Land of Israel, or parts of it from which the people have been disinherited or removed by force. The extant part of one of the Qumran commentaries on the Psalms is devoted mainly to an exposition of this Psalm that envisions the vindication of the community against their enemies (4QpPs[a] 1–4). Following this line of interpretation, the Parables of Enoch make the point in negative form, "thereafter it will not be the mighty and the exalted who possess the land" (1 Enoch 38:4). The beatitude ascribed to Jesus in Matthew 5:5 is a veritable quotation of Psalm 37:11, declaring the meek as fortunate because they will inherit the land/earth. Common to all of these texts is the belief that the locus of eschatological blessing and salvation is not in heaven, but on the earth and, it would seem, in the Land of Israel.

earthquake of 31 B.C.E. In the spring of Herod the Great's seventh year of rule, an earthquake caused great destruction and loss of life among people (30,000 killed in Josephus's estimate) and cattle. Evidence of the earthquake can be seen in a cracked cistern and other destruction at Qumran. The earthquake demoralized Herod's army, which was fighting a war against the Nabatean Arabs in Transjordan, until Herod rallied them and successfully routed the Arabs.

Eastern Aramaic *see* ARAMAIC, EASTERN

Eḇel Rabbati *see* SEMAḤOT

eḇer min haḥai a limb [severed] from that which is alive, which, according to rabbinic law, is forbidden for consumption, the eating of which renders one culpable for forty lashes. The restriction applies to any amount of meat taken from a living domesticated animal, wild animal, or fowl (T. Zaḇim 5:12; B. Ḥullin 101b–102a). Flesh from a living human being is clean, while bone matter is unclean as though it were from a corpse (M. Ḥullin 9:8). Rabbinic Judaism understands the proscription against eating a limb severed from a living beast to be one of the seven obligations incumbent upon all humanity.

eḇer min hamet a limb from that which is dead. This category is of interest in a case in which a creature had a dangling limb while alive and then died (M. Ḥullin 9:8; B. Ḥullin 129b). At issue is whether or not, after the death, the dangling limb is treated under the category of a limb severed from a still-living creature (eḇer min haḥai). If it is, then in the case of an animal, it is forbidden for consumption but does not render unclean as carrion does. By contrast, if the limb is treated as separated after death, then if it is from an animal, it is carrion, and if it is from a human, it is corpse-matter, which is unclean in the minimum quantity of an olive's bulk.

Ebionites reference to Jewish Christians in early Christian literature. It is the Greek transliteration of the Aramaic "servant," or "poor." One finds the title "the poor" used at Qumran (Commentary on Ps. 37, 2.9; 3.10; Commentary on Habakkuk 12.3), in the Septuagint, and in the New Testament (Gal. 2:10; Rom. 15:26) with various positive religious overtones. The first Christian author to use the name Ebionites as a direct reference to Jewish Christians is Irenaeus of Lyon in his five-volume work *Adversus haereses* (I.26.2), written in the latter part of the second century. He notes that they reject Paul as an apostate from the law, and read only Matthew's gospel; they profess a special veneration for Jerusalem and keep true to the law, the observance of circumcision, and a Jewish way of life. In their beliefs they refuse the legend of Jesus' virgin birth; in their eucharistic liturgy they use unleavened bread and substitute water for wine. Soon after Irenaeus, Tertullian of Carthage (*De carne Christi* 14) reported that they recognized Jesus as a "mere man." Origen of Alexandria (c. 330–350) added that the Ebionites of Egypt observed the Passover; he knew of one group of Ebionites who accepted the virgin birth of Jesus. Tertullian (*De praescriptione haereticorum* IV.8) and Hippolytus of Rome spoke of a heretical leader, Ebion, and this allowed them to categorize the Ebionites as a sect. Their lead was followed by Latin antiheretical writers, such as Epiphanius of Salamis, who quoted excerpts from a gospel identified by modern scholars as the Gospel of the Ebionites (*Panarion* 30.3.7). Origen mentioned the same gospel several times and cites it in his commentary of the Gospel of John (*In Johannem* II.12). Epiphanius also knew of a book of the Ebionites called the *Periodoi* of Peter (*Panarion* 30.15.1) and a work entitled *Anabathmoi* of James (30.16.6–7). The last two writings were familiar to the anonymous authors of the so-called Pseudo-Clementine *Homilies* and *Recognitions,* which date from the third century. The Ebionites must have appropriated the *Homilies* at an early stage and interpolated them with additions that stressed Peter's prominence over Paul. Later in the third century the *Recognitions* corrected the anti-Pauline bias in conformity with what was then orthodox dogma. But the leadership of Peter and James, of Ebionite origin, became a common tradition. Near the end of the third century, Eusebius of Caesarea theorized that the Ebionites were among the Christians who fled Jerusalem for Pella shortly before 70 C.E. (*Onomasticon* 138, 24–25).

Ebr. *see* DE EBRIETATE

Ecclesiastes, Targum to *see* KOHELET, TARGUM

Ecclesiasticus *see* SIRACH, WISDOM OF

ecstasy (from Gr.: *ekstasis,* astonishment) often used in a technical sense to mean a state of trance, especially when undergoing a mystical experience. It is thought that prophetic revelations sometimes or often came to the prophet in a condition of ecstasy.

Eden the garden that was the home of the first human beings (Gen. 2:15; 3:23, 24). The word has been traced back to the Sumerian *eden,* meaning "steppe." More likely the Hebrew *eden* has its regular meaning of delight or luxury and refers to the food in the Garden (Gen. 2:9). Thus, the Septuagint translators regularly render *eden* by the Greek *tryphē* (luxury). In Isaiah 51:3, Ezekiel 36:35, and Joel 2:3, Eden or the Garden of Eden symbolize fertility in contrast to desolation, and the first two of these passages anticipate a time in the future when God will turn the desolate land into a place of luxury and fertility. Ezekiel 28, which presents a variant form of the story in Genesis 2–3, identifies "Eden, the garden of God" as "the mountain of God" (Ezek. 28:13–14).

In its retelling of Genesis 2–3, Jubilees 3:9–35 employs the name "Garden of Eden" eight times. Jubilees 4:26 mentions it as one of God's four holy places on earth. Since the other three are mountains, the mountain identity of the place in Ezekiel 28 seems to be implied. According to Jubilees 4:23, the Garden of Eden is the place where Enoch permanently dwells (cf. 1 Enoch 106:8; 1QApGen 2:23). The mythic geography of 1 Enoch 20–32, in effect, divides Eden into two locales. According to chapters 24 and 25, the tree of life stands on a high mountain in the far northwest, where God will descend in the end-time, while, according to chapter 32, "the garden of righteousness" (32:3), the place of the first parents' sin, is located in the far northeast and contains "the tree of wisdom" (cf. Ezek. 28:2–7, 12, 17), which is identified with the tree of knowledge in Genesis 3:3–6. 2 Esdras 3:6 states that the garden to which the first human was brought had been created before the earth appeared. In time, the Septuagint translation *paradeisos tēs tryphēs* (garden of delight) gives way to the Jewish and Christian use of *paradeisos* as a proper name for the primordial home of the first humans and the place of eschatological bliss. *See also* PARADISE.

Edessa present-day Urfa, a city in the Euphrates Valley, in Asiatic Turkey. Until the first century C.E., it was a border area, frequently changing between Parthian and Roman control. The Palestinian Targum has Edessa for Erech at Genesis 10:10. Despite a paucity of references in Jewish sources, Jews appear to have lived in Edessa early on. In the second century C.E., Edessa was ruled by Abgar VII, son of the previously converted Izates of Adiabene. In this period, the apostle Addai is reported to have stayed there with a Jew named Tobias and to have converted him and other Jews to Christianity. The Syriac Edessa Chronicle reports an order of the emperor in 411 C.E. to build a convent on the site of a synagogue, though other sources suggest that the bishop of that period was friendly toward Jews. In the wars of 610–642 C.E., Edessan Jews supported the Persians against Heraclius, the Byzantine emperor.

Edom a land southeast of the Land of Israel, encompassing Mount Seir (Deut. 1:2) or "the land of Seir" (Gen. 36:30); in rabbinic writings, an enemy of the people of Israel, specifically, Rome. This may be because the Herodians were descended from converts to Judaism of Edomite origin. In scripture, Edom is described as having taken advantage of Israel's defeat to seize parts of the land (Ezra 25:12, Obad. 11:16) and also as having participated in the destruction of the Temple (Ps. 137:7). Edom is compared to a pig and to an eagle, as is Rome, and Edom, Seir, and Esau all are symbols for Rome.

Eduyot (Heb., testimonies) Mishnah tractate formed out of collections of testimonies in the names of major authorities. The tractate is organized in the following form: Shammai, Hillel, and their Houses (chap. 1); authorities of Yab̲neh (chaps. 1–2); the Houses of Hillel and Shammai, with the House of Hillel in the stricter position on the law (chaps. 4–5); authorities of Yab̲neh (chaps. 6–7); and unit organized around the use of a common form (chap. 8). Every composition in the tractate has a primary location in some other Mishnah tractate.

Efa amora of the fourth century C.E.; in the Jerusalem Talmud, also cited as Hefa. Little of his teaching is preserved, although at B. Sanhedrin 17b (which calls him Efa b. Raḥba) and at B. Menaḥot 17a he is referred to as one of "the ingenious scholars of Pumbedita."

Efes one of the last Tannaitic authorities, active in the third century C.E. Genesis Rabbah 75:5 reports of his serving as secretary to Judah the Patriarch. Later, he headed an academy in the south, leading to his designation as Efes Daromi (the southerner). B. Shabbat 59b and B. Ketubot 103b report the unusual circumstances surrounding his appointment as head of the academy at Sepphoris.

egg's bulk measure of volume equal to one-sixth of a *log; see also* LOG

eglah arufah rite of breaking a heifer's neck in atonement for the neglect of a corpse (Deut. 21:1–9); *see also* SOTAH

Egypt traditional independent state known from the biblical period as the country of the Exodus and in later times as a province with a very large Jewish population. Most of the Jewish population of Egypt was concentrated in Alexandria from about the middle of the sixth century B.C.E. For the fifth and fourth centuries B.C.E. a plethora of papyri and ostraca in Aramaic attest to a Jewish military settlement near the first cataract of the Nile at ancient Elephantine. These literary sources witness to a large and thriving Jewish community that first worked as mercenaries guarding the south of Persian Egypt from its southern neighbors. They built a temple to YHWH on the island of Elephantine in the Nile. It was rebuilt after being damaged or destroyed, by what agent we do not know. They maintained Aramaic as their language for everyday life and also for international correspondence in the Persian empire, which was normal for the time. After the rise of the Ptolemies in 305 B.C.E., Jews spread into many communities, particularly from the time of Ptolemy VI Philometor (181–145 B.C.E.). Since the Ptolemies allowed them to live as observant Jews, they would quickly develop indigenous Jewish traditions and associations, particularly in Alexandria. Thus they maintained their own councils of elders precisely at a time when other ethnic groups were denied that privilege. Philo Judaeus, the philosopher of the first century C.E., says that Alexandria contained one million Jews in his day, though it is doubtful that the city as a whole contained that many citizens.

Jews also maintained their own burial societies and burial grounds. Hundreds of Jewish epitaphs, principally in Greek, are known from Alexandria, mainly from about 250 B.C.E. to about the second century C.E. Other sites with large Jewish populations include Leontopolis (modern Tell el-Yahoudiyeh) about 35 miles north of Cairo, where there seems to have been a Jewish temple or other worship center. Other towns and villages with a Jewish population, according to the papyri, include Pelusium and Daphne in the eastern Delta, Schedia near Alexandria, Athribis, Bubastis and Heliopolis near Leontopolis, Memphis, Philadelphia (south of Memphis) with its cloud of at least ten Jewish villages, Arsinoe, Tebtynis, and Heracleopolis (all three close together on the west bank of the Nile), and Oxyrhyncus. There is a gap of 300 kilometers from Oxyrhyncus to Abydos before Jews are again encountered, then we find Jews again at Thebes, Diospolis Magna, Apollonopolis Magna, Ombos, and Elephantine.

Jews were to be found at every level of society. Some of those who could afford it in Alexandria took advantage of their special status and were admitted to the gymnasia. They worked as soldiers, artisans, laborers, traders, and landowners. Many of them frequented Greek courts instead of Jewish courts, and most of them appear to have spoken solely Greek by the Roman period. Many have Greek names, but Hebrew or other Semitic names are recognizable in their epitaphs.

In 38 C.E. a bloody slaughter broke out against the Jews of Alexandria fed by the jealousies of Greeks and native Egyptians. Rival delegations of Jews and Greeks appealed to the emperor Caligula in Rome. Within a few months of his accession as the new emperor, Claudius in 41 C.E. was visited by similar delegations. He responded with an edict ordering both sides to live at peace and to preserve the status quo.

Certain Greek inscriptions from Egypt reveal that a synagogue was normally called a place of prayer or a *proseuchē*. For example, an inscription of 246–221 B.C.E. says, "On behalf of King Ptolemy and Queen Berenice his sister and wife and their children, the Jews [dedicated] the proseuchē." A fragmented second century B.C.E. inscription from Alexandria reads ". . . to the highest God . . . the sacred precinct and the proseuchē and the appurtenances." This was evidently a dedicatory inscription.

After the two Jewish revolts of the first and second centuries C.E., Jewish privileges were curtailed in Egypt. It was ironic, however, that Vespasian was crowned emperor on 1 July 69 C.E. in Alexandria by the prefect Tiberius Julius Alexander, a distinguished member of an old Jewish family that included Philo Judaeus. Vespasian had left the prosecution of the Jewish War against Rome to his adopted son Titus, while he traveled to Egypt to accept the acclamation as emperor.

In 115 C.E., a Jewish revolt against Rome erupted in Egypt and Cyrene and quickly found sympathy among certain Jewish elements in Cyprus, Judaea, and Mesopotamia. It was not suppressed until shortly after the accession of the emperor Hadrian in 117. Thus for three years Egypt was locked in a ferocious struggle that ended in Roman victory. Nearly a century later, a letter from Oxyrhyncus reveals that this Roman victory was still being commemorated in Egyptian households and was looked upon as a time when native Egyptians and Romans fought side by side. About eighteen years later, the Bar Kokhba Revolt was broken in Judea, and by that time the Jewish community in Egypt may have been all but annihilated, though Jewish inscriptions of the third century C.E. are known.

The Jews of Egypt make an appearance again in the polemical writings of the Christian fathers in the fourth and fifth centuries C.E. By this time it appears that the Jews had made a comeback, for the Christian clergy issue warnings to the Christian population not to attend synagogues. Evidently some Christians found Jewish worship attractive and insisted on visiting synagogue worship. This resentment against the Jews came to a head in 391 C.E. and again in 412–415 C.E. On the first date, Christian mobs destroyed the Serapeum, the great temple devoted to the worship of Serapis. On the second date, another Christian mob murdered Hypatia, the pagan teacher of philosophy. On the latter occasion, the Christian mob first attacked the Jews in the theater on the Sabbath and then expanded their atrocities not only against Jews but also against Hypatia and other pagans. Monks streamed in from the desert to take part in the rioting and other disturbances. A few epitaphs from Jaffa in ancient Palestine are of Jews from Alexandria, all of whom had Greek forms of Hebrew names: Hezekiah, Isa (Jesse or Joshua), Thamoum (Tanhoum), Simonos (Shimon), Beniamin (Benjamin), and Aa (Aha). These could be refugees, though not all the Jews fled Egypt. When the Muslims first appeared to conquer Egypt in the early seventh century, Jewish communities were again well established. *See also* ALEXANDRIA, JEWS IN.

Eighteen Benedictions *see* AMIDAH

Ekah Rabbati *see* LAMENTATIONS RABBAH

ekpyrosis (from Gr., conflagration) technical term used for a belief important to Stoics and others. According to this belief, the universe followed a preordained cycle, leading up to a final conflagration, after which everything began anew. This belief is also found in some Jewish Sibylline Oracles.

el (pl., *elim;* Heb., god) *El* was the title of the chief god of the Canaanite pantheon and later of Israel's god YHWH. At its simplest level, *elim* just means "gods"; however, given Israel's tendency to monolatry, the *elim* early degenerate into lesser deities or angels, members of YHWH's heavenly court (cf. Ps. 29:1, Deut. 32:8 [NRSV]). A strange story in Genesis 6:1–4 relates how the "sons of God," the *elim,* mate with the daughters of men to produce a race of giants. In the Second Temple period, this story became the seed that germinated many stories about the fallen angels and their counterparts, the holy angels.

Many texts from the Second Temple period preserve speculation about the nature of the heavenly beings, and the finds from Qumran indicate how important this speculation was in this strand of Judaism. 1 Enoch, Jubilees, and the Testaments of the Twelve Patriarchs, all found at Qumran although not composed there, feature stories about the angels (especially the fallen angels) and their role in the divine plan. In Qumran texts such as the Testament of Amram, the angels are divided into two camps, good and evil, each governed by an archangel (Michael and Belial, respectively), and each encompassing humans as well. This notion of humanity being governed by the actions of angels passes later into certain speculative branches of Judaism and also into various groups in the early Christian community (cf. Revelation).

Ela Palestinian amora of the late third and early fourth centuries C.E.; also cited in the Jerusalem and Babylonian Talmuds as Hela, Ila a, Ilai, Ili, and La. Ela is primarily referred to in legal contexts, and Zeira I refers to him as "builder of the law" (Y. Gittin 7:3, 48d).

Elagabalus *see* HELIOGABALUS

Elchasai, Book of apocalyptic work named for the angel in the writing who reveals the message of the book. According to recent study, the surviving fragments suggest that the book was written c. 117 C.E., at the time of the revolts under Trajan. A male angel and female angel of enormous proportions reveal that after three years, a war will break out among the wicked angels, which will affect the kingdoms of the world. The recipient is promised protection, however, and is called on to swear to sin no more before seven witnesses (heaven, water, holy spirits, various angels). Beyond this, the contents are debatable.

Elchesaites Christian group that flourished in the first few centuries C.E. It was allegedly a baptismal group, though this has recently been disputed. What is clear is that the group used the Book of Elchasai, though the book was probably adopted by them rather than being written by them. This suggests that the idea of a founder named Elchasai or Elxai was only imagined by the antiheretical writers and that no such individual ever existed. Other beliefs are less certain, though they seem to have included the requirement of marriage and rebaptism for serious sins. *See also* ELCHASAI, BOOK OF.

Eleazar, son of Ananias first-century-C.E. captain of the Temple guard; grandson of Nedebaeus. His father had been high priest (47–59 C.E.). In 62–64, Eleazar had to ransom his secretary, who had been captured by the Sicarii. In the procurator Florus's last days in office, Eleazar instigated the suspension of the daily sacrifice for the emperor at the Temple, a clear act of rebellion. This led to the burning of the houses of the wealthy, including his father's house, and the siege of the Roman garrison. After Jerusalem had been secured in 66 C.E. he was sent with Jesus ben Sapphias, another high priest, as military commander in Idumea.

Eleazar b. Arak Tannaitic authority active at the end of the first century C.E. He was one of the five disciples of Yoḥanan b. Zakkai, who called him "a surging spring" (M. A̲bot 2:8). He is known for a very few aphorisms reported in his name, including that found at M. A̲bot 2:14: "Be constant in learning of Torah; and know what to reply to an Epicurean; and know before whom you work, for your employer can be depended upon to pay your wages for what you can do." According to B. Ḥagigah 14b, he had expert knowledge of mystical speculation.

Eleazar b. Azariah Tannaitic authority of priestly descent, active at Yab̲neh in the first and second centuries C.E. While active in both legal and exegetical studies, he is cited much more frequently in the latter area. He is known particularly for the exegetical devices of juxtaposing biblical verses so that they illuminate each other and of *a fortiori* arguments. He is recalled for his great wealth (B. Berakhot 57b) and wisdom (B. Sotah 49b).

Eleazar b. Azariah served as patriarch during the period in which Gamaliel II was deposed. Talmudic tradition holds that he was only eighteen years old upon appointment but that overnight his hair turned gray, giving him an appearance appropriate to his position of authority. Upon Gamaliel's reinstatement, Eleazar b. Azariah served as *ab̲ beit din*.

Eleazar b. Dinai first-century C.E. brigand described in rabbinic literature and referred to as son of Deinaeus by Josephus. He operated in the mountains for many years. During the governorship of Cumanus (48–52 C.E.), he led the Jewish people in a retaliatory raid against Samaritan villages after some Galilean pilgrims had been killed in Ginae (present-day Jenin). He was captured and sent to Rome by the procurator Felix. M. Sotah 9:9 describes him as having caused so many murders that the rite of breaking a heifer's neck when a corpse was found was discontinued. A late midrash (Song of Songs 2, 7, 1) uses Dinai as an example of someone attempting to hasten the end rather than wait for the Messiah.

Eleazar b. Eleazar haKappar *see* BAR KAPPARA

Eleazar b. Ḥarsum high priest listed at B. Yoma 9a. His mother reportedly made him a tunic worth 20,000 minas that the other priests would not allow him to wear, because in it, he looked as though he were naked (B. Yoma 35b; Y. Yoma 3:6, 40d). While Eleazar is mentioned numerous times in the rabbinic literature, it is impossible to determine when he lived.

Eleazar b. Judah Tannaitic authority of the beginning of the second century C.E., often referred to as "of Bartota," an unknown locality. He is remembered for his generosity (see M. A̲bot 3:7 and, e.g., B. Taanit 24a) and his admonition against neglecting the separation of dough offering (B. Shabbat 32b).

Eleazar b. Parta Tannaitic authority of the early second century C.E., arrested by the Romans for the capital offenses of publicly teaching Torah and observing Jewish law. The Talmud holds that he was saved because of his dedication to Torah (B. A̲bodah Zarah 17b).

Eleazar b. Pedat (d. 279 C.E.) Palestinian amora, referred to always without the patronymic. In the Palestinian Talmud, he generally is called Lazar. He was born in Babylonia, where he studied with Samuel (B. Erub̲in 66a) and Rab̲ (B. Ḥullin 111b). According to the Babylonian Talmud, he was also Yoḥanan's student in Tiberias (B. Bab̲a Batra 135b), although the Jerusalem Talmud presents the relationship more as that of associates. After Rab̲'s death, Eleazar traveled to the Land of Israel, where he studied under Ḥanina in Sephoris (Y. Kilaim 9:4, 32c). Additionally, he studied in Caesaria under Hoshayah Rabbah, whom he calls "father of the Mishnah" (Y. Kiddushin 1:3, 60a). Y. Kiddushin 1:4 (60b) also refers to him as a student of Ḥiyya Rabbah.

Eleazar is a frequently cited authority whose approach to interpretation of the Mishnah had a significant impact upon talmudic study. He evaluated mishnaic passages in light of nonmishnaic Tannaitic statement (*beraitot*) and showed a particular concern for determining which authority stands behind individual mishnaic rules. As an aspect of this approach, he often identified contradictory mishnaic statements and rejected rules whose source he could not determine (B. Ba<u>b</u>a Metzia 51a). In addition to his legal study, Eleazar is cited frequently in midrashic settings and is known for statements such as "Even when a sword rests on a man's neck, he should not give up hope of mercy" (B. Berakhot 10a).

Eleazar b. Shamua Tannaitic authority active in the mid-second century C.E., generally referred to without the patronymic. A priest, he was one of the last students of Aki<u>b</u>a (B. Ye<u>b</u>amot 62b) and, after the Bar Kokhba Revolt, was one of the scholars ordained by Judah b. Ba<u>b</u>a. The confusion between the names Eleazar and Eliezer makes it difficult to determine the extent or exact content of Eleazar b. Shamua's teachings. He was, however, highly regarded by early talmudic masters. Ra<u>b</u> called him the happiest of the sages (B. Ketu<u>b</u>ot 40a), and Yoḥanan recalled him in similar terms (B. Eru<u>b</u>in 53a). Eleazar b. Shamua is listed among the ten martyrs of the Hadrianic persecutions.

Eleazar b. Simeon b. Yoḥai Tannaitic authority of the late second century C.E.; son and student of Simeon b. Yoḥai, with whom he is said to have hidden in a cave for thirteen years (B. Shabbat 33b). Later, Eleazar accepted a Roman administrative position (B. Pesaḥim 112a), which led to his being censured by Joshua b. Karḥah, who referred to him as "vinegar, son of wine" (B. Ba<u>b</u>a Metzia 83b). After his death, however, he was praised as a master of scripture and Mishnah, a writer of liturgical supplications, and a poet (Lev. Rabbah 30:1).

Eleazar b. Tzadok I Tannaitic authority at the beginning of the second century C.E. Along with Abba Saul b. Batnit, he was a Jerusalem shopkeeper reputed for his honesty. He would fill measuring vessels with oil and wine, to be picked up on a festival (M. Betzah 3:8). T. Betzah 2:13–14 reports his activity at Ya<u>b</u>neh in the house of the patriarch, Gamaliel II.

Eleazar b. Tzadok II Tannaitic authority of the late second century C.E.; grandson of Eleazar b. Tzadok I. He appears in controversy with the later disciples of Aki<u>b</u>a. He spent many years as a teacher in Babylonia, where his approaches to specific religious obligations served as legal precedents (see, e.g., B. Sukkah 44b).

Eleazar b. Yose **1.** Tannaitic authority of the late second century C.E., known for his trip to Rome (with Simeon b. Yoḥai) to persuade the emperor to abolish edicts against Jewish religious practices (B. Meila 17a)

2. Palestinian amora of the early fourth century C.E.; perhaps the son of the head of the academy at Tiberias

Eleazar Ḥisma Tannaitic authority of the second century C.E. He was a student of Joshua b. Ḥananiah and Gamaliel II, in whose academy Eleazar reportedly held a post.

Eleazar of Modiim Tannaitic authority at the end of the first and beginning of the second centuries C.E. Except for one legal statement, he is known only for his exegetical comments, which were praised by Gamaliel II (see, e.g., B. Shabbat 55b). Y. Taanit 4:8, 68d, reports that Eleazar was Bar Kosiba's cousin and was in Betar during the final stages of the Roman siege. According to this story, as a result of a Samaritan's conspiring with the Roman enemy, Bar Kosiba was led to suspect Eleazar's loyalty and to strike and kill him. Based upon this story, some scholars conjecture that the Eleazar the priest referred to on coins from the revolt was Eleazar of Modiim. *See also* ELEAZAR THE PRIEST.

Eleazar the High Priest third-century-B.C.E. high priest mentioned in the Letter of Aristeas to Philocrates (1, 35, passim) as having been approached by an embassy from Ptolemy II Philadelphus requesting a translation of the Jewish law for the library in Alexandria. Josephus (*Ant.* 43) says that he succeeded Simon the Just, but the identity of Simon and the story are dubious. Eleazar, like Simon, is a common name for a Jewish hero and leader.

Eleazar the Priest mentioned on coins of the Bar Kosiba War (132–135 C.E.), either alone or with Bar Kosiba. Presumably Eleazar was a coleader, analogous to the high priest as leader while the Temple stood. Perhaps Eleazar's office and role imply a hope for the rebuilding of the Temple. Nothing else is known about him, though some try to identify him with Rabbi Eleazar of Modiim, described in some stories as the uncle of Bar Kosiba (B. Git. 57a), or with Rabbi Eleazar ben Azariah. *See also* BAR KOSIBA, SIMON; BAR KOSIBA WAR; ELEAZAR OF MODIIM.

Eleazar the Scribe second-century-B.C.E. priest (4 Macc. 5–7) and heroic martyr during the Maccabean persecutions (2 Macc. 6). He is described as an old and respected community leader who refused to eat pork or even appear to do so at the command of Antiochus IV, endured cruel tortures, and gave exhortatory speeches, counseling loyalty to God and Judaism and pointing out the irrationality of his oppressors. The passages about him in 2 Maccabees stress the hope of immortality, and those in 4 Maccabees stress the strength of Stoic reason in the face of suffering.

election the act or result of selecting an individual or group to carry out a particular task. In the Bible and in later Jewish texts, the election intended is almost always God's choice of Abraham and his descendants to be his special people among all the nations. Genesis tells the story of how God selected Abra[ha]m and promised him the land of Canaan and numerous descendants. These promises were renewed to Abraham's son Isaac and his grandson Jacob. The twelve tribes who arose from Jacob's twelve sons became the people who fulfilled both promises when their population exploded in Egypt and the next generation gained the promised land. They are identified as the people whom the Lord chose from all the nations to be his prized, unique possession—the people whom he particularly loved, despite their modest size in comparison with other nationalities (Deut. 7:6–8). Israel, if it remained within the covenant with the electing God, would continue to be his treasured possession and serve as a kingdom of priests, a holy nation (Exod. 19:5–6). It would be set apart from other nations but also serve among them, just as was the case with priests in relation to the general populace. Later, Israel's unique status was called into question when the nation violated the laws of God (Amos 2 and 3:1–2), and eventually both the northern and southern kingdoms experienced defeat and exile. However, after some time, the anonymous prophet called Second Isaiah (Isa. 40–55) again used the language of election for the people who would return to the Land of Israel following their temporary displacement (Isa. 41:8–10, 44:1–2). The same prophet speaks of Israel's role as a light to the nations (51:4) and conduit of God's law to the peoples (42:1). In the last chapters of Isaiah (56–66), which are often attributed to a third prophet, it seems that a group within Israel is being called the chosen (e.g., 65:9).

The concept of election, whether for the larger group or an individual or both, remained alive in Early Judaism and in the New Testament. In the Apocalypse of Weeks found in 1 Enoch 93 and 91, the elect are pictured as arising in the last period of history, when they will receive special wisdom. The Dead Sea Scrolls, too, evidence the concept. The Manual of Discipline orders that the members of the group are to love all whom God has chosen and hate those He has rejected. God has elected the "sons of light" for an eternal covenant; others he did not choose. One text refers to an unknown individual as the elect of God. There is an interesting development of the theme of election in the Similitudes of Enoch (1 Enoch 37–71). There, a figure of the end-time is designated the Chosen One, and the ones whom he vindicates at the judgment are the elect.

The belief that God had elected some also plays an important role in the New Testament. Jesus himself, the Son of God, is called his Chosen One (Luke 9:35) and chosen Messiah (Luke 23:35), and his followers are designated as the ones whom God has selected. In the Gospel of John, Jesus says of his disciples that they have been chosen out of the world (15:19), and elsewhere, the members of the church are so addressed (1 Pet. 2:9). God's elect ones will endure throughout the final tribulation (e.g., Matt. 24:22–24), and eventually the Son of Man will come to gather them (24:30–31). Similar language is present in Revelation 17:14. The best-known presentation of election is found in Paul's Epistle to the Romans, chapters 9–11 (8:28–39 treat related matters). There, he speaks of the divine election of Jacob (the ancestor of Israel) rather than Esau, defending it as having its own reason in God's plan. He rejects the idea that God has nullified the election of Israel by extending his call and grace to non-Israelites who believe in Christ. The purpose is to incite the Jewish people to jealousy so that they, the original recipients of God's promises and covenants, will finally be saved. The author of Ephesians writes that God has chosen believers to be holy, while the writer of James notes that he chose the poor so that they could become rich. *See also* CHOSEN ONE; CHOSEN ONES; CHOSEN PEOPLE.

Elephantine, Jews in A large batch of Aramaic papyri discovered in or near the island of Elephantine, on the upper Nile opposite Aswan, revealed the existence of a Jewish military colony on the island, settled there to defend the southern frontier of Egypt. The beginnings of the settlement antedate the Persian conquest of Egypt in 525 B.C.E., and it continued in existence throughout the fifth and perhaps the early years of the fourth century B.C.E. The papyri consist of letters, including a batch written by Arsames, satrap of Egypt; contracts dealing with loans, sale of land, legacies, and marriage; a copy of the Bisitun (Behistun) inscription of Darius I; and an Aramaic version of the Words of Ahikar the Sage. The community was organized in military units and had its own temple, which was destroyed in 410 B.C.E. as a result of friction with the local Egyptian population. The temple was dedicated to the cult of YHW (Yahu?), God of Heaven, but the names of other deities—Anathbethel, Herembethel, Eshem, the Egyptian goddess Sati—appear in votive offerings and oaths, attesting to a certain degree of syncretism, no doubt furthered by intermarriage. The contracts, including the archive of a much-married matron named Mibtahiah, throw considerable light on the daily social life of the community.

eleutheria (Gr., freedom) The term implied political rights, the difference between being a slave or a free person. In the Hellenistic age, debate centered on philosophical freedom, that is, the ability to control and master the self—rather than be a slave to passion. This concept was important to such Jewish writers as Philo.

Eleutheropolis *see* BETH GUVRIN

Eliashib fifth-century-B.C.E. high priest. He was the son of Joiakim and the grandson of Jeshua, the priest who returned from Babylon with Zerubbabel (Neh. 12:10). He was high priest during the governorship of Nehemiah in the mid-fifth century B.C.E. (Neh. 3:1) and assisted in the rebuilding of the walls of Jerusalem.

Eli, Eli, lama sabachtani a somewhat hebraized form in Matthew 27:46 of the Aramaic *elohi, elohi, lema shevaḥtani* ("My God, my God, why have you forsaken me"), which is ascribed to Jesus of Nazareth during his crucifixion. The words are a quotation of Psalm 22:1, and the evangelists' use of the expression, along with other quotations and allusions to this Psalm and others, such as 34 and 69, identifies Jesus as a righteous sufferer who pleads for vindication. His use of the prayer suggests that, in the evangelists' view, Jesus believed that God would deliver him, as the psalmist had believed (Ps. 22:22–31).

Eliezer b. Hyrcanus Tannaitic authority at the end of the first and beginning of the second centuries C.E. He is generally referred to without the patronymic and sometimes is called Eliezer the Great. He wished to preserve early legal traditions (see Y. Yeḇamot 3:3) and hence stood in conflict with other authorities at Yaḇneh, who, in the face of the destruction of the Temple, worked to revise and revitalize the Jewish legal system. By contrast, Eliezer worked to limit the use of hermeneutical principles to derive new rules (see, e.g., T. Teḇul Yom 1:8 and 1:10). He rejected the growing acceptance of intention as a factor in determining whether or not an individual has fulfilled his religious responsibilities. Eliezer held instead that only a physical action has legal weight (see, e.g., M. Keritot 4:3). Eliezer's conflict with his contemporaries is reflected in a story that describes the other sages' rejection of his position in an issue of cultic cleanness, a rejection they maintained despite Eliezar's demonstration of divine evidence that he was correct (B. Baḇa Metzia 59b). This argument led to Eliezer's excommunication, the decree being annulled only after his death (Y. Shabbat 2:6, 5b).

Eliezer reportedly was born of a wealthy family but left home in his twenties to enter the academy of Yoḥanan b. Zakkai, where he quickly rose in stature. A different story suggests that he had studied and had been recognized for his potential since his youth. B. Gittin 56a reports that it was Eliezer, along with Joshua b. Ḥananiah, who carried Yoḥanan b. Zakkai in a coffin out of Jerusalem for his meeting with Vespasian during the war with Rome.

Eliezer b. Jacob I Tannaitic authority of the first century C.E., active in the period of the destruction of the Temple. He is known for his descriptions of the Temple and its rituals (see, e.g., M. Middot 1:9 and M. Arakhin 2:6). Later talmudic tradition credits him with the authorship of Mishnah Middot—on the structure and measurements of the Temple—in its entirety (B. Yoma 16a). It is difficult sometimes to differentiate the teachings of this Eliezer b. Jacob from those of Eliezer b. Jacob II.

Eliezer b. Jacob II Tannaitic authority of the second half of the second century C.E. Along with Judah b. Ilai, Meir, Simeon b. Yoḥai, and Yose the Galilean, he was among Akiḇa's younger students who survived the Hadrianic persecutions.

Eliezer b. Yose the Galilean Tannaitic authority of the second century C.E., a younger disciple of Akiḇa (B. Berakhot 63b). After the Bar Kokhba revolt, he had an important role in establishing the center of rabbinic learning in Usha (Song of Songs Rabbah 2:5). Eliezer was known for his exegetical sayings (B. Ḥullin 89a), which comprise the bulk of the materials found in his name in the talmudic literature. His expertise in this area resulted in the attribution to him of a posttalmudic compilation of exegetical principles known as the Beraita of the Thirty-two Rules. This text is known only from citations in medieval commentators, including Rashi.

Elijah (Heb.: Eliyahu; Gr.: Ēlias/Hēlias) Judean prophet during the reign of Ahab (1 Kings 17–19; 2 Kings 1–2), around whom traditions developed of his eschatological return (Mal. 4:5–6). The sequence of miraculous and agonistic episodes about Elijah in 1–2 Kings suggests that stories of the hero Elijah had already become a folklore cycle before their addition in the biblical texts. The association between Elijah's status as charismatic leader and his performance of miracles suggests further that the Elijah cycle reflected a model of ideal charismatic leadership in ancient Israelite society (cf. Deut. 18:15–22) based in traditions of Moses (e.g., 2 Kings 2:8). Out of this model of ideal prophet evolved speculations about an eschatological prophet (Mal. 4:5) who would serve as restorer of the social order (Mal. 4:6; Ecclus. 48:10). By the Tannaitic period the eschatological Elijah was thus imagined as the ultimate arbiter of unsettled legal and ritual questions (M. Eduyyot 8:7; M. Baba Metzia 1:8, 2:8, 3:4–5; cf. 1 Macc. 4:46, 14:41); for whether scholastic, familial, or social, discord was viewed as an obstacle to the Messiah. As eschatological speculations developed during the Roman period and both Jewish and Christian scribes focused upon the signs of the end-times, Elijah assumed a more esoteric role as the revealer of the eschatological adversary, with whom (in some texts) he would engage in actual combat (usually in combination with Enoch; cf. Apoc. Elijah 4:7–19, 5:32–34).

Two other important traditions developed in connection with Elijah's eschatological return. Through the similarity of one form of his Greek name *Hēlias* to *hēlios* (sun), the image of Elijah in his heavenly chariot (2 Kings 2:11) came to be conceived after the traditional Greek image of the sun on its chariot (cf. Sib. Or. 2:187–189). Thus, it has been suggested, Elijah appears in the center of the zodiac on the floor of the sixth-century synagogue of Beth Alpha. In another tradition that probably developed to explain the relationship between Jesus of Nazareth and John the Baptist, some early Christians came to fix Elijah as the precursor to the Messiah (Mark 9:11–13; Matt. 11:13–14) and even the one who annoints him (Justin, *Dial.* 8.4, 49.1).

In times of religious ferment the Elianic model of ideal prophet became actualized in prophetic movements led by Elijahs *redivivi* (cf. Mark 6:15). Historical prophet figures who have been recognized as expressing Elianic characteristics in dress, speech, and location vis-à-vis society include John the Baptist (Mark 1:4–6; Luke 3:7–9 [Q]) and Jesus ben Hananiah (Josephus, *War* 6.5.3, secs. 301–309), both of early Roman Palestine (cf. also Origen, *Cont. Cels.* 7.9). Jesus may also have been viewed at an early stage after the model of Elijah (Mark 6:15; cf. Luke 12:49; Mark 5:35–43 [after 1 Kings 17:17–24]).

Since he was translated to heaven alive, Elijah was believed in early Jewish (and some Christian) traditions to be a perennial representative for humans, both in his status as citizen of the heavenly paradise (1 Enoch 89:52, 90:31; B. Der. Er. Zut. 1:18) and as a heavenly mediator, helper, and revealer for mankind. He assumes different forms in order to instruct or help the righteous or to punish the wicked. He is the master interpreter of Torah and the revealer of its hidden meanings; and in this latter function he continued to be venerated in the Kabbalistic tradition.

Elijah, Apocrypha of including variously the following: Books of Elijah, Book of Elijah, Sefer Eliahu, Prophecy of Elijah, Apocalypse of Elijah. At least three individual texts framed as revelations of Elijah were in circulation in antiquity.

(1) A Christian eschatological discourse (perhaps based on prior Jewish and Egyptian oracular fragments) that is entitled Apocalypse of Elijah in one manuscript and cited as the Prophecy of Elijah in Didymus the Blind's *Commentary on Ecclesiastes* (235, 26–28; on Eccl. 8:4–5). It is preserved in four incomplete Coptic manuscripts (Sahidic[1] and Achmimic: Berlin staatl. Mus. P. 1862 + Paris Bibl. nat. copte 135; Sahidic[2]: B.M. 7594 colophon; Sahidic[3]: P. Chester Beatty 2018) and a Greek fragment (PSI 7), the latter implying a Greek original. Whereas the manuscripts derive from the fourth and fifth centuries, the contents of the text strongly suggest a date of composition in the second half of the third century; attempts at earlier, pre-Christian dates have been highly tendentious. Geographical details in the text and its early diversification into two Coptic recensions imply an Egyptian provenance of authorship. The text consists largely of a protracted narrative of the end-times, including deceptive leadership, social and political chaos, the advent and activities of an eschatological adversary, and the destruction and reconstitution of the world.

(2) A Hebrew Book of Elijah preserved in at least one manuscript and dated to the seventh century. Moses Buttenweiser (1897), its first serious student, argued for a third-century *Vorlage,* but this has not been generally accepted. Framing the revelation as part of the prophet Elijah's encounter with God on Mount Horeb (1 Kings 19:5–9), the book briefly describes Elijah's tour of the four directions (e.g., "a high place in flames such that no one could enter there") and then turns to a series of prophecies of eschatological events in Jerusalem.

(3) A lost book of revelations ascribed to Elijah that is cited by Didymus the Blind (*Commentary on Ecclesiastes* 92, 5, with respect to a vision of hell) and known by Origen (*Commentary on Matthew* 27:9). Its latest date of composition would be the beginning of the third century, and its language would almost certainly have been Greek. It apparently contained a tour of different heavenly regions.

There are also fragmentary narratives of Elijah's

tours of hell preserved in the Epistle of Pseudo-Titus (Latin) and the Chronicle of Jeraḥmeel (Hebrew; paralleled in Elijah de Vidas, *Reshit Ḥokhmah*). Whereas the three Elijah apocrypha above show no literary relation to each other, the details of infernal torments in Pseudo-Titus and Jeraḥmeel reflect the growth of a common tradition about measure-for-measure punishments in hell. These latter narratives may derive from a section of the lost Elijah apocryphon (3) cited by Origen and Didymus. The physiognomies of an antichrist figure in both Hebrew and Coptic Elijah texts, as well as another attributed to Elijah in a Greek fragment (Paris Grk 4, f. 228[r]), suggest a general ascription of this kind of knowledge to a revelatory Elijah (the three physiognomies are too different to derive from a single original).

Traditions of Elijah's apocalyptic revelations undoubtedly arose in connection with his intimate encounters with God, his assumption to heaven, and the signs that would surround his eschatological return. Whereas the Hebrew Book of Elijah and the lost Elijah apocryphon seem to have crystallized around the first two motifs, the Coptic Apocalypse of Elijah, which concerns the signs of the end-times and of an eschatological adversary, probably developed in connection with the third. The eschatological concerns of both the Hebrew and the Coptic Elijah texts may also reflect a tendency in both Judaism and Christianity of the Roman period to associate times of historical and social stress with the appearance of Elijah. Josephus retrojects to the time of Joram (or Jehoram), the king of Judah, the notion that a vengeful "letter from Elijah" might appear in situations of gross misrule (*Ant.* 9, sec. 99). In the subsequent evolution of Elianic revelations that is evident in the Epistle of Pseudo-Titus and the Chronicle of Jeraḥmeel, Elijah's authority becomes particularly associated with tours of hell and physiognomies of an antichrist figure; and under his pseudonymous authority the specific details of these traditions continue to evolve.

The Egyptian Christian provenance of the Coptic Apocalypse of Elijah, the text's prophetic self-presentation, and its overall eschatological urgency together suggest a context among one of the many millennialist movements that arose in third-century Egypt (cf. Eusebius, *Hist. Eccl.* 7.24), perhaps in connection with one of the many "prophetic" holy men in activity there (cf. Eusebius, *Martyrs in Palestine* [Syr.] 11.8; *Historia monachorum in Aegypto* 7).

The continuing tradition of ascribing visions of hell or physiognomies of Antichrist to Elijah demonstrates the established nature of his pseudonymous authority from late antiquity through the Middle Ages in both Judaism and Christianity. There is no evidence in this continuing tradition, however, for the direct legacy of a particular Elijah apocalypse such as the lost Greek apocalypse of Elijah (3 above) that apparently contained a vision of hell.

The Coptic apocalypse of Elijah itself did achieve some renown in late antiquity. In Greek form the text was used approvingly by Didymus in Alexandria; by the Greek editor of the Tiburtine Sibyl (early sixth century) in Syria, who used it for composing details of the last days; and probably by the author of the Irish apocryphon, the Two Sorrows of the Kingdom of Heaven. In Coptic it provided eschatological details for a vision ascribed to the abbot Shenoute of Atripe in a seventh-century Arabic version of his life.

Elisha b. Abuyah Tannaitic authority born prior to the destruction of the Temple and active in the late first and early second centuries C.E.; an apostate, referred to as Aḥer (the other) to avoid explicit mention of his name. Talmudic sources report that he had a broad education both in Jewish learning and in Greek thought (B. Ḥagigah 15a–18b) and suggest that his heresy had its origin in a mystical experience, in which he, along with Ben Azzai, Ben Zoma, and Akiḇa, entered paradise (B. Ḥagigah 14b).

Elohim *see* GOD, NAMES OF

El Shaddai *see* GOD, NAMES OF

Elul twelfth month of the Jewish calendar (August/September); season for repentance prior to the New Year, at the beginning of the next month, Tishrei

Elvira, Council of early-fourth-century synod. Elvira, the Roman Illiberis (modern Granada in southern Spain), was still a predominantly pagan city in the early fourth century C.E. Its Jewish community was ancient and outnumbered the local Christian church until the ninth century. Elvira was the site of a first national synod, dated between 295 C.E.—the ordination of Hosius of Cordoba, one of its most famous participants—and 314 C.E., the date of the Council of Ares that refers to it. There were nineteen bishops, twenty-six priests, some deacons, and laymen as delegates from thirty-seven Spanish church communities. A more precise dating would be between 306 and 314. The Council of Elvira's collection of eighty-seven disciplinary canons, handed down in its entirety, without any apparent order, is famous because it is the oldest such collection known in the Western church. It also reflects the major problems faced by the earliest flourishing of Christianity in Spain. Rigorous measures, in the form of penalties excluding reception of the sacraments, were taken by the synod. The canons aim at a complete separation of church members from the pagan way of life. The regulation of the clergy was at the top of the synod's priorities: fornicators are excluded from communion, even on their deathbeds (canon 18); continence is imposed on married bishops, priests, or deacons (canon 33); trade is tolerated only in strict limits (canon 19); usury is forbidden (canon 20). The common believers are warned against offering sacrifices to an idol in a pagan temple, the penalty once again being privation of communion until death (canon 1). Apostasy, without such sacrifices, entails ten years of penance. Magical practice, causing death, also imposes privation of communion until death (canon 6). A heretic's return to orthodoxy requires ten years of penance (canon 22). Lay people missing Sunday liturgy three times consecutively face a temporary exclusion from the communion (canon 21). The synod recommends attendance at the Pentecost liturgy in particular (canon 43). Canons 23 and 26 urge monthly fasts, except in July and August. Pictures of Christ or the saints are excluded from the walls of churches (canon 36), satirical or defamatory pamphlets are forbidden (canon 52), and gambling is punished by one year's excommunication (canon 79). Twenty canons deal with marriage. Engagements undertaken by parents in the name of their children should not be broken without a serious reason (canon 54). No marriage is permitted between brother-in-law and sister-in-law (canon 61). A widower cannot marry his former wife's daughter whom she had conceived in a former marriage (canon 66). Christian parents who allow their daughter to become the wife of a pagan priest are excommunicated until death, but no such sanction is imposed if the pagan groom is not a priest. Marriage with heretics and Jews is severely punished: five years of excommunication for the parents of the bride (canon 16). Adultery is equally punished for either husband or wife, with five years of excommunication (canon 69). A wife's adultery, with the agreement of her husband, entails perpetual excommunication, even in the case of death, particularly if the husband is a cleric (canon 70). Divorce is treated with the same rigor (canon 8). Canon 78 forbids Christian women from being concubines of Jews. Canon 50 excommunicates, for an undetermined period, church members for taking meals with Jews. Canon 59 forbids landowners to ask for a Jewish blessing on their fields.

embryo *see* FETUS

Emmanuel (Heb., God is with us) name of a child to be born of an unnamed young woman (*almah*), according to Isaiah 7:14 (also 8:8). The name is applied to Jesus in Matthew 1:23, which interprets the Greek *parthenos* (virgin), the Septuagint translation of *almah* in Isaiah 7:14, to refer to Jesus' virgin mother.

Emmaus town 20 miles northwest of Jerusalem; site of a Seleucid camp overtaken by Judas Maccabeus in 166 B.C.E. (1 Macc. 3:40). In 66 C.E., Vespasian stationed the Fifth Macedonian Legion there; during the Bar Kokhba Revolt, Roman detachments were posted there. Abot deRabbi Natan 14:59 refers to Emmaus as "a pleasant place with good and sweet water," referring, presumably, to the presence there of hot springs. According to Luke 24:13–16, Jesus appeared on the road to Emmaus after his crucifixion.

The evidence for the presence of a Samaritan synagogue in Emmaus is a set of four inscribed stones. (1) An Ionic capital found in the ruins of a Crusader church is inscribed on one side in Samaritan Hebrew, "Blessed be his name forever" and is inscribed on the other side in Greek, "One God." (2) On a block of limestone appears Exodus 15:3–13 (from the Song of Moses), Genesis 24:31 (the invitation to the chief servant of Abraham by Laban), and Deuteronomy 33:26 ("the God of Jeshurun"), according to the Samaritan text. (3) A limestone doorpost is inscribed with the text of Exodus 13:22, "Neither the pillar of smoke by day nor the pillar of fire by night departed from before the people." (4) A limestone block is inscribed with the text of Exodus 15:3–11 (also from the Song of Moses). It is assumed that the Samaritan synagogue was in the vicinity of the Crusader church where most of these architectural fragments were found. The date usually assigned to the inscriptions is the fifth century C.E.

employers, employees those who hire salaried workers and those who work for a salary, with the rights of the latter generally taking precedence over those of the former. God is described as the original laborer, so the Torah shows great concern for workers. Employers must pay day laborers, whether Israelite or foreign, on the same day, because the laborers are needy; employers will incur guilt if they fail to do so. The prophets decry the infringement of this rule. By stating that "whoever withholds an employee's wages is as if he had taken his life," the rabbis expand the biblical command. Because no one should be held in servitude to another person, employees are free to withhold their labor at will. The Talmud details both employers' responsibilities for feeding their employees and the benefits to which employees are entitled. Nonetheless, the Talmud expresses suspicion toward employees' tendency to shirk their tasks, and designs some laws in the interests of the employer—for example, employees may not become ascetics because the physical weakness that results will rob their employers of their labor.

encyclia latinized form of the Greek term *enkyklia* (lower school studies). It was used in reference to the first phase of the traditional Graeco-Roman education in rhetoric, in which a broad learning was emphasized. Philo of Alexandria, in *De Congressu quaerendae Eruditionis gratia,* lists the subjects as grammar, music, geometry, rhetoric, and dialectic. *See also* DE CONGRESSU QUARENDAE ERUDITIONIS GRATIA.

end of days, times, age the conclusion of the present age brought on by the great judgment, which is to be followed by the age to come. This eschatological concept is expressed through a variety of Hebrew, Aramaic, and Greek words with different connotations. Hebrew and Aramaic *sof* means simply "end" and can designate the conclusion of a period of time (1 Enoch 91:13). Hebrew and Aramaic *ketz* is derived from *katzatz, ketzatz* (cut off) and designates either a fixed, limited time (1 Enoch 91:15, *ketz dina rabba,* time of the great judgment) or the end of such a time (Dan. 12:9, *et ketz,* time of the end [of the age]). The normal Greek words for the expression (*telos, synteleia, pleroma*) emphasize that this is the "goal" toward which time is moving, or the "consummation" or "fulfillment" of the days, times, or age(s) that preceded this moment (Mark 13:7; Matt. 28:20; Gal. 4:4). *See also* AGES, TWO; ESCHATOLOGY; FULLNESS OF TIME.

endogamy marriage within one's ethnic, tribal, family, religious, or geographical group; contrasted with exogamy or intermarriage. While the Bible and postbiblical Judaism promote endogamy, intermarriage was common and often accepted. It is recounted without condemnation in the cases of Joseph, Moses, and Esther, all of whom lived outside the land of Israel. Kings such as David, Solomon, and Ahab married foreign women for political purposes, and, as a general rule, Israelites were permitted to take wives from prisoners of war (Deut. 21:10–14). At the same time, intermarriage is viewed negatively at Genesis 24:3, 37, 27:46, 28:1, and Numbers 36:8, and marriage with the indigenous people of the land is forbidden for fear that it will lead Israel away from worship of God alone (Exod. 34:11–17; Deut. 7:1–4; 1 Kings 11:1–4).

In postexilic Judaism, endogamy became a helpful means of retaining community coherence threatened by diaspora existence, assimilation, and Hellenism. Ezra 9–10 and Nehemiah 10:28–30, 13:3, and 23–31 require endogamy and explicitly condemn exogamy, viewed as a path to idolatry and loss of Jewish solidarity in the face of an often hostile environment. In the second century B.C.E., on the basis of Genesis 34 (the rape of Dinah), Jubilees 30 prohibits exogamy as a matter of law (see also 20:4, 22:20, and 25:1–10). Similarly, endogamy is insisted upon throughout the Book of Biblical Antiquities (Liber Antiquitatum Biblicarum), is a major theme in Tobit, and provides an underlying motif in the Additions to Esther (see also Test. Levi 14; Test. Job 45:3; and 2 Bar. 42). Interpretations of Tamar, Ruth, and Asenath eliminate suggestions of mixed marriages by transforming the women into proselytes. In the first century C.E., Philo prohibits intermarriage because it leads to assimilation of the children of the marriage (*Leg.* 3:29); Josephus, speaking of Solomon, connects intermarriage with idolatry (*Ant.* 8:190–196).

The rabbinic literature does not treat intermarriage extensively. The Mishnah has no discussion of it and rejects an exegesis that applies Leviticus 18:21 to sexual relations with Gentiles (M. Megillah 4:9). The Talmud contains a few discussions of intermarriage (e.g., Jerusalem Talmud Megillah 4:10 (75c); B. Kiddushin 68b). While these argue for the invalidity of marriages with Gentiles, the matter is disputed because of the lack of a clear biblical prohibition forbidding intermarriage.

endurance a virtue much praised in literature of the Second Temple period. Two kinds of endurance are prominent. The first appears in hortatory contexts and is equivalent to patience or perseverance. Job in the *Testament of Job* (1:5) is a model of the patient endurance of misfortunes and suffering. Job is compared to the athlete who endures the rigors of training and competition (*Testament of Job* 27:4). Joseph similarly was presented as a figure who endured a series of tests (*Testament of Joseph* 2:7). Philo of Alexandria exemplifies the same general hortatory approach, linking endurance, in the fashion of Stoic moralists, to courage and steadfastness. Once again athletic imagery abounds (*On the Immutability of God* 12; *On the Change of Names* 197).

The second major context in which endurance is treated is a special application of the more general notion. 4 Maccabees illustrates the endurance of the martyrs who persevered in their fidelity to Torah through the worst sufferings. The martyrs' courage and endurance (1:11) amazed all who saw it. The endurance of Eleazar won him glory (7:9). That of the seven martyred sons enabled them to win the prize of virtue and be with God (9:8). Here again the athletic overtones of the image are clear, particularly in summary reflection on the martyrdoms (17:4, 10, 12, 17, 23).

En Gedi (Arab.: Ein Geddi) Jewish oasis town on the west shore of the Dead Sea. A translation of the town's name, "the spring of the kid," reveals the abundant water supply that flowed though this ancient site. The town was famous in antiquity for its cultivation of balsam. The most prominent archaeological feature is Tell Goren, which was occupied more or less continuously from 630 B.C.E. through the middle of the sixth century C.E. Tell Goren consisted of an artificial mound built up over centuries, on top of which stood a fort and associated housing. The fort was renovated and used many times by the occupying powers, including the Jewish kings John Hyrcanus (r. 135–104 B.C.E.) and Alexander Jannaeus (r. 104–76 B.C.E.). This fort and its associated village were destroyed in about 40 B.C.E. On the plain east and northeast of the tell there developed a Jewish town from about the same time, or from the days of Herod the Great onward. This town extended to the northeast to the Nahal David and to the east to Nahal Arugot. A testimony to the conforming power of Roman culture and to the abundance of water at En Gedi is a Roman bath, which was built in the middle of town between 60 and 70 C.E. En Gedi was the capital of its district, and a new fortress was built on Tell Goren during the first century C.E. This settlement seems to have disappeared early in the second century C.E., possibly as a result of the Second Revolt. En Gedi is frequently mentioned by Bar Kosiba himself in his correspondence with his field officers at En Gedi, namely, Yehonathan and Masabala. These papyri were found in the "Cave of Letters" in the Nahal Hever about 4.5 kilometers south of En Gedi. *See also* EN GEDI SYNAGOGUE.

En Gedi Synagogue At the ancient Jewish town of En Gedi are remains of a spectacular, white limestone synagogue built in the late second to early third century C.E. The synagogue was built in three stages. In its first stage, a simple, rather rectangular building faced north toward Jerusalem. Three entrances in its north wall gave entry to worship space. The floor was a white mosaic pavement of large tesserae, or cubes, of stone. A black rectangular frame in the floor was divided into three squares, and a black swastika appeared in the south square.

In its second stage, around the beginning of the fourth century C.E., the building underwent several transformations and renovations. Square pillars resting directly upon the pavement divided the interior space into a nave, a narrow east aisle, and a south aisle across the back. A narthex, separated from worship space by pillars, was added to the west. Entrances were moved to the west of worship space off the narthex, and three tiers of benches were added on the south wall. The blocked north entrance was transformed into a niche, and a "chair of Moses" was added on its east side. While a new colored mosaic, mainly with geometric and floral designs, was added in the nave, two pairs of birds appeared in a central medallion, and pairs of peacocks holding bunches of grapes in their beaks were depicted in each corner of the surrounding square.

In its third and last stage, around 450 C.E., a new narthex, paved with mosaics, was added on the west. A monumental staircase may have led to a gallery. The niche of stage two was closed, and a large wooden Torah shrine projected into the hall. A semicircular niche was built into the shrine and a raised *bimah* was located in front of it. The *bimah* was paved with a mosaic portraying a bird and three small menorahs. On the floor near the Torah shrine was found a bronze seven-branched menorah, though its base was missing. In the floor of the west aisle appeared an eighteen-line Hebrew and Aramaic inscription that cites 1 Chronicles 1:1–4 (the genealogy from Adam to Yapheth), then lists the twelve signs of the zodiac, the twelve months of the year, and then the names of the three patriarchs and the three companions of Daniel. This section ends with the words "Peace upon Israel." The second section mentions major patrons of the synagogue and utters a curse on anyone who "slanders his friends before the Gentiles or steals the property of his friends or anyone revealing the secret of the town to the Gentiles." The "secret" is usually understood to be balsam growing. The find of a coin hoard in a destruction layer seems to date the synagogue's violent end during the persecutions of Justinian I about the middle of the sixth century C.E.

En Natosh (Arab.: En Nashut) ancient Jewish village and synagogue site in the northern Golan Heights about 1 kilometer southwest of the Danqalle synagogue site and 2 kilometers north of Qatsrin. The site is a small hill protected on three sides by deep valleys. In surveys, two stone slabs with reliefs of lions and then a lintel stone with a seven-branched menorah in low relief were discovered. Excavation revealed a large prayer hall that had a porch with Ionic columns. Its inner space was highly decorated and was divided into a nave and two aisles by two rows of columns. Three-tiered benches ran along the walls of the hall. The base of a Torah shrine lies west of the entrance. The pedestals of the columns were decorated with various reliefs, including a rosette, a menorah, and geometric patterns. The Ionic capitals of the columns were decorated with a nine-branched menorah, a seven-branched menorah, and an altar or incense shovel. Other motifs, such as a bird pecking a cluster of grapes, a spoked wheel, a Hercules knot ending in snake heads, and a wreath tied in a Hercules knot with a rosette within, appear on the stone beams and other members. A Hebrew inscription on an architrave or beam says, "Amen, Amen, Selah. Shalom." An Aramaic inscription lists a benefactor, "Abun bar Yose." The ruins are dated from the fourth or fifth centuries C.E.

Enoch the seventh descendant from Adam, according to Genesis 5. Because of his unusual characteristics (Gen. 5:21–24), he became an object of speculation as the putative author of several revealed books. Unlike all other characters in the genealogy of Genesis 5, he is said to have "walked with God" during his lifetime, to have lived a total of 365 years—a number with great potential for calendrical elaboration—to have "walked with God" again at the end of his earthly days, and not to have died because God took him. The repeated phrase "walked with God" was taken by early interpreters to mean that he spent time with the angels during and after his stay on earth (1 Enoch 12–36). They revealed to him information about the structure of the universe and the course of world history until its end. The five parts of the book called 1 Enoch (a collection of booklets written from the third to the first century B.C.E.) center about him as the recipient of angelic revelations. At first, he seems to have been associated with astronomical and geographical topics: the lunar and solar years, the seasons and months, the geographical divisions of the earth. He also became connected with the story of the angels who left heaven and mated with women (Gen. 6:1–4; 1 Enoch 1–16). These fallen angels, who had made their ill-fated descent in the days of Enoch's father, Jared, asked Enoch to plead their case before God; he, however, was ordered to condemn them for their actions and to predict their immediate and final punishments. The final judgment became a major focus of the revelations to Enoch: he warned the wicked about it and assured the righteous that their vindication was coming soon. Angels also disclosed to him in two dreams or visions what had and would happen throughout history from the beginning until the great judgment and beyond (1 Enoch 85–90, 93 and 91). The special information that was revealed to him allowed him to serve as a preacher to his children and his contemporaries. In the Similitudes of Enoch (1 Enoch 37–71), he is given the exalted title of the Son of Man who will play a major part in the last judgment; he is particularly closely associated with the righteous and chosen ones. The books of Enoch were highly regarded by the authors of the Dead Sea Scrolls; twelve copies, all in Aramaic, have been found in cave 4, attesting all parts of the book except chapters 37–71 (the Similitudes). This high esteem was shared by some early Christians, who considered Enoch's books to be inspired (see Jude, chaps. 14–15 [= 1 En. 1:9]). Two later books of revelations are also ascribed to him: 2 Enoch, an apocalypse (preserved only in a Slavonic translation), which develops many of the themes found in 1 Enoch; and 3 Enoch, a revelation (written in Hebrew) about the heavens and their occupants.

1 Enoch (Ethiopic Apocalypse of Enoch) a collection of revelatory traditions ascribed to the patriarch Enoch (Gen. 5:21–24). Composed in the fourth to first centuries B.C.E., the accreting Aramaic traditions were translated into Greek and from Greek into Ethiopic. The whole collection is extant only in this secondary translation, in a multitude of biblical manuscripts. Although some of its contents had been known through a quotation in Jude 14–15, some allusions in the church fathers, and some excerpts in the Byzantine chronographers, the collection as a whole was recovered for the West only when copies of the Ethiopic version were brought to Europe in the early nineteenth century. Later two sections of the Greek translation were found in Egypt. The Qumran scrolls have yielded fragments of eleven Aramaic manuscripts.

The contents of 1 Enoch orbit around two myths. Enoch's walking with God (Gen. 5:24) is interpreted as his heavenly and cosmic journeys. An elaboration of the myth in Genesis 6:1–4 describes how the mating of the watchers (sons of God) and mortal women (daughters of men) bred a race of malevolent giants who devastated the earth and brought on the flood. A secondary mythic motif blames the watchers for revealing forbidden heavenly mysteries, which caused other havoc on earth. In this double myth of the watchers, the flood is a prototype for the final judgment revealed to Enoch during his journeys and dream visions.

1 Enoch consists of five major parts. The Book of the Watchers (chaps. 1–36) opens with an oracle about the imminent judgment (chaps. 1–5); it then narrates the myth of the watchers (6–11) and recounts Enoch's ascent to heaven, where he is commissioned as a prophet of judgment (12–16), and his journeys to places in the cosmos where aspects of that judgment will be enacted (17–36). The Book of Parables (chaps. 37–71), the latest section, features visions about the Son of Man, the heavenly vindicator of the persecuted righteous. The Book of the Heavenly Luminaries (chaps. 72–82), the oldest section (fourth century B.C.E.), recounts Enoch's travels through the heavens and describes celestial mechanics. Two dream visions (chaps. 83–84, 85–90) predict the flood and the course of human history from creation to the final judgment. The fifth major part of the book (chaps. 92–105) contains exhortations to the righteous and woes against their oppressors, based on Enoch's knowledge of the judgment gained through his visions and journeys. A story about Noah's miraculous birth provides a portent of the coming salvation of the righteous (chaps. 106–107), and a final appendix summarizes the book's themes (chap. 108).

This five-part collection expands on a smaller collection that claimed to be Enoch's testament delivered to his son Methuselah (see chaps. 81:1–82:3) as an exhortation to the righteous to endure as they await eschatological vindication. Its authority lay in its appeal to the seer's revelations of the hidden matters related to the judgment. Suggested at a number of points is the belief that the community that generated this literature would survive the judgment because they possessed the true interpretation of the Torah, notably the solar calendar revealed in chapters 72–82. The imitation of Moses' blessing (Deut. 33) in chapter 1 and the omission of any reference to Moses' receipt of the Torah in 89:29–35 may indicate that the Enochic authors saw Enoch as a prophet superior to Moses, who received revelation long before Moses appeared on the scene.

The Enochic literature was significant for sectors of early Judaism, and its form of apocalypticism preceded the Book of Daniel. Its influence in Christian circles of the first three centuries C.E. was considerable, and its ideas linger in the Gospels' teachings about Jesus the son of man. It remains canonical for the Ethiopian church.

2 Enoch (Slavonic Apocalypse of Enoch) an extensive pseudonymous account of the revelations that Enoch received while traveling through the ten heavens. An analysis of 2 Enoch is complicated by the condition of its text. The work is preserved in a Slavonic translation of the Greek original. Only a few of the twenty manuscripts contain the text from start to finish, and its individual components have been transmitted in three textual recensions of different length. There is no consensus as to which recension in general or which readings in particular may be original. Although it has been transmitted in Christian circles, 2 Enoch very likely stems from a Jewish group in the first century C.E.; however, there is much uncertainty about its date and provenance.

The major part of 2 Enoch is shaped as a testamentary apocalypse narrated in the first person. Two heavenly beings approach Enoch, instruct him to take leave of his family (chaps. 1–2), and escort him through the nine heavens (chaps. 3–21) to the presence of God in the tenth heaven. There he sees the enthroned deity (chap. 22), is instructed in the mysteries of the universe, which he writes in 360 books (chap. 23), hears God's account of the creation (chaps. 24–32), learns of the coming flood, and is sent back to earth to instruct his children (chaps. 33–38). Chapters 39–66 contain his testamentary admonitions, and chapters 67–73 are a set of narratives about Enoch's removal from the earth, Methuselah's priestly activities and death, Melchizedek's conception without benefit of a biological father and birth to the sister-in-law of Noah, and his removal from the earth before the flood.

2 Enoch draws on traditions related to those in 1 Enoch. Strikingly similar are the testament form (chaps. 33, 36; cf. 1 Enoch 81:1–82:3), Enoch's escorted visits to places of eschatological significance (5–12; cf. 1 Enoch 17–36), the astronomical visions and instruction (13–16, 23), reference to the myth of the watchers (18; cf. 1 Enoch 6–11), his vision of the enthroned deity (22; cf. 1 Enoch 12–16), his extensive instructions to his sons, often in the form of beatitudes and curses that are reminiscent of the exhortations and woes in 1 Enoch 92–105, and the concluding narrative, which parallels the story of Noah's birth in 1 Enoch 106–107. Different from 1 Enoch, this text features a vertical cosmology, which locates the places of reward and punishment in the various levels of heaven rather than on earth's disc, and it individualizes eschatology by placing the moment of reward and punish-

ment after each person's death rather than at the cosmic conclusion of the present age.

Special aspects of 2 Enoch are its emphasis on the oneness of God the creator, its concluding focus on a non-Jerusalem priesthood and cult, and its detailed instructions about responsible conduct toward other human beings and animals. While it contains much material that is Jewish in origin, its complete lack of reference to Israel's history (contrast 1 Enoch 85–90, 93:1–10) and some of its peculiar ideas suggest a provenance in a group whose identity is not bound up with the Jewish people and whose purview is that human beings in general (and animals) are creatures of God who are entitled to love and deeds of kindness.

3 Enoch (Hebrew Apocalypse of Enoch) a Hebrew apocalypse pseudepigraphically attributed to the early-second-century-C.E. Palestinian scholar Rabbi Ishmael; also known as the Book of the Heavenly Palaces (Sefer Hekhalot). It tells how Rabbi Ishmael ascends to heaven and meets the archangel Metatron (chaps. 1–2), who reveals that he is the biblical patriarch Enoch (Gen. 5:18–24) transformed into an angel. Having described in detail the process of his elevation and transformation (chaps. 3–16), Metatron discourses to Ishmael on the angelic hierarchies and their involvement in the heavenly law court and in the performance of the celestial Kedushah (chaps. 17–29). He then shows Ishmael certain heavenly wonders: the cosmic letters by which the world was created, the storehouses of souls, and the right hand of God waiting impatiently to bring the messianic redemption to Israel (chaps. 41–48A). An appendix (chap. 48A–D) contains a miscellany of Metatron traditions, borrowed from the Alphabet of Rabbi Akiḇa, which lists the seventy names of God and of Metatron, contains a short acrostic on the elevation of Enoch, and has an account of Metatron's role as the Prince of Torah (Sar Torah).

3 Enoch is a compendium of motifs and traditions, some of which go back to late Second Temple times. However, its reuse of Talmudic material indicates that, as it now stands, it cannot have been compiled much earlier than the sixth or seventh century C.E. Though many of its apocalyptic elements originated in Palestine, 3 Enoch's close literary relationship, specifically with the Babylonian Talmud (as in its reinterpretation in chap. 16 of the story of the humbling of Metatron, attested elsewhere only in Babylonian Talmud Ḥagigah 15a), suggests that its final editing took place in Babylonia.

Different versions of 3 Enoch are extant in the manuscripts and early printed editions. The longest is attested in Vatican 228 and Oxford 1656. The differences between the versions are essentially a matter of length. The order in which the material appears is always the same. It is unclear whether the shorter versions are extracted from the longer or represent earlier stages in the evolution of the text. 3 Enoch is one of the major works of the Hekhalot literature that emanated from the circles of the Hekhalot mystics in Palestine and Babylonia in late antiquity. It is the main early source relating to the archangel Metatron, whom it describes in highly exalted terms as The Lesser YHWH and God's vice-regent in the world. Along with a number of other Hekhalot writings, 3 Enoch was copied by the Haside Ashkenaz, and strongly influenced their mystical theology. Hekhalot traditions were also known to the Kabbalists of Provence and Spain. Knowledge specifically of 3 Enoch, however, has not been proved. The references to Books of Enoch in the Zohar, if they are not totally fictitious, do not appear to be to 3 Enoch.

eparchy term derived from Greek, used in reference to a province or a similar political entity governed by an official called an eparch in Greek terminology (the Roman equivalent was a prefect). An eparchy was not precisely defined and might refer to anything from a major entity, such as a satrapy, to a relatively minor one.

ephebate term used in reference to a group of young men who were candidates for citizenship in a Greek polis (city). The rules for who might be a citizen were rather strictly defined in most Greek cities. Only the children of two citizens were normally allowed to become candidates for citizenship. After preliminary and middle education, between ages 15 and 20, the youth would be placed on the list of the gymnasium, where he would receive training in Greek literature, rhetoric, athletics, and other skills needed for someone who would later participate in both military and political activities as a citizen.

Ephesus, Jews in Jews in Ephesus were citizens from the mid-third century B.C.E. and had their privileges reaffirmed by the Romans. Acts of the Apostles (18:19, 26; 19:8) refers to a synagogue, and a fragmentary inscription may refer to synagogue officials. Other inscriptions of the second and third centuries C.E. seem to mention Jewish names.

ephphata transliteration of the Aramaic *etpattaḥ,* meaning, "be opened" (Mark 7:34); a word of healing or exorcism spoken by Jesus to a deaf and mute man.

Ephrem (306–373 C.E.) Christian poet, exegete, and theologian. He was born in Nisibis, where he eventually established a theological school. When the city was taken by the Sassanids in 363, Ephrem was forced to move to Edessa where he continued teaching for ten years, until his death. He appears not to have been a monk, contrary to the views of some scholars, but to have practiced sexual abstinence as an aspect of having dedicated his life to Jesus. He was a master poet, creating numerous hymns, liturgical poems, and sermons in hymnal form. He is one of the earliest Syriac writers, and his poetic liturgical style finds echoes throughout Syria and Palestine. He seems not to have known Greek, and he rejected religious rationalism. His exegeses of the Old Testament have close parallels to midrashic and targumic traditions, and like Afrahat, he often employs methods of argumentation that closely parallel rabbinic arguments. Three of his "Hymns of Faith," composed in Syriac, are biting polemics against Arians and Jews. Like Afrahat, Ephrem argues that Christianity has replaced Judaism as the means through which God works out his plan of salvation. God rejected the Jews because they voluntarily rejected his son, making it possible for the Gentile nations to receive the blessing from God. The destruction of the Temple and the dispersion of the Jews constrast with the fact that God has gathered the nations into his church. Observation of the Sabbath, circumcision, and the purity laws were designed to prevent Israel from adopting paganism, so that they are no longer necessary for Christians. Ephrem repeatedly argues that Jewish customs such as unleavened bread and synagogue prayer have no legitimacy at all. He compares the unleavened bread to "the sacrament of Judas." He characterizes the Jewish hands as "stained with blood." Ephrem states that he hated the Jews, whom he terms "crucifiers," because Israel "persecuted Moses in his time and it crucified its Lord in his time." Like Afrahat, Ephrem viewed Passover in typological terms. Passover was given to the Jews, but its reality became obvious within the church only with the appearance and sacrifice of the True Lamb, Jesus. Ephrem also warns that Jews were trying to enslave Christians under the law, and several of his poems are warnings to Christians to avoid the Jews and their practices. Several scholars have argued that Ephrem's vehement anti-Jewish rhetoric resulted from the attempt by Syrian Jews to convert Christians. They claim that his repeated characterization of Jewish rituals as being unnecessary for and even harmful to Christians reflected the reality that some Christians were following these rituals either as Jews or as their form of Christianity.

Epictetus (c. 55–135 C.E.) Greek Stoic philosopher who taught in Rome. His work was evidently aimed at the layperson rather than the Stoic sage. His teachings include ideas on the brotherhood of all people, and his references to the Jews show no hostility to them. He mentions the different dietary restrictions among Jews, Syrians, and Egyptians. When commenting on conversion to Judaism in one of his discourses, he mentions baptism. Some have thought he was confusing Judaism with Christianity, but others think baptism was a necessary part of conversion to Judaism at that time.

Epicureanism philosophical school founded by Epicurus (341–271 B.C.E.), which believed that the source of happiness is pleasure, that nothing exists after death, and that death is not to be feared. The basis of Epicurus's philosophy was the scientific theory ascribed to Democritus and Leucippus, which stated that nothing exists but atoms and space. According to this view, the world and life in it are all an accidental conglomeration of atoms, and the gods (though they exist) have nothing to do with human life. The goal of life is pleasure (*hedone*), which was defined as "absence from pain." Therefore, death is not to be feared, since there is no pain in death. Epicurianism was often condemned for being hedonistic in the modern sense, as well as being atheistic, but this criticism is inaccurate. In fact, Epicurus taught a life of moderation, since he believed that increasing pleasure also increased pain; the orgiastic lifestyle was therefore not for him. He also accepted the honoring of the gods. Nevertheless, the charge of atheism is somewhat understandable because the Epicureans thought that the gods were not involved with human beings, and thus their acceptance of the gods' existence made no difference to anything. Josephus compared the Sadducees to the Epicurians. The term "Epicureanism" also surfaced in rabbinic literature, where it reflected popular misunderstanding and served as the equivalent of godlessness. *See also* EPIKOROS.

Epikoros in the Mishnah, an Epicurean, listed at M. Sanhedrin 10:1 along with those who deny resurrection or reject the divine origin of the law as having no share in the world-to-come. In later rabbinic parlance, the term has a broader meaning, referring in general to a heretic or apostate (see, e.g., B. Sanhedrin 99b–100a).

epiphany appearance of a divine figure to a human being. Most often the deity or the angel of YHWH appears in order to make an announcement or to commission the person to a task or role. In the Hebrew Bible, stories of epiphanies are recounted in a stereotyped literary form that includes most or all of the following narrative elements, sometimes in a different order: circumstances; an appearance of the Deity or an angel; the person's fearful reaction and God's response, "fear not"; a message that one is to serve a particular role (as a prophet or the parent of an agent of God); a protest that one is not fit for the office or an expression of doubt; a divine reassurance such as "I am with you" or, again, "fear not, do not be dismayed" or a reiteration of the message; the disappearance of the divine being; the person's acquiescence to the message or the occurrence of the announced birth.

The Book of Tobit offers an interesting example of how an epiphany can structure a narrative and serve a variety of functions. In chapter 3 both Tobit and Sarah pray for death as release from their troubles. God responds by sending the angel Raphael to heal their ills. Raphael appears in human form (5:4; the disguise motif is typical), guides Tobias across Mesopotamia (serving the traditional function of the accompanying and interpreting angel of apocalyptic literature; cf. 1 Enoch 20–32), heals Sarah and Tobit, reveals himself as an angel (chap. 12), commissions Tobit to write a book about his experiences (1 Enoch 81:5–82:2; Dan. 12:9; Rev. 1:11), and disappears suddenly.

New Testament epiphanies include annunciation stories about the birth of John and Jesus (Luke 1:5–20, 26–38; 2:8–20), accounts of post-Resurrection appearances of Jesus for the purpose of commissioning apostles (Matt. 28:16–20; Luke 24:36–53; John 20:19–29, 21:1–19; Acts 9:1–9, 22:6–22, 26:4–18; and the Book of Revelation as a whole). In Gnostic literature, the Apocryphon of John claims to be a revelation given by Jesus to John on the Mount of Olives. Its epiphanic narrative frame (1:1–2:10, 31:25–32:5) is reminiscent of the Book of Revelation and authenticates the book's message. *See also* ANGELOPHANY; BIRTH, MIRACULOUS; CALL; THEOPHANY.

epispasm physical removal of the signs of circumcision. At certain times, a few Jews wanted to remove their particular Jewish identity, especially those who might participate in athletic contests, though the number has probably been exaggerated. The operation would have been traumatic and required considerable motivation to undergo.

epistles (after the Gr.: *epistole,* letters) literary genre attested in nonbiblical Jewish texts, which became the dominant genre in the New Testament. Some scholars distinguish between the personal, informal "letter" and the more literary "epistle," which was designed for publication; but since ancient use of the term "epistle" is quite broad, others use the words interchangeably. Nonbiblical Jewish letters are extant from as early as the seventh century B.C.E. (e.g., letters from the Jewish colony at Elephantine in Egypt from the 5th c. B.C.E.). There are eleven short letters embedded in the Tanakh (Old Testament), such as 1 Kings 21:9–10 and Jeremiah 29:4–23. Among the texts of early Judaism (2d c. B.C.E.–2d c. C.E.) several works of other genres have been erroneously labeled epistles: the Epistles of Jeremiah and Aristeas, the Epistle of Enoch (1 Enoch 91–105), and 1 Baruch. Other works contain letters: 1, 2, and 3 Maccabees, the Epistle of Aristeas, 2 Baruch, Paraleipomena of Jeremiah, Josephus's *Antiquities of the Jews,* and later, the Palestinian and Babylonian Talmuds. Many of these letters are official communications, for example, three letters from the Seleucid ruler Antiochus Epiphanes in 2 Maccabees. Some are fictionalized (e.g., a letter by Baruch the scribe to Jeremiah, with Jeremiah's reply, in the Parleipomena of Jeremiah).

Twenty-one of the twenty-seven books of the New Testament are called "epistles." Most are real communications written by individuals to individuals or to Christian communities, which combine theological instruction with personal greetings. Two other books include short letters (Rev. 2–3 and Acts 15). Best known are the fourteen letters attributed to Paul, which scholars classify into three groups: (1) seven letters generally thought to be written or dictated by Paul (Romans, 1 and 2 Corinthians, Galatians, 1 Thessalonians, Philippians, Philemon); (2) six "Deutero-Pauline" letters, which claim to be written by Paul but were probably composed by his followers (Colossians, Ephesians, 2 Thessalonians; and the three "pastoral" letters: 1 and 2 Timothy, Titus); and (3) Hebrews, which makes no claim to be composed by Paul but was attributed to him in the ancient Church. Most of Paul's letters, which are the earliest surviving Christian texts (written in the 50s) were addressed to churches he had founded, except for Philemon, sent to an individual, and Romans, sent to prepare the way for Paul's first visit to the church in Rome. Intended for public reading, the letters function as a substitute for the presence of the apostle. They respond to questions (1 Cor. 7:1: "Now concerning the things about which you wrote") and treat problems and disputes that have arisen in Paul's absence (Gal. 1:6: "I am amazed that you are so quickly deserting the one who called you . . . and are turning to a different gospel"). Several epistles dispute interpretations of the Christian message that differ from Paul's own. The remaining seven New Testament letters are traditionally called "catholic" (universal) letters, because they were thought to be addressed to the church as a whole. Scholars now think, however, that these, too, were intended for specific churches or groups of churches. Some of these works, which date from several decades after Paul, are real letters (2 and 3 John, 1 and 2 Peter), while others seem to be sermons (1 John) or treatises (James, Jude) put into letter form. In early Christianity, letters to churches continue to be an important genre (e.g., Ignatius, 1 Clement), and the correspondence of the church fathers (e.g., Basil, Gregory of Nazianzus, and John Chrysostom in the 4th c.) served as a vehicle for theology.

epithymia (Gr., desire) Although it could be used in reference to natural desires, it often had a negative connotation, implying "wrong desire" or "lust." Both Greek philosophers and Jewish and Christian writers in Greek were opposed to irrational desire and thought that it should be strictly controlled by the mind.

equality with God This expression or its equivalent is used in a variety of texts about human attempts to attain divine status or prerogatives, or divine attempts to exceed one's assigned place. In Genesis 3:5 the snake tempts the woman to seek the knowledge that will make her and Adam "like God." In context it is a subtle perversion of the motif that humans were created in God's likeness and image (Gen. 1:26–27). The motif recurs in the Eden story in Ezekiel 28:1–19, with reference to the hybris of the king of Tyre. Isaiah 14:12–15 employs an old Semitic myth about heavenly rivalry to describe how the king of Babylon seeks to be "like the Most High." These texts are employed with reference to other royal figures: Antiochus IV, who seeks to be "equal to God" (2 Macc. 9:12; cf. Dan. 8:9–11); Pompey (Ps. Sol. 2:26–30); and Herod Agrippa I (Acts 12:20–23). The motif also informs the account of Satan's fall in the Life of Adam and Eve 12–16. In every case the attempt to storm heaven or the pretension be like God meets with disaster. In a parody on the motif, Philippians 2:5–11 asserts that the preexistent figure who became Jesus eschewed divine equality and was exalted because he humbled himself.

equestrian *see* EQUITES

equites (Lat., equals) used to refer to the class of knights in Rome. Although almost equal in rank to the senatorial class, the knights did not enter the Senate, as a rule, and were excluded by law from the office of consul. There was always a certain rivalry between the knights and the senatorial class.

ereb̲ evening, sunset; beginning of a holy day

Eretz Yisrael *see* ISRAEL, LAND OF

eroticism, in Jewish literature the treatment of sex and sexual love in Jewish writings. Jewish literature has not been known for its erotic content; nevertheless, one of the most famous—as well as one of the most beautiful—examples of love poetry is the Song of Songs in the Hebrew Bible. It became common to allegorize the Song as representative of the relationship between Israel and God. Despite this interpretation, its origin as poetry celebrating physical love is not in doubt. Exactly when the Song was first allegorized is not known, though the earliest-known allegories of it are quite late (e.g., Christian writers such as Origen, the Targum, and the Midrash Rabbah). It is often asserted that the book was accepted into the canon only because it had been allegorized, but we do not actually know enough about the process of canonization to assume this. For all we know, the book was taken into the canon because it was valued for its expression of human love.

Erotic imagery is also found in other writings, and particularly in wisdom literature, when it deals with Dame Wisdom. We see examples of this theme in the following citations: Proverbs 4:6–8, which discusses the acquisition of wisdom in terms of physical love; Proverbs 8:1–4 and 9:1–6, in which Dame Wisdom calls to the simple in seductive terms reminiscent of the loose woman of chapter 7; and the Wisdom of Solomon 8:2–16, in which Solomon courts Wisdom as a bride.

Ecclesiasticus 51 constitutes a poem on wisdom. For many centuries, only the Greek version was known. When the Hebrew text was rediscovered in the twentieth century, some scholars felt that it used much more explicit and erotic language than was found in the Greek text or in the Book of Proverbs. If their interpretation is correct, the Hebrew writer was not afraid to make use of erotic imagery, even though he was writing about a strictly religious subject.

Other biblical images, while perhaps not intended to be erotic, lent themselves to erotic interpretation, especially in the visual arts. In one of these images, David observes Bathsheba bathing (2 Sam. 11:2); in the other, found in the story of Susanna and the Elders in the Septuagint version of Daniel, the elders spy on Susanna in the bath.

These narratives were interpreted by many renowned painters, including Rembrandt.

Talmudic rabbis present a largely negative view of eroticism and erotic behavior. Within the context of marriage, sexual intercourse was viewed as a positive and natural aspect of human behavior, required in the relationship between husband and wife (M. Ketubot 5:6, B. Nedarim 15b). But the rabbinic legal system assured that this behavior occurred only within strict parameters established by rules of purity (see Lev. 19:19, 20:18) and defined by restrictions that prevented what the rabbis deemed lewd and lustful. Sexual intercourse was to take place only at night (B. Niddah 64b), clothed (Lev. Rabbah 21:8), and using the "missionary" position (Pesikta deRab Kahana 11:6; B. Nedarim 20a). One was not to gaze upon the sexual organs (B. Berakhot 1), and sexual satisfaction had a negative connotation (M. Sotah 3:4; B. Sotah 21b). Irregular sexual positions and other erotic behaviors, including cunnilingus and talking during intercourse, were held to cause the birth of maimed children (B. Nedarim 20a); in general, one who indulged in sexual fantasies was held to have no place in the "precincts of God" (B. Niddah 13b). Only one passage proposes an opposite view to this usual rabbinic attitude. Yoḥanan (B. Nedarim 20b) rejects the notion that sexual behavior within marriage should be limited, stating that all sexual behaviors are permitted and should be used according to each individual's personal taste.

error, to err (Heb.: *to ah, ta ah;* Aram.: *ta ut, te a;* Gr.: *plane, planesis, planao*) to stray, to wander; a moral or religious wrong. The metaphor implies the scheme of the two ways and denotes straying from the path of uprightness and truth. Although the concept appears in the Hebrew Bible, the terms come into wide currency in Judaism and Christianity, often with an emphasis on false teaching. At Qumran the noun and verb frequently denote sinful conduct (1QS 3:21, 5:4). False teachers are described as "those who lead many astray" (1QpHab 10:9–12; cf. 4QpNah 2:8; see also 1 Enoch 98:15), and in this context the words can describe the activities of false interpreters and deceitful seers (cf. also 1QH 4:5–25). Mark 13:6 describes false messiahs as those who "lead many astray." In the targums the noun and verb are regularly substituted for other biblical words that denote idolatry.

ẹrub (Heb.) symbolic fence constructed around a number of dwellings, forming of them all a single domain, so that on the Sabbath it is permitted to carry objects around the courtyard shared by dwellings joined by the symbolic fence. *See also* ERUBIN.

Erubin Mishnah tractate devoted to the interplay between holy time and space, addressed to the rule that one may not leave one's abode on the Sabbath (Exod. 16:29–30). This is taken to mean that one remains in one's village, not in one's house; a village consists of the settled area and its natural environs. One may establish residence for purposes of travel on the Sabbath elsewhere than one's normal abode by making provision for eating a meal at that other place; this allows one to measure one's alloted area, 2,000 cubits, for travel from that other place. In order to establish a symbolic place of residence, one sets out, prior to sundown on the Sabbath, a symbolic meal or makes a verbal declaration to the same effect. One may furthermore form into a single domain, for purposes of carrying on the Sabbath, all the houses that open up onto a common courtyard, or an alley into which many courtyards open, through a symbolic meal, or through the construction of a common boundary. The tractate deals with the delineation of a limited domain; the symbolic meal and the Sabbath limit of a town; the symbolic meal and commingling of ownership of a courtyard or an alleyway; and the public domain in general, all in relationship to travel or carrying on the Sabbath.

erub tabshilin (Heb., fusion meal) fictive meal, with a symbolic portion of food for all householders who share in the meal, that effects the blending of domains into a single domain, thereby permitting carrying of objects in a common courtyard shared by several householders. *See also* ERUBIN.

Erucius Clarus, Gaius Sextus consul in 170 C.E. and legate in Judaea sometime thereafter. His father, Sextus Erucius Clarus, had been consul from 117 until his death in 146 and earlier had been the protégé of Pliny the Younger, who had helped him secure a magistracy (97) and, a few years later, senatorial status from Trajan. Gaius married Junius Rufinus's daughter, Pomponia Triaria. Pomponius Erucius Triarius and perhaps Gaius Julius Erucius Clarus Vibianus (consul in 193) were their children.

erusin (Heb., agreement to betrothal) in rabbinic Judaism, the agreement of a woman to wed a man, representing the first step toward marriage. The rite of betrothal involves the drinking of a cup of wine after reciting the following blessing: "Blessed are You, our God, king of the world, who creates the fruit of the vine. Blessed are You, Lord our God, king of the world, who has sanctified us by his commandments and commanded us concerning proper sexual relations, forbidding to us betrothed women but permitting to us married women through the rites of the huppah and sanctification.

Blessed are You, Lord, who sanctifies his people Israel through the marriage canopy and the rite of sanctification." Then there is a gift of a ring to the bride, with this formula: "Behold, you are sanctified to me by this ring in accord with the tradition of Moses and Israel." *See also* BETROTHAL.

Esau son of Isaac and Rebekah; elder twin of Jacob. He sold his birthright to Jacob for a bowl of stew (Gen. 25:29–34). Jewish and Christian tradition portray Esau as evil and jealous. In Malachi 1:2–3, God loves Jacob but hates Esau. The Book of Biblical Antiquities (LAB 32:5) attributes God's hatred to Esau's deeds. In the Book of Jubilees 35:13, God explains the divine love for Jacob and anger at Esau by reference to Esau's deeds (cf. 15:30). Throughout his works, Philo sees Esau as a figure who symbolizes evil passions. In the New Testament, Paul takes Esau's loss of his birthright as proof that election is through grace, not birth (Rom. 9:10–13). Hebrews 12:16–17 says that Esau's selling of his birthright makes him "immoral and godless." Esau is the eponymous ancestor of the Edomites (later the Idumeans), traditional enemies of Israel. In some accounts, Jacob kills Esau in war (Test. Jud. 9:1–8; Jub. 37–38).

eschatology teaching about the end-time. This word of modern Christian coinage captures a central theme in the later texts of the Hebrew Bible, much Second Temple Jewish literature, and almost all of the New Testament writings. From this perspective, an end to present history is in sight and beyond that the beginning of a new day.

The end of the old and a new beginning. Jeremiah 23:7–8, 31:31–34, and Ezekiel 34–37 imply the notion of an end as they predict a new beginning that repeats the foundational events of Israel's history, the Exodus and the institution of the covenant, and even creation itself. For Second Isaiah (that is, Isa. 40–55), these hopes for an end and a new beginning are already being realized in the present event of the return from exile. Writing a few decades later in a more sober vein, Third Isaiah (Isa. 56–66) projects the fulfillment of these promises into the future, announcing that God will soon appear in glory to "execute judgment on all flesh," dividing between righteous and wicked humanity (66:15–16). At that time, God will create new heavens and a new earth and a new Jerusalem where the quality of life will replicate the situation in paradise (65:17–25). Isaiah 24–27 develops the motif in its references to cosmic upheaval and resurrection of the dead. In these texts are sown the seeds of an eschatology that will become prominent in apocalyptic writings, a view of the world and history that is governed by a sharp division between the present troubled time and a future time of bliss described by reference to the myths of origins.

The fulfillment of prophecy. When these prophetic promises were not fulfilled, belief in God's faithfulness led Jews in the Graeco-Roman period to posit a future time when these things would in fact happen. One looked toward the goal to which prophecy pointed; eschatology was teleology. A number of texts in the wisdom tradition express this point of view. Ecclesiasticus 36:1–16 appeals to God to vindicate those who wait for the fulfillment of the ancient prophecies. According to Tobit 14:5 the time of that fulfillment is fixed, and both Tobit 13 and Baruch 4–5 reiterate Second and Third Isaiah's promises of the new Jerusalem.

In some circles it was believed that prophecy was already being fulfilled. The author of the Testament of Moses assumed the prophet's voice and rewrote Deuteronomy 31–34, filling out its historical scheme with specific references to the details of contemporary history. The Qumran Community believed that God had revealed to the Teacher of Righteousness when the consummation of time predicted by the prophets would occur (1QpHab 7:1–5), and Qumran sages composed commentaries on prophetic scripture (the Prophets and the Psalms) that expounded in detail how specific predictions were being fulfilled in the events of their own time and with relation to their community.

Apocalyptic eschatology. The writers of Jewish apocalypses from 1 Enoch (third to first centuries B.C.E.) and Daniel (c. 165 B.C.E.) to 2 Baruch and 2 Esdras (late first century C.E.), also reflect on current tragic events and their disparity with God's justice and the ancient prophecies, and like Third Isaiah they posit an imminent judgment, a sharp break with the present, and new age depicted in mythic terms that recall primordial events and circumstances. Their special contribution to eschatology—which draws on "scientific" speculation in Greek, Mesopotamian, and Jewish wisdom circles—is the development of a dualistic world view and a complementary claim to revelation, which guarantee their scenarios for the future. A spatial dualism between earth and heaven and between the inhabited world and the outer edges of the universe enables them to posit the present existence of the mechanisms of judgment and the places of future punishment and blessing. The created structure of the cosmos, the existence of heavenly tablets containing the order of the ages and the details of future history, and the present intercessory activity of the holy ones all ensure that the judgment will occur when God has determined that it should. The apocalypticist's worldview is anchored by a claim to special revelation. The seer has traveled to heaven and through the cosmos and has seen the things of which he speaks. His revelatory writings transmit this information and enable the eschatological community of the elect to stand fast as they await the consummation that they are certain will take place.

Realized eschatology. This term, which scholars coined with reference to the New Testament, describes the belief that eschatological events have taken place. In fact, already the Jewish texts indicate many degrees of eschatological realization. 1 Enoch's spatial dualism emphasizes that the present accomplishment of God's will in heaven guarantees its execution on earth. The historical reviews in 1 Enoch, Daniel, and the Testament of Moses, as well as the Qumran commentaries, define current events as eschatological events. Certain Qumran hymns express a more radical view: the Qumranite's entrance into the community of the elect is depicted as resurrection from the realm of the dead and exaltation to the heavenly sphere, where one stood among the heavenly hosts (1QH 3:19–23, 11:3–14). Nonetheless, this sense of realization is nuanced by the recognition that a final consummation has not yet taken place and the powers of Belial still present a real danger (3:28–36).

Variety and coherence in Jewish eschatology. Jewish eschatological texts are remarkable for the variety of their expression. These writings are populated with disparate eschatological figures: a restored Davidic king; a pair of anointed figures from the tribes of Levi and Judah; an eschatological prophet; Michael the heavenly prince; a transcendent savior who combines the qualities of the Davidic king, Second Isaiah's servant, and the one like a son of man in Daniel 7. They posit, variously, resurrection of the body or the spirit, assumption to heaven, immortality of the soul, and eternal life on earth or in heaven. They await the eschaton at various times, sometimes revising old timetables, or they believe that it has already begun to happen.

Thus, the coherence of Jewish eschatological texts does not lie in a set of beliefs that can be harmonized. It consists in three general characteristics. First, the texts attest their authors' pessimistic assessment of their present situation. Second, the authors tenaciously embrace traditional belief in the faithfulness and justice of the God of the covenant and thus posit a substantial turn for the better in the imminent future, when the end of this age gives birth to the beginning of a new age in which God's royal reign is realized finally, fully, and forever. Third, the texts share a common function—to exhort and encourage their readers to share their faith and to endure present suffering as they await God's vindication.

The absence of eschatology. Eschatology flourished among Jews where eschatology was needed. The disparity between the belief in God's justice and the perceived experience of injustice gave rise to eschatological hopes and speculation. Where such experience did not exist, eschatology was not present or was not a vital part of one's world view. The situation of the wealthy and powerful demonstrated to their satisfaction that they were already the beneficiaries of divine blessing and not in need of adjudication at the bar of God's justice. The fact that these same people might create the need for eschatology among the people they oppressed, or whose needs they ignored, simply demonstrates how the shape of theology was bound to the specifics of one's circumstances. Although much Jewish literature of the Graeco-Roman period had an eschatological bent, a full picture requires that we give careful attention to the situations that gave rise to a text's eschatology and make allowance for texts that express no eschatological hopes because their authors required none. The hymn to Simon the Hasmonean in 1 Maccabees 14 provides a helpful example in this respect. The author's allusions to scripture suggest that the high priest's conquests and treaties have initiated a time in which prophecy is fulfilled and the glories of the Davidic and Solomonic kingdoms have been restored. This protagonist and beneficiary of the Hasmoneans does not need eschatology, because prophecy has been fulfilled. The fact that the Hasmoneans caused their aggrieved and disenchanted opponents to espouse eschatological hopes is something we must learn from the Qumran literature.

Cross-cultural currents. Scholars debate the extent to which Jewish eschatology was influenced by parallel currents in other religions. Iranian texts (of late date in their present form) attest dualistic notions and schemes of world eras. The Stoics described eschatological conflagrations. Oracles and divinations of many sorts abounded. In diverse ways and different cultures, people in the Graeco-Roman period matched a sense of anxiety and exhaustion with hopes for a better time. The relationship of eschatological Judaism to its native traditions and to the religious and philosophical speculation of its gentile neighbors was complex.

Eschatology in the New Testament. Early Christianity rode the crest of a wave of eschatological hope and speculation. The church came into existence as a Jewish eschatological sect that was constituted by the revelation that the ministry, death, resurrection, and imminent glorious return of Jesus embodied the fulfillment of hopes sown by Israel's prophets and nourished by Jewish sages and apocalypticists. The experience that the end already permeated the present was the air that early Christians breathed. If this is not immediately evident on any given page of the New Testament, this is due to an author's taking the fact for granted. In general, the situation is clear. In Paul's view, Jesus, God's son and the Messiah, appeared at the consummation of time (Gal. 4:4), his resurrection and exaltation in heaven initiated the new age which is manifested by the Spirit's presence in the church (1 Cor.), and his defeat of the demonic powers and glorious return, in Paul's own lifetime, will bring about the general resurrection of the dead (1 Thess. 4; 1 Cor. 15). The gospels depict Jesus' message of the coming kingdom as an eschatological proclamation, and see Jesus as the fulfillment of prophecies and the exalted son of man who will soon return as the agent of God's judgment. Colossians, the pastoral epistles, and some of the general epistles warn about the false teaching that is characteristic of the end times. The Book of Revelation expounds its consoling eschatology in a traditional apocalyptic genre reminiscent of 1 Enoch and Daniel.

Christians differed from other eschatologically oriented Jews primarily in the orientation of their eschatological beliefs and hopes to the historical figure of Jesus. They differed among themselves in their espousal of various Jewish eschatological notions. They identified Jesus variously as royal Messiah, anointed high priest, servant of the Lord, son of man, son of God, the earthly eschatological epiphany of heavenly Wisdom or a high angel, and various combinations of the above. They interpreted the meaning of Jesus' death and the manner of his resurrection according to a whole range of options available in Jewish eschatological and non-eschatological literature.

The white heat of eschatological fervor waxed and waned within the first-century church according to circumstances. Although Paul anticipated a consummation in the imminent future, he also saw dangers in the ecstatic experience of the eschaton in a spirit-filled church (1 Cor. 12–14). The Pseudo-Pauline author of Ephesians emphasized the accomplished facts of salvation. Using conceptions reminiscent of 1QH 3:19–29, he spoke of the Christians' exaltation to heaven and warned of the dangers presented by "the evil one" (Eph. 1:15–23, 6:10–18). John believed that eternal life was already the possession of believers (John 5:24) and interpreted the presence of the spirit as the fulfillment of the promise that Jesus would return (1 John 5:1–12). Luke awaited the coming of Christ but he allowed for an extended timetable (Acts 1:6–8). The authors of James 5:7–11 and 2 Peter 3:1–10 encouraged their readers to wait patiently for the fulfillment of God's promises.

Part of the first-century controversy between Christians and Jews turned on eschatology. The variety of Jewish eschatological beliefs, or their absence in a given case, could be an important factor in a Jew's response to the Christian proclamation. Did one's experience call for eschatological resolution? If so, did one await a messiah? Was it a scion of David, an anointed priest, a heavenly savior? What did one make of Jesus' ministry? Was his death unjust and the proclamation of his resurrection plausible? In these and other respects, differences between Christians and Jews mirrored differences among Jews during the whole Graeco-Roman period.

Eschatology in rabbinic Judaism. Like Third Isaiah and the Apocrypha, the rabbis envision a future fulfillment of God's promises at a time when He will judge all human beings and initiate a messianic age. This age, called "the world to come," will be introduced by a distinct period, referred to as "the days of the Messiah." This period will occur in a time of devastating political and social upheaval (M. Sotah 9:15), leading ultimately to the destruction of the current world (B. Sanhedrin 97b). In light of the travail to accompany the coming of the Messiah, some rabbinic masters declared that, however much they longed for messianic redemption, they wished not to be alive at that time (B. Sanhedrin 98b).

Rabbinic masters show some interest in calculating the advent and duration of the days of the Messiah and world to come. According to different rabbis, the former would last 40, 70, 365, or 400 years (B. Sanhedrin 99a; see B. A<u>b</u>odah Zarah 9b). Similar attempts to reckon the messianic age held that the world will exist for six thousand years: "For two thousand it will be desolate, two thousand years will be the time of Torah, and two thousand years will be the days of the Messiah" (B. Sanhedrin 97a–b). The same source holds that, on account of the Israelites' sins, the Messiah has tarried and part of what should have been the messianic age has been lost.

While speculation concerning the exact date on which the Messiah will come occurs (see Mekhilta Pisha 14), the rabbis in general condemn those who engage in such predictions. The exact date is listed among things God has hidden from the people (B. Pesaḥim 54b; B. Sanhedrin 97a). Since the failure of messianic expectations might lead people to deny that the Messiah ever will come, those who make predictions are cursed. Instead of being predetermined, the rabbis held that the coming of the Messiah depends upon the Israelites themselves. When they conform to the will of God—repenting and performing good deeds, or even simply correctly observing one Sabbath—the Messiah will come (B. Sanhedrin 97b; Y. Taanit 4:8, 68d; Exod. Rabbah 25:12). In the meantime, the people are admonished not to attempt forcibly to hasten the coming of the end of time (B. Ketuḇot 111a).

In the days of the Messiah, the priesthood and sacrificial worship would resume in a rebuilt Temple, differentiated from the current age by the fact, for instance, that the harps played by the Levites will have more strings (T. Arakhin 2:7). The riches of the days of the Messiah will lead people to sin (Sifre Deut. 318), and modes of expiation such as study and observance of the law will still be required. In this period, the transplantation of the Babylonian rabbinic academies to the Land of Israel is imagined (B. Megillah 29a).

Coming after the final judgment and the resurrection of the dead, the conditions in the world to come will be very different from those of current life. According to Raḇ, "The world to come is not like this world. In the world to come there is neither eating nor drinking nor procreating nor business negotiations nor envy nor hatred nor competition. But the righteous are enthroned with their crowns on their heads, enjoying the splendor of the Presence of God" (B. Berakhot 17a). This age will be like a continual Sabbath (Aḇot deRabbi Natan 1:13), and there will be no death, sorrow, or tears (M. Moed Katan 3:9). What will remain is study and observance of the law, taught now by God himself (Tanḥuma, Yitro 13; Tanḥuma Vayigash 12).

Despite the rabbis' limited speculation regarding the nature of the messianic age and world to come, they generally discouraged concrete messianic thinking, seen as a threat to communal stability and as a promoter of potentially deadly political insurrection. When Akiḇa declared Bar Kokhba to be the Messiah, Yoḥanan b. Torta reportedly responded to him, "Akiḇa, grass will grow from your cheeks and He will still not have come" (Lam. Rabbah 58; Y. Taanit 4:8, 68d). Similarly, one who, while plowing his field, hears word that the Messiah has arrived is admonished to complete his work and only then to investigate. *See also* AFTERLIFE; APOCALYPTICISM; JUDGMENT, DIVINE; ZOROASTRIANS.

1 Esdras known as First Esdras or Esdras A, now part of the Apocrypha; closely parallels the biblical accounts in 2 Chronicles 35–36, Ezra 1–10, and Nehemiah 8. It provides a continuous account of Israel's history from the great Passover celebration of King Josiah (died in 609 B.C.E.) through the destruction of the Temple and Jerusalem (586 B.C.E.), to the return from exile (beginning in 538 B.C.E.), the reconstruction of religious and political life under the Judean officials Zerubbabel and Ezra, and concluding with the festive reading of the Torah (probably 444 B.C.E., although 398 or later, the time of Artaxerxes II, has also been proposed). The book's structure is as follows:

(1) Ideal state of affairs: the period of King Josiah (1 Esdr. 1:1–23; 2 Chron. 35:1–27)

(2) Decline and destruction (1:24–55; 2 Chron. 36:1–21)

(3) Return and restoration (2:1–9:55)

- First return under the Persian king Cyrus and the Jewish court official Sheshbazzar (2:1–30; 2 Chron. 36:22–23, Ezra 1 and 4:7–24)
- Second return under King Darius and Zerubbabel (3:1–7:15; Ezra 2–6 and additions that are without parallel)
- Third return under King Artaxerxes and Ezra (8:1–9:55; Ezra 7–10, Nehemiah 8)

The earliest extant version of First Esdras is in Greek. Although it reflects a Hebrew original (probably 2d c. B.C.E.), no Hebrew manuscripts have survived. The book modifies parallel biblical accounts by amplifying the role of Zerubbabel, the descendant from the house of David, and by highlighting the role of the prophets. Although some scholars debate this point, it is most likely that the book is a deliberate reworking of the biblical books of Chronicles and Ezra-Nehemiah (rather than a source for either) expressing a later, Hellenistic ideology, one that resembles Chronicles in its emphasis on the Davidic monarchy and the Temple. One of this book's most striking additions is the story of the three guardsmen (1 Esdr. 3–5), in which young Zerubbabel rises to prominence in the Persian court of King Darius by winning a contest in which he praises the power of women and of truth. First Esdras emphasizes Zerubbabel's Davidic ancestry and his heroic role in shaping Israel's destiny (granting him the longest and most dramatic narrative), in contrast to Ezra-Nehemiah which uses similar material to emphasize the role of the community and diminish Davidic importance. Furthermore, First Esdras envisions a restoration of earlier patterns and institutions whereas Ezra-Nehemiah expresses discontinuity. The antiquity and authority of this book are attested by the use that the first-century Jewish historian Josephus makes of it in his account of the return and restoration.

2 Esdras (4 Ezra) an ancient religious writing—today included among the Apocrypha—that is actually a compilation of three separate and independent works: 5 Ezra (transmitted as 2 Esdras chaps. 1–2); 4 Ezra (2 Esdras 3–14); and 6 Ezra (2 Esdras 15–16).

5 Ezra is a document of Christian prophecy that dates from the second or third century C.E. Pseudonymously attributed to Ezra, it first indicts the people Israel for their sins and disregard for God's beneficent acts, and predicts the transfer of God's allegiance to a "coming people" (1:4–2:9). In the second part (2:10–48), the "coming people" are exhorted, and the blessings that they will receive are described. 5 Ezra was composed by an unknown author, in Greek or (more probably) Latin.

4 Ezra is a sophisticated pseudepigraphic Jewish apocalypse that was written in Hebrew in the 90s C.E., probably in the Land of Israel. The purpose of the book is to come to terms with the theological issues raised by the Roman destruction of the Jerusalem Temple in 70 C.E. As an apocalypse, 4 Ezra consists mainly of the revelation of heavenly information by a divine agent, here an angel, to a human seer, here Ezra.

The book is made up of seven visions of Ezra. The first three (3:1–9:25), which are similar in form and content, consist mainly of theological dialogues between the distressed Ezra and an angel of God. The dialogues, which focus on questions of theodicy, generally conclude with the angel's offering eschatological solutions to Ezra's queries.

In the fourth vision (9:26–10:59), which is pivotal, Ezra encounters a distraught woman, who is then transformed into the heavenly city of Jerusalem. In the first part of the vision, Ezra adopts the role of comforter and adviser to the woman, just as the angel had previously done to him. This transitional vision constitutes a "conversion" experience, in which Ezra moves from distress to consolation.

The fifth and sixth visions (chaps. 11–13) are symbolic dream visions which again posit eschatological and messianic solutions to the problem of theodicy. The hated Roman Empire will be destroyed and replaced by God's messianic kingdom. In the seventh vision (chap. 14), Ezra receives a revelation from God which culminates in his inspired recitation and transcription of public and esoteric religious scriptures. Finally, Ezra is taken up to heaven.

6 Ezra is an anonymous writing of eschatological prophecy, probably Christian in origin, dating from the second or third century C.E. It was written in or around Asia Minor or Egypt. Although probably composed in Greek, the book survives in full only in Latin.

The first section of 6 Ezra (15:1–16:34) describes calamities that will soon take place on earth as punishment for human sin. In the second section (16:35–78), God's people are exhorted to withdraw from worldly activity and abstain from sin if they wish to be saved.

It is not known precisely when or by whom the textual associations between 4, 5, and 6 Ezra were made. The first connection occurred when the Latin version of 6 Ezra was appended to the end of a Latin text of 4 Ezra, probably before 400 C.E. Next, a Latin text of 5 Ezra was joined to the end of the 4/6 Ezra corpus, probably before 450 C.E. At a later date, 5 Ezra was moved to the beginning of the corpus. The earliest extant full Latin text of 2 Esdras is in a ninth-century Bible manuscript from France.

None of the three parts of the 2 Esdras corpus exerted substantial influence individually in either Jewish or Christian tradition. As a collection, however, the corpus did stand on the fringes of the medieval Roman Catholic canon, and as such did have some prestige. 2 Esdras, like the other writings of the Apocrypha, is regarded as noncanonical by Protestants; Catholics since the Council of Trent (1546) consider it noncanonical, but place it in an appendix to the Vulgate.

Eshtemoa (Arab.: as-Samu and variants) ancient Jewish town and synagogue site identified with biblical Eshtemoa (Josh. 15:50, etc.), about 15 kilometers south of Hebron. Stones carved with two seven-branched menorahs were reported in reuse in the village a century ago. Now the synagogue is excavated and partially restored. The original walls have withstood natural disasters and still stand at a height of 8.5 meters. The synagogue was built and remodeled in two stages. (1) A rectangular building was erected with its long, north wall oriented to Jerusalem. Three entrances in the short, east wall opened into worship space from a town square through a raised narthex or porch. An Aramaic inscription in the mosaic floor of the narthex reads, "Remembered be for good Eleazar the Priest and his three sons who donated one tremissis [a gold coin] to the synagogue. [last line broken]." The tile roof of the porch was held up with Corinthian columns. The worship space was without internal columns, and the center of worship was on the hall's long, north wall. This kind of orientation on a long wall is termed "broadhouse" orientation. Two tiers of benches ran along the two long walls, and other benches may have rested against the west wall. The floors were paved with multicolored geometric and floral mosaics. Three large niches, formed of carefully cut stone, graced the interior of the north wall above head height. (2) In the Byzantine period, presumably during the late fifth or early sixth centuries C.E., a stone *bimah* was added in front of the niches. The *bimah* included steps to ascend to the niches, and the Torah shrine presumably stood in the central niche. In several village stones, apparently from the synagogue, are remnants of Jewish and other art. One lintel fragment shows a menorah on a tripod base with a rosette to the right. A second stone fragment shows a menorah flanked by a column to the right. A fragment of a capital has a seven-branched menorah in relief. Yet another lintel is decorated with a spoked wheel, an amphora, a grapevine, and a six-pointed star. Several shell motifs appear on cut stones, including the lintel over the central entrance. Another lintel displays a wreath tied with a Hercules knot. It appears that the synagogue was transformed into a mosque during the seventh century C.E.

Essenes a Second Temple Jewish sect that flourished from the second century B.C.E. to the first century C.E. The meaning of the name is uncertain; it may mean "pious ones" or "healers," but other derivations have been proposed. Extended accounts in Philo and Josephus, along with a notice by Pliny in his *Natural History,* furnish enough details to identify the Essenes with the inhabitants of Qumran, who wrote many of the Dead Sea Scrolls. Essenes were also found in many cities and villages in Israel; thus there were various branches or related sects of Essenes. Like the Pharisees and Sadducees they were a Second Temple reform movement.

The Essenes based their way of life on an enthusiastic and strict adherence to God's covenant with Israel, understood according to their interpretation of the law. They kept a clear distinction between priests and lay people and stressed living a life of holiness and ritual purity. Those who retreated to Qumran did so in rejection of what they perceived as wicked behavior and improper observances by the priesthood in Jerusalem. They were an apocalyptic group who awaited divine intervention for the destruction of wicked Jews and Gentiles and the restoration of a perfect Temple, city, and people. In the meantime, the Qumran Community and Essene communities in Israel stressed strong, generous, and loving ties among members of the community, careful observance of all the requirements of Biblical law, and a pure worship of God. They were instructed to avoid contact with less observant Jews, who were condemned as wicked and unfaithful to the covenant.

The Qumran Community went through several stages of development. The community was ruled by a guardian and probably a fifteen-person council. The most important governing body was a council of the whole community, which met frequently and discussed all matters of importance. Members were organized hierarchically according to seniority and the evaluation of their spiritual progress. They prayed, ate, and studied scripture together. Detailed rules governed their behavior at meetings and with one another. Infractions against these practices and biblical laws were punished with a graded series of sanctions, culminating in expulsion from the group. All property was held in common and used for the upkeep of the community and of guests. At Qumran, the community seems to have been celibate, at least for most of its history. Essenes in villages and cities married, however. An applicant to the group had to become acquainted with the members and leaders and be examined by the guardian. If he (all members were male) was found acceptable, he underwent a two-year probation, which, if successfully completed, led to his and his property's integration into the life and practices of the group.

The history of the Qumran group and other Essenes must be deduced from allusions based on biblical interpretations and from archaeological excavations. The Covenant of Damascus and the presence of other sectarian literature at Qumran suggests that the movement may have derived from earlier sectarian movements and taken shape in the early second century B.C.E. After twenty years, a period that included the Maccabean revolt, a so-called Teacher of Righteousness led the sect. During this period, in the middle of the second century B.C.E., Qumran was settled by a small group. At the beginning of the first century B.C.E., during the rule of Alexander Jannaeus, the community was enlarged. It was destroyed during the time of Herod the Great, perhaps because of the Parthian invasion or an earthquake in 31 B.C.E. The settlement was rebuilt in the first century C.E. It was finally destroyed in the War with Rome (c. 68 C.E.). According to Josephus, some Essenes took part in public life. They were noted for their integrity and ability to predict the future. *See also* COMMUNITY RULE; DEAD SEA SCROLLS.

Esther, Book of part of the section of the Hebrew Bible known as the Writings. Esther is a Hebrew novella by an unknown author, written in the eastern diaspora of the Persian Empire. Although no firm date for the book can be established, a date of the early fourth century B.C.E. is reasonable, based on the book's familiarity with the court of the Persian Empire and lack of Hellenistic elements.

The Book of Esther is the story of a young Jewish girl named Esther who, because of her beauty and charm, becomes the wife of the Persian emperor Ahasuerus and, with the help of her cousin Mordecai, saves the Jewish people from destruction at the hands of the evil Haman, counselor to the emperor. At the end of the book, Esther and Mordecai inaugurate the popular festival of Purim to commemorate this event. The story is fast-paced and exciting; it is well told and all ends happily. However, most scholars do not view Esther as an original composition, but rather a compilation of two (or possibly three) tales: one a story of Esther and a conflict between Jews and Gentiles in the provinces of the Persian Empire, and the other a tale about the royal courtier Mordecai and the court intrigue that almost leads to his downfall. In addition, the link between the story of Esther and Mordecai and the festival of Purim is seen as doubtful; the association was probably made to legitimate a (possibly pagan) festival already being celebrated by diaspora Jews.

Esther was written for an audience of diaspora Jews. This is demonstrated by the assumption of the book that Jews must and should live in a cooperative relationship with their gentile overlords (for example, Mordecai overhears a plot against the king and informs Esther, thus saving the king's life). In fact, the book is mostly sympathetic to Gentiles; the evil in the book is caused by one Gentile, Haman, and the other Gentiles, such as the king, are his dupes. The Book of Esther, and the characters of Esther and Mordecai, give Jews a model for successful living in the diaspora, which helps to account for its popularity in the diaspora.

The Book of Esther, in spite of its popularity, was not accepted into the canon by the Jews until the third century C.E., by the Western Christian church until the fourth century C.E., and by the Eastern Christian church until the eighth century C.E. The chief difficulty the authorities found with the book was its perceived lack of religiosity: there is no mention of God, no acknowledgment of the law or the convenant, and no prayers. Esther, the heroine of the story, is married to a non-Jew, does not follow the dietary laws, and, in fact, lives a completely gentile life. Her Jewish identity seems to be more ethnic than religious. However, popularity among its Jewish audience eventually earned the book canonical status. Christian churches were slow to follow, however, because of what they saw as Esther's anti-Gentile bias (this charge was still being leveled in some twentieth-century Christian commentaries). This perceived basis is, however, a misunderstanding of the book's audience and function. Esther remains one of the most popular biblical books among Jews today, due mainly to its association with the Purim festival.

The Additions to the Book of Esther are found in the Septuagint, or Greek translation of the Hebrew Bible, and were produced with the translation of Esther in the late second or early first century B.C.E. The additions are six passages not found in the Hebrew text whose purpose is to add a specifically religious element (for example, the prayers of Esther and Mordecai), to heighten the dramatic interest, and to lend a note of authenticity to the events of the book (e.g., the royal edicts of Haman and Mordecai). God is mentioned over fifty times, as well as prayer, the Temple and its cult, and the dietary laws. However, most readers find the Additions gratuitous to the main plot, and thus the Additions do not find a wide audience within Judaism or Protestant Christianity.

Esther, targums to There are three known targums to Esther. The first two contain much additional and expansive material. They were probably composed in the early Middle Ages (seventh or eighth centuries). The third targum to Esther, published in the Antwerp Polyglot, is quite literal. It was created by sixteenth-century Christian scholars, who simply removed the additional material from the first targum, leaving a literal third targum. The value of this third targum to Esther for the study of Judaism is thus nil.

Esther Rabbah I exegesis of the Book of Esther, compiled c. 500–600 C.E. The exegesis concerns (1) the relationship between Israel and God, with special reference to the covenant, the Torah, and the land; (2) the relationship between Israel and the nations, with focus on Israel's history, past, present, and future, and how that cycle is to be known;

(3) Israel on its own terms, with focus upon Israel's distinctive leadership; and (4) the Book of Esther in particular. Esther Rabbah presents a single message: the nations are swine; their rulers, fools; and Israel is subjugated to them, though it should not be, because of its own sins. But just as God saved Israel in the past, so the salvation that Israel can attain will recapitulate the former ones.

eternity a concept that undergoes a distinct shift in meaning between the time of the Hebrew Bible and that of early Judaism. In the Hebrew Bible, the idea of eternity is most commonly connected with God. God is the "eternal God" (Deut. 33:27), the "everlasting God" (Gen. 21:33), the "everlasting King" (Jer. 10:10). The early writings of the Hebrew Bible depict God as a God *of* time, of the remotest past, and of the longest spans of time. "Eternity" is coextensive with the duration of the world.

In the postexilic period, the conception of God's eternity begins to shift from being equivalent to the time of the world to transcending that time. Eternity becomes a truly unlimited span that extends both before and after the "time of the world" (cf. Ps. 90:2; Isa. 44:6, 60:19–20).

Early Jewish literature continues this trend. Here, in many contexts, eternity is the antithesis of time, a timelessness that surpasses the duration of the world (see especially 2 Enoch 65). An important development here is the rise in Jewish eschatology of the idea of two distinct "ages" or "aeons": the "present age," which constitutes this world and its time; and the "future age," an ideal eschatological era that will be incorruptible, eternal, and perfect (cf. 1 Enoch 71:15; 2 Enoch 66:6–7; 2 Esdras 6:9). Within this framework, the idea of "eternity" is extended to various aspects of the eschatological age, for example, "eternal life," "eternal light," and "eternal torment."

Early Jewish notions of time and eternity are taken over in early Christianity. A new development here is that notions of God's eternity and preexistence are extended to Christ (cf. John 17:24; Heb. 13:8). The eschatological doctrine of the "two ages" is expressed in a wide variety of contexts (e.g., Mark 10:30; Rom. 12:12; 1 Tim. 6:17).

Jewish rabbinic literature also expresses similar notions of "eternity," including the idea of the "two ages" (e.g., Gen. Rab. 14 on 2:7). *See also* AGE, THIS; AGES, TWO; AGE TO COME.

Ethiopia kingdom in northeastern Africa. Egypt ruled the country from 2000 B.C.E. to 1000 B.C.E. Isaiah prophesied the doom of Egypt and Ethiopia, and 2 Kings and Isaiah name the pharaoh Tirhakah as Ethiopia's king in the eighth century B.C.E. Ethiopia's first independent kings descended from an Arabian dynasty. The country's Semitic language and culture stems from this dynasty, which traced its origins to Menelik and claimed to be descended from the son of Solomon and the Queen of Sheba. Medieval legends state that this son brought Jewish customs and law to Ethiopia. The Jewish nature of the Coptic Monophysite Christianity of Ethiopia may be the result of pre-Islamic contacts between the Ethiopians and the Jews.

ethnarch (from Gr.: *ethnos* [people] and *archon* [ruler]) ruler over a native people. Under the Romans, such rulers (e.g., Hyrcanus II and Archelaus) were not officially kings, though they might be so regarded by their people. The term might also be used for the head of a *politeuma* in a Greek city.

ethnos (Gr., people) In Jewish writings in Greek, the word is sometimes equivalent to "Gentiles," especially when used in the plural (*ethnoi*). On the other hand, the Jews themselves also formed an ethnic community in many areas outside Palestine, that is, an *ethnos* in the strict sense.

etiquette specific social rules concerning banquets, religious festivals, and gatherings of private associations. At formal meals such as those depicted in Esther, Daniel, Ben Sira (Ecclesiasticus), the Qumran scrolls, the Gospels, and 1 Corinthians, placement was usually based on social rank: the more privileged sat closer to the host and often received more food (cf. 1 Cor. 11:17–22). Ben Sira's counsel includes accepting one's placement, eating in moderation and being the first to stop, avoiding argument, not deriding those who are drunk, and leaving quickly (31:12–32:13). Other areas of etiquette depicted in wisdom literature include proper speech, clothing, treatment of family members, and behavior in the business world.

etrog citron or yellow, thick-skinned citrus fruit; an important motif in ancient Jewish art that often appears with a menorah, shofar, and lulab. The etrog is not often carved in detail but may simply be depicted as a round object. In these depictions, if it did not occur with other species, it would be impossible to identify. On other occasions it may be shown with a "waist" and a point at the end. The etrog occurs unambiguously on coins of year four (69 C.E.) of the First Revolt, where it appears with the other three species of the Feast of Sukot: lulab, willow, and myrtle. The etrog also appears with the same group of symbols in coins of year one (132 C.E.) of the Bar Kokhba War. It also appears on glass and lamps and in synagogue art in relief or in mosaic art. We have more than twenty etrogs portrayed in ancient Jewish synagogue art from the third to the sixth century. *See also* CITRON.

etymology, in exegesis Hebrew and Aramaic names are often transparent in meaning; for example, Abimelekh means "[the] father [is] king." Already in the Hebrew Bible, we find plays on names, even though some of these represent only folk etymologies rather than scientific ones. In Jewish literature of the Graeco-Roman and rabbinic periods, names often played a part in exegesis. In rabbinic literature, this was usually fairly straightforward; for example, a name might indicate a particular characteristic of the person bearing the name. This does not differ significantly from the wordplay found in the Bible. In some of the Jewish exegetes writing in Greek, however, we have some quite sophisticated exegeses based on etymologies. This occurs as early as Aristobulus the Exegete, who uses the etymology of "sabbath" in his discussion. The height of etymological exegesis is reached in the works of Philo of Alexandria, who often incorporates etymologies into his allegories; Philo gives an etymology to 166 different names in the Hebrew Bible, some of them rather obscure. Josephus also gives occasional etymologies, which resemble those in rabbinic literature.

etzba *see* FINGERBREADTH

eudaimonion (Gr., happiness) Originally used in a broad sense, *eudaimonion* became a technical term in ancient philosophy for the goal of life. Although philosophers were ready to see happiness recognized as the proper goal, there was much debate about the proper means to achieve it.

Eudaimonis mother of Apollonis, military magistrate in Upper Egypt; author of letters written during the Jewish revolt in Egypt, 115–117 C.E. In one letter to her son, Eudaimonis, having heard of atrocities perpetrated by the Jews, offers a prayer to "the gods, especially the invincible Hermes, that they may not roast you." In the summer of 117 Eudaimonis laments the poor economic conditions resulting from the war, believing that she will have to go through the winter "without a stitch to wear." A letter from Eudaimonis to her daughter-in-law written in July 117 indicates that the situation still was not stable enough for Apollonis to return home.

euhemerism belief that gods were only men or heroes who were deified. The term is taken from the name of the Greek writer Euhemerus (fl. c. 300 B.C.E.), who wrote a novel of an island on which the gods were actually rulers who had been promoted to gods in thanks for their benefits to the people. Euhemerism is often found with reference to pagan gods in Jewish writings of the Graeco-Roman period. For example, Artapanus states that Moses set up the Egyptian worship, including gods in the form of animals, in order to keep order for the king. As a result, the Egyptians honored him as divine and named him Hermes.

eulabeia (Gr., caution, awe, fear of God) In Jewish writings in Greek, it is used with two main meanings. It can refer to the caution or prudence of the sage. More often in Jewish literature, however, it has the meaning of "piety." These concepts are not mutually exclusive, however, as an examination of Ben Sira (Ecclus.) shows. Here, the prudence or caution of the wise man is also equal to fear of God. This fits very much Ben Sira's general development of the wisdom tradition, in which wisdom is ultimately equated with the Torah.

eunuch a castrated male. In cultures in which the king maintained a harem, the bodyguards who protected and looked after the harem were often eunuchs. Sometimes the word in Hebrew (*saris*) or Greek (*eunuchos*) indicated an important officer or official who was not a physical eunuch, as, for example, Potiphar in the Joseph story.

Eupolemus one of the Fragmentary Hellenistic Jewish Writers of the second century B.C.E. He is often identified with the important official of 1 Maccabees 8:17 whose father John had negotiated terms with Antiochus III and who himself was sent on a mission to Rome. Only fragments of a history, *On the Kings of Judah,* are preserved in the writings of Josephus and Eusebius, though one fragment ascribed to him is now usually assigned to another writer referred to as Pseudo-Eupolemus. A good deal of his narrative is taken from the Hebrew Bible but with much interpretation and extrabiblical aggadic material included. He claimed that Moses taught the alphabet to the Jews, from whom the Phoenicians acquired it. His narrative of the rise and rule of David seems to have been sanitized (unless the preserved account is heavily abbreviated). His section on Solomon gives a series of supposed letters to and from the kings of Egypt and Tyre. There is also a detailed description of Solomon's temple, which does not always agree with the biblical account or other accounts. He claims that one of the Judean kings attempted to burn Jeremiah alive. He calculates the age of the world to his own time as just over five thousand years.

Eupolemus, Pseudo- also known as the Anonymous Samaritan. Two of the fragments of the Fragmentary Hellenistic Jewish Writers once attributed to Eupolemus are now generally thought not to be by him. These fragments are all found in Eusebius. Pseudo-Eupolemus was probably a Samaritan, since his account of Abraham's meeting of Melchizedek, described in Genesis 14, does not take place at Salem (i.e., Jerusalem), but at Argarizin, the sacred temple of the Samaritans. The use of the name Argarizin instead of Gerizim is also a sign of a Samaritan writer. The two surviving fragments have come through Alexander Polyhistor; this and other factors suggest a dating for the work in the early second century B.C.E. The fragments both focus on Abraham, who was a hero to the Samaritans as well as to the Jews. Pseudo-Eupolemus was a proponent of euhemerism; he wrote that Enoch (identified with Atlas) discovered astrology and that Abraham taught astrology and mathematics to the Phoenicians and Egyptians. He also wrote that the Tower of Babel was founded by a race of giants, from whom Abraham was descended. Where the Hebrew text refers to Canaan or Canaanite, Pseudo-Eupolemus uses the term Phoenicia or Phoenician.

eusebeia (Gr., piety, or worship) one of a group of related words, including *sebomai* and *eulabeia,* which have a similar meaning. These words were often used by Jewish writers who were writing in Greek in reference to Jewish religion and worship. For example, the word *sebomai* is often translated as "God-fearers."

Eusebius (265–339/340 C.E.) bishop of Caesarea, born perhaps at Caesarea, Palestine. He was taught by Pamphilus, Origen's leading disciple. In response to Diocletian's persecutions, he fled to Tyre and then to Egypt. He returned to Palestine as a result of the Edict of Tolerance of 311. He was one of Arius's early supporters. He composed historical works, exegetical tracts, philological studies, theological tractates, and apologetic compositions; however, his historical works are the major reason for his importance today. His *Chronicon* has two parts. The first summarizes the history of the most famous peoples of the ancient world, while the second provides synchronic tables arranged in parallel columns with brief notes on the important historical facts from Abraham's birth to 303 C.E. Following a well-developed argument, Eusebius demonstrates that Judaism is the oldest religion. Interestingly, he does not consider Adam to have been a historical figure. His *Ecclesiastical history* demonstrates that Christianity's final victory testifies to its divine origin and legitimacy. In the *Evangelical Demonstration* he refutes the Jewish claims that the Christians had distorted and corrupted Judaism. He argues that the law of Moses was temporary and merely a transitional period between the patriarchs and Jesus. He also argues that the prophecies found in the Hebrew Bible were fulfilled in Jesus' incarnation, passion, and death.

Eutychius ibn Batriq (877–940 C.E.) Melchite patriarch of Alexandria and historian. He states that Constantine prohibited the Jews from living in or passing through Jerusalem. He reports that twenty thousand Jewish warriors helped the Persians during their invasion of Palestine in 614 C.E. and records the attacks on Acre and Tyre.

Eve (Heb.: Havva; Gr.: Zoe) meaning "life" and defined as "mother of all living," the name bestowed on the first woman by Adam (Gen. 3:20). The Assumption of Moses 15–30 (Latin: Life of Adam and Eve) offers Eve's lengthy recounting of the Eden story, her accepting responsibility for sin (18:1, so also Sir. 25:24 and contrast 4 Ezra), acts of repentance, witnessing of the return of God after Adam's death, and her own death and burial. Jubilees 3–4 expands on Genesis 2–4 by including such material as women's postpartum purity instructions. According to 1 Enoch 69:6, she was misled by an angel. In 2 Enoch 30, in an interesting word play, she is named by God. The Pauline tradition (2 Cor. 11:3; 1 Tim. 2:11–15) makes her the archetype of women's sinfulness: because the first woman was deceived by the serpent, disobedient to divine command, and the cause of the expulsion from paradise, all women share her fate of subordination to her husband (Gen. 3:16). The writer of 1 Timothy 2 insists that to overcome Eve's sin, women must be modest, faithful, and bear children. Other references to Eve include Sibylline Oracles 1:40–45 (on the fall); Apocalypse of Abraham 23–24 (an Eden scene, with both Adam and Eve of extraordinary height and with the serpent awakening Eve's sexual desire); and the Greek Apocalypse of Ezra 2 (the seer holds God responsible for creating Eve and thereby causing the fall). A figure of substantial speculation for Gnostic writers, Eve is frequently associated with Sophia, is presented as an instructor of heavenly wisdom, and is Adam's teacher. *See also* ADAM; ADAM AND EVE, BOOKS OF.

evening prayer (Heb.: *arbit;* later: *ma ariḇ*) vesper prayers of Judaism, comprising recitation of the Shema with its preceding and following blessings, the Prayer and Aleinu

evidence *see* TESTIMONY

evil, origins of The Hebrew Bible devotes relatively little space to speculation about the origins of evil and the causes of sin. Human suffering is generally construed as punishment for sin; human beings are responsible for their own evil deeds.

There are a few exceptions. The myth of Eden traces the enmity between humans and animals, the sterility of the earth, women's pain in childbirth, and the necessity of death back to a primordial rebellion by the first human beings. Some of the psalmists protest against unjust suffering. The present form of the Book of Job carries the protest to great lengths and explains Job's suffering as the result of a test instigated by the heavenly accuser (Heb.: haSatan). For Second Isaiah the innocent suffering of the righteous servant of YHWH is expiation for the people (Isa. 53:4–6, 10–11).

Different from the biblical texts, Jewish documents from the Graeco-Roman period present a range of explanations for the origins of evil and the causes of sin which posit the existence of a world of evil spirits whose activities will continue until God ends the present evil age. Especially prominent are a set of myths about a primordial heavenly revolt. 1 Enoch 6–16 has three variations of the myth. (1) Shemihazah and his associates descend from heaven, mate with women, and beget bellicose giants who ravage the earth and its inhabitants. Like many myths, the story narrates primordial events in order to explain present conditions; specifically, it inverts claims that the successors of Alexander the Great were sons of the gods and explains the origin of violence in the early Hellenistic period by identifying the divine parents as rebels against the high God. (2) Asael reveals heavenly secrets about metallurgy and mining, which enable humans to forge weapons and fabricate seductive cosmetics and jewelry; other watchers reveal the secrets of magic and astrological prognostication. (3) Because the giants are partly divine, their death at the time of the flood releases their spirits into the world to constitute a realm of evil demons who will continue to wreak havoc until the end-time.

The Book of Jubilees adds a new twist to the Enochic myths. The Prince of Mastema, the chief of the evil spirits bred by the watchers, makes a pact with God that permits one tenth of his subordinates to have their way with the earth and humanity (chap. 10). They obstruct God's purposes, fostering idolatry, spreading sickness, and inciting humans to commit sin.

In the Life of Adam and Eve 12–16, the devil (Lat.: *diabolus*) recounts a myth of heavenly revolt based on Isaiah 14. The angels are ordered to worship the image of God in Adam. The devil refuses and proposes to set his throne above the stars and be like the Most High. He and his angels are hurled down to earth, and in revenge the devil tempts Eve and Adam—the cause of the devil's fall—to sin.

The Qumran Community Rule (specifically 1QS 3:13–4:26) traces the origins of evil back to the dualistic structure of creation itself rather than to a primordial heavenly revolt. Truth and perversity have been generated from a "spring of light" and a "fountain of darkness," and God has set "the Prince of Light" and "the Angel of Darkness" over the children of righteousness and the children of perversity. Although human beings are responsible for their actions and receive appropriate rewards and punishments, their deeds are functions of these two spirit powers and their hosts of good angels and evil spirits, who dwell in human hearts. Thus, different from 1 Enoch, both Jubilees and the Community Rule suggest that, for unstated reasons, God permits evil and sin to take place. In 1QS 3–4 the cosmic spirits of good and evil are explicitly located within human beings; cosmology has merged with anthropology.

The move toward an anthropological explanation of sin is completed and radicalized in 2 Esdras. The seer charges that "a grain of evil seed was sown in Adam's heart from the beginning," which continues to produce wickedness until the present time (4:30–32). All descendents of Adam are born with an inclination to sin, and God is responsible for not removing this propensity (3:20–26). Later, rabbinic texts will develop the ideas in 1QS 3–4 and 2 Esdras into a teaching about the *yetzer* or the two *yetzer*s."

The Apostle Paul in Romans 7–8 works with notions especially close to 1QS 3–4 and 2 Esdras. The problem of sin is anthropological; human beings since Adam have a kind of genetic defect. "Flesh" is generically the locus of "sin," which is the functional equivalent of the evil spirit, and the Torah is impotent to effect the obedience it commands. Paul's solution is the appearance of the Son of God, whose obedience, substitutionary death, and resurrection release into the world the equivalent of the Qumran Prince of Light—the spirit of the Risen Christ—who facilitates the obedience that brings eternal life.

The most radical explanation for the origin of evil and sin appears in the Gnostic texts of the second century C.E. (e.g., the Apocryphon of John; the Origin of the World). The heavenly revolt took place before creation, and, indeed, the creation of the world and humanity are the result of that revolt. Thus, the creator is demonized, and the creation is essentially evil.

Fundamental to all of this speculation is an attempt to explain the existence of sin and evil while maintaining the justice and power of God. The ongoing existence of sin and evil is explained by the apocalyptic and Gnostic generational myths: the watchers literally bred their malevolent spiritual substance into the world, and the Gnostic demiurge created the universe from the substance that derived from Sophia's miscarriage. In both cases, an eschatological divine intervention will obliterate evil and sin. The anthropological explanations for sin in 1QS 3–4, 2 Esdras, and Paul also posit an eschatological solution.

Myths concerning the origins of evil and sin draw motifs from their gentile environment. The Enochic myths reflect Greek myths about the mating of gods and mortals and about the revolt of Prometheus. The devil's narrative in the Life of Adam and Eve derives, ultimately, from Canaanite mythology. The radical dualism in 1QS 3–4 has significant parallels in Iranian texts. *See also* DEVIL; DUALISM.

evil eye, in rabbinic Judaism jealous gaze cast upon a person or object to cause harm through magical means. Rabbis believed that biblical figures cast it upon one another and that their own contemporaries, too, could exercise this power. It can be warded off by modesty and restraint, or it can be counteracted by wearing a talisman, by magical gestures, or the recitation of verses specified in the Talmud (B. Ber. 55b).

exaltation raising of one to a position of high authority. Biblical stories set in royal courts describe how Joseph, Mordecai, and Daniel and his three companions are persecuted, condemned to death, and then rescued, vindicated, and installed as viziers or royal counselors (Gen. 37–47; Esther; Dan. 3, 6). Isaiah 52–53 describes "the servant of YHWH" as a persecuted prophet (also 50:4–9) who is exalted in the presence of the kings and the nations (52:13–15). Wisdom of Solomon 2–5 recounts the case of the righteous and wise spokesman of God, employing the form of the court stories and describing the sage's exaltation in the language of Isaiah 52–53. Daniel 12:3 attributes the Deutero-Isaianic pattern of suffering and exaltation to the teachers of the Torah during the persecution by Antiochus IV, and later Jewish texts democratize the notion of glorious heavenly exaltation (2 Bar. 49–51). The tradition in Daniel 12:3 and Wisdom of Solomon 2–5 becomes a model for describing Jesus' death and his exaltation to heaven. Its influence is evident in the hymn in Philippians 2:6–11, in credal formulas elsewhere in the Pauline epistles, and in the literary shape of the gospel narratives about Jesus' suffering, death, and resurrection, which also employ motifs from biblical Psalms about the humiliation and exaltation of the righteous one. More broadly, the pattern of death and exaltation is applied to persecuted Christians (Rev. 20:4–6). *See also* SERVANT OF THE LORD.

excommunication expulsion from the religious community. The preservation of institutional integrity and orthodoxy requires communal self-discipline. In addition to restriction of ritual privileges, silencing, and temporary banishing, excommunication, or severance from the group, proved an often effective means of maintaining internal peace. Ezra 10:8, the earliest biblical attestation of excommunication, bans from the congregation those who refuse his summons. The Qumran scrolls mandate separation either on a temporary or permanent basis; permanent excommunication would result from infractions such as speaking the divine name, complaining against congregational authority, deliberately transgressing Mosaic law, and sharing food with an excommunicate (see 1QS6:27–9:2; Josephus, *War* 2.8.8). Matthew insists that a church member be forgiven "seventy times seven" times (18:22) but notes as well that after three warnings against misconduct, the Church treat the wrongdoer "as a Gentile and a tax collector" (18:17). Regarding a man cohabiting with his father's wife, Paul advises excommunication; the Church should "deliver him to Satan for the destruction of the flesh that his spirit may be saved in the day of the Lord Jesus" (1 Cor. 5:1–5). Rather than depict excommunication, Acts presents the death of those who would cheat the Church (5:1–11). John 9:22, 12:42, and 16:2 (see also Luke 6:22) mention synagogues that excommunicate (Gr: *aposynagogos*) those who confess Jesus; the Birkhat haMinim or Benediction against Heretics, the twelfth benediction in an early version of the Shemonah Esreh (Amidah), is frequently adduced as independent testimony to John's claim, although the prayer makes such severance the voluntary act of the (apostate) worshiper.

The rabbinic literature speaks of two types of excommunication, the rebuke (*nezifah*), which applied for a minimum of seven days, and the ban of excommunication (*niddui*), which applied for a minimum of thirty days (B. Moed Katan 16a; Y. Moed Katan 3:1, 81a). During these periods of punishment, members of the community were forbidden to have contact or do business with the offender, who was expected to engage in acts of penitence and to show signs of remorse. Once in effect, a ban of excommunication could be released only by a court or individual of greater stature than the one who had imposed it. Similarly, an individual placed under a ban by a student or lower court was not treated as excommunicated by a superior court or authority of higher stature (B. Moed Katan 17a).

The Babylonian Talmud depicts excommunication as a broadly applied punishment for social or religious misconduct that seems also to have been a tool used by individual rabbis to protect their personal honor. A learned person might excommunicate someone who insulted him (B. Moed Katan 17a); a teacher could excommunicate a student who decided a law in his presence (B. Shabbat 19a) or who asked silly questions (B. Menaḥot 37a); and excommunication applied to those who treated lightly the washing of the hands, who told stories about departed sages, or who acted in a familiar way toward heaven (B. Berakhot 19a). The Jerusalem Talmud speaks narrowly of the use of excommunication, reserving it for individuals who lead the community into improper religious belief or practice, for instance, by preventing people from performing their religious obligations or by inducing the community as a whole to commit blasphemy (Jerusalem Talmud Moed Katan 3:1, 81b).

execution in rabbinic law, the death penalty. While generally rejecting the biblical theory of retaliatory punishment, preferring instead monetary compensation, rabbinic law retains the punishment of death for homicide. In this, the rabbis apparently hold that only in a case of murder is the corresponding punishment—execution—always equitable (B. Ba_b_a Kamma 84a). While retaining execution as a punishment applied whenever called for by scripture, however, the rabbis advanced the general theory that courts should do everything possible to ensure that a death sentence would never be imposed. This entailed enacting strict guidelines defining the conditions under which the death penalty could be used; for example, murderers had to have been warned that their actions made them subject to execution. Additionally, judges could ask questions the witnesses were unable sufficiently to answer. This rendered their testimony unreliable and thus precluded execution as a punishment for the crime (B. Makkot 7a). Simeon b. Gamaliel held that hesitating to impose capital punishment caused the number of murderers to multiply within the people of Israel (M. Makkot 1:10). The apparently normative view, however, was that execution was not appropriate in any case. Tarfon declared that a court that imposes the death penalty more than once in seventy years is "murderous" (M. Makkot 1:10). Eleazar b. Azaria and Aki_b_a stated that no court on which they presided would impose execution (ibid.).

Where scripture does not indicate the method of execution, the rabbis assign one of the four biblical methods. Stoning, considered the most severe punishment, was applied in eighteen circumstances, including bestiality, blasphemy, cursing a parent, idolatry, and witchcraft. Strangulation, deemed the mildest form of execution, applied in five cases, including false prophecy and kidnapping. The other methods are burning, applied in ten cases of inappropriate sexual activity, and decapitation, applied in cases of communal apostasy and murder.

exilarch Resh Galuta, the head of the Babylonian Jewish community from the Parthian Empire through the Sassanid dynasty and for several centuries in the period of Arab control as well. Designated in Aramaic as "chief of the diaspora," the exilarch was recognized by the state as the ruler of the Jewish community. He had a place on the king's council, was responsible for governance and collection of taxes in the Jewish community, and was in charge of the Jewish criminal and civil courts. While enjoying the backing of the government, within the Jewish community the exilarch legitimated his power by tracing his lineage back to David, implicitly claiming that he, or one of his descendents, would be the Davidic Messiah (see, e.g., Jerusalem Talmud Ketu_b_ot 12:3; 35a). The exilarch thus was a political figure who, through a messianic myth, claimed rightfully to rule the Jewish community in Babylonia.

No evidence exists regarding the founding of the exilarchate or the earliest exilarchs. The office likely was created by the Parthians in the first century C.E. as an aspect of their reorganization of the empire and in response to the need to secure the loyalty of the Jewish population that lived in substantial and strategically vital territories. While the nature of the early exilarchate is unknown, it is clear that by the time of the Bar Kokhba Revolt and especially in the period of Judah the Patriarch, a Babylonian exilarchate existed as a central governing office. The exilarch had direct access to the Parthian throne, wore insignia of Parthian nobility, and controlled a military force to execute his edicts. The exilarch appears to have been substantially more powerful and independent than the patriarch in the land of Israel, who was subordinate to Roman officials and ruled at their pleasure.

The exilarch ruled the Jewish community through the appointment of judges and community officials. For this purpose he used the rabbis, who enhanced the exilarch's power through their knowledge of the oral Torah, recently codified in the land of Israel in the form of the Mishnah. B. Sanhedrin 5a suggests that a rabbinic judge could indemnify himself against financial responsibility for errors by securing appointment from the exilarch. In the face of such appointment, that individual would be a representative of the secular government and exempt from the rabbinic rule that deems judges personally culpable for errors.

Beginning in the late third century C.E., the rabbis' growing power and prestige increasingly came into conflict with the exilarch's authority. The conflict is typified in the rabbinic stories of Geniva, who, in about 275 C.E., apparently asserted the superiority of rabbis over the exilarch and who was executed by the state. Similarly in this period, rabbis began to contend that as communal leaders they should be exempt from the head tax, a claim that the exilarch rejected. The talmudic literature additionally relates the mistreatment of rabbis by members of the exilarch's staff (see, e.g., B. Gittin 67b; B. Shabbat 121b). Through the remainder of the Talmudic period and almost to the end of the exilarchate, the relationship between exilarchs and rabbis varied depending upon the extent to which the exilarch accepted, supported, and at times participated in rabbinic culture, learning, and the system of rabbinic academies.

After the Arab conquest, the Muslim government for a time continued to recognize the exilarch as the political head of the Jewish community, responsible for taxation, appointment of judges, and administering of the Jewish courts. By the time the exilarchate ceased to exist, in the eleventh century C.E., the title passed on dynastically but carried with it no special authority nor responsibility within the Jewish community.

exile an idea occurring in two main contexts in early Jewish thought. One is the exile of the ten northern tribes of Israel imposed by the Assyrians under Sargon II in 722 B.C.E. The other is the exile of the inhabitants of Judah to Babylon in 598 and 587 B.C.E. under Nebuchadnezzar and the Neo-Babylonian Empire. Since it was the Judahites who returned to and restored the land of Israel, the Babylonian exile plays by far the more important role in Jewish theology.

The Babylonian exile is one of the major foci of theological reflection in early Jewish thought and, like the destruction of the Second Temple by the Romans in 70 C.E., constituted a severe challenge to the idea of theodicy, the justice of God. Why had God allowed his earthly abode, the Jerusalem Temple, and the holy city of Jerusalem to be destroyed, and the people of God to be exiled? This problem was answered, in deuteronomistic fashion, by interpreting the destruction and exile as punishment for the sins of the Jewish people. When these sins were absolved, God would remember the covenant with Israel, allow mercy again to reign, and permit the restoration. The Babylonian exile ended in 538 B.C.E. when Cyrus and the Persians conquered the Babylonians and allowed the Jews and other captive peoples to return to their homelands.

The Babylonian exile thus functions in early Judaism as a major manifestation, or testing ground, of deuteronomistic theology. The event and its lessons are recalled in numerous early Jewish writings. It plays a dominant role, for example, in 1 Baruch, 1 Esdras, the Letter of Jeremiah, 4 Ezra, 2 Baruch, and 4 Baruch. Many other documents mention the exile or include it in the context of a historical review (1 Enoch 89:66–72; Jub. 1:13–18; Pss. Sol. 9:1–2; Sib. Or. 3:265–294; Test. Moses 3–4; and Lad. Jac. 5:16).

The exile of the ten northern tribes (cf. 2 Kings 17) is less significant theologically, but is mentioned in early Jewish literature. The first significant use is in the book of Tobit, which alleges to tell the story of a Galilean Israelite exiled to Ninevah. At a later period, the legend grew up that the northern tribes, whose actual fate was a mystery, resided in untold numbers in an unknown land east of the Euphrates. According to 4 Ezra, after their initial exile, these tribes removed themselves still further to a remote land where they devoted themselves to the law. At the time of the eschaton, they would return to the land of Israel (4 Ezra 13:12–13, 39–50; cf. 14:33). Related references appear in the Testament of Moses 2–4; Josephus, *Antiquities of the Jews* 11.133; 2 Baruch 1:2–3; chaps. 62–87; Sibylline Oracle 2:168–176; Ascension of Isaiah 3:2; Testament of Joseph 19:1–7; Testament of Naphtali 6; Commodian, *Carmen apologeticum* 941–973 and *Instructiones* 1.42; and rabbinic literature, for example, M. Sanhedrin 10:3.

In Christian sources, the motif of exile usually functions in a different manner. In 1 Peter, the Christians of Asia Minor are depicted as "exiles of the dispersion" (1:1), probably reflecting the idea that Christians, while on Earth, are exiles from their heavenly home (cf. 1:17, 2:11). This idea is made explicit in Hebrews 11:13; 2 Clement 5:1; and Diognetus 5:5. The Testaments of the Twelve Patriarchs depict an exile directly preceding the eschaton (Test. Levi 10:3–4, 15:1–3; Test. Jud. 23:3–5; Test. Issa. 6:2–4; Test. Zeb. 9:6–7; Test. Naph. 4:2–5). Matthew 1:11–12 and 17 refer historically to the Babylonian exile. *See also* BABYLON.

exile, return from return of the Jews from the Babylonian exile in the late sixth century B.C.E. As a result of successive deportations by the Babylonians in the early decades of the sixth century B.C.E., several thousand Judeans were settled in the Nippur region of southern Mesopotamia, where they were able to maintain their separate identity as an ethnic minority. The prospect of return to the homeland, encouraged by the early military successes of Cyrus II, became a reality for those who could afford it and had the necessary motivation after the conquest of Babylon by the Persians in 539 B.C.E. The Cyrus cylinder inscribed in the following year announced a policy of tolerance, including repatriation of peoples deported by the conquered Babylonians. The same policy is reflected in the imperial decree recorded in Ezra 1:1–4 (cf. 5:13–15, 6:1–5), according to which Babylonian Jews were encouraged to return and rebuild the Temple; the version in Ezra 6:1–5 even states that the cost of rebuilding will be defrayed by the imperial treasury and orders the return of the sacred vessels confiscated by the Babylonians. The authenticity of these documents is disputed, but they are at least consistent with Persian policy with respect to other parts of the empire.

The sequel to these decrees is unclear in several respects. Ezra 1–2, records that a caravan of about fifty thousand Jews returned at once, bringing the sacred vessels and rich offerings for the Temple. The returnees set up an altar on the site of the former Temple and reinstituted the daily sacrifice under the leadership of Jeshua, the chief priest, and Zerubbabel, the grandson of the deported king, Jehoiakhin (cf. 1 Chron. 3:19). However, the list in Ezra 2:1–67 (= Neh. 7:6–68) may date from a later period in the history of the province, the roles of the civic leaders Sheshbazzar and Zerubbabel remain unclear, and in any case no substantial progress was made toward the rebuilding before the reign of Darius about two decades later (Hag. 2:15). In the sixth year of Darius's reign (515 B.C.E.), the Temple was finally completed and dedicated; later still, in the seventh year of the reign of Artaxerxes (probably Artaxerxes I, and therefore 458 B.C.E.), Ezra arrived at the head of another caravan, with a mandate to enforce traditional law in the province (Ezra 7–8). In the following decade the province of Yehud (Judah) achieved a degree of autonomy and relative stability under the governorship of Nehemiah, c. 445–430 B.C.E. The Babylonian returnees and their descendants formed the dominant elite in the province by virtue of their superior wealth and education and their control of the Temple. It was this group that imparted to nascent Judaism its most characteristic institutions and expressions.

Prophetic texts from the time of the exile and restoration provide different religious viewpoints on the political disaster—the Babylonian conquest and the destruction of Jerusalem and its Temple—and hold out different prospects for the future. Ezekiel, taken to Babylon with the first deportation, rejected the argument that the deportees were being punished for the sins of their forebears; he emphasized the moral failure of the nation as the cause of the disasters, but held out the possibility of a new dispensation, following on divine judgment (chaps. 33–37). His vision of the chariot-throne by the Chebar canal in the Nippur region assured the deportees of the possibility of worship in a land polluted by idolatry (cf. Ps. 137), while the Temple vision (chaps. 40–48) provided a kind of blueprint for the restoration of worship, led by the legitimate (i.e., Zadokite) priesthood, in the purified and repopulated Land of Israel. A more specific program of restoration, probably elaborated in Babylon and in Judah shortly after the return, can be deduced from the priestly narrative and legal material in the Pentateuch, with its emphasis on the sanctuary, cultic and ritual institutions, and the life of holiness in general. Somewhat different is the viewpoint of the Deuteronomists, apparent in the exilic edition of Deuteronomy and of the national history set forth in Joshua and 2 Kings, as well as in Deuteronomic additions to and expansions of prophetic books, especially Jeremiah. The point is to place responsibility for the disasters squarely where it belongs, since the people had not heeded prophetic warnings, and to inculcate a change of heart, a "seeking of YHWH," in response to the new opportunity offered to them by their God.

The clearest expression of the hope for return and restoration is to be found in the exilic Isaiah, for whom Cyrus is to be YHWH's agent in bringing this hope to fulfillment (Isa. 44:24–45:7). For this prophet, judgment is in the past (e.g., Isa. 40:2), and the way is being prepared for a new exodus and occupation of the land (Isa. 51:9–11, 52:11–12). For many at that time in both Judah and Babylon, hope for the future focused on the exiled

Davidic dynast Jehoiakhin, who had been released by the Babylonians after thirty-seven years of captivity (2 Kings 25:27–30). Occurring often in prophetic texts from the exilic period (Jer. 23:5–6, 30:8–9, 33:14–26; Ezek. 34:23–24, 37:24–25; Isa. 55:3), the dynastic theme was transferred to Jehoiakhin's grandson, Zerubbabel, in the early years of Darius's reign, when it seemed that the Persian Empire might fall apart (Hag. 2:20–23; Zech. 3:8–10, 6:9–15). The disappointment of this hope, together with the harsh reality of life as a subject people in an impoverished land, finds expression in the final chapters of Isaiah (chaps. 56–66).

Within rabbinic literature the concept of return from exile pertains primarily to the future event by which God will gather the dispersed of the nation of Israel and return them to the promised land. The rabbis depict this return as an event of even greater magnitude than the exodus from Egypt, holding that, in the messianic age, it will comprise the focus of Jewish recognition of God (B. Berakhot 12b). Unlike the exodus from Egypt, the messianic return will entail neither haste nor flight (Mekhilta Bo 7); the Israelites will return to their land with song and everlasting joy (Mekhilta Beshallah 1).

Exodus narrowly defined, the "going out" of the Hebrews from Egypt; according to most scholars, the three events narrated in Exodus 11:1–15:21: the Passover, the abandonment of Egypt, and the encounter at the Reed Sea. Unfortunately, most of the "historical" details were obscured in the compilation/composition of the Book of Exodus. The Passover, in its present form connected with the last plague inflicted on Egypt, most likely originated as an older rite that later became attached to the account of the plague in Exodus. The two major questions of the date of the Exodus and the route the Hebrews followed continue to be matters of dispute. The Bible nowhere names the pharaoh who reigned at that time; the two periods most vigorously defended by scholars are the mid-fifteenth century B.C.E., under Thutmose III, and the mid-thirteenth century B.C.E., under Rameses II. The mention of the cities of Pithom and Rameses (Exod. 1:11) and the inclusion of "Israel" on a commemorative stele of Pharaoh Merneptah, erected 1221 B.C.E., incline most scholars to support the latter date. The location of the encounter at the Reed Sea (Exod., chap. 14) is usually situated somewhere in the Bitter Lakes, a region north of the Reed Sea in the area of the modern Suez Canal. None of the proposed routes from the Reed Sea to Sinai are without problems, including the location of the mountain itself, and a route across the northern half of the Sinai peninsula toward the Gulf of Aqaba seems most probable.

The remembrance of the Exodus became one of the central elements of Israelite and Jewish piety, and the event still is recalled annually in the Passover Seder, where God's salvation is appropriated by each member of the community. As a consequence of these events, YHWH became Israel's God, and the Law was given to Israel. Subsequent Israelite and Jewish literature has at its heart ideas and language of deliverance, redemption, salvation, and election grounded in God's deliverance of Israel from Egypt. In several psalms, God's acts in the Exodus contrast with the faithlessness of his people, even as they witnessed the events (Ps. 78:12–53, 106:7–46). The biblical prophets indict the sinfulness of the people of Israel by explicitly recalling the magnitude of God's salvation in the Exodus events (Hos. 11:1–2; Amos 2:9–12; Ezek. 20:5–26).

Both Jeremiah and Deutero-Isaiah view the Exodus as paradigmatic for understanding the Babylonian exile. Jeremiah 16:14–15 looks forward to the time when God would be seen as the one who brought his people out of Babylon, rather than out of Egypt. The beginning of Deutero-Isaiah (especially Is. 43:16–19) is replete with Exodus imagery that equates God's deliverance of his people from Egypt with that of his people from Babylon.

In Second Temple Jewish literature, the Exodus events continue to be pivotal to understanding God's relationship to his people. In rehearsals and rewritings of Israel's history, such as those in The Wisdom of Solomon, Jubilees, 3 Maccabees, and Judith, the Exodus occupies a central place. For Philo of Alexandria these events are not only about the history of Israel but also an allegory about the destiny of the human soul.

The Exodus was also a focal point for Greek and Roman perceptions about Jews and Judaism. Several versions of an Exodus story circulated in the Greco-Roman world, some anti-Jewish and some more neutral, which claimed that the Jews had been expelled from Egypt as lepers. In *Against Apion,* Josephus attacks those who use such a tradition against Jews. Various aspects of the Exodus story influenced New Testament writers, especially the gospel writers who infuse Jesus' life with allusions to the Exodus (cf. Matt. 2:13–15; John, chap. 19).

Exodus Rabbah midrashic compilation on the Book of Exodus, divided into fifty-two sections.

Sections 1–14, on Exodus chapters 1–10, resemble later medieval midrashic compilations and appear to derive from the tenth century C.E. These sections depend heavily upon earlier midrashic compilations, including Genesis Rabbah, Leviticus Rabbah, and Lamentations Rabbah, and have as their chief source materials from versions of the Tanḥuma.

Sections 15–52, on Exodus chapters 12–40, are earlier than sections 1–14, probably having been compiled in the ninth century C.E. In addition to the Mishnaic Hebrew that is primary throughout all sections of the text, sections 15–52 contain Greek and Latin words as well as some Galilean Aramaic. These sections contain numerous parables and, unlike sections 1–14, some legal expositions.

Both sections are based on the divisions of Exodus in the Palestinian triennial lectionary cycle and feature proems. Sections 1–14 are primarily exegetical, interpreting successive verses and individual words. Sections 15–52, by contrast, are homiletical and include epilogues often referring to a coming redemption. The two bodies of material seem to have been combined in the eleventh or twelfth century. They are first referred to by Nahmanides, in the thirteenth century.

Exodus Rabbah was first printed in Constantinople in 1512, in an edition that included the five Rabbah midrashic compilations on the Pentateuch. That edition serves as the source for all subsequent printings of Exodus Rabbah.

Exodus, Targum to *see* PALESTINIAN TARGUMS; ONKELOS, TARGUM

exogamy *see* ENDOGAMY

ex opera operato (Lat., let it work from the work) often found as a technical term in scholarly references to mean that a particular religious or cultic act is itself efficacious. For example, a sacrifice might remove sin or make pure simply because the act is carried out, without regard for personal attitude or repentence.

exorcism the practice of casting out evil spirits that possess a person or, in some cases, an immaterial object, such as a house. In antiquity, Jews had a reputation for the ability to do this. The ability allegedly goes back to Solomon, who was credited with casting out demons and forcing them to do his bidding, even building the Temple.

expiation making amends or atoning for something. In English translations of biblical and Jewish texts, "expiation" and "atonement" are often used interchangeably, with "atonement" more common in recent translations. Both words are used to translate Hebrew terms derived from the root *kpr* (e.g., Yom Kippur, the Day of Atonement) and Greek terms derived from the root *hilaskesthai,* which translate the Hebrew *kpr* in the Septuagint. The Hebrew derives from a root metaphor meaning "cover over," and the Greek, from "making amends." Depending on context and on the translator's theology "propitiation" and "purification" are also used to translate these words. More properly, "atonement" should be used for terms associated with reconciliation.

In the bible, "expiation" refers primarily to sacrifices offered regularly to purify the Temple sanctuary from the effects of sin. (Deliberate personal sin was expiated by repentance and punishment.) On Yom Kippur, the priest sprinkled blood on the "cover" above the ark to "cover over" all the ill effects of Israel's sins on the sanctuary. Similarly, after Heliodorus had violated the Temple and been flogged by angelic emissaries, the high priest offered an expiatory sacrifice for him (3 Macc. 3:33). In 1 Esdras, the priests who had taken foreign wives offer rams in expiation of their error.

In Second Temple Judaism, cultic metaphors are common. God can make amends for sinners, that is, He forgives sins (Sir. 5:6, 16:7). Various ethical actions, such as almsgiving or honoring one's father, can atone for one's sins (Sir. 3:3, 30). The Qumran Community members expiate their sins and are purified by "the spirit of true council concerning the ways of man" and "the spirit of uprightness and humility" (1 QS3:4–8, 8:1–3). The Community also conceives of itself as expiating the sins of Israel and the land (1 QS 8:4–8). Frequent mention of expiation at Qumran testifies to the priestly and cultic orientation of the Community and to its ideal of creating a pure and holy Israel. Finally, martyrdom was also understood in terms of expiation. Though heavily influenced by Stoicism, 4 Maccabees understands the painful deaths and blood of the mother and her seven sons as an expiatory sacrifice because of which God preserved Israel (17:22).

New Testament authors took up sacrificial terminology, including expiation, in order to explain the execution of Jesus. Thus Jesus is an expiation or makes expiation for the sins of the people (Rom. 3:25; 1 John 2:2, 4:10; Heb. 2:17). The metaphor of expiation is also used for being merciful or reconciled with a sinner (Luke 18:13). *See also* ATONEMENT; ATONEMENT FOR THE LAND; RECONCILIATION.

expulsions of Jews from Rome events occurring three times, according to various ancient historians whose accounts are not always clear or consistent with one another. In 139 B.C.E., the Roman authorities expelled some Jews for proselytism. This would be consistent with the Roman policy of resistance to eastern religions in order to preserve Roman practices and virtues. In 19 C.E., the emperor Tiberius punished the Jewish community because some members had defrauded an aristocratic Roman woman out of a large sum of money and perhaps because of the enmity of his adviser Sejanus toward Jews. He expelled the community from Rome and impressed four thousand men into the military. Finally, the emperor Claudius either expelled the Jews from Rome or forbade them to assemble because they "constantly made disturbances at the instigation of Chrestus." This passage from the historian Suetonius seems to indicate that the community contained members who were followers of Jesus Christ (Latin *Christus,* meaning anointed one) who were causing trouble. The historical sources disagree on the date for this decree from Claudius, placing it either in 41 or 49 C.E. *See also* ROME, JEWS IN.

Ezekias the Brigand Chief first-century B.C.E. leader of a group of dispossessed people in Galilee, along the Syrian border, according to Josephus. In the course of defeating his opponents, Julius Caesar appointed Herod the Great's father, Antipas, as a ruler in Judea (47 B.C.E.); Herod the Great was sent to Galilee as governor, where he captured and killed Ezekias and many of his followers. This vigorous activity brought Herod to the notice of Sextus Caesar, governor of Syria, and won him praise from villagers.

Ezekiel, Apocryphon of Several ancient sources claim knowledge of an apocryphal book that circulated under the name of the biblical prophet Ezekiel. The Jewish historian Josephus (*Ant.* 10.5.1 [10.79]) provides the earliest testimony when he says that Ezekiel left behind two books of predictions. The fourth-century-C.E. church father Epiphanius of Salamis (*Panarion* 64, 70.5–17), writes of finding a story about a lame and a blind man "in Ezekiel's own apocryphon." Finally, the Canon List of Nicephorus lists a pseudepigraphon in Ezekiel's name.

Unfortunately no apocryphal Ezekiel book has survived, although it seems certain that some book or books did exist. What remain extant are quotations in early Christian writers that are not in the biblical book, but that are attributed to the biblical prophet, and several fragmentary manuscript discoveries, including some at Qumran, that are clearly associated with the prophet Ezekiel.

The language and character of the surviving materials are varied, and they obscure the issues of the original language and form of these sayings. Thus, questions about language, provenance, and mechanism of transmission remain open. Five passages in the Christian Church Fathers, however, are usually claimed to belong to this apocryphon because of their explicit attribution to Ezekiel, although several additional citations have been suggested. The earliest attestations of these five are listed below. Neither Clement of Rome nor Justin Martyr give explicit attribution to Ezekiel; his name appears only in later quotations of these passages. The story related by Epiphanius also occurs in several Hebrew versions in rabbinic literature, while the material in Clement of Alexandria appears in more extended form in a papyrus manuscript, Chester Beatty 185. The traditional "fragments" of apocryphal Ezekiel are (1) Epiphanius, *Panarion* 64; (2) Clement of Rome 8.3; (3) Tertullian, *De Carne Christi* 23; (4) Justin Martyr, *Dialogue with Trypho* 47.5; and (5) Clement of Alexandria, *Paedagogus* I.9.84.2–4.

In addition to these passages, four copies of a text that contains revelatory dialogues between God and Ezekiel have been discovered among the Qumran scrolls. Dubbed "4QPseudo-Ezekiel" by its editors, this text appears to be based primarily on the biblical Book of Ezekiel. The fragments published thus far contain the vision of God's chariot-throne (*merkabah*) (Ezek. 1) and the vision of the dry bones (Ezek. 37). Their relationship to the fragments listed above is not yet clear.

Ezekiel, Targum to *see* TARGUM TO THE PROPHETS

Ezekiel the Tragedian one of the Fragmentary Hellenistic Jewish writers. He wrote the *Exagoge,* a drama on the Exodus in Greek style. Only fragments of the work are preserved in Eusebius, but these consist mainly of monologues and dialogues. Since he was quoted by Alexander Polyhistor in the first century B.C.E., we know his period must have been earlier than this, but he cannot be dated more exactly. There seems to have been some desire in his work to resolve difficulties in the biblical text. For example, he explains how the Israelites obtained their weapons after leaving Egypt (from the corpses of the Egyptians drowned in the Red Sea).

Ezel Moshe ("Go Moses") poem written in an alphabetic acrostic style. It appears earliest in two targum manscripts and a fourth–fifth century papyrus fragment. It concerns Moses' encounter with the Red Sea. In the Paris Fragmentary Targum, the poem appears after Exodus 14:29, but in the Hamburg manuscript of Targum Onkelos, it is interspersed with the verses of Exodus 14:16–25, the reading for the seventh day of Passover.

Ezra priest and scribe who was sent on a mission to Judah in the seventh year of the reign of Artaxerxes (probably Artaxerxes I, and thus 458 B.C.E.), with a mandate to put observance of law on a firm basis and bearing rich offerings for the Temple (Ezra 7–8). He arrived at the head of a large company of immigrants in the fifth month (Ezra 7:8); the public reading and explanation of the law took place, followed by the celebration of Sukkot, in the seventh month (Neh. 7:72–8:18), and the dissolution of foreign marriages took place two months later (Ezra 9–10). The failure of this last measure would explain why at this point the record comes to an abrupt end. In rabbinic tradition, Ezra is presented as a second Moses, who restored Torah after the fall of Jerusalem (e.g., B. Sanhedrin 21b). Josephus (*Ant.* 11.120–83) follows 1 Esdras and does not seem to have any independent source of information. He is also confused on the chronology of the Persian period, placing the activity of both Ezra and Nehemiah in the reign of Xerxes. In his encomium of the great figures of Israel's past, Sirach passes over Ezra in silence, probably by design. Our only sources of information therefore are Ezra-Nehemiah, a continuation of 1–2 Chronicles, and 1 Esdras (Esdras alpha in LXX), a Greek version beginning with the reign of Josiah, ending with the public reading of the law (Neh. 8), and omitting entirely the Nehemiah material.

Ezra does not figure prominently in Jewish literature between the Bible and the destruction of the Second Temple in 70 C.E., or in early Christian literature. Ezra is, however, adopted as the pseudepigraphic hero by the author of the Jewish apocalyse 4 Ezra (2 Esdras), written around 95 C.E. About fifty years later, the Christian apologist Justin Martyr cites a nonbiblical tradition that Ezra was associated with a Passover celebration (*Dialogue with the Jew Trypho* 72). 5 Ezra, a Christian writing of the second or third century, also is pseudonymously ascribed to Ezra.

4 Ezra circulated widely in Christian circles and served as a literary base for several later Christian apocalypses, including the Greek Apocalypse of Ezra, the Vision of Ezra, the Questions of Ezra, and the Apocalypse of Sedrach. *See also* EZRA, BOOK OF; EZRA, REFORM OF.

Ezra, Book of biblical book that depicts the return of the people of Israel from the Babylonian exile to Judah and their rebuilding of the Second Temple and the community in accordance with the Torah (538–457 B.C.E.). The book has three parts: chaps. 1, 2–6, and 7–10.

Ezra 1:1–4 records that King Cyrus of Persia, in fulfillment of divine command, decreed that the house of God in Jerusalem should be built (538 B.C.E.). Ezra 1:5–6 claims that the children of Israel promptly went up to the Persian province of Judah from Babylon to build it. The rest of the book (Ezra 2–10) identifies two stages in the fulfillment of the decree.

Ezra 2–6 describes how the Jewish returnees built the altar, renewed the sacrificial cult, and laid the Temple's foundations, all according to the Torah of Moses and under the leadership of a Jewish governor Zerubbabel (a Davidic descendant) and the priest Jeshua (or Joshua; chap. 3). Opposition from some "people of the land" and from officials in Samaria temporarily disrupted these efforts (chap. 4). However, due to the urging of the prophets Haggai and Zechariah, work on the Temple resumed (chap. 5). After extensive correspondence between Judah and the new king of Persia, Darius, the Temple was completed with Persian support (516/515 B.C.E.) and then duly dedicated (chap. 6).

Ezra 7–10 depicts the shaping of the community in accordance with the Torah, under Ezra's leadership. As scribe and priest, and commissioned by the Persian king Artaxerxes I, Ezra and his entourage arrived in Jerusalem in 458 B.C.E. (The year 398 B.C.E. has been proposed by scholars who connect Ezra's work with Artaxerxes II. However, the evidence for such a late date, which reverses the order of the missions of Ezra and Nehemiah, is insufficient; the canonical sequence seems more probable.) Ezra's goal was to "study the Torah of YHWH, and to do it, and to teach its statutes and ordinances in Israel" (Ezra 7:10). His activities included bringing Temple personnel and contributions to Jerusalem (chaps. 7–8), implementing the Torah, and supervising communal efforts to resolve the sensitive matter of mixed marriages (chaps. 9–10). The result was an ethnically and religiously separated Jewish community of returned exiles, living according to the teachings of the Torah. The book contains Hebrew and Aramaic sources, official Persian correspondence, lists and "memoirs," combined probably by 350 B.C.E. Scholars debate the authenticity of some of the material. Extra-biblical evidence, however, generally supports the basic contours of the biblical account. Although Ezra is never mentioned in other contemporary sources, the Cyrus Cylinder presents Cyrus as a temple restorer, excavations show increased settlements in Judah during this era, and Persian policies favor resettlement programs in Judah at this time in light of threats to the empire from Greece.

The Book of Ezra, along with Nehemiah (which

together originally formed a single work), offers the only clear biblical witness to postexilic history. It reflects a major religious and political shift: the Judean monarchy is replaced by Temple and Torah as central authorities, and the community has a greater role. Although several leaders emerge (Zerubbabel, Jeshua, and Ezra), the book emphasizes the people's role by preserving numerous other names (chaps. 2, 8, and 10) and showing how Ezra, the exemplary leader, transfers privileges and responsibilities to others. *See also* EZRA, REFORM OF.

Ezra, Reform of the events (458–444 B.C.E.) that consolidated postexilic Jewish settlers in Judah under Persian rule into a Torah-centered community. Commissioned by Persian authorities, Ezra established structures through which a distinctive Jewish identity and life were cultivated and sustained religiously, ethnically, and socially even under foreign rule. In doing so, he forged patterns that enabled subsequent Judaism to withstand recurrent periods of subjugation. Ezra's reforms were a turning point in that they defined (possibly redefined) Israel as a community separated from "the peoples of the land" and centered around the book of Torah. Although guidelines for such a community appear in the Torah itself, thus ascribed to the time of Moses, it is with Ezra that these teachings became normative and applied concretely, creating a distinctive community and enduring patterns for subsequent Judaism. Our source for these reforms is Ezra-Nehemiah, originally considered one book until at least the third century C.E.

There are two interrelated steps to Ezra's reforms. First, Ezra influenced the forming of a distinct community within the ethnically diverse province of Judah, separating Jews (mostly those who came back from exile) from other inhabitants of the land and confining the term Israel to them (Ezra 7–10). Second, Ezra publicly proclaimed, reclaimed, and implemented the book of the Torah as the document to govern all aspects of Jewish life (Nehemiah 8; see below for what this "book" might have been). According to Ezra-Nehemiah, "Ezra has prepared his heart to seek the Torah of YHWH, and to do it, and to teach in Israel its statutes and judgments" (Ezra 7:10). In 458 B.C.E., Ezra as priest and scribe came to Judah from Babylon, authorized by Artaxerxes I to supervise legal and cultic matters in Judah and to bring them into conformity with Persian and Jewish law (Ezra 7:12–26). When informed that community leaders had married women from among the "peoples of the land" (Ezra 9:1–2), Ezra campaigned to exclude such persons from the congregation. In a crucial exegetical move, he applied Deuteronomy's prohibitions of marriage with indigenous peoples (Deut. 7:1–4) to the postexilic situation. Under Ezra, the entire community was convened in order to reach consensus and exert pressure on violators, and a committee was appointed to investigate the matter and adjudicate cases. Ezra 10 ends with a report that 113 men were guilty of foreign marriages. The decision to maintain ethnic and religious separation has had long-term consequences for Judaism, as did the very process used to arrive at this decision.

Less controversial (and more enduring) was Ezra's establishing the Torah as a publicly accessible document governing the life of the entire community. According to Nehemiah 8, the climax of the return and reconstruction after the exile was reached in 444 B.C.E. when Ezra, in his role as priest and scribe, brought the Torah to the assembled congregation. This public ceremony echoed the giving of the Torah at Sinai. This time the people (men, women, and children) immediately obeyed the Torah's teachings. As later generations understood, this moment marks the transformation of Israel into Judaism centered around the book as the source of authority (replacing king, prophet, or even priest as ultimate spokespersons for God). Although the Torah, according to the Bible itself, goes back to Moses, it had played, at best, a marginal role in Israel's public life as depicted in the books of Judges through 2 Kings. Josiah's reforms (2 Kings 22–23) are the exception that proves the rule. In contrast to Josiah's reforms (which were of short duration and initiated by the king), Ezra's reforms are cast as the spontaneous response of the community (they ask Ezra to bring the Torah), and proved to be formative for subsequent Judaism.

It is no longer possible to determine whether Ezra's Torah comprised the entire Pentateuch, portions of it (such as the Priestly or Deuteronomic sections) or an altogether different document (Ezra-Nehemiah's references to the Torah do not consistently reflect the Pentateuch as we now have it). What is certain, however, is that Ezra succeeded in firmly placing the Torah at the center of communal life, where it has remained. Ezra's reforms parallel reforms in Egypt under Persian auspices and are best construed as a reflection of Persian imperial policy seeking to secure support among subject peoples in sensitive regions of the empire. Such reforms were also economic and political in nature, not merely religious, for the purpose of preserving Jewish land in the province of Judah from transfer to other ethnic groups.

Ancient rabbis and modern historical critics have acknowledged the significance of Ezra's reforms. The rabbis saw Ezra practically as a second Moses who brought the Torah after it had been forgotten (T. Sanhedrin 4:7). They attributed to him additional rulings, such as certain synagogue ceremonies and the practice of reading Torah publicly on market days (Monday and Thursday). The Pseudepigrapha likewise magnifies his role (4 Ezra maintains that God dictated to Ezra the entire Bible after all versions of it had been destroyed). Historical critics have credited Ezra with directly shaping the Torah that he brought, identifying him either as its author (so Spinoza) or its chief redactor, a task he would be qualified for as a skilled scribe and influential priest (Ezra 7:1–10).

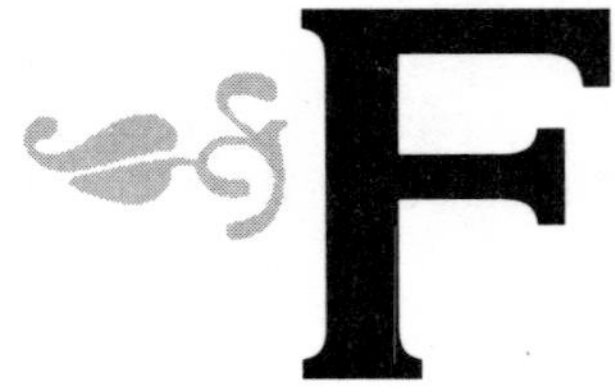

fables, rabbinic animal tales used to transmit an ethical or political message, often called *meshalim* in Hebrew. Rabbi Meir allegedly knew three hundred "fox fables," and legend has it that Bar Kappara after him knew hundreds more. Fables in the major Midrash collections are used in a formulaic manner to elucidate biblical verses.

Fadus, Cuspius procurator of Palestine (c. 44–46 C.E.), appointed when Agrippa I died. He resolved a dispute between the city of Philadelphia in Transjordan and the Jews of Peraea, suppressed brigands, and destroyed the movement of Theudas, a prophet, who promised to part the waters of the Jordan. This Theudas is anachronistically mentioned in Acts of the Apostles 5:36. Fadus's attempt to take control of the high priestly vestments was reversed by the emperor Claudius. Josephus praises him as generally respectful of local customs.

faith, faithfulness translates the Hebrew root *'mn* and the Greek noun *pistis,* whose basic meanings are trust, loyalty, and obedience. In the Tanakh (Old Testament), "faithfulness" is a characteristic of God. Used together with "grace" and "love," it describes God's loyalty to his covenant people (Deut. 7:9) and his reliability in fulfilling his promises (Ps. 89:1–2, regarding the promises to David). The "faith" of human beings is the faithful response to God's promises (Gen. 15:6), which involves trust (Hab. 2:4, Isa. 7:9), loyalty, and obedience to the commandments. The emphasis is not on belief or intellectual assent but on acts of "remembering" and "keeping." The opposite of faith is not doubt but apostasy, serving other gods.

The texts of Early Judaism (2d c. B.C.E. to 2d c. C.E.) use the root *'mn* and its Greek equivalent *pistis* with a similar range of meanings. It designates trust in God (Wisd. of Sol. 12:6) and obedience to his law (2 Bar. 54:5). Ben Sira praises Moses' "faithfulness" (Ecclus. 45:4) and celebrates the "faithful" Abraham for his willingness to sacrifice his son (44:20). In 4 Maccabees, "faith" means loyalty to God and his law in the face of trial and persecution: those who face martrydom during the Maccabean times are exhorted to have the "same faith" as Abraham and Daniel (16:20–23). Among the Dead Sea Scrolls, a commentary on Habakkuk interprets verse 2:4b ("but the righteous shall live by faith") to refer to those who observe the law, whom God will deliver because of "their faith in the Teacher of Righteousness" (1QpHab 8:1–3).

"Faith" is a central concept in the New Testament, especially in the letters of Paul, which greatly influenced later Christian usage. Paul follows Jewish tradition in using "faith" to refer to the loyalty of God to his promises (Rom. 3:3; cf. "faithful" in 1 Cor. 1:9). But when Paul speaks of human faith, he departs radically from his Jewish heritage in that he sunders the link between faith and the law: "We reckon that a person is justified by faith without works of the law" (Rom. 3:28). "Faith" for Paul is acceptance of the "gospel," namely, the Christian preaching of Jesus as the crucified and resurrected Messiah who redeems from sin and brings reconciliation with God (Rom. 1:17, where he cites Hab. 2:4b; Rom. 3:21–26). As with Ben Sira and 4 Maccabees, Paul holds up Abraham as a model of faith; but instead of claiming that he observed the law (Ecclus. 44:20; cf. Jub. 24:11), Paul cites Gen. 15:6 ("Abraham believed God and it was reckoned to him as righteousness") to argue that Abraham's faith was before, and therefore apart from, the law (Rom. 4, Gal. 3). Thus Abraham is not the model for faithful observance of the Torah, but for reliance upon God's promise (Rom. 4:14). Paul also uses "faith" in the absolute sense for what was later called Christianity (Gal. 3:23). In the pastoral Epistles, written by followers of Paul, "the faith" has the meaning of correct teaching (in contrast to that of the heretics; 1 Tim. 1:19). Hebrews defines "faith" as "the substance (or assurance) of things hoped for" (11:1) and cites Abraham, Moses, and other biblical figures as examples of those who earned God's approval "by faith" (11:1–40). The Gospel of John does not use the noun *pistis* but makes frequent use of the verb "to believe." As in Paul, believing is the response that allows humans to accept salvation (here usually called "eternal life"; John 3:16). Readers are exhorted to believe that Jesus was sent by God (16:27) and that he is God (14:1, cf. 1:1). More frequent are references to simply believing "in Jesus," where the character of faith as personal trust is evident (3:15–16, 4:39, 14:10).

Falco, Quintus Pompeius governor of Judea and Syria and commander of a legion in the area, about 104/105–107/108 C.E. He served in the first war against the Dacians, an agricultural people living in the lower Danube, from 101 to 102 and was legate of Lycia-Pamphylia. After serving in Syria-Palaestina, he was legate of Moesia Inferior, legate of Britain, and proconsul of Asia.

family (Heb.: *bayit* [house]; *beit a<u>b</u>* [house of the father]; *beit am* [house of the mother]; or *mishpaḥa* [extended family, clan]) The primary source of religious identification in the diaspora and apart from the Temple, the family became an increasingly important institution in formative Judaism. Family membership affected priestly responsibilities and benefits, marital options, inheritance, and social status. "Father of the synagogue" and "mother of the synagogue" appear in several inscriptions and so demonstrate the importance of familial designations. Moreover, concern for relationships between spouses and among parents and children and other family members appears in such diverse texts as Esther, Tobit, Ben Sira, Joseph and Asenath, the Testament of Job, and the Book of Ahikar. The descriptions encompass all facets of domestic life: love, disputes, the joy of infants, the problems of wayward sons and daughters, the difficulties of betrothal, questions of heirs, the sorrow of death. Family life was, like that of its biblical predecessor, generally patriarchal: husbands were to be the rulers of the household (see especially Ben Sira). This structure is still maintained, although enriched by the addition of the names and descriptions of various wives and mothers, in Liber Antiquitatum Biblicarum. Several texts may be interpreted as criticizing the patriarchal family structure (Esther, Judith, the depiction of the relationship between Tobit and Anna, Joakim's absence from Susanna's defense, and the pathetic portrait of Sitidos in the Test. Job). The strong roles accorded women are comparable to those played by such figures as Rebekah, Jael, the wife of Manoah, and the Great Woman of Shunem (2 Kings 4:8–37).

Greek texts employ two terms: *patria,* for biological lineage, as in the families of the earth to be blessed by Abraham (Acts 3:25); and *oikos* for one's immediate household (cf. Acts 10, the conversion of the "family" of Cornelius; Gal. 6:10, the "family [lit., household] of faith"; Eph. 2:19–20; 1 Tim. 3:15; Heb. 3:2–6; 1 Pet. 4:17).

As expressions such as "children of Israel" locate the covenant community within an extended family united by common concerns and belief, so the Church defined family/household beyond biological ties to include all those within the new confession. This affiliation established a new set of kinship obligations for the new "houses and brothers and sisters and mothers and children" (Mark 10:29–30; Matt. 19:29; Luke 18:29–30) that included financial support, loyalty, and teaching. Membership in this new household could cause disruption within the traditional household or family (Matt. 10:35–37; Luke 12:52–53). Yet the Gospels also follow the Decalogue in teaching that one should honor one's parents (Matt. 19:19; Luke 18:20). The household codes (Col. 3:18–4:1; Eph. 5:22–6:9; 1 Pet. 2:18–3:7) institutionalize domestic life in the form of benevolent hierarchies: husbands and wives, masters and servants, parents and children. Jesus' biological family is accorded substantial interest in Church tradition: James, "the brother of the Lord," directs the Jerusalem church (Acts 15; Gal. 2); the Epistle of Jude is traditionally assigned to another brother; Mary and "his brothers" are described by Luke as among those who pray together in Jerusalem (Acts 1:14).

Rabbinic texts are concerned with the family's

role in the observance of the laws and traditions of Judaism and its place in the transmission of these values to future generations. In Judaism, marriage and procreation accordingly are seen not simply as a normal state but as required by divine law. The rabbis disapproved of celibacy and held that a man who does not marry by the age of twenty has sinned (B. Kiddushin 29b).

The rabbis recognized the family as a transmitter of traits of character and piety. Alongside the hereditary priesthood, the Talmudic literature knows of aristocratic lines of descent, representing families upon which God's spirit rests (B. Kiddushin 70b). The importance attributed to lineage is reflected in the report that on the two occasions in the year on which the young men of Jerusalem would go to the vineyards to choose brides, the young women would admonish them to gaze not upon physical beauty but upon a prospective wife's family (M. Taanit 4:8).

fasting refraining from food and drink, normally for twenty-four hours from sundown to sundown; often accompanied by refraining from sexual relations and from wearing leather shoes

fate *see* TYCHE

Father, God as The motif of the heavenly Father appears throughout scripture (Deut. 14:1, 32:6; Hos. 11:1; Jer. 3:4, 31:9; Ps. 103:13, etc.). Like earthly fathers, the Deity loves, blesses, and corrects the children of the worshiping community. The title became increasingly popular in the Second Temple period in prayers for protection and forgiveness (1 Chron. 29:10; Jub. 1:24, 28; 19:29; throughout 3 Macc.; Jos. Asen. 12:14–1; Sir. 23:1, 4; Wis. 2:16–20; 14:3; Tob. 13:4; 4Q372; 1QH 9:35, etc.). Application of "Father" to God also mirrors the title's increasingly prominent secular use: *pater* (Latin: father) is increasingly identified with the emperor who rules over the extended "family" of Rome. Although "Mother" is not applied to the Deity, maternal images are (Num. 11:12; Deut. 32:11; see also Matt. 23:37).

The Gospels depict Jesus often referring to God as "Father" (e.g., Matt. 6:9/Luke 11:2, the "Lord's Prayer"), and Paul employs the formula "Father of our Lord Jesus Christ" (2 Cor. 1:3; Rom. 15:6; see also Col. 1:3; Eph. 1:3). The Odes of Solomon frequently addresses God as a personal "father" as well as providing maternal depictions such as lactation (Ode 19). The Prayer of Jacob opens with a threefold invocation to the Father of the patriarchs, all things, and cosmic powers. Father language also appears in such texts as the Testament of Abraham, Testament of Isaac, Testament of Job, Apocalypse of Elijah, and the Greek Apocalypse of Ezra. *See also* ABBA.

Fathers According to Rabbi Nathan, The (Heb.: Abot deRabbi Natan) an amplification, compiled c. 400–600 C.E., of the tractate Abot (c. 250), adding fresh materials in the names of the authorities who appear in the earlier document, and also providing a large number of stories about those authorities, as well as sayings in their names. The Fathers According to Rabbi Nathan contains amplifications of sayings in Abot (The fathers) as well as materials not related to anything in the original document, in that order. Thus The Fathers According to Rabbi Nathan first of all presents itself as continuous with the prior document, and then adds compositions that are new both in rhetoric and in logic. The Fathers According to Rabbi Nathan provides citations and glosses by providing proof-texts, illustrative stories drawn from lives of sages, parables, and exegeses of scripture found pertinent to the sentiment at hand. Moreover, details in the exegetical materials trigger secondary accretions; at numerous points, for example, exegesis of a proof-text is supplied, names mentioned in a story serve as the framework for the inclusion of further stories, none of them pertinent to the point of the original, or a vast anthology on a theme is inserted because the theme has made an appearance in another context altogether.

fathers of uncleanness principal sources that render a person unfit to enter the areas of the Temple restricted to males who are ritually clean. The twenty fathers of uncleanness are set forth in the Mishnah tractate Kelim, chapter 1, as follows:

> The fathers of uncleanness are (1) the creeping thing, and (2) semen of an adult Israelite, and (3) one who has contracted corpse uncleanness, and (4) the leper in the days of his counting, and (5) purification water of insufficient quantity to be sprinkled. These render man and vessels unclean by contact, and earthenware vessels by presence within the vessels' contained airspace. But they do not render unclean someone who carries them without directly touching them. Above them: (6) carrion, and (7) purification water of sufficient quantity to be sprinkled. For they render man unclean through carrying, to make [his] clothing unclean. But clothing is not made unclean through contact. Above them: (8) he who has intercourse with a menstruating woman, for he conveys uncleanness to what lies [far] beneath him [in like degree as he conveys uncleanness

to what lies] above. Above them: (9) the flux of the *zab*, and (10) his spittle and (11) his semen and (12) his urine, and (13) the blood of the menstruating woman, for they render unclean through contact and carrying. Above them: (14) the saddle, for it [the saddle] is unclean under a heavy stone. Above the saddle: (15) the couch, for touching it is equivalent to carrying it. Above the couch: (16) the *zab*, for the *zab* conveys uncleanness to the couch, but the couch does not [convey equivalent uncleanness to] the couch. Above the *zab*: (17) the *zabah*, for she renders him that has intercourse with her unclean [for seven days]. Above the *zabah*: (18) the leper, for he renders unclean by his coming [into a house]. Above the leper: (19) a bone about the size of a barley seed, for it renders unclean for a seven [days'] uncleanness. Weightiest of them all: (20) the corpse, for it renders unclean by overshadowing [a mode of rendering uncleanness by] which none of the rest conveys uncleanness.

See also FLUX.

Faustus of Byzantium fourth- to fifth-century-C.E. historian of Armenia. His *History of Armenia* is our only source for Armenian history during the fourth century. The name "Byzantium" is attested in the fifth century and refers to the location of his scholarly training, not to his place of birth. Faustus wrote in Greek, but the work survives only in an Armenian translation from the fifth century. The work pays particular attention to the relations between the Church and the nobility, the moral conduct of individuals, and the family intrigues of the nobility. He reports Shapur II's deportation of the Jews from Armenia in 365 C.E. and their resettlement in Isfahan.

fear of God In the Bible, fear of God refers to a range of responses to God, from terror at signs of his presence (thunder, lightning, clouds, shaking of a mountain, trumpet blast) to a solemn sense of responsibility toward God and conformity to the divine purpose. A prime example of the former occurs when God descends to Mount Sinai to give the law to his people through Moses (Exod. 20:16–25). The latter attitude characterizes the patriarchs—like Abraham (Gen. 22:12)—whose fear of God leads them to obedience and conformity to his purpose. Fear is evoked by those who have been in God's presence or have been commissioned by Him, such as Moses (Exod. 34:30), Joshua (Josh. 4:14), Samuel (1 Sam. 12:18), and Solomon (1 Kings 3:28). The place of his presence evokes fear (Lev. 19:30; 26:2), as does his quality of holiness (Isa. 8:13), so that the Lord of Hosts becomes a source of fear and dread. God's deliverance of Israel from Egypt is regarded by his people as "signs and wonders," but fills their enemies with great terror.

In the tradition of Deuteronomy, fear of God by his people comes from having heard his commands and by teaching them to their children (Deut. 4:7–10), but even here there is a recollection of the awe that overcame Israel when God came down to the mountain in their midst. In the wisdom tradition, fear of God is equated with knowledge of God, and both qualities come to those who earnestly seek wisdom through accepting God's words and commandments. Those who seek the Lord are those who "fear" and obey him (Ps. 34:9–11), and they will experience happiness and divine provision for their needs. They will live in confidence and safety, experiencing a full and rewarding life (Prov. 14:26–27), and will join in praise of the God who cares for those of his people who are in need (Ps. 22:13–26).

This understanding of "the fear of the Lord" is found in later Jewish writings from the second and first centuries B.C.E. In the Testaments of the Twelve Patriarchs from this period, those who fear the Lord are careful to avoid doing evil or offending God but are filled with love and obedience to God's will. Members of the Dead Sea community manifest their fear of God by earnest commitment and full obedience to his commands, which derive not only from Moses and the Torah tradition, but also from their own founder, the Teacher of Righteousness. On the other hand, the Dead Sea documents teach that God will act in a fearful way to punish and destroy the "children of darkness," who are those outside, and hostile to, this community. But his own faithful people are able to see beyond the impending time of terror as they await in confidence the time of fulfillment of God's purpose for and through them.

References in the New Testament Book of Acts to those who "fear God" relate to Gentiles who were drawn to Judaism, the God of Israel, and belief in one sovereign God, but who did not accept circumcision or agree to obey the Jewish ritual and dietary laws. These Gentiles in Acts serve as a major source for converts to Christianity. Some scholars in the past have questioned whether such a group of Gentiles actually existed, but recent discoveries and analyses of inscriptions from Asia Minor—especially one from Aphrodisias—show that there were such groups and that they were recognized by the ethnic Jewish community. At

Aphrodisias there is a list of sixty-nine Jews who contributed to the synagogue followed by fifty-four "God-fearers," whose occupations ranged from workmen and craftsmen to city councillors. The individuals in the latter group share in the worship life of the Jewish community but are not full members and apparently were not strict in their obedience to Jewish dietary laws or Sabbath observance. The city councillors would have been involved in pagan civic ceremonies, but abstinence from pagan worship and sexual promiscuity and conformity with the dietary law against eating or drinking blood (Lev. 17:10–14), which Acts 15:20 indicates are the minimum obligations for the God-fearers, fit well with the information conveyed by the Aphrodisias inscription. Apparently there were no uniform rules for God-fearers in the Jewish communities scattered throughout the Roman world, but the basic pattern of expectations for these committed Gentiles is clear.

Whereas the Hebrew Bible sees fear of God and love of God as essentially equivalent (see Deut. 10:12: "And now, Israel, what does the Lord your God demand of you, but to fear the Lord your God, to walk in all his ways, to love him . . ."), the rabbis distinguish these two concepts, deeming the obedience that comes from fear to be a lesser form of piety than obedience that comes from love. Simeon b. Eleazar makes this explicit, arguing that "the merit attained through fear suspends punishment for a thousand generations, while the merit attained out of love suspends punishment for thousands of generations" (B. Sotah 31a). The same passage suggests that, while scripture states that Abraham and Job both served God out of fear, they actually did so out of love.

Despite this elevation of love of God, the rabbis generally viewed fear of God as an essential element in human beings' acceptance of divine sovereignty. "Everything," the Talmud states, "is in the hand of Heaven except the fear of Heaven" (B. Megillah 25a, B. Berakhot 33b), and "Any man who has Torah but not fear of Heaven is comparable to a treasurer to whom they handed over the keys to the inner treasury but to whom they did not hand over the keys to the outer door. So how is he supposed to get in?" (B. Shabbat 31a–b). That fear of God comprises the proper foundation for religious practice is explicit in the statement of Antigonos of Sokho (M. Abot 1:3): "Do not be like servants who serve the master on condition of receiving a reward, but be like servants who serve the master not on condition of receiving a reward. And let the fear of Heaven be upon you."

Felix, Marcus Antonius procurator of Judea (52–60? C.E.). He was appointed procurator by the emperor Claudius through the influence of his brother, Pallas, a court favorite. Felix was a freedman who married first a granddaughter of Mark Antony and then Drusilla, the daughter of the late King Agrippa I. According to Tacitus, he ruled cruelly, and according to Josephus, uprisings against unjust Roman rule became continuous during his term of office and led to the rebellion against Rome in 66 C.E. Acts of the Apostles, chapter 24, reports a hearing concerning the guilt of the apostle Paul before Felix in Caesarea and a private meeting of Felix and Drusilla with Paul. Felix kept Paul in jail for two years, hoping for a bribe.

fence, symbolic *see* ERUB

fertility a sign of prosperity and divine favor, affecting plant, animal, and human life. In Genesis 1:28 and 9:1 and 7, humankind is blessed with fertility, and Israel in particular is noted for being prolific (Exod. 1:7). The Valley of Eshcol (Heb., cluster) produces individual grape clusters that must be carried by two men (Num. 13:23). Blessings for adherence to the Sinaitic covenant include "the fruit of your body . . . ground . . . beasts, and increase of your cattle, and the young of your flock" (Deut. 28:4). Parables find the motif fertile ground: The sower, for example, speaks of hundredfold yields (Matt. 13:23 and pars.). *See also* BARRENNESS.

festival offerings animal sacrifices in the Jerusalem Temple presented on festival days in addition to those required on an everyday basis

Festus, Porcius procurator of Judea (60?–62 C.E.). He was appointed procurator by the emperor Nero, and he died in office two years later. Josephus has less complaints against him than against the other procurators of the prewar period, but his term was marked by violent activities of the Sicarii and an uprising under a popular leader. Acts of the Apostles, chapters 25–26, recounts that at the hearing before Festus, the apostle Paul, as a Roman citizen, appealed to the imperial tribunal in Rome and that Festus, with Agrippa and his sister Berenice, had a further hearing with Paul.

fetus human being in the womb of the mother, regarded after forty days from conception as possessing a soul. Abortion for any purpose other than saving the life of the mother is not permitted. Until the baby is born, the life of the mother takes precedence over the life of the embryo; once the baby is born, the baby's life takes precedence. A guardian can be appointed to protect the rights of the embryo.

Fifteenth of Shebat day for planting trees, especially in modern Israel. Originally, however, this was the annual inventory date for trees, according to which the determination of the tithe on fruit was computed.

fig's bulk (Heb.: *gerogeret*) a measure of food volume. If on the Sabbath one carries food in the volume of a fig from private to public domain, liability is incurred.

fig tree Common in the Mediterranean, the fig tree has multiple shadings in biblical literature. Its leaves provided clothing for Adam and Eve (Gen. 3:7); its fruit had medicinal value (2 Kings 20:7/Isa. 38:21); it symbolized prosperity and safety (1 Kings 4:25). According to Mark 11:12–14 and 20–21 (see also the parable in Luke 13:6–9), Jesus curses a fig tree that lacks fruit, enters Jerusalem, and returns in the morning to find the tree dead. The interrelationship of his actions suggests that the Temple and city will suffer the same fate as the unproductive tree. Matthew 21:18–19 undermines the symbolism produced by the encapsulation but heightens Jesus' power by having the tree wither immediately.

fine (Heb.: *kenas*) in Rabbinic Judaism, extrajudicial penalty imposed by rabbinic sages, over and above the fines required by scripture, for example, as a precautionary measure

fingerbreadth (Heb.: *etzba*) a measure of length equivalent to the breadth of an ordinary man's finger

fire Fire can be both useful, as in cooking food, or destructive, as in burning homes and fields. This ability to help or harm—to purify and to destroy—made it an ideal symbol for the divine world.

The divine world as fire. YHWH had appeared to Moses in a burning bush (Exod. 3:2), led Israel through the wilderness in a pillar of fire by night (Exod. 13:21–22), and appeared as fire at Mount Sinai (Exod. 19:18, 24:17). Ezekiel's vision of God's chariot is full of images of fire (Ezek. 1:4–28), and so too are Daniel's vision of the Ancient of Days (Dan. 7:9–10) and the vision of Enoch (1 Enoch 14:8–25). Angels are formed out of fiery matter (2 Enoch 29:3; 2 Bar. 21:6; 3 Enoch 7.15), and fire can come out of their mouths (2 Enoch 1:5; 3 Enoch 18:21, 22:4). The Messiah will destroy his enemies with his fiery breath (4 Ezra 13:10–11). Christ is described as having "eyes of fire" (Rev. 1:14, 2:18), and the Holy Spirit appears as "tongues of fire" (Acts 2:3). The continual presence of God is symbolized by the ever-burning fire on the altar (Lev. 6:12–13). The element fire must not be identified with God, however, as it was created by Him (Wisd. of Sol. 13:2; 2 Enoch 29:1).

Fire as purification. As Isaiah's lips were purified when touched with a burning coal (Isa. 6:6–7), so the angels, before praising God, bathe in a river of fire (3 Enoch 36). As gold is tested in fire, so God tests humans (Sir. 2:5; cf. Jdt. 8:27). God will refine his people when He appears (Mal. 3:2–3; 1 Cor. 3:13–15; 1 Pet. 1:7; Rev. 3:18). The references to a baptism of fire (Matt. 3:11; Luke 3:16), as well as later descriptions of Jesus' baptism as fiery (Sib. Or. 6:6, 7:84) have this sense of purification. Fire is a symbol for the law (4 Ezra 13:38), and the book of judgments is fiery (3 Enoch 32:1).

Destructive fire. Most of the references to fire are to its destructive use. God used it in the past as an instrument to punish the wicked (Wisd. of Sol. 16–17); the Book of Jubilees claims all women who fornicate should be executed by fire (20:4, 30:7). The wicked use fire as a means of torturing the pious (2 Macc. 7; 4 Macc. 6:24–30, 10–14), but often this backfires on them (Dan. 3:19–22; Lives 21:9–15). Frequently it is predicted that the world will be destroyed by fire (Sib. Or. 2:196–213, 3:80–90, 7:118–131; Apoc. Elijah 1:4, 5:22–23), resonating with ideas in Stoicism. For the wicked is reserved fiery torment (1 Enoch 10:13–14, 18:11, 21, 90:23–27; Dan. 7:11; Sib. Or. 2:283–305; 1 QS 2:8, 4:13; 1 QM 11:10, 14:1; CD 2:5), which occurs frequently throughout the Christian scriptures (e.g., Matt. 25:41; Rev. 19:20, 20:10).

Fire in talmudic sources. Like earlier Hellenistic and Christian sources, the talmudic literature imagines all that derives directly from God to be represented in fire. The Torah is described as having been given as a white fire scroll with letters engraved in black fire. It was "fire, surrounded with fire, engraved out of fire, and set in fire" (Y. Shekalim 6:1, 48d). At the time of creation, the primordial fire was the source of light (Exod. Rabbah 15:22). The fire of the altar in the first Temple had originally come down from heaven in the time of Moses. It was transferred to the stone altar of the Solomonic Temple, where it continued to burn until the period of Manasseh (B. Zebaḥim 61b). This is distinguished from the fire of the altar of the second Temple, which the rabbis understood to be of human origin (B. Yoma 21b).

Other numerous talmudic references to fire concern its use on Sabbaths and festivals. Kindling fire is one of thirty-nine categories of labor prohibited on the Sabbath. Unlike the Sadducees, the rabbis, however, permitted the use for light and heat on the Sabbath of a fire lit before the Sabbath. Along with carrying, lighting a fire is the only work prohibited on the Sabbath but permitted on other festivals. Outside of its place within holiday law, fire is significant within rabbinic jurisprudence as one of four principal categories of damage.

fire and brimstone a dual torment, in which brimstone is now generally translated as "sulfur." The classical place for this double punishment is the divine retribution rained on Sodom and Gomorrah (Gen. 19:24; Luke 17:29; 3 Macc. 2:5). In other references, it is used against the wicked and apostates (Deut. 29:23; Job 18:15; Ps. 11:6), the king of Assyria (Isa. 30:33), Edom (34:9), and Gog (Ezek. 38:22). In the Qumran documents, the Wicked Priest will suffer it (1QpHab 10:5). The Book of Revelation tells us that it is used to punish idolaters (14:10), the beast and the false prophet (19:20), the devil (20:10), and sinners in general (21:8).

Firmilianus governor of Palestine (308–310 C.E.). Eusebius mentions Flavianus, Urbanus, and Firmilianus as the governors of Palestine during Diocletian's persecution of the Christians. Virtually nothing is known about these three other than the fact that Urbanus and Firmilianus were executed while in office. Eusebius also mentions Firmilianus in his *Martyrs of Palestine.*

First *for works numbered* FIRST, *see under the substantive name of the work*

firstborn (Heb.: *bekor*) the firstborn son or beast, accorded special status; *see also* BEKOROT; FIRSTBORN, RIGHTS OF

firstborn, rights of The laws of primogeniture mandate for firstborn sons a special blessing and a double portion of inheritance (Deut. 21:15–17; see also Gen. 25:29–34), regardless of the father's greater affection for another wife and/or her children. The firstborn also receives authority over other family members (Gen. 27). Firstborn males are dedicated to the Deity because, according to Exodus 13:12–16, they were preserved from death in Egypt. Such sons were then redeemed from service by means of an offering (Num. 3:45–51, 18:15–16). Biblical narrative provides several examples of younger sons inheriting blessing and authority (Isaac, Jacob, Ephraim, David, Solomon). The metaphorical extension of these conventions presents the Davidic ruler as the firstborn of God (Ps. 89:27; Heb. 1:6). Luke 2:22–24, which cites Exodus 13:12, is the evangelist's version of a *pidion haBen,* or redemption of the firstborn. However, this ceremony did not require presentation in the Temple. *See also* BEKOROT.

firstfruits the first part of the harvest presented to God to acknowledge that He owns the soil and all its produce. The Israelite farmer was ordered to make a pilgrimage to the sanctuary with the first part of the wheat harvest at the Festival of Weeks (also called the Festival of the Firstfruits [Exod. 23:16; Num. 28:26]). The Hebrew Bible also contains the general requirement that the first part of all produce from the soil should be brought to the Lord's house (Exod. 23:19, 34:26; Deut. 26:1–4). Nehemiah 10:35–37 indicates that the practice was reaffirmed after the return from exile. Jeremiah used "firstfruits" in a related sense: Israel was holy to the Lord, the firstfruits of his harvest (2:3). The Book of Tobit reports that the hero, Tobit, formerly presented to the Jerusalem priests the initial yield of his land and animals (1:6–7).

The Temple Scroll, one of the Dead Sea Scrolls, adds several other firstfruits festivals to the biblical legislation: perhaps the ceremonial waving of the first of the barley harvest (col. 18); the new wine festival (col. 19); and that of new oil (col. 21). Several New Testament authors, however, use "firstfruits" in the sense that certain things or people were the first part, and the remainder were to follow. Paul speaks of Jesus as the firstfruits of those who have died but will rise (1 Cor. 15:20, 23). Elsewhere Paul writes that believers have the firstfruits of the Spirit now and eagerly await the full gift (Rom. 8:23). He also calls two groups of believers "firstfruits," that is, the first converts in an area (Rom. 16:5; 1 Cor. 16:15). James refers to those whom God has chosen as the firstfruits of his creation (Jas. 1:18), and Revelation calls the 144,000 the firstfruits of God and the Lamb (14:4).

Unlike in early Christianity, firstfruits in rabbinic Judaism do not have a metaphorical or theological significance. Rather, within Tractate Bikkurim in the Mishnah and Jerusalem Talmud, the rabbis treat firstfruits solely within the framework of the Hebrew Bible's requirement that the first part of the harvest be brought to the Temple. The rabbis held that firstfruits were to be brought only from the seven species for which the land of Israel was noted: wheat, barley, grapes, figs, pomegranates, olives used for oil, and dates used for honey. At the Jerusalem Temple, the donor would express gratitude to God for having redeemed the Israelites from Egypt. The firstfruits themselves were given to the priests, who could eat them. Bringing of firstfruits was suspended when the Temple was destroyed in 70 C.E.

First Revolt *see* REVOLT AGAINST ROME, GREAT

first tithe a tenth of the crop given to the Levite, who then gives a tenth of that to the priest

fiscus Judaicus imperial treasury. The Jews from throughout the world paid a half-shekel tax to support the Temple in Jerusalem. When the Temple was destroyed, Vespasian required the Jews to pay an annual tax of two drachmas or dinars to Capitoline Jupiter, the temple he had built in Jerusalem. The tax was paid into a special imperial treasury, known as the *fiscus Judaicus*. In reality, the tax was used by the emperors any way they wished. Domitian required even those who followed the Jewish way of life but did not openly profess Judaism to pay into the *fiscus Judaicus*.

fish minor motif in ancient Jewish and synagogue art that appears on various items. The fish is usually represented simply in outline with the eye as a circlet. In mosaic art a fish may appear in detail sufficient to identify its species, particularly in certain zodiacs. One fish other than the Pisces sign is known from the synagogue zodiac of Beth Alpha. Fish in relief appear in the Golan Heights at Dabbura and Dikke. Others are known from amulets, lamps, and tomb paintings. *See also* DOLPHIN.

fishing the occupation of Simon (Peter) and Andrew, James and John as well as their father, Zebedee (Mark 1:16–20; Matt. 4:18–22; Luke 5:1–11; John 21:1–11). Since the third century B.C.E. the Galilee had a strong fishing industry. Methods included use of dragnets and hand nets (Matt. 4:18, 13:47; John 21:8), fishhooks (Job 41:1; Amos 4:2; Matt. 17:27), and harpoons and spears (Job 41:7). By catching a miraculous fish, Tobias is able to exorcise the evil demon plaguing Sarah and to cure his father's blindness (Tobit). In the Gospels, the language of fishing provides a setting for parables and a model for Jesus' followers to become "fishers of people" (Mark 1:17; Matt. 4:19; Luke 5:10).

Five Megillot *see* FIVE SCROLLS

Five Scrolls (Heb.: Ḥamesh Megillot) the biblical books of Lamentations, Ruth, Esther, Song of Solomon, and Kohelet (Ecclesiastes), read in the synagogue on special occasions

Flacc. *see* IN FLACCUM

Flaccus, Aulus Avillius Roman prefect of Egypt (32–38 C.E.). His role in the pogrom against the Jews of Alexandria in 38 C.E. is narrated by Philo of Alexandria in his treatise *Against Flaccus*. With the accession of Caligula as emperor in 37 C.E., Flaccus allowed himself to be used by the anti-Jewish Greeks in Alexandria in support of an anti-Jewish policy, which led to a pogrom and rioting in 38 C.E. Flaccus fell out of favor with the emperor the same year, and he was executed in 39 C.E. *See also* IN FLACCUM.

Flavianus governor of Palestine, 303 C.E. Eusebius mentions Flavianus, Urbanus, and Firmilianus as the governors of Palestine during Diocletian's persecution of the Christians. He states that Flavianus was governor during Easter of Diocletian's nineteenth year. Possibly Flavianus is the same person as Junius Flavianus who was prefect of Rome for a few months in 311–312.

Flavius Boethus legate of Palestine (162–166 C.E.). He was an educated person who dabbled in philosophy and medicine. He was from Ptolemais on the Palestinian frontier near Syria. His friend Galen often refers to him and is virtually our only source of information about him.

Flavius Silva *see* SILVA, LUCIUS FLAVIUS

flesh most basically, the muscle and tissue beneath the skin, or the skin itself, of a human or animal. This term carries various other connotations in the Hebrew Bible. It is often used by synecdoche to signify the human body as a whole, or any living human or animal being (thus "all flesh" denotes all human, or all human and animal, beings). The term also signifies a blood relative; the mortal, earthly world of humans; and a symbol of softness and sensitivity. Thus, in biblical usage, the term describes human life and experience generally, especially in contradistinction to the world of God.

In Jewish intertestamental literature, the term tends to retain its biblical usage. In some cases "flesh" carries a distinctly negative connotation, describing the inherent physical or moral weakness of humans. Generally this usage serves to contrast human life with the realm of God, indicating a cosmological dualism. With time, however, the anthropological dualism of "flesh" (or "body") and "spirit" so characteristic of Hellenistic thought influenced Judaism. Thus, in some of the later pseudepigrapha and in Philo and Josephus, "flesh" describes the physical human body that contains, and sometimes imprisons or holds down, the inner "spirit." This view is also characteristic of rabbinic Judaism.

Early Christian usage, while in many instances retaining the biblical paradigms, also markedly reflects the Hellenistic anthropological dualism of the period. In some senses, Paul combines these two ideas, using "flesh" to signify the "lower" element and "spirit" to denote the "upper" element in a dualism that embraces cosmological, anthropological, eschatological, existential, and ethical spheres. Paul portrays "flesh" as that aspect of the human condition that keeps humans bound to sin and separates them from God. "Flesh" for Paul also symbolizes the efforts of humans to "justify" themselves by following the written Jewish law, including such practices as circumcision.

Rabbinic Judaism also recognizes the distinction, found in biblical and Hellenistic literatures, between flesh, defined as the source of human moral weakness, and the incorruptible, divine spirit with which all people are endowed. Accordingly, talmudic literature routinely distinguishes the traits of "flesh and blood," that is, human traits, from those of God. The Hebrew word for flesh (*basar*) is itself interpreted as an acronym for shame (*busha*), stench (*seruḥah*) or death (*sheol*), and worm (*rimmah*; B. Sotah 5a). Similarly, the corruptibility of flesh is a frequent theme: "The more flesh, the more worms" (M. A̱bot 2:7), and "Whither are you going? To a place of dust, worms, and maggots" (M. A̱bot 3:1).

Despite these negative views of flesh, rabbinic Judaism discouraged mortification of the flesh or severe asceticism. An individual's vow to engage in self-castigation entailed "afflicting the soul," not the flesh. If such a vow prevented the individual from carrying out normal societal or familial responsibilities, it was deemed invalid (Y. Nedarim 11:1, 42c). Fasting and afflicting the soul were in general limited. Self-affliction on the day of atonement, for instance, comprised only one day of abstention from eating and drinking, washing, using ointments, wearing shoes, and cohabitation (M. Yoma 8:1).

flogging in rabbinic law, the punishment of a maximum of thirty-nine stripes or lashes inflicted on the bare upper torso with a whip of calfskin. Such punishment was carried out especially for the violation of prohibitions of the Torah where monetary or capital punishment was not involved or where biblical law imposed the punishment of extirpation. *See also* CORPORAL PUNISHMENT.

flood the universal punishment that God brought on all living things because of their sin (Gen. 6–9). Belief in a universal deluge can be traced back to ancient Mesopotamian sources of the third millennium B.C.E. and appears in the literature and lore of many peoples.

In the biblical account, Noah alone of the human race is found righteous, and he and his family are preserved in a great ark, along with representatives of the animal species. When the flood subsides, God makes a covenant with Noah never again to bring such a deluge upon the earth, and the postdiluvian situation is described as a reestablishment of the created order, except that the animals—previously forbidden as food—may now be eaten by human beings (9:2–6).

Beyond Genesis, the Hebrew Bible makes few allusions to the flood. An exception is Isaiah 24–27, a relatively late text that has much in common with 1 Enoch, which is the chief source of Jewish traditions about the flood. In 1 Enoch the flood is a prototype of the final judgment. Chapters 6–11 selectively retell the Genesis story with some major revisions. The source of the problem is not the universal wickedness of all flesh, but the rebellion of the heavenly watchers and the violent deeds of the sons, the giants, who sin against the human race and animal world and then cannibalize one another. The description of the judgment in chapter 10 is both an allusion to the primordial event and a prediction of the final judgment, which will cleanse the earth (10:20). Employing language from Genesis 9:11, it promises that this will be the final judgment, which will be followed by a new creation that will last forever (10:16–11:2). The Parables of Enoch (1 Enoch 37–71) contain other narrative material about the flood that focuses primarily on Noah, and 1 Enoch 106–107 recounts the story of the patriarch's miraculous birth (cf. 1QapGen 2). Other pieces of a broader literature about Noah have been preserved in very fragmentary form in the Qumran scrolls and in Jubilees 5–8. The notion that the final judgment will be a repetition of the flood occurs in the New Testament in a saying about the son of man ascribed to Jesus (Matt. 24:36–39) and, perhaps, in 1 Peter 3:20–21. *See also* EVIL, ORIGINS OF; NOAH.

Florilegium Found in Cave 4 at Qumran in 1952, this fragmentary Hebrew manuscript consisting of two damaged columns of text dating from the end of the first century B.C.E. was published by J. M. Allegro in DJD V (1968); the manuscript's title is abbreviated as 4QFlor. Since a florilegium is a collection of selected passages from the writings of previous authors, in this sense the title is a misnomer, for this manuscript is a collection of biblical texts (2 Sam. 7:10–14; Ps. 1:1, 2:1) around a common theme (the "last days"), accompanied by a *pesher*-like interpretation; as such it is an example of the thematic *pesher*. Florilegium's importance lies in the information it provides on the beliefs concerning the eschatological age and the Messiah held by the community that produced the manuscript.

The *pesher*, or interpretation, of 2 Samuel 7:10–14 is divided into two parts. The first, 7:10–11, understands the biblical text as referring to three temples. The first is the eschatological temple (2 Sam. 7:10a), which will be built by God and will be undefiled. The second, from 7:10b, is the Temple of Israel, which has been desolated by foreigners and refers to the First Temple or the Temple of Solomon. The third is the Temple of Men, which seems to refer to a temple made up of men, where deeds of Torah take the place of burnt offerings. This would appear to be the sect itself, which saw its own way of life as a substitute for the (defiled) Second Temple, in anticipation of the eschatological temple.

The second section of the *pesher* (2 Sam. 7:11b–14) is an interpretation concerning the coming of the Davidic Messiah (the Branch of David) and his colleague, the "Interpreter of the Law," which apparently is a reference to a priestly Messiah, who also appears in other Qumran sectarian documents (e.g., the Community Rule). After this section, the last two biblical passages interpreted—Psalms 1:1 and 2:1—are concerned with the last days (the eschaton) and the sect's role during that time. The sect sees itself as the remnant that, on account of its righteousness, shall be saved from the conflagration of the last days. Florilegium serves to illustrate the Qumran sect's belief that most biblical passages were, in fact, eschatological, and that the sect itself, living as it was in the last days, was the focus of these prophecies concerning the end-time.

Florus, Gessius *see* GESSIUS FLORUS

flower motif in Jewish art, often carved in relief in stonework associated with Roman and Byzantine synagogues; painted on frescos, struck on coins (especially the lily), and depicted in mosaic floors. The flowers carved in relief on lintels and moldings of the Capernaum and Chorazin synagogues are justly famous. None of them can be identified, as they are stylized, but they typically appear in high relief. A popular way to depict flowers is as a garland, either in a straight line above a lintel or as swags on a sarcophagus. The lily appeared on Yehud coins of the Persian period, but it is not at all clear that it functions there as a Jewish symbol. On the other hand, the lily appears so often on coins of the Hasmonean rulers that it appears to have functioned somewhat as a symbol of royalty. By the time of Herod the Great, floral motifs are de rigueur in low relief in stone and plaster in the Second Temple. At this stage they are not so much Jewish symbols as they are aesthetic devices to fill space. At a much later period, abstract flowers were delicately carved into the marble screens used in Byzantine synagogues, the most famous of which is from the synagogue at Gaza. At the most conventional level of decoration, flowers of various types, including water flowers, appear on mosaic floors as in those of the House of Kurios Leontis at Beth Shean.

flux (Heb.: *zob*) source of uncleanness affecting male (Heb.: *zab*) or female (Heb.: *zabah*), described at Leviticus 15. For females, flux is the flow of vaginal blood outside of the fixed days of the menstrual cycle; these days are called zibah-days (the eleven days ritually defined as being between one menstrual cycle and the next), during which any flow of vaginal blood is classed as flux and a mark of uncleanness. For males, it is the flow of semen from a flaccid penis. *See also* ZABIM.

food taboos (Heb.: *kashrut*) biblical and rabbinic regulations defining permitted and prohibited foods and methods of food preparation. The outline of the Jewish dietary system derives from scripture, which distinguishes animals that are forbidden or permitted for consumption, defines basic requirements for slaughter of animals for meat, and indicates how food must be prepared in order to be permitted for consumption. Rabbinic writings dramatically expand the legislation in each of these areas.

To be permitted for consumption, animals must chew the cud and have cloven hooves; fowl must have an extra toe and a gizzard, the sac of which can be peeled, and fish must have fins and scales that can be removed without tearing the skin. According to the Talmud, insects and reptiles are uniformly forbidden except for certain locusts that have four legs and wings. So long as they are prepared without any meat additives, dairy products are permitted, as are all fruits and vegetables. Wine, a special category, is permitted only if prepared under Israelite jurisdiction, lest a Gentile pour some of it out as a libation and thereby dedicate the vat to a pagan deity.

Special rules apply to the preparation of permitted food for consumption. Of particular concern is the slaughter of animals for meat, which is subject to intricate regulations designed to assure that the animal is killed quickly and painlessly, that it has no internal defects, and that all of the blood is drained prior to consumption. The slaughterer uses a knife to sever the animal's esophagus and trachea, making one swift cut without chopping or tearing the flesh. After slaughter, this cut and all of the animal's organs are examined to assure that there are no defects. The lungs are examined for proper structure, coloration, and texture, and to be certain they are free of perforations, blisters, cysts, or swelling. The other internal organs, the skull, spinal column, ribs, and legs are also examined for blemishes. The Talmud understands the presence of such defects as a likely indication of the animal's death within a year (B. Ḥullin 11a–b) and renders the meat impermissible for consumption by Jews.

Final preparation of meat assures compliance with scripture's prohibition against consuming blood, the symbol of the animal's life that belongs to God (Lev. 7:26–27, 17:10–14). Certain veins are removed and the meat is soaked and salted. The lungs, liver, and other parts of the carcass that contain significant amounts of blood require special attention, including perforation or being sliced open to allow all blood to drain. Meat that is not salted and drained of blood within seventy-two hours of slaughter may be consumed only if it is roasted over an open flame, deemed an effective method of removing blood.

Food preparation is governed by the principle that meat and dairy products may neither be cooked together nor even prepared in nor served on the same utensils. The Talmud even prohibits the consumption of milk after meat during the same meal (B. Ḥullin 105a). The rule requiring separate dishes intends to prevent the actual mixing of the food or the imparting of a dairy taste to meat or vice versa. In the earliest formulation of the law, such mixing of utensils renders the food prohibited only if the taste of milk actually is detectable in meat or vice versa (T. Terumot 8:16). In later practice, even in a case in which no impermissible flavor is imparted to the other food, that food is deemed forbidden.

Talmudic authorities generally understand the food taboos to promote moral conduct and do not attempt to explain them philosophically. They view it of no concern to God how an animal is killed, but they recognize the human significance of observing divine edicts for their own sake (Gen. Rabbah 44:1; Lev. Rabbah 13:3; Sifra 11:22). In later periods, the dietary restrictions have variously been explained as a system of health and disease prevention, as methods of assuring the humane treatment of animals, as a system of social differentiation, or in line with the talmudic view, as an aspect of adherence to the divine will that requires no philosophical or social explanation. *See also* DIETARY LAWS.

fool (Heb.: *kesil*; Gr.: *aphrōn*) person whose conduct and attitude in practical, moral, and religious matters (often called "folly") are wrong-headed because he or she has no insight into divinely revealed wisdom or because this attitude and conduct result in harmful consequences, often divine judgment. The term is at home in the Israelite wisdom tradition, which often contrasts wisdom and folly, the actions of the wise and the fool, and their respective consequences. Later wisdom texts often focus on the judgment that befalls those who deny God's sovereignty (Wisd. of Sol. 3:2, 5:4; 1 Enoch 98:9; cf. also Luke 12:20).

In a specific usage, the terms "fool" and "folly" are associated with idolatry (Deut. 32:6; Jer. 5:21; Wisd. of Sol. 12:23–24, 13:1; Rom. 1:22–23). The idolator fails to understand the unique reality of the true God and as a result falls under divine condemnation. The notion that idolatry is folly—even if the term does not occur—also appears in polemical texts that ridicule idolatry and the inability of idolators to understand the nonsense of their religious activity (Isa. 44:9–20; Bel and the Dragon, Letter of Jeremiah; Apoc. Abr. 1–7). *See also* WISDOM LITERATURE.

forbidden targum biblical passage deemed unsuitable for translation into Aramaic. In the rabbinic period, synagogue worship services apparently included weekly readings of scripture in Hebrew followed by a translation of each verse into Aramaic. Lists of forbidden targums appear in the Mishnah (Meg. 4:10), the Tosefta (Meg. 4[3]:31) and the Babylonian Talmud (Meg. 25a–b). There were two types of forbidden passages. Some passages, such as Genesis 35:22 and Exodus 32:21–25 and 35, were to be read in Hebrew, but not translated into Aramaic, while others, including Numbers 6:24–6, 2 Samuel 11:2–17, 2 Samuel 13:1–9, and Ezekiel 1:4–28, were considered so offensive or difficult that they were to be neither read in Hebrew nor translated. Several of these were forbidden because they concern illicit sexual activity, but others were forbidden because of their religious or mystical nature. *See also* SCRIPTURE READING IN THE SYNAGOGUE.

forgiveness Forgiveness of repentant sinners by God is a common theme in the Bible, which continues in postbiblical Jewish literature and the New Testament. Forgiveness is embedded in the context of God's mercy and love for Israel and God's care for the humble and needy who pray for help (Ecclus. 2:11). It is associated with a lively sense of human imperfection and sinfulness and depends on human admission of need or sin and on repentance (Ecclus. 18:12). In Jubilees, Judah repents of having slept with Tamar (41:23–24). When the people of Israel sin, they are punished so that they will repent and can then be saved by God's mercy at the judgment (Pss. Sol. 3:3–4, 10:4; 2 Bar. 13:10). Righteous gentile proselytes, such as Asenath, are also saved by repentance (JosAs 11:10–14).

Voluntary Jewish sects put a great emphasis on obtaining God's forgiveness. In the Dead Sea Scrolls, people become members of the community by repenting and being forgiven by God (CD 2:3,

3:18; 1QH 4:37, 7:30). Forgiveness is closely associated with cleansing and sanctification (1QS 3:1–6). In the New Testament, John the Baptist, Jesus, and his disciples all urge their audiences, Jewish or Gentile, to seek forgiveness of sins by repentance and baptism (Mark 1:4; Luke 24:47; Acts 2:38). In the post-Pauline tradition forgiveness of sins is seen as an effect of Jesus' redemption from sin of those who believe in him (Col. 1:14; Eph. 1:17). In the Gospels, Jesus' claim to forgive sins provokes controversy because in the biblical tradition only God can forgive sins (Mark 2:1–12). In addition, a series of metaphors of salvation, redemption, and expiation connect Jesus' death with God's forgiveness of sins.

Humans are also called to be like God in forgiving one another (Sir. 28:2; Matt. 6:12, 18:21–35). God's forgiveness of sins becomes unavailable in apocalyptic literature only at the end of the world. The unrepentant wicked are destroyed by the eschatological upheavals or condemned at a judgment. No further opportunity for repentance and forgiveness is allowed. *See also* ATONEMENT; REDEMPTION; REPENTANCE.

Former Prophets the books of Joshua, Judges, 1 and 2 Samuel, and 1 and 2 Kings; called the Former Prophets because they are placed before the Latter Prophets in the arrangement of the Hebrew Bible. These books are also called the Deuteronomistic History because they present a consecutive narrative ("history") beginning with the period of the judges, moving through the establishment of the Israelite monarchy, the division into the two countries of Israel and Judah, and finally the destruction of each country. The prophets play roles as actors in this history, which chronicles more of their deeds than their words. The prophets who appear in these books range from Deborah and Samuel to Nathan, Elijah, Elisha, and Isaiah.

fornication general term for illicit sexual behavior (Gr.: *porneia*) and frequently indicating sexual intercourse outside of wedlock or with a legally unacceptable partner; examples often cited include the fall of the watchers (1 Enoch 6–16, 40, 54; 2 Enoch 18; 2 Bar. 56; Test. Reuben 5 [blaming the women]). Fornication, defined broadly to encompass various sexually based transgressions, is a staple in vice catalogs and lists of legal prohibitions (Jub. 20; 1 Cor. 6:9; Rev. 18:3; *Mart. Asc. Isa.* 2:5, 3:28; Sentence of Syriac Menander 49). *See also* ADULTERY; HOMOSEXUALITY; INCEST; MARRIAGE; VIRGIN.

foundation (Heb.: *yesod, musad;* Gr.: *themelion*) element in a complex metaphor that depicts the community of the righteous as a building. Two relevant Qumran texts do not identity what the foundation(s) of the community are (1QS 5:5, 8:7–8; 1QH 6:26–27). However, a fragmentary commentary on Isaiah 54:11, 12 may identify the priests (among the laity) as shining sapphires among the stones of the foundation (4Q164 1:1–3), thus indicating that the founding members of the community were its foundation. This is the function of the term in Ephesians 2:19–22, which identifies the apostles and prophets as the foundation of the church. *See also* BUILDING.

fountain, well vital sources of fresh water. A fountain usually denotes a "spring" of water, whereas a well is a pit dug to reach an underground water source. Since the Land of Israel receives little rainfall during much of the year, fountains and wells were extremely important there, and their location often determined the placement of towns and settlements. Israel was known as a land with many wells and springs (Deut. 8:7).

Wells and springs are especially important in nomadic societies, which need dependable sources of water both for humans and for large herds of animals. Several stories in the Book of Genesis, for example, revolve around wells and how they were named. Genesis 26 depicts controversies over wells involving Abraham and Isaac, and their enemies or rivals. In Genesis 29, Jacob meets Rachel at a well.

Fountains are often used in a figurative sense in early Jewish literature to symbolize a source of refreshment or life-giving power. In Psalms 68:26 and Jeremiah 17:13, God is Israel's "fountain." The Proverbs often use the term "fountain of life," which describes the "mouth of the righteous" (10:11), the "fear of the Lord" (14:27), and "wisdom" (16:22). Baruch 3:12 warns that Israel has "forsaken the fountain of wisdom," whereas 4 Ezra 14:47 states that the apocryphal Jewish writings contain the "fountain of wisdom." In the Parables of Enoch (1 Enoch 37–71), the seer sees in heaven "numerous fountains of wisdom," from which "thirsty ones" drink to gain a place among the elect (1 Enoch 48:1).

In early Christian literature, the most significant application of these terms occurs in John 4, where Jesus meets a Samaritan woman at "Jacob's well." After asking the woman for a drink, Jesus tells her that he can give her "living water" that will satisfy thirst forever, and that will become in a person "a spring of water welling up to eternal life" (4:10–14). *See also* WATER.

four cups (Heb.: *arbah kosot*) four cups of wine drunk at the Passover seder, one at the start, with the Kiddush, one at the end of the narrative, one at the end of the Grace after Meals, and the fourth at the end of the liturgy of the seder

Fourth Philosophy the historian Josephus's name for the teaching of Judas the Galilean (also identified as Judas the Gaulanite from Gamala) and Sadok, a Pharisee. In 6 C.E. these teachers responded to the imposition of direct Roman rule and to a Roman census by calling for the people to acknowledge only God as their ruler, to resist Roman rule and taxation, and to expect divine help. Josephus disapproved of this teaching because he blamed it for much of the unrest and rebellion that led eventually to the war against Rome in 66. Josephus testifies to the willingness of the followers of this philosophy to undergo incredible suffering and torture to achieve liberty. He contrasts this radical Fourth Philosophy with the more stable and "respectable" teachings of the other three philosophies of Judaism, those of the Pharisees, Sadducees, and Essenes.

Many scholars have claimed that Judas the Galilean was the son of an earlier resister, Ezekias the Galilean, but his son Judas, who raided the armory in Sepphoris in 6 C.E., is a different person. Some say that Judas led a revolt against Rome in 6 C.E., but Josephus only says that Judas's teaching incited others to revolt and to resistance. Judas and his family are sometimes understood as part of the long-lasting Zealot movement, since two of his sons were later executed by Tiberius Julius Alexander, the Roman procurator of Judea (46–48 C.E.). Others have connected him with the Sicarii since his son Menahem led the Sicarii in the capture of Masada during the war against Rome. The Zealots, however, are best understood as several groups of peasant revolutionaries driven off their land by the Roman armies in 66–67, not as an intergenerational movement.

Josephus makes clear that Judas and Sadok were teachers who attracted followers and that their teachings led to active resistance to Rome. He relates their teaching to that of the Pharisees, except that Judas and Sadok were more active, and they were less adaptive in relating to the foreign regime. They taught people to trust in divine providence and also to be responsible for their actions and lives, as did the Pharisees in Josephus's paradigm of Jewish groups.

fourth-year fruit (Heb.: *rebiit*) produce in the fourth year after the planting of a fruit tree; subject to the rule governing second tithe

Fragmentary Hellenistic Jewish writers fifteen or so Jewish authors from the last three centuries B.C.E., described as fragmentary because only short excerpts of their work have survived and as Hellenistic because these excerpts show the influence of Greek civilization on non-Greeks, in this case on the Jews. They lived in Egypt and Palestine, and include the earliest named Jewish writers of Greek. Among them are poets, a dramatist, a philosopher, and historians with interests of a scientific type.

Most of the fragments were collected by Eusebius in the fourth century C.E., who quoted earlier authors to prove the antiquity of the Jews. If (as was claimed) the birth of Christianity was foretold in the history of the Jews, Christianity could then show a well-established past. Since excerpts in general are unlikely to give an accurate picture of an author's work, especially those chosen for the Christian cause, the work of these writers is not easy to assess.

But one trend is clear. The fragments bridge the Jewish background of the authors and their Hellenistic milieu. Based on a detailed knowledge of the Jewish Bible, they describe biblical personalities, subjects, and themes. We encounter such persons as Abraham, Jacob, Joseph, Moses, David, and Solomon, references to Jerusalem, and discussion of such subjects as the Jewish Sabbath and the date of Passover. There are also examples of Midrashic-style tales that are not found in rabbinic texts. For example, Eupolemus the Historian says that Solomon gave Hiram a golden pillar for the Temple of Zeus at Tyre, and quotes letters from Solomon to King Sauron of Phoenicia and to King Vaphres of Egypt on building the Temple. Ezekiel the Dramatist includes a dream of Moses, and states that the wife of Moses had a brother called Chum.

But Greek influence pervades. Many details of Greek mythology appear; for example, the writer Artapanus claims that Moses was called Hermes because he interpreted sacred texts. More significantly, the methods of expression and trends of thought could have come only from a Greek milieu. The poets Theodotus and Philo the Elder composed Homeric hexameters, and Ezekiel wrote a drama in iambic trimeters, inserting phrases from Euripides' plays. The fragments in prose explore such subjects as ethnography, chronography, etymology, and historiography, already familiar from the Bible but now more rationally pursued. The sequence of events in the historical work of Demetrius the Chronographer shows an overriding concern with pure chronology, a topic developed by the Greeks, rather than evidence of the role of God, as occurs in the historical books of the Bible or in the chronology of other Hellenistic Jewish work, such as the Book of Jubilees. In fact, chronology was a popular pursuit, and the fragments include several attempts to rationalize the chronology in different biblical books. A rational approach can also be seen in answers to questions (often implied) that arise from a detailed study of the biblical text. How old was the world? How big was the Temple? What was the meaning of biblical names? How did Jacob acquire twelve children in seven years? How could Moses have married Zipporah, when they were three generations apart? How did the Israelites obtain weapons in the desert, having left Egypt unarmed?

This factual analysis may partly account for the lack of meaningful references to God. Exceptions include the drama of Ezekiel, where God, probably unseen even by Moses, foretells and directs events. Similarly, Aristobulus the Philosopher stresses the nonhuman nature of God and his role in the creation of the world. But even here Greek influence intrudes. The claim of Theodotus that the murder of the Shechemites fulfilled a divine command is in accord with a theme in Greek mythology, in which crimes can be ordained by a decree from the gods, as when the Delphic oracle sanctioned the murder of Clytemnestra by Orestes, her son. Similarly, the Orphic fragment describes a Jewish God ("He is one . . ."), who is called Zeus.

Greek influence on these writers can also be seen in their personal names, which, apart from Ezekiel and Artapanus (a Persian name), are all Greek. On balance, however, it appears that the Jewish identity of these authors was preserved. This emerges not only from their positive use of Jewish sources and themes, but also because many fragments are "apologetic" in tone; that is, their authors had sufficient self-confidence to explain Jewish concepts, account for potentially embarrassing events in Jewish history, and even attack anti-Semitism in society at large. This may have been especially necessary after the official translation of the Pentateuch into Greek, probably in 281 B.C.E. Accordingly, in answer to the charge that the Jews "despoiled" the Egyptians (Exod. 12:36), Ezekiel claims that the Egyptians donated their valuables to compensate their former slaves. Similarly, Theodotus justifies the murder of the "impious" Shechemites by Jacob's sons (see Gen. 34) because this fulfilled a divine decree. Theodotus thus implies that just as Jacob did not condemn the act (contrary to the biblical text), neither should the (Hellenistic) reader of the tale. The frequent encomia to biblical heroes, who often acquire nonbiblical roles, may also relate to apologetic needs. For example, the claim (if believed) that Abraham learned astrology from the Chaldeans, and then taught it to the Phoenicians and Egyptian priests, would have increased veneration for the Jewish patriarch in the non-Jewish world.

The work of the Fragmentary Hellenistic writers thus offers glimpses of the variety of Jewish achievements and concerns over a considerable period of time, which, despite Hellenism's lure, were not pursued at the expense of faith. *See also entries on individual writers mentioned herein.*

Fragmentary Targums (also known as Fragment Targums) The Fragmentary Targums belong under the rubric of the Palestinian Targums to the Pentateuch. Rather than providing a continuous text, the Fragmentary Targums translate only selected verses—sometimes only selected words—into Jewish Palestinian Aramaic. Usually the selections contain either additional material common to the Palestinian Targums or updated references to technical terms, forgotten words, *hapax legomena,* or otherwise obscure language; sometimes, though, the translated verses are simply literal translations. There are at least five different recensions of the Fragmentary Targums; manuscripts of the two most complete ones are found in Paris (the Paris Targum) and the Vatican. Scholars currently think that these targums were developed during the time when Targum Onkelos was replacing the Palestinian Targums among eastern Mediterranean Jewry (seventh to tenth centuries). Although the Jews changed the type of translation they used, they still wished to retain the interpretive traditions of the Palestinian Targums. So they compiled collections of those traditions to be used alongside Targum Onkelos. In the earliest references to this text, it is called Targum Yerushalmi, or Targum of Jerusalem.

fragments of targums *see* CAIRO GENIZA, TARGUM FRAGMENTS FROM

free will the ability to make choices for oneself, without external constraints. The issue of free will versus determinism is not treated in any systematic way in the Hebrew Bible. There are, nevertheless, a few passages or themes that raise the problem, such as the repeated references to God's hardening of the pharaoh's heart during the time of the plagues in Egypt (Exod. 7–12). In later literature, more attention is paid to free will. The community that wrote and copied the Dead Sea Scrolls denied that humankind possessed the ability to choose. They believed that God had determined everything that would happen in history before it took place.

Most scholars identify this group as a branch of the Essene party, which, according to the first-century C.E. Jewish historian Josephus, rejected the view that humans are free to choose. This is one of the issues on which, again as Josephus reports, the major Jewish parties differed: the Sadducees believed it was within human power to choose, the Pharisees thought some decisions were made freely and others were not, and the Essenes attributed all things to fate. In the New Testament, Paul deals with similar topics and maintains that believers have been chosen by God to be his people and others have not (see Rom. 9–11); it is not, in the first place, a matter of human will. The books 2 Esdras and 2 Baruch (written in about 100 C.E.) struggle with the same issue as the authors try to explain the destruction of Jerusalem at the hands of pagans. While rabbinic literature does not systematically treat the issue of free will, it appears to offer a largely deterministic point of view, expressed in its maxim that "All is in the hands of Heaven except for the fear of Heaven" (B. Megillah 25a; B. Berakhot 33b; B. Niddah 16b).

free-will offering (Heb.: *nedabah*) gift made out of benevolence and not in fulfillment of a vow or other obligation. Such offerings were used to construct and furnish the wilderness tabernacle, First Temple, and Second Temple (Exod. 35:29; 1 Chron. 29:5–9; Ezra 1:4). Additionally, when the Temple stood, they took the form of burnt offerings or peace offerings (Lev. 22:18–21), which, alongside the burned fat, provided meat to the priesthood and donor.

Friends (of the king) these were honored advisers to the Ptolemaic, Seleucid, and other Hellenistic kings (*philoi* in Greek). They seem to have been of various ranks, with kinship terms such as "cousin" or "brother" indicating higher status. Jonathan Maccabee was made a Friend of Alexander Balas (1 Macc. 10:20).

friendship Friendship between men is infrequently observed by narrative texts; more rare is friendship between women. While David and Jonathan, Jesus and Lazarus, Ruth and Naomi provide idealized examples, more attention is dedicated to didactic prescriptions. Wisdom literature notes loyalty and fidelity as the hallmarks of a true friend, but warns against those who would take advantage (Ecclus. 6, 12:8–18, 13:21, 37:4–5; Prov. 19; Pseudo-Phocylides 91–96). Sentence of Syriac Menander comments extensively on friendship; the treatment of friends; lifelong models; and its relation to wealth. The Letter of Aristeas 228 addresses the honor due friends. More theologically oriented literature draws upon the model of friendship to describe the relation between the Deity and select individuals; Abraham (Isa. 41:8; 2 Chron. 20:7; James 2:23) and Moses (Exod. 33:11) are both called friend of God. The Gospels depict the charge that Jesus is a friend to tax collectors and sinners (Luke 7:34; see also Matt. 9:11; Luke 15:1–2). John 15:13 states that the greatest love is to give one's life for one's friends; in John 15:14 Jesus states that those who follow his commandments are his friends. On an ironic note, Luke 23:12 claims that their mutual dealings with Jesus caused Pilate and Herod Antipas to become friends. Enigmatically, Luke 16:9 advises making friends by means of "unrighteous mammon."

The talmudic literature defines true friendship as a relationship through which neither party hopes to advance his or her own interests. This contrasts with selfishness, which destroys friendship (M. Abot 5:16). The rabbis note that true friendship is rare, for, "At the gates of shops you have many friends and kin; at prison gates, you find no friends or kin" (B. Shabbat 32a). The greatest value of friendship is in the desire of true friends to improve each other's moral and intellectual stature. Thus, Abot deRabbi Natan 19 states that one should love the person who corrects him and hate the one who offers only flattery.

fruit a major motif in ancient Jewish art, particularly in mosaic floors and carved in relief in synagogues. Fruits also figure heavily on Jewish coins, particularly on coins of the Jewish War and of the Bar Kokhba Revolt, and also on lamps. Fruits appear individually, in groups, or in baskets with many other fruits. Fruits are among the seven kinds of bounty indigenous to the land (Deut. 8:8) and grapes, dates, figs, and pomegranates are often depicted in various media. The etrog, though it is a fruit, is treated separately, as it occurs with menorah, lulab, shofar, and incense shovel with regularity. The pomegranate appeared as early as the Hasmonean period on coins of John Hyrcanus I, John Hyrcanus II, Judas Aristobolus, Mattathias Antigonus, Herod the Great, and the coins of the Jewish War. The palm tree bearing fruit is a popular motif in mosaics and on Jewish coins, especially the coins of Herod Antipas. Dates alone also appear on the coins of Herod Antipas. Baskets of figs, dates, or other fruits are known on Jewish lamps of the first to the third century C.E. In the synagogue floor from Hammath-Tiberias, the figure of Spring (Nisan) holds a bowl of fruit in her right hand. The Beth Alpha figure of Summer (Tammuz) is associated with fruit and field produce, but it is not in baskets.

FT *see* FRAGMENTARY TARGUMS

Fuga *see* DE FUGA ET INVENTIONE

fulfillment of prophecy *see* PROPHECY, FULFILLMENT OF

fullness of time (Gr.: *plērōma tou chronou*) technical term employed in Jewish eschatological literature to refer to the end of the old age, which ushers in the new age (e.g., 2 Bar. 30:3). Paul uses the expression in Galatians 4:4 with reference to the coming of Jesus, as part of an extended argument to prove that obedience to the Torah is passé due to the coming of the Messiah and the new age (Gal. 3:15–29). *See also* ESCHATOLOGY.

full-time, perpetual students *see* ASARAH BATLANIM

furnace, fiery the instrument of punishment for people refusing to worship Nebuchadnezzar's massive image (Dan. 3). The story portrays the three youths' refusal to participate in the idolatrous exercise as an ordeal that tests the power of Israel's God, which is vindicated when the youths are delivered without harm and Nebuchadnezzar must acclaim their God and praise their trusting obedience. The story may be a narrative elaboration on Isaiah 43:2. The Septuagint version of Daniel 3 enhances the story through the addition of Azariah's prayer for deliverance and the youths' song of thanksgiving. The Book of Biblical Antiquities 6–7 identifies the plain of Dura in Babylon (Dan. 3:1) with the plain in Shinar, where the Tower of Babel was erected (Gen. 11:1–9) and where Abram is cast into a fiery furnace because of his refusal to participate. Thus Abram is chosen by God, and the fire is the *ur* of the Chaldeans from which the patriarch goes forth (Gen. 11:31).

fusion meal *see* ERUB̲ TABSHILIN

Gabara (or Gabaroth) Jewish village in Galilee on the north edge of the Beit Netofa Valley. The Hebrew name of the village is Arav in the Talmud, though there are at least two villages of that name. The village was known to Josephus in the first century as a town attacked by Vespasian near the outset of his march into Galilee (*War* 3.7.1, p. 132, reading Gadara as Gabara). He also knew it as a town hostile to John of Gischala in Upper Galilee (*Vita* 10:44). First-century-C.E. tombs are known in the modern village, called Arraba. It is the place where the priestly course of Pethahiah fled from Jerusalem in 70 C.E. Fragments of a Byzantine church are also known in the modern village.

Gablan an area in the northern Transjordan, known for its fertility (B. Ketubot 112a). The area's fertility is stressed by M. Sotah 9:15, which states that with the approach of the Messiah, even Gablan will be made desolate.

Gabriel (Heb., power [or man] of God) one of the four or, in some cases, seven holy ones (angels) who stand in God's immediate presence. Gabriel is mentioned in all lists of these angels of the presence in the Pseudepigrapha (1 Enoch 20, 40) and Qumran scrolls (1QM 9:15–16). Along with Michael and Raphael, he is one of three who appear by name in canonical and deuterocanonical texts. In Daniel 8–9 and Luke 1:26, he functions as God's messenger to Daniel and Mary, explaining the divine mysteries and deeds of salvation.

Gaggot-Tzarifin location mentioned at M. Menaḥot 10:2, referring possibly to Sarafand, near Lydda. When the crop near Jerusalem did not ripen in time, the barley required for the *omer* was brought from there. An alternate reading is Gannot-Tzarifin, that is, the gardens of Tzarifin.

Gaium *see* DE LEGATIONE AD GAIUM

Gaius Roman emperor (r. 37–41 C.E.). Gaius Julius Caesar Germanicus was born in 12 C.E. to Germanicus (the adopted son of the emperor Tiberius) and his wife Agrippina. As a young child living with his parents in a military camp on the Rhine he was nicknamed Caligula (Little Boots) by the soldiers. After the death of his father in suspicious circumstances in Syria, he lived in Rome with his mother. As declared heir he joined Tiberius at Capri and was proclaimed emperor by the Praetorian Guard on the latter's death in 37. However, after only a few months in office he suffered a severe illness that may have left him somewhat deranged. He turned on his former supporters, including Gemellus, and had them executed. His dealings with the Senate became more autocratic as he adopted a lifestyle more in keeping with an eastern potentate than that of his predecessors in the office of the principate. It was this policy that brought him into direct confrontation with the Jews, whose religious beliefs did not allow the use of human representations. The refusal of the Alexandrine Jews to worship his image was partly responsible for the troubles in Alexandria, which gave rise to the delegation that Philo writes about in his *Legatio ad Gaium*. He was a close friend of Herod the Great's grandson, Agrippa, and bestowed on him the title of king together with the territories of his uncle Philip in Batanea and Trachonitis and, two years later in 39, the territories of the deposed Antipas (Galilee and Perea). Jews had destroyed a votive altar to the emperor at Jamnia and Gaius responded by ordering the governor of Syria, Petronius, to have his statue erected in the Temple in Jerusalem. Petronius was aware of the dire repercussions that such an action would likely have in Palestine, especially after receiving a threat of an agricultural strike from the Jews. Agrippa approached the emperor and succeeded in having the matter postponed until Gaius himself could visit the east. Gaius and his family were murdered in 41 C.E. before the proposed visit took place. The Jews were spared an open confrontation with the might of Rome for another thirty years.

Galen (131–197 C.E.) physician and philosopher, born in Pergamum. A medieval Jewish legend identified Galen with the patriarch Gamaliel II, who was supposed to have written a handbook of medicine for Titus after the destruction of Jerusalem. Galen often expressed disapproval of the centrality of uncritical faith and authority in Judaism. He compared incompetent physicians to Moses, whom he criticized for stating positions without offering proof, saying only that "God commanded" or "God spoke." Galen viewed Moses as a philosopher and in his writings engaged in philosophical debates with the latter concerning the causes of creation, rejecting the doctrine of *creatio ex nihilo*.

Galerius Roman emperor (r. 293–311 C.E.). Diocletian appointed him Caesar of the East in 293 as part of Diocletian's tetrarchy. He was born the son of peasants at Serdica, Thrace, in 250. He led a successful campaign against the Persians. His religious views were similar to those of Diocletian, and he may have been the ideological force behind the Christian persecutions of 303. He became Augustus of the East upon Diocletian's abdication in 305. After suffering a major illness, he issued an edict of partial toleration to the Christian church, perhaps to placate their god.

Galilean Aramaic *see* ARAMAIC, GALILEAN

Galilee the northernmost area of the Land of Israel; also known as Gelil. In the first century C.E., Galilee was governed as a province of Judea. In 66 C.E. its Jewish inhabitants joined the war against Rome, with Josephus in charge of its defense. The area was ceded to Vespasian in 67 C.E. The Jewish character of the area during the mishnaic period is subject to dispute. The absence of references to Galilee in Second Temple biblical sources and the lack of any specifically Jewish archaeological evidence support the view that Galilee was home to only a small Jewish minority. By contrast, some scholars point to the rabbinic traditions of a distinctively Galilean Judaism, found as early as the Mishnah, as evidence for a significant Jewish population in the area. Comparably, the schism between Samaria and Galilee may suggest a much more Jewish Galilee than the opposing view recognizes. Scholars also dispute whether the citizens of Galilee participated in the Bar Kosiba revolt.

Galilee, archaeology of *The Persian period.* The western part of Galilee was influenced by and may even have been an integral part of the Pheonician kingdom of Sidon, as shown by finds from the cemeteries at Ahziv and excavations at Tell Akko and Tell Kisan. Other parts of Galilee were part of a district which had the town of Meggido as its center. On top of Tell Hazor a large fortified building was found, built perhaps to control the main road in the valley. Many farmhouses were located in Galilee, together with small sites, indicating that Galilee played a smaller role than the coastal area during this period.

The Hellenistic period. Two large and important centers grew up around Galilee during the Hellenistic period. In the west, Ptolemais became the most important city between Dora and Tyre. Remains of a strong city wall, private buildings with fresco walls, temples, inscriptions, and a tunnel for an aqueduct have been excavated. Fortresses and army camps were built around the town to protect its hinterland. The second city, to the southeast, is Skithopolis, founded in the third century B.C.E. Remains of large Hellenistic neigborhoods have also been uncovered at Tell Istabah on the north bank of the river. A large fortress was built on top of Mount Tabor; along with many others, it was used in the Syrian wars.

The remains of Persian temples, with mainly Hellenistic features, were uncovered at Beer Sheba and in small villages in central Upper Galilee. Another enigmatic cult site was uncovered at Tell Dan. Above the remains of the large Israelite cult center, a Hellenistic temenos was found, including an altar, liquid basin, and an inscription in Greek and Aramaic about the "Great God of Dan."

In the Hulla Valley, the remains of an unusual Hellenistic palace were uncovered at Tell Anafa, with very early examples of golden frescoes and stucco. No archaeological evidence for Jewish life was found from that time up to the Hasmonean conquest around 100 B.C.E. The destruction layers of Tell Anafa, the temple at Mizpe Yamim, and the

Hellenistic residential areas at Skithopolis can be attributed to the conquest of Galilee by the Hasmoneans. Numerous Hasmonean coins have been found all over Galilee, indicating the extent of the Jewish population. From that time Jewish Galilee, detached from Jerusalem by Samaria, developed mainly in Lower Galilee, with Sepphoris as its capital, and in central and eastern Upper Galilee.

The Roman period. During Herod Antipas's reign, the new capital of Tiberias was built; archaeological finds, such as a gate with round towers and perhaps a theater, show the Roman style of urbanization. It is possible that Sepphoris was built in a similar way.

Galilee was surrounded by Gentile towns, including Tyre Qedesh, and Paneas, where excavations of the cult center for Pan and the remains of monumental buildings dating to the first century C.E. are found. On the north, there is Ptolemais; on the west, Hipos and the small town of Philoteria; and on the east, Skithopolis, where excavations have uncovered mainly the large buildings of the civic center and paved, pillared streets.

Evidence of daily life during the first century C.E., together with actual remains from the First Jewish Revolt in Galilee, were uncovered at the small town of Yodfat. The remains of a Roman asphalt ramp, arrowheads, ballista stones, and the city wall attest to the heavy battle described by Flavius. Private houses, cisterns, baths, oil presses, clay vessels, stone vessels, and coins all shed light on life in Galilee in the early Roman period. Layers of the same period were also uncovered at Sepphoris and Tiberias. Remains of Roman-period layers at both capitals of Jewish Galilee reveal well-organized cities with paved streets, public bathhouses, aqueducts, simple private houses, and some large, well-designed buildings.

Five Jewish villages were partly unearthed in Galilee: Capernaum, Chorazin, Meiron, Naburaya, and Horvat Shema. The private houses, mostly one story high, were built of local stones and covered with simple plaster. Roofs were made of wooden beams covered with mud or, very rarely, of roof tiles. Most villages were not planned, but had an organized structure; some of the alleys were paved and had sewage-water channels below them. At Chorazin and Horvat Shema, two water installations were found and identified by the excavators as ritual baths.

Twenty synagogues from the late Roman to the Byzantine period were excavated in the Galilee and about twenty-five more were identified at the survey according to their architectural elements. The architectural origin of the synagogue in Upper Galilee was Roman public architecture. The synagogue was the largest and most impressive building in the Jewish village. Most synagogues had two stories and were covered with gabled, tiled roofs. The synagogues are the main evidence of Jewish life, since almost all the Hebrew inscriptions from Galilee have come from synagogues. The inscriptions from Upper Galilee are mainly in Hebrew, though some are in Aramaic and one is in Greek. In Lower Galilee, most inscriptions are in Greek; some are in Hebrew and Aramaic. Much evidence comes from the funerary world. The large public cemetery at Beth Shearim, which has provided many inscriptions and names, demonstrates the diversity of Jewish burial customs in the late Roman period.

The Roman imperial road system was constructed mainly in Lower Galilee. A major road connected Ptolemais with Tiberias; another ran from Legio north to Sepphoris. Milestones with inscriptions were found along these two roads and experimental excavation sections revealed that they were built by Roman methods. Upper Galilee was surrounded by Roman roads but none of them cut through it.

Early Christianity: the fourth century. Some of the earliest remains of Christianity were found in Galilee. At Capernaum are the remains of the Domus Eclesia, which was built, according to tradition, above the house of Saint Peter. An early chapel, dated to the fourth century, was uncovered below the remains of the large "church of fish and loaves" at Tabha (Heptapegon). Two uncertain fourth-century-C.E. churches were unearthed in western Galilee, one at Hebron and the other at Savei-Zion.

The Byzantine period. Most of the Jewish villages continued their way of life throughout the Byzantine period. In spite of the Christian laws against building synagogues, new ones were constructed. In Upper Galilee they were built in the Roman tradition, as at Naburaya and Meroth. In the valley they were built in the Byzantine style in the plan of churches; the synagogues at Beth Alpha and Maoz Hayim are examples. Some villages were abandoned for various reasons, and there is no doubt that Christian pressure was an important factor. In Lower Galilee, churches and monasteries were built between Jewish villages and in one case, at Capernaum, beside a synagogue.

Galilee, Sea of large fresh water lake in the northern rift valley of ancient Palestine, also known as Lake Tiberias (from one of its largest cities) or in

Hebrew as Yam Kinneret (Num. 34:11). Josephus refers to it simply as "the lake" (*Vita* 96), though he knows that the locals also called it the Lake of Genesareth (*War* 3.10.1, p. 462), probably because of a town of that name on the northwestern plain beside the lakeshore. Today the lake is about 12.5 miles by 7 miles, though in antiquity it may have been larger. Josephus, in particular, thought it extended about 16 miles north to south, but he believed it was only 4.5 miles wide. In the Hellenistic period the site of Philoteria was built on its southwestern shores on the site of biblical Beth Yerah. The town of Hammath stood at the hot springs one Roman mile south of Tiberias and north of Philoteria, the site of a Jewish town. In the early first century C.E., Herod Antipas built Tiberias north of Philoteria. On the northwest shore stood Magdala (also known as Taricheae) and Ginnosaur. Just west of Magdala are the imposing cliffs of Arbel where Herod the Great killed the last rebel in his resolution of the civil war. Just west of the entrance of the Jordan into the lake stood ancient Capernaum, and west of the Jordan stood Bethsaida-Julias. On the west shore stood Gerasa (Gergesa of Matt. 8:28). To the southeast stood a city of the Decapolis, Hippos-Susitha.

A series of harbors and anchorages have been identified around the lake, as it was well exploited by the fishing industry. In fact, the Greek name of Magdala, Taricheae, means salted or pickled fish. The towns of Capernaum and Magdala figure in the ministry of Jesus, who called his first disciples from among its fishermen (Matt. 4:18–22). The lake was the scene of a pitched maritime battle between the Jews and the Romans in the First Jewish War (*War* 3.10.9: 522–542). This battle was disastrous for the Jews. In the Roman and Byzantine periods synagogues were built around the lake at Hammath, Tiberias (at least two), Magdala, Capernaum, and Beth Yerah. Doubtless others were built and remain to be found. In the Byzantine period there was great interest on the part of the Christian emperors and of local Christian citizens to build memorial churches to the memory of Jesus' ministry around the lake. Great churches were built at Heptapegon west of Capernaum, at Capernaum, and at Hippos, and a great monastery was built at Gerasa (Kursi).

Galilee boat (also known as the Kinneret boat, after the Hebrew name for the Sea of Galilee) two-thousand-year-old fishing boat recovered intact in 1986 from the Sea of Galilee. The vessel was discovered buried in sediment during a severe drought that caused the lake's waters to recede and revealed vast expanses of the lake bed. To prevent the hull from imminent destruction by treasure hunters, the Israel Department of Antiquities and Museums mounted an exceptional, around-the-clock salvage excavation. Once the hull had been cleared of overburden and studied in situ, it was encased in a fiberglass and polyurethane "cocoon," and sailed down the lake to the Yigal Allon Center at nearby Kibbutz Ginosar, where it is currently undergoing conservation.

The boat is 26½ feet (8.2 meters) long, 7½ feet (2.3 meters) in breadth, and was preserved to a height of 4½ feet (1.2 meters) in the stern. The hull was built in "shell-first" technique; its planks were edge-joined and fastened together with mortise-and-tenon joints. The hull appears to have been built to a large degree of timbers that had seen use in earlier vessels. Most of the boat's planking was made of imported Lebanese cedar, and the frames of locally available oak. Single timbers of five other types have also been identified in the boat's structure: Aleppo pine, hawthorn, redbud, sidder, and willow.

A study of the construction techniques, related pottery, and radiocarbon dating places the boat's lifetime sometime around 100 B.C.E. to 70 C.E. This was a workboat that would have been used for fishing, as well as transporting passengers and cargo. The boat had a long lifetime of service on the lake; when it was old and decrepit it was brought ashore to have all of its reusable timber removed for secondary use. The remaining hull, no longer of any commercial use, was pushed out into the lake where it was soon covered with sediment, which preserved it.

The Galilee boat gives us a unique and intimate view of life on the Sea of Galilee in the waning years of the Second Temple period, a time of demographic expansion when the Kinneret was ringed by Jewish fishing settlements. In 67 C.E. Jews, apparently using boats of this type, were defeated by Roman soldiers in the Battle of Migdal. Josephus gives a detailed account of this conflict, which left the lake's waters crimson with Jewish blood (*War* 3:522–531).

gall Like liver or, more usually, its product (bile), gall carries the metaphorical associations of bitterness, anger, or, most commonly, poison (Lam. 3:19; Job 20:14, 25; Acts 8:23). It functions apotropaically when Tobias cures his father's blindness by anointing his eyes with a paste made from the gall of a miraculous fish (Tob. 11:8); gall was believed to have some medicinal properties. Some suggest that the "gall" offered to Jesus while he was being crucified (Matt. 27:34) may have been myrrh or a narcotic.

Gallus, Cestius *see* CESTIUS GALLUS, GAIUS

galut *see* DIASPORA

Gamala Jewish city of the northern Golan Heights destroyed in the First Revolt and never rebuilt; the site of possibly a first-century-C.E. synagogue. The city of Gamala is well known from Josephus (*War* 4.1ff). There the inhabitants resisted the Romans under Vespasian as long as they could, but finally all but two women were slain by the Romans. Identified with a ridge known as as-Salam in Arabic that is about 10 kilometers east of the northeast shore of the Sea of Galilee, the site was built on a natural, steep ridge so that its appearance closely resembles a camel's hump (hence the Aramaic name). The excavators at Gamala have traced the city wall and identified a total area of about 75 acres within the walls. Furthermore, they have excavated a ritual bath, several rooms of residences, and a possible synagogue. Other installations brought to light include a town gate, cisterns, the lower city, and an aqueduct to the lower city.

Whether the building identified as a synagogue is indeed correctly identified has absorbed the debating energies of many scholars. The building in question is a rectangle with one wall against the city wall and one wall cut from bedrock. Its interior columniation was arranged in a rectangle around all four walls, with double columns or "heart-shaped" columns at the corners of the rectangle. The column capitals were carved with meander decorations. The central space between the columns steps down lower than the aisles between the columns and the walls, rather like benches, which is the strongest evidence that this is an assembly area. The central space was divided visually into two spaces by at least two columns across the space. This assembly area is entered from two doors to the southwest, where the doors give entry from a short hallway rather than directly from the street. Another door in the northeast corner opens outward to a staircase down to the side street. The aisles are paved with basalt flagstones, though the lower, central area is paved with pressed earth. A square niche, which some have identified as the place of the Torah shrine, is to be found in the corner to the left of the entrances.

Since the building is built against the city wall, its orientation is southwest to northeast. It was not built to orient to Jerusalem, though the facade does more or less point in that direction. Decoration within the building is confined to geometric motifs, such as rosettes, swastika meanders, and vines, which are in low relief or incised. The community ritual bath (so called because of its large size) was found only a few meters southwest of the putative synagogue and has been interpreted as part of the synagogue complex. That the building was used for some kind of gathering seems clear, though whether it is a synagogue in the narrow sense is still debated. It was probably built in the first century B.C.E. and destroyed during the First Revolt in 68 C.E. Huge ballistae from Roman siege engines and arrow heads from Roman archers littered its floors, as they litter the floors of all areas within the city that have been excavated.

Gamaliel I also known as Gamaliel haZaken (the Elder); president of the Sanhedrin, active in the first half of the first century C.E. He was a grandson of Hillel. He is known for letters he wrote, while the Temple still stood, to Jewish communities in the land of Israel and, during the diaspora, regarding the separation of tithes and the intercalation of the year (T. Sanhedrin 2:6). He was responsible as well for a number of ordinances aimed at improving the status of women (M. Gittin 4:2–3; M. Yeḇamot 16:7). He is referred to at Acts 5:34 as tolerant of followers of Jesus and at Acts 22:3 as a teacher of Paul.

Gamaliel II also known as Gamaliel of Yaḇneh. A grandson of Gamaliel the Elder, he followed Yoḥanan b. Zakkai as patriarch around 80 C.E. He played a significant role in the development of the center of rabbinic learning at Yaḇneh and in the struggle to establish that center, its patriarch, and court as the center of Judaism. The result was a struggle for power with elder rabbis of his generation, a fight which led him to excommunicate his own brother-in-law, Eliezer b. Hyrcanus (B. Baḇa Metzia 59b). Of special concern was Gamaliel's establishing of his court's right to set the calendar. He clashed with Joshua (M. Rosh Hashanah 2:8–9) over this issue and, as a result, for a time was removed from the office of patriarch (B. Berakhot 27b–28a).

Gamaliel's legal statements are cited frequently in the Mishnah, and he was recognized as one of the greatest authorities of his generation. He is known for ordinances aimed at shaping Judaism in the face of the destruction of the Temple, for instance, by formulating the ritual for Passover eve (M. Pesaḥim 19:5) and by establishing individual prayer as normative.

Gamaliel's knowledge of and participation in Hellenistic culture are clear from his positive attitude towards the study of Greek (T. Sotah 15:8; B. Sotah 49b) and his use of a bathhouse of Aphrodite in Acre (M. Abodah Zarah 3:4). At the same time, he was a fierce proponent of Judaism against heresy and idolatry. Later sources associated him with the Amida's benediction that excluded Christians from membership in the Jewish community (B. Berakhot 28b).

Gamaliel III son of Judah the Patriarch; also called Gamaliel b. Rabbi; active in the first half of the third century C.E. While few of his dicta are preserved, he was a teacher to important authorities of the first Amoraic generation, including Samuel, Yoḥanan, and Ḥanina. His father appointed him patriarch (B. Ketubot 103b). At M. Abot 2:3, Gamaliel preaches suspicion of the Roman government.

Gamaliel IV son of Judah II Nesiah; active in the second half of the third century C.E.; father of Judah III. He is infrequently cited, and his exact period of activity is unclear.

Gamaliel V son of and patriarch following Hillel II. Little more than his name is known.

Gamaliel VI the last patriarch. He defended Jews against Christians and, without governmental approval, built a synagogue. As a punishment, in an edict dated 415 C.E., the emperors Honorius and Theodosius II deprived him of the post of patriarch and of its associated honorific titles. His death in 426 C.E. marked the end of the patriarchate.

gambling frowned upon in Jewish law and considered a form of theft. Professional gamblers were disqualified from serving as witnesses or judges in court. Playing dice and betting on pigeons were specifically denounced by the rabbis. However, gambling for entertainment was not prohibited, as illustrated by the popularity of the game of dreidel on Hannukah.

gaon (pl., geonim) title of the head(s) of the Babylonian academies at Sura and Pumbedita, beginning in the sixth century C.E. The geonim determined the educational activity of the academies and sat as heads of a court system modeled after the Sanhedrin. The gaon generally was elected by the academy. Occasionally he was appointed by the exilarch, from whose office the gaonate was distinct.

garments, rending of ritual act of mourning. The act might be a reaction to death (2 Sam. 3:31, 13:31; Jdt. 14:19; 2 Macc. 4:38) or acute personal loss (2 Sam. 13:19). It was also a sign of repentance (Joel 2:12–13; Ezra 9:3–5) and a ritual response in a trial for blasphemy (Mark 14:63; M. Sanh. 7:5). *See also* SACKCLOTH AND ASHES.

gathering together of the exiles (Heb.: *kibbutz galuyot*) eschatological hope that all Israel will be restored to the Land of Israel by the Messiah at the end of days; the gathering of all the Jews into the Holy Land

Gaton Kabrath Gaton, referred to at T. Shebiit 4:11 as demarcating a border area of the Land of Israel

Gattung *see* GENRE

Gaza coastal city of importance from the biblical period, but also throughout the period from the sixth century B.C.E. to the sixth century C.E. Gaza formed a major port and formed the west end of a caravan route across the Negeb toward the eastern desert kingdoms. In the Persian period Gaza belonged to the Fifth Satrapy. At the end of the Persian period, Alexander the Great conquered the city after a two-month siege. The city wall of this siege was excavated in 1922. After Alexander's death, the city changed loyalties back and forth between Greek Egypt and Greek Syria. Gaza was under Ptolemaic rule from 301 to 198 B.C.E. It was a major economic center, forming the last staging point for goods imported to Egypt from Palestine and vice versa. From this point onward, Gaza gradually developed more and more autonomy, though this was threatened by the conquest of Gaza by Jonathan the Hasmonean in 145 B.C.E. and by John Hyrcanus I about 125 B.C.E. The Jewish king Alexander Jannaeus destroyed and annexed Gaza at the beginning of the second century B.C.E. Gaza came under Roman rule in 63 B.C.E. and began to mint its own coins in 61 B.C.E. The city passed to Herod the Great in 40 B.C.E. Herod did not trust Gaza to remain loyal to him, probably because of its small Jewish population and because of the economic connections Gaza maintained with Egypt and with the Kingdom of the Nabateans east and south of the Dead Sea. At the death of Herod, the city was almost an independent polis under the authority of the Roman governor at Damascus.

Gaza flourished under the Romans and became the major slave market of the region. Captured Jewish slaves from the Bar Kokhba Revolt were sold in the markets of Gaza. Archaeological evidence from the Roman period suggests that the city was decorated and maintained as a Roman city, with sculpture everywhere. Gaza ceased to mint its own coins about 238 C.E. These coins feature Marnas, a local deity identified with Zeus, but also Tyche (Fortuna), and Io. The Jewish population of Gaza must have grown during the late Roman and Byzantine periods, for a beautiful synagogue was built there in 508 C.E. and has been recently excavated. A Byzantine dye works also came to light west of the synagogue. The dye works or industrial complex was surrounded by a mud brick wall on a stone foundation. It consisted of only two rooms with reservoirs, presumably for dyes. The Christian population of the Roman and Byzantine periods also flourished and built churches of note. Christian and Jewish epitaphs are known from the ancient cemeteries of Gaza. Gaza also figures in the sixth-century-C.E. mosaic map from Madaba in Jordan, its harbor shown with the name Maiumas Neapolis. The city wall of Byzantine Gaza has also been partially excavated.

Gaza Synagogue Byzantine synagogue with an elaborate mosaic floor. This synagogue was found accidently in 1965 when Gaza was under Egyptian administration. Its position near the sea shore suggests that it belonged to the Byzantine port city of Gaza called Neapolis Maiumas or Constantia Maiumas Neapolis. Emergency excavations by the Israelis in 1967 yielded much additional data. This was a large building about 30 meters by 26 meters in extent. The form of the building was a basilica with double rows of columns on two sides, that is, a nave and four side aisles. The building has its facade on the west side, probably with three portals. The excavator believes that an apse stood at the opposite, east end of the building, probably for the Ark of the Law. Fragments of an exquisite marble chancel screen of openwork in a floral motif revealed that such a screen stood around the ark at the east end. Carved into one fragment of the chancel screen was a menorah with lulab and shofar.

The earliest floor of the synagogue was a splendid mosaic that depicted King David dressed as Orpheus playing the harp. Above the harp is a single Hebrew word, David, so the interpretation is unambiguous. King David wears royal Byzantine garb and a gold crown or wreath. Around the king stand several animals, apparently soothed by his music: a lion cub, a giraffe, and a snake. The whole is surrounded by geometric designs. The south aisle is an inhabited scroll with representations of two peacocks, a hind, a nursing lioness, a feline chasing a deer, a wading bird, a bird in a cage, two giraffes, and foxes. This mosaic is in the same style as the synagogue of Maon, not far away.

The dedicatory inscription of the synagogue is in Greek and reads, "Menachem and Jeshua, sons of the Blessed Jesse, wood merchants, being thankful, give to the holy place this mosaic floor as an offering. . . ." "Holy place" refers to the synagogue. The date corresponds to 508 C.E. A bilingual inscription within a wreath carved on a white marble column, now in reuse in the modern mosque, mentions Hanania bar Iaakov in Hebrew and Anania the son of Iako in Greek. From the interior of the building came pottery lamps of the late Byzantine period. The excavator theorizes that the building was destroyed in the Arab conquest.

Geba city along the northern boundary of the tribe of Benjamin (Josh. 18:24), about 5 miles north of Jerusalem. In some biblical passages, confusion among the names Geba, Gibeah, and Gibeon, and the existence of more than one Geba, render it difficult to determine with certainty which city is meant. The Geba referred to at M. Kelim 17:5 and T. Kelim Baba Metzia 6:10 as inhabited by Kutim is the present-day Jaba, 4 miles north of Samaria.

Gebiha of Be-Katil Babylonian amora of the fifth century C.E.; during the last fourteen years of his life (419–433), head of the academy at Sura

Gedaliah, Fast of commemoration of the death of Gedaliah. Gedaliah was the son of Ahikam, son of Shaphan; he was appointed by Nebuchadnezzar to be governor over Judah and subsequently was murdered at Mizpah by rivals for control (2 Kings 25:22ff.). Scripture states that the assassination took place in the seventh month (Tishrei) but does not specify the date. Rabbinic sources place it on the third of Tishrei (B. Rosh Hashanah 18b). Medieval sources hold that the assassination took place on the New Year itself, that is, the first and second of Tishrei. Since fasting is prohibited on those dates, the fast takes place on the third or, in the event that the third is the Sabbath, on the fourth.

Gedara *see* GEDOR

Gedor talmudic name for Gedara, a Hellenistic town on a hill in Transjordan; one of the stations on which flares were lit to signal the occurrence of the new moon (B. Rosh Hashanah 23b); believed to have been fortified by Joshua (M. Arakhin 9:6; alternative reading: Gedod); the capital of Perea (Josephus, *War* 4:413). In scripture, the name Gedor also refers to other cities, including one in Judah (Josh. 15:58), one that is probably identical with Gederah (1 Chron. 4:18), and one in the area of Simeon (1 Chron. 4:39).

Gelil *see* GALILEE

Gemara the part of the Talmuds devoted to the commentary on the Mishnah. The Mishnah and Gemara constitute a Talmud.

gematria exegetical technique in which words are explained through reference to the numerical value of their constituent letters. The method was known to the Babylonians and Greeks and is referred to in rabbinic statements from the second century C.E. and on. In the talmudic literature, gematria occurs almost exclusively in homiletical settings, appearing only occasionally in legal contexts, for instance, in the creation of mnemonic devices. An example of gematria occurs at B. Shabbat 70a, where Nathan interprets the statement "these are the words (*eleh haDebarim,* Exod. 35:1) to refer to the thirty-nine categories of work forbidden on the Sabbath. He derives this number from the numerical equivalent of *eleh*—thirty-six—plus two for the plural form *debarim* and one more for the definite article *ha*.

gemilut ḥasadim (acts of loving kindness) supererogatory acts of humanity, over and above the religious duties of service to fellow human beings that the Torah requires

gender roles, in rabbinic Judaism Men are the principal active force in the law of rabbinic Judaism, and women are acted upon, an arena for concern in particular when women represent points of danger, for example, when their status is unclear. In such instances, the law focuses on them, for example, when a woman is betrothed and married, when the marriage comes to an end, and at similar turning points. The principal focus of a social vision framed by men, such as that of the Mishnah, not only encompasses but focuses on woman, who is perceived as the indicative abnormality in a world in which men are normal. But to place into perspective the Mishnah's vision of woman, we have to locate woman within the larger structure defined by the household. This is for two reasons. First of all, as a matter of definition, woman forms the other half of the whole that is the householder. Second, since the household forms the building block of the social construction envisioned by the Mishnah's framers, it is in that setting that every other component of the social world of the system must situate itself. In this conception, which sees Israel as made up, on earth, of households and villages, the economic unit also frames the social one, and the two together compose the political one—hence, a political economy (joining the Greek words for city and household, i.e., *polis* and *oikos*), initiated within an economic definition formed out of the elements of production. This explains why women cannot be addressed outside of the framework of the economic unit of production defined by the household, for, throughout, the Mishnah makes a single cogent statement that the organizing unit of society and politics finds its definition in the irreducible unit of economic production. The Mishnah conceives no economic unit of production other than the household, though it recognizes that such existed; its authors perceive no social unit of organization other than the household and the conglomeration of households, though that limited vision omits all reference to substantial parts of the population perceived to be present, such as craftsmen, the unemployed, the landless, and the like. The framers of the Mishnah, for example, do not imagine a household headed by a woman; a divorced woman is assumed to return to her father's household. The framers make no provision for the economic activity of isolated individuals, out of synchronic relationship with a household or a village made up of householders. Accordingly, women, as much as craftsmen and day laborers or other workers, skilled and otherwise, enter the world of social and economic transactions only in relationship to the householder. The upshot, therefore, is that the social world is made up of households, and, since households may be made up of many families (e.g., husbands, wives, children, all of them dependents of the householder), households in no way are to be confused with the family. The indicator of the family is kinship, that of the household, "propinquity or residence." But even residence is not always a criterion for membership in the household unit, since the craftsmen and day laborers are not assumed to live in the household compound at all. Accordingly, the household forms an economic unit, with secondary criteria deriving from that primary fact.

The mishnaic law of women defines the position of women in the social economy of Israel's supernatural and natural reality. That position acquires definition in relationship to men, who give form to the Israelite social economy. It is effected through both supernatural and natural, this-worldly, action. What man and woman do on earth provokes a response in Heaven, and the correspondences are perfect. Thus the position of women is defined and secured in Heaven and here on earth, and that position, always and invariably relative to men, is what comes into consideration. In the Mishnah, the principal point of interest is the time at which a woman changes hands, that is, when she becomes or ceases to be holy to a particular man by entering or leaving the marital union. These are the dangerous and disorderly points in the relationship of woman to man and therefore to society. Five of the seven tractates of the Mishnah that pertain to women and family are devoted to the transfer of women—the formation and dissolution of the marital bond. Of these, three (Kiddushin, Ketubot, and Gittin) treat what is done here on earth by man, that is, formation of a marital bond through betrothal and the marriage contract, its dissolution through divorce, and the consequences. One of them (Sotah) is devoted to what is done here on earth by woman. Yebamot, greatest of the seven tractates in size and in informal and substantive brilliance, deals with the corresponding heavenly intervention into the formation and dissolution of marriage: the effect of death upon the marital bond, and the dissolution, through death, of that bond. The other two tractates, Nedarim and Nazir, draw into one the two realms of reality, heaven and earth, as they work out the effects of vows—generally taken by married women and subject to the confirmation or abrogation of the husband—to heaven. These vows make a deep impact upon the marital relationship of the woman who has taken such a vow.

genealogy The Hebrew scriptures record over twenty genealogies; they appear as early as the primeval history and as late as the Chronicles. Emphasized in the postexilic period, especially in considerations of priestly purity (Ezra 2, 10:18–44; Neh. 12:22–23), the genealogy became increasingly important with the growth of diaspora communities and the consequent loss of geographical indicators of family and caste membership. Descent determined permitted marriages, priestly privileges, and social status. The Apocrypha provide genealogies for Tobit, Mordecai (in Additions to Esther), and, with the longest list, Judith. Josephus records that priestly genealogies were preserved in public archives (*Vita* 1).

The Gospels provide Jesus with two genealogies: Matthew's is divided into three cycles of fourteen generations (the last preserves only thirteen names) and underscores Jesus' Jewishness by highlighting Abraham, David, and the Babylonian expulsion. Matthew also explicitly names four women along with Mary: Tamar, Rahab, Ruth, and "she of Uriah" (Bathsheba) may prefigure the sexual irregularities of Jesus' own birth, the exercise of higher righteousness by those in weak positions, and/or the welcome of Gentiles into the Church. The Lucan genealogy traces Jesus' line back to Adam and so locates Jesus within the context of world history. While both genealogies name David, the lines pass through different sons and so are not consistent (Solomon and so the royal line in Matthew; Nathan in Luke). Both genealogies are those of Joseph, although the Gospels teach a virgin birth. Later Christian teaching made both Mary and Joseph Davidides. *See also* DAVID, SON OF.

Genesis Apocryphon a compilation of narratives about the patriarchs. This Aramaic text is extant in one damaged manuscript, discovered among the first Dead Sea Scrolls of Qumran Cave 1, but its revision of the Genesis stories reveals no tendency that indicates that it was composed in the Qumran Community. The date of its composition seems to have been around the turn of the era.

The extant portion of the scroll covers the period from Lamech to Abraham, but its badly deteriorated condition permits substantial reconstruction of only five of its twenty-two columns (2, 19–22). Columns 2–5 contained the story of Noah's birth. A series of episodes from the life of Abram probably began in column 18, and columns 19–22 retell the events in Genesis 12:8–15:4.

In freely recasting the events in Genesis, the author employs novelistic devices, the first-person singular voice, and some independent genres to create a running narrative that is richer and more complex than its Genesis counterparts. In general, the document focuses on the characters in the story, their human emotions and reactions to their circumstances.

The story of Noah's birth closely parallels the account in 1 Enoch 106–107 and emphasizes Lamech's suspicion that his wife has conceived a son by one of the fallen watchers. The story's genre is known from accounts of the conception of such biblical heroes as Samson and Samuel, and some of its details recall the story of Melchizedek's conception and birth in 2 Enoch 71 and Jesus' conception in Matthew 1:18–25.

The story about Abram's sojourn in Egypt is interpolated with a dream predicting the events to come, a lengthy description of Sarah's beauty cast in a traditional genre, and Abram's prayer for Sarah's release. Thus, picking up characteristics associated with Joseph and Daniel in the Bible, the author depicts Abram as a seer and interpreter of dreams, a sage, an effective intercessor with God, and a healer, who is set in opposition to the magicians and physicians of Egypt.

The Genesis Apocryphon is one of a range of texts often described as "rewritten Bible," but it differs from its counterparts in the Book of Jubilees and the Testaments of the Twelve Patriarchs in its lack of emphasis on the Torah and moral instruction and its interest in the humanity of its characters. A few elements of its chronology appear to be dependent on Jubilees; its focus on individuals is somewhat paralleled in the Book of Biblical Antiquities as well as in Josephus's *Antiquities of the Jews*.

Genesis Rabbah systematic verse-by-verse reading of the Book of Genesis, compiled about 400 C.E., against the background of the historic change represented by the conversion of the Roman

Empire to Christianity. Rome now claimed to be Israel, that is, Christian and heir to the testament of the founders. Sages of Genesis Rabbah affirmed that Rome is Esau, or Moab, or Ishmael. That concession—that Rome is a sibling, a close relative of Israel—represents an implicit recognition of Christianity's claim to share the patrimony of Judaism, to be descended from Abraham and Isaac. Sages in Genesis Rabbah represent Rome as Israel's brother, counterpart, and nemesis, and as the one thing standing in the way of Israel's, and the world's, ultimate salvation. It is not a political Rome but a messianic Rome that is at issue: Rome as surrogate for Israel, Rome as obstacle to Israel. By rereading the story of the beginnings, sages discovered the answer and the secret of the end. Rome claimed to be Israel, and, indeed, sages conceded, Rome shared the patrimony of Israel. That claim took the form of the Christians' appropriation of the Torah as "the Old Testament," so sages acknowledged a simple fact in acceding to the notion that, in some way, Rome, too, formed part of Israel. But it was the rejected part—the Ishmael, the Esau, not the Isaac, not the Jacob. Rome, then, marked the conclusion of human history as Israel had known it. Beyond lay the coming of the true Messiah, the redemption of Israel, the salvation of the world, the end of time.

Genesis, Targum to *see* PALESTINIAN TARGUMS TO THE PENTATEUCH

Geni<u>b</u>a Babylonian scholar active in the late third century C.E.; referred to without the title "rabbi." Geni<u>b</u>a is called a man of contention (B. Gittin 31b, 62a), and B. Gittin 7a reports his execution at the hand of Mar Ukba, possibly as a result of Geni<u>b</u>a's teaching that rabbis (not exilarchs) appropriately should rule the Jewish nation.

genius (pl., genii) also known as a *nike* (victory) in the singular; a very minor motif in Jewish art, usually confined to late synagogue art. The few times that we can identify them, genii are represented as winged figures. Apparently, two genii or *nikae* flank either side of a wreath from a synagogue window lintel at Ramah. Two such *nikae* are known from a synagogue lintel at ed-Dikke in the Golan Heights, and apparently two pairs were chiseled off two large, handsome synagogue lintels at Baram. The same fate befell two genii in a beautifully cut lintel from the synagogue at Capernaum. Both at Baram and at Capernaum, these genii flanked a wreath, perhaps with a flower at the center. It is possible that these fell to Jewish iconoclasm; it is at least equally possible, however, that the iconoclasts were Muslims.

geniza the Aramaic loan word for a storeroom in a synagogue. Linguistically, the word *geniza* comes from the Hebrew and Aramaic root meaning "to hide, or store up," and means simply a place of "hiding" or "storing up." The *geniza* developed out of a need for a place to retire old, sacred manuscripts. Since the worshipers at these synagogues did not want to desecrate old manuscripts of the Torah and other sacred writings that contained the holy name of God, the practice arose of permanently consigning these documents to a spare room or space in the synagogue. This same type of meaning for the word *geniza* is found in the Talmud Sabbath text. The rabbis teach that sacred objects that were no longer fit for worship (Sabb. XVI.1) most be removed. It seems, from the storerooms that have been discovered to date, that the practice of storing biblical and other sacred manuscripts that contained the holy name of God was carried over to any document, either printed or handwritten, that contained the name of God.

By far the most famous *geniza* is the Cairo Geniza. This *geniza* from the Old Synagogue at Fustat in Cairo was discovered in the late nineteenth century and contained tens of thousands of documents in Hebrew, Aramaic, Arabic, Samaritan, and Greek. The documents ranged from legal texts concerning the synagogues or its members to biblical documents and rabbinic interpretations. Perhaps the most famous document from the Cairo Geniza is an example of the Damascus Rule, a text in many ways similar to the document among the Dead Sea Scrolls found at Qumran known as the Damascus Document. There are, however, some salient differences in references to the Damascus Document's founder and its ideology. In any case, its rules referring to the "Sons of the Zadok" are important for understanding early Jewish movements contemporary or even earlier than Qumran. *See also* CAIRO GENIZA.

genre a particular type of literature. The term, from the French, is widely used in scholarly writings; the German equivalent is *Gattung*. A genre might comprise only examples of a very short literary form, such as songs, proverbs, or letters, or it might embrace a very large work, even containing subgenres, such as history or tragedy.

Gentiles (nations; Heb.: *goyim*; Gr.: *ethnē*) generic Israelite expression for all of humanity except Israel. Most often this common biblical expression has a pejorative connotation that parallels the Greek use of "barbarians." By virtue of its covenantal relationship to YHWH and its observance of the Torah, Israel is contrasted with the rest of humanity, which stands outside the scope of God's covenantal love. A number of biblical voices sing a different tune, however. In the earliest stratum of the Pentateuch, Abraham's election from the Gentile people of Chaldea has implications for a blessing on "all the families of the earth" (Gen. 12:3). Second Isaiah sees "the servant of YHWH" as a "light to the nations" (Isa. 49:6). The Book of Jonah sharply criticizes the prophet who refuses to seek Nineveh's repentance. The touchy matter of intermarriage between Jews and Gentiles receives very different treatments in Ezra-Nehemiah and Ruth.

Jewish literature of the Graeco-Roman period attests a whole spectrum of beliefs between these extremes. The Letter of Aristeas and the Jewish Sibylline Oracles assert that Gentiles can obtain God's favor if they avoid the major sins of idolatry, murder, and sexual promiscuity. Stories about Abraham's conversion from idolatry may have encouraged the kind of conversation depicted in Aristeas to Philocrates (Jub. 11:14–12:24; Apoc. Abr. 1–8). The tales in Daniel 1–6 describe Gentile kings acclaiming the unique sovereignty of Israel's God. 1 Enoch envisions divine blessing for "all of the children of the whole earth," providing they adhere to the Torah as expounded in Enochic circles (10:21, 90:38, 91:14, 100:6, 105:1). Its stories about Abraham notwithstanding, the Book of Jubilees sees the covenant and Torah as the distinguishing mark of Israel and warns its readers to avoid the Gentiles. Some works written in response to the persecution by Antiochus IV are especially bitter in their anti-Gentile invectives and explicit in their expectation that God will destroy them in the coming judgment (e.g., Dan. 7–12; Testament of Moses). 1 and 2 Maccabees distinguish between Gentile persecutors and others who are friendly to Israel. The two major apocalypses written after the trauma of 70 C.E. (4 Ezra and 2 Baruch) are wholly antagonistic to the Gentiles.

Although Jesus of Nazareth seems to have confined his ministry to Jews, early Christians, experiencing Jewish resistance to their proclamation that Jesus was the Messiah, rapidly developed a mission among Gentiles. Conceiving themselves as the eschatological community of the elect, they proclaimed their gospel to the Gentiles, to different degrees abandoning the Torah as the source and criterion for righteous contact. The position developed by Paul (Romans and Galatians) is analogous to the viewpoint in the Sibylline Oracles and Aristeas, but he differs in that he claims that Gentiles who follow his gospel are true children of Abraham. In Romans 9–11, he expresses the expectation that Israel would eventually come to faith in Christ. In the succeeding decades, Mark, Matthew, Luke, and John were becoming increasingly pessimistic about this prospect. By the mid-second century a mainly Gentile church was claiming, ironically, that its christological faith defined it as the true Israel, over the Jews for whom Torah observance was the criterion to covenantal fidelity.

The rabbinic sources do not exhibit an interest in Gentiles as Gentiles. They deal with them only in relation to those matters that are important to Jews: the holiness of the Land of Israel, the observance of the Jewish holidays, especially the Sabbath and Passover, the Temple and the sacrificial cult, the purity laws, and the social and legal institutions that function within Israelite society. In each of these areas of concern, the Jewish sources sharply distinguish between the activities of Jews and those of Gentiles. Even when Jews and Gentiles do similar things, such as offering sacrifices at the altar in Jerusalem, they are required to do them in different ways. While the Jewish documents state that Jews and Gentiles lived in the same neighborhoods and courtyards, jointly owned fields of produce, traded with one another in the market, and even ate at one another's homes, the same documents go to great pains to demonstrate that in those areas that define Judaism, Jews and Gentiles do not interact in normal ways. This results from the fact that 613 obligations are placed upon Jews, while only seven commandments are assigned to the Gentiles.

Although some Jewish documents argue that YHWH treats the Jews in a special manner, others stress that Gentiles should be allowed to live as Gentiles, especially outside of Israel. The Jewish texts speak of Gentiles who study Torah, those who honor their parents, and those who observe many of the other commandments. While those who observe the laws because they are commanded (Jews) receive a greater reward than those who merely observe them (Gentiles), those who observe the laws are more honored than those who do not do YHWH's will. While Gentiles are often pictured as sexually uninhibited and untrustworthy, they are also described as righteous and the progenitors of rabbis and even kings of Israel. The biblical Job is often identified as a righteous Gentile. Rabbi Joshua maintained that righteous Gentiles would receive a share in the world to come. Others claimed that a Gentile who studied Torah was like the Jewish high priest.

ger (pl., *gerim*) convert. The Bible does not have a concept of conversion. The idea arose around the first century C.E. Apparently, Jews did not engage in missionary activities among Gentiles (Matt. 23:15 is probably an exaggeration). Several sources state that Gentiles outside of the Land of Israel should be allowed to worship their own deities. Some rabbis were vehemently opposed to accepting converts, claiming that they were the source of the troubles that often plagued the Jews. Many other sages, however, favored accepting converts into the community, describing Abraham as the first Jew to seek converts and teaching that all Jews should follow his lead by attempting to win over Gentiles to the worship of YHWH. Several sages believed that Gentiles would be attracted to Judaism by the spirituality of the Jews worshiping at the Temple or their honesty in their business transactions. For the most part, converts were equated with native-born Israelites. However, some theoretical distinctions were maintained. Apparently converts could not marry into a priestly family, especially into the high priest's clan. Also, several sages believed that converts could not own a parcel of the Land of Israel, and some held that they could not address YHWH as "the God of our ancestors" in public worship. *See also* CONVERSION; PROSELYTIZATION.

Gerasa ancient city in Transjordan, north of the Jabbok River. The Hellenistic city was founded by Antiochus IV Epiphanes. Later, Gerasa was captured by Alexander Yannai and remained a Hasmonean possession until the time of Pompeii. Under Roman rule it was a center of the caravan trade, which reached the peak of its development under the emperor Hadrian in the early second century C.E.

Gerasa Synagogue synagogue with an elaborate mosaic pavement, located today in the Hashemite Kingdom of Jordan, in the city of Jerash. The synagogue is located on the west side of the ancient city on high ground. The synagogue is part of a complex composed of a colonnaded atrium, a narthex, and a prayer hall. The atrium is a square, open courtyard with columns. The narthex of the synagogue is entered from the atrium and up a flight of steps through three doorways in the eastern wall of the narthex. The narthex was paved with an elaborate mosaic floor depicting Noah and his family leaving the ark after the flood. Animals, birds, flowers, and plants are depicted in great detail, and the animals march two by two with one of each sex. The arrangement is in three ranks of birds, animals, and creeping things. Directly opposite the main entryway in the floor is a menorah flanked by lulab, etrog, shofar, and incense shovel. A Greek inscription around the menorah reads, ". . . the [holy] place. Amen, Selah, Peace to the synagogue."

The prayer hall is a basilica type with two rows of columns dividing the interior into a nave and two side aisles. The interior space was about 10 meters by 7 meters in extent. Stone benches extended along the walls of the two aisles. There was likely a *bimah,* but it is not clear whether it had an apse. The nave was paved with a mosaic of geometric patterns, though it was mostly destroyed by later building. The north aisle was paved in similar fashion and bears an Aramaic inscription in five lines: "Peace upon all Israel. Amen, Amen, Selah. Phinehas bar Baruch, Jose bar Shmuel, and Judan bar Hezekiah." These were apparently donors.

In 530 C.E. the synagogue was destroyed and a church was built on top its ruins; this was during a period of extensive church building at Gerasa. Thus it appears that the Jewish community went out of favor during the reign of Justinian I. We otherwise know almost nothing of the Jewish community of ancient Gerasa.

Gerim (Heb., Proselytes) a minor tractate published with the Babylonian Talmud. The first chapter describes the initial procedures for accepting proselytes. The second provides regulations for a proselyte's circumcision, immersion in a ritual bath, and offering of a sacrifice. The third chapter contains a dispute between Meir and Judah concerning the status of a resident alien. The fourth and final chapter exhorts Jews to maintain friendly relations with proselytes.

Gerizim, Mount now called Jebel et-Tor, a sacred mountain facing Mount Ebal. A. M. Schneider began excavating Zeno's Theotokos Church in 1928. Hadrian's temple at Tel er Ras, one of Gerizim's three peaks, was discovered as a result of Robert J. Bull's careful evaluation of the evidence (Drew University expeditions, 1964, 1966, and 1968). This in turn led to the discovery of an altar of the Samaritan temple at the same site.

The Samaritans, under the leadership of Sanballat (c. 330 B.C.E.), built their Hellenistic period temple to YHWH on Mount Gerizim at a site now called Tel er Ras. Antiochus Epiphanes in accordance with an alleged Samaritan petition renamed their temple for the Greek god, Zeus Xenios. The Samaritan temple was destroyed by John Hyrcanus in 128 B.C.E. although he did not destroy the city of Shechem until 107 B.C.E.

According to Josephus, during the Jewish Revolt, the Romans surrounded Mount Gerizim in 70 C.E. and killed over eleven thousand Samaritans. In the second century C.E., Hadrian rebuilt the temple to Zeus. During the fifth century C.E., Zeno built a church, subsequently destroyed by the Samaritans, on Mount Gerizim. This church was rebuilt by Justinian, but it was demolished during the Arab invasion.

gerogeret *see* FIG'S BULK

gerousia (Gr., council of elders) In the Second Temple period this council seems to have had the high priest at its head and was probably an advisory body to him. But it was also a body with some authority, at least at certain times. Many equate it with the Sanhedrin and *boulē*.

Geshem an opponent of Nehemiah, who, together with Sanballat of Samaria and Tobiah the Ammonite, opposed the rebuilding of the wall of Jerusalem, tried in vain to trap Nehemiah in order to assassinate him, and spread rumors that he was planning to rebel against the Persian imperial authorities (Neh. 2:19, 6:1–7). The name (also spelled Gashmu) occurs on a silver bowl found at Tell el-Maskhuta in lower Egypt ("Qaynu, son of Gashmu, king of Kedar") and in a Lihyanite inscription, both of which may refer to the biblical Geshem, a Kedarite Arab prince of the fifth century B.C.E., following the Kedarite expansion into the Transjordanian region.

Gessius Florus the last Roman procurator of Judea (64–66 C.E.) before the war with Rome. He was from Clazomenae, a city in western Asia Minor north of Ephesus. He owed his appointment to his wife's friendship with Nero's wife, Poppaea. He is charged by Josephus with unparalleled and open venality, injustice, and inability to keep order in Judea in an increasingly turbulent situation. He robbed individuals and cities and took a share of brigands' spoils.

get *see* DIVORCE

Gezer (Tell Jezer) ancient city located about 8 kilometers south-southeast of Ramleh. This site is the last city located in the Judean range before it runs into the Shephelah. It guarded one of the most important trade crossroads in antiquity. Because of this prominent location, there are archaeological remains at Gezer from the Caltholithic period through the Roman period. The site seems to have been fortified as early as the Middle Bronze Age (c. 1800 B.C.E.).

Since Gezer was such a prominent site in ancient Near Eastern history, there are many references to Gezer in both the Hebrew Bible and the extrabiblical material. The earliest biblical references are found in Joshua 10:33, 12:12, 16:10, and Jude 1:29, which mention Gezer in conjunction with the Israelite conquest of the Canaan. The name Gezer or its Greek equivalent, Gazara, is mentioned in numerous other passages in the Hebrew Bible and in 1 Maccabees 4:15. The city name is also attested in the Egyptian records of Thutmose III from the fifteenth century B.C.E., the Egyptian Amarna letters from the fourteenth century B.C.E., and from Assyrian records. Extrabiblical references continue down through the writings of the Greek historian Josephus in the first century C.E. The identification of Tell el-Jazar with ancient Gezer was made certain by the discovery of numerous boundary markers from the Herodian period which mention the name Gezer in both Hebrew and Greek.

Recent archaeological excavations found twenty-six strata at Gezer. Most of these levels are earlier than the Persian period. There are four strata from the Persian period through the early Arab period. Stratum IV contains small finds from the Persian period, but, there is not sufficient evidence from the city itself to reconstruct much of its history during this period. Strata III and II are Hellenistic and show remains from both the third and second centuries B.C.E. There is evidence that the city gates and walls were rebuilt during this time period. Gezer seems to have served as a fortress guarding this important travel route for the Judean kingdom down through the Hasmonean period. With the destruction of Stratum II during the end of the second century B.C.E., Gezer was never rebuilt to anywhere near its former strength or size.

Stratum I contains remains from the late first century B.C.E. through the first century C.E. This corresponds roughly to the Herodian period. During this era, Gezer was not rebuilt as a fortified city, but rather seems to have functioned only as a large private estate. The name of the owner or administrator (Alkios) is known from several Greek inscriptions, but it is uncertain if this man was a Jewish leader or not. This stratum seems to have died out around the end of the first century C.E. Evidence is found from some tombs, nonetheless, indicating that the site had some sparse occupation through the Byzantine period, but the city does not seem to have been rebuilt.

gezerah decree; often a precautionary decree, beyond the strict requirements of the law; may also mean an analogy or parallel

ghost the "spirit" of a dead person, thought to survive death as a discrete, and potentially active or sentient, being. Belief in ghosts was widespread in the ancient world, as was the idea that ghosts knew the future and could thus be used for necromancy. Common in the Hebrew Bible is the idea that ghosts, or the "shades" of the dead, reside in Sheol, a dark and shadowy underworld realm, where they exert little or no influence on the living. Also frequent in the Bible and in Jewish tradition in general is a polemic against necromancy.

While belief in ghosts was commonplace in the Graeco-Roman Mediterranean world, ghosts as such never became a substantive part of Jewish tradition and did not play a major role in early Jewish thought or literature. The New Testament Gospels do, however, contain several references of interest. When Jesus walks across the water of the Sea of Galilee, his disciples mistake him for a ghost (Mark 6:48–50; Matt. 14:25–26). In the Gospels of Luke and John, the resurrected Jesus demonstrates to his disciples that he is not a ghost by having them handle his body and by his eating a piece of fish (Luke 24:36–43), displaying the bodily marks of his resurrection (John 20:19–20), and preparing a meal for the disciples (John 21:9–14).

giant person whose great stature is usually associated with military prowess (Deut. 3:1–11, Og; 1 Sam. 9:2, Saul; 1 Sam. 17:4–11, Goliath; 1 Macc. 3:3, Judas Maccabee). Genesis 6:4 suggests a similar notion. According to 1 Enoch 6–7, which is closely related to this passage, the mating of the sons of God (also called watchers) and the daughters of men produced three classes of giants, whose great stature is doubtless related to the heavenly origin of their fathers, but whose bellicose deeds threaten the earth and its inhabitants. The story may be a polemic against the claims of Alexander's successors (the Diadochi) that they are children of the gods. The description of their bloody deeds fits well with the Jewish experience of the wars of the Diadochi, who repeatedly led armies through Palestine during the last decade of the fourth century B.C.E. The stories are also reminiscent of Greek myths about the primordial wars of the giants (Gigantomachia). The Qumran scrolls included multiple copies of an Enochic text known as the Book of the Giants, which described the exploits and fate of the children of the watchers. It later became popular among the Manichaeans. *See also* WATCHERS.

Gibeonites people of a Hivite city who, alarmed by the Israelite advance, formed an alliance with Joshua (Josh. 9:3–27). Because of the false pretense under which they achieved the agreement, Gibeonites were made "hewers of wood and drawers of water for all the congregation [of israel]" (Josh. 9:21). Rabbinic authorities deemed the *netinim* to be descended from the Gibeonites and granted them a reduced status within the Israelite nation, together with impaired priests, converts, freed slaves, *mamzerim,* and others (M. Kiddushin 4:1). *See also* NATIN.

Giddel Babylonian amora of the late third century C.E.; one of the best known of the younger disciples of Rab̲. Most of his statements are in the name of his teacher.

gift in contemplation of death bequest made by an individual on his or her deathbed. In the talmudic literature, this "gift of one lying sick" (*mattenat shekib mera*) serves as a substitute for a last will and testament. Under rabbinic law, a dying person's gift of all of his or her property is valid only if death in fact ensues, in which case the individual's words effect the transfer of real property, chattels, and commercial paper. The dying person's words thus take the place of the deed through which real property normally is transferred, the act of pulling (*meshikhah*) used in the transfer of chattels, or the meeting of the creditor, debtor, and proposed assignee needed for the transfer of demands. If in designating the gift, the individual retained sufficient property to support himself or herself upon recovery, the act is treated as an outright gift, unrelated to the person's illness. This gift is valid and irrevocable even if the person should live (M. Bab̲a Batra 9:6).

Gig. *see* DE GIGANTIBUS

gird one's loins to steel or ready oneself; literally, to tighten a girdle that was worn folded up and around the waist (loins). Since this girdle was evidently worn loosely at leisure, one tightens it, or "girds up the loins," before going out. Hence the expression came to mean "to get ready" or "to prepare oneself" (cf. 1 Kings 18:46; Jer. 1:17). The usual English phrase, "to gird one's loins," actually represents several different Hebrew expressions in the Bible. In later Hebrew literature, such as the Qumran scrolls, a different phrase, "to strengthen one's loins," occurs, an idea related to the biblical idea of "girding loins" (cf. 1 QS[a] 1:17, Hodayot 2:5). In other Second Temple period Jewish literature, "to gird one's loins" occurs in the Greek translation of the Jewish Bible, the so-called Septuagint, but rarely elsewhere in its figurative sense. In several cases, the phrase literally describes the girding of someone's waist (cf. Jos. Asen. 10:14, 14:12, 14).

Giscala *see* GUSH ḤALAB̲

Gittin Mishnah tractate on writs of divorce. The tractate describes how the writs are prepared and delivered (chaps. 1–3); the law of agency in receiving and handing the writs over (chaps. 6–7); stipulations and conditions in the writs (chap. 7); and invalidity by reason of improper delivery, improper preparation, improper stipulations, or invalid witnesses (chaps. 8–9).

Glabrio, Manius Acilius consul in 91 C.E. Dio mentions that Domitian executed his cousin, Flavius Clemens, and Acilius Glabrio for atheism, a charge leveled against those who were "drifting into Jewish ways," and exiled Clemens's wife, Domitilla. Glabrio was also charged with fighting as a gladiator. Suetonius mentions the executions of Clemens and Glabrio without any reference to either atheism or Jewishness. He claims that Glabrio was executed along with two others as a suspected revolutionary. Many scholars in the past have claimed that Domitilla, Glabrio, and Clemens were possibly victims of Domitian's persecution of the Christians. However, Domitilla is identified as a Christian martyr only in the fourth century, and Clemens is mentioned first in the eighth century. The evidence from the catacombs indicating that Glabrio and Domitilla were Christians should probably be discounted because it comes from the second and third centuries. Most likely Dio's mention of "Jewish ways" refers to Judaism and not to Christianity.

glass, gold an artisan-made decorative element in which a piece of gold leaf design or art was sealed on both sides by blown glass. Gold glass was often placed with a corpse in the graves of Jews and Christians during the early part of the common era. Though the exact function of gold glass is not certain, its use in burials and inscriptions found on the various examples indicates that it was associated with some sort of liturgical drinking that brought a blessing or life to the deceased.

The technique for making gold glass originated in Egypt. A decorated piece of gold leaf was first placed on a flat, hot-blown glass surface, sometimes with colors added to highlight the design in the gold leaf. Next, more hot-blown glass was added on top of the gold leaf, so that the gold leaf was sealed and protected by the glass, but the design was still visible.

Some of the examples could be either Christian or Jewish, because the symbols found on them are known to be used by both groups. Such examples include representations of Moses striking a rock, Adam and Eve, Abraham sacrificing Isaac, Jonah, and the spies carrying a hoard for grapes. Another group contains motifs that can only be Jewish. This group consistently exhibits an upper and a lower register, with the Torah shrine displayed prominently in the center of the upper register. Various other symbols were used on differing pieces of gold glass belonging to this type. One contains two lions guarding each side of the Torah shrine. Another also contains lions in the upper register with a menorah in the lower register. Other symbols include lulabs, lamps, shofars, etrogs, doves, and a tree of life. In every case, though, it is the Torah shrine in the center of the upper register that is emphasized—thus indicating the importance of the Torah.

The fact that many of the examples of gold glass are found in burials leads to the conclusion that these items carried an eschatological significance. Inscriptions found on various specimens indicate that they were used for a liturgical blessing that involved drinking. One intriguing example contains an inscription that reads, "O sweet spirit, Auxanon: drink and you will live," indicating some sort of libation bringing life. Other examples with inscriptions describe this drinking as a blessing. One reads, "House of Peace [the grave itself]: Take the blessing with all who are yours." Another simply reads, "A blessing to all."

These inscriptions and others are intriguing but somewhat mystifying, because they are too short to allow for a definitive interpretation. Further clarity is suggested by an inscription that reads, "Take the Eulogia with all who are yours." From a drinking pitcher with the label "eulogia" now in the Jewish Museum of New York, it seems that this is a reference to some sort of pitcher used in worship and in blessing the dead. If this interpretation is correct, gold glass would have been used in a liturgical blessing of the dead that involved drinking or libations.

glassmaking the art of manufacturing glass in antiquity. Ancient glass was made by mixing soda and lime and bringing them to a high temperature in a wood-fired furnace until they melted. The glassmakers added both colorants and agents to make the glass easier to work. By the Persian period, glassmaking was an established industry in the ancient Near East, as core-formed vessels were manufactured in Egypt as early as 1500 B.C.E. These vessels were made by winding molten glass around an organic core, which was later removed to make the vessel hollow. Vessels continued to be made in this manner up through the first century B.C.E. Very early in the history of glassmaking, in addition to making vessels using molten glass, glass was made into beads, jewelry, and bowls using the cold-working processes. Cold-working is the method of changing the shape and appearance of glass that has cooled down. Cold-working includes cutting, working the glass on a lathe, and some types of polishing. The lathe was used to make bowls from a solid piece of cold glass. These lathe-cut bowls, and ones similar to them, appear in the Mediterranean area from the fifth century B.C.E. to the mid-first century C.E. The earliest known glass-blowing factory was excavated in the Old City of Jerusalem and dates to the middle of the first century C.E.

There is no conclusive evidence as to the structure of ancient glass furnaces. Some appear to have been built upon stone that could withstand large amounts of heat. Some used fired ceramic bricks built into an arch over the furnace area to retain the heat created by a central, wood fire. Glassworkers likely received their glass ready-made from a glassmaker who sent it to them in large pieces. If they were engaged in cold-working, they would have broken the glass into the appropriate sizes and shaped it using the aforementioned techniques. Glassblowers placed the pieces of glass in a crucible, which is a deep bowl of limestone or perhaps clay, and placed crucible and raw glass in the furnace, where it would melt into a workable liquid. The glass was removed from the crucible by winding it around one end of a metal or possibly ceramic pipe, and then the glass was inflated by the worker blowing into the other end of the pipe. The glass could be shaped using a number of tools made of metal or wood. Soon glassblowers learned to blow glass into molds to make four-sided and six-sided vessels. Because the glassblowers usually had to rely on an outside source for their glass supply, they recycled broken pieces by simply remelting them in their crucibles. Glass continues to be blown in much the same manner today.

glass vessels containers and objects manufactured of glass in antiquity, such as bowls, bottles, cups, lamps, jewelry, and other forms. The first glass containers were made about 1500 B.C.E. and became commonplace during the sixth and fifth centuries B.C.E. Long cylindrical, round, or small two-handled flasks were common forms continuing into the Roman period. The casting industry of the Persians continued to influence the tableware of the next century. In the latter half of the third century B.C.E., a purely Hellenistic style of cast glassware emerged, the most popular being large- to medium-sized plates with outsplayed (outturned) rims and sides, broad dishes with upright sides and rounded bottoms, large hemispherical and footed bowls, jars, and two-handled cups. By the late 30s B.C.E., the Syro-Phoenician coast was identified as an important glassmaking center. These craftsmen produced cast monochrome and naturally colored ribbed and pillar-molded bowls. Aside from the lack of ribs, most linear-cut bowls are identical, representing two of the earliest Mediterranean styles of early imperial cast tableware. These were replaced by large intentionally or naturally colored monochrome bowls, which gave way to a succession of natural, bluish-green ribbed bowls. This was the last type of Roman cast glassware.

During the third to second century B.C.E., with the popularity of monochrome open shapes, glass became an everyday item resulting in a continuously developing style. In each period new forms, decorative motifs, handle types, and color combinations replaced those of the previous period. In addition, the Mesopotamian millifiori glass (a style of glass that resembles thousands of flowers fused together) was revived again by the Greeks, in the third century B.C.E., in the form of bowls and cups that endured into Roman times.

By the first century B.C.E. in Phoenicia or Palestine, the need to mass-produce led to the development of inexpensive glass. Mold-blown glass was both opaque and translucent. Deep blues, emerald greens, browns, and opaque whites were popular. Decoration was added by applying threads of different colors. By the middle of the first century B.C.E., drinking glasses were a natural green or were intentionally colorless. Quality glass was colorless.

During the first four centuries C.E., throughout the Roman Empire, the standardized needs of daily life for eating and drinking dictated shapes. Bottles, bowls, dishes, jars, jugs, and cups looked much the same everywhere. Glass had other specific uses as well, such as window glass, lamps, bracelets, faux gemstones, amulets, religious articles, gaming pieces, and small sculptures. Romans valued glass containers as shipping and storage vessels, as they were transparent, reusable, odorless, and imparted no taste. Utilitarian glass was commonplace, but beautiful luxury pieces were being produced as well. Decorations were varied in method and motif to enhance the beauty of the product.

When the western provinces of the Roman Empire fell in the fifth century C.E., all but the simplest forms seemed to be forgotten, but mold-blown wares continued in production in Syria, Palestine, and Egypt. Nevertheless, the golden age of Roman glassmaking died throughout the Mediterranean.

West of Palestine in the Sassanid Empire, Persian craftsmen applied thread decoration on cut glass from the mid-third to the mid-seventh century C.E.

Some of the Sassanid forms found their way into Byzantine Palestine in the sixth and seventh centuries C.E. Other local forms, both free-blown and mold-blown, continued in production.

glorify, magnify, sanctify God To glorify God is to declare that God is glorious; to magnify God is to declare that God is great; to sanctify God is to declare that God is holy. Verbs such as these are grouped together by linguists into a special category called delocutive verbs. When human beings are the subject and God is the object, the verb is not denominative as are most verbs in a language; that is, the intent is not that humans "make God glorious or great or holy." Rather, the verb indicates an act of speech, a declaration that God is such or such. A number of other verbs are used in a similar way in a liturgical context, including "to exalt," that is, to declare that God is high" (e.g., Ps. 113:4), and "to praise," that is, to declare praise, perhaps with music or instrument.

Often in hymns there are a series of imperative verbs summoning the addressee to glorify, magnify, and sanctify God (e.g., Ps. 29:1–2, Ps. 34:3, Ps. 96:1–3; Ecclus. 43:30; Song of the Three Children). Similarly, the worshiper can fulfill the injunction by a declarative statement, for example, "O Lord, you are great and glorious" (Jdt. 16:13) and "glorious is your name forever" (Prayer of Azariah 1:3). In the Thanksgiving Hymns (Hodayot) from Qumran, the community is commanded "to proclaim and say: Great is God who does [wonders]" (4QH[a] 7 ii. 4).

God is sanctified especially by the pronouncement, "Holy, holy, holy," modeled upon the triple acclamation of the angelic beings in Isaiah 6:3. The Hymn to the Creator, found in 11QPs[a] xxvi, begins, "Great and holy is the Lord, the holiest of the holy ones for every generation." Later the sanctification of God is embodied explicitly in the Kedushah of the daily synagogue liturgy.

glory (Heb.: *kabod*) Judaism asserts that God in himself is without form or image (e.g., Isaiah 40:18) and therefore beyond the range of the human senses, and yet he has created the world and reveals himself in it. One important term for the manifestation both in the physical world and in history of God's invisible nature is "the glory of the Lord" (*kebod haShem*). This concept is already well developed in the Bible (Ps. 19:1: "the heavens declare the glory of God, and the expanse shows his handiwork"). God's glory is seen here as a power diffused through creation, but in other texts it takes on a more concrete, localized character and is associated with particular moments of divine revelation. In these theophanies it is often depicted in terms of light or fire, and it is sometimes associated with a cloud that signalizes the presence of God. Thus when Israel received the Torah, "the glory of the Lord abode upon Mount Sinai, and the cloud covered it . . . and the appearance of the glory of the Lord was like devouring fire" (Exod. 24:16–18). Individuals could also have specific experiences of God's glory: Ezekiel was called to the prophetic office with an overwhelming vision of the glory of God (Ezek. 1:1–28).

In the literature of the Graeco-Roman period, the glory was especially associated with God's heavenly throne. Thus, in the vision in 1 Enoch 14, the seer describes God as "the great Glory," who is seated on the throne (v. 20), and in the parables of Enoch (1 Enoch 37–71), the son of man, the chosen one, is seen seated on the throne of (his) glory (61:8, 62:2–3, 69:27–29).

In later Jewish literature the doctrine of God's glory was closely bound with the doctrine of the Shekhinah, God's presence in the world, and in some contexts the two terms became interchangeable. The tendency towards hypostatization was accentuated by the Merkabah mystics. When the adepts ascended to heaven and stood before God's throne, called the throne of glory, what they saw on the throne was not God himself but the divine glory. In certain circles (following Ezek. 1:26), the glory was given human shape and the dimensions of its limbs became the subject of speculation in the esoteric tradition known as Shi ur Komah, "the measurements of the body [of god]." The transformation of the glory of God into an entity or being, mediating between the transcendent God and the world, was completed by the philosopher Saadia (882–942), who defined it as "a special light which God creates and makes manifest to his prophets that they may infer therefrom that it is a prophetic communication emanating from God that they hear" (Book of Beliefs and Opinions I, 13). Maimonides (1135–1240) distinguishes between God's glory in the sense of "the created light that God causes to descend in a particular place in order to confer honor upon it in a miraculous way," and God's glory in the sense of his "essence and true reality," which is beyond human perception. The latter sense he sees reflected in Exodus 33:18–20, where Moses asks to see God's glory and is told that no one can see God and live (Guide of the Perplexed I, 64). Similar ideas were taken up by the Haside Ashkenaz and married with the speculations of the Merkabah mystics. In some texts the manifestation on the heavenly throne was depicted as an angelic being called "the special cherub" or "the holy cherub," which represented the hidden glory of God. Through two hymns, the Song of Glory (Shir haKaḇod) and the Song of Unity (Shir haYihud), both composed in the circles of the Haside Ashkenaz, elements of this teaching entered the synagogue liturgy and were popularized.

The term "glory" occurs frequently in the liturgy in another context, that of giving glory to God (already in the Bible, e.g., Ps. 29:1–2). Here "glory" is used in the sense of respect, honor, or reverence. The difference between these two senses of the term is clearly recognized by the classical authorities, though there is some attempt to link them (note, e.g., Maimonides: "Glory is sometimes intended to signify the honoring of God. . . . The true way of honoring him consists in apprehending his greatness" [Guide of the Perplexed I, 64]).

glossolalia speaking in tongues, from the Greek *glossa* (tongue) and *lalia* (speech); a form of ecstatic speech mentioned in three books of the New Testament (Mark 16:17, Acts 2:3–11, 1 Cor. 12–14) and practiced in certain Christian groups today. Paul describes glossolalia as one of the gifts of the spirit (1 Cor. 12:4–11). As practiced in the Corinthian church, glossolalia consisted of babblings intelligible to the speaker but not to the hearers (14:2, 6–11). Although Paul claims for himself preeminence in this gift (14:18), the main force of his discussion of glossolalia is to deemphasize its importance: prophecy, namely inspired speech uttered in intelligible Greek, is preferable because it benefits not only the speaker but also the rest of the community (14:1, 19, 22). Paul exhorts the Corinthians to limit this spontaneous and potentially chaotic practice, advising those who speak in tongues to speak one at a time and only two or three at each service (14:27). Accounts of the early Christian mission in Acts present glossolalia as a sign of conversion associated with the gift of the Holy Spirit (2:1–13, 10:44–46, 19:6). The story of the first Christian Pentecost in Acts 2:1–13 differs from Paul's presentation of glossolalia in that the "tongues" are not unintelligible babblings but foreign languages: Jews from throughout the world who were assembled for the feast were able to hear the words of the Spirit in their own languages (2:5–12).

While inspired speech is common in antiquity (e.g., the prophets of the Tanakh or Old Testament and Greek oracles such as the one at Delphi), there is no known parallel for unintelligible babblings and only one known example, outside the New Testament, of inspired speech given in a foreign language: when Mys the Carian consulted the oracle of Ptoan Apollo, the prophetic priest uttered an oracle that no one but Mys could understand, as it was in Carian (Herodotus 8.135; Plutarch, *Mor.* 412a). *See also* ANGELS, TONGUES OF.

gnosis (Gr., knowledge) Although it could mean knowledge in general, in the Graeco-Roman world *gnosis* was often used to refer to esoteric knowledge. In some religions and cults, possession of secret knowledge was essential for salvation, as in Gnosticism.

Gnosticism (from Gr., knowledge) a diverse group of religious movements that developed within the Roman Empire during the second through fifth centuries. In one way or another Gnostic movements affirmed the superiority of the spiritual, heavenly world over the visible material world, which was regarded as evil. The human spiritual soul, trapped in a material body, must gain revealed knowledge (hence the name Gnosticism) in order to escape the material world and return to its home in the heavenly world. According to Gnostic mythology, the heavenly world originated from a divine unity that produced various heavenly powers, often called aeons. The heavenly world called the All (Gr.: Pleroma) is associated with spirit, light, intellect, and goodness. The material world, associated with matter, darkness, passions, and evil, is produced because of a flaw or fall of a heavenly being, most often identified as Wisdom (Gr.: Sophia). Her desire and passion produces an offspring who is cast out of the heavenly world and creates its own material, human world. The Gnostic drama consists in the struggle of Wisdom, who also has fallen from the heavenly world, and of enlightened humans to escape the evil world of the evil creator god (Gr.: *demiurge*) and return to the heavenly world.

Many Gnostic groups and teachings have clear links to Christianity, some to Graeco-Roman religion and philosophy, and some to Judaism. In a large number of cases the Gnostic stories have been based upon exegesis and parody of the biblical narratives, so much so that some theories locate the origins of Gnosticism among Jewish circles that had moved from apocalypticism or mysticism toward a more radical type of speculation about the divine and the universe. There is no explicit historical evidence, however, for the existence of such groups. The Gnostic texts depict a conflict between the true God and the evil creator god. A heavenly Adam/Eve figure is vivified by the divine light, a force that had fallen with the creator god. The fall of Eve and the flood story in Genesis 3–9 are understood as attempts by the creator god to prevent Adam/Eve from recognizing his or her heavenly nature and origin. Some Gnostics identified themselves with Seth and his sister Norea who embodied for them the spiritual seed of Adam. Through revelations from the heavenly Seth, the Sethians hope to return to the spiritual heavens. Other traditions are built around Enoch, heavenly and fallen angels, David, Wisdom, and others. Some Gnostic works, found in manuscript at Nag Hammadi in Egypt in the late 1940s, contain material closely related to Judaism. Others combine such material with Christian figures, such as Jesus who is identified as the heavenly revealer of Wisdom. Still others use biblical imagery in a thoroughly Graeco-Roman thought context. The most famous Christian Gnostic group was founded by Valentinus, an Alexandrian who moved to Rome in 140 and taught there for twenty years after being expelled from the Christian community.

The writings of many second- and third-century Christian teachers testify to the grave threat Gnostic movements presented to Christians. Rabbinic literature is more reticent concerning its opponents, but a number of passages may be polemics against Gnostic tendencies. By the fifth century imperial and ecclesiatical opposition and cultural change led to the demise of most Gnostic groups.

God a general designation for the deity presented as the central figure in the Hebrew Bible, who created and sustains the world, who guides the course of history, and who maintains a special relationship with the people of Israel. Earliest Christianity, which began as a Jewish sect, held that this same deity had revealed himself in a special way through Jesus of Nazareth and expanded the special relationship with Israel to include people of all nations and races. The general term for god or gods in Hebrew is *el* or *elim,* but when used for the God of Israel it is often used in the longer plural form *elohim,* a designation that occurs more than 2,600 times in the Hebrew Bible. The personal name for the God of Israel was YHWH (of uncertain etymology), often vocalized today as "Yahweh," and referred to as the Tetragrammaton because it consists of four consonants. This name was held with such sanctity that the name Adonai (Lord) was orally substituted when the Torah was read in synagogue services. Since the name YHWH was so rarely pronounced, its original vocalization was forgotten. In Christian versions of the Septuagint (the Greek translation of the Hebrew Bible), the name YHWH was translated Kyrios (Lord), a title that was also applied to Jesus in the New Testament (Rom. 10:9; Phil. 2:11). Elohim and YHWH are usually considered synonymous in the Hebrew Bible, and sometimes occur together as the compound name YHWH Elohim (Gen. 2:4; Exod. 9:30; Josh. 7:7).

God's role as creator is emphasized in the title "the one who made heaven and earth" (Gen. 14:19, 22; 2 Kings 19:15; Pss. 115:15, 146:6), while competitive deities could be dismissed as "gods who did *not* make heaven and earth" (Jer. 10:11). The special relationship between God and Israel was emphasized by referring to the legendary figures of the patriarchs, the traditional ancestors of Israel, in the title "the God of Abraham, Isaac and Jacob" (Exod. 3:6; 4:5; 1 Kings 18:36; 2 Chron. 30:6), or more generally as "the God of our fathers" (Deut. 1:11; Josh. 18:3; Judg. 2:12; Ezra 7:27). God's control of history together with his special relationship to the people of Israel was commemorated by the frequent reference to him as "the one who brought Israel out of the land of Egypt" (Lev. 19:36; Num. 15:41; Deut. 5:6; Josh. 24:17; 2 Kings 17:36; Jer. 2:6; Amos 2:10; Mic. 6:4).

The sovereignty of God was understood through the metaphor of divine kingship. Just as an earthly king is surrounded by courtiers, so God was conceived of as enthroned in his heavenly court attended by a host of angelic beings standing in his presence (1 Kings 22:23; Job 1:6–12, 2:1–6; Isa. 6:2–3). God was also understood as one who tempers justice with compassion (important qualities in earthly monarchs), and as the champion of those for whom society made no provision, for example, strangers, widows, and orphans (Exod. 22:21–22; Deut. 10:18). The relationship between God and Israel was also formalized as a covenant, that is, a legal relationship with the responsibilities of the people of Israel stipulated in terms of the 613 laws found in the Pentateuch, believed to have been revealed to Israel on Mount Sinai. Monotheism, in the strict sense of belief in one unique God, was one strand of thought that emerged only tentatively in postexilic Israel (Isa. 45:14–25). Henotheism, the belief that one deity presided over a particular people and territory, was more common in ancient Israel. It is in this sense that God is occasionally called a "jealous" God (Exod. 34:14), that is, he requires exclusive devotion and is intolerant of competing deities, as underscored by the First Commandment (Exod. 20:3–5; Deut. 5:6–10).

It is often claimed that Jewish writings of the Graeco-Roman period, especially the apocalypses, increasingly depicted God as remote from the world and humanity, enthroned in heaven among myriads of angelic attendants. While such a tendency may be observed in some texts, it is also the case that the gap between heaven and earth is bridged by a special class of heavenly beings who function both as intercessors in the divine throne room and agents who carry out divine missions on earth and bring messages from God to humanity. *See also* EL; GOD, IN HELLENISTIC JUDAISM; GOD, IN RABBINIC JUDAISM; GOD, NAMES OF; I AM.

God, in Hellenistic Judaism Belief in and fidelity to God was the heart of Jewish religion in the Hellenistic period, although the interaction with Greek traditions introduced new accents. God was, first of all, the Creator (Sibylline Oracles 1.5–60; 3.20) and this fundamental affirmation came to be expressed in terms of a doctrine of creation from the invisible or "from nothing" (Joseph and Asenath 12:1–2; Wisdom of Solomon 11:25; 2 Enoch 24:2; 48.5; Philo, *On the Special Laws* 187 and *On Dreams* 76). As creator, God was understood to be responsible for and involved in the world. Hellenized Jews understood this involvement as divine "providence" and took the side of those Greek philosophers, primarily Stoics, who argued for the reality of divine supervision of human affairs. In the words of Philo, whose *On Providence* consists of philosophical theodicy, God is a "king invested with a kindly and law-abiding sovereignty who governs the whole heaven and earth with justice" (in Eusebius, *Preparation for the Gospel* 8.14.2). The historian Josephus can present his *Antiquities of the Jews* as a lengthy illustration of divine providence at work in the world (*Ant.* 1.14). Contrary data, such as the suffering of the righteous, could be explained as divine chastisement (2 Macc. 6:12–17). Prayers addressed God as the caring Father and Savior (Tobit 13:1).

Hellenistic Jews affirmed that the Creator alone was God and, perhaps inspired by the prophets (e.g. *Isa.* 45:20; 46:5–7), they polemicized against idolatry (Wisdom of Solomon 13–15; Sibylline Oracles 3.545–49; 4.6–11; 8.375–98) and Greek mythology (Josephus, *Ant.* 1.15). Scriptural anthropomorphism could be embarrassing, but apologists from Aristobulus in the second century B.C.E. (in Eusebius, *Preparation for the Gospel* 7.10; 13.12) took pains to interpret them allegorically.

A common affirmation of Hellenistic Jews was that God is self-sufficient, in need of nothing (Letter of Aristeas 211; Philo, *On the Change of Names* 27 and *On the Virtues* 9; Josephus, *Ant.* 8.111). This exalted deity worked through various intermediary powers. Popular stories featured angels, such as Raphael (Tobit 12:11–15). In the sapiential tradition, the figure of divine Wisdom, Sophia in Greek, performs that role. Still a personification of a divine attribute in Sirach 24, Wisdom becomes a more serious ontological principle in Wisdom of Solomon 7, influenced by Stoic notions of the pervasive spiritual force that holds all things together.

Philo of Alexandria combines the sapiential tradition with Greek philosophy. God the Creator now bears the title of Demiurge or Craftsman used in Plato's *Timaeus*. God's Wisdom is also called the Logos or Word (*Allegory of the Laws* 1.65). The roots of that concept are complex. Popular traditions play a part and the Logos can be called an archangel (*On the Confusion of Tongues* 146; *Who is the Heir* 205). Yet the title is reinterpreted in philosophical categories, as the Platonic realm of ideas or forms in the mind of God (*On the Creation* 20, 24) and as the divine spirit immanent in the world (*On the Cherubim* 36). Some of Philo's language for the Logos, "a second to God" (*Allegory of the Laws* 2.86) or "son of God" (*On the Immutability of God* 31), could be taken to compromise monotheism, although Philo considered himself a strict monotheist. The category provided a useful conceptual framework for Christians when they began to reflect on their claims for Jesus' special status.

God, in rabbinic Judaism the divine Being, one, sole, and unique; the creator of heaven and earth; the giver of the Torah to Moses. God is known through self-revelation in the Torah, in which he appears in various forms: "with a stern face, in Scripture. When a man teaches his son Torah, he has to teach him in a spirit of awe; with a neutral face, in Mishnah; with a friendly face, in Talmud; with a happy face, in lore. Then said to them the Holy One, blessed be He, 'Even though you may see all of these diverse faces of mine, nonetheless: *I am the Lord your God who brought you out of the land of Egypt*'" (Exod. 20:2). God is represented as "an icon that has faces in all directions, so that if a thousand people look at it, it appears to look at them as well. So too when the Holy One, blessed be He, when He was speaking, each and every Israelite would say, 'With me in particular the Word speaks.'" The reason for God's variety is made explicit. People differ, and God, in whose image all mortals are made, must therefore sustain diverse images—all of them formed in the model of human beings: "And it was in accord with the capacity of each one of them to listen and understand what the Word spoke with him."

God is known in the Judaism of the dual Torah as premise, presence, person, and personality. As premise, God created the world and revealed the Torah to Israel. As presence, God is present in discourse and in making a decision. He constitutes a person in certain settings, but not in others. As a "You," God hears prayer; also, when the Torah is studied among disciples of sages, God is party to the discussion. As a personality, God emerges as a vivid and highly distinctive personality, actor, conversational partner, and hero. God is given corporeal traits. God looks like God in particular, just as each person exhibits distinctive physical traits. When God participates as a hero and protagonist in a narrative, He gains traits of personality and emerges as Godlike humanity: God incarnate. In the unfolding of the canonical writings of the Judaism of the dual Torah, God gained corporeality and personality and thus became incarnate, just as the Hebrew scriptures had long ago portrayed Him, in richly personal terms: God wants, cares, demands, regrets, says, and does—just like human beings. In Judaism in the age of the Bible, God is not merely a collection of abstract theological attributes and thus rules for governance of reality or a mere person to be revered and feared. God is not a mere composite of regularities, but a very specific, highly particular personality, whom people can know, envision, engage, persuade, and impress. Sages painted this portrait of a personality by making up narratives, telling stories in which God figures as do other (incarnate) heroes.

The unfolding of this account of God is to be traced from the Mishnah through the Babylonian Talmud. As Israel strives to form a kingdom of priests and a holy people, its way of life is shaped by its generative anthropology: humanity is like God. The Torah has revealed, and through sages continues to reveal, whatever it is about God that humanity is going to know. Therefore it is the task of humanity to study the Torah in order to strive to imitate God, which means conforming to the ways of God as the Torah defines those ways. Accordingly, through the successive documents of the oral Torah, we trace the history of the Torah's account of what it means to be "in our image, after our likeness." Israel knows God through the Torah, which reports to Israel exactly what God has told and what sages have handed on from the revelation at Sinai. In the first of the documents that make up the oral part of the Torah, the Mishnah, we may accurately speak of what Israel knows about God. But in later compilations, Israel no longer knows only *about* God. God is set forth as more than the principle and premise of being that is apprehended by philosophers and more, even, than the presence that is experienced by pious people through prayer. Rather, Israel knows God as a person and, at the end of the formation of the oral Torah, as a fully embodied personality.

In the first document of the oral Torah (the Mishnah and its related writings), God makes an appearance as principle or premise and also as presence; the God of Judaism is never merely the God that followers must invoke to explain how things got going and work as they do. In the next stage in the unfolding of the oral Torah, represented by the Talmud of the Land of Israel (the Jerusalem Talmud) and related writings, God is portrayed not only as principle and presence, but as a person. In the third and final stage, God emerges as a fully exposed personality, whom we can know and love. Since God is known through the Torah, sages recognize no need to prove the existence of God. The Torah proves the existence of God, and the glories of the natural world demonstrate the workings of God in the world. What humanity must do is explore what it means to be "in our image, after our likeness," that is, to be "like God." That fact explains why through its account of God, rabbinic Judaism sets forth its ethics, the account of the proper way of life. The sages bear the task of setting forth, through the oral Torah that they transmit, the answer to the question of how humanity should form itself to be "in God's image," "after God's likeness," and precisely what that means.

In the oral part of the Torah, as much as in the written part, God, who created the world and gave the Torah to Moses, encounters Israel in a vivid and personal way. But while some of the documents of the oral Torah portray God only as a premise, presence, and person, not as a personality with whom human beings may identify, others represent God as a personality, specifically, like a human being, whom people may know, love, and emulate. The categories of premise, presence, and person hardly require much explanation. As premise, God forms (in philosophical terms) the ground of being. That is how God plays a principal part in the Mishnah. Otherwise uncharacterized, God may form a presence and be present in all things. As a person, again without further amplification, God is a "You," for example, to whom people address prayers. When He is portrayed as a personality, God is represented in an incarnate way, not merely by appeal to anthropomorphic metaphors, but by resort to allusions to God's corporeal form, attitudes and emotions like those of human beings, and capacity to do the sorts of things mortals do in the ways in which they do them, again, corporeally. In all of these ways, the incarnation of God is accomplished by treating God as a personality.

The Babylonian Talmud (Ba<u>b</u>li) represents God in the flesh in the analogy of the human person. Prior to the Ba<u>b</u>li, the faithful encountered God as abstract premise, as unseen presence, as a "You" without richly defined traits of soul, body, spirit, mind, or feeling. The Ba<u>b</u>li's authorship, for the first time in the formation of Judaism, presented God as a fully formed personality, like a human being in corporeal traits, attitudes, emotions, and other virtues, in actions and the means of carrying out actions. God then looked the way human beings look, felt and responded the way they do, and did the actions that they do in the ways in which they do them. And yet in that portrayal of the character of divinity, God always remained God. The insistent comparison of God with humanity, "in our image and likeness," comes to its conclusion in one sentence that draws humanity upward and does not bring God downward. Despite its treatment of the sage as a holy man, the Ba<u>b</u>li's characterization of God never confused God with a sage or a sage with God. Quite to the contrary, the point and purpose of that characterization reaches its climax in a story that demands, in the encounter with the sage of all sages, that God be left to be God.

God, living an expression that explicitly or implicitly contrasts the God of Israel with the nonexistent or impotent deities of the Gentiles. The term appears in propaganda stories, where it may be placed on the lips of Gentiles who confess the power and uniqueness of Israel's God (Dan. 4:34, 6:26). In Bel and the Dragon, a contrast between the dead Bel and the living God is central to the narrative (vv. 5, 24–25). Major anti-idol polemics in Jubilees 12:2–5, the Letter of Jeremiah 24–27, Joseph and Asenath 11:8–10, and the Apocalypse of Abraham 1–8 employ exhortative, argumentative, and narrative forms to contrast the deadness of idols with the true and living God (cf. also Acts 14:15; 1 Thess. 1:9).

God, names of The personal and cultic name of the God of Israel has always been YHWH, although throughout the millennia there have been many other ways of referring to God: titles, circumlocutions, and general names. In ancient Israel, the name YHWH, which scholars refer to as the Tetragrammaton (today vocalized as Yahweh), was the specific name of Israel's God. When the high priest addressed God in the Temple's Holy of Holies on the Day of Atonement, he uttered this name. When the priests blessed the people in the Temple, they used this name. By the third century B.C.E., God's name had become so hallowed that it could not be pronounced outside of worship, and the term *adonai* (my lord) was regularly substituted. In the Middle Ages, scribes developed a reminder for substituting *adonai*: when copying biblical manuscripts, they placed the vowels for *adonai* under the consonants for YHWH, resulting in YeHoVaH. Christian scholars misunderstood this practice and considered it God's name: Jehovah. In ancient Israel, the general word for a god was *el,* which was usually combined with a location, such as *el Bethel,* or an epithet. The most frequently used epithets are *el elyon* (God Most High), *el shaddai* (God Almighty), and *el olam* (Everlasting God). The word *el* provides the linguistic base for one of the most common general names for YHWH—Elohim—which constitutes a plural form of *el.* Next to YHWH, Elohim forms the most frequently used name of God in the Hebrew Bible, even though it has no personal or cultic associations.

The rabbis developed several new titles for YHWH, which they often used in place of the name: *haKadosh Barukh Hu* (the Holy One, Blessed be He), *Ribbono Shel Olam* (Lord of the World), and *haRaḥaman* (the Merciful One). They also developed several circumlocutions to avoid God's name: *haMakom* (the Place), *Shekhinah* (the Presence), and *Memra* (the Word). In a similar vein, orthodox Jewry later developed the terms *elokim* (for *elohim*), *haShem* (the Name), and *adoshem* (for *adonai*).

During the rabbinic period, the idea developed that if a document containing one of God's holy names was discarded, the name would be profaned. To avoid this possibility, the rabbis prohibited the writing of God's name exactly and ruled that any document that might contain God's name should be thrown into a *geniza* (a special storehouse) rather than be discarded as mere trash. *See also* ABBA; EL; GOD; I AM; TETRAGRAMMATON.

God, unknown translation of the Greek term *agnostos theos*. The expression has been found in various Greek inscriptions dedicated to "unknown gods," that is, deities not otherwise identified (cf. Acts 17:23). The Jewish God was also often treated as unnamed and not identified with any known god.

God-fearers a common translation of the Greek expressions *theosebeis* and *phoboumenoi tou theou*. Among Jews in the Graeco-Roman period, "God-fearer" could be used to describe anyone who was pious or feared God. Many scholars believe that this term also had the technical meaning of Gentile sympathizers who followed many Jewish practices without becoming full converts (especially males for whom circumcision would have been a difficult step to take). Some scholars oppose this definition, however, arguing that the term refers only to pious Jews. Although proselytization was not a major activity among Jews, as it was among Christians, Judaism was willing to accept converts from an early period. *See also* PROSELYTIZATION.

Gog and Magog Gog may reflect Gyges, a seventh-century-B.C.E. king of Lydia, and Magog possibly means "land of God." In Ezekiel 38 and 39, Gog symbolizes the enemy of Israel who marches from the north and ravages Israel before being destroyed by God. The War Scroll from Qumran refers to Gog and his assembly, whom God will chastise at the end-time (1QM 11:6). In Revelation 20:8, Magog is no longer a land, but is someone alongside Gog at the final battle after Satan is loosed after one thousand years. Gog and Magog fight with Israel in the days of the Messiah (3 Enoch 45:5). Gog and Magog are situated in the midst of the Ethiopian rivers in Sibylline Oracles 3.319–22, perhaps because Cush is mentioned in Ezekiel 38:5.

golah *see* DIASPORA

Golden Rule a rule of the highest value. The name Golden Rule has been used by Christians during the last three centuries to identify Jesus' summary teaching, reported in Matthew 7:12 and Luke 6:31: "Do unto others as you would have them do to you." The point of this saying is similar to that of the command in Leviticus 19:18, "Love your neighbor as yourself," which is quoted often in the New Testament (Matt. 5:43, 19:19, 23:29; Mark 12:31, 33; Luke 10:27; Rom. 12:9, 13:9; Gal. 5:14; James 2:8). The same point is expressed in another way in a second-century B.C.E. Jewish writing, the Letter of Aristeas, which reports advice given to the king of Egypt about what divine wisdom teaches: "Since you do not wish for evil to overtake you but to share in every blessing, act in that way toward your subjects, even toward those who do wrong" (207). In the same period, Sira 31:15 advises, "Judge your neighbor's feelings by your own, and be thoughtful in every way," and Tobit 4:15 commands, "Do not do to anyone what you hate." Later rabbinic tradition tells of the Jewish teacher Hillel (70 B.C.E.–10 C.E.) being challenged by a prospective convert to Judaism to recite the essence of the law while standing on one foot. Hillel replied, "Do not do to your neighbor what you hate. That is the whole of the Law, everything else is commentary."

To the simpler form of Jesus' saying in Luke 6:31, Matthew adds, "For this is the law and the prophets" (Matt. 7:12). Other early Christian writers repeat this idea in various ways. Clement of Rome (1 Clem. 13:2) and Tertullian (*Against Marcion* 4.17) give the rule in the same positive form as Luke does; in an early Christian book of instruction, the Didache, and in a few ancient manuscripts of the New Testament's Acts of the Apostles (15:20), the negative form of the command is given: "Whatever you don't want done to you, don't do to anyone." The gnostic Gospel of Thomas, written in the second century C.E., reports Jesus as saying, "What you hate, don't do."

Gorpiaios name of a Macedonian month; appears in a number of Jewish sources, such as the writings of Josephus. Unfortunately, there was not a uniform usage; sometimes it corresponded to the Hebrew month of Ab̲ (July/August) and sometimes to the month Elul (August/September).

gospel (Gr.: *euangelion*) The verbal form, "to announce good news," appears particularly in Isaiah 40–55, where the messenger proclaims the good news of return from exile. In the Roman emperor cult in the eastern empire, the good news of Caesar's salvation, peace, and prosperity was proclaimed, known particularly from inscriptions by urban elites. The "Gospel (of God/Christ)" quickly became a technical term for the Christian message about redemption through Christ's death and resurrection, as can be seen in Paul's letters (e.g., Rom. 1:1; 15:16, 19; 1 Cor. 15:1). The term is used in other Christian literature for the "good news (of God/the kingdom)" preached by Jesus and his followers (e.g., Mark 1:14–15; Matt. 4:23; 9:35). Thence developed the literary forms about Jesus and his gospel and the canonical and other Christian Gospels (e.g., Matthew, Mark, Luke, John, and Thomas), although there is ironically little internal indication that "gospel" is an appropriate term for this literature.

governor general term used for rulers of Roman provinces. Provinces were of three types from the reign of Augustus on. Senatorial provinces were governed by Romans of senatorial rank and were divided into two kinds: more important provinces, governed by former consuls, and less important ones, governed by former praetors. These governors were called legates. A small number of lesser provinces were governed by Romans of the lesser equestrian rank, who were called prefects (later procurators). The province of Syria, which guarded the troubled eastern border of the empire, was ruled by a consular legate, who had command of substantial military forces, including legions. Judea was an equestrian province, ruled by a prefect who had at his command auxiliary units and who was to a certain extent under the authority of the Syrian legate.

grace the favor God displays to human beings; an essential part of the biblical idea of God. In the Tanakh or Old Testament, the term "grace" translates two different Hebrew roots (*ḥsd* and *ḥnn*), which characterize God's freely given, benevolent action toward his people Israel. The noun *ḥesed* appears about 250 times. Having no exact equivalent in English, it is also rendered as "steadfast love," "loyalty," and "kindness." The election of Israel and the covenant formed at Mount Sinai are primary examples of God's grace: "Know therefore that the Lord your God is God, the faithful God who keeps his covenant and shows grace (*ḥesed*) to those who love him and keep his commandments" (Deut. 7:9, cf. Exod. 34:6–7). The law is understood as a gift of divine grace, as is the ability to fulfill it (Ps. 119:19). *Ḥesed* can also refer to an action of God in response to a specific need, a use which is particularly common in the Psalms: "I will exalt and rejoice in your steadfast love (*ḥesed*), because you have seen my afflictions, you have taken heed of my adversities" (Ps. 31:7). Many Psalms of lament contain pleas to God to "be gracious to me," that is, to come to the petitioner's aid (Ps. 119:58). Praise of God's *ḥesed* occurs frequently in fixed liturgical formulae: "But you, my Lord, are a God of mercy and compassion (*ḥanun*), slow to anger and abounding in steadfast love (*ḥesed*) and faithfulness" (Ps. 86:15, cf. Exod. 34:6). In the sense of loyalty to the covenant relationship, *ḥesed* can also designate human acts: thus the prophet Micah describes what God requires of Israel as "loving *ḥesed*" (6:8), and Hosea indicts the people for their lack of *ḥesed* (4:1).

In the texts of early Judaism (2d c. B.C.E.–2d c. C.E.) God's grace to Israel, expressed in election and covenant, is generally presupposed but not often the subject of discussion. Much more attention is given to obedience to God's law and to the division of "sinners" from the "righteous" in the judgment of God. But there is in general no antithesis between law and grace, for it is recognized that even the "righteous" are not perfect and will withstand the judgment of God only through his grace or "mercy" (Gr.: *eleos*): "The souls of the righteous are in the hand of God, . . . and the faithful will abide in him in love, because grace (Gr.: *charis*) and mercy (*eleos*) are upon his holy ones" (Wisd. of Sol. 3:1, 9; cf. the use of the term "mercy" in the Psalms of Solomon 2:33–36 and 13:9–12). Only one text, 4 Ezra (2 Esdras) insists that obedience to the law must be perfect, that "the elect" are thus very few, and that the imperfectly righteous cannot rely on the mercy of God (7:120–8:3).

If early Judaism said little on grace, the Dead Sea Scrolls provide an exception to the general pattern, in their strong emphasis on the need for God's *ḥesed*: extreme devotion to God's law is coupled with an acute awareness of human inadequacy. The Rule of the Community, which sets forth the polity of the ascetic group from which the Scrolls come, is addressed to those who wish "to practice the precepts of God in the covenant of grace" (*ḥesed,* 1QS 1:7–8). Noncanonical Psalms contained in the Hymn Scroll make frequent reference to God's graciousness: "Blessed are you, O God of mercy and grace (*ḥaninah*), because of . . . the abundance of your favors (*ḥesed*) in all your works. . . . Cleanse me by your righteousness, even as I have hoped in your kindnesses (*ḥesed*) and have put my hope in your favors" (1QH 11:29–31).

The Greek word for "grace," *charis* (cf. *eleos,* mercy) is of fundamental importance in the New Testament, where it usually designates the gift of salvation given through Jesus Christ. The gospel, or basic Christian message, is characterized as "the word of (God's) grace" (Acts 14:3, 20:32, cf. 1 Pet. 5:12, Rom. 1:5). The Christian idea of grace is set forth most clearly in the letters of Paul, who maintains that Christians are "justified by [god's] grace as a free gift" through the death and resurrection of Christ (Rom. 3:24). For Paul, *charis* has broad application: it designates the gift of salvation (Rom. 5:2–20), the sphere or realm in which Christians live (Rom. 5:21, 1 Cor. 10:30), and a personified power which rules over Christian life (Rom. 6:14–15). Paul views his call and mission as gifts of divine grace: "By the grace of God I am what I am, and his grace to me has not been in vain" (1 Cor. 15:10, cf. Rom. 12:3). Grace works in and through Christian believers, supplying them with "gifts of grace" (Gr.: *charismata*; Rom. 12:6, 1 Cor. 12:4–31) such as prophecy, speaking in tongues, and love. One index of the centrality of *charis* to Paul's understanding of the Christian message is the fact that it appears as an opening and concluding greeting in most of his letters (1 Cor. 1:3; 16:23; 2 Cor. 1:2; 13:13; Rom. 1:7; 16:20, 24; Gal. 1:3; 6:18; 1 Thess. 1:1; 5:28; Phil. 1:2; 4:23 Philem. 3, 25).

In Paul's letters, as in the Dead Sea Scrolls, divine grace is contrasted to human unworthiness; no human being, even the most pious, can merit the grace of God (Rom. 1:18–3:20, 5:1–11). But Paul differs markedly from the Scrolls when he sets grace against law: Christians are not "under the law" but "under grace" (Rom. 6:14). He sternly warns his gentile converts in Galatia not to bow to pressure to take on the obligations of the Torah: "You who want to be justified by the law have cut yourselves off from Christ; you have fallen away from grace" (Gal. 5:4, cf. 2:21). God's grace (salvation) is appropriated by faith, not by "works" of the law (Rom 3:24–4:16).

While "grace" is particularly emphasized in the letters of Paul, the term is by no means limited to him, but occurs in most books of the New Testament (e.g. Acts 11:23, 15:11; Eph. 2:8–9; Heb. 2:9, 4:16, 13:9; 1 Tim. 1:13–16; 1 Pet. 1:10). In the Gospel of John, *charis* appears only three times, all in the prologue: "The Word became flesh . . . full of grace and truth" (1:14). As in Paul, "grace" is here contrasted to law: "the law was given through Moses, but grace and truth through Jesus Christ" (1:18). *See also* DEEDS, WORKS.

grace after meals *see* BIRKAT HAMAZON

grace prior to meals *see* BIRKAT HAZAN; BLESSING

grain, five kinds in rabbinic culture, wheat, barley, spelt, oats, and rye (M. Ḥallah 1:1)—the kinds of grain from which bread normally was prepared. Dough made from these grains is subject to the dough offering (Num. 15:18–21).

grammateus (Gr., scribe) term used for not only those individuals trained in writing and drawing up legal and business documents, but also for administrators. Like the English word "secretary," it could mean anyone from a clerk to the secretary of a governmental department. In Jewish writings in Greek, the word generally has this normal sense of "scribe" or "secretary." The Gospels, however, use the term to apply to what seem to be experts in the Torah, regardless of profession; the historicity of the use of this term in pre-70-C.E. times is debated.

grapes, grapevines a major motif in Jewish art of the Roman and Byzantine periods. The grapevine appears on coins of Herod the Great, but it also appears on the decorations of the Second Temple itself. Herod placed a golden grapevine at the entrance to the Temple. Furthermore, grape clusters, grapevines, or grape leaves appear on the coins of other Jewish rulers, in the art of Jewish tombs, on lamps, and in synagogue decorations. Since grapes are one of the seven kinds of fruits growing in the land (Deut. 8:8), they naturally appear in Jewish art. Often the vines and fruit are naturalistically depicted, but just as often the vines and fruit appear in stylized configurations. In synagogue mosaic floors, the grapevine is used as a border or, as a vine scroll, to form medallions or inhabited scroll patterns. Grapes are also associated with the festivals of Sukot, Pesach, and Pentecost. During the periods of heightened Jewish nationalism, namely, during the two revolts against Rome, grape clusters or grape leaves appear on Jewish coins. On First Revolt coins the grape leaf appears, and on Bar Kokhba coins grape clusters appear. Jewish sarcophagi and tomb facades of the Second Temple period are most commonly decorated with grapevine tendrils, bunches of grapes, and grape leaves. This motif persists in Jewish art until the Arab conquest.

Gratus, Valerius Roman prefect of Judea (15–26 C.E.) appointed by Tiberius. He deposed and appointed several high priests, including Joseph Caiaphas, who held the office from 18 to 36 C.E.

Great Assembly, men of *see* MEN OF THE GREAT ASSEMBLY

Great Khuray Kabrath-al-Kura, referred to at T. She<u>b</u>iit 4:11 as demarcating a border area of the Land of Israel

Great Revolt *see* REVOLT AGAINST ROME, GREAT

Grecism word or expression borrowed from the Greek language or culture. This might be an actual borrowing of a Greek word or phrase; however, the term is also often used for an expression in Hebrew or Aramaic that has been literally translated from Greek. Many terms relating to the area of literary criticism are actual Greek words (e.g., *notariqon, gematria*) or loan translations. It has been argued, for example, that some of the peculiar Hebrew vocabulary of Ecclesiastes (Kohelet) resulted from Greek terms being imitated. This is a controversial topic, however, and has yet to be settled.

Greek cities The classical Greek city-state (or polis) was autonomous and self-governing. On the Athenian model, the main governing body was the assembly, which was open to any citizen (a citizen being a person born of free parents who were both citizens). A council presented matters to the assembly. Each city also concerned itself with the preparation of its citizens, most often done through the gymnasium, a preparation that included physical, military, religious, and intellectual training. Such an ideal changed with the rise of the great kingdoms after Alexander the Great. The power of the king now restricted the autonomy of the older

Greek cities, although they still retained some rights and often kept their traditional form of government. The Greek and Macedonian settlers in the newly conquered territories wanted to bring with them some of their institutions, and existing large cities, particularly in the Seleucid kingdom, wanted to gain the status of a Greek polis, even if this did not entail a change in their traditional civic organization. Thus, numerous Greek cities were founded throughout Syria, Babylonia, and Asia Minor. For example, under Jason the high priest, Jerusalem became Antiocheia-in-Jerusalem and a gymnasium was built there (see 2 Macc. 4:7–22). Greek city-states dotted the area around Judea, for example, at Caesarea-Philippi and in the Decapolis.

Greek language With the spectacular success of Alexander the Great, Greek-speaking rulers reigned from Greece to Afghanistan, including Coele Syria and Egypt. While Greek traders and mercenaries had certainly traveled in these countries before, Alexander's achievement brought many changes. The language itself developed as it became the common (Gr.: *koine*) language of the Mediterranean world for ordinary and commercial speech. It is in this common language that the Septuagint and the Greek New Testament are written. Greek, as the language of the ruling class, also became a desirable language to learn for the ruling elite of all the cities now subject to Greeks. The spread of the Greek language particularly affected Judaism. The legend of the miraculous translation of the Hebrew Scriptures into Greek evidences not only a desire of Greek-speaking Jews to read the Torah but also to claim that the Bible in Greek was as good as the Bible in Hebrew, a claim challenged by others. Fragments of Jewish writers in Greek show an attempt to interpret and understand this Greek Bible, while Philo of Alexandria's learned treatises evidence how a Greek-educated Jew might read the Bible. The high priest Jason in the early second century B.C.E. set up a gymnasium in Jerusalem where Greek would have been taught, and Eupolemus of Jerusalem in the second century B.C.E. and Josephus in the first century C.E. rewrote the Bible in Greek. No doubt many Jews in the diaspora wrote in Greek, but only fragments of their work are extant.

Gregory of Nazianzus (c. 330–389 C.E.) sometime bishop of Constantinople, widely referred to as "the Theologian." In his *Theological Orations* (*Or.* 27–31), Gregory defended the orthodox doctrine of the Trinity against the Arians, who denied the full divinity of Jesus Christ. He also defended the doctrine of Christ's full humanity in his arguments against the Apollinarians (*Epistles* 101, 102, and 202). Apart from being a theological controversialist, well trained in classical rhetoric, Gregory was also a poet of considerable skill. Of note are his two long poems, one entitled *The Passion of Christ,* and the other an autobiographical narrative in verse. His many surviving letters testify to Gregory's being a wise pastor and one who at the same time was drawn to a life of contemplative asceticism, often despairing of ecclesiastical politics. Gregory seldom referred to the Jews, but he did raise one interesting question: how is it that Christians celebrate a feast day in honor of the pre-Christian Maccabean martyrs? Although they died before Christ, Gregory wrote, it was the divine Logos (Word) who was with them in their struggle—the same Logos that would subsequently become incarnate in Jesus Christ. He is also a source of information about the emperor Julian and the Jews.

guardian *see* APOTROPOS

Gush Ḥalab Hebrew name for Giscala, north of Meiron in the Upper Galilee; home of John b. Levi, a leader in the Jewish revolt against Rome in 68–70 C.E. Gush Ḥalab is the site of synagogue remains dating from the mid-third through mid-sixth centuries C.E. *See also* GUSH ḤALAB SYNAGOGUE.

Gush Ḥalab Synagogue Excavated in 1977 and 1978, the building gives us important information about Jewish life and faith in Roman-Byzantine Galilee. First built about 250 C.E., the synagogue was extensively damaged in an earthquake in 306 C.E. The building was immediately rebuilt and beautifully renovated. It remained in use until another earthquake shattered it in 363 C.E. The structure was once again rebuilt. This time, however, the restored building was more modest, suggesting a decline in the size of the community or its financial resources. This building shows signs of periodic refurbishing and repair. It was destroyed, again by an earthquake, in 551 C.E. Whether a Jewish community continued to occupy Gush Ḥalab following this destruction is uncertain; the synagogue was not rebuilt and lay in ruins until excavated and restored to its present condition by the Meiron Excavation Project.

The building itself was a beautiful structure. Although it has many unique features (described in detail in Meyers et al., 1990), like most synagogues of this period it was basilical in form with a central nave separated from side aisles by two rows of columns along the building's longitudinal axis. The southern facade, built of impressively large and carefully cut limestone ashlars, was oriented toward Jerusalem. A series of rooms, perhaps used for storage and other purposes, surrounded the main hall on the other three sides.

The synagogue was attractively, if simply, appointed. In all phases of its use, a *bimah,* perhaps with a Torah shrine, was located at the front of the sanctuary, west of the central entrance. In the restoration following the destruction of 306 C.E., benches were built along the east, north, and west walls, although apparently not along their entire length. Nicely shaped column bases, capitals, and architraves were used. Most notable, however, is the lintel from the front entrance. Decorated with a beautifully carved eagle and garland on its underside (those entering the synagogue had to look up to see the decoration) this lintel is uncommon among the synagogues of the period. Also interesting is a column with an inscription in Aramaic, which reads, "Jose Bar Nahum / made this. . . / may it be for him / a blessing."

Although it is unclear how the lower synagogue, described here, is related to the remains of another synagogue, still unexcavated, in the upper city, there is no doubt about the importance of this building. The synagogue at Gush Ḥalab̲ is one of the most striking in the region and provides eloquent, if silent, testimony to the importance of this city in the Upper Galilee throughout the Roman and Byzantine periods.

Gvat Horvat Jabata Synagogue possible synagogue site and ancient Jewish village site about 9 kilometers west-southwest of Nazareth. The site has been known since the late nineteenth century C.E. as a ruined medieval village. Recently, however, a building stone was found that was decorated with a five-branched menorah, lulab̲, and etrog. A roughly cut Ionic capital was also found in the ruins. A stone wall about 15 meters long and as much as 3 meters high was also found, perhaps the outer wall of a synagogue building. Rock-cut tombs in the vicinity appear to be medieval.

gymnasium an institution of a Greek polis (city). Although the word has passed into English, the meaning is not the same; the Greek gymnasium was more than just a place for exercise. It was the educational center for the young people known as *ephebates,* who were candidates for citizenship. The purpose of the gymnasium was to train and educate future citizens in the essential requirements for Greek identity (even when the young people were in fact members of the native population rather than of actual Greek descent). Thus, the training and activities of the program included language, literature, and rhetoric, as well as physical exercise and military skills (the last required since citizens often served in some sort of militia). Any Jew wanting to become a citizen would have attended, though this seems to have seldom occurred. Not only were Jews not normally citizens or candidates for citizenship, but participation in the gymnasium usually meant taking part in some sort of pagan rites. A gymnasium was established in Jerusalem during the Hellenistic reform, though there is no evidence of pagan rites in this case.

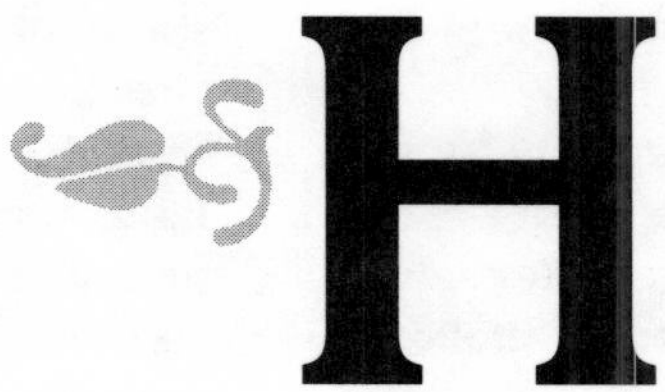

Habakkuk, Targum to *see* TARGUM TO THE PROPHETS

Habakkuk Commentary (also known as the Pesher Habakkuk; abbreviated as 1QpeshHab) one of the continuous *pesharim* from Qumran. It was found in 1947 in Cave 1 in one copy, dating between 30 and 1 B.C.E. Since no other copies were found, it has been argued by some that this is the autograph, but since there is evidence of copying (particularly the fact that the scroll was copied by two different scribes), this seems unlikely. The manuscript is almost complete, containing thirteen columns and presenting a running commentary on the first two chapters of the Book of Habakkuk. The events described fall under the end of Hasmonean rule and the beginning of Roman rule in Palestine, indicating a date of composition not long before the date of the manuscript.

The commentary indicates the distinctive Qumranian *pesher* form of commentary: the biblical verse is quoted, the phrase "its interpretation is" follows, and then an interpretation of the verse, referring to contemporary events intimately connected with the Qumran sect, concludes the text. Several important figures emerge: the Teacher of Righteousness, the sect's leader and its inspired interpreter of scripture; the Wicked Priest, clearly to be identified with one of the Hasmonean high priests, probably Jonathan or Simon; the Spouter of Lies, a rival figure to the Teacher, who flouts the teaching of the sect and sets up a congregation in opposition to the sect; and the Kittim, a fierce warlike people from "the islands of the sea," who are the instruments of God's vengeance on the sect's opponents. (They should be identified with the Romans.) It is therefore possible to reconstruct some history of the sect: the Teacher of Righteousness was the leader of a group of adherents, which espoused his particular interpretation of scripture; the Wicked Priest opposed the Teacher and his group; the Spouter split away from the Teacher and formed an opposing group; and these events took place in the time immediately prior to the appearance of Rome on the scene as a world power. The identification of the figures, however, remains obscure.

What is striking about the Habakkuk Commentary is the conviction of the author and his audience that biblical prophecy is chiefly concerned with the eschatological age, that they themselves are living in that eschatological age, and that the small events surrounding their group and its opponents are at center stage in the events of the last days. Thus we are presented with a clear picture of the sect's self-image and its eschatological fervor.

haḇdalah (Heb., division) rite marking the end of the Sabbath day at sunset on Saturday

ḥaḇer (Heb., fellow, associate) one who meticulously tithes his food and eats his meals in a state of ritual cleanness

Hadas ancient Edessa; the present-day Urfa, in Turkey. "Hadas" appears in the Jerusalem Targum to Genesis 10:10 for the Hebrew place-name Erech. No other rabbinic mention of the name is extant.

Hades Greek word for the underworld. In classical Greek lore, it is shorthand for "the House of

Hades," who is the god of the underworld. Thus, *hadēs* is the regular Septuagint translation for Sheol. In Jewish thought, Sheol comes to be identified as the place of post-mortem punishment, and thus the New Testament uses Hades to refer both to the place of the dead and the place of punishment. *See also* HELL; SHEOL.

Hadrian (76–138 C.E.) Roman emperor (r. 117–138 C.E.). Publius Aelius Hadrianus was born in 76 C.E. to the senator Publius Aelius Hadrianus Afer and Domitia Paulina, Spanish Romans from Italica, Spain. His grandfather married Trajan's aunt, and when his father died, Hadrian became the ward of the future emperor, who was childless. He eventually married Trajan's great-niece Vibia Sabinia. Hadrian began a successful military career under Nerva and held a succession of military, political, and religious positions under Trajan. Kinship and exceptional advancement marked Hadrian as Trajan's successor, and doubtless Trajan intended Hadrian to succeed him, although no formal adoption took place. Hadrian was governor of Syria when Trajan died at Selinas in Cilicia, and the suspicious circumstances surrounding Trajan's deathbed adoption of Hadrian should not overshadow the compelling logic of Hadrian's succession. When Trajan died, those with him, including Plotina, Trajan's wife, and the legions, all favored Hadrian and named him emperor. The Roman Senate soon followed suit.

Hadrian generally continued Trajan's policies, although he was more interested in consolidating the empire than he was in expanding it. He made peace with the Parthians and abandoned Trajan's plan of eastern conquests. In the Near East and in the territories of present-day Scotland, Hadrian replaced the often ill-defined frontier system with stone walls and fortifications; in the north, he replaced the old frontiers with wooden barricades and forts, which served more as checkpoints and tax centers than as barriers against enemies. Several other trends continued under Hadrian: foreign auxiliaries were increasingly indistinguishable from regular Roman soldiers in the legions; operations were increasingly tied to fixed fortifications; and detachments of legions (*vexillationtes*) were dispatched along an improved road system to answer emergencies. Under Hadrian, the army was made more alert, disciplined, and efficient by continuous training and maneuvering; the frontier and the peace were further secured by the emperor's frequent inspection tours, his keen interest in all aspects of frontier and military life, and his apparent willingness to share the life and routine of the common soldier.

Hadrian's journeys fill more than half his reign and clearly document his interest in all parts of the empire and his desire to administer it personally rather than to delegate responsibility. He was educated in Athens and fascinated by things Greek; some of his trips (the four years spent visiting Greek and Asian cultural centers, for instance) resemble sightseeing tours. Hadrian did not neglect Italy, but, cosmopolitan by nature, he wanted to organize and regulate imperial life, both domestic and provincial. One of his most enduring contributions was legal reform, particularly his codification of the earlier praetorian edict and his humanitarian edicts protecting the interests of children and slaves.

Hadrian's rich architectural legacy included refurbishment of the Pantheon, his mausoleum (Castel San Angelo), and his villa at Tibur (Tivoli). He also rebuilt Jerusalem, renaming it Aelia Capitolina. His construction of a temple to Jupiter on the spot of the old Temple precipitated the Zealot revolt of 132–135. Hadrian's designated successor, Lucius Ceionius Commondus, died before he did; Hadrian then selected Titus Aurelius Antoninus (Antoninus Pius), an elderly senator, as his successor.

haftarah (Heb., prophetic reading) passage of a book classified as prophetic, for example, Joshua, Judges, Samuel, both Kings, Isaiah, Jeremiah, Ezekiel, or the Twelve Minor Prophets, read in the synagogue on the Sabbath and festival days, following reading from the Torah. The one who reads it is called the maftir.

Hagar Sarah's Egyptian servant and mother of Abraham's first son, Ishmael; recipient of God's miraculous care. (Gen. 16, 21:8–21, 25:12). Hagar symbolizes in Galatians 4:22–31 the Sinaitic covenant of slavery to the law; Paul opposes her to Sarah, the heavenly Jerusalem, and freedom in Christ. Sarah's treatment of Hagar in Genesis 16 is suppressed by Jubilees (but see Jub. 17:4–14 on Gen. 21) and the Book of Biblical Antiquities.

haggadah *see* AGGADAH

Haggadah of Passover book containing the liturgy and ritual for Passover Eve; a narration of the story of the Exodus from Egypt, illustrated through symbolic foods and expressed through a midrashic interpretation of Deuteronomy 26:5–9. The ritual found in the Haggadah is first referred to in M. Pesaḥim, chapter 10, which describes a festival meal marked by a set order of foods and a required liturgy (seder). At the heart of the meal is an explanation of the significance of three foods (unleavened bread, bitter herbs, and the Passover offering) and recitation of the Hallel-psalms. In early Amoraic times, this basic ceremony was embellished through the addition of a discussion of Israelite history, leading up to and including captivity in Egypt. In later developments, continuing to the present, liturgical poems and other homilies have been added to the basic format set in talmudic times.

The Haggadah is introduced with the Kiddush, the blessing over wine that introduces all festivals. The ritual particular to Passover begins with a statement associating unleavened bread with "the bread of affliction" consumed by the Israelites in Egypt. This passage expresses the hope that all who participate in the Passover will, in the coming year, enjoy freedom in the Land of Israel. Next comes a set of questions, based upon M. Pesaḥim 10:4, regarding the ways in which the night of the Passover seder differs from all other nights (Mah Nishtanah, or the Four Questions, traditionally recited by the youngest child). The answers to these questions, found initially in the passage beginning "Avadim Hayinu" (We were enslaved by Pharaoh) introduces, first, several stories regarding the obligation to recount the story of the Exodus and, second, a recitation of the story itself. The recitation is introduced by Deuteronomy 26:5–8, interpreted in the Haggadah to mean "an Aramean would have destroyed my father" and embellished by homilies that focus upon the inability of the Egyptians to break the spirit of their Israelite captives. These passages expand as well upon the miracle of the plagues and the dividing of the sea that allowed the Israelites to escape the pursuing Egyptians.

The shift from the recitation of the story of the Exodus to the Passover meal itself occurs through a passage cited in the name of Gamaliel, which relates that the obligation of the Passover meal is to explain the significance of the Passover sacrifice, the bitter herbs, and the unleavened bread. The meal proper is followed by the usual grace and then a medieval creation, Shefok Ḥamatkha (Pour out your wrath), a compilation of scriptural verses that urge God to take vengeance on nations that oppressed the people of Israel and to bring Elijah the prophet, the precursor of the Messiah. The Hallel-psalms follow, and the Haggadah is completed by a number of passages that praise God as the source of all life.

Haggadat Megillah *see* ESTHER RABBAH I

Haggai Palestinian amora of the third century C.E., born in Babylonia. A pupil of Zeira, whose sayings he transmitted, he was a prominent member of the academy at Tiberias.

Haggai, Targum to *see* TARGUM TO THE PROPHETS

Ḥag haKatzir *see* SHAḆOUT

ḥagigah (Heb., festal offering) an additional animal offering presented by pilgrims to Jerusalem on the pilgrim festivals of Passover, Pentecost, and Tabernacles, to provide additional meat for the pilgrim family to eat.

Ḥagigah Mishnah tractate on the festal offerings. Pilgrims are to bring three animal sacrifices: an appearance offering, which is a burnt offering and yields no food for the priest or the pilgrim; a festal offering (*ḥagigah* proper), which is in the class of peace offerings and yields meat; and a peace offering of rejoicing, which also yields meat. The appearance offering is required at Deuteronomy 16:14–17; the festal offering, at Deuteronomy 16:15. The tractate describes the liability and cost of the appearance offering, festal offering, and peace offering of rejoicing (chaps. 1–2) and their presentation on the Sabbath (chap. 2). Since these offerings bring common folk to the Temple, the rules of ritual cleanness as they affect ordinary folk and Holy Things of the cult are laid out (chaps. 2–3): first come gradations of strictness of rules of ritual cleanness. This starts from the lowest, which is unconsecrated food eaten in accord with the rules of cleanness covering sacred food; then tithe and heave offering; and then Holy Things (e.g., sacrifices, which yield meat for the priest and the pilgrim) and rules of strict cleanness affecting these.

Ḥag Shaḇuot *see* SHAḆUOT

hair Hairiness and long hair represent a variety of themes: nature as opposed to settled life (Esau vs. Jacob); deception (Gen. 27); Nazirite vows (Num. 6:5, 18; Judg. 13:5; 1 Sam. 1:11; Acts 18:18, 21:24); effeminacy (Philo, *Spec. Leg.* 3.37). Perhaps to reinforce gender roles threatened by such teachings as Galatians 3:28, Paul advises women worshipers to be veiled and to not loose their hair: "any woman who prays or prophesies with her head unveiled dishonors her head—it is the same as if her head were shaven" (1 Cor. 11:5). Pseudo-Phocylides 210–212 and 1 Corinthians 11:14–15 exhorted men to keep their hair short and women to keep theirs long. While priests were not to have loose hair (Lev. 21:10), the test for adultery (Num. 5:18; Sus. 32) includes the loosing of the woman's hair and so presents her as if she had been caught in the act. In Testament of Solomon 13, loose, disheveled hair is a sign of the female demon Obyzouth. Masada evidence indicates some women wore long, single braids (see also 1 Tim. 2:9).

hairesis (Gr., sect, or party) Although the English word "heresy" is derived from it, it was widely used in the Graeco-Roman world to mean any religious group without necessarily implying anything pejorative, though in Christian usage it did come to mean "heresy," or "heretical group."

haKnasat Kallah (Heb., bringing in the bride) referring to the entry of the bride to the wedding canopy; by extension, the wedding ceremonies in general. In rabbinic Judaism, *haKnasat Kallah*—enabling a woman to marry—is an important religious obligation.

haKnasat Orkim (Heb., bringing in the guests) providing hospitality, especially to those in need. In rabbinic Judaism, *haKnasat Orkim* is an important religious obligation, often viewed as modeled on Abraham's welcoming of his divine visitors, described at Genesis 18:1–21.

Ḥalafta Tannaitic authority of the late first and early second centuries C.E.; head of the academy and leader of the community at Sepphoris. Only a few of his statements are preserved, some of them under the name Abba Ḥalafta. T. Shabbat 13:2 preserves a statement of Ḥalafta to Gamaliel II recalling the actions of Gamaliel the Elder in the final years of the Temple. This points to Ḥalafta's presence in Jerusalem while the Temple stood and suggests that he lived to an advanced age. Ḥalafta was the father of the well-known Tannaitic authority Yose b. Ḥalafta.

halakhah, in Jubilees and at Qumran Although the term *halakhah* (Heb., way; more generally, law) tends to be associated primarily with Pharisaic and rabbinic Judaism, these were not the only Jewish groups in the Second Commonwealth to systematize and observe Jewish law. The literature that survives in the Dead Sea Scrolls, including Jubilees (which has long led an independent existence), contains a sizable amount of prescriptive legal material, as well as texts that imply the observance of a form of what modern scholars would term halakhah. Even among the prescriptive texts, one ought to distinguish between the sort of prescriptions that are found in Jubilees and those that are found in more "codelike" documents from Qumran.

The halakhah in Jubilees (note that neither Jubilees nor Qumran literature employs the term in this "rabbinic" sense) consists primarily of a series of commandments interspersed with the narrative by which these laws are connected with events in the lives of the earliest generations of mankind through the patriarchs. They include the observance of the appointed times such as the Sabbath (2:17–33, 50:6–13), Yom Kippur (34:18), Passover (49:1–23), Shab̲uot (6:17–22, 22:1), and Sukkot and Aseret (16:20–31, 32:27–29); agricultural laws such as firstfruits (Heb.: *bikkurim*) (7:36, 15:1–2, 22:1, 44:1–4), the sabbatical year (Heb.: *shemitah*) (7:37), tithes (13:25, 32:10); and circumcision (15:11–14 and 25–29). In most of these cases, only the bare outlines of the law are mentioned, with few details of its observance supplied. The major exception is the Sabbath law, which, in both of its appearances, supplies a list of activities that are prohibited on the Sabbath under penalty of death. It should be stressed that the laws in Jubilees are often more stringent than the parallel regulations in rabbinic literature. Thus, it is a capital offense to lie with one's wife or make business plans for the following week on the Sabbath (50:8). For the rabbis, sexual activity is not forbidden on the Sabbath, and anticipation of business affairs, while prohibited, is not a capital offense. The section on the Passover also provides some of the details of the procedure of the festival. A variety of other commandments and injunctions is listed in Jubilees: not to go naked (3:31, 7:20); not to commit incest (16:8, 33:10, 41:25) or fornicate (7:20, 20:3–4); not to eat blood (6:12 and 38, 7:28–33, 21:6); not to intermarry with the Gentiles (20:4, 30:7–17); and to cover the blood of slaughtered animals (7:30, 21:18).

The observance of none of these laws is particularly unique to the Book of Jubilees, and it is its pervasive stress on the 364-day calendar and the accompanying effect that the calendar has on the festivals that makes Jubilees' halakhah most strikingly different from any other late Second Temple views. Other than the calendrical emphasis and the laws of the Sabbath, however, there are very few details of how the halakhah is to be observed. Even in the case of those commandments and injunctions, such as circumcision and the prohibitions of intermarriage with the Gentiles, where the focus of the halakhah is the preservation of Jewish identity and separateness, the details of the laws are not paramount for Jubilees. Most of the laws are merely restatements of pentateuchal material relocated into the earlier biblical narrative. The reason for this is presumably generic; Jubilees is not a work in which halakhah is intrinsic to the structure and movement, no matter how important it may appear to be theologically. As a result, even though Jubilees, including its halakhic material, claims to be divine revelation, one cannot know whether the goal of the Book of Jubilees was to be a prescriptive work for any group.

Qumran halakhic literature includes works of disparate genres, such as the Damascus Document (abbrev. CD; its 4Q ancestors are 4QD[a,b], etc.), 1QS (and related fragments), 11QTemple, and 4QMiqsat Maase haTorah (4QMMT). The former two provide insight into the way of life of the community whose members authored them, integrating a discussion of the theology and beliefs of the group with some of the practices that they maintained. We perhaps ought to differentiate between them and 11QTemple, which belongs to the genre "rewritten Bible," focusing almost completely on legal material. 4QMMT, in contradistinction to all the aforementioned, contains a list of halakhot regarding which the author is in disagreement with his correspondents, presumably some member(s) of the Jerusalem establishment. From its appearance in such a broad generic spectrum, it is clear that halakhah is central to Qumran practice and ideology.

Some of the halakhot at Qumran are of the same nature as those found in Jubilees or in the Mishnah, but one could also consider all of the unique rules (e.g., 1QS cols. 5–7) for the conduct of the members of the sect as halakhot. The author or compiler of CD/4QD does not distinguish between those sectarian laws whose observance is unique to the Qumran sect and other halakhot that were commonly held in Israel at that time. He integrates both types side-by-side in the portion of the Damascus Document that is usually termed "The Laws." Thus columns 15–16 (which follow col. 8 and precede col. 9 in the Qumran versions of CD) begin with the laws of oaths in general and proceed to uniquely Qumranic aspects of the law, returning to a discussion of other laws of oaths, some pentateuchally based and some novel. The laws of testimony, judges, purification, and Sabbath follow with no overt distinction between legal issues that are viewed as common Judaism of the Second Temple period and those that might be termed sectarian. The details of the laws are much more prominent in the Damascus Document than those in Jubilees because this portion of the text is fundamentally a law code.

The Temple Scroll contains a broad spectrum of halakhot pertaining to the construction of the Temple and its vessels, the sacrifices for a variety of occasions, laws of purity, laws of the king, as well as many others. Following biblical order on the whole, but departing from it in order to consolidate material on specific topics, the text presents itself as the product of divine revelation. Because the formulation of the laws generally is biblical, the legal exegesis of this text can frequently only be understood inferentially. Some of the laws have parallels in other Qumran texts, but there is still some dispute as to 11QTemple's being a native Qumran composition.

4QMMT (a fragmentary text, which survives in several Cave 4 manuscripts, whose official publication by Elisha Qimron and John Strugnell finally appeared in 1994; see "An Unpublished Halakhic Letter from Qumran," *Biblical Archaeology Today* 1985: 400–407) shows that some of the primary halakhic concerns of its authors and their differences with others were in the areas of sacrificial and purity laws, as well as laws dealing with the sanctity of Jerusalem and the Temple. The well-known disputes between the Pharisees and the Sadducees over the halakhic procedure to be followed in the preparation of the red heifer is reflected in 4QMMT (as well as other Qumran texts). This fact, among others, has led some scholars to assert that the halakhah of the sect is Sadducean in content (and, concomitantly, to reopen the whole question of Qumran origins).

In fact, it is extremely important for the history of the halakhah in the Second Temple period that in eight instances where rabbinic literature presents the Sadducean halakhah in the context of Pharisaic/rabbinic-Sadducean controversy, 4QMMT confirms that the position that the rabbis describe as Sadducean actually existed and, moreover, indicates that it was held by the authors of this document. As we observed of Jubilees, the halakhah at Qumran tends to be more stringent than that of the rabbis, as can be observed clearly from a casual study of the Sabbath laws in the Damascus Document and the laws of purification (e.g., *tebul yom*) in 4QMMT, 11QTemple, and several other texts. 4QMMT, in addition, demonstrates explicitly the significance of halakhah at Qumran and the fact that the separation of its authors from mainstream Israel took place over halakic disputes. It calls for its addressee (whoever that may have been) to rethink his halakhic positions and to come around to the views expounded in MMT.

In addition to the major compositions alluded to, there are other fragmentary Qumran texts such as 4Q159 and 4Q513–514 (Ordinances) that detail laws on a variety of topics, such as the rights of poor gleaners in the field, the payment of the half-shekel, cleansing from impurity, and a variety of other laws. Some of these seem to be of scriptural origin, but are rephrased in the rewriting, while others are of a more sectarian nature. It is clear from its appearance in so many different sorts of texts that the system of purity was of paramount concern to the Qumran Community in their daily behavior (as it was to the rabbis; note that Seder Tohorot, dealing with purity, is the longest order of the Mishnah). The presence at Qumran of a variety of texts dealing with the calendar points to the importance of that aspect of halakhah at Qumran, a concern that the Qumran Community shared with the author of Jubilees.

It is evident that the recording and copying of halakhic material must have been very fundamental to the Community at Qumran since a number of halakhic texts appear in several copies. This can only point to a community whose behavior was guided by the texts that they composed and wrote. An eventual study of the principles of composition of halakhic documents may shed further light on the roles that halakhah played in Qumran narrowly, on the broader issues of the development of Jewish legal and exegetical thinking in the Second Temple period, and perhaps even on the mode of literary composition of rabbinic literature.

half-shekel small coin, paid by Israelites as their share in the daily whole offerings, presented in the Temple as atonement for the entire people of Israel

ḥalitzah *see* RITE OF REMOVING THE SHOE

ḥallah *see* DOUGH OFFERING

Hallah Mishnah tractate on dough offering. The tractate defines bread from which dough offering is required (chap. 1); kinds of grain that yield bread, kinds of dough, and the process of separating the dough offering (chaps. 2–3); the liability of mixtures of a dough that is liable to dough offering and a dough that is exempt (chaps. 3–4); and the liability to dough offering of bread prepared from grain grown outside the Land of Israel (chap. 4).

ḥallal *see* PRIESTHOOD, UNFIT MALE

Hallel Psalms of thanksgiving, Psalms 113–118, chanted in the synagogue on Tabernacles, Hanukkah, Passover, Pentecost, and New Moon

hallelujah translated "praise Yahweh," from the Hebrew root *hll* (praise) and *Yah* (a shortened form of the divine name). In the Hebrew Bible it occurs only in the Book of Psalms. In most cases it opens or closes the psalm, and in Psalms 146–150 it does both. Its position in psalms of praise and its plural imperative form attest to its formulaic, liturgical nature, as does the fact that it is left untranslated in the Septuagint and the Vulgate. In Tobit 13:17, 3 Maccabees 7:13, and Revelation 19:1, 3, 4, 5 it appears untranslated as an expression of delight.

Ḥama Babylonian amora; head of the academy at Nehardea (356–377 C.E.); apparently a native of Nehardea, referred to under the designation "Amoraim of Nehardea" (B. Sanhedrin 17b). B. Ba̱ba Metzia 65a reports that he made a living as a merchant.

Ḥama b. Bisa Palestinian scholar of the late second and early third centuries C.E., at the nexus of the Tannaitic and Amoraic periods; a contemporary of Judah the Patriarch. At times he is referred to simply as the father of Hoshaya Rabbah (i.e., Hoshayah I). He lived in the south of the Land of Israel (Y. Niddah 3:2, 50c).

Ḥama b. Gurya Babylonian amora of the late third or early fourth century C.E.; infrequently cited in the Babylonian Talmud. He serves as a tradent of Abba Arikha, in whose name he says: "[let me live] under Ishmael but not under a Roman; under a Roman but not under a Magus; under a Magus but not a disciple of a sage; under a disciple of a sage but never under a widow and orphan" (B. Shabbat 10b).

Ḥama b. Ḥanina Palestinian amora active in the third century C.E.; the son of Ḥanina b. Ḥama and, like him, for a time head of the academy at Sepphoris (see Y. Shabbat 6:2, 8a, referring to "the courtyard of Ḥama b. Ḥanina in Sepphoris"). He apparently was of a wealthy family (Y. Peah 8:9; 21b).

Ḥama b. Raba Babylonian amora, referred to in Seder Tannaim veAmoraim, which says that he died in 471 C.E.

Ḥama b. Ukba Palestinian amora active at the end of the third century C.E.; a contemporary of Levi

Ḥamesh Megillot *see* FIVE SCROLLS

ḥametz *see* LEAVEN

Hamisha asar beShe̱bat *see* FIFTEENTH OF SHE̱BAT

Hamman-Lif Synagogue a site about 17 kilometers from Tunis, Tunisia. The synagogue dates from the sixth century C.E. and is known for its mosaics as well as its "broad-house" architectural style. Only fragments of the mosaics are known today because of the nature of their discovery. The synagogue was discovered by chance in the late nineteenth century by French army captain de Prudhomme. De Prudhomme uncovered the entire synagogue before a proper plan could be prepared. An amateur made several sketches, but there are some discrepancies between these sketches and later drawings by professionals. All of the mosaics were sold, and twenty-one fragments were eventually purchased by the Brooklyn Museum in 1905; the location of the rest of the fragments, if they survived, is unknown. All of these conditions complicate the interpretation of this important site.

Architecturally, the synagogue is classified as a

"broad-house" type, as it is entered on the long side. This type of architecture is not concentrated in one particular geographic location, but is found scattered throughout ancient Israel, Near Asia, and northern Africa. Parallel broad-house type synagogues are found at Horvat Shema in eastern Galilee, Horvat Susiya and Eshtemoa in southern Judah, and Dura-Europos on the Euphrates in Syria. The synagogue at Hamman-Lif has three entrances. The entrance at the rear left leads to a room isolated from the rest of the synagogue. Some have interpreted this as a women's chamber, but it is also possible that this room was used as a guest house. A second entrance is found on the right side, leading into a corridor with doorways into various rooms as well as into the central chamber at the rear of the synagogue. The front entrance leads through several halls paved with mosaics and into the same central chamber at the rear of the synagogue. At the threshold of the last hall before the central chamber, there is a short Latin inscription with a dedication.

The mosaics from the central chamber are particularly important. As reconstructed from early sketches and from the remaining fragments found in the Brooklyn Museum, several salient features can be noted. There are explicit Jewish motifs (a pair of menorahs and the inscriptions) as well as other artistic motifs, such as fish, a cup, peacocks, and animals placed in a vine design. In addition, there is an emphasis on the number four, as seen by the placement of an amphora in each of the four corners and by the iconographic representation of the Four Seasons or Winds. Some hold that this imagery represents various aspects of salvation. This interpretation is confirmed by the central inscription, which reads, "Thy servant Juliana P[. . .] at her own expense paved with mosaic the holy synagogue of Naro for her salvation."

Hammath-Gadera Synagogue synagogue and village site on the Yarmuk River about 7 kilometers east of the Sea of Galilee. The modern Arabic name of the site is el-Hammeh (the hot spring) and the name of the mound upon which the synagogue was found is Tell Bani, or the mound of the bath. (Bani is possibly a shortening of the Greek word *balaneion,* or bath.) The baths were mentioned by Origen, the Christian author writing at Caesarea after 200 C.E. In this and other Greek sources, the site is known by the Greek form of its name, Emmatha. Names of rabbis are identified with discussions of the boundary between Hammath and the city of Gadera, about one Roman mile to the south (Y. Shabbat 7a). The synagogue was found in 1932 and proved to be a complex of a dozen rooms measuring 32.5 meters from east to west. The prayer hall was not entered directly but through rooms on the west and east that opened into the sides of the worship area. A third entrance was in the southeast corner beside the apse area that opened from a long, narrow corridor leading outside the building. A fourth entrance was at the southwest on the other side of the apse and led into a corner room of the complex.

The apse of the building points south. Interior space of the prayer hall measures about 13 by 13.9 meters and is divided into three aisles and a central nave by three rows of columns around the central space. The floors of the aisles are paved with geometric mosaics. The nave is paved with mosaics divided into three panels. The first panel to the north contains a pattern of diagonal intersecting lines with an Aramaic inscription off center to the right (probably because there was once another to the left). The inscription honors Ada bar Tanhum bar Monikos, who contributed one tremissis, and Yoseh bar Qarosah and Monikos, who contributed one-half denarius toward the mosaic. The central panel was a repeated pattern of fleurons (flowerlike devices) with roses and pomegranates. Two long Aramaic inscriptions appear at the south end of this panel. One honors Rab Tanhum the Levite, bar Halfa, who had donated one tremissis; Monikos of Susitha the [Se]pphorite, Lord Patricius of Kefar Aqabayah, Yose bar Dositheus of Kefar Nahum [Capernaum], all three of whom donated three scruples; Yudan the architect [?] of Emmaus who donated three [scruples?]; and the people of Arbela, who donated their cloths (perhaps for the curtain in front of the Torah shrine). The second inscription honors Lord Leontis (who is known from a synagogue inscription at Beth Shean) and Lady Kalonike, who donated one or more denarii, a certain "righteous woman" who donated one denarius, and the inhabitants of the town who donated one tremissis.

The south panel next to the raised platform, or *bimah,* featured a central wreath with an Aramaic inscription; facing the viewer are two lions with tails up and tongues out. On either side of the guardian lions, cypress trees complete the frame. The central inscription reads as follows: "And be remembered for good Lord Hoples and Lady Protone, and Lord Sallustius his son-in-law, and Count Pheroros his son, and Lord Photios his son-in-law, and Lord Haninah his son—they and their children—whose acts of charity are constant everywhere and who have given here five golden denarii, may the King of the Universe bestow the blessing upon their work. Amen. Amen. Selah." A marble chancel screen enclosed the *bimah* and raised apse area. One fragment of a marble chancel screen was decorated with a seven-branched menorah in relief within a wreath. Surely a Torah shrine stood within the apse, though no fragment of it was found. Twenty-two coins of Justin II (r. 565–578 C.E.) found within the complex appear to date the last use of the synagogue, though it seems to have been founded in the fifth century C.E. The complex was destroyed in a fire. Recent excavations have suggested that two fourth-century phases of the synagogue exist farther down.

Hammath-Tiberias a site on the west side of the Sea of Galilee, about 200 meters south of the city wall of ancient Tiberias. Its existence was known from rabbinic literature for the hot springs that flow out of the ground nearby. Two excavations at the site uncovered one of the most interesting and controversial synagogues found in ancient Palestine. It was found in one of the strata of a series of superimposed buildings dating from the second through the sixth centuries. The latest building is a large, apsidal synagogue dating from the late Byzantine period, which apparently served the needs of the community up to the Arabic period.

The earliest building was a large public structure, which excavators indicated might be a gymnasium. Directly over this public building, a synagogue of the broad-house type was erected (stratum IIb), which, according to the director of the 1961–1963 excavations, was destroyed in the 306-C.E. earthquake that affected several sites in the Galilee. A second synagogue (stratum IIa) was built on top of this structure, which functioned throughout the fourth and into the early decades of the fifth century. It is the synagogue of stratum IIa, the Synagogue of Severos, that represents one of the remarkable finds in the history of synagogue research in Israel.

The initial construction of this "fourth-century" synagogue was allegedly occasioned by earthquake destruction in 306 C.E. Excavations, however, at adjacent Tiberius and at nearby Lower Galilean sites have turned up no such destruction. Moreover, the pottery published in the final report as illustrative of fourth-century usage contains clear examples of fifth- and sixth-century fine ware. Coins found in the excavations (latest coin, 395 C.E.) sustain a fourth-century date, as does a dating based on iconography of the main mosaic in the floor. Thus, the fourth-century dating of this synagogue is conjectured on grounds other than that of stratigraphic archaeology.

The synagogue structure itself is a nearly square building, containing a broad-house synagogue (one oriented by the long wall facing Jerusalem), whose interior space contained three rows of columns, which divided the main hall into four aisles with a conjectured exterior entrance on the north side. Just outside the nave on the southeast was a series of communicating rooms. The floor of one of these rooms (room 35) was raised, suggesting to the excavator that this was one of the earliest examples of a Torah repository outside the main room of a broad-house synagogue.

It is the polychrome representational mosaic, which covers the floor of the main nave, that sparked scholarly debates. In the top panel is an Ark of the Covenant (representation of the synagogue Torah shrine), flanked by menorahs and Jewish ritual objects (etrog, lulab, incense shovels with glowing coals represented). In the lower panel are Greek donor inscriptions flanked by rampant lions. The central panel, though, contains a zodiac executed in the Hellenic style, with the Four Seasons depicted as human figures in the corners of the mosaic. The discovery of a zodiac in a Jewish synagogue at first clouded discussions of the Jewishness of this synagogue's congregation, but subsequent discoveries of zodiacs in synagogues have removed this as an important factor.

What remains notable is the degree to which this zodiac represents an extremely Hellenic or gentile execution. Helios is portrayed as the young beardless youth with long hair driving the quadriga. Signs of the zodiac that surround this central Helios figure contain both animal and human figuration, including uncircumcised nude males. Although each sign has its name written next to it in Hebrew, the Hebrew for Deli-Aquarius is written in reverse and backwards lettering, showing that the congregation that paid for this mosaic knew no Hebrew. In fact, though extensive mosaic inscriptions are found at various places in the floor in Hebrew, Aramaic, and Greek, it is clear that Greek overwhelmingly was the language of this congregation.

Thus, Severos's synagogue is an important piece of evidence in breaking down the last generation of scholars' contentions that Hellenized Jews lived in the diaspora, but Jews in Israel were highly Semitic. It also has joined a growing body of evidence helping to distinguish between the Aramaic-speaking region of Upper Galilee and the Hellenized, Greek-speaking Jews of Lower Galilee.

Hamnuna **1.** Babylonian amora of the third century C.E.; a student of Ra<u>b</u>, he reportedly excommunicated an authority who had contradicted Rab̲'s opinion (B. Shabbat 19b)

2. rabbi of the late third and early fourth centuries C.E., sometimes referred to as Hamnuna Saba (the Elder), who was a student of Ḥisda

Hamza Isfahani historian and chronologer of Persia. In 961 C.E., he composed his *Annals,* which testify to his skills as an original researcher and his critical approach to his sources. He reports that in 468 C.E. the Jews of Isfahan, Persia, flayed two magi alive, and that as a result of this incident, Peroz, the Sassanid emperor ordered that half the Jewish population of Isfahan be slaughtered and that the Jewish children should be delivered to the fire-temple of Surusch Adzeran in the village of Hervan. This seems to confirm the Jewish sources, which also report the seizure and forced conversion of Jewish children.

Ḥana Babylonian amora active at Pumbedita in the early fourth century C.E.; a contemporary of Abayye and Raba; the son-in-law of Adda bar Ahab̲ah. He was born in the Land of Israel.

Ḥanamel high priest in the Jerusalem Temple in 37/36 B.C.E.; according to M. Parah 3:5, an Egyptian in whose time a red heifer was sacrificed. According to Josephus, Ḥanamel was a Babylonian, appointed by Herod the Great in place of the more logical choice, the Hasmonean Aristobulus. As a result of protests from Mariamme and Alexandra, Herod subsequently deposed Ḥanamel in favor of Aristobulus, restoring Ḥanamel to office only after Aristobulus was murdered.

Ḥanan b. Abishalom judge named at M. Ketub̲ot 13:1–9 as a judge of robbery cases in Jerusalem, alongside Admon (b. Gadai). B. Ketub̲ot 105a names a third judge, Ḥanan the Egyptian. The fact that, at M. Ketub̲ot 13:9, Yoḥanan b. Zakkai discusses these individuals' decisions suggests that they lived while the Temple stood. Little more is known about them.

Ḥanan b. Rabbah Babylonian amora active at Sura in the late third and early fourth centuries C.E.

Ḥananiah Tannaitic authority of the second century C.E.; the nephew and student of Joshua b. Ḥananiah; usually cited as Ḥananiah, nephew of Joshua b. Ḥananiah. He was born in Babylonia and returned there some time before his death, having spent much of his life in the Land of Israel. His name is absent from the Mishnah but appears in several Tannaitic statements recorded in the Babylonian Talmud. Ḥananiah reportedly was a highly respected and powerful authority of his day.

Ḥananiah b. Akabiah Tannaitic authority of the second century C.E. His first name is also cited as Ḥanina and his patronymic, probably incorrectly, as Akiba. Rab̲ reportedly admired his legal acumen (B. Shabbat 83b).

Ḥananiah b. Gamaliel II *see* ḤANINA B. GAMALIEL

Ḥananiah b. Ḥakinai Tannaitic authority of the mid-second century C.E.; a student of Akib̲a at Bnai-Berak. He is cited infrequently in the Mishnah. Y. Shekalim 5:1, 48d, reports that he knew numerous languages. He is also referred to simply as Ben Ḥakinai.

Ḥananiah b. Ḥezekiah b. Garon early Tannaitic authority. M. Shabbat 1:4 reports that in his upper room, the Houses of Hillel and Shammai voted on eighteen laws concerning Sabbath observance.

Ḥananiah b. Judah Tannaitic authority of the second century C.E.; a contemporary of Akiba. He is cited only twice in rabbinic literature, both times in exegetical contexts (Sifra, Tzav 2:3; Sifra Shemini 2:3).

Ḥananiah b. Teradyon Tannaitic authority of the second century C.E. For continuing to teach and hold public gatherings, he was martyred during the Hadrianic persecution that followed the Bar Kokhba Revolt. Few of his legal or exegetical statements have been preserved.

Ḥananiah of Sepphoris Palestinian amora active in the mid-fourth century C.E.; sometimes referred to as Ḥanina. He often is cited in conjunction with his contemporary, Mani.

Ḥanan the Egyptian Tannaitic authority of the second century C.E., reported to have "argued before the sages" (B. Sanhedrin 17b). Except for one statement in his name (B. Yoma 63b), nothing is known of him. He is different from the Ḥanan the Egyptian named as a judge in Jerusalem (B. Ketub̲ot 105a); that Ḥanan lived prior to the destruction of the Second Temple.

handbreadth (Heb.: *tefaḥ*) a measure of length made up of five fingerbreadths

hands, laying on of (Heb.: *semikhah*) the act of laying hands on a person's head to bestow a spiritual blessing. Through this deed, Jewish leaders were empowered to perform judicial functions. The concept of *semikhah* is based upon Moses' laying of hands on Joshua (Num. 27:22–23), thereby transferring to Joshua a portion of the divine spirit that rested on Moses. Rabbinic sources claim that Moses similarly ordained the elders (Num. 11:16–17, 24–25), who in turn laid hands on their successors. In this view, an unbroken chain of authority existed from Moses through early rabbinic times. Beginning in the fourth century C.E., the practice of laying on hands as a rite of ordination fell into disuse. Documents of appointment, certifying the individual's legal knowledge, replaced this rite.

In early Christianity, laying of hands similarly signified an extension of particular authority and blessing (see Acts 13:3; 1 Tim. 4:14; 2 Tim. 1:6). In the Gospels, the gesture accompanies healing (Mark 5:23) and blessing (Mark 10:13–16). In Acts 8:17–18, 9:17, and 19:6, it imparts the Holy Spirit (see also Heb. 6:2). The Genesis Apocryphon (11QapGen) depicts Abraham as exorcising a demon by the laying on of hands.

Ḥanina Palestinian authority at the end of the third and beginning of the fourth centuries C.E. Born in Babylonia, he emigrated to the Land of Israel and studied with Yoḥanan. Ḥanina explained his failure to achieve ordination by noting a family tradition that he was of the line of Eli the Priest and that none of this family was destined to be ordained. For this reason, like Hoshayah, who also was of the line of Eli and who might have been Ḥanina's brother, Ḥanina is referred to as "colleague of the rabbis."

Ḥanina, Prefect of the Priests Tannaitic authority active in the final years of the Second Temple. In the Mishnah, he speaks about the Temple service and customs of Temple days (see, e.g., M. Eduyyot 2:1–2).

Ḥanina b. Abbahu Palestinian amora of the fourth century C.E.; the son of the renowned Abbahu; active at Caesaria and, for a time, at Tiberias, where he was involved in charity (Y. Pesaḥim 3:7, 30b).

Ḥanina b. Dosa Tannaitic authority of the first century C.E.; a resident of Arab̲ and student of Yoḥanan b. Zakkai. He is noted for his piety (see, e.g., B. Berakhot 61b) and concentration in prayer, which reportedly saved him from a scorpion's bite (T. Berakhot 3:20). M. Sotah 9:15 states that when he died, wonder-workers came to an end. Few of his legal or exegetical statements are preserved.

Ḥanina b. Gamaliel son of Gamaliel I and brother of the patriarch, Simeon b. Gamaliel; a Tannaitic authority of the second century C.E. His first name occasionally is cited as Ḥananiah.

Ḥanina b. Ḥama rabbi of the early third century C.E., at the nexus between Tannaitic and Amoraic authorities. Born in Babylonia, he emigrated to the Land of Israel, where he studied in Sepphoris with Judah the Patriarch. There is a question whether Ḥanina was ordained by Judah himself or by Judah's son (see Y. Berakhot 5:1, 9a; B. Ketub̲ot 103b). Ḥanina worked as a merchant (Y. Peah 7:4, 20b) and practiced medicine (B. Yoma 49a). He lived to an old age (B. Ḥullin 24b).

Ḥanina b. Isaac Palestinian amora of the fourth century C.E.; a contemporary of Samuel b. Ammi; cited several times in exegetical contexts

Ḥanina b. Pappai Palestinian amora of the late third and early fourth centuries C.E.; a student of Samuel b. Naḥman; active at Caesaria with Abbahu. His name appears variously as Ḥanina, Ḥananiah, and Ḥinena. Reports of his life (Y. Shekalim 5:4, 49b) and death (B. Ketub̲ot 77b) claim that Ḥanina had intimate connections with the supernatural, including direct contact with the angel of death.

Ḥanina of Sepphoris *see* ḤANANIAH OF SEPPHORIS

Hannah the mother of Samuel (1 Sam. 1–2). She is one of several women in the Bible whose conception after barrenness results in the birth of an Israelite hero. In Jewish and Christian tradition she becomes a model for other mothers of notable sons. Language from the song of Hannah has informed the story of the mother and her seven sons in 2 Maccabees 7 (cf. 1 Sam. 2:5–6 with 2 Macc. 7:9, 11, 22, 23, 29). In retelling the story, the medieval historian Joseph ben Gorion (Josippon) gives the mother the name Hannah and has her recite a paraphrase of Hannah's song. The stories of the conception of John the Baptist and Jesus and the account of Jesus' youth (Luke 1–2) parallel the stories of Samuel's conception, birth, and youth, and the Magnificat, the song of Mary, Jesus' mother, imitates Hannah's song (Luke 1:46–55). *See also* BIRTH, MIRACULOUS.

Hansen's disease *see* LEPROSY

Hanukkah festival of lights, falling on the eighth day after the twenty-fifth of Kislev (corresponding to December), commemorating the victory of the Maccabees over the Syrians, the purification of the Temple, and the reestablishment of the cult

hare a minor motif in Jewish art, particularly in ancient synagogue mosaic floors. Hares are part of the fauna of the Land of Israel, so it is no surprise that they should appear in Byzantine Jewish art. Most commonly the hare appears in mosaics decorated with inhabited scrolls. For example, two running hares appear in the inhabited scroll in the synagogue of Maon, one on either side of the long axis. This pavement features fifty circles, most of which are inhabited by birds or animals found in ancient Palestine. An animal frieze in the Beth Shean synagogue depicts a hunt, with a dog chasing a hare and a bear chasing a deer.

harvest a metaphor for God's judgment. It appears in the Hebrew Bible at Jeremiah 51:33 and Joel 3:13 and in Second Temple Jewish texts in 2 Esdras 4:28 and 2 Baruch 70:2. The image is frequent in the New Testament, explicitly so in

Matthew 3:11–12 (and its parallel in Luke 3:16–17), Matthew 13:36–43, and Revelation 14:14–16, and less obviously in Matthew 9:37–38 and John 4:35–36. Paul's language about sowing and reaping may also be related (Gal. 6:7–9, cf. 1 Enoch 62:8). The connection in Matthew 3:8–12 and Luke 3:8–17 between harvest imagery and the cutting down of trees suggests another biblical source of the idea, the image of God wielding an axe against the trees of the forest (Isa. 10:33–34). This passage is applied in 4QpIsa[a] 8–10 to the activity of the Davidic Messiah and seems to be alluded to in 2 Baruch 36–40. *See also* JUDGMENT, DIVINE.

Ḥasdai name of four Babylonian exilarchs: (1) Ḥasdai b. Bustanai, in the late seventh century C.E.; (2) Ḥasdai b. Bardoi, at the beginning of the eighth century C.E.; (3) Ḥasdai b. Natronai, during the first half of the ninth century C.E.; and (4) Ḥasdai b. David, in the twelfth century C.E.

Ḥashem *see* GOD, NAMES OF

Hasideans Jewish military group in the 160s B.C.E. Their name derives from the Hebrew word for "devout ones" or "pious ones" (*ḥasidim*). In 1 Maccabees 2:42, they offer to cooperate with the Maccabees in fighting the Seleucids: "mighty warriors of Israel, all who offered themselves willingly for the Law." In 2 Maccabees 14:6, the high priest Alcimus claims that Judas Maccabeus was the leader of the Hasideans. According to 1 Maccabees 7:13–14, the Hasideans were fooled into accepting Alcimus as the legitimate high priest, with the result that sixty of them were killed. Attempts to link the Hasideans to the Essenes, the "early pious ones," and the Pharisees have not been successful.

Ḥasidim *see* HASIDEANS

Hasmoneans the family name of Judas Maccabeus. It was used as the dynastic name of his brother Simon and his descendants, who ruled Judea and its expanding kingdom in the second and first centuries B.C.E. According to Josephus's *Antiquities* (12, sec. 265), the priest Matthathias, the father of Judas Maccabeus, was the great-grandson of Asamonaios, a priest of the course of Joarib. The so-called Maccabees are usually referred to as the Hasmoneans from the time Simon secured independent rule over Judea from 142 to 140 B.C.E. *See also* MACCABEAN REVOLT.

ḥatimah (Heb., seal) the final line that seals or concludes a statutory benediction. It begins, "Blessed art Thou . . . ," and concludes with a phrase that summarizes the theme of the benediction.

ḥattunah (Heb.) wedding. In rabbinic law, the marriage ceremony is designated *kiddushin* (sanctification), reflecting the understanding that through marriage, a woman is made sacred to her husband and forbidden to all other men. In talmudic times, a marriage was formalized through two separate events, often performed months apart. The betrothal ceremony (*erusin*) formalized the decision of the parties to wed and marked their families' agreement to the financial details of the proposed union. The marriage proper, marked by the *nissuin* ceremony, took place later, once arrangements for establishing a common home could be completed. Once a woman was betrothed, she was prohibited to all other men and required a divorce in order to marry someone else. Connubial relations, however, were prohibited until the marriage proper, signified by the *nissuin* ceremony.

In posttalmudic times, *erusin* and *nissuin* are performed consecutively. Only the reading of the *ketubah,* the marriage contract specifying the financial and other obligations of the husband to the wife, comes between them. The *erusin* ceremony begins with the blessing over wine and a benediction praising God for instituting marriages. The groom then recites to the bride, "You are sanctified to me in accordance with the law of Moses and Israel" (B. Kiddushin 5b). Since the seventh century C.E. a ring, symbolizing fidelity, has been given by the groom to the bride as part of this ceremony. The *nissuin* ceremony follows, comprising seven benedictions, the first of which is a blessing over a second cup of wine. These blessings, referred to at B. Ketubot 8a as Birkhat Ḥatanim (blessings of grooms), then reflect upon God's creation of the world and the perpetual renewal of human beings in the divine form. The final benedictions pray for the restoration of Jerusalem and for the happiness of young couples. The seventh benediction cites Jeremiah 33:10–11 and prays for the restoration of a joyful Jewish community in the cities of Judah.

Since the fourteenth century, the wedding ceremony has taken place under a *ḥuppah* (canopy), symbolizing the couple's future home. The custom of breaking a glass at the conclusion of the wedding ceremony is based upon B. Berakhot 31a, where, during the course of his son's wedding celebration, a rabbi breaks an expensive vase in order to warn those present against excessive joy. *See also* ERUSIN; KIDDUSHIN; MARRIAGE; MARRIAGE CONTRACT.

Haustafel (Ger., household list, or domestic rules) used as a technical term in scholarship to refer to lists of duties or responsibilities found in moral instructions. In the Graeco-Roman world, there were certain expectations of conduct in the family and in society, depending on one's station in life. The idea is also found in the Hebrew Bible, elaborated on by Jewish writers, and in the New Testament. Pseudo-Phocylides gives a long section on family relations. Philo of Alexandria and Josephus both record the duties toward God and humans that were expected of all pious Jews.

ḥazakah (Heb., squatter's rights) presumption of right of possession or ownership through extended utilization of property; taking possession through long-term use

Hazkharat Neshamot (Heb., memorial of souls) a medieval custom of memorializing the dead. It is often mistakenly traced to biblical and rabbinic times because of putative precedents in 2 Maccabees 12:44 and a late interpolation into a Tannaitic midrash (Sifre Deut. 210:8). *See also* YIZKOR.

Hazor a major biblical city in Upper Galilee about 18 kilometers north of the Sea of Galilee. Hazor comprises the mound itself and a large rectangular enclosure of 70 hectares or nearly 175 acres. The mound or upper city was occupied in the Persian and Hellenistic periods, though not the huge enclosure. The southwestern part of the city had been dominated after the Assyrian conquest by a large fort, evidently built by the conquerors. This fort, with exterior walls nearly two meters thick, continued to be used during the Persian period (stratum II at Hazor), presumably by Persian forces. This fortress consists of an inner courtyard surrounded on four sides by rooms. On the east side a second courtyard was enclosed by a wall. Many walls of poorer construction than those of the Assyrian builders divided the rooms and some of the courtyard into smaller spaces. Pottery imported from Greece or the Greek islands, so-called Attic wares, were found here and there with the indigenous pottery. In the Hellenistic period the fort was again used during the second century B.C.E., evidently by the Hasmoneans in their attempts to secure Galilee. The fort would overlook the major commercial arteries to the north that passed through this valley. Graves of the Persian and Hellenistic period attest to the presence of a garrison within the fort, but as yet there appears to be no attached support village.

healing In the Torah, Psalms, and prophetic books, God is often pictured as a healer and as one who inflicts diseases on those who are disobedient or who seek to thwart his purpose. Just after the people of Israel cross the Red Sea and enter the desert, they are given the assurance that God will not inflict on them the diseases that He had sent to the Egyptians and that he is "YHWH who heals you" (Exod. 15:26). The same theme is heard in Deuteronomy 32:39: "There is no god beside me. I kill and I make alive; I wound and I heal." The psalmist celebrates God's forgiving his people all their iniquities and healing all their diseases (Ps. 103:3).

In the biblical narratives, God's healing activity occurs regularly in response to prayer. Thus when Abraham prays for Abimelech (who had taken Sarah when she and Abraham assured him that she was Abraham's sister), Abimelech is healed and his wives and slaves regain their ability to bear children (Gen. 20:1–18). For her jealousy of Moses, Miriam is stricken with a dread skin disease, but is healed in response to Moses' prayer to God on her behalf (Num. 12:10–15). In 2 Kings 20 and in Isaiah 38 the story is told of the sickness that overtakes King Hezekiah and of his prayer to the Lord, which results not only in his recovery but in the extension of his life for fifteen years and in the deliverance of Jerusalem from the Assyrians. The Aramaean king sends Naaman, the commander of the royal army, to Israel in the hope that he will be healed by the prophet Elisha (2 Kings 5). After first scorning Elisha's instruction to wash in the Jordan, he does so and is healed, which leads him to declare that the only true God is in Israel.

In the Torah, physical healing is linked with the maintenance of ritual and dietary purity. This is especially clear in Leviticus 11–15, where there are extended descriptions of skin diseases and instructions for gaining physical and ritual cleanness. There are also warnings aginst trying to use divination, exorcisms, or sorcery in an attempt to regain one's health (Lev. 18, 19:31, 20:6).

God's healing work aims at far more than regaining physical health: it involves the wholeness and moral strength of the covenant community and the souls of its members. In the Psalms, there are appeals to God to heal body and soul: "Be gracious to me, O Lord, for I am languishing; O Lord heal me, for my bones are shaking with terror. My soul is also struck with terror" (Ps. 6:2). In Psalms 30:2 there is praise to God for having helped and healed one who "cried to you for help." The link between sin and sickness is evident in Psalms 41:3–4, where the depiction of God as sustaining those who are ill and infirm is followed by the appeal, "Heal me, for I have sinned against you." Job shows the connection between the pain of God's disciplinary action and his power to heal: "For he wounds, but he binds up; he strikes, but his hands heal" (Job 5:18). The same prophet who mourns that there is no physician to ease the hurt of God's disobedient people (Jer. 8:22), that their "wound" is incurable and that they lack any adequate medicine or healing (Jer. 30:12–13) goes on to promise that God will restore health and heal their wounds (30:17).

By the middle of the second century B.C.E. the belief had arisen that disease is the result of penetration by evil spirits or demons. But in Jubilees 10:7–14 Noah's prayer for the ability to combat the effects of the evil spirits and the illnesses they cause leads to his receiving a book that gives details for healing the sick "by means of the herbs of the earth." The author of this book has clearly been influenced by the emergence in the Greek world of medical practice based on natural remedies. In the Dead Sea Scroll Genesis Apocryphon (1QapGen. 20:12–29), Pharaoh is possessed by an evil spirit that brings "scourges and afflictions" the Egyptian magicians are unable to expel, but Abram lays his hands on Pharaoh's head and drives out the demon. In the Gospels of the New Testament, Jesus' ability to heal and drive out demons is said to be evidence of the power of God (Luke 11:20), and the diseases Jesus cures—blindness, lameness, and deafness—are justified by him through an appeal to the words of the prophets (Luke 7:21–22; see Isa. 29:18–19, 35:5–6), where the renewal of human beings is a sign of the fulfillment of God's purpose for the world.

While the rabbis perceive of the healing powers of Torah and God (see, e.g., B. Ketuḇot 103a: "the sayings of sages heal"), they tend to view disease as a consequence of natural processes or the result of people's failure to take proper care of themselves. Accordingly, the interests of the biblical and Hellenistic literatures in the role of God or magic in healing is not frequently found in the talmudic literature. The rabbis indeed hold that one who attempts to bind God to offering a cure, for instance, by whispering over a wound the verse, "I will put none of the diseases upon you which I have put on the Egyptians, for I am the Lord who heals you" (Exod. 15:26), has no place in the world to come. The rabbis rather focus on natural cures for diseases, especially foods and herbs held to remedy specific maladies (see, e.g., B. Shabbat 109b; Pesikta deRab Kahana 18:4; B. Baḇa Metzia 107b).

Hear O Israel (Heb.: *Shema Yisrael*) the proclamation of the faith and theology of Judaism. This is in three parts: two introductory blessings, then the recitation of the Shema itself, and then a concluding blessing. The introduction speaks of creation of the world and revelation of the Torah; the Shema proper speaks of the unity of all being in God; and the concluding blessing speaks of the redemption of Israel, the holy people.

The blessings recited before the Shema are as follows. (1) *Creation of the world, attested by sunrise and sunset.* "Praised are You, O Lord our God, King of the universe. You fix the cycles of light and darkness; You ordain the order of all creation. You cause light to shine over the earth; your radiant mercy is upon its inhabitants. In your goodness the work of creation is continually renewed day by day. O cause a new light to shine on Zion; may we all soon be worthy to behold its radiance. Praised are You, O Lord, Creator of the heavenly bodies."

(2) *Revelation of the Torah as the expression of God's love for Israel.* "Deep is your love for us, O Lord our God; bounteous is your compassion and tenderness. You taught our fathers the laws of life, and they trusted in You, Father and king. For their sake be gracious to us, and teach us, that we may learn your laws and trust in You. Father, merciful Father, have compassion upon us: Endow us with discernment and understanding. Grant us the will to study your Torah, to heed its words and to teach its precepts. Enlighten our eyes in your Torah, open our hearts to your commandments. Unite our thoughts with singleness of purpose to hold You in reverence and in love. You have drawn us close to You; we praise You and thank You in truth. With love do we thankfully proclaim your unity. And praise You who chose your people Israel in love."

Next comes the proclamation of the faith: "Hear, O Israel, the Lord our God, the Lord is one." This proclamation of the Shema is followed by three scriptural passages. The first is Deuteronomy 6:5–9: "You shall love the Lord your God with all your heart, with all your soul, with all your might." The passage goes on to say that one must diligently teach one's children these words and talk of them everywhere and always, and place them on one's forehead, doorposts, and gates. The second scripture recited is Deuteronomy 11:13–21, which emphasizes that if Jews keep the commandments, they will enjoy worldly blessings; but that if they do not, they will be punished and will disappear from the good land God gives them. The third scripture recited is Numbers 15:37–41, the commandment to wear fringes on the corners of one's garments. The fringes are today attached to the prayer shawl worn at morning services by Conservative and some Reform Jews and worn on a separate undergarment for that purpose by Orthodox Jews; they are intended to remind the Jew of all the commandments of the Lord.

The theme of God, not as creator or revealer, but as redeemer, concludes the twice-daily drama. The blessing recited after the Shema is as follows: "You are our King and our fathers' King, our redeemer and our fathers' redeemer. You are our creator. You have ever been our redeemer and deliverer. There can be no God but You. You, O Lord our God, rescued us from Egypt; You redeemed us from the house of bondage. You split apart the waters of the Red Sea, the faithful you rescued, the wicked drowned. Then your beloved sang hymns of thanksgiving. They acclaimed the King, God on high, great and awesome source of all blessings, the ever-living God, exalted in his majesty. He humbles the proud and raises the lowly; He helps the needy and answers his people's call. Then Moses and all the children of Israel sang with great joy this song to the Lord: Who is like You O Lord among the mighty? Who is like You, so glorious in holiness? So wondrous your deeds, so worthy of praise! The redeemed sang a new song to You; they sang in chorus as the soar of the sea, acclaiming your sovereignty with thanksgiving: The Lord shall reign for ever and ever. Rock of Israel, arise to Israel's defense! Fulfill your promise to deliver Judah and Israel. Our redeemer is the Holy One of Israel, The Lord of Hosts is his name. Praised are You, O Lord, redeemer of Israel."

heart (Heb.: *leb̲, leb̲ab̲, leb̲ah;* Gr.: *kardia*) Different from modern technical usage, texts in the Hebrew Bible, late Second Temple Judaism, and the New Testament refer to the heart almost exclusively in psychic and religious rather than physical terms. The heart is the seat of the emotions and can, therefore, be glad, troubled, fearful, or filled with hatred or love. It is also the locus of the intellect, the place where knowledge and understanding reside. In a related sense, the heart is the seat of the will and the moral life. One may have a clean, upright, or pure heart, and in one form of Qumranic anthropology, the heart is the battleground where the spirits of truth and perversity struggle for the individual's loyalty (1QS 4:23; cf. Test. Judah 20). Thus, the heart can be identified as the meeting point between God and humans (Ps. 27:8; Rom. 5:5). Remarkably, these ancient views of the heart as the emotional, noetic, moral, and religious center of a human being persist in modern popular usage. *See also* HEART, HARDNESS OF.

heart, hardness of the failure or refusal to understand God's will and purposes or to accede to them. In ancient Semitic thought, the heart was the seat of knowledge and volition. To harden the heart is to surround it with a shell that resists revelation or to determine not to obey God's will. Most often, the expression is applied to Israel's disobedience.

Hardening of the heart may originate with God, who accomplishes the divine purposes in spite of human resistance; the story of the Exodus is a notable example of this (Exod. 4–11) and a rare application of the expression to a non-Israelite. Humans are also culpable for hardening their own hearts (Ps. 95:8; Jer. 7:24–26). In Mark 8:17, Jesus criticizes his disciples for hardening their hearts, by not perceiving and understanding even though the secret of the Kingdom of God has been revealed to them (4:11–12) and they have seen God's power in Jesus' miracles (chaps. 5–8). Two related terms include "uncircumcision of heart" (Acts 7:51; cf. Deut. 10:16) and "heaviness of heart" (1QS 4:11). These texts underscore the notion of stubborn refusal by combining the present expression with reference to stiffness of neck (cf. also 1 Enoch 98:11). *See also* STIFFNESS OF NECK.

heaven the part of the universe above the earth, including the firmament (a dome separating the waters above the earth from those on the earth; Gen. 1:6–8; cf. 4 Ezra 4:7) and everything above it. The firmament rests on pillars (Job 26:11) and foundations (2 Sam. 22:8). In the firmament are set the sun, moon, and stars; it has windows through which rain falls (Gen. 7:11–12; 8, 2; Isa. 24:18) and God's blessings (Gen. 49:25; Deut. 33:13; Ezek. 34:26; Mal. 3:10) and help (1 Macc. 12:15; 16:3) descend.

Although God is said to dwell in the Temple (1 Kings 8:12–13; 2 Chron. 6:1–2; Ps. 68:5, 35; Ezek. 43:7; Hab. 2:20), in Zion (Ps. 9:11, 76:2; Isa. 8:18; Joel 3:17, 21; Zech. 8:3), and at Sinai (Deut. 33:16; Ps. 68:17), heaven is God's dwelling place par excellence. Solomon's dedicatory prayer for the Temple claims that not even heaven and earth, much less the Temple (1 Kings 8:27), can contain God. Nonetheless, the rest of Solomon's prayer assumes that God lives in heaven (1 Kings 8:30, 34, 36, 39, etc.), a belief shared by the rest of the Hebrew Bible, postbiblical Judaism, and Christianity. In the Hebrew Bible, several mortals are privileged to see into or to visit heaven: The prophet Micaiah ben Imlah sees God's heavenly court and learns God's plans (1 Kings 22:19–23); Elijah ascends into heaven in a fiery chariot (2 Kings 2:11), and Enoch is thought to ascend as well (Gen. 5:24); Zechariah has a vision in which the high priest Joshua stands in the heavenly court and is accused by Satan (Zech. 3); and Daniel has a vision of the heavenly courtroom (Dan. 7).

Biblical Hebrew always uses the plural form *shemayim* (heavens). The Septuagint uses the singular form, and the New Testament uses both. Postbiblical Jewish thought conceives of several—often seven (the number can vary)—heavens. The various heavens contain meteorological phenomena such as wind, rain, snow, and hail, as well as angels, the righteous dead, and even, in some depictions, places of punishment for the wicked. Postbiblical Judaism is fascinated with heaven and its secrets. Because decisions made in heaven determine what happens on earth, and the unseen world dominates the seen, to learn heaven's secrets is to know the course of history and the future. Seers, including Enoch (1 Enoch, 2 Enoch), Abraham (Test. Abr.), and Baruch (3 Bar.), journey to heaven to learn the workings of the universe and to gain insight into human life.

Paul claims to have visited the third heaven (2 Cor. 12:2–4). The Gospel of John says that Jesus descended from heaven; only he has seen God or can speak of the world above (1:18, 3:11–15); and at his death he returns to heaven (14:28). In Luke 24:51 and Acts 1:9, Jesus ascends to heaven after his death and resurrection. The seer of Revelation learns of the cosmic powers at work behind the struggle between Christianity and the Roman Empire through a trip to heaven, where he observes the triumphant Jesus and other heavenly figures. Revelation 21:1 and 2 Peter 3:13 expect a new heaven and earth at the eschaton, a prospect probably based on Isaiah 65:17, 66:22. Early Judaism and Christianity see heaven as the place of reward for the righteous (Test. Abr. 11:10; 4 Ezra 7:88–99; 2 Bar. 51:8–10; Dan. 12:2–3; John 14:2; 2 Cor. 5:2; 1 Thess. 4:16–17; Heb. 10:12–19, 11:16, 12:22–24; Rev. 4:4, 6:9, 11:12).

The rabbinic literature develops the conception of heaven found in scripture and the Hellenistic period, in particular defining heaven as the seat of God. As the focus of human prayer and the place in which people's destiny is decided, the term heaven is equated with the name of God. This is seen in common rabbinic expressions such as "in the name of heaven," "from heaven it is decreed," "by the hand of heaven," and "fear of heaven." The expression "kingdom of heaven" refers to God's sovereignty over the people of Israel (see M. Berakhot 2:5) and to the messianic age, when God will be the sole ruler over all of the people of the earth (Pesikta deRab Kahana 5:9).

heavenly Jerusalem Jerusalem located in heaven. In Exodus 25:9, God tells Moses to construct the sanctuary according to the pattern (Heb.: *tabnit*) shown him on Sinai. Later traditions attest to a constellation of ideas related to this concept: the existence of heavenly measurements of the sanctuary or of Jerusalem; an eschatological Jerusalem to be constructed on earth, often without human agency; a city actually located in heaven. In 2 Baruch 59:4–11, God tells Baruch that on Sinai, Moses received the Torah and the measurements of Zion and the sanctuary, along with other, more apocalyptic revelations (see also LAB 19:10).

The image of an eschatological Jerusalem is common in Second Temple Judaism and expresses hope for Zion's renewal (1 Enoch 26–27, 90; 2 Bar. 32:2–4; 4 Ezra 8:52, 10:27, 38–55; Tob. 14:5–7). It occurs in several Qumran texts (1Q32; 2Q24; 5Q15). In 1 Enoch 90:28–29, God removes the old Temple (or city) and sets up a new one; the text may imply that the new one comes from heaven. The point is that God builds the eschatological Zion (cf. 4 Ezra 10:53–54; Mark 14:58; Acts 7:48–49; Heb. 11:10). In 4 Ezra 8:52, the eschatological realities, including a city, are already in existence and are waiting to be revealed. Ezra receives a vision of the city to come in chapter 10.

The heavenly Jerusalem can be used to place earthly trials in perspective. In 2 Baruch 4:2–6, God proclaims that the promise of divine protection (Isa. 49:16) did not apply to the earthly Jerusalem, but only to the heavenly one, previously revealed to Adam, Abraham, and Moses. In Testament of Job 18:6–8, Job says that he is willing to leave everything behind to enter the heavenly city. In 4 Baruch 5:35, Abimelech blesses an old man with the wish that God guide him to the heavenly city, Jerusalem.

In Christian sources, statements about the heavenly Jerusalem occur in contexts that devalue the earthly one. In Galatians 4:21–31, Paul uses allegory to assert the superiority of the new covenant (the heavenly Jerusalem) over the old covenant (the earthly Jerusalem). In Hebrews, Platonic categories are used to argue that the Jewish cult deals with the shadows of the heavenly realities to which Christians have direct access through Jesus, the high priest (see esp. chap. 9). Christians are said to have approached the heavenly Jerusalem (Heb. 12:22; cf. 11:10, 16). In Revelation 21:1–22:5 (cf. 3:12), a new Jerusalem descends from heaven to replace the old. Unlike the old, it has no temple but instead has the presence of God and Jesus.

The concept of a heavenly Jerusalem does not occur in talmudic writings.

heave-offering (Heb.: *terumah*) priestly rations; the portion of the crop in the Land of Israel that is raised up for the priest; the first gift separated from produce, given to the priests, who are to eat it in a state of cultic cleanness; any amount permitted, a fiftieth is average

heave-offering of the tithe *see* TITHE OF THE TITHE

Hebrew Bible (or Hebrew scriptures) terms coined by scholars to refer to the collection of texts that Jews call the Tanakh, Torah, or Bible, and Christians call the Old Testament. These terms refer to Jewish texts composed in Hebrew (except for a few passages written in Aramaic, e.g., Dan. 2:4–7:28; Ezra 4:8–6:18, 7:12–26) that are regarded as scripture by both Jews and Christians. The Hebrew Bible does not include the Jewish texts called the Apocrypha, which are included in certain Christian Bibles (e.g., the Roman Catholic Bible) but not in the Jewish canon. In referring to this collection as the Hebrew Bible or Hebrew scriptures, scholars are seeking to avoid the confessional overtones of its Jewish or Christian names.

Hebrew language primary language of the Jewish people throughout the ages; more specifically, a dialect of the Canaanite language, mutually intelligible with other dialects such as Phoenician, Ammonite, Moabite, and Edomite. The oldest attested specimens of Hebrew date to around 1100 B.C.E.

Like all languages, Hebrew changed throughout the centuries. Scholars divide the Hebrew of the Bible into three main phases: (1) Archaic Biblical Hebrew (c. 1100–1000 B.C.E.), represented by various poems embedded in the Pentateuch and the Former Prophets (Exod. 15, Num. 21:14–15, Judg. 5, etc.); (2) Standard Biblical Hebrew (c. 1000–550 B.C.E.), represented by the majority of the Bible (virtually the entire Pentateuch and Former Prophets, most of the Latter Prophets, most of Psalms, Proverbs, etc.); and (3) Late Biblical Hebrew (c. 550–200 B.C.E.), represented by the latter books of the Bible (Ezra, Neh., Chron., Esther, Dan., etc.), as well as the Book of Ben Sira. The Hebrew of the Dead Sea Scrolls, known also as Qumran Hebrew, is a continuation of Late Biblical Hebrew, and is attested c. 200 B.C.E.–c. 70 C.E.

Alongside the written Hebrew used to compose the aforementioned literary works, there existed a spoken variety of Hebrew throughout ancient times. Thus Hebrew is characterized by what scholars call diglossia, the coexistence of spoken and written varieties of the same language, each marked by separate morphological and syntactic (perhaps also phonological and lexical) traits.

The evidence for this spoken variety of ancient Hebrew in the early period consists of departures from the grammatical norms of Biblical Hebrew that reflect colloquial development. Eventually, Jewish scholars began to compose works in this colloquial Hebrew. Thus collections such as the Mishnah, the Tosefta, and some early Midrashim (as well as the letters of Bar Kokhba and his comrades) are composed in the spoken dialect, known to scholars as Mishnaic Hebrew. Since these collections include material that was transmitted orally and/or record the discussions of the rabbis in their academies, it makes sense that the Mishnah and related works were written down in the colloquial dialect and not in the literary standard.

Hebrew died out as a living, spoken language in the third century C.E., when it was replaced by Aramaic as the language spoken by the Jews. Aramaic, the lingua franca of much of the Near East in late antiquity, had exerted influence over Hebrew for about 750 years. Thus it was only natural that eventually the Jews, like many others in the region, came to speak Aramaic.

But Hebrew, specifically a fossilized form of Mishnaic Hebrew, continued to be used for literary purposes for the next several centuries. Thus many later Midrashim and some portions of the Gemara were written in Hebrew, even though their authors now spoke Aramaic. With the passing of late antiquity, this phase of ancient Hebrew came to an end as well.

Early Hebrew was written in a twenty-two-letter alphabet derived from the Canaanite (Phoenician) alphabet. In c. 400 B.C.E. the Jews adopted the script of the Aramaic (or square) alphabet for writing the Hebrew language.

Except for the Dead Sea Scrolls and the Bar Kokhba letters mentioned above, all the literary works referred to in this article (the Bible, Mishnah, etc.) are known from manuscripts copied centuries after the original compositions. We do, however, possess numerous inscriptions (most extremely short) from throughout the period of ancient Hebrew.

Hebrews term used in Greek writings as the national name for the people of Israel, usually referred to by outsiders in the postexilic period as Jews. It is used by Josephus for Jews in the biblical period. Paul uses it when he affirms the authenticity of his Jewish ancestry (2 Cor. 11:22; Phil. 3:5). The term also refers to linguistic usage and groups. In the New Testament, words identified as "Hebrew" may be Hebrew (Rev. 9:11, 16:16) or Aramaic (John 19:17, 20:16), the common language of many Jews in the Near East. In Acts 6:1,

Hebrews are Hebrew- or Aramaic-speaking Jewish followers of Jesus in Jerusalem, and Hellenists are Greek-speaking Jewish followers of Jesus. Philo, too, makes a distinction between the Hebrews and "us" (Greek-speaking Jews; *De Conf. Ling.* 129).

Hebrews, Epistle to the an early Christian text that interprets the death of Jesus as a sacrifice replacing the cult of the Temple. A midrashic homily rather than simple epistle, Hebrews was composed in the last third of the first century as an exhortation to Christians, perhaps in Rome, to maintain their faith in Jesus. The work is included among the Pauline epistles, but is clearly not by Paul. Various authors have been proposed, including such Christian missionaries as Barnabas and Apollos, but none is certain.

Hebrews likens Jesus to the high priest who enters the Temple once a year to effect atonement. Jesus as both heavenly high priest and perfect victim is seen to have entered the true, heavenly Temple by his death. There the offering of his sacrificial death, an act of conformity to the divine will, effects true atonement for sins by cleansing the consciences of his followers (chaps. 8–9). The sacrifice of atonement is also a sacrifice that inaugurates a new covenant for those who follow Jesus in faith (chap. 11).

The biblical texts that play a prominent role in the work are Psalm 110, a description of a royal investiture that is understood, as often in early Christianity, to be a description of the exaltation of Jesus to heaven. That Psalm also attributes to its royal addressee a "priesthood after the order of Melchizedek." In chapter 7 Hebrews claims that the priesthood of Jesus fulfills that oracle because Jesus, like Melchizedek, is a figure of the ideal, eternal realm. The covenant relationship established by the sacrificial death of Jesus allows his followers access to that same ideal realm (chap. 10).

Hecataeus, Pseudo- writer quoted by Josephus as being Hecataeus of Abdera; however, many scholars feel that he is a Jewish pseudepigrapher trying to cloak his statements in the genine Hecataeus's authority. The question is debated, and some eminent scholars argue for authenticity. He notes the Jews' loyalty to their laws, for example, their refusal to fight on the Sabbath, which allowed Ptolemy I to take Jerusalem. He also makes reference to the high priest Ezekias (Hezekiah), who was brought to Egypt by Ptolemy I. Some have identified this Ezekias with Hezekiah the Governor, who is known from a Jewish coin.

Hecataeus of Abdera Greek writer of the early third century B.C.E. His work or works are preserved only in fragments, especially in Diodorus Siculus. One of his most important writings was *On Egypt,* in which he attempted to describe Egyptian history and culture to the Greeks. He also mentioned the Jews and gave important insight into Jewish society in Palestine at the beginning of the Ptolemaic era. It is debated as to whether his references to the Jews were in a separate writing on the Jews or in his work on Egypt. According to Hecataeus, the Jews of Palestine formed a priestly state (though under Ptolemaic control), governed by about 1,500 priests, with the high priest at its head. Hecataeus evidently knew nothing about the Israelite monarchy, since he states that the Jews had never been governed by a king. His comments are mainly positive, and he sees the Jewish state as, in some sense, an idealized entity of which he approves. It has been suggested that his sources were Jews, perhaps even priests. Josephus also gives quotations in the name of Hecataeus, but many feel these are not genuine but belong to another writer referred to as Pseudo-Hecataeus.

ḥeder (Heb.) room; elementary school for early education

hēdonē (Gr., pleasure) a philosophical term in Epicureanism, which regarded pleasure as the goal of life. The word came to have a pejorative sense for many, both in Greek philosophy and in Jewish literature, even when pleasure was not an end in itself. The English word "hedonism" is derived from it.

Hefa *see* EFA

hegēmon (Gr., governor) a general term for a governor. Like its Hebrew equivalent, *peḥah*, it could be used for both major and minor ruling officials. More specific terms included "satrap," "eparch," and "toparch." The English word "hegemony" is derived from *hegēmon*.

Hegesippus a Latin version of Josephus's *The Jewish War* in various recensions. The name Hegesippus suggests a patristic writer of the second century C.E., but it is probably a version of Josephus. The real author is uncertain, though the work is generally thought to date from the fourth century C.E. Although clearly based on *The Jewish War,* the text is more of a paraphrase than a strict translation and includes some material not found in Josephus's work, drawing on a number of Roman historians, such as Tacitus and Suetonius. It served as a major source for Josippon.

heikesh a principle of scriptural exegesis that holds that if an analogy can be established between one classification and another, then the rule governing the one applies to the other; *see also* MIDRASH

heimarmenē (Gr., that which has been allotted, or destiny) Greek historians often use it to refer to impersonal fate; thus in a sense it is basically equivalent to *tychē,* but Josephus and other Jewish writers use the term as the equivalent of "God's providence." It is also a term important to many systems of Gnosticism.

hekdesh (Heb.) property consecrated as holy to the Temple in Jerusalem. Items were dedicated either for general use or specified for use in sacrifice on the altar.

hekhal *see* HEKHALOT; TEMPLE

hekhalot the plural of the Hebrew *hekhal,* which in the Bible denotes both a palace and a temple and thus combines the ideas of majesty and holiness. In early Jewish mystical literature the term *hekhalot* designates God's heavenly abode. The plural is used because God is envisaged as dwelling in seven concentric *hekhalot,* his throne being located in the seventh, innermost *hekhal.* This concept, which fundamentally expresses the inaccessibility of God, was associated with a doctrine of mystical ascent. The mystic who wished to see God's glory had to penetrate the doors of the seven palaces. These were guarded by fierce angels who would let him pass only if he had the correct spells, called seals. The *hekhalot* play an important role in a number of treatises (e.g., Hekhalot Rabbati, Hekhalot Zutarti, and Sefer Hekhalot [= 3 Enoch]), which comprise the Hekhalot literature. This literature emanated from a movement that flourished in Palestine and Babylonia in the Talmudic era (second to sixth centuries C.E.). The rabbinic authorities classified its teachings, which have certain affinities to Gnosticism, as belonging to the Account of the Chariot (Maaseh Merkaḇah) and therefore as unsuitable for public discussion. The demise of the movement in the early Middle Ages was precipated in part by the Karaites, who exploited its extreme anthropomorphic language about God to attack the orthodox Rabbanites. It left, however, a rich literary legacy, which was taken up by the Haside Ashkenaz and by the Spanish Kabbalists. Moreover, its hymnology influenced that of the synagogue liturgy (e.g., the Kedushah deYoser).

Hela *see* ELA

Ḥelbo amora of the late third century C.E., frequently cited in both Talmuds. He appears at Sura in Babylonia, where he studied under Ḥuna, and, later, in the Land of Israel. He frequently transmits exegetical statements of Samuel b. Naḥmani, and is referred to as a teacher of ethics. He may be identical with Ḥelbo b. Ḥilfa (Gen. Rabbah 51) or Ḥelbo b. Ḥanan (Y. Berakhot 7:1, 11a).

Helena mother of Izates, the king of Adiabene (1st c. C.E.). The royal house converted to Judaism. Helena had a palace in Jerusalem, aided the people during the famine under the Roman emperor Claudius, gave gifts to the Temple, and was buried in a large, well-known tomb north of the city.

Heliodorus an official of Seleucus IV (r. 187–175 B.C.E.) who was sent to Jerusalem in an unsuccessful attempt to confiscate funds deposited in the Temple. 2 Maccabees, chapter 3, recounts that he was prevented from entering the Temple and was flogged by heavenly beings. He subsequently assassinated Seleucus.

Heliogabalus Roman emperor (r. 218–222 C.E.), born Varius Avidius Bassianus in 203 C.E. He was the son of Julia Soaemias and a Syrian senator, Sextus Varius Marcellus. His maternal grandmother was Julia Maesa, sister of Julia Domna, the second wife of Septimius Severus and the mother of Caracalla and Geta. The family filled the hereditary priesthood of the sun-god, Heliogabal, in Emesa, Syria. As priest, Avidius called himself Heliogabalus. In order to win popular support, his mother spread the false rumor that he was Caracalla's son and, to gain military support, promised monetary rewards to the army, which in turn hailed Heliogabalus as emperor and acclaimed him Marcus Aurelius Antonius. Marcus Opellius Macrinus, Caracalla's immediate successor, was routed and killed. Heliogabalus's short reign is portrayed as filled with perverted, excessive, and strange religious activities, on which he was encouraged to concentrate. To this end he adopted a young cousin, the future emperor Severus Alexander, to share imperial power, but within a year, both Heliogabalus and his mother Soaemias were assassinated.

Helios one of two Greek sun gods. He is of uncertain paternity and is said to be the son of Hyperion, Zeus, or Hephaestus. Throughout antiquity, Helios had been depicted with rays emanating from his head. Although Helios can be traced back as far as the Homeric *Odyssey,* his cult became a significant popular Graeco-Roman religion only after the Julian calendar reform. Many of the children of Israel had worshiped YHWH as the Sun throughout the pre-exilic era. The Sun as a deity, with whom God's wisdom is favorably compared, was of importance in Second Temple Judaism. According to Daniel (2d c. B.C.E.), the Sun together with the Moon is asked to praise God. Philo of

Alexandria calls the Sun the great king, with whom he compares God.

The Therapeutai may have worshipped the Sun. There is strong evidence of Sun worship at Qumran, where in addition to attested astrological thought, the solar calendar was used as opposed to the lunar one used in Judah and Jerusalem. There is also evidence of Jewish Sun worship during the rabbinical era. A mosaic pavement in the third (or possibly fourth) century C.E. synagogue at Hammath-Tiberias depicts the Sun (some form of syncretization of Apollo and Helios) and his chariot in the center of the zodiac.

hell a word of old Germanic origin designating the underworld, either as the abode of the dead or the place of punishment. In the King James Version of the Bible, "hell" normally translates "Sheol" in the Hebrew Bible and "Hades" and "Gehenna" in the New Testament. Gehenna (or the Valley of Hinnom), the ravine south of Jerusalem, was widely thought to be the place of eternal punishment (1 Enoch 26–27; Matt. 5:22, 23:33). The apparent setting of Isaiah 66:18–24 in Jerusalem suggests that the punishment pictured in verse 24 occurs in the Valley of Hinnom. However, some believed that Sheol, the realm of the dead, would be turned into the place of punishment (1 Enoch 103:5–8; Luke 16:23 [Hades]).

Hellenistic period the era in Palestine from about 333–323 B.C.E. to about 63–30 B.C.E. or even later. The different beginning and ending dates reflect the fact that the Hellenistic period of Palestinian archaeology is not uniform in nature, particularly since different portions of the land had been incorporated into the "state" at different times. Prior to the Hellenistic era, only a small region in the central portion of Palestine had formed the Persian province of Judah. The boundaries of Judah altered during the early part of the Hellenistic period. Although it was different from the Persian province, Judah (= Judea), at first it still was restricted to the central region of Palestine. During the Hellenistic period, different regions, some of which are characteristically considered part of Palestine, others that are not, became incorporated into the developing state of Judah at different times, particularly during the Hasmonaean period, and under different circumstances.

Small regions to the west and northwest of Judea were conquered by Jonathan (c. 160–142 B.C.E.). A small region extending to the Mediterranean Sea in the region of Joppa had been conquered by Simon (c. 142–134 B.C.E.). Idumea, Philistia, and Samaria in "the land" and to the east of the Dead Sea was the region that had formerly been part of Ammon and extended as far as the Wadi Arnon in what had been Moab. It was captured by John Hyrcanus (c. 134–104 B.C.E.). Galilee, in the far north of the land and east of the Jordan had been conquered by Aristobulus I (c. 104–103 B.C.E.). Alexander Jannaeus (c. 103–76 B.C.E.) conquered Galaaditis, an area east of the Jordan and east by northeast of Judea and Gaulantis; a region north of that; a region in the extreme south (below Idumea to the west of and circling the southern end of the Dead Sea and incorporating portions of what had been Moab as far north as the Wadi Arnon), and additionally a small strip of land in which the cities Dora and Strato's Tower are located that bordered the Mediterranean in the northern part of Palestine. Land incorporation was not the only thing that makes it difficult to give an exact temporal specification to the Hellenistic period in Palestine, specifically in Jewish Palestine.

Because of sectarian differences between those inhabitants who were Yahwistic, it is also sometimes hard to characterize sites as belonging to Jewish Palestine or even to define what is meant by Jewish Palestine. Moreover, the artifactual evidence make the distinctions less rather than more clear. All we can really say is that some places had been inhabited mainly by Yahwists, who defined themselves as Israelites. Others were partially inhabited by Yahwists, who defined themselves as Israelites, and partially by those who worshiped other gods. The latter were usually people of Greek or Macedonian Greek origin, but they may also have been eastern natives, and sometimes they were Yahwists who did not worship YHWH alone. The Yahwistic portion of the population of any of the sites may have been Hellenized, non-Hellenized, or mixed. Some places were mainly inhabited by those of Greek origin even when they had been inhabited by Yahwists at some earlier time and possibly again at some later time. Moreover, because of the almost all-pervasive nature of Hellenism, even when people repudiated it, the archaeological findings may, but do not always, reflect this divergence.

In any case, the Hellenistic archaeological era began and ended at different times in different parts of Palestine. It is characterized by what has come to be known as the Rhodian type of jar handle, which reflects trade within the Mediterranean region. Larger architectural structures, when available for study, sometimes evince a melding of Oriental and Greek characteristics and art forms.

Despite great and continuing excavations, many

places cannot be fully excavated or sometimes excavated at all, because they are currently inhabited. Nevertheless, the following are foci of archaeological investigation.

(1) Jerusalem, the capital of the Hasmonean state of Judah and Jerusalem. It extended over the Judahite city of David, and over the Upper City as well. Because of its theological importance to both Christians and Jews today, Jerusalem is always a focus of archaeological interest. Various sites in Jerusalem were excavated by different teams at different times. Among the most important artifacts are some remains of two different city walls, the second of which may be Herodian rather than Hellenistic/Hasmonaean; remains of two towers associated with the "first wall"; remains of a Hasmonaean building on top of the Israelite wall; the foundations of a building; a relief that may have been part of a Hasmonean palace; a column base as well as an Ionic capital; Hellenistic tombs such as "Jason's Tomb," c. 200–175 B.C.E. (although some would place it in the first century B.C.E. on the basis of numismatic data; the tombs in the Kidron Valley; and Ptolemaic I coinage.

(2) Qumran and Ain Feshka, the regions to the southeast of Jerusalem, situated in the region on the northwestern shore of the Dead Sea. One of the most important sites of the Hellenistic era is that of Qumran, a settlement located on the northwest shore of the Dead Sea. It was comprised of one or more communities that rejected the Jerusalemite cult, left Jerusalem, and moved to the area near the Dead Sea. We do not know exactly when the communities migrated to Qumran. All we can say is that it was some time during the latter part of the first half of the second century B.C.E. The building complex at Ain Feshka is closely related to and most likely part of the complex of the communities from Qumran. Although Qumran was occupied well into the Roman era, there was an archaeological "break point" at Qumran in 31 B.C.E. due to earthquake and fire. The most meaningful artifacts are the remains of the fortress, sometimes called the monastery, Khirbet Qumran, a rebuilt seventh-century-B.C.E. building, and the Dead Sea Scrolls, in which all the books of the scriptures except for Esther are represented. Additionally, and meaningfully, there are sectarian documents that have allowed us to learn something about the communities themselves. So far, scrolls have been found in eleven caves. It seems likely that no more "scroll caves" will be found. The cemetery, the pottery found in many of the caves, and coinage, particularly from the period of Alexander Jannaeus, are also important artifacts of the region.

(3) Samaria (modern Sabastiyah) and Wadi ed-Daliyah. Samaria is the city built by Omri to serve his state as Jerusalem served David. Wadi ed-Daliyah is the location of a cave to which some of the upper class inhabitants of Samaria fled in 332. At the beginning of the Hellenistic era, Samaria was inhabited by Yahwists. After its inhabitants had been driven out by Alexander the Great in 332 B.C.E., Samaria became a Graeco-Macedonian military colony. Although many of Samaria's inhabitants escaped to Shechem in 332 and some fled to Wadi ed-Daliyah, where they died of starvation, not all were able to get away from Samaria itself. Samaria did not remain Graeco-Roman. It was conquered by John Hyrcanus in 107 B.C.E., and its inhabitants were forcibly "Judaized." We do not know, however, whether those whom he Judaized had been Greek or Hellenized Semites. Among the important Hellenistic era artifacts from Samaria are round (Hellenistic) towers (inside an Israelite wall) and remains of a fortification. There are Aramaic legal and administrative papyri from the fourth century B.C.E., some of which are actually dated, but these attest to the pre-Hellenistic rather than the Hellenistic era. What is important for the archaeology of the Hellenistic era is the more than three hundred skeletons of escapees from Samaria found in the cave in Wadi ed-Daliyah. Artifacts such as jewelry suggest that these skeletons are those of members of the upper classes.

(4) Shechem, a city southeast of Samaria between Mount Gerizim and Mount Ebal. Shechem is the city to which the inhabitants of Samaria migrated after Alexander made Samaria into a military colony in 332 B.C.E. The escaping upper-class Samarians may have been responsible for the rebuilding of Shechem, which had been deserted for the prior hundred and fifty years. Literary data suggest that there was also a Hellenistic Samaritan temple on Mount Gerizim. The author/redactor of 1 Maccabees 6:2 treats it as non-Yahwistic, calling it the temple of Zeus Xenius. On the basis of numismatic data, we believe that the Shechemites may have had ties to Egypt, but the Ptolemaic coin collection may simply reflect trade. Shechem was destroyed by John Hyrcanus. Although the date in which he destroyed Shechem is not firmly established, it is probable that he did so in 107 and not 128 B.C.E. Excavators have found third-century-B.C.E. potsherds in an area that may have contained a type of sacrificial altar. A coin collection dating to the second century B.C.E., containing coins of

Ptolemy I through Ptolemy V, was also found at the site.

Other sites of archaeological investigation include Acco/Ptolemais, Alexandrion, Araq El-Emir, Ashdod, Beth-Zur, En Gedi, Gezer, Joppa, Jericho, Lakish, Marisa/Maresha, and the Decapolis.

Hellenistic reform term applied to the transformation of Jerusalem into a Greek city (polis) in the mid-second century B.C.E., preceding the Maccabean revolt. At this time, Jason, the high priest, obtained permission to build a gymnasium and draw up a list of citizens. *See also* HELLENIZATION.

Hellenization the process in which Greek culture was spread to the Near East and elsewhere outside Greece proper. Hellenization was a complex process that continued over many centuries. It had actually begun before the conquests of Alexander, especially in such areas as Asia Minor and Phoenicia. All aspects of the civilization were eventually involved: language, literature, government, administration, art, architecture, and religion. Hellenistic culture was different in many ways from Hellenic culture (i.e., the culture in the Greek homeland).

The Hellenistic kingdoms that arose after the death of Alexander differed in many aspects from the city-states of classical Greece and had many features in common with the old Near Eastern empires. For example, kingship, empire, much of the administration, and even war in the Hellenistic period were Near Eastern in form. The royal courts were host to many Greek artists, poets, literati, and philosophers; nevertheless, the conduct of the royal courts followed the Near Eastern pattern, and the monarchies in many cases adopted native models and imagery. For example, the Ptolemaic kings adopted many aspects of the pharaonic kingship. The Ptolemies were still thoroughly Greek, and Greeks were privileged over the natives, but the old bureaucracies continued to operate. It is often stated that Greek replaced the native languages in administration, but this is only partly true. Although Greek was widely used, so were the native languages. Thus, documents continued to be written in cuneiform in Babylon and in Demotic in Egypt, alongside Greek. The native languages continued to be spoken by the common people.

What did change with time was the number of native peoples who sought to improve their station by obtaining a Greek education. In the Greek cities and colonies that were established throughout the East, the Greek citizens enjoyed the most privileges, and they guarded these jealously. However, the aristocrats among the native peoples had the money and connections to obtain Greek scribes for their own use and a Greek education for their sons. As decades and centuries passed, the old barriers began to break down. To be "Greek" became a matter not of physical descent but of language and education; to be Greek was to speak and write good Greek and to be at home in the culture of Greece, regardless of one's origins. Some local people, especially among the aristocracy, became citizens of the old Greek cities. In other cases, new Greek cities were founded in which many of the natives were citizens from the start.

Thus, Hellenistic culture was very complex. The Greek and the native existed side by side. It was not a case of "melting" together into some kind of homogenized form but of both sorts of culture coexisting. For example, Greek and native architecture began to influence each other and to produce mixed forms only to a limited degree and only after a long period of time. Each tradition was able to maintain its integrity and flourish alongside the other.

In the same way, the old and the new coexisted among the people. The average man and woman lived their lives as they had for centuries; the only change from life under the Persians (or Babylonians or Assyrians) was in who collected the taxes. However, some people, such as traders, found it useful to acquire some Greek. Others, who had the opportunity, especially among the upper classes, found Greek culture attractive and attempted to follow Greek ways in some or many aspects of their lives.

In this respect, the Jews were no different from anyone else. Those among the peasantry probably had little direct contact with the culture of Greece. Many others lived in or near Greek cities, however, or came to speak Greek as their first language. Those who were wealthy and had the opportunity often gave their sons a Greek education. This is hardly surprising, since adopting Hellenistic culture, to a lesser or greater extent, did not have to affect one's Judaism. Culture was one thing; religion and ethnic identity was another. The one area where Jews could not be fully at home, however, was in the religious area. No doubt some did compromise, but the number who are recorded as having abandoned their Judaism is very small. Even in the Hellenistic reform, when Jerusalem became a Greek city, no actual laws of the Temple or Torah were clearly broken. An individual such as Philo of Alexandria, who obviously had a good Greek education and participated in Hellenistic culture and life in Alexandria, was also a loyal Jew who was apparently ready to die for his religion.

When the Jews revolted against the Greeks, it was over religion, not culture as such. Some of the best expression of the Jewish resistance against Antiochus IV's attempt at religious suppression is found in 2 Maccabees, a thoroughly Hellenistic work. The Hasmoneans themselves show no inclination to remove Greek cultural elements from the society of Judea. It is also a mistake to assume that only the Jews were interested in maintaining their own culture. As noted above, the native cultures continued to thrive, and they did so because the natives wanted this. The Jews very much wanted to maintain their identity, but so did most other peoples of the Near East.

Hellenization had several possible meanings: (1) the new world situation after Alexander, in which the Near East and all its peoples had become a part of the Hellenistic world; (2) the culture of the Near East after Alexander, a complex mosaic of Greek and native, which continued to change and develop and included everyone; and (3) the individual adoption of Greek ways, which could vary enormously. Only in this third sense can one talk of some being "more Hellenized" than others.

Hellenization, resistance to It could take one of several possible forms, though many writers talk of "resistance" without being very specific. The most direct form of resistance would be to fight militarily against Greek domination. Although a number of peoples revolted against Greek rule at one time or another, only the Jews of Palestine had any real success, in the Maccabean revolt. Some resisted more passively by circulating anti-Greek literature. The main form this took was the production of counterfeit oracles in Greek or a native language. Several such oracles have been preserved, including the Oracle of Hystaspes from Persian and various Egyptian oracles (e.g., the Potter's Oracles). However, such resistance was often more symbolic than real; that is, some specific and overt symbols of Hellenization were attacked, such as Greek cults by Jews, but the continual process of Hellenization often proceeded unnoticed. Nor is there evidence that much of Hellenization was disliked, much less resisted. The complexity of the phenomenon meant that much that happened could be measured only over large areas and lengths of time.

Hellenizers term applied to those who adopted Greek ways; however, it is frequently used without clear definition, or a proper understanding of the process of Hellenization, to mean those who abandoned the Jewish religion. In 1 Maccabees it seems to mean those who did not agree with the Maccabees.

Hemerobaptists (Gr., daily baptizers) Jewish or Jewish-Christian baptismal groups mentioned by Patristic writers, such as Epiphanius; little is known of them. Apparently some Jewish groups practiced regular washings as a religious ritual, as some think the Essenes did.

Hephthalites inhabitants of an eastern Asian kingdom. They were Shapur II's confederates, but by the fifth century C.E., they posed a threat to both India and Persia. Bahram V was the first Persian to fight them. Peroz died battling them in 484. Balash was a Hephthalite tributary. Khusro I destroyed them in the sixth century C.E.

Heraclitus, Epistles of the name for a group of epistles that have been passed down in the name of Heraclitus, a philosopher of the sixth century B.C.E.; however, they are most likely pseudonymous. They exhibit a Cynic view of life and are probably to be dated to the first century C.E. It has been suggested that at least some of them are Jewish writings, because of such themes as the rejection of images of the gods and of eating animal flesh (because of blood?). The problem is that even these alleged Jewish elements have parallels in popular philosophy of the time, while there is little specifically Jewish about them.

Heraclius (c. 575–641 C.E.) Byzantine emperor (r. 610–641). The son of the exarch of Carthage, he overthrew the emperor Phocas. In 628 he defeated the Persians and forced them to leave all of the Byzantine provinces in Syria and Palestine. In 630 he conquered Jerusalem, returning to the Church of the Holy Sepulcher the relics he had taken from the Persians. Upon invading Palestine, he forgave the Jews for their support of the Persians. However, the Jerusalem Christians accused the Jews of killing more Christians than had the Persians, and he eventually expelled all the Jews from Jerusalem and its environs. A series of trials began for Jews accused of killing Christians and destroying churches.

Hercules knot a minor element in Jewish art, namely, a decorative knot normally used to bind a crown wreath commonly found in low relief on lintels of synagogues from Palestine. Today, the knot would be called a square knot. Other symbolic items were commonly found inside the crown wreath or on either side of the Hercules knot. The knot is normally depicted as loose as opposed to tight.

The Hercules knot is an example of an adaptation of Graeco-Roman symbolism by contemporary Jewish communities. In the Graeco-Roman world, the crown wreath symbolized victory. The Hercules knot was used on the lintels in the Roman world to create a concrete example of eternal victory by showing that the binding of victory (the crown wreath) would never come undone. In a similar manner, the items held within and adjacent to the crown are given eternal status as well. Symbolic items found either inside or adjacent to the crown wreath include menorahs, lulabs, shofars, birds, and fish. A particularly common type depicts a wreath bound by the Hercules knot and enclosing a menorah. Hercules knots have been found at synagogue sites such as Caperaum, Charazim (Khirbet Keraze), Kefar Birim, Nabratein, Khirbet ed-Derih, Joppa, and Gadara.

Heres *see* QUIS RERUM DIVINARUM HERES

Hermaiscus a Greek from Alexandria, Egypt, prominently featured in a papyrological document found at Oxyrhyncus now part of the collection known as the Acts of the Pagan Martyrs. This fragmentary act records the sending of a delegation of Alexandrian Greeks to Rome during the reign of Trajan around 108–113 C.E. The dozen or so delegates included priests, gymnasium officials, and teachers, but it is not clear if Hermaiscus was a delegate or was already in Rome facing unspecified charges. The act reported that when Alexandrian Jews heard about the Greek delegation they sent seven envoys of their own and that both delegations carried their own gods, the Greeks bringing a bust of Serapis.

The papyrus apparently depicts a judicial procedure before Trajan and is probably a fabrication composed for the edification and indoctrination of aristocratic Greeks in the gymnasium. Hermaiscus complained about the emperor's unfair treatment of Alexandrian Greeks and protested that Trajan's senatorial advisers included too many Jews. We are told that Plotina, Trajan's wife, conspired with senators to favor the Jews, and Hermaiscus impudently warned Trajan that he ought to support his own people and not side with the ungodly Jews. The bust of Serapis then broke into a sweat and struck terror into one and all. Like so many of the acts, the fictional record of the trial of Hermaiscus displays both anti-Roman and anti-Semitic sentiments, reflecting disenchantment with the position of Greeks in the Roman Empire and with the empire's perceived favoritism toward Jews, with whom Greeks had long been in conflict.

hermaphrodite a person having both male and female reproductive organs. In rabbinic law, a hermaphrodite is not deemed to have participated in God's bequeathing of land to the people of Israel. The hermaphrodite accordingly is excluded from reciting the confession that accompanies the bringing of firstfruits (M. Bikkurim 1:5), which refers to God's gift of land to the Israelite people.

Hermetica *see* POIMANDRES

Hermetidius Campanus *see* CAMPANUS, SEXTUS HERMETIDIUS

Hermon, Mount massive series of peaks at the south end of the Anti-Lebanon range. Its snow-capped prominence (2814 m.) made it sacred to Canaanites, Israelites, Greeks, Itureans, Christians, and Muslims. Judges 3:3 refers to Baal Hermon, and Psalm 29:6 associates epiphanies with Sirion, an alternative name. In 1 Enoch 6–16, it is the point for the rebel watchers' descent and Enoch's heavenly ascent (cf. Test. Levi 2–6). At Caesarea-Philippi, on one of its terraces, Jesus' messiahship was revealed to Simon, who is then commissioned as Peter, the rock (Matt. 16:13–20; Mark 8:27–30). Devotees to Pan erected a sanctuary there, and Herod the Great constructed a temple to Augustus. *See also* DAN.

Herod, son of Herod the Great son of Herod the Great and Mariamme, the daughter of Simon, the Alexandrian priest appointed high priest by Herod the Great. He was the first husband of Herodias, who later married Herod Antipas. In Herod the Great's first will, he was named heir if his half-brother Antipater did not survive.

Herod Antipas son of Herod the Great and his wife Malthace, a Samaritan; full brother of Archelaus, with whom he was involved in a bitter fight over succession to his father's kingdom. His name is an abbreviation of his grandfather's name Antipater, but in the writings of the New Testament, Josephus, and on his coins he is simply called Herod, a name that obviously had already become dynastic in the second generation of the family. In his father's original will Antipas had been designated the principal beneficiary, but this was changed later. As a result he went to Rome to contest the final will, which favored Archelaus. He was confirmed as tetrarch—though the New Testament loosely calls him king (Mark 6:14; Matt. 14:9)—of Galilee and Perea by Augustus in 4 B.C., with the right to revenue of two hundred talents. Antipas's achievements both inside and outside his territory were modeled on those of his father. He restored Sepphoris in Galilee, which had been destroyed by the Romans in putting down the disturbances on the death of Herod the Great. Antipas shared his father's interest in building on the grand scale. This is indicated by Josephus's comment that Sepphoris was the ornament of all Galilee, by the founding of Tiberias on the Sea of Galilee, and by the refurbishing of the fortress of Betharamphtha in Perea. By naming his new city Tiberias (founded in 19 C.E.) and the Perea fortress Julias he sought to honor the emperor Tiberius and his wife as his patrons.

Antipas's building projects should not be seen in isolation from his desire to develop the full potential of the region he had inherited. Sepphoris is the heart of lower Galilee, overlooking the fertile Beth Netopha Valley. Tiberias, together with nearby Tarichea, was well situated to exploit the fishing resources of the lake. Antipas's first marriage to a Nabatean princess, the daughter of Aretas IV, had definite political ramifications since Perea bordered the territory of the Nabateans and relations between them and Herod the Great had been anything but cordial. When Antipas divorced his first wife in favor of Herodias, his brother's wife, hostilities were renewed and the Nabateans inflicted a severe defeat on him. Many Jews attributed this defeat to divine retribution for the murder of John the Baptist, whom Antipas had executed as a subversive (*Ant.* 18:116–120; but cf. Mark 6:14–28). Antipas's standing with the emperor was such that the legate of Syria, Vitellius, was ordered to exact retribution on the Nabateans. A further example of his international stature can be seen in his promoting a peace accord between the king of Parthia and the Romans, by arranging a meeting at a specially erected bridge over the Euphrates. He used the occasion to ingratiate himself with the emperor, much to the annoyance of Vitellius.

Like his father, Antipas showed some sensitivity to the religious views of the mainly Jewish inhabitants of his territory. His building of Tiberias over a Jewish burial ground created problems for the Jewish inhabitants who were compelled to live there because of the purity regulations. His murder of John the Baptist was also unacceptable on religious grounds as both Josephus and the gospels make clear in different ways. Yet the fact that his coins are aniconic and that Jesus was able to conduct a ministry in the region that was openly critical of the court values without any serious repercussions, other than the threat reported in Luke 13:31, is significant. At the same time the absence of any mention of a visit by Jesus to either Sepphoris or Tiberias are best explained on the basis of reported Herodian opposition to him (Mark 3:16). Antipas's presence in Jerusalem for the feast of Passover may be attributed to continued Herodian concern with the Jewish religious institutions, instead of religious reasons.

Antipas probably retained hopes of eventually succeeding to his father's title and territory. The deposition of Archelaus in 6 C.E. and the introduction of direct Roman rule in Judea was, probably, a source of great disappointment to him. Prompted by Herodias, he went to Rome in the hopes of being given the title king, on hearing that his nephew and brother-in-law, Agrippa, had been given that title together with the territory of his brother, Philip, by the new emperor Gaius in 37 C.E. However, Agrippa had previously won the ear of the emperor and Antipas was banished to Gaul (Herodias choosing to join him in exile). Antipas's territories were now also added to those that Agrippa had already received.

Herodians an expression found in some Gospels in reference to the supporters of the Herodian family, most immediately, Herod Antipas, ruler of Galilee. They appear as opponents of Jesus and in Mark as allies of the Pharisees (Matt. 22:16; Mark 3:6, 12:13).

Herodias granddaughter of Herod the Great, daughter of his son Aristobulus, who was executed in 7 B.C.E. According to Josephus, she first married Herod, son of Herod the Great. The Gospel of Mark (6:17) says that she was married to Philip, brother of Herod Antipas, but this is probably an error; her daughter Salome married Philip. Herodias left her first husband for his half-brother, Herod Antipas. According to the New Testament, Herodias had Salome request the head of John the Baptist from Antipas after she pleased him with a dance (Mark 6:17–29; Matt. 14:3–12).

Herodium Herodian palace and monument on the summit of a partly artificial, isolated hill on the edges of the southern Judean mountains and the Judean Desert. This unusual structure was built with a circular double wall, 62 meters in diameter, which begins on both sides of a round tower on the east and with three half-rounded towers on the other sides. Around this construction, an earth and stone rampart was poured to cover it to the depth of about 12 meters, while the upper parts of the wall and towers were raised to a significant height. This rampart gave the hill its "volcano" shape. In its "crater" a palace was built which was divided into two sections. The eastern section was occupied by a large garden with a peristyle, and the western part held some dwellings, service rooms, a bathhouse on the north, and a reception hall on the south. As in all other Herodian palaces, luxurious elements, such as mosaic floors, frescoes, stucco plaster, and opus-sectile paving, decorated the building.

A developed water system was built at the site. Cisterns were cut in the palace itself. A series of tunnels that led into large, well plastered pools, which can be reached without going outside the palace, were also cut deep below the palace. As at Masada, the Jewish rebels took over the palace and made some changes, the most significant of which was the addition of simple benches along the walls of the triclinium, probably transforming it into a synagogue. Next to the entrance, a stepped pool was found that almost certainly was used as a ritual bath. A hoard of eight hundred bronze coins, as well as pottery vessels from the time of the Bar Kosiba Revolt were found at the site, showing that it was used by the rebels. This was proved later by the Bar Kosiba letters from the Judean Desert. According to the letters, Herodias (the name for Herodium) was the headquarters for Bar Kosiba in the last stage of the revolt.

A very large section of a public building and constructions were spread at the foothill and called by the excavators "lower Herodium." Some of them were excavated. The largest construction is an artificial pool 46 by 70 meters with a pavilion at the center. A large rectangular area of about 110 by 145 meters surrounds the pool and was used as a garden. North of the pool, a large complex of buildings was found, including a long storage room with hundreds of typical storage jars. To the southwest, a bathhouse was uncovered, the largest in all Herodian palaces. It was decorated with beautiful mosaic floors and frescoes. A beautiful rare marble washbasin was found that was decorated with the figure of a silenus, the only example of figurative art in Herod palaces.

A long artificial course (350 m) was constructed within the whole area. At its western end, a monumental building (14 × 15 m) was exposed, partly cut from the natural rock. Its unusual plane, some unusual decorated elements, and its context hint that it could be part of the monumental royal tomb and that the course was erected for the great funeral. The mountain-fortified palace and lower Herodium were parts of a huge summer palace used also for two other purposes: an administrative center for southern Judea and the tomb and memorial for the king.

Herod of Chalcis grandson of Herod the Great, son of Aristobulus, who was executed in 7 B.C.E., and brother of Agrippa I and Herodias. He was appointed ruler of Chalcis, in the Bekāa Valley of Lebanon, by the Roman emperor Claudius in 41 C.E. After the death of Agrippa I in 44 C.E., he was given superintendency of the Temple and the high priest's vestments and the right to appoint high priests. He died in 48 C.E.

Herod the Great king of the Jews (r. 40–4 B.C.E.). Herod first came to prominence while his father, the Idumean Antipater, was in charge of the affairs of state under Hyrcanus II. As a young man he was made governor of Galilee (c. 47 B.C.E.), and because of his achievements against alleged brigands (possibly ousted Hasmonean nobles) he was further rewarded with a supervisory role in Coele Syria by the Romans. His betrothal to Mariamme, a Hasmonean princess, was a further sign of his political ambitions. Even though his father was murdered in 43 B.C.E. by disaffected Hasmoneans who felt excluded by this half-Jew and his family, Herod continued to curry Rome's favor through the troubled period of civil war following Caesar's assassination. However, the ousted Hasmonean Antigonus encouraged the Parthians to resist Roman advances in the east by invading Judea and installing him as the rightful king under their patronage. Herod, having secured his family in the fortress Herodium, fled to Rome in 40 B.C.E., where he was declared king of the Jews by the Roman senate. Thus began Herod's long reign, which can be divided conveniently into three periods: consolidation, 40–27 B.C.E.; peak, 27–13 B.C.E.; and intrigues and decline, 13–4 B.C.E.

Consolidation. With the aid of the Roman legate, Herod succeeded in ousting the Parthians from Judea by 37 B.C.E. The next ten years were spent overcoming his internal enemies, the remnants of the Hasmoneans, and negotiating his way amid the changing fortunes of Antony and Octavian at Rome. His first act was, however, one of apparent friendship to his enemies. Hyrcanus II was recalled and treated with honor despite the fact that he was no longer fit for the high priesthood because of mutilation by the Parthians. His appointment of a Babylonian Jew, Hananel, should also be seen as an offering of peace to those Jews who were living as loyal subjects within the Parthian empire and on whose support Herod might have wanted to call in the future. The remaining supporters of Antigonus were executed, and eventually also those in the direct line, including Hyrcanus himself, his wife Alexandra, and eventually their daughter, Mariamme, his own wife. During this early period Herod also had to contend with Cleopatra, who had supported the Hasmoneans against him and who had influenced her suitor, Mark Antony, to insist that Herod cede to her the coastal plain as well as the valuable palm and balsam groves in the Jericho region. In addition Herod was charged with collecting revenues on her behalf from the Nabatean king. Unsuccessful at first, Herod was actually engaged in a campaign against the Nabateans when Antony suffered his defeat at Actium in 31 B.C.E. This circumstance was important in exonerating him in the eyes of Augustus when eventually Herod sought to make his peace with the new ruler. Augustus was quite willing to accept Herod's declaration of loyalty as a trusted client king of Rome. The territories previously ceded to Cleopatra were restored and Augustus was suitably feted as he passed through Herod's kingdom on his tour of the east. It was at this time, when he was secure in his external relations, that Herod ordered the murder of Mariamme, goaded by his sister, Salome. The affair had a deep effect on Herod, who became seriously ill and was himself close to death. Though he recovered and had many subsequent achievements of note, a legacy of intrigue remained that would return to haunt his declining years.

High point of Herod's reign. Herod had been quick to show his absolute control of affairs in Palestine by making the institutions of the theocracy subordinate to him. He appointed his own candidates, often from abroad, to the high priesthood, ignoring the hereditary character of that office, usually for political reasons. The council, or Sanhedrin, was totally subservient to him, and the Pharisees, who had once been an influential political force, were now effectively silenced. Dissent on the basis of religious grounds was impossible. At the same time his rebuilding of the Jerusalem Temple on a grand scale was intended to placate Jewish religious sensibilities, while also providing much-needed employment in Judea. In addition he was careful to insist on certain external aspects of Jewish religious practice, despite his own thoroughly Hellenized lifestyle. Thus there are no human representations on any of his coins or on any of the many lavish buildings which he had erected and that have so far been excavated. In this regard the incident of the golden eagle over the entrance to the Jerusalem Temple, which gave rise to violent reaction from pious Jews toward the end of his life, was atypical. He insisted on circumcision for any non-Jewish male who would marry into his household. Furthermore, despite the heavy burden of taxation that he imposed on the people as a whole he was also conscious of his image as a philanthropic dictator in the best traditions of a Hellenistic monarch. On two different occasions (24 and 20 B.C.E.) when the crops failed he imported grain from Egypt and reduced taxes.

Herod's reign must be seen as a period of active Hellenization in Palestine. His immediate court had a preponderance of non-Jews, foremost of whom was Nicholas of Damascus, the court historian and adviser whose works Josephus used in compiling his own account. Greek philosophers and tutors were also employed for members of the royal household and the Greek language was actively propagated. Greek games and shows were organized even in Jerusalem, despite the objections of pious Jews. His army comprised Jews as well as non-Jews, including the four hundred Gauls who had been Cleopatra's bodyguard and who had been bequeathed to him by Augustus after they had made peace. Many of the inhabitants of the Greek cities of Palestine had bitter memories of the Hasmoneans and were therefore natural allies of Herod in the early years when he was establishing his kingdom. Herod had always had good relations with the Samaritans and he built a new city on the site of ancient Samaria called Sebaste, dedicated to the emperor, settling it with his veterans. He also established another veteran colony at Gaba on the borders of Galilee. He built a temple to Augustus at Banias (Paneion) at the famous grotto of Pan in the foothills of Hermon. He established a new seaport on the coast at the site of Straton's Tower and dedicated it also to Caesar as Caesarea Maritima. It was appointed magnificently with a temple adorned with huge statues representing Rome and the emperor, a theater, an amphitheater, an aqueduct, and a harbor. It became an important source of revenue as trade from the east was diverted from the Phoenician ports to the north, and it honored his imperial patron. Elsewhere throughout the land there are many remains of Herodian buildings on a grand scale—fortresses like Herodium, Masada, Alexandrium, Hyrcania; palaces like Jericho and Jerusalem; and many other lesser buildings, many of them dedicated to Augustus, as Josephus observes.

In order to finance these projects at home as well as his benefactions abroad—such as support for the Olympic games and the rebuilding of a temple on the island of Rhodes to the Pythian Apollo, in addition to many other acts that were intended to show his magnanimity—Herod needed financial resources. As a client king he was of course liable to an annual tax for the emperor from his own total personal income. In addition he was expected to assist with special subventions and the billeting and provisioning of troops as the occasion arose. In such instances Herod was always at pains to show his loyalty by acts of great generosity, which had to be paid for. On the basis of the income allowed to his successors in their different regions, the annual tax in Herod's kingdom was about one thousand talents. This was comprised of the land and poll taxes for which every citizen was liable as well as sales taxes and those imposed on various municipalities within the realm. In addition Herod was able to raise considerable revenue from his private domains, some of which were inherited, others confiscated from ousted Hasmoneans, and others still the result of imperial bequest. The most important of these private holdings was undoubtedly the gift by Augustus to Herod of the regions of Batanea, Trachonitis, and Auranitis in Transjordan in 23 B.C.E. Zenodorus, the Iturean monarch in the region, had exploited their location to engage in acts of brigandage on the caravans passing from the east. On his death in 20 B.C.E. the rest of his territory, including Banias and the Huleh, also passed to Herod's control. These bequests meant that Herod was able to avail himself of the revenues both from the lands and the trade routes and at the same time take the opportunity to court further the Babylonian Jews, whom he planted in Batanea with a view to successfully policing the region on behalf of Rome.

Intrigue and decline. Though Herod was highly successful in political terms, especially under Augustus, his personal and family life was marked with tragedy. The murder of Mariamme had been traumatic for him and returned to haunt him when his sons by her, Alexander and Aristobulus, who had been brought up in Rome, returned in 17 B.C.E. to be reintegrated into the Herodian family through marriage. At first Herod favored them, but the attitude of the young men as well as the intrigues of Herod's Idumean family, especially his sister Salome and brother Pheroas, turned him against them. Eventually they were both executed following a trial in Berytus in 7 B.C.E. Antipater, Herod's oldest son by his wife Doris of Jerusalem, was now the favored successor, only to be exposed for intriguing with Pheroas against Herod. Antipater was executed in 4 B.C.E. after trial on his return from Rome, where he had sought to ingratiate himself in imperial circles.

Herod was now in serious decline. His first will favored Antipas, his older son by Malthace, a Samaritan, but on his deathbed this was again changed in favor of Archelaus, Antipas's younger brother. Herod died in 4 B.C.E. and was buried in the fortress of Herodium. His final disposition of his kingdom gave rise to bitter disputes among the various brothers. Augustus decided that none of them should have the title king, and instead appointed Archelaus tetrarch of Judea, Antipas tetrarch of Galilee and Perea, and Philip, a son by Cleopatra of Jerusalem, as tetrarch of Gaulanitis, Batanea, and Trachonitis. The fact that there were serious disturbances not just in Jerusalem but in Galilee and Idumea on the death of Herod shows that despite his efforts to placate the Jewish people he had not really won their allegiance.

Herod's style, ambition, and policies had brought about a major social change in Palestine, even in the sphere of Jewish religion. His distrust of the Hasmoneans and their supporters was a constant factor in his dealings with the religious institutions, but ironically it was because of this that his latter years were so unhappy. The opulence of his court life, his manner of treating his enemies (echoed in the story of the slaughter of the children in Bethlehem in Matthew), and his use of the resources of the people for outside benefactions were all contrary to the spirit of the Jewish people and their ethos. The apocryphal work The Assumption of Moses, written shortly after his death, sums up the feelings of pious Jews against Herod. On the other hand, at the height of his career Herod was an important figure in terms of Roman administration in the east. His political astuteness can be seen in his ability to negotiate successfully the transition from supporter of Antony to friend of Augustus. He played an important part in Roman policy, not just in Palestine and the east but also in Asia Minor. This role did help in consolidating the position of the Jews of the diaspora with whom Herod seems to have remained on excellent terms.

ḥesed *see* GEMILUT ḤASADIM

Ḥeshvan second month of the Jewish calendar, corresponding to October/November

Hesychius governor of Palestine, fifth century C.E. From Jerome we learn of a quarrel between Hesychius and the patriarch Gamaliel VI. The governor attempted to connect Gamaliel to a group of conspirators against Theodosius I. The governor bribed Gamaliel's secretary to deliver the patriarch's correspondences to him; however, his plan failed. Gamaliel complained to the emperor, who condemned Hesychius's plot and had him executed. This is one instance in a long battle between the church leaders and the patriarchs. Both John Chrysostom and Jerome remind the emperors of the patriarchs' wealth in order to encourage them to decrease the power of the Jewish leader.

hetaireiai *see* COLLEGIA

Hexapla the six-column work of Origen, which he produced to use as the basis for "correcting" the Septuagint. He thought the translation had become corrupted, and he hoped to restore its original purity with the help of other translations and textual resources. In column 1 was the Hebrew text; column 2 (Secunda) was a transliteration of the Hebrew text in Greek; column 3 was Aquila; column 4 was Symmachus; column 5 was the Septuagint; and column 6 was Theodotion; occasionally, there were seventh and eighth columns. Only a few fragments of the Hexapla have been preserved.

Ḥezekiah **1.** son of Ahaz; king of Judah (r. 715–687 B.C.E.); 2 Kings praises him because of his cultic reforms. In an Assyrian campaign against Judah during Ḥezekiah's reign, the Assyrian general Sennacherib reduced most of Judah but did not capture Jerusalem (701 B.C.E.). 2 Baruch 63 says that God spared Jerusalem because of Ḥezekiah's righteousness and wisdom, contrasted with the wickedness of the Judahile king, Manasseh (chap. 64). The two kings are also contrasted in the Martyrdom of Isaiah 1–5, a Christian work that may have been based on a Jewish legend. In 2 Kings 20:16–19 the Babylonian exile is blamed on Ḥezekiah's political involvement with Babylon.

2. Palestinian amora active in the third century C.E.; the son of Ḥiyya; sometimes referred to as Ḥezekiah beRibbi. Born in Babylonia, he was praised along with his father and brother, Judah, for restoring the Torah (B. Sukkot 20a).

3. Palestinian amora active in Caesaria at the beginning of the fourth century C.E.; a student of Jeremiah

Ḥezekiah b. Ḥiyya *see* ḤEZEKIAH

hidden furnishings and vessels sacred equipment hidden by God in a time of trouble and preserved until the end-time. Legends dealing with this topic are found in both Judean and Samaritan tradition.

According to 2 Maccabees 2:4–8, before the destruction of Jerusalem, Jeremiah hid "the tent and the ark and the altar of incense" in a cave on Mount Nebo (cf. Deut. 32:49), where they would remain "until God gathers his people together again and shows his mercy." A similar story appears in the Paraleipomena of Jeremiah 3:8–19 and 2 Baruch 6:7–9, where the the sacred equipment is consigned to the earth.

According to Samaritan tradition, God, with the help of the Samaritan priest Uzzi, hid the sacred vessels on Mount Gerizim when the priest Eli moved the sanctuary from Gerizim to Shiloh. The vessels will be recovered when the messianic Taheb arrives to initiate the Period of Divine Favor (Rautah).

According to the fourteenth-century chronicler Abul Fath, the priest Eli sought to usurp the priesthood from the descendants of Pinḥas. Eli withdrew to Shiloh and recreated a sanctuary to which he lured many followers. God, angered by Eli's action, vacated the sanctuary at Gerizim and left all in blackness. The high priest Uzzi, who had remained at Gerizim, placed the sacred vestments and vessels of gold and silver into a newly revealed cave, sealed it, and placed an inscription on the seal. Returning the next morning, Uzzi found no trace of the cave nor the inscription. According to the Samaritans, this was the beginning of the age of Divine Disfavor, the Fanutah.

Josephus (*Ant.* 18.4.1–2) tells a story regarding the sacred vessels in New Testament times. An unnamed Samaritan leader summoned an armed group of Samaritans to Mount Gerizim where he promised to show them the hidden sacred vessels. For unknown reasons, perhaps reflecting the form of the tradition in 2 Maccabees, Josephus ascribed the original hiding of the vessels to Moses rather than the priest Uzzi. The group assembled at a nearby village, Tirathaba, and prepared to ascend the mountain. Pilate, the governor, sent a military force to prevent access to the mountain. The troops slaughtered many Samaritans outright and captured others whom they later executed. The Samaritans complained to the Roman authorities and convinced them that they had not assembled to revolt. As a consequence, Pilate was recalled from his post in 36 C.E.

ḥiddush (Heb.) in Rabbinic culture, new point or insight, given as a comment on a classical text, often ingenious and sometimes hairsplitting

Ḥidka Tannaitic authority of the mid-second century C.E., mentioned a few times in Tannaitic statements in the Babylonian Talmud. His name appears in the Jerusalem Talmud (Shabbat 16:3, 15d) as Hundakas.

hieros gamos (Gr., sacred marriage) Sacred marriage is believed by many scholars to have been practiced in Mesopotamia. In this rite, the king enacted the marriage of god and goddess with either the queen or a priestess. Some have suggested that it was also practiced in ancient Israel. Sacred marriage imagery is often used in mystical texts.

hieros logos (Gr., sacred word, or sacred saying) It is used in reference to divine sayings or utterances. Many of the prophetic passages of the Hebrew Bible are oracles placed in the mouth of God and qualify as holy words. Thus, the expression is often the equivalent of "revelation."

high priest *see* PRIESTS, CHIEF

Ḥilfa Palestinian amora of the third century C.E.; referred to in the Babylonian Talmud as Ilfa; a student of Judah the Patriarch and Judah b. Ḥiyya. Because of poverty, Ḥilfa and Yoḥanan determined to go into business. Yoḥanan quickly returned to the academy, becoming its head. Upon his return, Ḥilfa was chastised for forsaking study, despite the fact that he, instead of Yoḥanan, could have headed the academy. In response he proved his complete knowledge of Tannaitic teachings (B. Taanit 21a).

Hillel II son of Judah the Patriarch; a Tannaitic authority and patriarch active in the mid-fourth century C.E. Hillel II is known for fixing the calendar so that determination of the date no longer depended upon the physical sighting of the new moon. He did this in response to the Roman government's limiting of the rights of the patriarch to proclaim new moons.

Hillel and Shammai, Houses of (Beit Hillel and Beit Shammai) academies developed by and existing for some time after the deaths of the legal scholars Hillel and Shammai. These schools of rabbinic thought flourished in the first century C.E. and were known for their foundational role in the development of rabbinic thought. After the destruction of the Jerusalem Temple in 70 C.E., the House of Hillel was known for its ascendancy over the House of Shammai, its chief disputant. The Talmud attributes the acceptance of the Hillelites' views as authoritative to heavenly intervention, in the form of a *bat kol*. The academy at Usha announced that in all matters the law follows the House of Hillel (Y. Berakhot 1:7, 3b). This contrasted with earlier practice, in which the views of the House of Shammai were deemed authoritative.

The Mishnah and Talmud attribute to the House of Hillel the proclivity to take the more lenient position. Mishnah Eduyyot chapter 4 and other talmudic sources illustrate this norm by pointing out the few occasions in which, to the contrary, the Hillelites have the stringent view. According to the Talmud, the tendency of Hillel's academy towards moderation was shaped by the personality of Hillel himself, who is recalled as a kind, gentle, and accommodating person. By contrast, members of the House of Shammai took on the characteristics of their teacher, Shammai, who is know for intemperance and severity (B. Berakhot 60a; B. Shabbat 31a).

Contrary to the talmudic generalization, the Hillelites do not consistently have the lenient position. The rabbinic literature itself identifies fifty instances, 20 percent of the corpus, in which the Hillelites rule stringently. This suggests that the Talmud's generalizing about the Houses and its attributing of populist motives to the House of Hillel, in particular, represent the attempt of later rabbinic Judaism to ascribe favorable traits to the group it promotes with presenting the foundation of rabbinic law.

The disputes of the Houses of Hillel and Shammai comprise the largest corpus of materials cited in the names of authorities active prior to the destruction of the Jerusalem Temple in 70 C.E. These materials are preserved in highly formalized literary constructions, generally consisting of a heading stating the legal problem followed by brief rulings that usually appear as single balanced words or short phrases. Frequently the houses state exactly opposite opinions, often distinguished only by the addition of the word "no" in one of the statements. The view of the House of Shammai always appears first in the more authoritative position. In a number of instances, these basic disputes are followed by debates in which each house explains and argues its position. In these debates, the House of Shammai always has the last word, again suggesting that when the material was first written down, its view was considered authoritative.

Talmudic stories about the Houses of Hillel and Shammai derive from the period of the House of Hillel's ascendancy and offer explanations for the House of Shammai's early authority. These stories refer to the Shammaites' violent behavior and occasional outnumbering of the members of the House of Hillel. It thus appears that the disputes attributed to the houses were given literary form in a period of the House of Shammai's predominance. When the House of Hillel gained greater influence, rabbinic masters produced stories that explained both the earlier and later circumstance. Most important, by positively characterizing Hillel and the academy that followed him, the rabbis offered a strong polemic in favor of their leadership, seen as founded on the views of a populist and sympathetic academic class. *See also* HILLEL THE ELDER.

Hillel the Elder legal scholar in Jerusalem at the time of Herod the Great, in the first century B.C.E.; founder of a school of rabbinic studies and recognized by later Judaism as a central ancestor of rabbinic Judaism. Born in Babylonia, Hillel went to the Land of Israel to study biblical exposition and is credited with developing a system of hermeneutics. He and Shammai are the final pair listed in M. Aḇot's chain of tradition.

In light of Hillel's importance in the history of

rabbinism, much has been written concerning his life and work. Dependent upon statements and stories recorded in rabbinic documents compiled one hundred to six hundred years after Hillel's death, our image of this master may or may not represent the actual individual. Indeed, to the extent that specific biographical materials appear primarily in the latest rabbinic documents, it seems likely that they are the creations of a mature rabbinism interested in fleshing out the image of its earliest forebears.

The earliest materials ascribed to Hillel are legal dicta and disputes, found in the Mishnah and Tosefta. Four areas of concern appear to derive from the earliest layers of rabbinic law and thus may be authentic to Hillel, as follows. (1) *Cultic cleanness*. Hillel argues that once a woman finds that she is menstruating, she is to be deemed unclean retroactively, back to the last point at which she was known to be clean. (2) *Agricultural tithes*. Hillel disputes with Shammai the quantity of dough one may make without incurring liability to dough-offering. (3) *Animal offerings*. In one of the best known of Hillel's legal debates, he argues that the paschal lamb may be sacrificed on the Sabbath. In talmudic sources, Hillel's treatment of this issue leads to his being appointed patriarch. Additionally, Hillel dictates that contrary to Shammai's position, one should lay hands on a whole offering. (4) *Economic rules*. Hillel rules that the buyer of a home within a walled city may not hide from the seller to avoid the right of repurchase mandated by scripture (Lev. 25:29). At the same time, Hillel stands behind a method of circumventing the scripture's Sabbatical remission of debts. Finally, Hillel proscribes trading in futures, which he deems a method of earning forbidden interest.

Unlike the legal statements, which appear in the earliest layer of rabbinic law, moral sayings and apophthegms are attributed to Hillel primarily in a later period, represented by M. A<u>b</u>ot and the midrashic and talmudic literatures. In M. A<u>b</u>ot, Hillel preaches conformity to the mores and rules of the community, condemns gossip, and impugns unfair judging of others. While praising study, piety, and patience, he maligns the body and things of this world.

A marked increase in the telling of stories about Hillel's life and character occurs in the latest documents of the rabbinic corpus. Here, we find a chronology of Hillel's life and anecdotes that reveal his personality. In many of these, Shammai functions as a foil, personalizing negative traits, just as Hillel represents the good. The overall picture is of a pious individual, who, for instance, studied Torah every day even as a poor man, giving half of the little he earned to the doorkeeper at the house of study. Two contradictory stories explain his move from Babylonia to Palestine. One holds that he went as a learned man in order to answer certain questions of law (Y. Pesaḥim 6:1). The other reports that he did not study at all until he arrived in the Land of Israel, at forty years of age. After his arrival, he studied for forty years, served as patriarch for forty years, and, like Moses, died at the age of one hundred twenty.

The rabbinic literature preserves a number of well-known stories that epitomize Hillel's wisdom and approach to Judaism and universal issues regarding the nature of God and humanity. Emblematic is his statement at M. A<u>b</u>ot 1:12, enjoining all Israelites to "be disciples of Aaron, loving peace and pursuing peace, loving people and drawing them near to the Torah." His broader understanding of the significance of Jewish thought and practice is revealed in the story found at B. Shabbat 31a, which recounts Hillel's response to a potential proselyte to Judaism. As is frequently the case in these stories, Hillel's personality—a model for all Israelites—is contrasted with that of his contemporary, Shammai:

There was another case of a Gentile who came before Shammai. He said to him, "Convert me on the stipulation that you teach me the entire Torah while I am standing on one foot." He drove him off with the building cubit that he had in his hand. He came before Hillel: "Convert me." He said to him, "What is hateful to you, to your fellow don't do. That is the entirety of the Torah; everything else is elaboration. So go, study."

ḥillul haShem (Heb.) in Rabbinic Judaism, profanation of God's name; doing something to bring disrepute either on Jews or on Judaism, particularly among non-Jews. Three deeds that one must not do even at the penalty of death are public profanation of the divine name, murder, or a forbidden sexual act.

ḥillul Shabbat (Heb.) in Rabbinic Judaism, the profanation of the Sabbath, for example, by an act of servile labor or a statement of a secular character on the holy day

hipparch Greek name for a commander of a cavalry troop. The term derives from the words *hippos* (horse) and *archon* (ruler or officer). The troop itself was called a *hipparchos* in Greek or an *ala* in Latin (from the word for "wing"). Under the Romans, an *ala* was made up of about five hundred mounted soldiers, commanded by a prefect.

Hippolytus bishop and antipope (rival pope) in Rome in the early third century C.E. (d. 235 C.E.). Although none of his writings is specifically about the Jews, a number of them are still interesting because of a certain Jewish connection. His was one of the first attempts to work out a way of calculating Easter in advance. Up until his time Christians were dependent upon the Jewish calendar if they wished to know beforehand when Easter would fall in a particular year. As it turned out, the sixteen-year cycle that he developed was too inaccurate to be practical. Hippolytus also wrote a world chronicle, which extended from creation to the year 234 C.E., with only a fraction of it still preserved in its original Greek, though the whole is available in a Latin translation. It draws heavily on the Bible and also on Julius Africanus, whose work has been largely lost but which may have depended on Jewish sources. A treatise ascribed to him, *Against the Jews,* is now thought to be a pseudepigraph. He also wrote a commentary on Daniel, making use of the so-called Theodotion text. It is evident that his version of the text had the deuterocanonical additions.

Ḥisda Babylonian amora active in the late third and early fourth centuries C.E.; a student of Rab and, later, Ḥuna, in the academy at Sura, which, after the death of Rab Judah, he headed for ten years. Together, he and Ḥuna are referred to as "the pious ones of Babylonia" (B. Taanit 23b).

Historia Augusta *see* SCRIPTORES HISTORIAE AUGUSTAE

historiography the study or art of writing history. It used to be argued that the first historians were the writers of the Hebrew Bible, such as the authors of the Deuteronomistic history (Deut. to 2 Kings) and the Chronicles. Although some still maintain this, others regard these biblical writings as only historylike, with the title of history proper reserved for the works of the Greek writers from Herodotus on. What is not in doubt is that Jewish history writing reached a quite respectable level of development during the Graeco-Roman period. A number of Jewish histories are known among the Fragmentary Hellenistic Jewish writers. These include Demetrius, who wrote on chronographical matters, and Eupolemus, who covered the kings of Israel and Judah. Both 1 and 2 Maccabees are two, somewhat different, histories of the Maccabean revolt. The main figure is Josephus, however, whose writings represent proper, full-fledged histories, modeled on the Graeco-Roman histories and fully the equal of most of them. Demetrius, Eupolemus, and the first part of Josephus's *Antiquities of the Jews* cover biblical times; however, much of Maccabees and Josephus's *The Jewish War* are devoted to contemporary history, as evidently was the writing of Justus of Tiberias.

history meaningful events, which form a pattern and therefore deliver God's message and judgment. The upshot is that every event, each one seen on its own, must be interpreted on its own terms, not as part of a pattern but as significant in itself. What happens is singular; therefore an event is to be noted and points toward lessons to be drawn for where things are heading and why. If things do not happen at random, they also do not form indifferent patterns of merely secular, social facts. What happens is important because of the meaning contained therein. That meaning is to be discovered and revealed through the narrative of what has happened. Thus for all Judaisms until the Mishnah, the writing of history serves as a form or medium of prophecy. Just as prophecy takes up the interpretation of historical events, so historians retell these events in the frame of prophetic theses. And out of the two—historiography as a mode of mythic reflection, prophecy as a means of mythic construction—emerges a picture of future history, that is, what is going to happen. That picture, framed in terms of visions and supernatural symbols, in the end focuses, as much as do prophecy and history writing, upon the here and now. History consists of a sequence of one-time events, each of them singular, all of them meaningful. These events move from a beginning somewhere to an end at a foreordained goal. History moves toward eschatology, the end of history. The teleology of Israel's life finds its definition in eschatological fulfillment. Eschatology therefore constitutes not a choice within teleology, but the definition of teleology. In other words, a theory of the goal and purpose of things (teleology) is shaped solely by appeal to the account of the end of time (eschatology).

History done in this way, then, sits enthroned as the queen of theological science. Events do not conform to patterns. They form patterns. What happens matters because events bear meaning, constitute history. Now, as is clear, such a conception of mythic and apocalyptic history comes to realization in the writing of history in the prophetic pattern or in the apocalyptic framework, both of them mythic modes of organizing events. We have every right to expect such a view of matters to lead people to write books of one sort rather than another. In the case of Judaism, obviously, we should expect people to write history books that teach lessons or apocalyptic books that through pregnant imagery predict the future and record the direction and end of time. And in antiquity that kind of writing was commonplace among all kinds of groups and characteristic of all sorts of Judaisms but one. And that is the Judaism of the Mishnah. Here we have a Judaism that does not appeal to history as a sequence of one-time events, each of which bears meaning on its own. What the Mishnah has to say about history is quite different, and, consequently, the Mishnah does not conform in any way to the scriptural pattern of representing, and sorting out, events: history, myth, apocalypse.

The first difference appears right at the surface. The Mishnah contains no sustained narrative whatsoever, very few tales, and no large-scale conception of history. It organizes its system in nonhistorical and socially unspecific terms: there is no effort to set its content into a historical context, such as a particular time or place, a circumstance defined by important events, or any of the laws of the Mishnah. Instead of narrative, which, as in Exodus, spills over into case law, the Mishnah gives descriptions of how things are done in general and universally, that is, descriptive laws. Instead of reflection on the meaning and end of history, it constructs a world in which history plays little part. Instead of narratives full of didactic meaning, the Mishnah provides lists of events in order to expose the traits that they share and thus the rules to which they conform. The definitive components of a historical-eschatological system of Judaism—description of events as one-time happenings, analysis of the meaning and end of events, and interpretation of the end and future of singular events—which are commonplace constituents of all other systems of Judaism (including nascent Christianity) of ancient times find no place in the Mishnah's system of Judaism. Thus the Mishnah finds no precedent in prior Israelite writings for its mode of dealing with things that happen. The Mishnah's way of identifying happenings as consequential and describing them, its way of analyzing those events it chooses as bearing meaning, its interpretation of the future to which significant events point—all those in context are unique. In form, the Mishnah represents its system outside of all historical framework. Yet to say that the Mishnah's system is ahistorical could not be more wrong. The Mishnah presents a different kind of history. It revises the inherited conception of history and reshapes that conception to fit into its own system.

When we consider the power of the biblical myth, the force of its eschatological and messianic interpretation of history, the effect of apocalypse, we must find astonishing the capacity of the Mishnah's framers to think in a different way about the same things. As teleology constructed outside the eschatological mode of thought in the setting of the biblical world of ancient Israel, the Mishnah proves amazing. By "history," as the opening discussion makes clear, is meant not merely events, but how events are so organized and narrated as to teach lessons (for the Mishnah's framers, theological lessons; for us, religious, historical, or social lessons), reveal patterns, tell us what we must do and why, and what will happen to us tomorrow. In that context, some events contain richer lessons than others; the destruction of the Temple of Jerusalem teaches more than does a crop failure, and being kidnapped into slavery teaches more than does stubbing one's toe. Furthermore, lessons taught by events—"history" in the didactic sense—follow a progression from trivial and private to consequential and public.

Ḥiyya rabbi at the end of the second century C.E., counted as both a Tanna and an Amora. He appears in disagreement with mishnaic rabbis but is cited in the Talmuds as a talmudic authority. Born near Sura, he moved to the Land of Israel late in life, living in Tiberias and supporting himself as a merchant. Ḥiyya was renowned for his knowledge of mishnaic rules. Zeira (B. Ḥullin 141a–b) states that any Tannaitic ruling not taught in the academies of Ḥiyya or Hoshayah is untrustworthy. He is also known as Ḥiyya Rabbah (Ḥiyya the Elder).

Ḥiyya b. Abba Amoraic authority active in the late third and early fourth centuries C.E. Born in Babylonia of a priestly family, he moved to the Land of Israel, where he was a student of Yoḥanan and Eleazar. B. Berakhot 38b speaks of the precision with which he reviewed and transmitted his teachers' words.

Ḥiyya b. Ashi Babylonian amora, student of Rab, active at Sura in the third century C.E.

Ḥiyya b. Gamda Palestinian amora of the late third and early fourth centuries C.E.; a student of Yose b. Saul. He transmitted sayings in the name of the collegium of sages, understood to represent the last of the Tannaitic authorities (see, e.g., B. Pesaḥim 64a).

Ḥiyya b. Joseph Palestinian amora active in the third century C.E.; born in Babylonia and later a student of Yoḥanan in the Land of Israel. In the talmudic literature, he frequently appears in dispute with Yoḥanan.

Ḥiyya b. Rab eldest and most distinguished of the many sons of Rab; active in the third century C.E.

He did not, however, succeed his father as head of the academy at Sura; that post went instead to his father's student, Ḥuna.

hodaah (Heb., admission) concession by a debtor as to a debt or by a defendant as to facts undertaken formally in court or in a document. If one concedes part of a claim, an oath is required only for the remainder of the claim.

Hodayot (Thanksgiving Hymns, abbreviated as 1QH) the first of the manuscripts of a Hebrew liturgical work found in Cave 1, Qumran, in 1947, and published by E. L. Sukenik in 1954. This manuscript, 1QH, is the largest of the Hodayot manuscripts, consisting of eighteen very damaged columns. Subsequently, two other fragments from the same Cave 1 manuscript were found, 1Q35:1–2, and in 1952 six more Hodayot manuscripts (4QH[a–e], pap4QH[f]) were found in Cave 4. In addition, five other manuscripts were found that resemble the Hodayot in style, but do not overlap with 1QH. The oldest of these Cave 4 manuscripts dates from c. 100 B.C.E.; thus the date of composition for the Hodayot cannot be later than the second half of the second century B.C.E.

The Hodayot (which means "thanksgivings") is a collection of liturgical compositions (hymns) united by style and themes. The majority of the hymns begin with the phrase "I thank thee, O Lord," and continue with expressions of thanksgiving and praise to God. The hymns are heavily dependent on the Hebrew Bible's Book of Psalms in imagery, language, and vocabulary, and they resemble in form those biblical psalms called individual thanksgiving psalms.

The major themes of the Hodayot are salvation and knowledge: "I thank thee, O Lord, for thou hast redeemed my soul from the pit, and from the hell of Abaddon thou hast raised me up to everlasting height" (Vermeš, *DSSE,* 5:1–4); "I thank thee, O Lord, for thou hast enlightened me through thy truth" (Vermeš, *DSSE,* 12:1–2). There is nothing unusual in these themes, but the Hodayot are clearly marked as sectarian by their use of motifs and language that has been recognized in other Qumran compositions as sectarian. Salvation is attained only in the Community, and knowledge is the special brand of knowledge known only to the members of the Community. Further, there is a strong sense of predestination in the hymns: God has chosen those who will receive salvation. A strict dualism emerges in the Hodayot, particularly an ethical dualism; this dualism is vividly portrayed in the metaphor of the two pregnancies (Vermeš, *DSSE,* 4); one pregnancy results in the birth of a "Marvelous Mighty Counselor," the other in wickedness. In addition, the hymns contain a reference to the controversy concerning the proper calendar, a mention of a "plant" that represents the beginning of the sect (cf. DAMASCUS DOCUMENT), and references to "those who seek smooth things" (cf. 4QpeshNah). These clearly mark the composition as sectarian.

Several of the hymns in the Hodayot have been claimed by various scholars as having been written by the Teacher of Righteousness himself. These are hymns 1, 2, 7–11 (numbered according to Vermeš, *DSSE*). These hymns are characterized by an exceptionally strong authorial personality; the author claims to be the recipient of special revelation by God, to be the leader of a community in which he acts as a father, and, especially, to have been persecuted both inside and outside the sect by others who challenge his authority, particularly by the leader of "those who seek smooth things" (identified in 4QpeshNah as the Pharisees). These features may point to authorship by the Teacher, but there is no final proof.

Ḥol haMoed (Heb., intermediate days) the days between the principal holy days of the festivals of Passover and Tabernacles, that is, between the first and second and seventh and eighth days of those festival celebrations. On those days it is permitted to do only light work, not to engage in heavy labor; it is further forbidden to do work on those days that are principally important after the festival season itself.

Holofernes Nebuchadnezzar's Assyrian general, whose siege of Bethulia ends when he is beguiled, besotted, and then beheaded by Judith. His head, returned in a food bag to Bethulia, causes his erstwhile compatriot Achior to faint. Possible models include Sisera (Judg. 4–5), the Seleucid Nicanor (1 Macc. 7:26–50), or the usurper Holophernes of Cappadocia (Diodorus 31.19.2–3).

Holy of Holies the area of the Jerusalem Temple regarded as having the highest degree of holiness, accessible only to the High Priest once a year, on the Day of Atonement. According to rabbinic sources, the Holy of Holies was demarcated by ornate veils (M. Shekalim 8:4–5; M. Yoma 5:1) and contained a stone on which, presumably, the original Ark of the Covenant rested.

Holy of Holies, representation of the depiction of the Ark of the Covenant. After the destruction of the First Temple, the Ark of the Covenant disappeared and the Holy of Holies in the Second Temple was an empty space. Its depiction by the Jews was in two ways, one as an ark and the other as a group of holy objects from the nave, the room in front of the Holy of Holies.

The earliest depiction symbolizing the Holy of Holies is the menorah on the coins of Antigonus in the first century B.C.E. The most complete depiction is the one that was found on two pieces of plaster in the Jewish Quarter, under the floor of a building that was destroyed by the Romans in 70 C.E. The dating of these fragments can be pushed back to the end of the Hasmonean reign or early Herodian period in first century B.C.E. Here the central object is the seven-branched Jewish menorah, with flames on top and a triangle base. To the right there is a description of an object standing on short legs, suggesting the table of showbread. Above it, the left lower corner of another object is visable, suggesting the golden altar. To the left of the menorah is another part of an object, suggesting a stepping stone on which the priest stood while fixing the menorah flames.

All these objects are mentioned in the Bible as placed in the nave, in front of the Holy of Holies, with the menorah on the left (south), the table on the right (north), and the incense altar above and in front of the curtain (Exod. 26:35, 30:6). It is not impossible that this representation decorated the walls for an important priest who wanted to show his holy furniture or, as has been suggested, to teach his young sons.

The table of showbread and the menorah are together in another scene at the Arch of Titus. It is not accidental that the artist chose these two objects. They were the most important holy objects of them all, as described by Josephus in the triumphal parade of Titus in Rome. The table of showbread is depicted again on the coins from the second Jewish revolt. The table stands inside a building that depicts the Temple. There is some similarity between the table on the coin and the fragment from the Jewish Quarter. According to some scholars, the table and the Temple on Simon Bar Kosiba coins express the aspiration for the liberation of the Temple from Gentile hands. From that time on, the table of showbread and the altar disapeared from Jewish art and symbolism and were replaced by the depiction of the Holy Ark.

One of the earliest appearances of the depiction of the ark is in the frescoes of the synagogue at Dura-Europos, dating to the third century C.E. The Holy Ark is seen a few times in its wandering in the desert or in its return from captivity by the Philistines. The ark is depicted as a small Roman-period temple or an aediculae, similar to the Holy Ark in the synagogue itself where the Torah scrolls were placed. Many other mosaic floors from Roman and Byzantine period synagogues were decorated with depictions of the Holy Ark, such as Beth Alpha, Hammath-Tiberias, Beth Shean, and others. The same depiction was found on architectural elements in synagogues such as Chorazin, Peqiin, and others. The Holy Ark at the synagogue was designed in a similar way and was a symbol and a hope for the Holy of Holies at the Temple.

holy ones (from Heb./Aram.: *kadash/kedash,* to be holy, i.e., separate) a major generic term for the inhabitants of the heavenly throneroom, emphasizing the quality that permits them to stand in the presence of the Holy One. 1 Enoch 1–36 and 92–105 emphasize this through their use of the divine title, “the *Great* Holy One.” Along with Daniel 4:13, 17, 1 Enoch also defines a class of these “holy ones” as “watchers and holy ones,” namely, holy ones who serve as “watchers.” According to Daniel 7, the one like a son of man, a high angel possibly to be identified with Michael, receives authority and kingship in behalf of his colleagues, the holy ones, who in turn are the heavenly patrons of Israel. 1 Enoch 39:4–5 attests a tendency to ascribe this angelic name to the righteous of Israel, although the idea of Israel as a holy nation is very old and is logically tied to its identity as a kingdom of priests (i.e., people who serve in God’s presence, Exod. 19:6). Paul capitalizes on the extended use of “holy ones,” repeatedly applying it to the members of his congregations (usually translated “saints” in modern versions). *See also* ANGEL; WATCHERS.

Holy Spirit a term used for the various ways in which God’s power was perceived to be active and influential in the world. It eventually came to be used in Christian thought as a term for one of the three persons in the divine Godhead, expressed in post-New Testament trinitarian creeds as God the Father, God the Son, and God the Holy Spirit. The Hebrew term *ruaḥ,* found nearly 380 times in the Hebrew Bible, basically relates to blowing or breathing and can be translated as either “wind” or “spirit.” When used of the living beings, *ruaḥ* refers to the essence of life and vitality in both human beings and animals that is manifested through movement and breathing (Gen. 2:7, 6:17, 7:15; Num. 16:22; Ezek. 10:17). Just as “spirit” was considered the essence of human life, so analogously the term “spirit” was used of the presence, activity and power of God, that is, characteristics that demonstrate that God is truly a “living God” (Deut. 5:26; Josh. 3:10; 1 Sam. 7:26; Isa. 37:4; Dan. 6:20; Matt. 16:16; Rev. 7:2). The divine spirit is referred to frequently in both the Old Testament as "the Spirit of God" or "the Spirit of the Lord." The phrase "Holy Spirit" itself occurs just three times in the Hebrew Bible (Ps. 51:11; Isa. 63:10, 11). The adjective "holy" (a frequent attribute of God in other contexts; see Lev. 11:44–45, 19:2, 21:8; Josh. 24:19; 1 Sam. 2:2; Isa. 6:3), suggests that God's spirit is a force that moves his people Israel, both individually and collectively, to obey the will of God as revealed through the Torah and the prophets. In several instances, individuals said to be "filled with the Spirit of God" manifest this filling through exceptional wisdom or skill (Exod. 31:3, 35:31). In some of the earlier biblical narratives, particularly Judges and Samuel, the Spirit of God is depicted as a powerful divine force that "comes upon," "falls upon" or "seizes" people, enabling them to win military engagements and perform astonishing feats of strength (Judg. 3:10, 6:34, 11:29, 14:6, 19, 15:14; 1 Sam. 11:6). Related to this is the notion that the Spirit of God was bestowed upon early kings of Israel when they were anointed (1 Sam. 10:1–8, 16:13–14). In the context of the experience of possession trance, the spirit of God is said to "come upon," "fall upon" or "seize" a person who then becomes a prophetic channel for divine revelation (1 Sam. 10:6, 10; 2 Chron. 20:14, 24:20; Ezek. 11:5). There are also references to the experience of vision trance, apparently involving out-of-body experiences, in which prophets are thought to be physically transported to other places by the Spirit of the Lord (1 Kings 18:12; 2 Kings 2:16; Ezek. 37:1; Acts 8:39).

In the New Testament, the terms "Spirit of God" and "Spirit of the Lord" occur only occasionally, while the most common designations are "Spirit" and "Holy Spirit," which are used in a variety of contexts. Early Christians designated the divine agency that spoke through the authors of the Hebrew Bible, such as David and Isaiah, as the Holy Spirit (Matt. 12:36; Acts 1:16, 4:25, 28:25; 2 Pet. 1:21; Heb. 3:7). Similarly, prophetic activity among early Christians is attributed to temporary manifestions of the Holy Spirit (Mark 13:11; Acts 13:2, 4, 21:11; 1 Cor. 12:3; Rev. 2:7, 11, 17). There was a widespread belief that God was present within individual believers, and this continuing divine presence was designated the Holy Spirit (Rom. 5:5, 8:9; 1 Thess. 4:8), the Spirit of God (Rom. 15:19; 1 Cor. 3:16). The conception of the Comforter or Paraclete, a special term for the Holy Spirit in the Gospel of John, as the alter ego of Jesus contributed toward the developing conception of the Holy Spirit as a divine person (John 14:26, 20:22). Baptism is frequently identified as the ritual moment when the Holy Spirit is thought to dwell in the individual (Matt. 3:11; Mark 1:8; Luke 3:16; John 1:33; Eph. 1:3), and it is in this context that the pretrinitarian formula in Matthew 28:19 refers to baptizing converts "in the name of the Father and the Son and the Holy Spirit." *See also* SPIRIT OF TRUTH; SPIRITS, TWO.

homosexuality Leviticus 20:13 names sexual intercourse between men a capital offense (see also Lev. 18:22); lesbian relationships are not mentioned, perhaps because the law code viewed sexual behavior as requiring a penis. Some scholars argue that the law was intended to combat cultic homosexual prostitution, but evidence for such a practice—Deuteronomy 23:17–18 is often cited—has been challenged. The reference to capital punishment might be viewed in the context of other behaviors so condemned by Leviticus: those who curse parents and those who consult mediums. Romans 1:26–27, appealing to nature, extends the condemnation of homosexuality to lesbians; similarly direct is Pseudo-Phocylides 190–192: "Do not transgress with unlawful sex the limits set by nature. For even animals are not pleased by intercourse of male with male. Let women not imitate the sexual role of men." Romans 1:26–27 is frequently explained as a condemnation of pederasty, but the reference to women compromises the thesis. Two other probable references in early Christian writing to homosexual practice, 1 Corinthians 6:9 (to "soft men" or the penetrated partner) and 1 Timothy 1:10 (to the penetrating partner), appear in vice lists. Condemnation of homosexual activities (some specifically designated as anal intercourse between men) appears in 2 Enoch 10 and 34, as well as, extensively, in both the Sibylline Oracles and Pseudo-Phocylides.

The rabbis deemed the biblical prohibition against homosexuality to be one of the Seven Noachide Commandments, which apply to all nations of the earth (B. Sanhedrin 57b–58a). Further, like Romans, rabbinic law explicitly extends to women the biblical prohibition against homosexuality, forbidding sex between women under the general prohibition against following the abhorrent practices of the Canaanites (Sifrei Aḥarei Mot Parashah 8). At the same time, at least as far as Jews were concerned, the rabbis apparently saw homosexuality and lesbianism as almost unthinkable and only infrequently referred to such practices. While Mishnah Kiddushin 4:14, for instance, prohibits two unmarried men from sleeping in the same cloak, Babylonian Talmud Kiddushin 82a rejects the idea that this might lead to homosexual intercourse, citing a statement of Judah that Israelites are not suspect of engaging in sodomy.

Ḥoni the Circle Maker pious wonder-worker of the first century B.C.E. During a period of drought, he drew a circle, stood in it, and refused to move until God produced rain of the exact quantity needed for the crops (M. Taanit 3:8). Josephus (*Ant.* 14:22) reports an abbreviated version of this story and continues by describing fighting between Aristobulus II and Hyrcanus II that led to Ḥoni's murder. B. Taanit 23a, by contrast, says that Ḥoni slept for seventy years, awoke, and, unable to convince anyone that he was Ḥoni, prayed for death and died.

Honorius, Flavius (384–423 C.E.) western Roman emperor (r. 395–423). He was the younger son of Theodosius, the last Roman emperor to rule both the eastern and the western halves of the empire. Theodosius gave his older son, Arcadius, control of the east and Honorius control of the west. Father and sons were united in their unrelenting oppression of paganism and superstition, but eventually both brothers became pawns of advisers and generals. Honorius and the west were controlled by the Vandal Stilicho. The eastern and western empires were in constant conflict with each other and both also were beset by internal struggles. Eutropius, Arcadius's adviser, convinced the Visigothic leader Alaric to go west, and for a decade Alaric attacked the west and forced Honorius to seek security at Ravenna. Stilicho was brought down by an internal plot and assassinated in 408, opening the way for Visigothic victory in the west; the Visigoths sacked Rome in 410. When Honorius's half-sister Placidia was taken captive and was married to Alaric's successor, Athaulh, the union symbolized the barbarization of the western government. Amid much turmoil, Honorius did not oppose those with real power and thus survived and died from natural causes in 423.

Horace (65–8 B.C.E.) Roman poet of the Augustan age. He wrote a large number of poetic works in his collections, *Satires* and *Letters*. He makes some brief references to Jews. In one satire, he mentions that some Romans will not do business on the "thirtieth day, the Sabbath" because of the Jews. Although the exact meaning of this phrase is uncertain, it suggests that some Romans respected Jewish customs, even if in a superstitious manner. Horace attests the fact of conversion to Judaism and even proselytization when he states that his band of poets would, "like the Jews," make the reader one of their number.

Horayot Mishnah tractate on the problem of collective sin, that is, erroneous decisions made by the instruments of government, as distinct from those made by individuals. Collective expiation of guilt is effected through public institutions of government and instruction; the explication is focused on Leviticus 4. The tractate defines the offering presented because of an erroneous decision by a court (chap. 1); the offering presented by a high priest who has unwittingly done that which is contrary to the commandments of the Torah; the ruler (chap. 2), the individual, the anointed priest, and the community (chaps. 2–3) and offerings required for inadvertent sin from each class.

Horeb, Mount an unidentified mountain. By the Second Temple period, Mount Horeb was equated with Mount Sinai, and the two names were used synonymously for the mountain of God. This assimilation of the two mountains to one another reflects a harmonization of those Pentateuchal traditions that use Horeb exclusively with those that use Horeb and Sinai indiscriminately.

From the Persian period onward, Horeb and Sinai are often treated as two different names for the same mountain of God on which Moses received the Ten Commandments and at which the Deity made the covenant with the Israelites. Ezra received his order from YHWH, who was on Horeb, to go to the Israelites. At the beginning of the second century B.C.E., Ben Sira takes a negative view of the events at the sacred mountain. He uses parallelism to suggest that the Israelites were rebuked at Sinai and were informed of their punishment at Horeb. Although this would seem to suggest he viewed the two mountains as different, the parallelism in the verse indicates that he may have thought of them as one and the same. But not everyone treated them as identical. As late as the fourth century C.E., Eusebius suggested that Sinai and Horeb were two different mountains.

Hormizd I Sassanid emperor (r. 272–273 C.E.); also known as Hormizd-Ardashir. In 262 C.E., Shapur I appointed him king of Armenia. The only thing that is certain about his rule is that he waged a war against the Sogians. He seems to have appointed Katir as high priest of Ohrmazda, beginning the latter's rise to power and decreasing Mani's support among the royal house. However, Hormizd did not prevent Mani from preaching in public. His name also appears as Ohrmazda, and on his coins, images of Mithra and Anahita are replaced by images of Ohrmazda.

Hormizd II Sassanid emperor (r. 301–309 C.E.). His father, Naresh, abdicated in his favor in 301. By the end of his reign, the Romans were entrenched in Armenia and in command of the Adiabenian highlands, the most direct invasion route into central Babylonia. There are no reports of Christian martyrdoms, and this appears to have been a period of stability and peace for the Church. There are no records of anti-Jewish acts during his reign. One source claims that he supported the Mazdean clergy, and another states that he did not listen to the magi.

Hormizd III Sassanid emperor (r. 457–459 C.E.). Upon the death of his father, Yazdagird II, Hormizd III had to contend with Peroz for the throne. Hormizd was favored by his father, and he ruled from Ctesiphon, while Peroz was made governor of Seistan. Peroz sought help from the Hephtalites, and with their help, he eventually defeated and captured Hormizd, won over his troops, and in 459 was established at Ctesiphon.

Hormizd IV Sassanid emperor (r. 579–590 C.E.). He declined to follow the magi's wishes that he persecute the Jews and the Christians. Like his father, he believed that a large empire should allow diversity of opinions and ways of living. He engaged in wars against Rome, the Arabs, and the Turks. In 588, his general, Bahram, suffered a major defeat at Lazica. Hormizd's public insult to his general caused the latter to revolt against the emperor. Eventually, Bahram, supported by a palace revolt, deposed Hormizd in 590 in favor of his son, Khusro II.

horn In addition to the literal meaning of a projection from an animal's head, in the Hebrew Bible, "horn" (Heb.: *keren*) can denote an object that holds liquids, especially oil for anointing (cf. 1 Sam. 16:13; 1 Kings 1:39); a trumpet (cf. Josh. 6:5); or one of the projections from the corners of the altar (Lev. 4:7, 18). The word is also used figuratively for power or salvation, particularly in such phrases as "horn of salvation" (Ps. 18:2) and "to raise one's horn" (Sir. 47:11), and it can refer to the Davidic king (Ezek. 29:21; Ps. 132:17). In apocalyptic literature especially, this meaning can be extended to symbolize a ruler or mythic being (cf. Dan. 7:7–8; Rev. 5:6, 12:3). *See also* SHOFAR.

horoscope astrological chart for an individual, found among the Jews from an early time. Horoscopes are already attested at Qumran at the turn of the era. A number have been found in the Cairo Geniza. Astrology clearly played an important part in the lives of Jews, as in the lives of the peoples around them.

Horvat Amudim (or Horvat ha-Amudim; Arab.: Umm el-Amud) ancient synagogue site on a raised plateau at the east end of the Beth Netofa Valley in Lower Galilee. The site is situated about 15 kilometers northwest of Tiberias. The synagogue is about 22.5 meters by 14 meters, with the inner space divided into a nave and two aisles by two rows of columns, with an extra row of columns across the back. Entry into the prayer space was through three entries in the narrow end, a characteristic of a basilica synagogue building. Stone benches were built against the walls on three sides. An Aramaic inscription on a stone found at the site reads as follows: "Yoezer the cantor and Simeon his brother made this gate of the Lord of Heaven." Some think that "gate" refers to the Torah shrine. The interior was furnished with a mosaic floor, in the northwestern side of which was a badly damaged Aramaic inscription. Enough was found to reconstruct the reading: "Be remembered for good . . . the son of Tanhum, who made this pavement of mosaic and roof. May he be blessed. Amen. Selah." Other synagogue art from the site includes a lion in relief from a lintel, probably one of a pair. Coins and pottery from the excavation confirm that the building was built about 300 C.E. and served the congregation during the fourth century C.E.

Horvat Kishor Synagogue Byzantine synagogue site in the southern Judean Shephelah, which is the line of low hills running north and south and lying between the coastal plain and the central Judean Hill country. The site is a large village of about 32 acres in extent with a cemetery. The only remains of the synagogue that have been identified are a large lintel of the fourth or fifth century C.E. In the center of the lintel in low relief stands a seven-branched menorah with hanging appendages at either end of the horizontal crossbar. To the right a vertical vine meander in low relief serves as decoration.

Horvat Rimmon Synagogue synagogue site in southwestern Judea. The earliest village was built about 100 B.C.E. and lasted to about 150 C.E. During the third century, there was a new Jewish population at the site who built a synagogue. The prayer hall of the building was divided into spaces by columns. This synagogue was entered from its long north wall and is therefore termed a broad-house synagogue. A niche in the northeast corner of the inner space was interpreted by the excavators as a room for the Torah shrine. During the fifth and sixth centuries C.E., this synagogue was extensively remodeled and enlarged. Two hoards of gold coins were found beneath the floor. One hoard dated to the fourth century and the second hoard dated to the sixth century C.E. The new synagogue was a basilica, entered at the narrow end; the interior was divided into a nave and two side aisles by two rows of columns. This synagogue was renovated at the end of the sixth century C.E. The prayer hall featured a finely paved interior. Two fragments of a bronze menorah were found in this synagogue. Another menorah was engraved into the stone floor close to some geometric rosettes.

Horvat Summaqa Synagogue (or Khirbet Summaqa) synagogue site on top of Mount Carmel, south of the modern village of Daliyyat el-Karmil. A synagogue was built here in the third century. The building was about 23.89 meters long by 14.8 meters wide on the interior. This inner space was divided by two rows of columns into a nave and two side aisles. An exterior narthex at the facade, which is on the north end of a north-south building, stood in front of three doorways that brought pedestrian traffic into the prayer space from the narrow lane that fronted the synagogue. This synagogue was deliberately destroyed during the late fourth or early fifth century C.E. The synagogue was rebuilt and renovated soon after its destruction. The floor was paved with a layer of thick, white plaster. The columns were replaced, which suggests that the roof had come down in the general destruction. Further renovations were carried out in the early seventh century C.E. just prior to the Arab invasion.

hosanna From the Hebrew imperative *hosa* (save) plus *na* (please/now), the expression was used in particular during Sukkot celebrations (Ps. 118:25). At Jesus' entry into Jerusalem, the Gospels echo Psalms 118:25–26 and associate "hosanna" with a royal or Davidic hope (Matt. 21:9, 15; Mark 11:9–10; Luke 19:38; John 12:13).

Hosea, Targum to *see* TARGUM TO THE PROPHETS

Hosea Commentary title of two fragmentary manuscripts (A and B) of a continuous *pesher* on the Book of Hosea that were found in Cave 4, Qumran, in 1952 and published by J. M. Allegro in *DJD* V; the title is abbreviated as 4QpHos. The commentary exhibits the *pesher* form: a citation of the biblical verse, followed by the phrase "its interpretation is," continued by a sectarian exegesis focusing on contemporary events. The present two manuscripts preserve Hosea 2:8–12, in which the interpretation understands the unfaithful wife to be the Jewish people, and 5:13–15 and 6:7, where the "furious young lion" appears. This figure has been identified in the Nahum Commentary as Alexander Jannaeus (r. 103–76 B.C.E.); here he is also called the "last Priest" who will strike "Ephraim" (identified as the Pharisees in the Nahum Commentary). If Jannaeus is the "last" priest, this may call for a composition date of the early first century B.C.E. for the Hosea Commentary.

Hoshanna Rabbah (The Great Hoshanna) the seventh day of Sukkot, marked especially by prayers for rain, circumambulations of the sanctuary (originally around the ancient temple's altar), cries for God's salvation (Hoshanna = Please save!), and beating the ground with willow branches (a natural symbol for rain, since willows grow by the water and droop as if heavy with rain).

Hoshaya I Palestinian amora active in the first half of the second century C.E.; referred to as Hoshayah Rabbah. The son of Ḥama, he was born in the south of the Land of Israel, where he studied with Bar Kappara and Ḥiyya. Later, he was in Caesaria (Y. Terumot 10:2, 47a). He was known for his collection of Tannaitic statements (Y. Horayot 3:5, 47d), which led Zeira (B. Ḥullin 141a–b) to state that any Tannaitic ruling not taught in the academies of Hoshayah or Ḥiyya was not trustworthy.

Hoshaya II scholar; a contemporary of Abbahu (late 3d c. C.E.); never ordained and thus referred to as "colleague of the rabbis." He is often mentioned together with Ḥanina, whose brother he may have been. Both are called priests of the house of Eli. Born in Babylonia, Hoshayah II was a student of Yoḥanan at Tiberias. A shoemaker, he married a daughter of Samuel b. Isaac.

Hoshaya Rabbah *see* HOSHAYA I

hospitality Providing comfort to visitors is esteemed throughout the ancient literature (Gen. 24; Sir. 29:25; Rom. 12:13; 1 Tim. 3:2; 1 Pet. 4:9; Heb. 13:2). Models include Job (Test. Job 10) and the women in his household (Test. Job 7); Abraham (Gen. 18 is extensively developed in Test. Abr. such that Abraham offers hospitality to Death; Test. Isaac 7); God (Ps. 23, 104; on the eschatological banquet, 1 Enoch 62:14); Jesus, who is depicted, especially by Luke, as participating in hospitality offered by others (Zacchaeus, Simon the Pharisee, Martha, and Mary) and as offering hospitality through meals and service (e.g., footwashing [John 13]); and even Pentephres, the Egyptian priest (Jos. Asen. 7).

House of Hillel *see* HILLEL AND SHAMMAI, HOUSES OF

House of Shammai *see* HILLEL AND SHAMMAI, HOUSES OF

house of study *see* SCHOOL

Huldah a site in the Judean coastal plain, 31 kilometers west of Jerusalem. A two-room building with mosaic floor was found in 1953; it at first appeared to be a synagogue, but now the northern of the two rooms is understood to have been used to store olive oil or wine. The north room has two niches in each of its other three walls, and the remains of storage jars littered the floor, which was paved with white mosaics. The south room, also paved with white mosaics, contained two Greek inscriptions. The first, in a panel outlined in black, shows on the right side a seven-branched menorah and shofar (ram's horn). To the left one sees an incense shovel, etrog (citron), and lulab (palm branch). Nested among these ritual objects one reads in Greek, "Blessing to the People." East of this panel is a square frame surrounding a circular panel in which is written in Greek, "Good luck to Eustochios and Hesychios and Evagrios, the founders." Left of center in the circular room is a circular pool 2.5 meters in diameter with plastered sides and three steps leading down into it. This circular pool is connected by a lead pipe to a second, square pool 1.1 meters square and paved with white mosaics. The south room is entered from the south, that is, from the outside, but the north room has no entry and is separated from the south room by a thin (30 cm. thick) wall or barrier, which is not pierced by a door. In general, the south room resembles a community ritual bath.

ḥullin (Heb.) secular produce for everyday use

Ḥullin Mishnah tractate devoted to the slaughter of secular, or noncultic, animals for everyday use and the preparation and use of meat for the table of the ordinary Israelite. Chapters 1–4 deal with the rules of slaughter of animals; then come other food rules: the law against slaughtering the dam and its young on one day (Lev. 22:28); the requirement to cover up the blood of a slaughtered beast; the taboo against the sciatic nerve (Gen. 32:32); the taboo against cooking meat with milk (Exod. 23:19, 34:26; Deut. 12:21); food uncleanness; gifts that are given to the priest, which include parts of an animal that has been slaughtered (Deut. 18:4) and the first fleece (Deut. 18:4); and letting the dam go from the nest when taking the young (Deut. 22:6–7). The Talmud of Babylonia provides a major commentary to this tractate.

ḥullin metukanim (Heb.) in Rabbinic Judaism, fully tithed produce that is not consecrated and is available for ordinary use

human sacrifice *see* CANNIBALISM, JEWS ACCUSED OF

Ḥuna I Babylonian exilarch and scholar; a contemporary of Judah the Patriarch, at the close of the Tannaitic period, the late second century C.E. Judah refers to Ḥuna's superior genealogy and, hence, authority (Gen. Rabbah 33:3). Ḥuna's remains were taken to the Land of Israel for burial.

Ḥuna II without a patronymic, generally a Babylonian amora of the late third century C.E., mentioned frequently in the Babylonian Talmud and often in the Palestinian Talmud as well. A student of Rab̲, Ḥuna was one of the most influential talmudic rabbis, represented in both homiletical and legal statements and through numerous details preserved about his life. After the deaths of Rab̲ and Samuel, Ḥuna served for forty years as head of the academy at Sura. Like Ḥuna I, and as had become customary, he was buried in the Land of Israel.

Huna b. Ab̲in fourth-century-C.E. Palestinian amora. Born in Babylonia, he studied with Joseph prior to emigrating to the Land of Israel (see Y. Rosh Hashanah 2:2, 58a), where he studied with Jeremiah. His homiletical and legal statements are found frequently in Palestinian midrashic documents and the Jerusalem Talmud. He is also known as Ḥunya or Neḥunya b. Ab̲in.

Ḥuna b. Ḥiyya Babylonian amora of the late third and early fourth centuries C.E. He succeeded Judah b. Ezekiel as head of the academy at Pumbedita.

Ḥuna b. Joshua fourth-century-C.E. Babylonian amora; together with Pappa, a disciple of Abayye and Raba. He served as head of the academy founded by Pappa at Naresh.

Ḥuna b. Nathan Babylonian amora and exilarch of the late fourth and early fifth centuries C.E.; a pupil of Pappa. He was esteemed for combining learning and high office (B. Gittin 59a). B. Zebaḥim 19a reports his high position in the court of Yazdegerd I, the Persian king.

Hundakas *see* ḤIDKA

Ḥunya b. Ab̲in *see* ḤUNA B. AB̲IN

ḥuppah bridal canopy; generally: marriage rite

Huzal town between Nehardea and Sura, known for its synagogue, reported to have been built by the exiles from Judah at the time of the First Temple and in which the divine presence dwelled (B. Megillah 29a)

Hyksos a group of "foreigners" who conquered Egypt in the second millennium B.C.E. Josephus refers to them in *Against Apion,* when trying to refute the anti-Jewish statements of Apion, from whom he probably took his information. From Egyptian sources, we know of such a group who established rule over Egypt from about 1750 to 1550 B.C.E. Their name probably means "foreigners" (rather than "shepherd kings," as Josephus says), though they may have long lived on the margins of Egyptian society. They preceded the Israelite settlement in Palestine by many centuries and probably had no connection with the Israelites.

Hymn Scroll *see* HODAYOT

Hyp. *see* HYPOTHETICA

hyparchy in the Graeco-Roman world, an administrative region governed by a hyparch. Often it seems to have been more or less equivalent to a province, that is, a subdivision of a kingdom or empire. Nevertheless, the exact size is not specific and seems to have varied considerably from time to time and place to place.

Hyperberetaios name of a Macedonian month; appears in a number of Jewish sources, such as the writings of Josephus. Unfortunately, there was not a uniform usage; sometimes it corresponded to the Hebrew month of Elul (August/September) and sometimes to the month of Tishrei (September/October).

hypocrite from the Greek term for an actor or one who performs behind a mask, "hypocrite" denotes one who advocates one practice but engages in another. The Psalms of Solomon 4:1–25 pray that God will "remove from the devout those who live in hypocrisy." The charge is leveled in the Gospel tradition against those—especially Pharisees—who practice external rituals but not internal repentance (see especially Matt. 23). The Matthean usage extends the connotations of the epithet to self-righteousness and general evil. Paul charges Jewish Christians such as Peter and Barnabas with hypocrisy (Gal. 2:13) because they began to insist on retaining practices such as dietary regulations in light of pressure from the "circumcision party." The charge is not uncommon in ancient polemic; therefore, one must exercise caution in reading the label "hypocrite" as having historical accuracy.

hypostasis the treating of an abstract quality as if it were a person or being. Thus, it is the next step above personification. For example, in the works of writers such as Philo of Alexandria, attributes of God (e.g., Wisdom and the Logos) might be treated as if they were actually separate beings.

Hypothetica the treatise, by Philo of Alexandria, that is also known as *Apologia pro Iudaeis (Defense of the Jews)*; its title is abbreviated as *Hyp.* Only a portion of this work is preserved in the writings of Eusebius, but one of the extant extracts discusses the laws given in the "Mosaic constitution" (the ideal community envisaged in the Mosaic legislation), while the other treats the Essenes.

Hypsistarians Jewish sect on the Bosphorus in the first century C.E. and found in Asia Minor through the third century C.E.; known from Christian sources of the third and fourth century C.E. Hypsistarians worshipped "the High and Almighty One" and observed some dietary restrictions and the Sabbath. They also followed certain pagan traditions and beliefs and did not practice circumcision.

Hypsistos (Gr., most high) In the Second Temple period, descriptive titles rather than the names of God became common, so that instead of YHWH or Shaddai, one might say "God of Heaven" or "Most High." The latter appeared as Hypsistos in Greek writings, where it sometimes translated the Hebrew Elyon of the Hebrew Bible. *See also* GOD, NAMES OF.

Hyrcania city in Persia, south of the Caspian Sea. Near the end of the Persian period (mid-fourth century B.C.E.) some Jews from around Jericho were deported to Hyrcania.

Hyrcanus II high priest, son of Alexander Jannaeus and Alexandra. Hyrcanus II served as high priest during the rule of his mother, Alexandra (r. 76–67 B.C.E.). After her death, he was displaced by his brother, Antigonus II, who took over the high priesthood and government. Prompted by Antipater the Idumean, father of King Herod the Great, Hyrcanus, with the help of Aretas, the Nabatean king, began a civil war against his brother. In 63 C.E. Pompey, the Roman general who had brought large areas of Asia Minor and Syria under Roman control, intervened. He besieged Antigonus, conquered Jerusalem, and reinstalled Hyrcanus as high priest. Jewish territory, however, was diminished and ruled directly by a Roman governor. In 40 B.C.E., the Parthians invaded Palestine, briefly reinstated Antigonus as ruler, mutilated Hyrcanus so he could no longer serve as high priest, and took him prisoner to Parthia. When Herod regained rule of Palestine in 37, Hyrcanus was returned. In 31 B.C.E., Herod had him killed to remove any possible claim against his throne.

Hyrcanus the Tobiad youngest son of Joseph of the Tobiad family; nephew of Onias II, the high priest. According to Josephus (*Ant.* 12.186–236), he supported the pro-Ptolemaic faction in Jerusalem during the reign of Seleucus IV (187–175 B.C.E.), but was forced to retire to the family home at Arak el-Emir, east of the Jordan, where he committed suicide. His property was confiscated by Antiochus IV Epiphanes, who succeeded Seleucus. 2 Maccabees 3:11 records that he deposited a large sum of money in the Jerusalem Temple treasury.

hyssop a small, aromatic plant, growing on or near walls (1 Kings 4:33); burned with the red heifer (Num. 19:6) and used in other purification rituals (see, e.g., Lev. 14:4ff.; Exod. 12:22). Early rabbinic authorities enumerated a number of different types of hyssop (M. Negaim 14:6) and detailed the correct use of this plant in ritual purification (M. Parah 11–12).

Hystaspes, Oracle of an oracle preserved in the name of an ancient Persian sage that circulated around the beginning of the common era. It is known only in a few quotations. It is commonly thought to have originated in ancient Persia and has a number of parallels with the Persian apocalyptic work Bahman Yasht; however, some scholars believe that it was actually Jewish in origin. It seems to have been a type of anti-Greek oracle, which served as an expression of resistance to Hellenization. It predicts the overthrow of the Roman Empire, and it seems to have used a six-thousand-year scheme of human history. *See also* WORLD YEAR.

I Am one of several biblical names for God; considered by some scholars to be the derivation of YHWH (the Tetragrammaton). In Exodus 3:14, God tells Moses, "I am who I am (*ehyeh asher ehyeh*)," and instructs him to say to the people of Israel, "I am (*ehyeh*) has sent me to you." Exodus 3:15 subsequently uses the name YHWH as an equivalent of "I Am" when God tells Moses, "Thus you shall say to the Israelites, 'The Lord (YHWH) . . . has sent me to you.'"

YHWH is the most important of several Hebrew names for God. The Bible provides two different accounts of its revelation to humankind. In Genesis 4:26, people begin calling God by this name in the time of Enosh. Exodus 6:2, however, introduces the name only after Moses has been rebuffed initially by Pharaoh. Although it is not certain when the Tetragrammaton ceased to be pronounced (Ecclus. 50:18–21 may describe the use of this name), ultimately lack of use resulted in uncertainty over the tradition of vowel sounds in the name and hence in its meaning. Instead of pronouncing the name itself, the word *adonai* (lord) was substituted for it. (Hence the modern "Jehovah" equals the erroneous combination of the vowel sounds for *adonai* with the Hebrew letters of the Tetragrammaton.) In some of the Qumran scrolls, this name is even written in paleo-Hebrew script rather than the more usual Aramaic square letters.

The connection with the "I Am" of Exodus 3:14 suggests that the Tetragrammaton may derive from the verb "to be" (although some commentators have suggested other verbs). Of those who derive the name from the verb "to be," some conclude that it means "He who is" (or, will be). Others see a causative meaning, "He who causes to be." Each of these possibilities emphasizes an important aspect of God's character in the Bible: one, his continual presence; the other, his status as creator.

In the Septuagint, the translator of Exodus 3:14 understood "I am who I am" to mean "I am the one who exists" (*ho ōn*). In other places in the Jewish Bible, however, God uses the phrase "I am" or "I am He" (*ani* or *anoki hu*) of Himself. In these cases the Greek translators, especially the translator of Isaiah, frequently rendered it in Greek as *ego eimi*. This phrase, which literally means "I am," can be understood in Greek not only as a claim about the oneness and existence of God, but also as a divine apellation. Thus, in Isaiah 43.25, the Hebrew, "I, I am He (*anoki, anoki hu*) who wipes away your sins for my sake" can easily be understood in its Greek translation as "I am, *I Am* (*ego eimi, ego eimi*), who wipes away your sins."

The appellative use of *ego eimi* in Second Isaiah, perhaps together with rabbinic uses of *ani hu* (I am; I am He) as a name, greatly influenced the christology of the Gospel of John, in which "I am" frequently comes from the lips of Jesus as a self-designation (6:35, 51; 8:24, 28, 58; 10:7, 9, 11, 14; 11:25; 14:6; 15:1, 5). For the evangelist, these "I am" sayings deliberately play on the connection with the divine name in the Jewish Bible, and he uses the phrase to make the important christological claim that Jesus is the revelation and manifestation of God to the world. This interpretation of Jesus is particularly clear in the "absolute" uses of *ego eimi,* that is, those passages where the phrase occurs with no predicate (John 8:24, 28, 58; 13:19). That the evangelist intends the connection is made even clearer by the reactions he attributes to the hearers of Jesus' statements. In 8:58, after Jesus claims, "before Abraham was, I am," the people try to stone him, undoubtedly because they understood the claim being made.

Even though the Fourth Gospel makes the most sophisticated use of the "I am" formula in the New Testament, several passages in the synoptic Gospels also have *ego eimi* emanating from Jesus' lips (Matt. 14:27; Mark 13:6; 14:62). These cases, however, are more difficult to assess and may simply mean "it is I" without christological overtones. *See also* GOD, NAMES OF.

Iao Greek name for the Jewish God, found in some literary sources and frequently in magical inscriptions. It probably represents a transliteration of the name Yahweh or perhaps some shortened form of it. The name is important because the vocalization of the Tetragrammaton (YHWH) was not preserved in the Masoretic text.

Ibn Ezra Synagogue *see* CAIRO GENIZA

Idi b. Abin I Babylonian amora active in the mid-third century C.E. at Shekanzib (B. Yebamot 85a; alternative reading: Hintzabu; a student of Ḥisda

Idi b. Abin II Babylonian amora; a student of Pappa; head of the academy at Sura, 432–452 C.E.

idolatry worship of the representation (image) of a god. The practice is forbidden in law (Exod. 20:4–5, 23; 34:17; Lev. 19:4; Deut. 4:15–18) and condemned in prophecy (Isa. 40:18–20, 42:17, 44:9–20, 45:16–20, 46:1–7; Jer. 10:3–5). However, not all images were proscribed by all Jews, as the cherubim in the Temple (Exod. 26:1, 36:8; 1 Kings 6:29; 2 Chron. 3:10–14) as well as the murals of Dura-Europos and the mosaics of Beth Alpha indicate. Less an actual threat in the postexilic period, idolatry came to represent any non-Jewish worship, and "idolater" became a synonym for Gentile. The Additions to Daniel, recounting the tales of Bel and the Snake, mocks idol worship as does the Apocalypse of Abraham, which uses the impotence of idols to underly Abraham's monotheism; Joseph and Asenath characterizes its heroine as one who "blesses with her mouth dead and dumb idols" (8:5), which she will then explicitly repudiate. Other condemnations include 1 Enoch 99; 3 Enoch 5; the Letter of Jeremiah; passages in Pseudo-Phocylides; The Book of Biblical Antiquities; Lives of the Prophets; 2 Enoch; the Sibylline Oracles; the Testament of Job; the Testament of Moses; the Testament of Solomon; and the Testaments of the Twelve Patriarchs, among others. The gentile writers Strabo and Varro praised the Jews for their imageless cult.

Acts 15:29 forbids eating meat offered to idols; Paul permits it, but advises the Corinthians to refrain in case the weaker member of the congregation believes the action to indicate idolatry (1 Cor. 8:7–13; 10:6–14). Paul fully condemns idolatry itself, which he associates with what he views to be unnatural sexual behavior (Rom. 1:22–27). Colossians 3:5 makes clear that idolatry is to be equated with covetousness: it distracts an individual from focus on God by setting up another object of worship.

Rabbinic Judaism deems idolatry to be one of three cardinal sins (along with deviant sexual practice and murder) in which one may not engage even at the cost of his or her own life. So central to Jewish belief was the rejection of foreign gods that rabbinic texts equate the renunciation of idolatry with an acknowledgment of the whole Torah and its acceptance with a denial of the entirety of God's teachings (B. Horayot 8a; B. Ḥullin 5a; Sifre Deut. 54). The rejection of idolatry was such a central distinguishing mark between Jew and non-Jew that a Gentile who renounced idolatry could be called a Jew (B. Megillah 13a).

While the prohibition against idolatry was central to all Jewish ideology, the rabbis did not treat idol worship as a real and immediate threat in their own day. They understood idolatry to have been entirely uprooted from the Jewish people; therefore, it was no longer the peril it had been in the First Temple period (Song Rabbah 7:14). While the rabbis included the prohibition against idolatry in the Seven Noachide Commandments, which apply to all nations of the earth, they were tolerant towards the idolatrous practices of non-Jews, whom they held acted out of ignorance (Y. Shabbat 16:9, 15c).

Accordingly, rather than focusing upon stemming Jewish acceptance of pagan gods, the rabbinic treatment of idolatry concerns the broader question of how to assure in their contact with non-Jews that Jews do not inadvertently participate in or contribute to idol worship. This is accomplished by placing strict controls upon all contact between Jew and Gentile. Within three days of gentile festivals, Jews are forbidden from having contact with Gentiles or selling them objects that might be used in idol worship (M. Abodah Zarah

1:1–2, 5). Before a pagan festival, even repaying money owed to a Gentile is forbidden, lest the money be used to support idol worship. The rabbis similarly deal with the problem of Israelite travel to and business in cities that contain idols. Business may not be done in an area containing an idol, and one is prohibited from using a road that leads to that city alone. Use of a road that also leads to other places is allowed (M. Abodah Zarah 1:4). As before, the rabbis' concern is preventing a Jew from inadvertently supporting idol worship or even creating an impression that he is himself involved in idolatry.

The rabbinic literature contains numerous references to specific deities, idolatrous rites, and products used in idol worship. Some actual practices and many familiar deities are mentioned, e.g., Peor, Aphrodite, Mercurius, and Asherah. Much of what is mentioned, however, seems idiosyncratic to the rabbinic understanding of pagan rites. Included in this category are M. Abodah Zarah's long lists of foods and animal products that may not be sold to or bought from a Gentile, lest they are to be used in idolatry.

The Talmud makes no specific mention of Israelites' obligation to destroy objects of idol worship or actively to prevent Gentiles from engaging in their worship. The Mishnah, however, provides a benediction to be recited when one sees a place in the Land of Israel in which idols previously were worshiped: "Blessed is he who uprooted idolatry from our land" (M. Berakhot 9:1).

Idumea a Second Temple geographical designation that included the southern Judean hills and the northern Negeb, extending from the coastal cities to the Dead Sea. Idumea was populated by Edomites, Nabateans, Jews, and other peoples. John Hyrcanus conquered Idumea in 129 B.C.E. and forced the population to be circumcised. Antipater the Idumean and his son, Herod the Great, eventually gained power over the last of the Hasmoneans and ruled all Jewish territory. During the Roman period, Idumea was a part of the province of Judea. Idumean forces participated in the revolt against Rome in 66 C.E.

Ifra Hormizd (early 4th c. C.E.) identified in the Babylonian Talmud as Shapur II's mother. The name does not appear in Persian sources. The Talmud records several encounters between her and the rabbis. Once she sent some denarii to Rabbi Joseph for his performance of "a great commandment." The rabbis concluded that the money should be used for redeeming captives from the Gentiles. In another passage, Rabbi Ammi, a Palestinian sage, refused a gift from her, while Raba accepted it in order to keep peace with the government. Eventually, Raba gave the gift to the gentile poor. A third account relates that she sent an animal sacrifice to Raba. In a fourth narrative she sent different types of blood to the same sage, which he successfully identified, testifying to the queen mother's recognition of the rabbis' extraordinary powers. In a fifth passage, she intervened when Shapur planned to punish Raba, whose court had executed a Jew for having intercourse with a gentile woman. The story claims that Ifra Hormizd acknowledged the rabbis' supernatural powers and the effectiveness of their prayers for rain. These accounts indicate that the rabbis believed that they had a friend in the Persian court in the person of the queen mother.

ignorant *see* AM HAARETZ

Ilai **1.** Tannaitic authority of the first century C.E.; a student of Eliezer b. Hyrcanus (T. Zebaḥim 2:17); the father of Judah b. Ilai. In Amoraic literature, he is sometimes referred to as Ilai the Elder.

2. Palestinian amora active at the beginning of the fourth century C.E.; a student of Yoḥanan in Tiberias. He was the teacher of Jonah and Yose.

Ilfa *see* ḤILFA

image of God a notion derived from Genesis 1:26 widely used in the Hellenistic period. Genesis affirms that human beings were created in the image of God. This affirmation, perhaps connected with the prohibition of graven images of the divine (Exod. 20:4; Lev. 26:1; Deut. 4:16; 5:8; 27:15), emphasized the immediacy of the relationship between God and human beings (cf. Ps. 8:5).

Some interpreters of the Second Temple period understood the image of God to be the human soul or spirit (Pseudo-Phocylides 106; Philo, *On the Creation of the World* 69). For others, however, the "image" of Genesis 1:26 was understood as a reference to an intermediary entity that served as a model for humanity. Inspired by the personification of Wisdom (Prov. 8:23), later interpreters would see Wisdom as that image. The Wisdom of Solomon (7:22–8:1) conceives of this "reflection of eternal light" and "image of God's goodness" as an all-pervasive spirit. Philo of Alexandria combined this sapiential notion with Platonic notions of a world soul, the locus of the ideal forms. He spoke of heavenly Wisdom or Word (Logos) as the image of God (*Allegory of the Laws* 1.33, 43; *On the Confusion of Languages* 97, 146–47; *On Flight* 101; *Who is the Heir* 230). Other exegetes found in the mysterious "human form" seen by Ezekiel (Ezek. 1:26) the image of God. These speculative traditions influenced early Christian affirmations about Christ (2 Cor. 4:4; Heb. 1:3; Col. 1:15).

images symbols of religious importance that were found in synagogal and funerary art and architecture. Various images found in synagogues and Jewish burials include menorahs, representations of the Ark, cultic elements from the Temple, and biblical scenes. The way in which a particular symbol came to be commonly adapted as a Jewish image is not altogether clear, but each image seems to have undergone development from particular to more general usage.

The probable development of the menorah from a symbol to a common Jewish image is instructive for understanding this process. The menorah was used as a vessel in the temple, and the act of lighting the menorah was an important function of the priest. Because of its importance, the menorah came to be seen as a professional sign of the priests during the Second Temple period. After the destruction of the Temple, the menorah developed into a symbolic representation of the function of the priest and in this sense became a widely adapted Jewish image.

The menorah is by the far the most common Jewish image to be found in the art and architecture of synagogues and Jewish burials. Probably as a result of the biblical prohibition against the veneration of images, the menorah was not depicted artistically before the second half of the first century B.C.E. In fact, Jewish images in general did not become widespread until after the destruction of the Second Temple in 70 C.E. The first known depiction of a menorah is from a coin of the last Hasmonean monarch, Mattahias Antigonus (r. 40–37 B.C.E.). The use of the menorah on his coins was probably an attempt to emphasize the king's Jewishness and to prove his legitimacy.

The menorah consisted of several parts, each of which might vary in form. Biblical sources do not describe the base of the menorah. As is known from an archaeological find from Second Temple Jerusalem, the base of the menorah used in the Second Temple itself was probably conical. Other examples from Beth Shean, Dura Europos, and Hammath-Tiberias depict a menorah base that consists of three animal legs. The most common form was a simple tripod.

The form of the branches was decreed in Exodus 25:33–36. These verses state that the branches should be composed of three cups fashioned as almonds and crowned with a capital and a flower. Many of the early menorahs appear to follow this directive, while some of the later ones follow the same pattern but become more ornate. Light fittings were found at the end of each branch, which varied in composition from glass to bronze to ceramic.

Noting that the menorah became a prominent Jewish image following the destruction of the Second Temple because it provided a concrete visual image of worship, it is no surprise that ritual objects often flanked menorahs in Jewish art. One prominent object was the shofar, or ram's horn, that was used in the temple during the New Year celebration (Rosh Hashanah) and the Day of Atonement (Yom Kippur). Other familiar images used in conjunction with the menorah were the lulab (a palm branch) and the etrog (a citrus fruit), both associated with worship during the Feast of Tabernacles. Incense shovels, used to clean the debris left from the menorahs, were also depicted.

Other prominent images that developed in synagogue art were the Ark of the Scrolls and the conch. The Ark of the Scrolls, the place where the scriptures were kept, was placed in a cabinet called a Torah shrine. As both these features were vital to the Jewish faith, they evolved into popular images in synagogue art. The development of the conch motif is somewhat different. The conch is known to carry sacred significance since the first millennium B.C.E. from Egyptian motifs. In Jewish synagogal and funerary art, the conch was initially used as a decorative motif. Later it became associated with the storage niche for the Torah shrine and finally with the Torah shrine itself.

Bible scenes are another well-attested type of motif found on Jewish art from synagogues and burials. Certain Bible scenes appear to have been especially meaningful to the various communities, and these were incorporated into the images of synagogal and funerary art. One example is the scene of the sacrifice of Isaac from the synagogues at Beth Alpha and Dura Europas. Both scenes portray the key parts of the narrative, though each one empahsizes different aspects of the story. This event becomes a symbol for the covenant between God and the Jewish people. Another biblical scene that signifies the preserving of the people of God is Noah's Ark; this scene is found in the synagogue of Gerasa. The synagogue of Naaran contains a depiction of Daniel, again containing the motif of salvation. Other scenes include a depiction of the twelve tribes at the Japhia Synagogue, King David at Gaza, and David and Goliath at Marous (in the Galilee).

Finally, what were commonly known as Hellenistic symbols developed into well-known images in Jewish works of art. Two examples are the peacock and the Hercules knot, which became minor symbols in Jewish art. In ancient Hellenistic art, the peacock could be purely decorative or it could be used as a symbol of the empress and of immortality. The latter identification arose out of a tradition associating the peacock with the goddess Hera (Juno). The Hercules knot was normally used to bind a crown wreath, which was commonly found in low relief on lintels of synagogues from Palestine. In the Graeco-Roman world, the crown wreath symbolized victory. Thus, the Hercules knot was used on the lintels in the Roman world to create a concrete example of eternal victory by showing that the binding of victory (the crown wreath) could never come undone. How much of the original connotations of these "pagan" images were preserved in Jewish adaptations is still debated. The dominant view is that they were adapted into Jewish images because the Jews lived in the Hellenistic world, but that these symbols did not compromise or transform the Jewish faith. *See also* ARK, REPRESENTATION OF; ETROG; HERCULES KNOT; HOLY OF HOLIES, REPRESENTATION OF; LULAB; MENORAH, REPRESENTATION OF; SARCOPHAGUS DECORATIONS; SHELL.

Ima Shalom (late 1st–early 2d c. C.E.) wife of Eliezer b. Hyrcanus and daughter of Simeon B. Gamaliel I. The Talmud reports that she had beautiful children (B. Nedarim 20b), and that after her husband's excommunication, she prevented him from prostrating himself in prayer, lest he utter a curse to punish his excommunicators, including her brother, Gamaliel (B. Baba Metzia 59b).

imbecile a person of severely limited mental capability. In the Mishnah and Talmuds, the imbecile is classified together with the deaf-mute and the minor and deemed to have no independent will. Accordingly, under rabbinic law, the imbecile is unable to perform religious obligations requiring the formulation of intention, such as the designation of agricultural offerings (M. Terumot 1:1) or the preparing of foods in a state of cultic cleanness (T. Terumot 1:1). The imbecile also is excluded from business transactions requiring comprehension (e.g., sale or purchase), and, since he does not understand the implications of his actions, the imbecile cannot be found liable under a claim of negligence.

imitatio dei (Lat., imitation of God) The term is found in modern scholarly writings rather than in ancient Jewish texts. The phrase is used in theological and ethical discussions to describe an attempt to live as God lives (or would live if He were a human being). The concept, if not the term, is well known from the Hebrew Bible and later Jewish literature. In Leviticus 19:2 and elsewhere, God states, "You shall be holy as I am holy." This idea occurs in later Jewish literature as well, especially in rabbinic Judaism.

The idea of imitation of God took on a special form in Christianity with the concept *imitatio Christi* (imitation of Christ). Although thought of by later Christians as divine, Jesus had by common consent been a man, and the Gospels seemed to describe his life on earth. Having "God in the flesh" as a model and trying to live as Jesus lived facilitated the imitation of God.

immersion the practice of immersing in a pool of water in order to cleanse a person (or vessel) of ritual impurity that derives from contact with a corpse, other defiling object, or bodily flux. The purpose of immersion is to achieve ritual and spiritual, but not physical, cleanness. By talmudic times, the primary function of immersion was to cleanse a woman of the impurity associated with menstruation, so as to render her permitted for sexual relations with her husband. Since talmudic law deems intercourse with a woman in the status of a menstruant to be a severe offense, rabbinic law insists upon meticulous observance of the ritual of immersion for this purpose.

Immersion is carried out in a mikveh, a pool carved into rock or otherwise built into the ground and containing a minimum of forty *seah*s of water (an uncertain amount, representing as little as 250 or as many as 1,000 liters). So as to represent the flowing water that scripture states is to be used for immersion, the water of the mikveh may never have been contained in a vessel. Rainwater, melted snow or ice, or other flowing water is used for this purpose.

immortality, incorruption (Gr.: *athanasia, aphtharsia*) the state or quality of being deathless or not subject to the corruption caused by death. From its first pages, the Bible denies that human beings are immortal (Gen. 3). Deathlessness is reserved for God and the heavenly entourage. The heavenly watchers who mate with mortal women and beget children are condemned because in their immortal state they do not need progeny (1 Enoch 15:3–7). The rise of a belief in resurrection and eternal life brings with it a notion of immortality. The terms immortality and incorruption tend to be limited to texts composed in Greek, but they do not posit the Greek notion of the soul's natural immortality. According to Wisdom of Solomon 2:23–24, sin and the devil caused humans to lose the incorruption of the divine image with which they had been created, but one achieves immortality through the righteous life (Wisd. of Sol. 1:15, 3:1–4, 5:15–16). Similarly, the martyrs in 4 Maccabees are transformed into immortality and incorruption through their deaths in behalf of the Torah (9:22, 14:5, 16:13, 17:12). In Joseph and Asenath 15:5 and 16:16, Asenath gains immortality, incorruption, and eternal life through her conversion, an idea paralleled in the Qumran Hymns (1QH 3:19–36, 11:3–14). The Second Book of Esdras 7:96–97 associates agelessness as well as immortality and incorruptibility with the future existence of the righteous in heaven, the realm of perfection.

According to Paul, at the return of Christ, all those in Christ, living and dead, will be transformed to receive immortal bodies in the image of the glorified Christ, the Second Adam (1 Cor. 15:42–57). In 2 Corinthians 4:13–5:5, he seems to say that the process of transformation is already underway, a notion consonant with some of the Jewish texts cited above.

Rabbinic authorities conceive of an immortal soul in a narrow sense. Created and bestowed upon the body by God, at the time of the body's death it is taken back to God, where it awaits the time of the resurrection and the world to come. Then it will be restored to that same body (see Y. Kilaim 8:4, 31c; B. Berakhot 60a) together with which it will be judged (B. Sanhedrin 90b–91a). Outside of the eternally existing soul, the rabbis imagined human immortality only in the context of their conception of resurrection. While no human being is immortal, the rabbis held that the righteous could anticipate bodily resurrection and a future life in the messianic world to come. *See also* LIFE, ETERNAL.

imperator (Lat., emperor) originally a title given to Roman commanders who had been successful in their campaigns. With Augustus, however, it came to refer to the head of the Roman Empire, rather like a quasi-king; the power in theory still lay with the Senate. *See also* IMPERIUM.

Imperial Aramaic *see* ARAMAIC, IMPERIAL

imperium (Lat., the power or right of ruling or administration) The term specifically applied to the responsibilities of waging war and upholding the law. The concept goes back to the time of the Roman kings and referred to the power held by them. Under the Roman Republic, it was a power held by the state but was given to consuls, dictators, and some others by authority of the Senate. Under the Roman Empire, this power was almost always held by the emperor and only exceptionally allowed to be exercised by others.

imprisonment not a prominent feature of Israelite or Judean society. Most occurrences of "imprisonment" in English Bible translations refer to the forced exile of (some of) the people, particularly the Babylonian deportation and "house arrest" of the Judean ruling elite after the destruction of Jerusalem in 587 B.C.E. But some ancient rulers used imprisonment as a means of controlling opponents and critics or disrupters of the established order. Rome usually either killed or enslaved the ordinary people they subjected and took military action against disruptions of any scope. But they used imprisonment to confine minor disrupters of the social order, such as small-scale bandits or vocal dissenters. The last kings of Judah confined the prophet Jeremiah, but were afraid to kill him. Herod imprisoned (and often executed) numerous critics and suspects, including his own sons. Antipas imprisoned and then killed John the Baptist, who had criticized him. Roman governors regularly rounded up and imprisoned bandits in Judea. In all of these cases, imprisonment was used simply for temporary holding rather than as a form of punishment, in contrast to the modern practice.

impure, pure *see* TAHOR, TAMEI

incense shovel device for containing hot coals and incense for use in worship; known in ancient Graeco-Roman, Jewish, and Christian contexts, but also as a major motif in Jewish art. The incense shovel typically was made of bronze or ceramic. Examples are known in most of the museums of the Middle East. The earliest incense shovels from a Jewish context are from the Cave of Letters west of the Roman town of En Gedi. These shovels were among the private possessions of Jews who fled advancing Roman armies during the Bar Kokhba Revolt. A typical incense shovel has a rectangular pan, open at the end opposite the handle, and measures about 13 centimeters by 16 centimeters by 1.6 centimeters deep. The pan has a grooved ornamental molding on the top edge that is wider than the thickness of the bronze. The hollow bronze handle is about 19.5 centimeters long and is equipped with two bronze "cups" mounted on the two corners of the pan near the handle. These shallow cups are round and about 7 centimeters in diameter, but only 2 centimeters deep. Four rings are mounted on the bottom of the pan near the corners to serve as feet, so that the pan and its hot coals will be elevated about 1.6 centimeters above a table. Of the four shovels found at En Gedi, only one was decorated with a floral motif on the handle and on the sides of the pan. To use such an incense shovel, one placed glowing coals in the pan and powdered incense in the cups. The powder could then be sprinkled on the coals as needed during worship. These rectangular pans with handles have been known in Jewish art for some time, though they were not always recognized as incense shovels. They appear especially frequently in low relief carvings on stone or in mosaic floors in synagogues with the menorah, lulab (palm branch), and etrog (citron).

incest Leviticus 18 and 20 and Deuteronomy 23:1 (MT), 27:20, and 21–23 prohibit men from engaging in sexual intercourse with specific individuals related by either blood or marriage; father–daughter incest is not included, perhaps because in the Hebrew legal structure the daughter's sexuality was classified as belonging to her father. Genesis 20:12 (Abraham and Sarah), Genesis 29 (Leah and Rachel with Jacob), and 2 Samuel 13:13 (Tamar and Amnon) provide accounts of relationships the law code would judge incestuous. The Qumran community extended the biblical list of prohibited relationships (see also Jub. 33). Judah's repentence for his "incest" with Tamar (Gen. 38) appears in Jubilees 41 and Testament of Judah 12–13. Other texts addressing incest include Pseudo-Phocylides 179–183; Psalms of Solomon 8; and the Sibylline Oracles 5:390–391; 7:43–45.

While some rabbinic authorities extended the prohibition in Leviticus 18:6–18 against intercourse to relationships not specified by scripture (see B. Yeb̲amot 21a and 22a), the general tendency within rabbinic law was to limit such developments and, indeed, to treat as permitted some relationships forbidden by Leviticus. Sifre Aḥarei-Mot 13:15 explicitly argues that Leviticus's list of prohibited unions is not subject to extension through analogies; B. Yeb̲amot 62b–63 permits marriage between cousins and even encourages a man to marry his niece, especially the daughter of his sister.

According to talmudic law, incest is a capital offense. Sexual relations with one's mother, stepmother, or daughter-in-law are punished by stoning (M. Sanhedrin 7:4), and intercourse with one's daughter, granddaughter, mother- or grandmother-in-law, stepdaughter, or stepgranddaughter is punished by burning (M. Sanhedrin 9:1). Other incestuous acts are punishable with flogging.

inclination, evil and good (Heb.: *yetzer haRa, yetzer Tob̲*) the two inclinations in every person, to do evil and to do good. They contend with each other; when the impulse or inclination to do evil prevails, a person sins, and the contrary is the case as well. These terms occur in the rabbinic literature. *See also* WAYS, TWO.

In Flaccum the treatise *Against Flaccus* by Philo of Alexandria; its title is abbreviated as *Flacc.* or *Flaccum.* This treatise is an account of the riots against the Jews in Alexandria in 38–39 C.E. According to Philo, not only did the Roman governor Flaccus fail to protect the Jewish community against the attacks of the Greeks, he positively encouraged the attacks.

inheritance Sons inherit a father's estate, and the firstborn son receives a double portion (Deut. 21:16–17). Should only daughters survive, then they inherit, provided they contract endogamous marriages; in their absence, the father's brother and then the nearest relative inherits (Num. 27:1–11; 36:6–12).

The testamentary genre frequently describes bequests. For example, the Testament of Job depicts the dying hero as bestowing miraculous girdles on his three daughters. Judith bestows her property on "all those who were next of kin to her husband Manaseh and to her own nearest relations" (16:24).

Inheritance also indicated the relationship between God and Israel (Deut. 9:26; Jer. 10:16; Ps. 28:9). In Sirach 24:23 and 1 Enoch 99:14, the law is Israel's inheritance. For Psalms of Solomon 14:7, 1 Enoch 40:9, 2 Enoch 50:2, and 2 Baruch 44:13, the inheritance is eternal life, and this bequest appears, as mediated through Jesus and as a replacement for family-based inheritance, in Matthew 19:29, Mark 10:29–30, 22, and Luke 18:29–30. Matthew 5:5 announces that the meek will inherit the earth (or the land) (see Ps. 37:11; 1 Enoch 5:7). In the Pauline tradition, the baptized are fellow heirs (Rom. 8:17; Col. 3:24; Eph. 5:5) with Christ to the reign of God. In Hebrews, Jesus is heir of all things (1:2); 1 Peter 1:4 promises the faithful "an inheritance imperishable, undefiled, and unfading." The various texts vacillate as to whether the inheritance is present or future, empirical or spiritual, focused on a covenant mediator (e.g., David, Jesus), a faithful individual, or the corporate community.

Like the biblical and Hellenistic literatures, rabbinic texts treat inheritance as a theological category, referring to Jews' acquiring of a special place in God's scheme of salvation. Individuals receive this inheritance by carrying out their obligations under the covenant, for instance, by showing kindness to the poor. As a result, God "will bind a crown upon them in the world to come" (B. Shabbat 104a). The Talmud is careful to note that this inheritance, embodied in the Torah, is the possession of the entire people. It is not a legacy only of scholars or their children (B. Nedarim 81a).

Elaborating the Bible's provisions for inheriting an estate, the rabbis held that sons are first in the line of succession, followed by daughters, the father of the deceased, the brothers of the deceased, the sisters of the deceased, the grandfather, and so on (B. Baba Batra 115a). Unique to the rabbinic approach is the principle that each individual in the order of succession transmits his right of inheritance to his own descendants. Even if an heir should die, the next relative in line inherits only if that preceding individual had no heirs of his own. The rabbis also differed from the Bible in placing in the line of succession the father of deceased, whom scripture does not list among the heirs.

According to rabbinic law, the deceased's property was divided equally among the sons, except for a father's firstborn, who received a double share. A mamzer or a son born after his father's death was treated as a regular heir among the other brothers (B. Yebamot 67a). According to the principle already explained, should one of the sons predecease his father, his sons receive his share in their grandfather's estate.

While a man inherits his deceased wife's separate property, she does not stand in his line of inheritance. Similarly, daughters inherit only if their father had no sons. The rabbinic system meets these women's needs by requiring that, so long as they remain unmarried, they be supported from the estate (B. Ketubot 22b). This claim for support is prior to that of all who stand in the actual line of succession, including the deceased's sons. Depending upon the size of the estate and the length of time for which the women receive support, they therefore may potentially receive a larger share of the estate than those who actually inherit and may even entirely exhaust the estate's value.

injustice (Gr.: *adikia*) actions that are unjust or, more specifically, not consonant with the righteousness required by the Torah. In the Septuagint, the term translates a whole range of Hebrew words denoting wickedness, transgression, and wrongdoing. The Greek negating prefix *alpha* before the root *dik* (right, just) gives the word an explicit connotation not necessarily present in the Hebrew, one that would have resonated with the Greek-speaking people who read the Septuagint, Greek translations of the pseudepigrapha, and Jewish and early Christian works composed in Greek against the background of Greek notions of justice and righteousness. In 1 Enoch 92–105 and the Psalms of Solomon, it is a common term for wicked deeds perpetrated against others. Like its synonym "lawlessness" (Gr.: *anomia*), it is sometimes combined with verbs and verbal nouns meaning "do, doer" to create an idiom meaning to do evil or sin, or to be an evildoer or sinner (cf. 1 Enoch 98:12; Ps. Sol. 4:24; 9:4, 5; Luke 13:27, quoting Ps. 6:8). *See also* LAWLESSNESS.

insanity Rabbinic law holds that an insane person is unable to formulate the intention to fulfill religious obligations or to comprehend the significance of his actions. Accordingly, he is precluded from participating in rituals that require intention, for example, leading the community in prayer or designating agricultural tithes. Additionally, one who is insane may not validly enter into contracts or other agreements. T. Terumot 1:3 refers to temporary insanity, holding that at any point at which the individual appears sane, he is treated in all respects like a person of sound mind.

inscriptions, Aramaic those ancient texts preserved in the Aramaic language in stone or mosaics, but also on pottery, metal, and small objects. The best-known inscriptions of the Persian period are ostraca, or potsherds with inscriptions in ink. For example, an Aramaic ostracon from Tel el-Farah in the south lists the amount of barley that is to be sown in two fields: "For sowing in the field which is near, 3 kors of barley, in the other field, 35 kors." Many Aramaic ostraca were found at ancient Beer Sheba, the largest administrative center of the Negeb, dating from mid-fourth century B.C.E. These are receipts for food and other materials. They are difficult to decipher, but typically they name the date and a commodity (wheat or barley), then its measure. One reads "On the 15th of Ellul, year four four, from . . . eight seahs of wheat." Similarly, distribution lists from Arad, also in the south of the country, direct someone to give to named persons so much barley for so many animals. One reads, "Give to Qos . . . for one horse and one ass, 4 seahs of barley and 3 kabs of . . . , on the sixth." On the other hand simple wine tags are known, as an example painted directly on the pot from Ashdod shows: "Vineyard of Zebediah."

In the Hellenistic period Aramaic continued in strong use. At Khirbet el-Kom, a site south of Bethlehem, a series of ostraca were found that were apparently the receipts or memoranda of two Edomite moneylenders, Qosyada and Qosbana. Five are in Aramaic and one is in Aramaic and Greek. One Aramaic example reads, "Qosyada to Jaaphat, two quarter-shekels. Qosbana to Malha, one shekel and two quarter-shekels." Evidently these transactions took place in 277 B.C.E.

Ossuaries, Roman period stone boxes for storage of bones in a tomb, are a rich repository of Aramaic inscriptions. These are most commonly names, but also include titles and other indicators for the family. One such ossuary from Jerusalem reads, "Simon, builder of the Temple." Others have similar laconic inscriptions: "Salome the wife of Shapir," or "Yehonathan the potter." A marble plaque of the first century C.E. contains an interesting Aramaic inscription: "Here were brought the bones of Uzziah, King of Judah, and not to be opened." This apparently refers to King Uzziah, of whom it is recorded in 2 Chronicles 26:23 that he died and was buried with his fathers, though the interpreters understand this to mean outside the city, as he was a leper. Another Aramaic inscription on the wall of a tomb in Jerusalem records the bringing of the bones of a certain Mattathai, son of Yehud, from Babylon to Jerusalem for reburial: "I, Abbah, son of the priest Elaz son of Aaron the elder, I, Abbah, the afflicted, the persecuted, who was born in Jerusalem and exiled to Babylon, and I brought Mattathai son of Yehud and buried him in a cave which I bought by deed."

Ancient synagogues provide by far the largest corpus of Aramaic inscriptions. For example, the mid-third-century synagogue of Dura Europos in ancient Parthia was found to have fifteen Aramaic inscriptions. Many of these were on the ceramic tiles in the ceiling. Most synagogue Aramaic inscriptions appear on lintels, columns, marble slabs, chancel screens, and in mosaic floors. Most are either dedicatory inscriptions or are longer texts for other purposes. The dedicatory inscriptions normally state, "Be remembered for good X the son of Y who donated the Z" or "X the son of Y made (donated) this Z. May it be for him a blessing." Sometimes the donation is a specific part of the synagogue, such as the mosaic floor, a column, or some other member, but on other occasions it is money that was donated. An example of an inscription mentioning a specific part of the synagogue is from Capernaum, inscribed on a column: "Halphe bar Zebidah bar Yohanan made (donated) this column. May it be for him a blessing."

An example of an inscription for other than donors was found in the mosaic floor of the synagogue at Hammath-Tiberias. It reads as follows: "Peace be upon everyone who has fulfilled the commandment in this holy place, and who will fulfil the commandment. May the blessing be his. Amen. Amen. Selah. And unto me. Amen." A dedicatory inscription from the synagogue in the House of Kurios Leontis in Beth Shean is less formulaic. It reads as follows: "Be remembered for good all the members of the Holy Congregation who endeavored to repair the holy place. In peace shall they have their blessing. Amen. Peace. Loving kindness in peace." One of the most famous of the textual types of synagogue Aramaic inscriptions is from Rehob, east of Beth Shean. This inscription is twenty-nine lines long and gives a detailed list of fruits and vegetables forbidden or permitted during the sabbatical year in specific regions of ancient Palestine. Of equal interest is the Aramaic portion of a long Hebrew and Aramaic inscription from the mosaic floor of the synagogue at En Gedi. The Aramaic portion begins with a formula: "Be remembered for good Yose and Ezron and Hizziqiyu the sons of Hilfi," then proceeds with a curse against those who would reveal the secret of the town to the Gentiles. It is usually assumed that this is the secret of balsam preparation.

Other important Aramaic inscriptions come from tombs, both within ancient Palestine and in the diaspora. A long tomb inscription from Zoar on the southwestern shore of the Dead Sea reads as follows: "This is the monument of Esther daughter of Adaio who died in the month of Shebat, year three of the sabbatical year 346 years after the destruction of the Temple. Peace. Peace on her." This date translates to 416 C.E. Many Aramaic tomb inscriptions are known from Jewish communities in Egypt; they reveal many of the details of community life.

inscriptions, diaspora texts inscribed, usually in stone, found outside of the Land of Israel. Inscriptions from various sites of the diaspora give insight into Jewish beliefs and customs outside of Israel. The most readily accessible inscriptions from the diaspora are from North Africa, mainly Egypt, but a smattering of archaeological inscriptions are found from other sites as well. These additional sites demonstrate that the inscriptions from North Africa provide an acceptable sample of diaspora inscriptions.

One important site with a Jewish inscription is the Naro Synagogue, located in modern Tunis, Tunisia. This synagogue contains a typical dedicatory inscription. The mosaics found in the central chamber of this synagogue are now kept in the Brooklyn Museum and contain typical Jewish and "pagan" symbols with dedicatory inscriptions. The Jewish symbols of menorahs are joined by more "pagan" symbols of a fish, a cup, peacocks, and animals placed in a vine design. It is commonly held that these images represent various aspects of salvation, and the accompanying inscription shows that this salvation was especially intended for the benefactor who paid for the mosaic. The inscription reads, "Thy servant Juliana P . . . at her own expense paved with mosaic the holy synagogue of Naro for her salvation."

The most accessible group of inscriptions from the diaspora are found in Egypt on burial inscriptions. Almost all of these inscriptions are written in Greek, though a few are written in Hebrew and Aramaic. Another set of inscriptions that are preserved are written in Aramaic with Hebrew proper names. The inscriptions are very important for understanding the use of Jewish names in the diaspora, as well as for illuminating Jewish beliefs in the diaspora about the afterlife and grief.

The most essential element of a burial inscription was the name of the deceased and, often, the age at death. Several simply read, Akabiah son of Elionenai," "Joanna Euphrosyne," "Simotera daugher of Heliodorus, a woman of Sidon," and "Philon, son of Hipp . . . , fifty years old." Another type of burial inscription shows that it was at times important to mention the king and queen. One of these inscriptions reads, "On behalf of King Ptolemy and Queen Cleopatra, Ptolemy son of Epikydes, chief of police, and the Jews in Athribis [dedicated] the attendant to the Most High God." Other burial inscriptions add a brief evaluatory comment about the deceased. One such inscription reads, "Mariame, excellent woman, farewell. In the thirty-third year."

Another similiar form is a group of inscriptions that develop the evaluatory comment and add a lament in order to encourage readers of the inscription to mourn for the deceased. This is a very interesting development among the Jewish inscriptions from the diaspora, because it shows that the mourning of others was an important aspect of proper grief. Another important motif is that of the figure of Hades serving as a bridegroom for a young woman of marriageable age. One typical inscription from this group reads, "Weep for me, stranger, a maiden ripe for marriage, who formerly shone in a great house. For, together with my bridal garments, I, untimely, have received this hateful tomb as my bridal chamber. For when the noise revellers are my . . . was going to make my father's house resound, suddenly Hades came and snatched me away, like a rose in a garden nurtured by fresh rain. And I, stranger, who was twenty years . . ."

A similar inscription also calls on the stranger to mourn the deceased who was even younger. It reads, "Look on my gravestone, passerby, and having considered it, weep. Beat with your hands five times for the five year old. For now I lie in the tomb, without even having shared marriage. My parents suffer likewise for the son who pleased them, and my friends look for their comrade and companion; but my body lies in the blessed place. Weeping say, Untimely dead, deeply mourned, you who were always renowned for all virtue."

These inscriptions provide different clues on beliefs and customs from the diaspora. Most of the inscriptions show that the Jews attempted to preserve their culture, while at the same time adopting some of the beliefs and customs of the non-Jews around them.

inscriptions, Greek From the period between Alexander the Great and Muhammad, more than fifteen hundred Jewish inscriptions on stone in Greek are extant, the vast majority of them being epitaphs. They are an important but much neglected source for the study of Jewish life and thought in late antiquity. Though there are several hundreds of Jewish inscriptions in Hebrew, Aramaic, and Latin, these amount to no more than some twenty-five percent of the total number. The heavy preponderance of Greek is an impressive testimony to the influence of Hellenistic culture on the Jews in this period, not only in the diaspora but also in the Land of Israel where a great number of Jewish Greek inscriptions have been found. Even rabbis and their families in the famous rabbinic center of Beth Shearim in Galilee wrote most of their tomb inscriptions in Greek. It is only from the sixth century C.E. onward that Greek was gradually replaced by Hebrew in epigraphic sources. Greek influence is visible not only in the language but also in the forms, formulas, and motifs in the epitaphs. That is only to be expected since there is little evidence of an Israelite tradition in composing tomb inscriptions. Indeed, it was the Greeks who had elevated funerary inscriptions to an art form. In these Jewish epitaphs we find many Hellenistic features: Greek forms like hexametric and iambic poems; Greek literary motifs like death as marriage to the god of the netherworld; Greek mythological figures such as Hades, Charon, Lethe, and others; numerous concepts and formulas of pagan origin (although probably filled with a new sense in some cases, e.g., Moira, originally the goddess of Fate); the Greek notion of astral immortality; and Greek epigraphical conventions, such as the dialogue of the deceased with the passer-by and threats or even curses aimed at potential tomb robbers. In Jewish inscriptions of a nonfunerary nature, we find, for instance, Greek honorary and dedicatory inscriptions (from synagogues) and Greek forms for declarations of manumission of slaves.

The geographical spread of these inscriptions

reveals, even more than the literary sources, that Jews were indeed living all over the ancient world, from Morocco and Spain in the West to Iraq in the East. This is especially true for the Roman period from which the majority of the inscriptions date; although from places such as Leontopolis in Egypt (with its rival Jewish temple) or the Greek island of Delos there is plenty of epigraphical evidence for a strongly Hellenized Jewry from as early as the middle of the second century B.C.E. onward. From many of the inscriptions it is apparent that Jews were often fully integrated into the surrounding society because, for instance, they are said to have been members of the local city council or to have exercised other important public offices. It seems, however, that it was especially in western Asia Minor that Jews reached these high positions; for the city of Rome and other major cultural centers there is no (or much less of) such evidence, although the Jews probably nowhere lived in isolation, as far as we can judge. It should be added, however, that functions in the religious community are mentioned much more often than secular professions and occupations, which is an important indication of the fact that the synagogal community played a major role in the life of ancient Jews. Often inscriptions are our only sources that provide information about the titles of synagogue officials in the diaspora. Moreover, they reveal that in a good many diaspora synagogues women had positions of leadership, which is another indication that it was not until the early Middle Ages that the rabbis began to dominate diaspora communities. On the whole, the more than two thousand inscriptions reveal surprisingly little influence of rabbinic ideas, even though laudatory epithets such as "loving the Torah," "loving the commandments," "loving the synagogue," and the frequent mention of synagogal functions leave us in no doubt about the religious commitment of many Jews.

The average age at death (mentioned in some 550 epitaphs) turns out to be about twenty-eight years. Although it is very hard to determine how representative this data is, it may be said that most probably the Jews shared with pagans both the fate of a short life expectancy—the average length of life for the Roman Empire as a whole lying somewhere between twenty and thirty years—and the fate of a high infant and child mortality, with probably not half of those born reaching adulthood. Even though one would expect in such a situation clear expressions of hope for some sort of afterlife, most of the epitaphs yield very little information concerning the ideas of either the survivors or the deceased about life after death. Only a handful of inscriptions testifies to a variety of forms of belief in afterlife (such as the traditional conception of the gloomy netherworld, immortality of the soul, or becoming a star), and there is only one inscription that explicitly confesses a belief in the resurrection of the body. This need not imply that it is only the few authors of these epitaphs who believed in afterlife—in early Christian epitaphs this belief finds expression relatively rarely as well—but neither can it be said on the basis of this evidence that Jews widely believed in life after death or resurrection. (It must be added that it is unclear what is implied by epitaphs that exhort the deceased to keep courage.) What one does find expressed often is grief about the untimely death of the beloved one(s), much as in pagan epitaphs. Frequently one finds laments over the loss of young persons who had died without having had the chance to marry or beget children, which was felt to be a particularly cruel form of unfinished life. In short, these inscriptions yield important information that is often not found in literary sources and, therefore, they deserve more serious scrutiny than they have received hitherto.

inscriptions, Hebrew those ancient texts preserved in the Hebrew language in stone or mosaics, but also on pottery, metal, and small objects. The best-known Hebrew inscriptions of the Persian period are simple jar handles with the word "Yehud" (Judea) or "Jerusalem" stamped upon them. These occasionally occur with a proper name, such as Hanana or Yehoezer the Governor. From fragments of a fourth-century B.C.E. pottery storage jar from Shikmona on the coast of Israel, we read "Ben Matton, 25 royal (measures) of wine of Gath Karmel (the Carmel Press)." Since this is a Phoenician script, it may be preferable to read this as Phoenician, a related language.

In the Hellenistic period, finds of inscriptions multiply, but most of them are in Greek. Hebrew inscriptions, however, usually of personal names, occur on storage jars from Qumran, the site famous for its association with the Dead Sea Scrolls. The names found in Hebrew include Roma and Yehohanan, the latter also found in its short form Yohanan. Other Hebrew words on other storage jars from Qumran record their contents, such as balsam, or its use, mikveh or ritual bath. Hebrew tomb inscriptions of the Hellenistic period include the inscription of the sons of Hezir, which is found on the facade of the monumental tomb in the Kidron Valley just east of the Temple Mount. The inscription reads, "This is the tomb and the memorial of Elazar, Hania, Yoezer, Judah, Simeon, and Yohanan, sons of Joseph son of Obed; Joseph and Elazar, sons of Hania, priest of the sons of Hezir." This inscription is often dated to mid-first century B.C.E.

The biblical city of Gezer apparently had become a country estate owned by a single man, Alkios, in mid-first century B.C.E. The boundary stones of the estate have been found around the ancient mound of the city inscribed directly into the bedrock in Hebrew and Greek. The Hebrew says "boundary of Gezer." The Greek says "of Alkios."

From excavations in Jerusalem a part of a leg of a small stone vessel has been found inscribed *qrbn* (qorban) or "sacrifice." This vessel was surely from the Temple worship. A large stone from the top of the southwest tower of the Temple Mount was inscribed "From the place of trumpeting . . ." in Hebrew.

Ossuaries for the reburial of the bones of the dead also occur with Hebrew inscriptions. These usually are to be dated from mid-first century B.C.E. to mid-second century C.E. Most often this is simply a name, such as Yehonan ben Hanania, a title, such as "mother," or a similar phrase, such as "the sons of Eliezer." Other variations on such inscriptions occur, such as "Martha, our mother" or "John the craftsman," or "Salome the proselyte."

Synagogues supply the largest body of Hebrew inscriptions during the Roman and Byzantine periods. The first group is made up of dedicatory inscriptions, of which there are surprisingly few examples in Hebrew. (Most are in Greek or Aramaic.) For example, from Dabbura in the Golan Heights comes the Hebrew inscription, "This is the school of R. Elezar ha-Qappar," usually dated to the second or third century C.E. A dedicatory inscription with a precise date was found at Naburaya in Upper Galilee: "The synagogue was built 494 years after the destruction of the Temple" (564 C.E.). On the lintel inscription from the small synagogue at Kefar Baram, before it was destroyed, one could read, "May there be peace on this place and on all the places of Israel. Yose the Levite, son of Levi made this lintel. May his acts be blessed. Shalom." A Hebrew inscription from Alma, also in Upper Galilee, was composed in a similar fashion: "May there be peace upon this place and upon all the places of His people Israel. Amen. Selah." One usually interprets the word "place" to mean "synagogue."

The second type of synagogue inscription is textual and may contain various elements. For example, two fragments of a marble plaque from the synagogue at Caesarea contained a list of the priestly courses and the localities in the Galilee to which they fled after the destruction of the Second Temple in 70 C.E. On the other hand, the eighteen-line inscription from the mosaic floor of the synagogue at En Gedi on the west shores of the Dead Sea contains both a Hebrew and an Aramaic section. The first eight lines are in Hebrew and list the thirteen ancestors of the world according to 1 Chronicles 1:1–4. Lines 3 and 4 list the twelve signs of the Zodiac. Lines 5 through 7a list the twelve months of the year. Lines 7b through 8 list the patriarchs Abraham, Isaac, and Jacob with the word "Peace." Then the three companions of Daniel appear in their Hebrew names: Hananiah, Mishael, and Azariah, and finally "Peace unto Israel." The remainder is in Aramaic. Other synagogues with zodiacs normally have the signs of the zodiac identified in Hebrew, as are the four seasons. In the synagogue at Beth Alpha west of Beth Shean, Hebrew was used to identify the figures in the presentation of the binding of Isaac in the first panel in the mosaic floor.

A few other Hebrew inscriptions are known from the third to the sixth centuries C.E. For example, sometime during the fourth century C.E. an anonymous person scratched Isaiah 66:13–14 on the western wall of the Temple Mount. It reads, "You shall see, and your heart shall rejoice; your house (shall flourish) like a garden." This may refer to the joy that greeted the emperor Julian's proclamation in mid-fourth century that the Jews were to be allowed to rebuild the Temple in Jerusalem. When Julian was killed in Parthia, the permission was rescinded.

inspiration term used to describe the supernatural influence exerted upon individuals that enables them to perform certain tasks, to produce oral or written messages (which are then considered to be supernatural revelations possessing divine authority), or to have supernatural wisdom and insight into the meaning of earlier revelations or revelatory writings. Modern Jewish and Christian communities typically regard the particular collection or canon of scriptures they revere as inspired and authoritative, though this judgment, often vague and undefined, is based primarily on each religious community's theological assessment of the religious value of the sacred texts, rather than on a general claim articulated within the texts themselves. In rabbinic Judaism the belief that the Torah was *min shamayim* (from heaven) was a major way of emphasizing its unique inspiration and authority.

Inspiration to perform particular tasks is sometimes expressed in the Hebrew Bible through the idiom "God placed it in the heart." In Exodus 35:34, for example, it is said of Betzalel the master craftsman (who was filled with the spirit of God, v. 31), that God "put it into his heart" to teach his skill to others. The same idiom is also used of the divine guidance given to Nehemiah in his plans for restoring Jerusalem (Neh. 2:12, 7:5). Divine inspiration is often associated with the two major types of altered states of consciousness, possession trance and vision trance, both involving temporary personality changes. When Saul was possessed by the spirit of the Lord and began to behave like a prophet, for example, the text says that he was "turned into a different person" (1 Sam. 10:6). Possession trance entails the belief that supernatural beings or spirits enter or control an individual's personality, while vision trance typically involves visions or out-of-body experiences. Both types of trance are attributed to prophets in the Hebrew Bible.

Israelite prophets claimed divine inspiration and authority for their messages in a variety of ways. Sometimes the revelations they received were attributed to the activity of the spirit of God (Judg. 3:10; 1 Sam. 10:10; Isa. 48:16, 59:21, 61:1; Ezek. 3:12–15), and for this reason an ancient designation for a prophet was "man of the spirit" (Hos. 9:7). Another type of claim to inspiration is involved in the prophet's assertion that "YHWH's hand" was upon him (Ezek. 3:14, 8:1, 33:21–22; Isa. 8:11; Jer. 15:17), an expression strongly suggesting divine control or possession. Yet another way of claiming divine inspiration was the frequent introduction of oracular speeches with the messenger formula "thus says YHWH" (Amos 1:1, 3:11, 7:17), and the proclamation formula "hear the word of YHWH" (1 Kings 22:19; Jer. 2:4; Ezek. 3:3), and conclusion of such speeches with formulas like "YHWH has spoken" (Amos 1:5, 8, 15, 2:3, 5:17). The revelatory trance could be experienced as a vision seen by the prophet (Amos 1:1, 7:1, 4, 7, 8:1). One distinctive type of prophetic visionary experience involved the prophet's perception of his presence at the deliberations of the heavenly court (1 Kings 19:22–33).

In early Christianity, the inspiration and authority of the Jewish scriptures, either in the form of the Hebrew Bible or in its translated and expanded form, the Greek Septuagint, was increasingly emphasized. The term *theopneustos,* meaning inspired by God, is used in 2 Timothy 3:16, where it is claimed that "all Scripture [i.e., the Jewish scriptures] is inspired by God." Another way of expressing the notion of inspiration is by claiming that biblical authors such as David wrote "in the spirit" (Mark 12:36; Matt. 22:43). While there is overwhelming evidence for revelatory experiences in early Christianity (Acts 2:1–21, 8:14–17, 10:44–46, 19:1–6; 1 Cor. 12–14; 1 Thess. 5:19), it is only in the Revelation of John that there is an explicit claim for divine inspiration (Rev. 1:1–2, 21:8–21).

intention the mental determination of an action's purpose or desired result. Rabbinic Judaism ascribes paramount importance to intention, holding that the meaning and significance of an action are determined by the individual's underlying purpose rather than by what he or she physically does or says. This idea appears in rudimentary form within scripture's priestly source, which distinguishes between intentional and unintentional desecration of holy things (Lev. 22:10–14) and between homicide and manslaughter (Num. 35:16–28). It is fully developed within later rabbinic Judaism, which deems intention central in many aspects of law and ritual.

Scripture generally understands the significance of an action to be inherent in its outcome. In Leviticus, for example, a priest's offering of a sacrifice is valid as long as he carries out the proper actions, regardless of what he is thinking while he performs them. Comparably, scripture deems foods to become subject to uncleanness when they are wet, whether or not an individual purposely moistens them. Physical condition alone determines status. Rabbinic writings by contrast generally hold that physical actions have no inherent meaning. An action's significance or an object's status, rather, must be determined in light of the intention and purpose of the person involved.

This rabbinic view holds that people inherit an incomplete world, which awaits human interpretation and ordering. This notion is familiar from the Yahwistic creation story (Gen. 2:4–20), in which Adam names the animals and thus completes Creation. But it is quite unlike the priestly conception (see Gen. 1:1–2:3), which understands humankind to have been placed in a completed and perfectly ordered world. In this view, classification and interpretation are based entirely upon outward appearances, established by God without regard to human cognition and purpose.

The mishnaic perspective imputes to Israelites the power to determine what is sacred and profane, to judge what actions conform to or break the law, and to establish the status of physical objects. For instance, the Mishnah holds that only intentionally moistened foods become susceptible to uncleanness. Similarly, the rabbis treat as foods, subject to tithes, only things someone actually intends to eat. If the individual plans to discard the substance, then even if it is edible, it takes on the status of refuse, exempt from tithing. Finally, the Mishnah's authorities hold that a priest—or any individual engaged in a ritual action—must formulate the intention properly to perform that act of worship. If he intends to do the wrong thing, his act is not valid, even if his physical actions conform to the rules. In all these cases, human intention and purpose are primary in establishing the significance and effect of actions.

The Mishnah's rabbis thus hold that human will and purpose impart meaning to a world that has no inherent order. In this way, Israelites share in what the rabbis perceive to be the continuing creation of the universe. They share with God the task of imparting meaning and order to what otherwise is chaotic. This idea represents a major distinction between the rabbinic perspective and that of scripture's priestly code, in which Israelites confront a world completed and perfected in the original events of creation and therefore unaffected by human thought and purpose.

intercession the pleading of humanity's case before God by human and divine beings. In the Hebrew Bible prophets intercede for the sinful nation (Exod. 33:12–23; Amos 7:2; Jer. 15:1), and priestly sacrificial rites mediate between God and humanity. Following the exile and the absence of a sacrificial cult, we see the priest Ezra offering a prayer of repentance in behalf of the people (Ezra 9:6–15), and later texts stereotype high priests in this role (2 Macc. 3:31; 3 Macc. 2:1–20).

At some indeterminate point, the role of intercessor is ascribed to members of the heavenly courtroom. It is suggested in Job 9:33, 16:19, and 19:25–27, but comes into full bloom in the apocalyptic literature of the early Hellenistic period. For the authors of 1 Enoch, four named angels relay the prayers of a decimated humanity (chap. 9), and other texts repeat the image (chap. 47, 89:59–90:17). Often these intercessors are associated with heavenly books that contain the names of the righteous and the record of their good deeds and their enemies' evil deeds (1 Enoch 97:2–3, 98:6–8, 104:1–3). Angelic intercession is pivotal in the action of the Book of Tobit (3:16–17, 12:12–15).

Although the notion of angelic intercession is not absent from the New Testament (Matt. 18:10), in general, the exalted Jesus has taken over the role of heavenly intercessor. The Epistle to the Hebrews expounds Jesus' heavenly high priesthood in great detail, but the idea appears earlier in Romans 8:34 with an allusion to the priestly Psalm 110. *See also* ANGEL.

interest the amount paid for the use of borrowed money. In contemporary usage, interest is distinguished from usury, which refers to a rate of interest higher than what is permitted by law or common practice. In dealings between Israelites, biblical and rabbinic law prohibit the payment of any interest whatsoever. In discussions of Jewish law, therefore, the terms interest and usury are interchangeable.

Rabbinic authorities clearly recognize the value of money over time. For instance, they distinguish between the worth of a note of indebtedness payable in ten years and the much greater value of such a note payable in thirty days (M. Makkot 1:1). Even so, rabbinic law consistently enlarges upon scripture's prohibition against interest, thereby foreclosing any possibility of a lender's receiving in return more than he lent. Within this rabbinic system, profit from all sorts of investments is categorized as forbidden interest and even the appearance of interest is to be avoided. This applies, for example, in a case in which one purchases a home and some months later sells it back to the original owner for the same amount of money. This is to be avoided since it creates the appearance that the purchaser enjoyed the use of the home in exchange for the original seller's use of his money (M. Arakhin 9:3).

The rabbinic approach to interest reflects a larger economic system, familiar from Aristotelian economics, in which barter is seen as natural and good, while profit—economic gain derived from money that has not been used in an exchange of commodities—is unnatural. In the rabbinic like the Aristotelian system, money functions as a means of exchange only. Interest violates money's essential purpose and creates opportunities for inappropriate economic gain.

intermediate days *see* ḤOL HAMOED

Ios. *see* DE IOSEPHO

Irenaeus bishop of Lyons (fl. 180 C.E.). In his major extant work, *Adversus omnes haereses* (Against All Heresies), written against the Gnostics, the Christian Bible takes recognizable shape as constituted of two Testaments. Irenaeus referred to an Old Testament, comprising the Septuagint, and coined the name New Testament for the collection of Christian documents, which he knew as including the four Gospels, a collection of Paul's Epistles, the Acts of the Apostles, Revelation, 1 Peter, and 1 and 2 John. Prior to Irenaeus's work, Christians had claimed the sacred writings of the Jews by reading them as witnesses to Christ. Decisions on which Christian writings to include rested fundamentally on whether a given writing gave a theologically correct interpretation of the Christian faith in general and of Christ in particular. Irenaeus's work marks crystallization of the almost complete Christian canon. It also includes reflection on interpretation; for example, *Adversus haereses* II.25.3–28 outlines conditions for the right use of the scriptures.

Isaac son of Abraham and Sarah; father of Jacob and Esau. God's promises are passed down through Isaac, rather than Ishmael, Abraham's firstborn. Paul sees this as proof that divine election depends on grace (Rom. 9:7–8; Gal. 4:28). The writings of the rabbis enhance the miraculous aspects of Isaac's birth.

In Genesis 27:1–40, Rebekah and Jacob trick Isaac into giving Jacob the blessing of the firstborn, even though Esau was born first. Jubilees 19:15–31 justifies this by saying Abraham loves Jacob because he is learned, in accord with Jubilees' interest in halakhic learning. Abraham blesses Jacob in Rebekah's sight, legitimating her deception of Isaac.

The sacrifice of Isaac (Gen. 22) is of particular interest to tradition. Jubilees 17:15–18:19 sees it as a test of Abraham's faith. Josephus (*Ant.* 1.13.1–4, secs. 222–36), Philo (*On Abr.* 32–36, secs. 167–207), and Pseudo-Philo (18:5, 32:1–4, 40:2) stress both Isaac's and Abraham's willingness that the sacrifice proceed. Philo and Pseudo-Philo consider it a real sacrifice, as does rabbinic tradition. In Pseudo-Philo, God chooses Israel because of Isaac's blood (18:5).

In Hebrews 11:17–19, the sacrifice of Isaac illustrates Abraham's faith. Isaac's faith is connected to his blessings for his sons (Heb. 11:20). James 2:21–24 considers Abraham's sacrifice of Isaac a "work," proving that both faith and works are necessary for justification. The Testament of Isaac is a Christian work picturing Isaac as an ascetic who teaches and tours the heavens before his death.

Isaac I Tannaitic authority of the mid-second century C.E.; a contemporary of Judah the Patriarch; not cited in the Mishnah, but mentioned frequently in the Talmuds, Mekhilta, and Sifrei

Isaac b. Abdimi Babylonian amora of the late third and early fourth centuries C.E.; known primarily for his biblical exegesis; often in dispute with Ḥisda. Regarding Isaac, Raba̱ (B. Zeba̱ḥim 43b) states: "Every passage of scripture that R. Isaac b. Abdimi did not expound, and every passage on Tannaitic authority which Zera did not expound, are not really explained." Isaac's teachings frequently are transmitted by Abayye or Raba̱.

Isaac b. Eleazar **1.** Palestinian amora active at the end of the second century C.E.; a relative of Yoḥanan, who delivered his funeral eulogy; the same individual as Isaac Ḥakola or Ben Ḥakola, found in both Talmuds (see B. Pesaḥim 113b).

2. Palestinian amora active in the second half of the fourth century C.E.; a native of Caesaria. Both legal and homiletical authorities cite sayings in his name.

Isaac b. Naḥman third-century-C.E. Palestinian amora; a contemporary of Jacob b. Idi, with whom, according to Y. Peah 8:9 (21b), he served as a lay leader of the community, possibly Tiberias

Isaac Ḥakola *see* ISAAC B. ELEAZAR

Isaac Nappaḥa third-century-C.E. Palestinian amora; a student of Yoḥanan; in sources other than the Babylonian Talmud, generally referred to simply as R. Isaac, without designation as "the smith." He was active at Tiberias and Caesarea with Ammi, Abbahu, and Ḥanina b. Pappa. He also traveled to Babylonia, where he transmitted teachings from the Land of Israel. Isaac is known for both his legal and exegetical teachings.

Isaac of Antioch (d. 459 C.E.) Syrian church father. In his homily against the Jews he argues that they should not feel a sense of pride for having the law because there were righteous people before Sinai—such as Abel, Enoch, Noah, and Seth—who were blessed even though they did not keep the law. The law was given to the Jews because they had rebelled and sinned through the golden calf. According to Isaac, Jacob had disinherited the Jews in his will, and Jesus "had revoked the curse of the law" on the cross. He argues that circumcision, an operation for removing the foreskin that is done by the hand, is replaced by baptism, which is a removal of sin accomplished by the Holy Spirit. Isaac accuses the Jews of encouraging the Christians to sin by inviting them to keep the Sabbath and to practice circumcision. He chastises the Christians for using Jewish amulets and charms. Isaac states that because God still loves the Jews, he will forgive them if they become Christians.

Isaiah prophet in Jerusalem in the second half of the eighth century B.C.E. Lives of the Prophets and Martyrdom of Isaiah relate the nonbiblical tradition of Isaiah's death at Manasseh's hands by being sawed in half (cf. Heb. 11:37). The explanation of this strange fate may lie in rabbinic legends that tell of Isaiah magically hiding in a cedar, which is then sawed in two. In Martyrdom of Isaiah 3:8–9, the prophet is charged with claiming to have seen God, contrary to Moses' words (Exod. 33:20; see Isa. 6). Martyrdom of Isaiah 6–11 is a Christian work telling of Isaiah's vision of a trip to heaven, where he foresees Jesus' career. *See also* ISAIAH, MARTYRDOM OF.

Isaiah, Ascension of *see* ISAIAH, MARTYRDOM OF

Isaiah, Martyrdom of a legendary account of Isaiah's death. Although elements in the legend are referred to in Hebrews 11:37 and in rabbinic texts (B. Yebam. 49b; B. Sanh. 103b; Y. Sanh. 10:2; cf. Lives of the Prophets 1), the story itself is preserved only as a part of the second-century Christian apocalypse, the Ascension of Isaiah.

The legend is set in the reign of Manasseh, who has turned Jerusalem into a center of apostasy, lawlessness, and the occult arts and a place where the righteous are persecuted (2:4–6). As a result, Isaiah and his friends flee to the Judean wilderness, where their hiding place is discovered by Isaiah's opponent, a false prophet named Bechir-ra, a descendant of Zedekiah ben Ḥenaanah, the opponent of Micaiah ben Imlah. Bechir-ra accuses the prophets of predicting the fall of Jerusalem and Judea and the captivity of the king and people, and he criticizes Isaiah for claiming to have seen God (Isa. 6:1ff.; cf. Exod. 33:20) and for calling Jerusalem "Sodom" and the princes "the people of Gomorrah." The king condemns Isaiah to be sawed in two.

Apart from the specific sins attributed to Manasseh (2 Kings 21), the parallels to the story of Ahab, Micaiah, and Zedekiah (cf. 1 Kings 22), and the reference to Isaiah's throne vision, the details of this narrative have no specific counterparts in the Bible and may be indicators of the story's origin. Details in chapter 5 recall the martyr stories in 2 Maccabees 6–7 and could point to a time of origin during the persecution by Antiochus Epiphanes; however, one would expect a foreign king as the antagonist, as is the case in several texts from this period which feature Nebuchadnezzar as the arch-villain. The polarity that sets Isaiah and his cadre of true prophets against Bechir-ra and his entourage suggests a situation in which a group of true believers oppose establishment leaders who are seen as false teachers. This narrative structure, as well as the retreat from the corruption of Jerusalem to the wilderness of Judea, parallels the circumstances of the Qumran Community, and the text could have emanated from such a group.

Elements in the actual account of Isaiah's death, especially his inspiration by the Holy Spirit at the moment of death and his refusal to recant, become common fare in later accounts that emphasize the martyr's ecstasy and transformation to immortality at the moment of death (cf. 4 Macc. 14–17; Gosp. Peter 4).

Isaiah, Targum to *see* TARGUM TO THE PROPHETS

Ishmael son of Abraham and Hagar, Sarah's Egyptian slave; Isaac's older half-brother. The promise of land is passed down through Isaac, not Ishmael (Gen. 17:1–22). Ishmael is considered the ancestor of the Arabs. In Gal. 4:21–31, Paul allegorizes Sarah and Hagar, interpreting them as old and new covenants. As Ishmael "persecuted" Isaac (Josephus, *Ant.* 1.12.3, sec. 215), so the present children of the slave Hagar (those under Torah) persecute those in Christ. For Paul, those under Torah are in slavery, and those in Christ are free (Gal. 4–5).

Ishmael b. Elisha one of the most important Tannaitic authorities, active at the beginning of the second century C.E.; generally referred to without the patronymic, often in dispute with Akiba. He is particularly known for the thirteen hermeneutical principles cited in his name. His school is held to stand behind the midrashic compilations Mekhilta deRabbi Ishmael (on Exodus), Sifrei to Numbers, and part of Sifrei to Deuteronomy.

Ishmael b. Yoḥanan b. Beroka Tannaitic authority of the middle of the second century C.E. He is frequently quoted in agreement with or opposition to Simeon b. Gamaliel II. He repeats the exegetical principle that scripture employs ordinary human idiom. While his name appears infrequently in the Mishnah, it is associated with about fifty statements in the Tosefta and Talmuds.

Ishmael b. Yose b. Ḥalafta Tannaitic authority at the end of the second century C.E. He transmitted teachings of his father, Yose b. Ḥalafta, and followed him in leadership of the academy at Sepphoris. At Y. Megillah 4:1, 77d, Ishmael reports that he can write out the entire scripture from memory. B. Baba Metzia 84a reports that Ishmael was forced to work for the government, and he is criticized for not having fled.

Isidorus Alexandrian opponent of the Jews in the period around the riots in 38 C.E., when the Jewish community suffered greatly. A version of the story is found in the Acta Alexandrinorum, according to which Isidorus brought a private lawsuit against Agrippa I and was tried and executed by Claudius.

Isis goddess originating in ancient Egypt whose worship and cult spread across the ancient world.

She was worshiped in Palestine and other parts of the Roman Empire as late as the sixth century C.E. In Egyptian religion, Isis was the wife of Osiris and the mother of Horus. From the earliest times of Egyptian religion, she was seen as the supreme mother goddess who possessed the ultimate creative powers of the soil. This control of the creative powers of the earth caused her to be assimilated into other cults throughout the ancient Near East, and she was identified with numerous other Semitic, Greek, and Roman deities.

Archaeological evidence of an Isis worship in Palestine dates back to at least the Late Bronze Age. A foundation tablet of an administration building at Tell Aphek (14 km from modern Tel Aviv) identifies the local governor with the epithet, "Beloved by Isis, the Great, mother of the god, the one of On." In the Hellenistic period, there is evidence of an actual Isis cult in Palestine. Remains of a third-century-C.E. temple to Isis were uncovered at Samaria underneath the ruins of a Roman temple to Kore. A Greek dedicatory inscription confirms that this temple was primarily devoted to the worship of Isis.

From the evidence of Jewish names formed from the name Isis, it is possible to deduce that the worship of Isis became familiar enough that the name was a choice for a child's name. For example, the name Eisas, from Isis, is attested in Catacomb 16 at Beth Shearim. The veneration of Isis probably continued in Palestine well into the first few centuries of the common era.

isopoliteia (Gr., equal citizenship) The term is often used by Josephus to imply an equality of citizenship of the Jews with the Greeks in a Greek polis (city). Despite Josephus's claim, it is now generally accepted that the Jews as a whole did not have such citizenship in most Greek cities. The Jews were usually given the right to practice their own laws, but this was as an ethnic community (*politeuma*), not as citizens. Josephus's statements represent a form of pro-Jewish propaganda, perhaps in support of those Jews who were arguing for rights of equal citizenship.

Israel (Heb., one who strives with God) the name given to Jacob after he wrestled with God (Gen. 32:28). It was used for his descendants, understood as the twelve tribes of Israel, and for the land given to them by God. They often refer to themselves as the sons of Israel and to God as the God of Israel. During the divided monarchy, Israel was the northern kingdom, in contrast to Judah, the southern kingdom. "Israel" is the name used by the authors and audiences of postexilic Jewish literature for themselves, in contrast to "Jews," a name used by or in address to outsiders. "Jews" is a Hellenized form of "Judeans," referring originally to the inhabitants of the Persian province of Yehud (539–332 B.C.E.), an area around Jerusalem roughly corresponding to the homeland of the tribe of Judah. The Greek term was used for adherents of the Jewish way of life in both Judea and the diaspora. True to this usage, Josephus speaks of Israel when he is recounting the biblical story in the first eleven books of his *Antiquities of the Jews,* and then uses "Jews" when he describes their part in the Hellenistic and Roman periods. In 1 Maccabees and Judith, which recount conflict with the gentile world, "Israel" is used frequently as a way of affirming Jewish identity. *See also* ISRAEL, LAND OF; ISRAEL, PEOPLE OF.

Israel, Land of **1.** in Second Temple literature, a designation that usually refers to the region of Israel; the term "land," however, can be used for territory owned or inhabited by any individual or group. The Bible contains legislation that protects the property rights of individuals. Land was not to be removed permanently from the control of the family to which it was allotted originally (see the story about Naboth's vineyard in 1 Kings 21). Land that had been sold was supposed to be returned to the first owner in the fiftieth year, that is, at the end of a jubilee period of forty-nine years (Lev. 25). There is no evidence that this concept was ever put into practice, but the Book of Jubilees dates Israel's regaining of its land (the conquest of Canaan) to end of the fiftieth jubilee period—a large-scale application of the biblical concept.

The Land of Israel plays a large role in biblical and Second Temple literature. In Genesis, God promises that his descendants will one day possess the Land of Canaan whose boundaries stretched from the river of Egypt to the Euphrates River (Gen. 15). The long story of their absence from that land, their return to it, and their conquest of it occupies much of the first six books of the Bible. The prophets threatened the nation with loss of the land if they were unfaithful to the covenant; after several centuries their words came true, when Assyria exiled many residents of the northern kingdom in 722 B.C.E. and the Babylonians deported thousands from the southern kingdom in 587 and 586 B.C.E. The prophet Ezekiel described a vision in which, prior to the destruction of Jerusalem, he saw the presence of the Lord leaving the Temple because of its impurity. Though not all residents left the land, the return to the land of a sizable number of Jewish people from Babylon and points east began in 538 B.C.E. and continued in different waves for some time thereafter. This, too, happened in accordance with prophecy (see, e.g., Jer. 32). The Jewish state in Israel remained small during much of the postexilic period, but during the time of the Maccabean, or Hasmonean, dynasty (152–63 B.C.E.), the borders were expanded considerably. The Second Temple, which stood from 515 B.C.E. to 70 C.E., remained the focal point of religion for Jews in Israel and to a certain extent for those in other lands. All males were required to make pilgrimage to the Temple three times in a year, and it is known that large crowds were present at those festive times (see, e.g., Acts 2). In the New Testament, the land is mentioned a number of times. It was the place where Jesus lived, died, and rose. In fact, the Gospel of Matthew (chap. 2) presents his brief departure from it to Egypt and his return to it as a repetition of the ancient Israelite Exodus. In Hebrews, the promise of land to Abraham and his offspring is reinterpreted as the assurance of a heavenly homeland (Heb. 11).

2. in rabbinic Judaism, the Holy Land, centered upon Jerusalem, extending to Judea and Samaria, with variable boundaries elsewhere. It is regarded as cultically clean; all other lands are cultically unclean, bearing corpse-uncleanness. The Holy Land is a central category in Judaism; it is where Israel, the people, belong, and it is owned uniquely by Israel, the people, in partnership with God. This joint ownership is expressed in a variety of concrete rules. First, Israel, as tenant on God's Holy Land, maintains the property in the ways God requires, keeping the rules that mark the land and its crops as holy. Next, the hour at which the sanctification of the land comes to form a critical mass, namely, in the ripened crops, is the moment ponderous with danger and heightened holiness. Israel's will so affects the crops as to mark a part of them as holy and the rest of them as available for common use. The human will is determinative in the process of sanctification. When Israel wants to use the produce of the land, at that moment God asserts the divine right to ownership of a share of the crop, which is parceled out among God's clients, the priests, Levites, poor, and the like.

What happens in the Holy Land at appointed times marks off spaces of the land as holy in yet another way. The center of the land and the focus of its sanctification is the Temple. There, the produce of the land is received and given back to God, the one who created and sanctified the land. At these unusual moments of sanctification, the inhabitants of the land in their social being in villages enter a state of spatial sanctification; that is, the village boundaries mark off holy space, within which one must remain during the holy time. This is expressed in two ways. First, the Temple itself observes and expresses the special, recurring holy time. Second, the villages of the Holy Land are brought into alignment with the Temple, forming a complement and completion to the Temple's sacred being. The advent of the appointed times precipitates a spatial reordering of the land such that the boundaries of the sacred are matched and mirrored in village and in Temple. At the heightened holiness marked by these moments of appointed times, therefore, the occasion for an affective sanctification is worked out. Like the harvest, the advent of an appointed time, a pilgrim festival, also a sacred season, is made to express the regular, orderly, and predictable sort of sanctification for Israel that the system as a whole seeks.

The Mishnah's economic theory regards land as the sole form of wealth and capital, and land in this sense means only land in the Land of Israel. Only the householder figures as an economic actor, and the householder is defined as one who owns land in the Land of Israel. As principal and head of so sizable a network of material relationships, the householder saw himself as pivot of the village, the irreducible building block of society, the solid and responsible center of it all. The householder controlled the means of production and held the governance of the basic economic unit of the village as such. Traders and peddlers and others outside the economy of the household also functioned outside the framework of the village as such; by definition, they were not settled, landed, stable. Their economic tasks required them to travel from place to place, for instance, to collect produce and resell it at the market. But so far as the Mishnah's picture of society in its economic relationships and productive aspects is concerned, the whole was held together through the householder. He who owns something is the only one who may sanctify it; in heaven, God sanctifies, and on earth, the householder does. Ownership of a slice of land in the Holy Land formed the center of the system.

Israel, people of **1.** in Second Temple times (c. 515 B.C.E.–70 C.E.), the Jewish people. During this long period, the nation of Israel was scattered into several centers of population, with the largest numbers being in Babylon (where some were exiled in the sixth century B.C.E.), Egypt, and the Land of Israel. In each place, the Jewish people established their own societal arrangements and wrote their own literature. The Jewish community in Egypt produced the first ancient translation of the Hebrew Bible by rendering it into Greek (the Septuagint). The process had already begun in the third century B.C.E. Jerusalem served as a center for all Jews in the sense that the Temple was there (Jews everywhere contributed to its expenses), and it was the goal of the three annual pilgrimages (the festivals of unleavened bread, weeks, and booths). At some point in the Second Temple period, synagogues appeared in different localities, including Israel.

There was little political independence for the people of Israel throughout these centuries. In fact, the most influential Jewish leader seems often to have been the high priest, although at several points in these centuries, there is mention of a council that exercised some administrative and judicial powers. When the Temple was rebuilt (515 B.C.E.) after the Babylonians had destroyed it, Israel was part of the immense Persian Empire; the central government ruled it by means of appointed officials—Nehemiah, for example—who were Jewish. Once Persia fell to Alexander the Great (about 330 B.C.E.), Israel became part of the Hellenistic world. First, it was ruled by the Ptolemies in Egypt; beginning in about 200 B.C.E. the Seleucid Empire, centered in Syria, took control. A brief period of native rule resulted when the Maccabean family led a revolt, which won the Jews in Israel a degree of independence from Seleucid control. Members of the Maccabean (or Hasmonean) family served as the political and religious heads of the state from 152 to 63 B.C.E., when the Romans, led by Pompey, captured Jerusalem. Roman control took different forms as time progressed (client kings, such as Herod the Great, or governors, such as Pontius Pilate), but it witnessed the rise of strong Jewish opposition, which eventually caused a revolt against Rome (66–70 C.E.). That revolt, to which a radical group called the Zealots made a significant contribution, ended with the demolition of Jerusalem and its Temple and immense loss of life.

During the Second Temple period, there were different parties or factions among the people. Josephus the historian mentions the three major parties, the Pharisees, the Sadducees, and the Essenes, and describes their varying beliefs and practices in some detail; he also says that the Zealots agreed with the Pharisees but were violently opposed to foreign rule. The spoken language of Israel seems to have been Aramaic throughout this period, though Hebrew was used and, later, some Greek.

2. in rabbinic Judaism, the holy people of God; the children of Abraham, Isaac, and Jacob; the group of which the Hebrew scriptures speak, deemed by Judaism to be the living people of Israel "after the flesh," the Jewish people. The doctrine of "Israel" implicit in the Mishnah (c. 200 C.E.) is that the community now stands in the place of the Temple of Jerusalem, which was destroyed in 70 C.E.—"Israel" now serves as had the Temple. As in the vision of Ezekiel, chapters 40 through 47, the Temple had marked the boundaries among the hierarchy of society, with the high priest going to the innermost sanctum, the other priests then going closest to the holiest place, and all others approaching in hierarchical distance: Levites, Israelite males, women, and outward to the Gentiles. "Israel" served this second task of social hierarchization, as well as the outer-facing task of political differentiation of "Israel" from everyone else, "the nations." In the second phase in the formation of the Judaism of the dual Torah, from the formation of the Talmud of the Land of Israel at the end of the fourth century, "Israel" became a historical entity, with traits that were intrinsic, not merely aspects of a relationship of comparison and contrast. "Israel" served not only as a classification but also as the hero of stories, the subject of sustained (if episodic) narratives. "Israel" in the writings redacted in the late fourth and fifth centuries gains flesh and substance, becoming not merely a category to be set into relationship with other categories, but the name of a palpable social group, living out a concrete historical existence in a world of material reality, about which people told important stories and made weighty comments—a different "Israel" altogether.

Israelite term for Jew; Hebrew; descendant of Abraham and Sarah, Isaac and Rebekah, Jacob and Leah and Rachel

Issi *see* ASSI

Issi b. Akabiah *see* YOSE B. AKABIAH

Issi b. Gamaliel *see* YOSE B. AKABIAH

Issi b. Gur Arye *see* YOSE B. AKABIAH

Issi b. Judah *see* YOSE B. AKABIAH

Issi b. Mehallel *see* YOSE B. AKABIAH

issur haNaah (Heb., prohibition against [deriving] benefit) prohibition against deriving any profit whatsoever from an object; distinguished from a less inclusive prohibition, which forbids, for instance, eating or drinking the thing but allows other benefit, for example, sale or use of a prohibited animal's skin (see B. Shebuot 24a–b)

Issus, Battle of battle at Issus, to the east of Tarsus and the Cilician Gates, in which Alexander the

Great defeated the Persian emperor Darius III in 333 B.C.E. When Darius fled east, Alexander proceeded south toward Egypt, receiving the submission of Jerusalem on the way, but fighting a difficult seven-month siege at Tyre.

ius gladii (Lat., law of the sword) term used by modern scholars (though the Romans may not have used the expression themselves) with reference to the right of passing a sentence of capital punishment and carrying it out. It is now generally agreed that the Jews under Roman rule did not have this right.

Iyon city, also called Tel-Dabin, in the north of the Land of Israel, in the area of Susita, east of the Sea of Galilee. According to T. Shebiit 4:10, produce that is cultivated in Iyon is subject to tithing, as though the city were part of the Land of Israel proper. T. Shebiit 4:11 explicitly lists Iyon as a border area.

Iyyar eighth month of the Jewish calendar, corresponding to April/May

Izates king of Adiabene during the reign of the Roman emperor Claudius (41–54 C.E.). His kingdom in northern Mesopotamia was dependent on the Parthians. Izates and many of his family became Jews and made many donations to Jerusalem and the Temple. His five sons were educated in Jerusalem.